# The
# Dark Side
# of Genius

## *THE LIFE OF ALFRED HITCHCOCK*

by Donald Spoto

Plexus, London

All rights reserved including the right
of reproduction in whole or in part in any form
Copyright © 1983 by Donald Spoto
Published by Plexus Publishing Limited
26 Dafforne Road, London SW17 8TZ
First Printing 1994

Spoto, Donald
  Dark Side of Genius: Life of Alfred
  Hitchcock. – New ed
  I. Title
  791. 430233092

ISBN 0 85965 213 0

The right of Donald Spoto to be identified as author of
this work has been asserted by him in accordance with
the Copyright, Designs and Patents Act, 1988

Printed in Great Britain by Hollen Street Press
Cover design by Richard Adelson ·

The author gratefully acknowledges permission to quote from the fol-
lowing previously published materials:
*Hitchcock* by Francois Truffaut. Copyright © 1967 by Francois Truffaut.
Reprinted by permission of Simon & Schuster, a division of Gulf and
Western Corporation. *The Defendant* by G. K. Chesterton. Reprinted by
permission of Arno Press. "The Americanisation of Alfred Hitchcock ...
and Vice Versa." © 1973 by *Performing Arts Magazine*, Los Angeles.
Reprinted by permission. "There's Just One Hitch," from *Women's Wear
Daily*, June 16, 1972. Articles appearing in the *New York Times*, by
Derrick de Marney, February 5, 1938; by Bosley Crowther, January 13,
1944; by A. H. Weiler, May 9, 1954. © 1938, 1944, 1954 by The New
York Times Company. Reprinted by permission. "Master of the
Macabre" by Rex Reed, July 30, 1972. Reprinted by permission of
Tribune Company Syndicate, Inc. "In the Hall of Mogul Kings" by
Alfred Hitchcock, June 23, 1969. Reprinted by permission of Times
Newspapers Limited.

10 9 8 7 6 5 4 3 2 1

*for Ned*

A friend may well be reckoned
the masterpiece of Nature.
— Emerson

# Contents

*Illustrations follow pages 189 and 427*

It takes the pity of God
to get to the bottom of things.
— Enid Bagnold,
*The Chalk Garden*

# Preface

My fascination with Alfred Hitchcock began over thirty years ago, while I was, a schoolboy and he was quickly becoming an international institution. Approaching the height of his popularity in the early 1950s, he was giving us a motion picture — and sometimes two — annually, and part of the fun was watching for his quick cameo appearance as he walked past an actor or boarded a train. Then, as if he wanted to extend his ample presence right into our living rooms, he became the host of his own weekly television series. With his nearly expressionless descriptions of the most antisocial conduct, he seemed to me like someone from another world, a land where murder was routine and betrayal the typical response of one person to another. At the same time, his face peered out from bookracks, where collections of tales were marketed as Hitchcock anthologies. His presence touched every medium of entertainment and communication; hardly a month passed without a Hitchcock interview in the local newspapers and national magazines.

Twenty years later — in 1975, to be exact — I met him for the first time. He invited me to watch him at work on *Family Plot,* his fifty-third feature-length movie — and, as it turned out, his last. I was near to completing a book about his films, and he took time between scenes to answer some technical questions. Then, a year later, he kindly acknowledged the publication of *The Art of Alfred Hitchcock* by inviting me to luncheon. By this time, he was firmly established as a legend, and I was firmly established in awe of him. The awe remained undiluted during subsequent meetings and luncheons. But we discussed at these times only what Hitchcock wanted to discuss, and I had the impression that he was directing conversations the way he directed his films — to include only what he wanted to include, to reveal as little as possible of

himself and as much as possible of others. He was always cordial, but
there was a cautionary coolness in his manner, as if he feared a sudden
unmasking of his real, carefully hidden feelings. This, I quickly learned
from earlier research, was an impression also left upon colleagues and
associates who had known him for years. Very easily, this most public
of popular cultural figures withdrew into a secret shell when one showed
interest in the deepest levels of his work, or in his background or family
or inner life or certain large periods of his career. He was smoothly
adept, at these times, in changing the subject.

When he died in 1980, I asked his daughter, Patricia Hitchcock
O'Connell — who also spoke for his ailing widow — about the possibility of an authorized biography. Very courteously, she told me of her
father's expressed intention that no further research or work on his life
be undertaken, and that therefore the family would not actively cooperate with or contribute to the preparation of such a book. This, of
course, was consistent with Hitchcock's obsessive secrecy. But he was,
after all, a world-renowned figure, a wealthy and powerful man; his
career touched millions, and his presence continued to fascinate and
invite reflection. As an admirer of his art I had for over a decade read
and cataloged scores of articles and interviews, in which there occurred
alarmingly contradictory statements about his life, and major gaps to be
filled.

And so I proceeded. I learned at once that Alfred Hitchcock was a
notoriously poor correspondent and that almost no personal letters survive. Nor did he keep diaries or journals or notebooks — a fact that
reflects his deep inarticulateness. This lack of written primary sources
at first seemed a crippling omission. But as the facts emerged, it became
clear that Hitchcock's films were indeed his notebooks and journals and
that his almost maniacal secrecy was a deliberate means of deflecting
attention away from what those films really are: astonishingly personal
documents. As my work continued — first in England, where he spent
half his life, and then in America — I turned to public records, county
and family registries, school archives and studio files, as well as to
those who knew him professionally and socially, to artists and writers
and actors who worked with him. With the exception of a small number
of people and one major studio, people felt freer after his death to summon memories, to contribute clues that led me further. Gradually, a
complex image appeared, more mysterious than any of the stories he
chose to film.

# Acknowledgments

GENEROUS assistance and considerable kindness were offered to me during the research and writing of this book.

At the Humanities Research Center of the University of Texas at Austin, Decherd Turner, W. H. Crain, and Edwin Neal smoothed my path through the vast materials of the David O. Selznick Collection and the Ernest Lehman papers.

Robert Knudsen, head of special collections at the Doheny Library, University of Southern California, enabled me to work in the Warner Brothers production archives.

The William Seymour Theatre Collection at Princeton University also contains important Warner Brothers material, and Mary Anne Jensen and John Hein provided help there. Access to all the Warner Brothers data was possible through the assistance of Georgiana K. Morrison and Bernard Sorkin.

John Hall, West Coast Manager of RKO Pictures, Incorporated, made it possible for me to work in the relevant files there. Similar help and access at Metro-Goldwyn-Mayer were extended by Herbert Nussbaum.

In the special collections of the Mugar Memorial Library at Boston University, Howard Gotlieb provided space and time to work in the Evan Hunter papers.

In Los Angeles and Washington, the American Film Institute provided help, and I am grateful to its director, Jean Firstenberg; to the chief librarian, Anne G. Schlosser; and to Monica Morgan, Betti Brown, and Ron Geatz.

Similarly, at the British Film Institute, London, my research was facilitated by the generous assistance of Elaine Burrows, Brenda Davies, Gillian Hartnoll, Peter Seward, Sandra Archer, John Gillett, Patricia

Coward, and Michelle Snapes. Adrian Turner, at the National Film Theatre, London, has been a welcoming host for my lectures on Hitchcock there.

At the Margaret Herrick Library of the Academy of Motion Picture Arts and Sciences in Beverly Hills, Terry T. Roach enabled me to pore over a vast and important collection of materials, and helped me sort oceans of newspaper and magazine clippings. The staff of the Billy Rose Theatre Collection at the Lincoln Center Library for the Performing Arts, New York, were equally helpful.

The Film Study Center of the Museum of Modern Art, New York, is an important source of material, and Ron Magliozzi and Charles Silver opened files and answered questions that made my work there easier.

The State Historical Society, on the campus of the University of Wisconsin at Madison, houses the United Artists and Walter Wanger papers. Josephine Harper welcomed me to that library and provided much help.

At the Newberry Library, Chicago, the Ben Hecht papers were opened up for me by an efficient and helpful staff under the supervision of Diana Haskell, Curator of Manuscripts.

Invaluable historical data came to light with the help of David Mander, Archivist of the Vestry House Museum in the London borough of Waltham Forest. He also provided photographs of Victorian and Edwardian England.

Daniel M. Selznick graciously gave permission for the publication here of previously unavailable letters and memoranda of his father, David O. Selznick.

Peter Bogdanovich offered kind encouragement, and permitted me to cite extracts from his important 1963 interview with Hitchcock.

During my many travels, warm hospitality was provided by David Thuesen and Jerry Murra; Herbert and Mary Belle Coleman; and Nathan and Linda Bernstein Stark.

Professional support and encouragement have always come from Allen Austill, Dean of The New School for Social Research, New York. I am grateful to him, and to Elizabeth Coleman, Dean of Undergraduate Studies, to the faculty and staff of the Department of Film Studies, and to the students of that university, all of whom followed the course of my work with enthusiastic interest.

Those who wrote screenplays for Alfred Hitchcock were of course among my most important sources. I am deeply indebted for the time, memories, and materials shared with me by Jay Presson Allen, Charles

Bennett, Hume Cronyn, Howard Fast, David Freeman, John Michael Hayes, Evan Hunter, Arthur Laurents, Ernest Lehman, Brian Moore, Samson Raphaelson, Anthony Shaffer, Joseph Stefano, and Samuel Taylor.

Hitchcock's legion of actors included many who gladly spoke of their work with him. My thanks are offered for interviews with Peggy Ashcroft, Martin Balsam, Laurinda Barrett, Anne Baxter, Ingrid Bergman, Karen Black, Joseph Cotten, Hume Cronyn, Doris Day, Bruce Dern, William Devane, Marlene Dietrich, Mildred Dunnock, Jon Finch, Henry Fonda, Joan Fontaine, Barry Foster, Princess Grace of Monaco (Grace Kelly Grimaldi), Farley Granger, Barbara Harris, Tippi Hedren, Tom Helmore, Isabel Jeans, Janet Leigh, Barbara Leigh-Hunt, Margaret Lockwood, Alec McCowen, Karl Malden, Anna Massey, Vivien Merchant, Bernard Miles, Reggie Nalder, Paul Newman, Gregory Peck, Suzanne Pleshette, Claire Griswold Pollack, Elsie Randolph, Michael Redgrave, Eva Marie Saint, James Stewart, Jessica Tandy, Rod Taylor, Ann Todd, Billie Whitelaw, Josephine Wilson, and Teresa Wright.

Among Hitchcock's artistic and personal associates, I was very warmly received and helped by John Addison, Saul Bass, Robert Boyle, Henry Bumstead, Herbert Coleman, William Dozier, Suzanne Gauthier, Edith Head, Anna Lee, Peggy Robertson, Leonard South, Jack Whitehead, and Albert Whitlock.

At Saint Ignatius College, Enfield, the Reverend Anthony Forrester, S.J., devoted himself to helping me find records of Hitchcock's school days in London. He also enabled me to contact a classmate of Hitchcock's, the Reverend Robert Goold, whose keen memory provided invaluable material.

Others whose kindnesses should not go unacknowledged are Denise Abramson; M. Amaral; Robert Anderson; John Baisi, Norman Schneider, and the staff at Copy-Line, Incorporated; John Belton; Yvette Biro; Mel Brooks; Katherine Brown; Royal Brown; John Darretta; Robert DePietro; Clare Derick; Vincent de Sola; Anthony De Vito; David B. Eisendrath; Harry Grant-Whyte; David Griffith; Otis L. Guernsey, Jr.; Cheryl Hart; Jonathan Heap; David Henry; Mary Hoffman; Pippa Johnson; Gabrielle Kelly; Norman Lear; Irene Mahoney; John Maxtone-Graham; Colleen Mohyde; Marvin Paige; Richard Plant; Joan Pollak; Dilys Powell; Ira Progoff; C. J. Rhodes; M. E. Rhodes; Meade Roberts; Andrew Sarris; the Reverend Laurence Skelly, S. J.; Tony Slide; Mark Small; Eugene Stavis; Eric Storey; Suzanne Taylor; Kathy Tiddens; Alexander Walker; and Robert Wise.

My agent Elaine Markson and her associates Geri Thoma and Raymond Bongiovanni have been keen and affectionate guides in my career, and I am grateful for their constancy and confidence.

At Little, Brown, William Phillips is the kind of editor every author hopes to have — warmly supportive and gifted with rare creative insights. He offered not only his special skills but also his friendship, and that has made this enterprise uniquely joyful and rewarding. And Leslie Gardner, in London, brought me to the publishing firm of Collins, where Christopher MacLehose and Hilary Davies have been very gracious and enthusiastic.

From the beginning of my work, I was helped by my research assistant, Matthew Bernstein. He located out-of-print literary sources for the Hitchcock films, hunted down obscure manuscripts, and assisted in turning up material on Hitchcock's association with Walter Wanger.

Finally, and most of all, I owe to my friends more than words can express. In the blessings of love and trust and companionship I am daily sustained; no work, no achievement, no real life is possible without those gifts.

*D.S.*

New York
Easter Day, April 11, 1982

# The
# Dark Side
# of Genius

# One

---

March 1979

REPORTERS and photographers, movie fans and autograph-seekers and guests at the Beverly Hilton Hotel clustered in the lobby all afternoon, and by five-thirty on March 7, 1979, the desk clerks and bellmen were finding routine duties almost impossible. The hotel, at the intersection of Wilshire and Santa Monica boulevards in Beverly Hills, California, was fully booked, and all day there was an increasingly clear feeling that an important event was about to occur and to be recorded for posterity.

Throughout the afternoon, ten-foot stands supporting lights of enormous wattage were strategically placed from the front door of the hotel all the way to the entrance to the grand ballroom; miles of thick black cables linked generators to cameras to lights to control-consoles; taping and editing machines and microphones were uncrated and tested. Technical directors supervised carpenters and electricians; young men and women from the television studio were directing traffic indoors and out; and members of the dinner committee were making last-minute adjustments to the seating arrangement.

Fifteen hundred people were to attend the formalities that evening, and millions more, thanks to technology, were to watch a taped and edited version on television within the week. Inside the ballroom, one hundred fifty tables were set for a four-course dinner, and a stage had been constructed, with a speaker's podium and with great, looming photos of film stars in a variety of dramatic situations and settings.

At six o'clock, as if on cue, the first limousines drew up to the entrance of the hotel, and the curious onlookers — restrained by blue-coated guards and velvet ropes — strained to watch the parade of those who arrived for a $300-a-plate dinner. Like footmen at a royal banquet, several youngsters in the crowd called out the names of arriving guests; this was not entirely inappropriate, since a Hollywood gala has for a long time been the closest American parallel to the appearance of crowned heads. "It's James Stewart! . . . Ingrid Bergman! . . . Cary Grant!" — and Charlton Heston, Jane Wyman, Olivia de Havilland, Barbra Streisand, Michael Caine, Mel Brooks, Walter Matthau, Diana Ross, Christopher Reeve . . . The list comprised the venerable senior citizens of Hollywood and the newest faces of popular television series.

On that warm, dry evening the American Film Institute was going to present its seventh Life Achievement Award. Everyone awaited the arrival of the honored recipient, but as usual he sabotaged their expectations. He had been quietly escorted to the hotel much earlier in the day and had been settled in a seventh-floor suite.

The staff for the event was acutely anxious, for although they had announced Alfred Hitchcock as their choice in the autumn of 1978, he had for months refused to cooperate in the press arrangements and interviews, and had declined to help with the complex preparations involved in selecting film clips and sending special invitations to colleagues and actors. He had also refused to divulge his preferences about how to handle many crucial details regarding the taping. During January and February, he had his vital signs monitored professionally every other day — far more often than the once-a-week habit of the past forty years. With a heart pacemaker in place for almost five years, and with an undiminished appetite for undiluted alcohol, his concern for a quiet, private life was understandable. And he delayed any involvement with an event that might unsettle him.

"He looked on the evening as his own obituary," according to David Freeman, a writer working with Hitchcock at the time, "and he didn't want to attend the funeral." Although only one of the previous recipients was no longer living, there was for Hitchcock something final about a life-achievement award, something that marked him for the unspeakable reality of death — a reality he had tried to dispel, as if by sympathetic magic, in all his films. He did not want to allude, even by a celebration of his career, to his no-longer-remote decline. "He was seventy-nine years old and one hundred fifty pounds overweight," Freeman said. "He was at the end and he knew it. But he didn't want others to know it." Finally, days before the dinner, he reluctantly agreed to see representatives of the press and to answer questions from the Institute staff.

On the morning of March 7, Alma Reville Hitchcock, his wife and most frequent collaborator for fifty-three years, read in the *Los Angeles Times* that she was not expected to attend because, after several strokes, she was partly paralyzed and bedridden. Small and frail, she had always appeared even tinier when placed next to her husband's outsize girth, and her illnesses had indeed sapped her energy. But as she had for decades, she made a remarkable stubbornness serve her physically, and on the spot she decided to go; by afternoon the nurse at home had helped her to bathe and dress, and she was ready to depart long before a car was sent to their home, which was only a five-minute ride from the hotel.

Her husband had preceded her hours earlier, for everyone connected with the event agreed that he should read his acceptance speech for videotape cameras in the afternoon. The chance to edit, correct, and rearrange his remarks electronically would be thus guaranteed, and they could avoid the risk of evening exhaustion on Hitchcock's part. In addition, they knew he had to be kept away from strong drink if he were to get through the evening at all. In fact they were not entirely successful in that regard, in spite of their vigilance. A bellboy delivered a basket of champagne to his suite, and over the objections of studio executives who guarded him all day, he ordered the gift package brought in and opened.

The diners' first glimpse of Alfred Hitchcock that evening was, aptly, on screen — an image of Alfred Hitchcock as he had been a quarter-century earlier. Those in the ballroom of the Beverly Hilton and those who watched on national television five nights later saw at the outset a calm, middle-aged gentleman — alert, detached, just a bit stocky. His words — recited in his measured, almost emotionless monotone — were excerpted from an old black-and-white film clip from his television show, but they were perfectly suited to the occasion that March 7:

"Good evening, ladies and gentlemen — and welcome to darkest Hollywood. Night brings a stillness to the jungle. It is so quiet you can hear a name drop. The savage beasts have already begun gathering at the water holes to quench their thirst. Now one should be especially alert. The vicious table-hopper is on the prowl and the spotted backbiter may lurk behind a potted palm. . . ."

At the crowded tables in the International Ballroom, a wave of laughter rose; then, as the real Alfred Hitchcock was announced, a swell of applause greeted his slow emergence from a door near the stage. What they saw was not the genial television host, but a distraught and distracted man, obese and unsteady, slowly and painfully inching his way through the crowd to the table of honor. His evident discomfort was occasionally leavened by a wink toward someone he recognized, or aimed at an attractive woman.

He sat at his place, Alma at his right and Cary Grant at his left, and

he acknowledged with a bland nod the others at his table: Ingrid Bergman, who had starred in three of his movies; James Stewart, who like
Grant had been in four; Sidney Bernstein, whom he had known from
his earliest movie-making days in London; Lew Wasserman, for a long
time his agent and then the chief executive of the parent company for
which Hitchcock made his last six films. Throughout the dinner, the
guest of honor confided his few comments only to Alma. He sat and ate
and watched and replied briefly if a question was asked by a table-mate.
When approached by a visitor, he drew back as if a deadly fear gripped
him. He gave everyone the impression of wanting to be left alone to
observe the proceedings, and to admire the ladies.

He and fifteen hundred others were served as gracefully as speed allowed, for the tribute, the speeches, the film selections, and the award
presentation had to be got through, and taped, that evening. No one
could return for a retake next day, for the stage set would be dismantled
along with its huge photos, and all the guests would have departed.

By eight-thirty everything was ready for the show, and the taping
began. John Houseman, who had been a producer, writer, and actor in
a long career that once intersected Hitchcock's, introduced the mistress
of ceremonies, Ingrid Bergman. She set aside the designated script and
supervised the program with admirable spontaneity. Between selections
from his movies, she introduced an array of actors and writers and directors, as well as the British ambassador to the United States, each of
whom spoke with words of formal praise for Alfred Hitchcock's genius
as a filmmaker.

But when the cameras turned to record Hitchcock's reactions, there
was no response, no obvious emotion — just a blank stare. Nothing
appeared on the surface, and it was difficult to know what might be
beneath the affectless gaze. That evening he was the extreme of what
he had been to the public all his life — an enigma. In earlier years he
had joked more, but now, with the debilities caused by arthritis, heart
disease, and a fierce indulgence in food and drink, his tone was more
somber.

The detached look was no surprise to those who had been associated
with him for any length of time. He was a man whose truest feelings
and fears and yearnings, and even his ordinary daily reactions, were
hard to gauge, and rarely expressed directly. They were controlled, calculated, measured out for greatest effect with smallest effort. And the
deepest areas of his inner life were always refracted through the angles
and shadows of a film narrative, focused and concentrated in an alternating series of violent and tender images.

By 1979 he had perfected a small supply of familiar anecdotes that

satisfied the press — one or two about the painstaking methods he applied to preparing a film, one or two about practical jokes he liked to
play in the early days. Of his parents and his childhood he said almost
nothing apart from a story that gave a neat explanation for his many
films about a man unjustly accused of a crime. He told the anecdote
once again that evening, but his speech was too slow and erratic for the
editors to use anything but the afternoon version:

"When I was no more than six years of age, I did something that my
father considered worthy of reprimand. He sent me to the local police
station with a note. The officer on duty read it and locked me in a jail
cell for five minutes, saying, 'This is what we do to naughty boys.' I
have, ever since, gone to any lengths to avoid arrest and confinement.
To you young people my message is — Stay out of jail!''

This single childhood event, he insisted for years and years, inspired
a body of work with the recurring motif of fear of prison and enclosure,
about the terror of authority at home and abroad. Otherwise, a forest of
privacy darkened the grounds of his early years. In his adulthood, there
was always the cultivated image of the bourgeois gentleman — a simple
man, he seemed, with one wife and one daughter and one interest. But
like the taped speech that day, the image was a carefully edited illusion.

There were in fact many sides to Alfred Hitchcock's complex character. There was the visual poet of anxiety and accident who avoided
both, and who, according to many, deserves a place with Kafka and
Dostoevski and Conrad and Poe. There was the obsessed technician who
worked at the business of pure cinema, trying for over a half-century to
make popular but perfect motion pictures. There was the shameless im-
personator of an English burgher. There was the publicist who devoted
himself to the advancement of his own cause. There was the modest
family man who seemed to embody middle-class values even while he
traveled first class. There was the magician, dealing in lights and mirrors with a blithe hand and black humor. There was the chronicler of
unusual emotional states. There was the bully commercial tycoon and
the suffering artist.

His life was a relentless pursuit of the best food and wine and comfort
and collaborators, but it was also a restless search for the ideal woman
to worship, the perfect complement to the frustrated fat boy he always
considered himself. Showman and artist, gloomy isolate and amusing
raconteur, gentle romantic and stern manipulator, he had become a repository of everything contradictory in human nature. His feelings were
poured into the creation of startling images, his disarticulate longings
onto the lips of many different characters; and his strongest and truest
impulses — those that partook of the demonic and those of the di-

vine — were transmuted from the stuff of his own frustrated and contradictory life.

This partly explains why he was so reticent about that life, for a few
injudiciously mentioned facts could set people to following the clues. It
was better to tell a few jokes over and over, better to tell the neat
psychological explanation of the jail cell in childhood, better to give the
impression of a rigidly proper professional and private life, where
everything was as tidy as a film production schedule. Even the most
presumably charmed life is never *that* tidy, of course, and from the
beginning Alfred Hitchcock's was in fact riddled with disappointments,
unhappy surprises, interjections of chaos and of cruelty.

# Two

1899–1920

LEYTONSTONE, a district in London's East End, is five miles from
the center of the city. Situated on a gentle slope between Epping Forest
and the river Lea, it is a suburb of small stores and houses built mostly
between 1870 and 1910, and even before World War I it had quickly
and quietly taken on a shabby, exhausted appearance. In a typical family dwelling — a ground-floor shop with private quarters above — the
third child of William and Emma Hitchcock was born on Sunday, August 13, 1899.

Alfred Joseph Hitchcock, as he was soon christened, always claimed
that his family had been both East End greengrocers and Roman Catholics for centuries, but this is a somewhat typical exaggeration and sim-
plification. In fact, it is possible to trace his lineage clearly only from
the middle of the nineteenth century. Up to that time family and local
records were neither complete nor reliable. What can be firmly established is that on December 22, 1851, Alfred's paternal grandfather, the
son of Charles Hitchcock, a Stratford fisherman, was married in the
parish church of West Ham, the center of the East End market trade.
This Joseph Hitchcock, who gave his occupation as "general dealer,"
was in his father's employment. With uncles and friends they fished and
sold. The bride for that wedding was Miss Ann Mahoney, a Stratford
girl, daughter of a dayworker named Silvester Mahoney.

Several things are noteworthy about this marriage. The Irish-born bride
was at the time unemployed (1851 apparently being a difficult year for
immigrants to find even domestic work), and she was still illiterate: the
marriage certificate is marked with her $X$, and her name was inscribed
by the officiating curate, Edward Cridge. Joseph Hitchcock was apparently the only literate member of the wedding party, for even the family

friends who stood witness (the brothers Cornelius and Michael Queenland) marked the certificate and had to have their names inscribed by another. But what is even more interesting is that in fact Joseph Hitchcock married Ann Mahoney not in a Catholic church or chapel, but "according to the rites and ceremonies of the Established Church."

Since the Roman Catholic population of Essex was generally confined to Irish immigrants at the time, and since there is no record of a Hitchcock family enrolled in the Catholic parishes of Stratford, it seems that it was not Joseph Hitchcock who was marrying outside his religious faith, but rather his bride. The Hitchcocks were Church of England people. There are numerous precedents for a Catholic quietly marrying in an Anglican ceremony in England, and there was very often a good social reason to do so. When Miss Mahoney was wedded to Mr. Hitchcock at least one social stigma was removed.

Joseph and Ann Hitchcock (Alfred's future grandparents) remained in Stratford, where they took up residence in a small cottage on Windmill Lane and at once began a family — a rather large one, as it turned out. There were nine sons and daughters, and by the time the youngest was born, Joseph Hitchcock had attained the official status of "master greengrocer." The term does not imply any particular success or wealth: it simply indicates that the man was by this time self-employed and dealt in the wholesale and retail grocery trade. On September 4, 1862, the Hitchcocks' son William was born, and his mother marked the birth certificate a month later, still unable to write her own name. In Stratford this was not a cause for shame. Quite the contrary, since literacy was often considered a characteristic of the much-resented leisure class, and of those second-generation Irish who had risen above their station and forgotten their roots.

Not all of the Hitchcock children stayed in the family business. One of the girls, Emma Mary, married and emigrated to South Africa, where her husband — aptly named Cecil J. Rhodes (but unrelated to the noted financier) — settled into business and raised his family. But one son, John, and eventually his wife Sophie were involved in the grocery enterprise at least for a time; and it was William, Alfred's father, who finally took over the business. By the 1880s it was operating from a storefront in Forest Gate, still part of the district of West Ham, Essex.

At this point the Catholic influence that was not felt by the marriage of Joseph Hitchcock to Ann Mahoney was for the first time activated, and apparently in all its fierce Irish splendor. Emma Jane Whelan, the daughter of literate, second-generation Irish parents, had grown up at 4 John Street in West Ham. Her father, John Whelan, was not only Irish and Catholic but also — and this made him especially unpopular in his

home area — a policeman, as her birth certificate indicates. Cock-
neys — the East End working class — traditionally hated and mocked
policemen because they saw them as defenders of a system that exploited the poor and the workers to make the rich and the privileged
more comfortable. In addition, police and detectives regularly abused
their powers, intimidated street folk, and were guilty of open bribery
and corruption.

At the age of twenty-four William Hitchcock married this Emma Jane
Whelan (a year his junior) in a Roman Catholic ceremony at the Church
of Saint Antony of Padua, Khedive Road, Upton. The officiating priest,
the Reverend Alfred McLaughlin, was also part of the local Irish community, as were William and Emma's witnesses, their friends William
Wilfred Trench and his wife Mary Josephine. Henceforth, the Hitchcocks would be firmly Catholic, and the laxity of Ann Mahoney Hitchcock would be corrected. Mrs. William Hitchcock and her parents, the
Whelans, would see to that, and the influence was strongly felt on at
least the youngest of their three children.

"Ours was a Catholic family," Alfred Hitchcock said years later,
"and in England, you see, this is in itself an eccentricity. I had a strict,
religious upbringing. . . . I don't think I can be labeled a Catholic
artist, but it may be that one's early upbringing influences a man's life
and guides his instinct. . . . I am definitely not anti-religious; perhaps
I'm sometimes neglectful." The emotional alchemy of early influence
and adult "neglect" would not only mark his work but also the major
pains and problems of his declining years.

William and Emma Hitchcock moved back to Stratford to find a suitable place to enlarge the grocery business and begin a family. After
three years of marriage, a boy, also christened William, was born in
1890, at their house at 29 Louise Road; and in the same room, on
September 14, 1892, there followed a girl they named Ellen Kathleen
but who was always known as Nellie. In 1896 the family moved to 517
The High Road, Leytonstone, leasing the modest premises from a grocer who retired to the quieter Chichester Road. By 1899, when Alfred
Joseph was born, the store had been somewhat enlarged and fronted the
family quarters: they lived behind and over the crates and shelves of
produce, and unless they went around through a back alley to a small
rear door, they had to pass through the shop to reach the family rooms.
In the middle of a small, dark, and unsuccessful garden was the family
outhouse. Privacy was even rarer than silence or sustained sunshine.

Life at 517 The High Road was a quiet rhythm of work for the parents and relative solitude for the youngest child, whose older brother

and sister were already packed off to school and with whom he would never develop any relationship at all. His father worked long hours in the grocery, supervising two and sometimes three assistants, as well as the multiple daily deliveries — some destined for retail sale to the people of Leytonstone, some sold wholesale and carted off to Covent Garden. Meager incomes and a bumper crop of potatoes in the early years of the century made that food the staple for local tables as well as for the market deliveries, and the Hitchcocks, like many middle-class English families, depended on potatoes for a cheap, filling, and nutritious (if somewhat monotonous) diet. Everyone who ever dined with Alfred Hitchcock knew that (except when he was on an unusually rigorous diet) potatoes accompanied every dinner. They were variously boiled, baked, double-baked, and — in later years, when he suffered some dental problems — mashed.

William Hitchcock, Sr., according to his youngest son, was a typical Cockney merchant who insisted on discipline, order, and simplicity in life as in diet. Some idea of the strictness of Alfred's upbringing and the ambivalence of his feelings are confirmed by the prison-cell story he told the press, colleagues, writers, and actors for decades. If the account is true, then William Hitchcock had an oddly cruel streak, no matter the offense for which the child was to be corrected. It is possible that behind the story are Alfred's mother and her father, the shadowy figure of the grandfather-policeman, but about this one can do no more than guess. Throughout his life, Hitchcock insisted that his brief boyhood jailing scarred him for life with a terror of the police, and he pointed to the recurring motif in his work of the innocent man, arrested and imprisoned, as an attempt to exorcise the childhood trauma.

But Alfred Hitchcock was always a master of the red herring, and he told interviewers just what they wanted to hear — a neat psychological explanation, connected to a facile anecdote, to justify a frequent plot device. He may also have invented the story quite naturally, given his Cockney family background in a society that hated policemen ("It must be said to my credit that I never wanted to be a policeman," he said years later).

The imprisonment story is, then, impossible to corroborate, impossible to negate, and it may have at its base a family incident involving some kind of punishment that, as a child, Hitchcock thought extreme and that his fantasy at once enlarged. But the anecdote certainly does tell what he *felt* about his father and the sting of memory that his childhood had inflicted. If the incident actually happened as he said, then his father certainly had a strange sense of correcting his son. If the account is pure Hitchcockian fiction, one is still left with an adult's impressions of his father and his childhood — or, at the least, the impressions of fear and guilt he wanted people to believe he endured.

Guilt, of course, is the predominant theme of Hitchcock's films. It derives not only from the complexities of his own inner life: guilt is also one of the great themes in all art, and especially in contemporary art and literature. When this theme is connected to some experience of a religious tradition, the situation and characters are informed with a rare human intensity. With Catholic artists as different as England's Graham Greene and Japan's Shusaku Endo, Hitchcock shared an intuition that one can, in the last analysis, be freed from corruption only *by* guilt — by standing condemned and accepting forgiveness and redemption freely or enduring punishment and hoping for a second chance. Such artists stand apart from the heady healthy-mindedness of our time that insists on the denial of all spiritual guilt; they resist the modern era's attempt to dismiss all moral responsibility as an infraction of manners, or as psychosis — or as a blunder along any less extreme part of the spectrum.

The Hitchcock household was not, it seems, very different from that of other working-class Cockney Catholics. Mr. and Mrs. Hitchcock called the boy Fred, which he detested and which was replaced with the even more repellent nickname "Cocky" in school. Once he was able to announce himself, rather than suffer an introduction by his parents, he would call himself "Hitch," which he preferred even before he met his future wife (who took credit for the nickname for years after).

Hitchcock's father, at the age of forty, began to decline in health. This, added to the natural predominance of mothers in the East End homes, the doting affection with which Mrs. Hitchcock surrounded her youngest child, and the apparently contradictory sternness of her Irish Catholic background, made inevitable the centrality of Alfred's mother in the boy's life. According to a cousin, Emma Hitchcock was "a smartly dressed, sedate person, very quietly spoken and with an aristocratic manner. She was very meticulous when preparing a meal, at which she was very good. She would not venture out of her room unless neatly, perfectly dressed, and she quietly conducted her affairs in a dignified manner."

Hitchcock himself only rarely referred to his mother — outside his films — and when he did so in conversation it was only in the briefest and most general way. We do know, however, that later she often accompanied her son — even in his adult life — on holidays with his wife, and that on these occasions he felt more compelled to satisfy her whims than to attend to his wife's comfort.

The town hall of Leyton was the place for weekend dances, and Alfred had to chaperone his sister Nellie. This could not have been a comfortable assignment for either of them: the practice began when she was fifteen and he was eight. The hours of such entertainments were carefully parceled out, and their father awaited their return at the prescribed hour. Uppermost in his mind was his duty to protect his children from bad influence. But if father watched the clock and set down the rules for socializing, mother gathered to herself the greater parcel of time.

Each evening, on his return to the house — whether from school or a dance or a stroll along The High Road — Alfred was made to stand at the foot of his mother's bed and answer her detailed questions about the business of the day with detailed replies. "It was something she always had me do. It was a ritual. I always remember the evening confession," he recalled fifty years later. This became something of a hallowed tradition and persisted even through the years after he left school and was employed in central London. It tells us something about the degree of their psychological intimacy, although there seems something overwhelming about it, something too intimate, a devotion exacted by a mother whose interest in her son's life imprisons rather than frees, investigates rather than encourages — and inculcates guilt of a scrupulous and neurotic type.

Yet whatever Emma Hitchcock's own needs might have been, they were complemented by those of her son. If she asked and gave too much, it might have been because of Alfred's own enormous needs and insecurities — needs and insecurities mysteriously present, in his own mind, from the beginning, and for which his parents, like any parents, are not entirely responsible.

Asked if he was ever really frightened about anything, Hitchcock would reply simply: "Always!" — and the brevity of the reply and the insistence with which he changed the topic are clues to the large truth of it. Any easy explanation of his dark fears, of his deep sense of dread, that would trace everything back to a single childhood incident (or even to a pattern of incidents) would also have to explain the talent that enabled him to transform real, imagined, desired, and dreaded experience into art. But human psychology is never simple. There is no doubt, however, that *he* traced a large dose of this fear back to his early years.

"Fear? It has influenced my life and my career. I remember when I was five or six. It was a Sunday evening, the only time my parents did not have to work. They put me to bed and went to Hyde Park for a stroll" — a considerable distance from The High Road, Leytonstone, one might add: at least an hour and a half each way by tram and train in the early 1900s. "They were sure I would be asleep until their return.

But I woke up, called out, and no one answered. Nothing but night all around me. Shaking, I got up, wandered around the empty, dark house and, finally arriving in the kitchen, found a piece of cold meat which I ate while drying my tears.''

How did this incident affect Hitchcock? Certainly by imparting a lifetime fear of being alone or in darkness; certainly by inflicting a terror — quite understandable, considering East End life at the turn of the century — that something deadly, unexpected, had happened or could happen; that his family had abandoned him or that he was prey to intruders. But the memory also indicates that he knew, even if subconsciously, that food could be his comfort against solitude — an association that has become in recent times a self-evident truth to both doctors and dieters alike.* And the link between suspense and food was acknowledged by Hitchcock himself in a curious analogy: "I've known fear since my childhood. . . . I myself hate suspense, and that's why I would never allow anyone to make a soufflé at my home: my oven has no glass door! We'd have to wait forty minutes to find out if the soufflé turned out right, and that is more than I could stand!'' As in his films, so in his life: the fundamental comparison with terror is the proper preparation of food, and the basic sign of unease is nausea.

As Roman Catholics, the Hitchcocks took their boy regularly to Sunday mass. Curiously, however, they did not attend the local churches or chapels, which were conveniently located. In nearby Leyton, there was Saint Agnes's Orphanage and School Chapel, Church Road, which was open to the public on Sundays; in Walthamstow there was Saint George's, Shernhall Street; and even closer, in the heart of Leytonstone, was Saint Joseph's, Vicarage Road. But Mrs. Hitchcock would have nothing to do with them, and young Alfred rode the few miles down to Stratford, to her own former parish church, Saint Francis. Mother's priests and mother's church would minister to the spiritual needs of her boy.†

At Saint Francis the Catholic ritual impressed the boy. "I was always interested in ceremonial,'' he recalled. "I once bribed a master of ceremonies at a high Mass to let me be an acolyte. Which he did. But what

---

*Conversely, for Hitchcock, being deprived of food was almost catastrophic. He often told of watching, unobserved, while his mother transferred a delicacy from his Christmas stocking to his sister's and replaced it with a mere piece of fruit.

†It was there that he saw, maybe for the first time, the romantic statues and images of Saint Francis, preaching to and taming the wild birds with gentle eloquence.

Perhaps this is behind an odd moment in *Strangers on a Train*, when the daffy mother shows her murderous son a grotesque figure that reminds him of his father. "But I was trying to paint Saint Francis!'' she protests.

I found out as soon as the Mass started was that I hadn't learned, or attempted to learn, the responses to the priest. It was only my childish anxiety to be a ceremonial figure.'' (Later Hitchcock would be able to gratify his desire to be part of the show without having to learn any lines: the famous Hitchcock wordless walk-on in his films became one of his magnificent methods of self-advertisement and a universally appreciated joke.) But if in later life he would admit to being "neglectful" of religious ritual, he certainly did not dare to be as long as he was in his family's care.

From his earliest years, Alfred Hitchcock was a loner and a watcher, an observer rather than a participant. "I don't remember ever having a playmate," he recalled as an adult. At family gatherings: "I would sit quietly in a corner, saying nothing. I looked and observed a great deal. I've always been that way and still am. I was anything but expansive. I was a loner — can't even remember having had a playmate. I played by myself, inventing my own games.''

The games seemed to have consisted mostly of map and timetable study, some reading (mostly about travel), and some wandering (mostly along the piers and quays of London when he accompanied his father for deliveries). By the time he was eight he had ridden every tram line in London and had taken the river steamers to the mouth of the Thames at Gravesend. At home he constructed a huge wall chart showing the positions each day of virtually every British ship afloat. When he was not charting these courses and checking them in the newspapers, he would thumb through magazines or amuse himself with a book called *Plotto,* which was divided into three flip-over sections so the aspiring writer could make up and then rearrange his own plot lines.

But most of all he loved timetables — "as literature,'' he said. Perhaps they corresponded to his training in tidiness and orderliness, everything regulated and on schedule; and perhaps, too, they corresponded to a wish to be somewhere else.

When he was seven it was time to think of school, but for some reason that may never be known, this was delayed — whether because of childhood illness or fear is impossible to say, and in any case the dates of entrance and departure were more flexible then. At home he continued to study timetables, and astonished his family by reciting from memory the schedules of most of England's train lines. In 1906 the electric tram was added to the horse tram in Leytonstone, and there was a great complicated junction just at the foot of The High Road. Crowds formed quickly here as the trams arrived and departed, and neighborhood children outguessed each other on the timing and distance and delays of the various lines.

Alfred's father continued to use the horsecart for deliveries to local customers and merchants, and frequently father and son loaded the cart and climbed aboard for a day's outing. Even when motorcars began to rumble through London and its boroughs, these horsecarts endured — an anachronism as awkward and dangerous as it was later thought charming. As a director, Hitchcock would insert these memories of his childhood into his films (even when they seemed ridiculously unsuited to a modern setting and were in fact no longer to be found); in *Stage Fright* the police are conveniently delayed by a passing merchant in horsecart, and a grocer's goods spill to the road as the horses go wild amid a fire in *The Birds*.

The passive observance of local life, the habit of watching rather than participating in children's outdoor games, the solitary child's inventive ways to amuse himself — these were the habits that helped to develop an active inner life, a life of fantasy. And an active inner life made it difficult for Alfred to be accepted by his peers, with whom he could share none of his fears and dreams. Even at school, he was a visually oriented child at a time when English society was insistently literary. Added to this, as a Cockney child he was, ironically, part of a subgroup (and the Catholic Cockney was an even smaller subgroup) that rigorously avoided the articulation of feelings.

But young Hitchcock confronted those unspoken feelings in other people's literary descriptions and dialogues. This may in part explain why he later always felt compelled to ask expert dialogue writers to give the proper expression to scenes he had already visualized completely in his own mind down to the last glance and gesture and detail. It may also explain why he was not given to much letter-writing; his letters were usually cryptic and formal and brief. His natural reticence and his Catholic-Cockney avoidance of emotional display made him shun demonstrations of any strong feeling — although those feelings were certainly unleashed in his films. "There the fantasist was set free," as one of his collaborating writers said.

This reticence, combined with physical fear, was perhaps accountable for the fact that Alfred Hitchcock, young or old, never took exercise. "I never walk when I can ride. My exertion is all from the neck up," he once boasted. "I watch." And so it was quite natural for him to become a filmmaker: film gave him control over situations and at the same time satisfied the desire to watch.

Leytonstone was thick with young athletes — Cockney boys playing cricket and lacrosse and football, and entering races in the cycling clubs, but Alfred took part in none of these. He was content with his books and his games, and especially with his mother's close and constant companionship. His life was safe, quiet, withdrawn — and friendless. The pattern increased with the years.

There were family outings, however — usually to the theater. The family loved theater, but Hitchcock later allowed that "we must have been a rather eccentric little group," and eventually he went, even to first nights, alone. As he grew older his attendance was more frequent. He loved to admire from the stalls the beauty and talent and posture of actors and actresses whom he would later engage for his own films and entertain with lavish dinner parties in order to be accepted into what he considered their polite and exciting world.

One of Hitchcock's earliest memories, in fact, was of a play he saw in 1905. The villain took the stage bathed in a green light, accompanied by sinister orchestra music. The heroine was, on the other hand, glorified by rose-colored lights, and he remembered the uncanny beauty that the stage could effect. "I remember the green light — green for the appearances of ghosts and villains."

Not all the popular theatrical or vaudeville entertainments of that time were mysteries or productions of Shakespeare or historical melodramas or premieres of new plays by Shaw. There was a good deal of rough-and-tumble comedy, spiced with a healthy dash of iconoclasm and suburban vulgarity. *Humanity,* a short play performed numerous times in variety theaters between 1900 and 1920, may well have been seen by Hitchcock in one of its East End versions, for in it there is a direct antecedent to one of the most famous scenes in his British films.* In the play, a quarrel between two rich gentlemen ends in the smashing of all the furniture in several elegant rooms. Working-class people watched the scene with a mixture of incredulity and amusement: it was a moment of shocking prodigality, and it gratified the audience's desire to see a little impropriety among those who were supposedly their betters.

The contrast between manners and mockery so evident in the common vaudeville entertainment is in fact a perfect reflection of the struggle that existed in Hitchcock's society and in his personal world. As a clever, lonely boy, pampered by a doting mother, he was caught between the Victorian world of class and privilege and the Cockney's inbred resentment of that world. A child of the East End who was not destitute but who was also not socially respectable, he was caught, too, between a desire for respectability and luxury on the one hand and, on

---

*The play was a great favorite of English schoolboys and general audiences from 1910 to 1920. If Hitchcock did in fact see it, it may have partly inspired the original (1934) version of *The Man Who Knew Too Much,* where there is a comic-violent scene of table and chair smashing in a nonconformist chapel.

the other, the carefully taught Catholic sense that respectability and luxury were not sufficient for happiness.

Toward the end of 1907 the Hitchcocks made plans to move from
Leytonstone. Their older son, William — described by a cousin as "a
well built man, always smartly dressed" — was ready to make a life of
his own, and it would not be long before Nellie would take the first of
two husbands. In addition, the heart of Mr. Hitchcock's business (now
enlarged to include a fishery) had shifted to the heart of the Cockney
world — to Poplar, a section of the East End that would suffer dreadful
bombings in the great wars to come. The relocation also allowed for the
education of Alfred. The Howrah House Convent, Poplar, enjoyed a
solid reputation for training boys and girls, and the Hitchcocks could
afford its modest fees.

Leytonstone and Poplar were distinctly and proudly middle-class
communities, but in Poplar being Cockney was more than a characteristic: it was a definition of personality and attitude. Poplar was smaller
and more crowded than Leytonstone, and the move threw the boy into
a crush of common humanity. Later Hitchcock would draw on that experience to enliven even the smallest roles — as well as the visual fabric — of his British films.

In the two districts of his childhood, he was a commoner among
commoners, but theater, then schoolbooks and movie magazines — and
very soon the cinema itself — showed him a different world, one with
which he was not entirely comfortable: a world of glamour and charm
and education and social grace, a world for which he always longed but
from which he would feel forever excluded. After two years in Poplar,
the family relocated again, this time to nearby Stepney, where at the
age of eleven the boy entered a new and often frightening environment.

Saint Ignatius College, Stamford Hill, London, was founded in 1894
by the Jesuits who staffed the parish church of the same name. By the
time Hitchcock was enrolled, as one of the 250 day students in the fall
class of 1910, the school was already widely known for the traditional
Jesuit insistence on order, discipline, and a rigorous curriculum.*

School records are incomplete for those early years — not because
the administrators were lax about files, but because the school was evac-
uated during the London bombings of the wars and a great deal of early
material was destroyed or lost. But the admissions register has survived,
and "Alfred Hitchcock, son of William Hitchcock, Fishmonger" is listed
as number 343 in volume two of the school's entrance file. Apart from

---

*Saint Ignatius was never, as some have thought, a boarding schoool.

the boy's dates of admission (October 5, 1910) and departure (July 25, 1913), there are only two items that official records tell about him. One concerns an academic honor he received in 1911; the other is a curious discrepancy about his date of birth — August 13, 1900, according to the admission book. It seems that this was not a slip of the pen or a secretary's error in copying a birth record. Apparently the Hitchcocks deliberately enrolled their son as a ten-year-old instead of an eleven-year-old. "The reason could only have been," according to a later headmaster, "that the boy was a year behind his classmates for some reason — illness perhaps, or a delay in entering the primary school.* In any case, he certainly did not want to be singularized as special — older and perhaps thought to be slow in the lower grades. The easiest thing was just to falsify his age." The exact reason for this odd fabrication will never be known, but certainly behind it is the Cockney appreciation for being one of the crowd, which prompted the Hitchcocks to take precautions against anything that might single out their boy for question or ridicule.

Alfred's first day at Saint Ignatius was a Wednesday (the senior boys had been admitted earlier in the week). The first activity of the first day of term was a visit to the church, a Victorian-Romanesque building that has hardly changed in almost a century. This initiation, as any child discovered at once, set the tone for everything that would follow, both in the classroom and in the schoolyard — and that tone could not accurately be described as cheerful. As the boys marched into the twin-spired, red-brick church and recited prayers for the success of the school year, what they saw (when their eyes became accustomed to the darkness) could easily depress any group of fidgety children. For like many English Roman Catholic churches, the interior was damp and gloomy and gave the impression that the religious life is not a happy pursuit.

The students gazed toward a cluttered sanctuary and side chapels with wall mosaics depicting a blank-faced Christ Triumphant. Below him, in orderly array, stood the company of the English saints and martyrs and the Church Fathers of the first centuries. The main altar, beyond the white marble communion rail that separated the congregation from the clergy, was embellished with a baroque delirium of winged angels; and from a Gothic reredos peeped the Jesuit saints Ignatius, Francis Xavier, and the young Aloysius Gonzaga, who died very young and very pure and was held up to the students as a model of piety and, above all, chastity ("the angelic virtue," as the teachers called it). Votive candles flickered along the right sidewalls, partially illuminating dark paintings

---

*Earlier, as mentioned, the Hitchcock's had indeed failed to enroll Alfred in school at the prescribed age of seven.

and yet more statues, casting over the interior of the church a dreamlike haze, and enlarging the shadows of the priests who paced back and forth, urging the boys to kneel up straight. A little natural light was filtered in through plain gray windows that were always coated with a layer of chalky grime.

But if the tenebrous waxworks solemnity reflected the common iconography of English Roman Catholic piety, what the students saw on the left wall indicated its moral rigor. A series of narrow, slightly pointed doors opened to the confessional booths, with the priests' names posted above. FATHER VAUGHAN, one of the signs announced in 1910, and another identified where the boys could find Father Newdigate — a famous and influential prefect of studies, a scholarly, serious man who traced his Catholic family for several centuries of English history.

There were students ranging in age from ten to seventeen at Saint Ignatius, and for the privilege of attending they had to pass an entrance test that selected only the highest achievers to receive letters of acceptance: just 25 percent of those who applied were admitted. The fee of three guineas would be, by the standards of seventy years later, about sixty pounds. A few of the less wealthy but more gifted boys were provided scholarship grants. For Alfred Hitchcock, there is no record of such exemption from tuition fees in the spaces provided on the admissions register.

The boys in the upper school with Hitchcock were led, under Father Newdigate's supervision, in a course of studies that was relentlessly demanding. The curriculum included Religious Knowledge, Latin, English, French, German, history, literature, geography, mathematics, natural science, drawing, essay, elocution, and choir. Report cards also graded the students on "conduct and application." It was a full schedule, and those who could not keep pace with the assignments were summoned, sometimes with their parents, to Father Newdigate's office and informed that their places at Saint Ignatius could not be guaranteed unless there was a swift and major improvement in academic standing. Ordinarily, a short conversation with the prefect achieved the desired effect. If not, or if the boy was guilty of poor conduct or several incomplete assignments, punishment could be exacted more swiftly.

Discipline in Roman Catholic schools has always attracted the scorn of liberals and the approval of conservatives. That it was for the most part based on a philosophy of "Spare the rod and spoil the child" — especially in the nineteenth and first half of the twentieth century, and especially in Europe — is widely known, even to those who have not read the more detailed accounts of it (for example, in the writings of James Joyce). Students who experienced even only once the penalty for a serious infraction of the rules of conduct or academic performance never forgot it. But colorful literary accounts have given a distorted image of the system of punishment. Many people have the mistaken notion that daily beatings or canings were the compensation merely for an incorrect answer to a teacher's question, when in fact corporal punishment was dispensed only for consistent failure or notorious recalcitrance. An old guidebook for the Jesuit schools comments on an earlier model and seems to show that, at least by the early twentieth century, the Jesuits leavened discipline with a certain wry humor:

### The Question of Punishment.

No one who understands children will undervalue the importance of corporal punishment. It is healthy and English. We read in a pre-Reformation instruction book some tonic advice to parents and guardians in regard to children who are troublesome. The writer says:

*"If any child be stiff-hearted, stubborn and froward, and if it be within age, let it be surely whysked with a good rod. And if the person be of forther age and past such correction let them have such sharp and grievous punishment as conveniently may be devised, as to sit at dinner alone and by themselves at a stool with only brown bread and water and every person in order to rebuke them as they would a thief and a traitor. I would not advise nor counsel any parent to keep such a child in their house without great affliccyon and punishment"* (*Christian Family Life in Pre-Reformation Days,* by Cardinal Gasquet).

For lesser faults the writer suggests "a gentle whysking." We do not urge quite such a spartan discipline in these days.

### The Rule in all Jesuit Colleges

is an excellent one, and might be recommended to the Board of Education, namely, that the Teacher who sentenced the child to punishment never administers it. There can be no fear of excess or anger. Correction should be calm, inevitable and dignified, in other words, "Justice."

### The Teacher's Temper

It's one thing to have money and another to lose it, and it's the same with one's temper. Loss of temper always means loss of power. The vast power of the locomotive is its pent-up steam — held in with such terrific restraint.

That shrieking, deafening whistle is the engine letting off steam and means loss of power. So it is with our temper. The Head Teacher should be calm, disciplined, patient, orderly and absolutely refined in thought, word and deed. When the furious virago — some unkempt parent — comes to the school to give the Teacher "a piece of her mind," receive her calmly, firmly and, rebuked, let her depart.

The teachers who followed this counsel certainly exerted influence on the Hitchcock boy, for the description could be literally applied to the filmmaker Alfred Hitchcock in his dealings with actors, staff, and colleagues, both on and off the movie set: "Loss of temper always means loss of power. The vast power of the locomotive is its pent-up steam — held in with such terrific restraint " It was precisely that detached calm, that monotonic temper that gave Alfred Hitchcock a manner and appearance — and a power — so different from the typical blustering mogul.

In spite of popular misconception and literary celebration, the discipline young Alfred was exposed to was not extraordinary. "In fact," recalled the Reverend Robert Goold, one of Hitchcock's schoolmates, "the discipline was quite fair, never really harsh. It was certainly strict, but in fact all of English life was strict — at home, in the shops and streets and public gathering places, and at school. A bit of the strap on the right hand was not unusual or cruel punishment, and I don't think any of us really thought we were badly treated. When punishment was exacted it was carried out swiftly and fairly — and, just as the guidebook said, never by the teacher who had assigned it. This assured that his anger would not intensify the appropriate punishment."

There is no doubt, however, that for many students (especially the sensitive ones who might not have been punished at home), even the remotest possibility of being summoned for corporal punishment induced a mortal terror. It was certainly such a specter for Alfred Hitchcock. More than a half-century later he told a student at Saint Ignatius:

The method of punishment, of course, was highly dramatic because the form master would tell the pupil of his wrongdoing and the pupil would have to go before the disciplining priest. It was left to the pupil to decide when he would go for the punishment, and of course he would keep putting it off. And then at the end of the day he would go to a special room where there would be a priest or lay brother who would administer the punishment — like, in a minor way, going for execution. I think it was a bad thing. It was not like they give boys the cane in other schools. This was a rubber strap. If by chance you had gone as bad as to be sentenced to shall we say twelve, you would have to spread it over two days because each hand could take only three strokes, as it became numb.

There were always warnings in school — warnings against laziness and warnings against frivolity were common English practice (just as corporal punishment was "healthy and English") — and within four weeks of Alfred's arrival he and his schoolmates read religious essays reminding them of the gravity of their lives as students. In November 1910 they heard a stern reminder: "With the various signs of frivolity all around us in the shape of skating rinks, pictures palaces and music halls, it is perhaps time that the towers of our church should begin to rise as representation of the serious side of life."

Lectures and sermons like this were usually followed by discussions on appropriate conduct, and it could not have been easy for Alfred to admit, nor to deny, his family's excursions to places of public amusement. For if the Hitchcocks' private life was certainly not frivolous — mainly concerned as it was with the father's business and his failing health — the family did attend music-hall performances, and the boy was permitted to go to the short films screened several afternoons each week at the skating rinks, where most movies were shown while the cinemas were being constructed. If he told the truth about this at school, he would be warned about "the spirit of the world"; if he lied, he would have to bear the burden of guilt for lying. "If you've been brought up by the Jesuits, as I was, these elements are bound to intrude," he explained. "I was terrified of the police, of the Jesuit Fathers, of physical punishment, of a lot of things. This is the root of my work. . . . But if you examine my films, I daresay you'll find very few where wrong has the ascendancy."

The required reading that helped to form Alfred Hitchcock's education and imagination in 1910/1911 included Dickens's *Great Expectations* and *A Tale of Two Cities,* and particular attention was paid to *Bleak House,* a novel that seems to have engraved itself on Hitchcock's memory. More than a simple treatment of political corruption and the injustices of the legal system (which the young Dickens and his family had experienced firsthand), *Bleak House* details a grim distrust in any public institution. This same sort of cynicism informs Hitchcock's films, where statesmen and judges and lawyers and policemen are venal, small-minded, driven by the most intense lust and greed, and not much better than the apparent villains. In addition to Dickens there were Walter Scott's *Ivanhoe* and the tragedies of Shakespeare — with large sections to be memorized for class recitation. Immediately after the Christmas holiday, the students sat through two performances of *Richard II,* performed by the senior boys, and studied the text in class. The tale of theft, imprisonment, murder, and penance not only provided the form masters with plenty of material for moral injunction but also helped to form Hitchcock's own sense of moral drama.

Alfred's first year at Saint Ignatius seems to have been devoted exclusively to studies, for the Distinction List singles out A. Hitchcock, in

form 1B, as third among six who received general honors. The report
was sent to his parents on July 24, 1911, and became a matter of public
record for the borough when the news was published in the parish bulletin the following month. The citation was for achievement in Latin,
English, French, and religious education — the major subjects, taught
by the form master.

In August 1911 Alfred Hitchcock observed his twelfth birthday. Four
days earlier, the temperature at Greenwich was 100 degrees, and workers fell at their benches and pedestrians fell in the streets. The incidence
of disease among the poor tripled overnight. Children fared especially
badly that summer, but Alfred thrived at home, content with his books
and his games and his school prize.

In November the superior of the Jesuit community, Father Donnelly,
announced on Prize Day that a major expansion of the school building
was to begin the following spring. The boys were asked to pray for the
success of this enterprise. Meantime, he reminded them, the term's work
summoned them once again to rigorous application of all their mental
powers: seven plays by Shakespeare would be read in the first three
months, and large selections from the American poet Longfellow, together with his translation of Dante's *Divine Comedy.*

Alfred's boyish frame was filling out quickly. "I remember him,"
schoolmate Robert Goold recalled, "as a solidly built dumpling of a
boy with a ruddy, smiling face and a mischievous capacity for getting
into trouble." Just how much mischief, and how much trouble, Goold
would not know until the following year, but right from the start Hitchcock impressed him as "a lonely fat boy who smiled and looked at you
as if he could see straight through you."

At school that year the students attended concerts of music by Bizet
and Mozart and Johann Strauss, and the winter term began with a detailed study of *Robinson Crusoe,* a book which certainly must have appealed to Alfred's wanderlust. With the Lenten season, a series of sermons and lectures was prepared for the boys and parishioners. The first
of these, dated February 1912, was called "Dread of Sin." It gives a
clear idea of the moral suspicions, the obsession with crime and sex,
sin and death, that characterized Hitchcock's spiritual background.

A true horror of sin is not natural to mankind in general. Of the vices of
others we have always a sufficient dread; the judgment of our own is apt to be
a very kindly and merciful one. Other men's crimes fill us with a certain fear,
because they may and sometimes do affect our personal safety. Few men need
to be convinced of the exceeding sinfulness of murder and theft, or of some

breaches of the sixth and ninth commandments. . . . But even men and women who are well instructed do not always succeed in exercising a true dread of sin. . . . We are expected to take supernatural views, and if we fail to do so we are, very rightly, condemned. So long as we take the worldling's view of vice we imperil our own souls and the souls of others.

This first Lenten sermon — virtually a moral outline for the collection of Hitchcock's scenarios — was followed by others hardly more jolly or positive in tone: on March 10 the weekly meditation for the students was on "Sin and the Justice of God"; on March 17, on "Sin and the Majesty of God"; on March 24, on "Sin and the Christian"; and on March 31, on "Sin and the Passion of Christ," which was intended to lead the hearers directly to a consideration of the Lord's death on Good Friday and the celebration of Easter. At the same time, a new book arrived at Saint Ignatius and was widely circulated — *Cases of Conscience for English-Speaking Countries*. It was by an American Jesuit named Father Slater, and it was instantly hailed as an important handbook on practical morality. The school purchased a dozen copies of the seven-shilling guide.

Such a typically nineteenth-century view of morality, with its strong emphasis on sin, was not, of course, proclaimed only to those who followed the rigidities of English Roman Catholicism. Boys throughout the empire were hearing similar sermons, with appropriate adjustments made for the denominational preference of the school. The British sense of propriety and "good form" demanded ethical conduct even from those who were unsure whether there was a judging and demanding God. Much less did anyone seem to consider that authentically free and mature morality derives not from fear of God or of man, but from the primacy of love. Artists and writers and even the man in the street admitted that moral values were certainly changing very quickly, and some people were questioning the old truths about what was right and wrong. The questions would have a forum not only in liberal meeting halls and university dormitories but, in the aftermath of the horrors of the World War, in the drawing rooms of Chelsea and Hampstead and Holland Park.

But the official English ethic — if it is not too schematic to speak of a common denominator in so vast and shifting a culture — was still, in 1912, a morality based on scriptural laws, the Commandments, the law of the realm, and the accepted convention of vigilance over the passions — especially sexual passion. Nice people honored the king, refrained from stealing, murder, fornication, lustful thoughts, lying, and drunkenness, and they had a positive horror of bad table manners. It

was taken for granted that there was an inevitable downward progress
to the worst of these once you had set yourself on the first step of the
course.

It is also true that Roman Catholics in England have been for five
centuries a minority group, one that not only struggled to assert its differences — in this case the strong religious (rather than merely social)
foundation for morality — but that also took a strong position against
moral relativism. First openly hated and persecuted, then reluctantly accepted, the Catholic minority in England has always been something of
a social embarrassment (Catholics are still, in some places, considered
much less desirable company, and maybe even philosophically dangerous). This has made the Roman Catholic in England a rather severe and
persistent defender of his faith, and sometimes quite a bigot (as in, for
example, the case of Evelyn Waugh). The blood of martyrs is not always required to fertilize the soil of Church life: a little social ostracism
will at times do just as well.

And so the insistence on a dread of sin, on moral probity, and on the
preservation of each jot and tittle of the law both ancient and modern
was designed to keep the ranks of Catholics strong and sturdy. And the
insistence, reiterated in sermons and lectures and magazines, was also
designed to show that English Catholics were no less English for being
Catholic: they backed up their support of moral strictures with promises
of reward and punishment that had, even here on earth, a frequently
instant reflection. It would take years of questioning and failure before
preachers felt free to link morality to a more profound Christian spirit-
uality than this.

Of course, in the meantime, while preachers snorted and school-
masters snarled, a few boys could always be expected to challenge the
rules. And in his last year at Saint Ignatius Alfred Hitchcock challenged
the rules, his teachers, and his schoolmates.

"Hitchcock became a notorious purloiner of eggs from the priests'
hen house, on the forbidden side of the presbytery garden," according
to Robert Goold. "He loved to steal the eggs and throw them on the
windows of the Jesuit residence. When an angry priest ran out, demanding to know who had dirtied the glass, Cocky affected an innocent look,
glanced at the sky, shrugged, and said, 'I don't know, Father. It looks
like the birds have been flying overhead.' That's how he got the nickname, even to junior boys, of Cocky." The clever fat boy who had no
friends was, it seems, overcoming his shyness. He was certainly a cocky
lad, this boy who smiled and looked as if he could see straight through
you. But the same schoolmate was in fact the victim of a more dangerous, and more cruel, practical joke.

In the early afternoon, between a lecture class and a quiet study time, the boys were free to gather in the schoolyard near the church. Goold, then nine, was suddenly yanked away from his peers by Hitchcock and an accomplice and dragged off to another forbidden area, the basement boiler room of the school. Before he could cry out or struggle — not much use in any case against two bigger boys — Goold was bound hand and foot. Once he was immobilized, he was prey to a carefully planned psychological torture that could have ended disastrously.

His trousers were pulled down, and Hitchcock quickly stepped behind him. Then there was the sound of a scratching noise, and the two bullies raced up the stairs. Young Goold must have thought he was attacked by a firing squad: at once the sound of gunfire exploded — but it was a string of firecrackers that had been pinned to his underwear and ignited. "It was a good job I wasn't burned," Goold remembered. "I stood there shaking and crying for I don't know how long, until finally someone found me and set me free. Of course I was too frightened to tell anyone who had done it. I was afraid of recrimination, and they knew it. I guess you could say Alfred Hitchcock had a sense of the macabre even at school."

After leaving Saint Ignatius, Hitchcock and Goold never met again, although professionally they might have found later contact interesting: Goold became a technical assistant to the famous handwriting expert Gerald Gurrin, who provided solutions that led to the capture of several of England's most dreaded murderers and spies. Then, during World War II, Goold was ordained a priest and served as a prison and reformatory chaplain for over thirty-five years. He claimed never to have seen a film by Alfred Hitchcock.

Hitchcock's interest in unconventional and unsavory behavior was satisfied in less antisocial but no less revealing pastimes. In addition to his theatergoing, he spent free days at the Old Bailey Court, watching murder trials and storing up material in notebooks as the young Dickens had done. Unfortunately none of these notebooks survive; but the films Hitchcock made later are sufficient evidence of his careful study of criminal behavior.

He also went often to the famous Black Museum at Scotland Yard, a police chamber of horrors that contains relics of famous crimes and criminals. "They've got all the shoes of prostitutes from the gaslight era," he recalled many years later. "Did you know that the color of every scarlet woman's shoes determined what her specialty was? If a man saw a prostitute walking along Waterloo Bridge at night he knew she did one thing in red heels, another thing in blue heels. I find that a fascinating bit of information.''

Later, he would visit the vice museum in Paris, where he fingered the blade that dispatched Marie Antoinette. His interest in patterns of murder and sadomasochistic behavior was also satisfied by a Sunday paper called *News of the World,* which had at the time a circulation of 7.5 million. It featured accounts of crimes committed all over England, and few of the unpleasant details were spared the reader.

''I have always been fascinated by crime,'' Hitchcock noted. ''It's a particularly English problem, I think. The British take a peculiar interest in the literature of crime. It goes back to reading Conan Doyle. Every time you read about a particularly grisly trial at Old Bailey you also read that some famous actor or director or writer is present. . . . There is even a club here that meets after every trial just so both attorneys for the defense and the prosecution can have lunch in a private dining room and discuss the case all over again. I have been to these meetings, and they are much more interesting than the actual trials. Of course it's not as exciting now because you can't hang anybody anymore.''

''There was a period in England when robbery with violence carried a mandatory sentence of fifteen strokes of the cat o'nine tails,'' he recalled later. ''It was nine knotted thongs at the end of a short stick and was administered by a guard to a man strapped to a triangle. They had a heavy leather collar around his neck so that the spine would not be hurt, and a doctor would examine him with a stethoscope after each stroke. The doctor would then decide after so many strokes, usually eight or nine, whether or not he'd had enough.''

Few artists of the macabre owned so complete a library of criminal cases as Hitchcock and, like the crime novelist who speaks for him in *Suspicion,* he always thought of his murderers as his heroes. But where he differed from most British crime-writers was in his obsession with the detail of suffering — perhaps because most of his personal life, from his oversensitive and protected childhood to his adult terror of illness and death, was spent avoiding physical suffering and pursuing physical comfort at any cost.

There is no doubt that Hitchcock absorbed some of his gruesome fascination, as he himself said, from a general British interest in crime. And there was at this time a particularly nasty series of murders that galvanized the public's attention. For years afterward, the hideous murder committed by Charles Peace in the East End of London in 1876 was sensationalized by the press, and immortalized in wax at Madame Tussaud's. Similarly, the unsolved case of Jack the Ripper, who terror-ized the same area in 1888, was still household gossip and a cause for fear (he figured prominently in Hitchcock's 1926 film *The Lodger* and was mentioned as late as 1972's *Frenzy*).

Just a few years before he was born, Mrs. Mary Eleanor Pearcey murdered her lover's wife and baby, then wheeled the broken bodies through Hampstead in a pram that was subsequently enshrined at Madame Tussaud's. (In Mrs. Pearcey's kitchen hung a wall plaque emblematic of the cruel irony of her madness: UNDERNEATH ARE THE EVERLASTING ARMS.) The infamous Dr. Hawley Harvey Crippen, who murdered his wife, was executed at Pentonville Prison just weeks after Hitchcock entered Saint Ignatius, and the London newspapers heralded the event with lengthy accounts. In August 1915 George J. Smith was executed for an unusually horrid series of crimes: he was the so-called Brides-in-the-Bath murderer who drowned his wife, Margaret Lofty, and three of his subsequent six wives, in his bathroom in Highgate.*

But the criminal who eventually made the greatest impression on Hitchcock was also a schoolboy at the time, a shy and mysterious lad just a year older named John Reginald Halliday Christie. While the filmmaker chose to sublimate in art whatever dark impulses may have lurked in his mind, Christie ultimately lived out his own. "Did you ever read the Christie case?" Hitchcock asked. "Christie the murderer. He murdered eight women! He was a bald, mild little man, very calm. He was impotent and could only reach his climax and get his satisfaction by strangling a woman while he was having sex with her. And then he hid the bodies — in cupboards, under the floorboards of the house. And went on living there with all those bodies!"

The late Victorian and the Edwardian eras were, like many societies in which there are social extremes and unhealthy repressions, times of frequent outbursts of monstrous violence. What the British reading public relished, of course, was the mystery aspect, the intellectual game of solving the crime and trading reports with friends about police progress in the grisliest cases. Hitchcock was right: from Wilkie Collins and Conan Doyle to Edgar Wallace and Agatha Christie, it was the mental approach that delighted and excited. A rationalization of what was horrific could somewhat defuse the panic by a kind of distancing. Newspapers of the time celebrated all these killings just as many urban tabloids do today, all over the world. Mrs. Pearcey and Crippen and Smith were only the most well known of those who were perhaps the first nonroyal and nonartistic "stars" — they were in fact the media's first

---

*These various events justify Rebecca West's felicitous reference to "the peculiarly cosy character of English crime" (in "Mr. Setty and Mr. Hume," an essay in *A Train of Powder*).

grotesque celebrities, and they achieved the status of notoriety in a society hungry for distraction from social problems and political turmoil.

In July 1913 Hitchcock left Saint Ignatius College and formal education, and from then until 1920 spent his adolescence in a monotonous
round of work, with some artistic diversion and some sporadic attempts
to find the kind of future that would appeal to whatever natural abilities
he might develop.* The lives of very many people include apparent
times of stasis, when there seems to be no growth or progress in their
lives at all. The rhythms of disengagement then seem to impose a great
gray haze of purposelessness on their lives, and for those with creative
talents these periods can be spiritually devastating. Fortunately for
Hitchcock, he seemed not to be aware of, nor to demonstrate as yet,
any artistic ability during his teen years, and his family (whose finances
were particularly strained because of his father's illness) certainly did
not encourage him to entertain any notions of the artist's precarious
livelihood.

In the autumn of that year there was not much of anything to occupy
his interest. There were four hundred movie theaters (or movie screenings in skating rinks) in London by this time, visited by almost eighty
thousand people weekly — a formidable number only if not compared
to the five million people in America who were similarly entertained
*daily* that same year. Movie admissions were cheaper than theater seats,
and by attending the cinema Hitchcock did not have to travel all the
way to the West End for an afternoon's diversion.

Since he was expected to contribute something to the family's income, and since he had no special skills, he was enrolled for a short
time in some evening lectures in navigation at the University of London.
Exactly what these lectures would fit him for was clear to no one, but
maps and wall charts were his hobby, and with the rumors of war there
might have been some thought of a naval career, or at least of a respectable position in a factory at home. At the same time, he attended a few
workshop courses and learned the elements of electricity, mechanics,
force and motion, draftsmanship, screw-cutting, blacksmithing, and lathe
operation. Of these courses and his attendance at them there are no
extant records in any of the divisions of the university system in London. This is disappointing, since it would be interesting to know precisely what sequence of courses he visited, but it is also understandable.

---

*There were no very specific regulations concerning uniform date of entrance or graduation at
this time. Diplomas and commencement ceremonies were instituted only later. Many students left
school, for example, to help support their families.

The University of London, the Workers Educational Association (which helped nonmatriculated students find classroom and workshop courses that might equip them for employment), and the City and Guilds Division did not keep records for any students who were not formally enrolled in a degree-granting program. Things were rather loosely structured at this time, and the educational system of central London was extremely generous to people who simply wanted to improve themselves. A young man could walk into any of the buildings in Bloomsbury or Paddington where evening courses were in progress, pay a few shillings, and find a bench where he could work under the helpful eye of an expert. The details of administration were quite subordinate to the needs of the moment, and in fact with the eruption of war attention was deflected from such details and toward easy admission of people who needed to learn a skill that would help Britain.

Throughout 1914 Hitchcock attended evening courses and an occasional play or film. But any uncertainty about the demands of his family on his future was abruptly ended when his father died on December 12 of that year. He had, it seems, worked right up to the last day. England was by this time at war with Germany, and London working people were putting in long hours. William Hitchcock's frail health was aggravated by the daily commute to Limehouse, where the family's fishery had grown and demanded more of his time than the grocery in Leytonstone. Work and worry about his family took their toll, and the result of his natural inclination to nervousness was a condition that added kidney disease to his chronic emphysema: the death certificate indicates that the primary cause of death was a perinephric abscess. William Hitchcock's older son and namesake, who was already living away from home in Southwark, was present when he died quietly at the age of fifty-two, at Guys Hospital.

Alfred had never been very close to his father, who left on his son an impression of nervous harshness. The father's death would understandably and quite predictably have had a devastating effect on the sensitive fifteen-year-old who feared and resented him and who may well have had the typical lonely child's fantasy: a death wish against his stern and repressive parent. He was the father who would be forever associated with the terror of imprisonment, and Alfred Hitchcock told the world of that for half a century.

Immediately, Alfred and his mother had to rearrange their lives, and this meant first of all that he had to find steady work. There is some evidence that they moved back to Leytonstone, perhaps because there were solicitous family friends there. But Hitchcock's lifelong secretiveness — especially about this period, and especially about his parents —

and the incomplete local records of the East End make it impossible to know for certain about the relocation.

"At the age of fifteen I was dropped off the wagon and had to walk." Hitchcock maintained. ". . . I was alone and practically penniless." In fact he was neither alone nor penniless, although he certainly had to provide for his mother, who apparently went into a considerable depression and demanded even more attention, care, and visits from friends and relatives, and more contact with the child who remained at home.

In early 1915 Hitchcock found an office job at the Henley Telegraph and Cable Company, and for fifteen shillings a week he put some of his night-class experience to good use. The hours were long at Henley's — the demand for war matériel had increased the firm's production and its need for workers — but the atmosphere was cordial, and the company encouraged after-hours socializing. At first he was assigned to calculate the sizes and voltages of electrical cables to be installed by the company. The work did not engage his interest, and it was about this same time that he returned to classes in other subjects one or two evenings a week in London; art-history, economics, and political-science lectures engaged him for a few months, and then some additional classes in drawing. The job as an estimator was to have been his stable form of endeavor, but his interest began to shift more toward the arts. Eventually he took a course in painting.

There may have been a vague idea of moving up the ranks at Henley's; the lectures in economics would have fitted him for an executive position in a technical company that the war had kept busy. But there was certainly something in his deeper self that was being tapped, too: the courses in art could not have been further removed from the demands or expectations of his employers. Something was opening up in him; a new part of his inner life began to flourish in late adolescence as he took up his sketch pad — usually at home, but sometimes during a break at the office. Could he possibly become an artist? How would he earn a living from it? The paintings he studied at night school were mostly English portraits and landscapes: how did the reality of London life, and the noise of war, prepare one for the life of an artist?

He need not have worried (if indeed he did), for his natural quietness and youthful eagerness at his job caught the attention of a supervisor, who soon transferred him to the advertising department of the company. There he could draw to his heart's content and help Henley's in the bargain. One of his first assignments was to design an advertising layout setting forth the merits of institutional wiring. "I'd write *Church Lighting* on the cover of a brochure and then draw two candles," he recalled. "And there would be darkness all round, suggesting that church lighting

by candles alone wouldn't be enough to light any service." The sense
of irony was clever — and so was the simplicity of execution, for he
showed that it was unnecessary to draw cables in order to advertise
them.

Meantime, the war raged, and the Hitchcock home was not spared.
Arriving from work one evening, Alfred found that artillery fire had
exploded quite near his house, and he ran to his mother's room to find
her in a state of fear and confusion, trying to struggle into her clothes
while still wearing her nightgown.* No one was injured, but the near-
ness of the danger must have caused continual upset and aggravated the
boy's fear of the unexpected, just as his father's death had given him a
sense of the fragility of life and relationships. Order was an important
value in Cockney life and in the Hitchcock home, and death and war
and financial uncertainty were breaking down that sense of order and
replacing it with a sense of chaos and the omnipresent possibility of
disaster. This became, with the years, an attitude toward life, and it is
perhaps the single most obvious situation in Hitchcock's films — the
sudden eruption of chaos and disorder into a life of apparent security,
and the psychological and emotional reactions this eruption evokes.

The threats to life were not usually so close, however, and the people
of London developed, as people in war do everywhere, a habit of dole-
ful but courageous insistence on trying to go on with life as normally
as possible. For Hitchcock this meant frequenting more often the local
movie theaters. He was a devoted film buff from the age of fifteen,
attending first screenings of the early French and German pictures. The
work of Griffith — *Birth of a Nation* and *Intolerance* especially — made
a great impression on him, as did the films of Keaton, Fairbanks, and
Pickford. He found that he preferred American films to the British ones,
for technical reasons. He had begun to study photography, and he noted
that while British films presented a flat image, with background and
foreground figures blending together, the American films employed
backlighting. This technique made the foreground figures stand out in
relief, heightened the drama of an actor's presence, and gave depth and
shading to what were mostly crude images.

"I would read not the fan magazines but the American trade journals," Hitchcock remembered, "to follow the real news of new productions and the filmmakers whose works excited me. . . . There used to
be a book shop just off Leicester Square, near the Leicester Galleries,

---

*The scene was etched into his memory, and it is recalled at the beginning of *Murder!*, when a
woman's frantic attempt to put on one set of clothes while taking off another leads to awkward
comedy, with legs caught in fabric and sleeves variously turned out.

and upstairs they had all kinds of American trade magazines as well. There was *Motion Picture Daily, Motion Picture Herald,* and then we had our own *Cinematograph Lantern Weekly* and there was the *Bioscope.*"

In 1915 and 1916 he also began to read more widely in fiction, but not, as far as can be determined, the latest works of the British novelists. (These were the years in which there appeared Lawrence's *The Rainbow,* Woolf's *The Voyage Out,* Maugham's *Of Human Bondage,* and Joyce's *Portrait of the Artist as a Young Man.*) Hitchcock's taste tended more to the detective fiction of the Catholic novelist G. K. Chesterton, whose sleuth Father Brown was delighting thousands of readers. And he also discovered John Buchan, whose novel *The Thirty-Nine Steps* was a great success; Hitchcock later returned to it for the basis of one of his best English films.

But it was the American author Edgar Allan Poe who fascinated him most of all:

At sixteen I discovered the work of Edgar Allan Poe. I happened to read first his biography, and the sadness of his life made a great impression on me. I felt an enormous pity for him, because in spite of his talent he had never been happy.

When I came home from the office where I worked I went straight to my room, took the cheap edition of his *Tales of the Grotesque and Arabesque,* and began to read. I still remember my feelings when I finished "The Murders in the Rue Morgue." I was afraid, but this fear made me discover something I've never forgotten since: fear, you see, is an emotion people like to feel when they know they're safe. When a person is sitting quietly at home reading a tale of terror, one still feels secure. Naturally you shiver, but since you're in familiar surroundings and you know it's only your imagination that responds to the reading, you then feel a great relief and happiness — like someone who has a cold drink after being very thirsty. And then you appreciate the gentle lamp and the comfortable armchair you're sitting in. . . .

Very likely it's because I was so taken with the Poe stories that I later made suspense films. I don't want to seem immodest, but I can't help comparing what I've tried to put in my films with what Edgar Allan Poe put in his novels [*sic*]: a completely unbelievable story told to the readers with such a spellbinding logic that you get the impression that the same thing could happen to you tomorrow. And that's the key thing if you want the reader or viewer to substitute himself for the hero — since people are, after all, interested only in themselves or in stories which could happen to them.

I never broke this rule. If "The Gold Bug" fascinated me then, it still does now, because I've always loved adventure, travel and the impression of somehow always being away from home. . . . I believe Poe has a special place in the world of literature. He's at the same time certainly a romantic and a herald of modern literature. He couldn't avoid being a romantic because no one can avoid the spirit of his own times. You can't forget that Edgar Allan Poe went to school in England in 1818, when Goethe had just published *Faust* and the first stories of Hoffmann had just appeared. This romanticism is perhaps even more obvious in Baudelaire's translation of Poe into French — these two authors, in fact, are very similar and I'd go so far as to call Baudelaire the French Edgar Allan Poe.

And surrealism? Wasn't it, too, born from the work of Poe as much as from Lautréamont? That school of literature certainly had an enormous influence on film, especially around the years 1925–1930, when surrealism was brought to the screen by Buñuel with *L'Age d'Or* and *Un Chien Andalou;* by René Clair with *Entr'acte,* by Jean Epstein with *The Fall of the House of Usher* and by Jean Cocteau with *The Blood of a Poet.* I was influenced by all this, as you can tell by certain dream and fantasy sequences in some of my films. . . .

But both Poe and I are prisoners of the suspense genre. If I made *Cinderella* into a movie, everyone would look for a corpse. And if Poe had written *Sleeping Beauty* they'd be looking for a murderer!

The influence of Chesterton must be assessed as well. Much admired and celebrated by the Catholic clergy, and read by Catholic schoolboys, Chesterton's popular essays "A Defence of Penny Dreadfuls" and "A Defence of Detective Stories" (published in his 1901 collection *The Defendant*) entertained the adolescent Hitchcock, and provided him with ideas for the formation of his own style and vision when he was an apprentice filmmaker. It was Chesterton who defended popular literature, Chesterton who pointed out the archetypal, fairy-tale structure of police stories, and Chesterton who defended exploration of criminal behavior.

"One of the strangest examples of the degree to which ordinary life is undervalued is the example of popular literature, the vast mass of which we contentedly describe as vulgar," Hitchcock read in "A Defence of Penny Dreadfuls."

Among these stories there are a certain number which deal sympathetically with the adventures of robbers, outlaws and pirates, which present in a dignified and romantic light thieves and murderers. . . . That is to say, they do precisely the same thing as Scott's *Ivanhoe,* Scott's *Rob Roy,* Scott's *Lady of the Lake,* Byron's *Corsair,* Wordsworth's *Rob Roy's Grave,* Stevenson's *Macaire* . . . and a thousand more works distributed systematically as prizes and Christmas presents. Nobody imagines that an admiration of Locksley in *Ivanhoe* will lead a boy to shoot Japanese arrows at the deer in Richmond Park; no one thinks that the incautious opening of Wordsworth at the poem on Rob Roy will set him up for life as a blackmailer. In the case of our own class, we recognise that this wild life is contemplated with pleasure by the young, not because it is like their own, but because it is different from it. . . . These publications have nothing evil about them. They express the sanguine and heroic truisms on which civilisation is built; for it is clear that unless civilisation is built on truisms, it is not built at all. Clearly, there could be no safety for a society in which the remark by the Chief Justice that murder was wrong was regarded as an original and dazzling epigram.

Chesterton and Hitchcock shared not only Catholicism but also a sense of irony. And what Chesterton wrote of the popular literature, Hitchcock took to heart, for it provided, if ever he needed, the justification for his apparently slight moral tales about all the garden varieties of villainy.

"Books recommending profligacy and pessimism," Chesterton charged,

lie upon all our drawing-room tables. And with a hypocrisy so ludicrous as to be almost unparalleled in history, we rate the gutter-boys for their immorality at the very time that we are discussing (with equivocal German professors) whether morality is valid at all. At the very instant that we curse the Penny Dreadful for encouraging thefts upon property, we canvass the proposition that all property is theft. At the very instant we accuse it (quite unjustly) of lubricity and indecency [Chesterton could have been speaking, prophetically, of Alfred Hitchcock's mature work] we are cheerfully reading philosophies which glory in lubricity and indecency. At the very instant that we charge it with encouraging the young to destroy life, we are placidly discussing whether life is worth preserving.

It was a deeply rooted Catholic sense of the pervasiveness of moral turpitude that also linked Chesterton and Hitchcock. "But it is we who are the morbid exceptions," wrote Chesterton, "it is we who are the criminal class. This should be our great comfort. The vast mass of humanity, with their vast mass of idle books and idle words, have never doubted and never will doubt that courage is splendid, that fidelity is noble, that distressed ladies should be rescued, and vanquished enemies spared." Although Chesterton did not formally embrace Roman Catholicism until 1922, he was a conservative traditionalist all his life, and his private belief and public image were those of a man who was a medievalist, a romantic hankerer after sobriety and asceticism; he was psychologically a Catholic long before he bent his capacious head over the font.

It was G. K. Chesterton who spoke to Hitchcock's concept of ordinariness and extraordinariness. "The romance of police activity," he wrote in the second essay, keeps in some sense before the mind the fact that civilisation itself is the most sensational of departures and the most romantic of rebellions. By dealing with the unsleeping sentinels who guard the outposts of society, it tends to remind us that we live in an armed camp, making war with a chaotic world, and that the criminals, the children of chaos, are nothing but the traitors within our gates. . . . Morality is the most dark and daring of conspiracies. It reminds us that the whole noiseless and unnoticeable police management by which we are ruled and protected is only a successful knight-errantry.

At the same time that he discovered Poe and Chesterton, Hitchcock began to read Gustave Flaubert, and afterward admitted that his favorite character in fiction was Emma Bovary. This is important, and not only because the story of a woman's fall from social respectability and grace to ostracism and finally death must have been exciting and a little shocking to his rather sheltered sensibilities. It is also noteworthy because it points to a strong creative affinity between Hitchcock and Flaubert. Each devoted a lifetime of discipline and subordination of the strongly romantic side of his nature to the demands of his art. Each practiced a furious attention to precision, planning, and detail. Each developed a rigorous sense of order and balance in his craft. And each had, parallel to this fanatical involvement in his life's work, a highly charged emotional sensitivity, carefully restrained in exterior life, carefully explored in art.

By the end of 1918, as Hitchcock later said, he was "very fat and very ambitious" — although just how ambitious would not be clear for several months. He had a reasonably secure position in Henley's advertising department and had managed to avoid the upset of conscription thanks to a medical deferment for obesity and because he was employed by a company contributing to the war effort. Henley's, soon to be merged with a larger corporation, encouraged the staff to contribute to its "social club magazine," *The Henley,* and in its first issue there was a short story on page one:

### Gas

She had never been in this part of Paris before — only reading of it in the novels of Duvain, or seeing it at the Grand Guignol. So this was the Montmartre? That horror where danger lurked under cover of night; where innocent souls perished without warning — where doom confronted the unwary — where the Apache revelled.

She moved cautiously in the shadow of the high wall, looking furtively backward for the hidden menace that might be dogging her steps. Suddenly she darted into an alley way, little heeding where it led . . . groping her way on in the inky blackness, the one thought of eluding the pursuit firmly fixed in her mind . . . on she went . . . Oh! when would it end? . . . Then a doorway from which a light streamed lent itself to her vision . . . In here . . . anywhere, she thought.

The door stood at the head of a flight of stairs . . . stairs that creaked with age as she endeavoured to creep down . . . then she heard the sound of drunken laughter and shuddered — surely this was — No, not that. Anything but that! She reached the foot of the stairs and saw an evil-smelling wine bar, with wrecks of what were once men and women indulging in a drunken orgy . . . then they saw her, a vision of affrighted purity. Half a dozen men rushed towards her amid the encouraging shouts of the rest. She was seized. She screamed with terror . . . better had she been caught by her pursuer was her one fleeting thought as they dragged her roughly across the room. The fiends lost no time in settling her fate. They would share her belongings . . . and she . . . Why! Was this not the heart of Montmartre? She should go — the rats should feast. Then they bound her and carried her down the dark passage, up a flight of stairs to the riverside. The water rats should feast, they said. And then . . . swinging her bound body to and fro, dropped her with a splash into the dark, swirling waters. Down she went, down, down. Conscious only of a choking sensation, this was death . . . then . . . "It's out, Madam," said the dentist. "Half a crown, please." — HITCH

The short story resembles an undergraduate's imitation of a Poe short story. But it has most of the characteristics of its author's later scene-treatments. Had it been rendered as a silent film, few title cards would have been necessary. There is a kinetic urgency, a sense of doom and dread and suspense that sweep the reader's attention past the naive diction. Half nightmare and half realistic depiction of a vaguely perceived danger, "Gas" shows the young Hitchcock's instinctive grasp of the mechanics of reader manipulation and the evocation of fear. It has no great literary merit, but neither is it boring — and there are plainly the images of sadism and of the woman plunged into water, images that would recur with increasing frequency and significance in his major films. Perhaps the only element in the story that Hitchcock would later abandon was the return to normalcy. But he was, after all, not yet twenty when he wrote the piece, and the memories of the war, of his father's death, of the chaotic and unpredictable and fragile nature of family and national life were still in his mind. He was not the only artist of promise who permitted in his inchoate craft the pleasant resolution that life so often denied.

Although the atmosphere at Henley's was cordial, Hitchcock once again seemed not to have participated in its social life. "I was an uncommonly unattractive young man" was how he later described his appearance during the years from 1920 to 1926. "And I had never been out with a girl in my life."

But with his maturity things would suddenly change. He read in the trade papers that an American film company, Famous Players–Lasky, was opening a studio in London at an old electrical powerhouse. He quickly found out what film they were planning, and with the assistance of Henley's advertising manager (who helped him arrange a portfolio and with whom he agreed to split any fee), he went along to the Islington offices.

It is no exaggeration to say that what happened that day altered the course of Hitchcock's life forever and would later affect the lives of many others. The executive at Islington opened the large, black brief-case and found sketches of people glimpsed in the underground, draw-ings of Londoners common and grotesque, designs for exotic movie scenes, and decorations for silent-film story-cards. Hitchcock was hired at once, on a part-time basis, to work at title designs. The portfolio was left behind at Islington, where amid the general disorder it soon vanished.

# Three

1920–1925

HE was almost twenty-one. And the film industry was not much older.

Louis Daguerre's still-photographic process was first publicly announced in 1839, and by 1872 there was already a stumbling progress toward the reproduction of motion in pictures: Eadweard Muybridge photographed the successive rapid movements of a trotting horse in a series of closely timed still shots. The illusion of motion was soon attempted in parlor-game devices, too, such as Emile Reynaud's diverting Praxinoscope (an arrangement of mirrors and hand-drawn or photographed figures that when quickly manipulated provided simple amusement). Thomas Alva Edison, who was much more interested in perfecting his light bulb and phonograph than in catering to what he considered the middle-class taste of those hungry for motion pictures, turned over to his assistant William Kennedy Laurie Dickson the task of working on a Kinetoscope. By 1891 Dickson had developed a crudely effective slot machine that projected a film loop for a solitary viewer. About the same time, George Eastman announced a perforated celluloid film, and this enabled Dickson and Edison to perfect their motion-picture camera and to standardize the thirty-five-millimeter film-stock ratio.

At this point fewer than sixty years had passed since the first photographs astounded those who sat for them, yet it was clear that cinema would have wide popular appeal. Edison, however, needed some convincing that it would be wise to allow more than one person at a time the privilege of viewing the film loops in individual Kinetoscope machines: he reasoned that if dozens of spectators crowded into one room to see images projected on a wall, a handsome income would be forfeited. His staff prevailed, however — as did the creative suggestions of several foreigners (among them the Englishman William Friese-Greene, who had taken out a patent on a projector in 1889 in London) — and on April 23, 1896, the first public projection of a motion picture in the United States was offered in New York City.

Audiences were quickly enthusiastic on both sides of the Atlantic. "Why did it arrive at this moment?" historian Ernest Betts has asked. "It arrived because the means existed. Every invention has its hour, and the hour for the cinema struck at the close of the nineteenth century. Its development beyond its circus origins can be traced to the social needs of the time. There was little amusement for the working class. The whole [British] nation yawned with boredom during weekends and was ready to put a fortune into the hands of anyone who could relieve the tedium."

But this was true not only for England. One of the curious facts about the birth of film was that this most democratic, mass means of entertainment had its origins simultaneously in several countries and in the hands of several creative individuals. In March of 1895, Louis and Auguste Lumière projected a film privately for the members of the Société d'Encouragement pour l'Industrie Nationale in Paris. On June 10, 11, and 12 they gave private screenings of short films to the Photographic Congress at Lyons. On June 15 they presented the first complete program of films at the Revue Générale des Sciences in Paris, and shortly afterward they took out a patent on their Cinématographe, a machine that shot, printed, and projected motion pictures.

Their short films were the first movies commercially shown anywhere in the world — on December 28, 1895, in the Grand Café of the Hotel Scribe, Paris. The films were short scenes of Paris life, bits of family business, and country and seacoast vignettes; by 1900 they had registered 1,299 films. Each lasted only a minute or less, and they were classified as *vues diverses, vues comiques,* or *vues militaires;* there were, for example, shots of local interest, street scenes, people at the zoo, and pictures of workers leaving the Lumière factory. But there was nothing like a narrative. A ship was seen leaving the port, a lion was fed and teased by a keeper, a baby was amused by his parents, men chopped wood in a side street. And a comic potential was recognized also: thus the famous visual gag of the unwary gardener sprinkled by his own garden hose through the mischief of a sly brat.

The Lumière brothers were as keen in matters financial as they were canny about what entertained the middle class, and they took small crews (headed by Félix Mesguich and Francis Doublier, the first cinematographers) all across Europe and America to shoot various historical events, as well as scenes of everyday life, from an artist's congress to soldiers marching in full dress uniform. At the same time, Georges Méliès, a French showman with a wildly creative mind, took film into the realm of fantasy and fiction. With tinting, stop-motion animation, and other kinds of trick photography, he satisfied the taste for diversion on yet another level: plants bloomed in seconds, a woman's hair turned into a garden of exotic blossoms, and, in *A Trip to the Moon* (1902), a crew of wacky scientists predated the modern astronauts. The Lumière brothers recorded reality; Méliès reordered it.

This was the period during which Alfred Hitchcock was born, and it was the most important for the nascent film industry. Between 1895 and 1905 political life was dominated in England by an extremely conservative government. The monarchy was prestigious, the state imperialistic, the sun never set on the realm, and Victoria's Diamond Jubilee was celebrated with great rejoicing in 1897. England was still a country with a sharp division between the rulers and the ruled. Shocking poverty still prevailed and was much more taken for granted than it is today. It was a land where, as J. B. Priestley observed, "a third of the population, living at the centre of this huge Empire, were below any humane level of subsistence. They were overworked, underpaid, and crowded into slum property."

Gradually, however, the working classes experienced some improvements in their lives. Laborers were forming unions, there was better education, and working hours were shortened — which meant more leisure time. The rich began to transport themselves in automobiles, while the poor could purchase bicycles more cheaply than ever. With the increase in literacy, public libraries multiplied, newspapers proliferated, and in 1896 the first halfpenny newspaper, the *Daily Mail,* was published. It made a "story" out of each news item. Nothing was so important as the reader's attention — and if the techniques of fiction were necessary to hold it, they were exploited at the drop of a printer's block.

This was also the era of the "spectator-worker." To the sports matches, the music halls, and the theaters were soon added the movie parlors, and then the movie palaces of London. Like the assembly line when it developed the possibilities of mass production, the astounding growth of the modern mass media fed on people's need for diversion and novelty and their willingness to pay for it. Manufactured by showmen and marketed by showmen, the cinema was born at a time when the arts — like the benefits of science — were becoming available to the masses.

Edison, Dickson, and the Lumière brothers had British counterparts in the rush for this burgeoning market. The dominant figure of the early

English cinema was Robert William Paul, who built copies of Edison's Kinetoscope machine when he was told that Edison, not yet convinced of its potential, had not applied for an international patent. Paul had a show of his Theatrograph (soon renamed the Animatographe) in London on February 20, 1896 — the same day, in fact, that the Lumière brothers' London representative projected short scenes at the Regent Street Polytechnic. From then on, things happened quickly. On March 9, 1896, a fifteen-minute show (which forever laid to rest Edison's fears that people would not sit still for more than sixty seconds) was screened at the Empire Theatre, London. It was not a fifteen-minute story with a continuous narrative, but rather a dozen disparate scenes of London life, not unlike the Lumière *actualités*.

A week later, still another major advance occurred when Birt Acres, a sometime partner of Paul, made a short dramatic tale and then a short comedy sketch for private presentation. Acres had already exhibited to a small group at the Royal Photographic Society the previous month. Soon, more interested in serious private demonstrations than music-hall exploitation, Acres would concentrate his time and talent on the development of equipment. But for almost a year (1895–1896) he and Paul made about a dozen short films; the Oxford and Cambridge boat races were documented and the running of the Derby was captured for audiences who had not attended. Scenes like this justified the presence of the upper classes at local screenings, and no less a sensitive soul than Miss Virginia Stephen herself, daughter of Sir Leslie, enjoyed Paul's Animatographe show during the Christmas holiday in 1896. By the end of that year, films were part of every music-hall show, and they were also being offered for a small fee at fairground booths, "penny gaffs" (nickelodeon parlors), and skating rinks.

The year Hitchcock was born, Paul opened England's first indoor motion-picture studio, at Muswell Hill in north London. "It comprised," as Rachael Low and Roger Manvell have documented, "a miniature stage, about 28 by 14 feet, raised above ground level and protected by an iron building with sliding doors and a glass roof facing north. At the rear of the stage was a hanging frame on which backcloths painted in monochrome could be fixed; the frame could be lowered through a slot to facilitate the work of the scene painter. Traps in the stage, and a hanging bridge over it, provided means for certain effects." Paul continued to make about fifty short films a year there between 1899 and 1905, but when film narrative became more complex, around 1910, he — like Acres — abandoned the cinema and returned to instrument-making.

If Acres and Paul were comparable to Edison and Dickson, the Englishman George Albert Smith was closer in spirit to Georges Méliès. Between 1897 and 1900 Smith developed special effects like superimposition and the close-up in his trick films, while his colleague Frank Mottershaw pioneered the narrative film with his brief tales of crime and adventure. Better known is Cecil Hepworth, a man of considerable ingenuity who attended the Lumière films in 1895. In short films made between 1899 and 1911 he exploited sophisticated tracking shots and revealed a creative use of editing. His *Express Train in a Railway Cutting* (1899), *How It Feels to Be Run Over* (1900), and *Rescued by Rover* (1905) advanced the possibilities of the mobile camera and the swift, suspenseful cut.

By 1910 (when Hitchcock began to join the crowds at the music halls and vaudeville houses) a few British films — taking their lead from *The Great Train Robbery,* the twelve-minute landmark film directed by the American Edwin S. Porter in 1903 — were as long as ten minutes. Most, however, were shorter; an advertisement for a 1908 matinee lists *The Fatal Sneeze, The First Quarrel, Baby's Dream of Toyland, The Onion Fiend, Tommy and the Police Whistle, Harry Lauder in a Hurry* — the entire program was screened in less than a half-hour (and was accompanied by a full orchestra).

At once, however, problems arose in England: the weather, the climate, the economy, and the curious philistinism that held the cinema to be fundamentally a lowbrow diversion were factors hostile to the development of a successful film industry. By 1906, most films shown in Great Britain were made in America or on the Continent: the native British industry was fading. Very quickly, American companies, especially, saw a fertile field in England for their operations, and Famous Players–Lasky Corporation, the parent company that controlled Paramount Pictures Corporation, opened the Islington studio that hired Alfred Hitchcock. By 1920 Robert Paul's studio had shut down, as had Cecil Hepworth's. It was clear that most of the early British filmmakers were inspired technicians but not artistically exciting storytellers. They could not combine technical expertise with an aesthetic sense or even the ability to sustain anything other than a grade-school kind of narrative. Although the commercial cinema in England owes its foundation to Hepworth's success at producing and distributing short films that were briefly arresting visually, his talent did not extend beyond the simplest material. There was in Great Britain no serious contender for comparison with America's D. W. Griffith until Alfred Hitchcock entered the cinema.

In 1915 Léon Gaumont's Paris-based company built its impressive Shepherd's Bush studio for thirty thousand pounds — a commitment to the reality of the industry in England. But actors' salaries were low, and

the most successful and persevering of the performers went to Hollywood as soon as they got an invitation. It was not long before Shepherd's Bush was crowded with English technicians and foreign actors.

By the time Hitchcock had left Saint Ignatius and was going more
often to the cinema (before he began to work full-time at Henley's), the
British two-reeler, usually based on a respectable literary source, was a
fact of entertainment life. There were films telling the story of Henry
VIII, of Rob Roy, Oliver Twist, Lorna Doone, and David Copperfield.
Also, by 1913, the industry was ready for feature-film directors. But the
most prolific men, like Maurice Elvey (who turned out over three hundred
features and an even greater number of shorts in four decades of work),
were not much better storytellers than their predecessors; in Elvey's case,
the sheer volume of product was the only thing of real note in a career
devoid of all but the most routine commercial aspirations.

Among the most popular and widely distributed British films at the
time of Hitchcock's youth, and among those that seem to have exerted
some influence on his imagination, was William Haggar's 1905 movie
about murderer Charles Peace. Haggar avoided primitive studio sets and
shot much of the action on real rooftops. Peace was depicted as an
ingenious, agile, high-spirited villain who managed to outfight and outwit half a dozen bumbling constables, and the East End teenagers ap-
plauded this cagey, imaginative scoundrel — much to the chagrin of
their parents. All came out right morally at the end, however. The gruesome execution was depicted with unusual force thanks to imaginative
editing and quick cutting: the camera focused on the details of tying the
villain's hands, recorded the fear in his eyes as the noose is placed
around his neck, and then cut to a long shot of the death drop. The
criminal paid his due to society, but hardly much honor was paid to the
police.

In 1913 William George Barker's production of *East Lynne,* directed
by Bert Haldane, attracted the patronage of thousands, and schoolboys
especially loved it. It was the first British six-reeler (running time over
an hour) and it told of a brutal murder. An innocent man was wrongly
accused of the crime, and this brought about a series of tragic misun-
derstandings, recourse to disguises, a humane and plausible villain finally unmasked, and at least two pathetic death scenes. The British taste
for murder and mystery was more than satisfied by *East Lynne,* and the
element of suspense was introduced with the device of the innocent man
in flight. Like almost every early film made in Britain, it survives only
in written précis, but as such it could be an outline for Hitchcock's

treatment of *The Thirty-Nine Steps*.* If he somehow missed seeing *East Lynne* (and the omission is unlikely, since it played often and was extremely popular among schoolboys), it can at least be said that he shared its spirit.

In both these early films there is considerable attention given to a crew of unsympathetic policemen; they are the more cynical, complex, adult versions of the successful imports starring Mack Sennett's Keystone Kops. They appealed to the audience's anarchic, antiauthoritarian fantasies, and they often looked just plain ridiculous — as in the Sennett films and Hitchcock's deliberate comic rendering of bumbling policemen in *The 39 Steps* and *Young and Innocent*.

During and after World War I, America cornered the market on film distribution in Britain, London closed down its native-owned studios, and Americans virtually took over the field. Between 1914 and 1916 imports of American films doubled, and Americans were able to schedule series of films in British theaters through "blind booking" contracts that bound exhibitors to show films they themselves had not seen in advance. Even so, there was rarely cause for alarm: the most modest American movie was ordinarily, by just about everyone's agreement, superior to the most ambitious British film.

Famous Players–Lasky Corporation, in an attempt to profit from the popularity of American films abroad and the failure of most of the native products to captivate audiences, came to London immediately after the Armistice. In a former power station of the Metropolitan Railway at Poole Street, the company built its studio. There were two stages, space for shops and offices, and, because of the preexisting wiring, splendid possibilities for lighting designs and configurations. The managing director, J. C. Graham, was responsible to the American partners who controlled the company, Adolph Zukor and Jesse L. Lasky. They had merged the former's Famous Players Film Company and the latter's Feature Play Company in 1916 to form the new company under Zukor's presidency. Soon Famous Players–Lasky acquired a distribution arm — Paramount Pictures Corporation. A 1917 advertisement proclaimed: "If it's a Paramount Picture it's the best show in town," and the copy that followed confirmed that modesty or understatement was not the company's strong suit:

Paramount Pictures were the first feature motion pictures ever made. In five years of progressive leadership, Paramount has built a library of motion picture

---

*John Buchan's novel was published as *The Thirty-Nine Steps*, but Hitchcock's film title was printed and released as *The 39 Steps*. That distinction is preserved (when appropriate) throughout this book.

classics — not one star or ten, but a hundred — commencing with Mme. Sarah Bernhardt — who under the Paramount banner have achieved their finest success. All of these great pictures are still available.

Paramount visualizes the plays and books of the past and present. More than a million followers of Paramount Pictures, in thousands of theatres in two hemispheres, daily renew acquaintance with the famous places and characters of classic and contemporary literature. Paramount Pictures preserve indelibly for all generations the world's greatest stories and plays, acted by the leading artists.

Alas, the preservation was not quite so indelible, for few of these early films survived a decade.

About the time Hitchcock was preparing a portfolio to present to Graham and his colleagues, Zukor and Lasky visited Islington (separately) between March and June 1920. They approved preproduction plans and budget for the first films the company would produce in England, and the trade papers reported that their first picture would be *The Sorrows of Satan*. Accordingly, Hitchcock read the novel on which the screenplay would be based, and included in his portfolio a series of designs appropriate to that story. By the time he was being considered for the part-time job of title designer, however, a decision had been made to cancel *The Sorrows of Satan* and to proceed directly with Hugh Ford's film *The Great Day*, to be followed by *The Call of Youth*. Eager to please his prospective employers, Hitchcock prepared designs for these films almost overnight, and was hired at once — but, as mentioned earlier, only on a part-time basis. He continued to work at Henley's, and provided the movie studio with title designs and graphics every few days. He was modestly compensated by Famous Players–Lasky for the piecework, which he produced on his own time. But when Hugh Ford's two films were successful (both were released in November 1920 for trade assessment), the studio decided to employ Hitchcock on a full-time basis, and he resigned from Henley's.

In the next two years he designed the title-card drawings and the lettering styles for all the Famous Players–Lasky films — and sometimes he also figured the dimensions of a frame or a set, for the crews at Islington were small and duties often overlapped without the constrictions of carefully regulated union policies. Donald Crisp, the Scottish actor-director who had had considerable success in America, was brought to England to direct four films (*Appearances, The Princess of New York, Beside the Bonnie Briar Bush,* and *Tell Your Children*), and Hitchcock worked on these also. The films seem not to have been very good either in content or in treatment, and in fact none of them survive. The same fate befell other projects to which Hitchcock contributed — two films by John S. Robertson (*Perpetua* and *A Spanish Jade,* presented for the trade in May and August 1922), and two films by Paul Powell, *Mystery Road* and *Dangerous Lies* (trade shown in September and October 1921).

The hours were long at Islington, and the shooting schedules were demanding. But Hitchcock, who was now putting on weight quickly and finding it harder to take off, was often the first to arrive in the morning and the last to depart at night. "I'm American-trained. . . . All of the personnel at the studio was American," he later recalled in an interview, "and as soon as you entered the studio doors you were in an American atmosphere. I started out as designer of titles, working with Mordaunt Hall, who was a critic later for the *New York Times,* and with Tom Geraghty, who had been a writer for Douglas Fairbanks."

If Hitchcock was not — as he always insisted he was not — ambitious to assume more responsibility, and if he did not hope to move along to positions of greater creative control as a director, then it is hard to understand the intense devotion to a very modest job and his insistence on learning everything there was to learn about film. When the studio executives or film directors ran into trouble with some part of a project, or if they required additional help in writing a scene or designing a costume or a set, Hitchcock was always at the ready with bright suggestions and an alacrity to try his hand at a new assignment. Graham and his team were not dealing with an indifferent or disinterested talent.

In 1922 George Fitzmaurice directed two films at Islington, and his methods had a profound influence on Hitchcock. Of the pair (*The Man from Home* and *Three Live Ghosts*) almost nothing is known, but of Fitzmaurice himself there is more information. Born in Paris, where he studied to be a painter, he saw art and sculpture as intimately related to film. When he began working in the cinema in America, he paid particular attention to character analysis, preparing detailed storyboards for each shot and supervising set preparations. During actual shooting he earned the respect and admiration of his cast by an apparently casual but really deadly serious approach to his craft. He said he never bothered about most things once he had left the storyboard-script stage of his work, and this is part of the legacy that he passed on to the young Hitchcock. Fitzmaurice's own description of his working procedure summarized exactly what Hitchcock's method would be later:

The public of today demands something more than mere action; it demands a well-developed theme, and when you enter upon this you enter the realms of psychology. To incorporate human nature into a picture you must understand the science of mental phenomena, for it is this science that is the guiding hand of realistic action.

I can only speak of my own individual method. First there is the purely technical work of designing the sets. I work out every detail of this in advance, even selecting the design and color of the wallpaper. Then I pick out my furniture and work out detailed plans of just how it will be arranged in the completed sets. I even carry out this initial supervision so far as to accompany the women of the cast to the stores where they purchase their gowns in order to be perfectly sure before I start work that everything is in harmony. During all this time I am thinking deeply of the play (i.e., the "photoplay") as a whole, not in a conscious detailed manner, but absorbing the theme, the atmosphere, in a subconscious manner.

From George Fitzmaurice, Hitchcock learned not only what to look for in painting, in lighting possibilities, in the development of a coherent script: he also learned about a quietly professional approach to the usually chaotic and undisciplined atmosphere of a film set. Fitzmaurice got what he wanted from his cast and crew by being calm, slightly detached, quietly insistent, and so well prepared that for virtually every alternative suggestion someone could offer, he had a reply ready. Hitchcock not only saw at first hand how successful this style could be but also sometimes had the chance to discuss technical matters with Fitzmaurice over a late supper at the local pub.

It was the occasional evening with Fitzmaurice that provided virtually the only social life Hitchcock had in these early years of the 1920s. Long hours at the studio, attentiveness to his mother at home, attendance at an occasional matinee when he had a day free — this was the business of his life. Though it was not social and full of diversions, it was intense, and the very elements that some might have considered restricting in fact nourished his single-minded purpose, his sense of discipline. He was working in film, seeing films, reading about films, studying other people's films. There was the studio, and there was the quiet of Leytonstone, and this rhythm of attentiveness and alertness established a pattern that would dominate the rest of his life. When he was directing films in the 1930s and living in central London, it was not so very different. And when he was directing films in the 1940s and later, and living in California, the pattern maintained. His marriage, and then the death of his mother, altered the supporting cast of his life somewhat. But his career was always the major element of the plot, and he was the leading player.

Facilities improved at Islington in 1922 and early 1923. Glass walls were installed on one side of the studio, and there were adjustable awnings to utilize natural light; darkrooms, printing and chemical labs, scenery shops, prop departments, carpenters' quarters, dressing rooms, engine rooms, writing and conference rooms, and executive offices were completed. The studio's appointments might have been satisfying for most employees, but those who worked in front of the camera would not have been entirely pleased by the working conditions. Because the film stock was so much less sensitive than it is today, the lighting had to be very strong indeed, as producer Michael Balcon later recalled: "The players (both sexes) wore heavy pancake make-up and everyone had to take care not to look into the arc lights, otherwise an attack of 'Klieg eye' — a particularly painful form of conjunctivitis — was likely. The camera was hand-operated, the lights were noisy and generated such heat that everybody was very uncomfortable."

But production continued, and apparently without any hint from the executives that the studio was in trouble. During this time it happened that Hitchcock stepped in to finish, with producer-actor-writer Seymour Hicks, the direction of a film called *Always Tell Your Wife,* a project that was undertaken for the sake of Hicks's beautiful wife Ellaline Terriss. Hugh Croise, the original director, had irreconcilable differences with Hicks and was summarily removed from the picture. The typical story was circulated: Croise was ill, and Hicks, with the assistance of a member of the crew, would himself complete the picture. Years later Hicks recalled:

In the days of silent pictures a one act play of mine called "Always Tell Your Wife" was being filmed at a small studio in Islington. Half way through the production the director was taken ill and I was at my wit's end to know what to do. Being on the verge of throwing the whole thing up, I was interested when a fat youth who was in charge of the property room at the studio volunteered to help me. It seemed a forlorn hope, but as I liked the boy and as he seemed tremendously enthusiastic and anxious to try his hand at producing, we carried on as co-directors and the picture was finished. Who do you think that boy was? None other than Alfred Hitchcock.

And shortly thereafter, a comedy script was prepared, called alternately *Mrs. Peabody* or *Number Thirteen,* and Clare Greet and Ernest Thesiger were signed to play the leads. Alfred Hitchcock undertook the direction, on assignment from the chief of production, but by this time the studio's dwindling funds were being diverted from production to pay debts and salaries, and the unfinished film was shelved. To this day nothing else is known about this aborted project apart from Hitchcock's assertion that it was not very interesting.

Just when he was learning the craft of film step by step, the studio was preparing to close down operations. The films made in England had a terrible reception, and there seems to have been something almost self-destructive about the industry after the war, as more than one historian has suggested. Film in Great Britain was regarded only as a business, whereas in Europe and America people realized it was an art form. "In the early 1920s," Ernest Betts has written of England, "our directors and studio executives can hardly be mentioned in the same breath with their continental rivals, or, for global success, with the Americans. They [the English] suffered a narrowness of outlook which was often to cripple the work." After World War I, "we forfeited our independence as an industry. The war had reduced our own studio output to a shadow, we needed foreign films, we needed the business, and we were ready to pawn our future to that need." And so the British exhibitors booked the popular American productions — the only films they could count on, and those they knew would ruin the British industry by reducing the call for native products. It is all, Betts concluded, "easily explained. Their films were better than ours." In addition, the climate had never been hospitable for location shooting, and Hollywood salaries were soaring in comparison with English salaries, which further declined.

"They started to close down the studio gradually," Hitchcock later said, "and began exporting people to America. Directors like John Robertson, George Fitzmaurice, Donald Crisp, big players like Anna Q. Nilsson, James Kirkwood, Evelyn Brent, Norman Kerry and Eddie Goulding, and Fitzmaurice's wife, who was also his writer — her name was Ouida Bergere, and she eventually married Basil Rathbone. But the rest of us who stayed around in London were temporarily unemployed. The empty studio became a rental studio and one hung around for the jobs. Eventually a group of independents came in." Among the group of independents was a man no one had heard very much about before then — Michael Balcon. He would change the shape of the British film industry, and one of the ways he would do that would be to give Alfred Hitchcock a chance to direct his first complete films.

In 1920 Balcon had formed, in association with Victor Saville, a small film rental company in Birmingham called Victory Films. It was a healthy partnership: Balcon had experience as a salesman, and his innate abilities enabled him to move swiftly as a business manager and producer. Victor Saville, on the other hand, had a showman's instinct for promotion and advertising that never became merely flamboyant, and to this he added a keen appreciation of the American market. In Birmingham they represented the local interests of the W. and F. Distribution Company as well, which had headquarters in London and was under the direction of financier C. M. Woolf. In 1922 Woolf invited them to London to produce advertising films. Soon they met director Graham Cutts, a former marine engineer who had entered films as an exhibitor and who was now working for independent producer Herbert

Wilcox. It was not long before Saville, Balcon, and Cutts were talking about making commercial feature films.

They decided to proceed at once, were joined by businessman John Freedman as additional partner, and embarked on an independent production of a successful play, *Woman to Woman*. As leading lady, the American star Betty Compson was brought over (at the astonishing salary of a thousand pounds a week); the cast also included Clive Brook and Victor McLaglen. Working with a small crew and with money raised by Woolf, the film was quickly but elegantly made at the Islington studio as a Balcon-Saville-Freedman production in the summer of 1923. It was first presented the following November, to instant acclaim. Balcon had hired Alfred Hitchcock as assistant director, and when the production needed additional help, Hitchcock volunteered to do the script and the art direction. Balcon, Cutts, and the rest were amazed that his talent matched his ambition. Hitchcock also told them he knew a good editor who had worked at Islington, a woman named Alma Reville. They gave permission for him to bring her onto the picture too.

Encouraged by the success of *Woman to Woman*, the Balcon-Saville-Freedman team rushed *The White Shadow* into production with Miss Compson as star once again. "The same Star, Producer, Author, Hero, Cameraman, Scenic Artist, Staff, Studio, Renting Company as *Woman to Woman*" ran the advertisements — but the results were far from the same. The film was a total failure. The agreement with C. M. Woolf was now in jeopardy, and the entire partnership was eventually dissolved after the completion of a third film, *The Prude's Fall*.

The trio of films had been a mixed stew, and Graham Cutts wondered if he had the right crew. His assistant director might have been spreading himself too ambitiously around the production, he complained to Balcon: Hitchcock was writing script and title cards, designing the sets, preparing the cast, supervising the costumes and props. Nonsense, Balcon replied: Hitchcock was capable, cheerful, and serious. And he was saving them considerable amounts of money. Cutts grumbled, and Balcon wondered how long he would be able to pacify his star director.

In January 1924, Famous Players–Lasky made it official that the Islington studio, which it had for over a year been renting out to independent producers like Wilcox and Balcon, was now for sale. "J.C. Graham announced," it was reported in the trade press, "that in the opinion of the American company the producers had failed to reach a quality comparable with [that of films] made in the States." Balcon now had the bold idea that instead of being just one of the occasional tenants he would try to buy the place. With a studio of his own he would have a better chance of producing a steady flow of films; only in that way could he see a real English industry emerge.

"I may have had the over-confidence of my youth in my ambitions," Balcon recalled,

but I was self-critical enough to be unable to see myself in the role of the shrewd, tough negotiator over a property deal with a major company. . . . So when I made an appointment to see J.C. Graham, the managing director of Paramount, I asked our accountant to accompany me. He could not do so but sent along a young man from his office called Reginald Baker. The meeting is clear in my memory:

GRAHAM: Yes, I'm willing to sell the studios. I want 100,000 pounds.
BAKER: We have a surprise for you, Mr. Graham. We can only raise 14,000.
GRAHAM: I have a bigger surprise for you — I'm going to accept your offer.
BAKER: Today is full of surprises, Mr. Graham. We shall have to spread our payments — 2,000 pounds a year for 7 years.

Graham accepted our terms. It was a day to remember.

The negotiations clearly had what Balcon later called "an Alice in Wonderland quality." Within weeks he owned the studio, the equipment, and the option on the jobs of the Islington employees.

The following month, Balcon registered "Gainsborough Pictures" — a major step that insured the survival of the British film industry. In the 1930s Balcon would be in charge of the vast Gaumont-British studios (the largest share of which was owned by the powerful Ostrer brothers); in the 1940s and 1950s, he would head Ealing Studios.

Gainsborough's first picture was to be *The Passionate Adventure,* a fourth Cutts-Hitchcock film, shot in the summer of 1924 and released in November. The partnership with Saville and Freedman was formally dissolved, and an arrangement for distribution was made with Gaumont, which since 1922 was a wholly British company.

Hitchcock attracted Balcon's attention "because of his passion for films and his eagerness to learn. He had no background in the entertainment world at all; his family owned a group of London fish shops. But apparently he never wanted anything but to work in films and I'm sure that if he never actually swept the floor at Islington he would have been ready and willing to do so. He was a clever draughtsman and he wrote and designed the subtitles which were so important to silent films."

From the beginning — from the first story conferences on *Woman to Woman* — Hitchcock wanted to advance rapidly in film work. He conceded later that although he was engaged as assistant director, he quickly filled other jobs as well — such as when he was asked to recommend a good scriptwriter: " 'I'll do it,' I said. 'You? What do you know about it?' So I handed them a sample script I'd written. They were suitably impressed and I got the job. Then my friend the art director left, saying he had a prior commitment. 'What are we going to do for an art director?' asked the executives. I said, 'I'll do it.' So for nearly three years — 1923 to 1925 — I did all these jobs: wrote the script, designed the sets and costumes, assisted the director and acted as production manager for each picture.''

Hardly anything is known about these films; no prints survive, no press materials or production files. But it is clear that the position and authority of director Graham Cutts was gradually reduced as Alfred Hitchcock moved from job to job, from strength to strength. Ten years later, Cutts would be looking for day work in any studio while Hitchcock was in the uncomfortable position of having to give not very significant employment to his former boss.

Among the reasons for this shift in the fortunes of the two directors beginning in the 1920s were the complicated distractions of Cutts's private life. Married and soon to be a father, Cutts was a handsome and sociable man who readily accepted both the attention of established actresses and the admiration of young fans. His involvement with one young woman in particular strengthened Hitchcock's position even further.

*"The Prude's Fall,"* Hitchcock remembered, "was to have been shot on the Continent. We all went off looking for the right locations — Paris, Saint Moritz, Venice — but Cutts's girl friend, an Estonian he'd picked up along the route, was unhappy wherever we went. So we all came back to London without a foot of film.'' Soon Cutts's life became desperate, and he used friends and colleagues (Hitchcock among them) to run interference between his mistresses and his wife; there were the subterfuges of double dinner parties, clandestine meetings as Hitchcock made excuses to Mrs. Cutts about late shootings, deceptive telephone calls — the usual ingredients of an "open secret.'' In addition (and perhaps because of his somewhat wild personal life), Cutts seems to have had, as Rachael Low said, "only a sketchy interest in film structure and he was, sadly, an uneven and unreliable film maker whose richness of imagination was not accompanied by discipline or control and whose work later fell off disappointingly.''

The crew for *The Prude's Fall* thus came back to England without a foot of film, and with no clear idea of how Cutts would fulfill his contractual obligations. Hitchcock, however, came back with some ideas of his own about helping Balcon plan the film in such a way that it could be made entirely in the Islington studio.

Balcon and his company were earnest workers for the most part, but at times, as Balcon observed, they were rather feisty London rakes. They were all, like Hitchcock, in their twenties (except for Cutts, who was almost forty), and some long days at the studio were followed by long nights in the private clubs of London. Hitchcock, who quickly earned Balcon's respect with his multiple talents and his quick wit, rarely joined them. His pleasures remained solitary — even the pleasures of the table, which he frequently indulged (at Simpson's, for example). He also continued his habit of attending the theater alone, and during these years he saw plays that intrigued him and piqued his curiosity about sexual activity, still a part of life that was unexplored territory to him.

From 1920 to 1925 Hitchcock saw most of the major plays performed in London, and there were echoes of many of them in his films years later. In 1920 he saw Fay Compton (who would later appear in his *Waltzes from Vienna*) in the title role of James M. Barrie's *Mary Rose* — a fragile and delicate fantasy with an unsettling, bittersweet tone. It was revived in 1926 and 1929; the fact that he was frustrated in his attempt to film it forty years later was perhaps the single greatest disappointment of his creative life. He also saw Galsworthy's *The Skin Game,* which he would later film for John Maxwell; and *The Last of Mrs. Cheyney,* Frederick Lonsdale's comedy about sex and theft. That play's bedroom scene, with its bold repartee about sexual blackmail, directly prefigures the bizarre situations of *To Catch a Thief* and *Marnie* (which Hitchcock would radically alter from the novels by David Dodge and Winston Graham).

There were also *The Beggar's Opera;* Gladys Cooper (later to appear in Hitchcock's *Rebecca*) in *The Second Mrs. Tanqueray;* Edmund Gwenn (who would play in four Hitchcock films) in *Old Bill, M.P.;* Conrad's dramatization of his own novel *The Secret Agent* (a theatrical event that apparently made so strong an impression on Hitchcock that he persuaded Balcon to let him film it, in 1936, as *Sabotage*); *Merton of the Movies* with Patricia Collinge (who would later play the mother named Emma in Hitchcock's *Shadow of a Doubt*); and *The Lady from the Sea* with Brian Aherne (later to appear in *I Confess*), Herbert Marshall (Hitchcock's star in *Murder!* and *Foreign Correspondent*), and Josephine Wilson (the false Miss Froy in *The Lady Vanishes*). Others who would appear in films by Hitchcock were seen in London's theaters in the 1920s (and when he came to work with them the director was able to recall their stage performances): Cedric Hardwicke, Ivor Novello, John Laurie, Malcolm Keen, Esme Percy, Edna Best, May Whitty, Leo G. Carroll, John Williams, Isabel Jeans, Sara Allgood, Cathleen Nesbitt, Henry Kendall. And the formidable Tallulah Bankhead.

Hitchcock first saw Tallulah Bankhead in 1923, when she was making her London debut in *The Dancers,* a play by "Hubert Parsons" (the joint pseudonym of Viola Tree and Gerald du Maurier). Bankhead played the role of Maxine, and she appeared only in the first and third acts. The play opened February 15, 1923, at Wyndham's Theatre and co-starred Nigel Bruce and du Maurier. It ran for 344 performances and was Bankhead's longest run until *The Little Foxes* in New York years later. On a bitter winter night Hitchcock saw Bankhead, was struck by her brassy charm and severe sensuality, and made some mental notes. Twenty years later he insisted that she play the lead in his film *Lifeboat.*

But Hitchcock came back to England from the European trip for *The Prude's Fall* with more than plans to redeem it: he also came back with a fiancée. The sudden shattering of everyone's presumption of Hitchcock's eternal bachelorhood was something none of his associates could have foreseen. It was, one might say, the first in a long series of surprises. The fiancée, he told them, was none other than the free-lance editor at Islington, Miss Alma Reville.

Alma Lucy Reville was born one day after Alfred Hitchcock — on August 14, 1899 — at 69 Caroline Street, Nottingham. Her paternal grandfather, George Edward Reville, was an ironsmith in that town, and his wife, Jane Bailey Reville, also came from a working-class family. They were living in Woolpack Lane when their son, christened Matthew Edward (Alma's father-to-be), was born on September 28, 1863.

Alma's mother, Lucy Owen, was born three years later, on November 3, 1866, to Hugh and Ann Dance Owen. Lucy's father was a retired military man, and her mother a gentlewoman who traced her family back many generations in Nottingham. The Owens, in fact, had lived for a long while at the aptly named Robin Hood Terrace. Lucy Owen married Matthew Reville in the Castle Gate Meeting House (a nonconformist chapel) on August 25, 1891, with Matthew's sister Annie attending the bride. Eight years later, their daughter Alma was born in the Caroline Street house to which they had moved during Mrs. Reville's pregnancy; shortly thereafter they took up residence in Twickenham, west of London.

On weekends, and during holidays from school, Alma was taken by her mother to the local cinemas at about the same time that, in the East End, Alfred Hitchcock enjoyed similar diversion. But young Alma's interest in film was extended more quickly than his: the studios of the London Film Company were a short bicycle ride from the Reville home, and Alma often went to watch the actors perform in short outdoor scenes. Her enthusiasm was so great that by the time she was ready to leave school, her father was able, through a neighbor, to find her a job in the editing room. "It was," Alma said, "the only place where it would be possible to work without any experience."

In 1915 film directors edited their own films with the assistance of a small crew who did the actual cutting and splicing; there was as yet no really creative work involved in the task of editing. Working in the cutting room from the age of sixteen (which gave her a four-year head start on her future husband), Alma was asked to supervise the continuity on a series of features. She had no idea what the term meant, but she, too, was anxious to move up the ranks as a filmmaker. She quickly learned the art of continuity, which involves responsibility for the logical progression of scenes, the consistency, from shot to shot, of clothing and background and gesture, and the general inherence of the film treatment. Eventually her father's friend and neighbor was hired away to Famous Players–Lasky, and Alma went along. It was in 1921, while doing both editing and continuity, that she first met Alfred Hitchcock.

He was still a part-time employee at the studio, and he walked in and out the front yard daily looking for assignments as the full-time crews went from office to office and set to set. On Hitchcock's second visit he introduced himself to Alma, and his calm, unruffled attitude struck her as unusual. His face a perfect deadpan, he asked for the location of a certain office, she pointed it out, he strolled across the lot as coolly as he might wander through Regent's Park, and he disappeared into the production office with his title cards. His nonchalant manner was an extraordinary exception to the chaos at Islington — a chaos generally aggravated by the ebullience of the youngest employees. Alma remembered that Hitchcock wore a draggy gray topcoat that seemed ludicrous, covering his girth like an Oriental gown, and she almost laughed in his face.

But she was even more puzzled as the weeks of 1921 passed. After the first meeting, they often crossed paths and were even assigned to the same films, but Hitchcock never acknowledged her presence, never initiated a conversation — not until Balcon put *Woman to Woman* into production and made Hitchcock Cutts's assistant. The telephone of her parents' home in Twickenham rang one evening and the voice at the other end, cool and distant, inquired: "Is that Miss Reville? This is Alfred Hitchcock. I have been appointed assistant director for a new film. I wonder if you would accept a position as a cutter on the picture?''

After she began working with him, she found out why he had ignored her for so long. "I'm very shy when it comes to women," he confessed one day over a cup of tea — and the matter was never again mentioned. His attitude toward her remained strictly businesslike. There was no sharing of free time, no formal or informal courting, no introduction of her to his mother. He later confessed that he watched her almost constantly when she was not looking. "But it was unthinkable for a British male to admit that a woman has a more important job than his, and I waited until I had the higher position — assistant director."

They worked together on several of the Balcon-Cutts films, and the marriage proposal finally came, aboard ship from Germany to England after the location scouting for *The Prude's Fall*. Hitchcock described the event.

The day I proposed to Alma she was lying in an upper bunk of a ship's cabin. The ship was floundering in a most desperate way and so was Alma, who was seasick. We were returning to London from Germany. Alma was my employee. I couldn't risk being flowery for fear that in her wretched state she would think I was discussing a movie script. As it was, she groaned, nodded her head and burped. It was one of my greatest scenes — a little weak on dialogue, perhaps, but beautifully staged and not overplayed.

Their engagement was substantially longer than such formalities usually are today: they were not married until December 1926, by which time Hitchcock had directed three films. "I had wanted to become, first, a movie director," he said, "and second, Alma's husband — not in order of emotional preference to be sure, but because I felt the bargaining power implicit in the first was necessary in obtaining the second."

In light of this curious and exceptionally revealing statement, it is important to note that, once they were married, Alma's future as a producer and director in her own right — which was more than a possibility in the minds of producers like Balcon and Basil Dean, and directors like Adrian Brunel and Henrik Galeen — was completely subordinated to her husband's career. The union was apparently based on a kind of professional symbiosis rather than a grand passion. Alma Reville, already proclaimed one of England's few brilliant editors and screenwriters, and Alfred Hitchcock, already proclaimed a cinematic wunderkind by 1926 — it is easy to imagine them deciding (for even then they were people who decided rather than merely hoped) that she would fashion great screenplays for him, and he would render them on film with unprecedented artistry.

But their loyalty went beyond that of working partners, and no one ever really doubted their lifelong devotion to each other. It was not unalloyed, however: there was always the tincture of mutual resentment that Hitchcock himself once admitted, and there would be something of childish hostility in their attitudes to one another. The shipboard proposal on a violent sea — straight from the pages of a cheaply sentimental romance — was a cliché to be explored in the pages of their future. They were to share more than a half-century of married life, but the journey would be often harsh, the storm of confusion mysteriously bitter.

During their engagement, however, there would be more trips to the Continent, the first in 1924 for an Anglo-German coproduction. The British film industry's crisis was deepening, and Michael Balcon made an arrangement with the Berlin producer Erich Pommer for shooting *The Blackguard* at Neubabelsberg, where the huge facilities of Universum Film Aktien Gesellschaft (UFA) were the grandest in the world. The film would be distributed by W. and F., and the profits shared. The preeminence of the German cinema after the war had helped to create a worldwide acknowledgment of its distinctive visual style, and because Hitchcock's experience assistant directing (and later directing) in Germany was so formative an influence on his life and career, it is worthwhile to summarize the place of that national cinema in the early history of the industry.

Although British and American directors were unable to match the German stories and acting styles, they did try to imitate Germanic styles of lighting and editing, the odd angles and dark, slanting shadows, and the morbid psychology that afflicted a country in social chaos. During the difficult period of the Weimar Republic, when inflation and unrest haunted the German people, there was an attempt in England to form coproductions for mutual benefit. It was this that motivated Balcon's partnership with Pommer.

The cinema of the Weimar Republic had its roots in prewar German culture, in particular in the theatrical influence of Max Reinhardt and in the uniquely stylized atmosphere of expressionism. It was above all a cinemà of the studio, designed to create a fantasy world more powerful than the real life of everyday. *The Cabinet of Dr. Caligari* (directed by Robert Wiene in 1919), a tale of lunacy enacted against deliberately distorted, artificial sets, established the renown of German films not only for their bizarre stories but also for their unprecedented and evocative design. The film portrayed the irrational subconscious in such a way that spectators were given the impression they were in fact dealing with the disorders and disillusionments of their time.

Quickly, however, the expressionist fantasy was succeeded by a new kind of film that, while retaining a distinctive visual style, treated parcels of recognizable daily life. *Kammerspielfilme* (intimate filmed dramas) dealt with realistic, limited situations, observed the unities of time and space, and strove to convey universal values without resorting to titles. Although there were earlier attempts, the most famous in this genre was F. W. Murnau's 1924 classic *Der letzte Mann* (released in English-speaking countries as *The Last Laugh*), in which Emil Jannings played an aging doorman who is demoted to lavatory attendant.

A subgenre within the *Kammerspielfilme* was the so-called street film, which contrasted the security of home life with the dangers outside. The best example is, aptly, Karl Grune's *Die Strasse* (1923), which pictorially and spiritually corresponded not only to something endemic in the German postwar spirit but also to something close to Hitchcock's own soul. The film concerned a man who escapes from the boredom of marriage by plunging himself into the seductive life of city streets. But there he finds only chaos and threats to his safety, and he finally retreats to his former security. The theme of security at home against outer social chaos provided the basis for other German street films, and Hitchcock's films (from *Rich and Strange* through *North by Northwest*) make it clear that he felt a spiritual kinship to this motif.

But this new realism of the German films in 1923, 1924, and 1925 was also short-lived. The Great Depression changed the themes and images once again. In the meantime, however, there was a great deal for Hitchcock to learn — both in technique and content — from the Germans. From his supervision of virtually everything in *The Blackguard* in 1924, through the direction of his own first two films in Munich, at the Emelka Studios, in 1925, Hitchcock absorbed the Teutonic spirit.

Cutts, Hitchcock, and the crew arrived in Berlin to find a city with diverse districts and great contrasts of population, but it was irreplaceable as a source of film apparatus and sophisticated craftsmanship. With its permissive, cosmopolitan atmosphere — rather shocking, one must imagine, for the rather naive young Hitchcock — no other city could offer artists a more conducive laboratory for experimenting with new techniques. Berlin was the Hollywood of the Continent, the magnet for the best technicians in the medium.

"Those were the great days of the German pictures," Hitchcock later recalled.

Ernst Lubitsch was directing Pola Negri, Fritz Lang was making films like *Metropolis,* and F. W. Murnau was making his classic films. The studio where I worked [UFA] was tremendous, bigger than Universal is today. They had a complete railroad station built on the back lot. For a version of *Siegfried* they built the whole forest of the *Nibelungenlied* [which Hitchcock promptly ordered torn down on his arrival to make room for his grand staircase in *The Black-guard*].

I arrived in Berlin knowing not a single word of German. My job was art director, and I worked side by side with a German draftsman. The only way we could communicate was by pencil — drawing things so we could understand each other. The other man looked a little bit like Harpo Marx. We were both designing titles and sets, and finally I was forced to learn the language.

Germany was beginning to fall into chaos. Yet the movies thrived. The Germans placed great emphasis on telling the story visually — if possible with no titles or at least very few. *The Last Laugh* was almost the perfect film. It told its story even without subtitles — from beginning to end entirely by the use of imagery, and that had a tremendous influence on me.

And during the weeks Hitchcock watched Murnau film *The Last Laugh* — just a studio away from where Cutts was huffing and puffing and delaying over details of *The Blackguard* — he was learning more about the craft of film than he had learned in the previous years in London (even considering the influence of Fitzmaurice). "My models were forever after the German filmmakers of 1924 and 1925. They were trying very hard to express ideas in purely visual terms."

One afternoon, Hitchcock stood watching Murnau shoot a particularly difficult scene in a film, and afterward Murnau explained the odd way things were constructed. The two men could not have been more different, but their passion for film united them. Murnau was almost seven feet tall, angular, graceful, and quite openly homosexual. He made no secret of his private life, but neither did he flaunt it for its own sake, and his apparent comfort with everyone's knowledge of him surprised many in the English crew. Next to him stood Hitchcock, well under six feet, fat, not terribly at ease with himself, and not even comfortable in the presence of women, let alone homosexual men. Yet the meeting was cordial, and Murnau proceeded to point things out to the English assistant director. A railroad sequence was being filmed, and the focus of the set was a large railway clock. All the lines in the set went toward the clock, emphasizing the element of time. The remainder of the scenery, in the background, was built in a drastically foreshortened perspective that gave the impression of great length.

"The locomotive, a whole stream of coaches, and the glass roof of the railway station were all in perspective," Hitchcock remembered.

"The set had one drawback: as the perspective diminished there was no light in it. They solved that by putting a real train at the point in the distance where the lines met, and they had people coming out of the train."

This single afternoon with Murnau influenced Hitchcock's designs for the sets of *The Blackguard* the very next day (and it later influenced the opening of his 1932 film *Rich and Strange* — the office of Henry Kendall, the expressionism of its huge clock and odd shadows and lines, and the sense of professional order disarrayed when the masses of workers crowd the halls and stairwells a few seconds later).

I picked up a great deal of insight into the techniques of set building and perspective of every kind. In *The Blackguard* I had a scene against the doorway entrance to Milan Cathedral. It's one of the biggest Gothic piles in Europe. I only had to have a shot of a man going through the door into the black interior, so I had to decide how I was going to do it. I would never have been able to build the entrance of the Milan Cathedral; the doors are probably a hundred feet high. What I did was to solve the problem by building, in actual scale, the real thing — but just one column on the left. . . . Its proportions were enormous, and I included half a dozen steps, accurately measured, so that we got this big base of a Gothic column and the lines of the set went out to the right. I went to the zoo there and asked for a few pigeons. So I had these few pigeons and they flew around and sat on the stonework, but the point was to do a little piece of the building accurately and well rather than to do a sort of cheaply built whole structure.

In addition to Murnau's sense of forced perspective, with its perfect union of architectural economy and visual suggestion, Hitchcock absorbed the prevailing images that German culture exploited to express its sense of postwar horror, social unrest, and the emotional dislocation and ubiquitous fear of madness that lurked just behind (in the experience of the war) and just ahead (in the awfulness of the depression and the tyranny that, many felt, it foreshadowed).

The fairground in *The Cabinet of Dr. Caligari* was among the era's most potent images, and was drawn from the tradition of circus grotesquerie, Goethe's demonic carnival in *Faust,* and the nightmare carnivals of Hoffmann's tales. It was the place where the forces of madness and deadly desires are magically acted out, where distortions are made real (and thus exorcised). The fairground is the carrier of precisely this meaning in Hitchcock's *Mr. and Mrs. Smith, Stage Fright,* and *Strangers on a Train.* In *The Ring,* he would very soon exploit the association of the fairground with freaks and grotesque distortions of physical as well as emotional life; and in *Saboteur* the fairground releases its freaks into outer "normal" society and questions that normality.

The year 1924, then, was a major one in the artistic life of Alfred Hitchcock: from Germany's filmmakers, technicians, history, and culture he learned the nature of tension in a sequence, the elements that create powerful expression within the framed image, the dynamics of the relationship between light and shadow and between characters and decor. But most important of all, he came to understand the nature and power of an unstable and distorted image. Each shot in the best German postwar cinema has a menacing, anxious, waiting quality, a quality of disequilibrium. And it is precisely this quality that informs the best moments of Hitchcock's later black-and-white work — the staircase scenes in *Shadow of a Doubt;* the scenes in the Sebastian mansion in *Notorious;* the entrances and exits to the courtroom and the visit to Hindley Hall in *The Paradine Case;* the final confrontation below the stage in *Stage Fright;* the interiors of the Anthony mansion and the final fairground sequence in *Strangers on a Train;* the oppressive interiors of the Balestrero home in *The Wrong Man;* the motel and the Bates house, a veritable kingdom of death in *Psycho.*

When he was not working with Cutts on *The Blackguard* or watching Murnau make films, Hitchcock indulged his favorite leisure-time activity: he attended the theater, although the German language of course prevented complete understanding. Schnitzler's *La Ronde* was already in revival after its 1920 premiere in Berlin, and the works of Wedekind, Hauptmann, Thoma, Halbe, and Gorki were always in repertory. It is impossible to know for certain which of them Hitchcock saw, since he could not recall specific titles years later. But drama in Berlin in 1924 and 1925 was serious, whether classical or romantic stagings of classical or romantic plays; and Hitchcock would not have seen — whatever in fact he saw — much that was not visually arresting.

What is known for certain, however, is that he became fascinated with the world of the Grimm brothers — not only the lavishly illustrated volumes, but also the stage and park-puppet versions of their tales that were so popular at the time. The world of the Grimms was crowded with grotesque creatures, hideous metamorphoses, imaginative turns of the moral screws. Their stories partook of the tradition of the *Volksmärchen,* or peasant tales — combinations of the grotesque and the ordinary that fascinated Hitchcock for the rest of his life. He also became acquainted with the symbolic *Kunstmärchen,* or art stories. Both types were short and moved easily from the real to the fantastic world, and they sometimes had tragic endings. One of the leading representatives of German romanticism in this regard was Ludwig Tieck, who combined elements of the psychologically horrific with the visually realistic in his verbal descriptions. And from E. T. A. Hoffmann's tales Hitch-

cock also learned the technique of blending humor and horror, inter-
weaving closely the nightmare world with the everyday world of office
and kitchen. The writings of both of these authors were newly popular-
ized in Germany after the war, and Hitchcock's library in England would
later contain several editions of Hoffmann in German and English.

With *The Blackguard* completed, the crew returned to London early
in 1925. Reports of Cutts's depression reached producer Balcon; the
director found it increasingly difficult to handle technical problems. And
Cutts also resented his assistant's skill. For a time there was serious
doubt as to who should do what on future projects. The Cutts-Hitchcock
team had once been a successful matching of a genial, extrovert director
with a serious, ambitious assistant almost fifteen years his junior. .Cutts
had been a kind of mentor to Hitchcock, and although the apprentice
may have welcomed the guidance, he also sensed that he could do more
if given the chance, and that his own style would be quite different.
Hitchcock also came to appreciate his own intelligence (he had picked
up a quite serviceable command of German in a short time), and he
knew the advantages of his quiet private life.

That private life was, in fact, a slow, measured process of preparing
to marry Alma — although just when this would occur neither of them
could say. Hitchcock's mother was still the center and focus of his life
at home, and he continued to live with her in Leytonstone while Alma
lived with her parents far to the west, in Twickenham. Their meeting
was restricted to suppers after the day's work, an occasional evening at
the theater, or attendance at one of the monthly afternoon screenings of
the London Film Society.

Some members of London's intellectual world were beginning to accept the cinema not only as inevitable and diverting but also as an art
form. With the emergence of the first film critics in the city, serious
treatment was at last accorded the newest craft, and this made it possible
for Mayfair to join Poplar in open enjoyment of the new films. As early
as 1919 the Stoll Picture Theatre Club had been founded, composed of
people who assembled to discuss film; Hilaire Belloc, G. K. Chesterton,
and St. John Ervine were among the first participants. Then, in 1925,
the London Film Society began to meet regularly. The guiding spirit
was Iris Barry, film critic for the *Spectator* and, from 1925 to 1930, for
the *Daily Mail*. (It was she who became librarian at the Museum of
Modern Art, New York, and was appointed its film curator in 1935.)

On the Society's council with Barry were filmmaker and critic Ivor
Montagu, distributor and theater proprietor Sidney Bernstein, director
Adrian Brunel, and critic Walter Mycroft of the *Evening Standard*. Other

members of the Society included Hugh Miller, Anthony Asquith, Lord Ashfield, Roger Fry, Lord David Cecil, Julian Huxley, George Bernard Shaw, H. G. Wells, John Maynard Keynes, Augustus John, Angus MacPhail, Dame Ellen Terry, and George Pearson. The meetings at the New Gallery Cinema, Regent Street, and at the Tivoli, in the Strand, were genial, sometimes politically radicalized sessions in which opinions were set forth and vigorously debated. It was here that Hitchcock met some of the regulars who would become important supporting players in the scenario of his future career.

When the meetings of the Film Society and its prestigious membership were publicized, polite society and even members of the royal family took notice. King George and Queen Mary saw a film in 1924 —on the Society's public recommendation — and the Prince of Wales quite casually attended the London Pavilion's screening of *Covered Wagon* the following year. The Duke of Kent made no secret of the fact that he saw Erich von Stroheim's *Foolish Wives* three times, and the Duke and Duchess of York took a party of friends to a regular public screening of *Beau Geste* at the Plaza Theatre in 1926.

But the Film Society insisted (and the public agreed) that most British films were of an awfulness that was a national embarrassment; American imports were so much better than an American release-title or an American company's name alone guaranteed box-office success. By 1927 Arnold Bennett could write: "All the new [British movie] stories . . . are conventional, grossly sentimental, clumsy and fatally impaired by poverty of intention."

In addition, a gaudy showmanship prevailed at the cinemas. For the screenings of D. W. Griffith's American film *Broken Blossoms* (starring Lillian Gish, Richard Barthelmess, and Donald Crisp), cages of singing canaries were suspended from the ceiling of one major London theater. Amateur impresarios were given license to stage bad ballets with what can only be called *danseurs manqués* who introduced films in local cinemas. Mediocre pictures were accompanied by live appearances of, for example, Paul Whiteman and his band, and Edward Elgar himself once agreed to conduct a musical interlude — an unfortunate rendering of Tchaikovsky's concert overture *1812* with a group of costumed performers in side-boxes, sporting makeshift Russian-peasant garb and blowing trumpets. No wonder that the Film Society attempted to repeat the 1923 booking of *The Cabinet of Dr. Caligari,* or that they supported with considerable publicity the London premieres of Fritz Lang's *Dr. Mabuse* and Paul Wegener's *The Golem.*

The problems at Islington reflected the problems in the British cinema at large: dissatisfaction with the annual crop of native films, the inability of British financiers to meet the salary demands of the highest paid American actors, and the lack of compelling material. The best of the British silent directors — Cutts, Pearson, and Hepworth — were no longer pleasing the masses, and Paramount's Cecil B. De Mille was only one of several Americans who began to attract audiences by the appearance of their names alone above the title. Hitchcock pointed this out at a meeting of the Film Society in 1925, when the group gathered to discuss just who made a film succeed — publicists or stars or producers or distributors or exhibitors or critics.

"*We* make a film succeed," Hitchcock insisted. "The name of the director should be associated in the public's mind with a quality product. Actors come and actors go, but the name of the director should stay clearly in the mind of the audiences." This, as will become clear, was one of the reasons why Hitchcock chose to make himself a visible presence in his own films, and this was also why he, like Dickens, insisted that intelligent showmanship, publicity, a certain rapport with the public were essential to the product's success. Before he ever directed a film, Hitchcock knew what would be responsible (at least in part) for wide public acceptance of a man's work. But he also knew that he had to prove himself to the public, and this could not happen soon enough.

The time was right to encourage new British talent, and Hitchcock's apprenticeship had served him well enough — and had served Balcon well enough — that he could let it be known that he was ready to sit in the director's chair himself.

Hitchcock always insisted that he never had any intention of becoming a director, that he was quite content writing scripts, designing sets, and assisting the man in charge. "I never volunteered to direct," he claimed. "I was the victim of studio politics. Graham Cutts didn't like me and complained to Balcon, and Balcon came to me and said, 'How would you like to direct a picture yourself?' It never occurred to me."

Balcon's account is rather different, however. Although the alacrity and cleverness of Hitchcock was felt by Cutts as a threat to his own directorial supremacy, the issue was not simply one of resentment and politics, as Hitchcock wanted people to believe. Having taken over virtually every key function on the Cutts films and demonstrated his ability to handle them with speed and accuracy, it was only natural, as Balcon wrote later, that "he wanted to be a director, but it was not easy to get a young man launched in so important a job." Hitchcock was ready, Hitchcock was ubiquitous — and if he did not actually demand a promotion to director status, he certainly made his hopes known. But Balcon was first faced with a dilemma. He had to depend on the support of distributors for finances, and they were very much resistant to new and untried talent at so precarious a time. Just when they should have been adventuresome, they grew timid and insisted on the old names with whom they felt comfortable. The promotion of an assistant struck them as needlessly risky.

And so Balcon turned once again to Germany. If he could send Hitchcock back there to direct a film or two, and if Hitchcock's work was successful, then perhaps an important new talent on Balcon's staff at Gainsborough Pictures would be launched. "I had to arrange to have these two subjects made in Germany because of the resistance to his becoming a director," Balcon wrote. And so at last he was able to approach Hitchcock with the news that his wish had been fulfilled. A crew was being readied (Alma Reville could go along as Hitchcock's assistant director), and negotiations were in progress for top American stars to act as leading ladies.

Hitchcock was twenty-five and engaged, but he was socially untutored and his only friends were colleagues at Islington. Grateful to have Alma by his side in this important venture — "my severest critic," he always called her — he set out for the Emelka Studios in Munich. Balcon gave them a hearty farewell: Mr. Hitchcock and Miss Reville had had so much solid experience, after all — and the crew, the cast, and the facilities (not to mention the beautiful location settings they would visit at Lake Como in Italy) were guaranteed ingredients of success. He assured them (or was he encouraging himself?) that Hitchcock would make a wonderful debut, that his first film would be a hit. Finally, he said that careful planning indicated everything would go smoothly. That was his only rash presumption.

# Four

1925–1927

THEY must have seemed an odd trio to the travelers on the night train to Munich — the angularly handsome and imposing Baron Giovanni Ventimiglia (the cinematographer appointed to the film), who looked and acted like the former Italian aristocrat he was; Alma Reville, tiny, alert, and quietly excited, her carrot-red hair in a fashionable bob, who shuffled through maps of France and Germany; and the dough-faced Alfred Hitchcock, not yet twenty-six, who read and reread the script Eliot Stannard had adapted from Oliver Sandys's novel *The Pleasure Garden*.

As the train rushed through the German countryside, they knew it would have been easier to go directly to the Emelka Studios to shoot the interiors: some initial control, some success with actors and sets would have fed their confidence. The atmosphere there would have been familiar to Hitchcock, who could at least have impressed the crew with his command of studio filmmaking. But the schedule (as usual dependent on the availability of the leading players, on the weather, and on the studio space available for the construction of various interiors) called for a violent discontinuity in the shooting. They were to begin with some necessary shipboard scenes, to be photographed in Genoa, then move to the Mediterranean shore at San Remo, and transfer over to Lake Como before returning to the German studio.

On Friday, June 5, 1925, they arrived in Munich, and almost at once Alma left the two men and went west again — to Cherbourg, where she was to meet the American leading ladies arriving on the *Aquitania*. The fact that the project would be a story of British people, played by Americans, acting in Italy and Germany as if the setting were England and the Far East, was par for the cinematic course; commercial considerations prevailed, and Balcon was insuring an American market for his films by using established Hollywood stars. As long as they could be made to look and dress "English," the silent film would not betray them.

Hollywood stars, however, were accustomed to accommodations worthy of royalty, so a major portion of the available cash went along with Alma for her double duty as hostess. Hitchcock and Ventimiglia, who were joined the next day by the leading man, Miles Mander, and a camera operator, figured they had just enough money to get them all to Lake Como, Genoa, and San Remo and back to Munich.

The train from Munich to Genoa was scheduled for departure at eight o'clock that Saturday morning, June 6. Twenty minutes prior, the men were settled on board. Panicky because he could not find his makeup kit, Mander dashed from the train while Hitchcock, equally panicky because he thought Mander would not return in time, shouted instructions to him about taking a later train. The makeup kit turned up in the waiting room, and moments later Mander leaped back onto the train. The suspense, however, disarrayed Hitchcock, who had, in the few intervening moments, imagined himself on location without a leading man. And before he could completely recover his equilibrium, there was another bit of discomfiting news, this time from the cameraman.

"He told me not to declare the camera or the 10,000 feet of stock as we crossed the border into Austria," Hitchcock said. "The studio wanted to save money on the customs. 'Where is the camera hidden?' I asked. 'Under your bed,' he told me." During the search at the border, the officials did not discover the camera. But the film stock was in the baggage car, and that was confiscated. The encounter with the authorities cannot have done much to diminish Hitchcock's resentment and fear of uniformed authority figures.

Before dawn on Monday, they arrived in Genoa and were informed that the ship to be photographed was scheduled to depart Tuesday at noon. Pounds and shillings and marks and pfennigs were changed into lire, and, at depressing postwar exchange rates, their budget was quickly and drastically reduced by the expenditure for fresh film stock. To make matters worse, when the men returned to their hotel from dinner that night, Hitchcock had to tell them his room had been robbed of cash he had unwisely left in his luggage. For a loan, Hitchcock prevailed upon Mander, who complied with an unctuous flourish; the amount was doubled by the camera operator, who also wondered how much confidence any of them should have in this young director: if he couldn't manage money, how would Hitchcock acquit himself with a film schedule and cast and crew?

As if these financial troubles were not disheartening enough, the hotel manager then announced that the police and customs officials had arrived with the confiscated film stock, which had been forwarded and on which there was now a considerable duty and fine. Hitchcock wired Munich for a small advance to cover unexpected technical expenses, and he looked forward to Alma's return with the balance of her cash allowance. The photographing of the ship in Genoa harbor was accomplished on schedule Tuesday. Ventimiglia and his technician, after waiting for uncooperative crowds and clouds to disperse, leaped from the moving boat's deck (where they filmed the receding shore) to the pier (where they filmed the reverse-angle shot of the departing ship).

San Remo had been chosen as the setting for several exotic beach scenes in the melodrama — scenes involving a drowning native girl and an antagonist crazed by the Oriental sun and an excess of rum. The schedule allowed two days' shooting in San Remo with Mander and a young actress. When the key scene was ready Hitchcock noticed the cameraman, Mander, and the girl in a hushed conference. "She can't go into the water," Mander announced. "Now what do we do?"

"You mean she's refusing to play her part? Afraid of the water?" Hitchcock asked.

"Not exactly," Mander replied, and left the matter to Ventimiglia, who, with the technician, explained the inconveniences occasioned by the woman's menstrual period.

"I was twenty-five years old and I had never heard of it," Hitchcock said years later with an odd touch of pride. "I had had Jesuit education, and such matters weren't included." The setups were then rearranged, the actress was sent away, a double was enlisted for the troublesome aquatic episode, and eventually yet another American actress — Nita Naldi — played the part of the native girl.

They arrived back in Munich to find Alma and the American stars anxious to begin studio work. Mander and the cameraman were also anxious — for repayment of the cash they had advanced the director. When Hitchcock pressed Alma for the unused funds, she replied that the actresses had insisted on luxury suites from Cherbourg through Paris, where they also selected certain additions to their wardrobe that had depleted Alma's expense account. There was just enough to repay the debts, with virtually nothing left (after paying for their own hotel rooms) for their support in Munich. Never again would the Hitchcock-Reville accounts be in such a frightening condition.

The project proceeded smoothly enough in the studio, where Hitchcock did not have to depend on weather, passersby, or the tides for the success of filming. He made substantial emendations in Stannard's script

and, with Ventimiglia's patient agreement, redesigned major portions of
several sets so that the movement of the camera would be facilitated.
Visitors to the studio found the agile director slipping off to a corner
for a few words with a technician, leaping back to the set for a rehearsal
with his actors, then vanishing to an adjacent room to instruct the extras
who would shortly be required for a crowd scene. He was clearly in his
element — although some of the excitement and activity was deliberately generated by Hitchcock to avoid too much contact with his cast.

Balcon's custom of bringing in handsome American stars for his European productions was never surpassed after *The Pleasure Garden,* for
it featured Virginia Valli — at the time Universal's stunning brunette
leading lady — who had an unusually affecting screen presence and a
porcelain innocence that, with her dark hair and distracted, almost sad
eyes, gave her the look of an ingenue saint. With her in the cast was
her good friend Carmelita Geraghty, whose pert, blond sassiness was a
perfect counterpoint.

Virginia Valli was thirty years old, and only five years away from
the start of what would turn out to be almost forty years of happy retirement after marrying her husband, actor Charles Farrell. "I was scared
to death she'd find out I'd never directed before," Hitchcock recalled.
He found that the Hollywood contingent had a breezy confidence, a
certain elegant haughtiness, and money; and they tended not to socialize
with Hitchcock, Alma, and the rest of the London crew. This apparently
suited the engaged couple, in any case, since their evenings were spent
drafting detailed preparations for the next day's shooting — Hitchcock
sketching storyboards for Ventimiglia to follow, while Alma made suggestions for script improvement and took charge of the financial details.

One member of the American group fascinated Hitchcock, however:
the formidable Nita Naldi. Exactly the same age as the director and his
fiancée, she was born Anita Dooley in New York City, but her sen-
suous gaze and dubious sense of timing quickly established her as the
quintessential vamp of the American silent cinema. With Rudolph Val-
entino in *Blood and Sand,* she had become, in 1922, an international
cause as much as a film star. Producers, directors, and audiences wanted
more of her more often, and she accepted Balcon's precipitous invitation to replace the native girl on condition she could extend her stay in
Europe for another role.

Hitchcock admired and was somewhat intimidated by Naldi's brassy
directness. But he was put at ease by her tough humor, and apparently
she accompanied him and Alma on one of their rare excursions into the
demimonde of Munich society — a tour of a brothel. Hitchcock swore,
ever after, that they had stepped into the place quite accidentally, and

that he had beat a hasty retreat with an embarrassed Alma clutching his sleeve. On at least one other occasion, he was invited to what seemed an innocent party that turned out to be a prelude to something like an orgy. When he refused consort with one of the women, she shrugged and bedded a female companion while Hitchcock stood by, compensating for his scant knowledge of matters sexual by making a prolonged observation of the lesbian encounter.

*The Pleasure Garden* was completed late in the summer of 1925, and the cast and crew disbanded. Hitchcock and Alma, reviewing the final cut of the film, saw a melodrama that dearly needed some original touches. As it stood, it was an unexceptional story of two London chorus girls (performers at The Pleasure Garden, a music hall) and their different fidelities to the men in their lives. One of them (Valli) follows her husband (Mander) to the Far East when she hears he is ill, but she discovers that he has taken up with a native girl. The other girl (Geraghty) forsakes her fiancé (John Stuart) — who is also in the tropics — and ruthlessly pursues a theatrical and a fast life in London. The deranged husband is shot after he drowns the native girl, and his widow finds consolation in the arms of her friend's jilted fiancé.

By a skillful rearrangement of several scenes in mid-picture, Hitchcock tightened up the ironic associations between the two couples, emphasizing the double-crossed friendship of the men and women. The famous opening shot — of leggy chorus girls rushing down a spiral staircase and onto a stage, where they are avidly inspected by spectators with opera glasses — is in many ways a primer for scenes and images and themes that would have, in the later films, considerable psychological resonance: the dizzying staircase, the impulse to voyeurism, the theater as a rehearsal for real-life drama. These were the director's own additions to a somewhat wooden story. And his experience as title-card designer made it easy for him to exploit the possibilities for appropriate designs; thus, the drawing of a snake around a tree gives, in one card, another meaning to the garden of the title.

Before Balcon arrived in Munich to inspect the finished film, Hitchcock knew he had to improve the pacing. And so from the American films of Griffith he took the technique of the chase and the nick-of-time rescue, combining them with his love story and effecting his first double-chase motif. "In the ideal chase structure," he said, "the tempo and complexity of the chase will be an accurate reflection of the intensity of the relations between the characters." And so the feelings of the women, and of their men, shift and change as the murder, the madness, and the rescue become emblematic of the characters' variations in passion. "Griffith was the first to exploit the possibilities of the physical chase, but I tend to multiple chases and a lot of psychology."

By the time Balcon arrived, Hitchcock had a print he was proud of. They sat in a stiflingly small screening room and watched together, and when the lights went on Balcon reflected aloud that it had the look not of a European but of an American picture — which meant not that it was inferior to the continental product, but that, on the contrary, it would have a wide marketability. He was sufficiently pleased, in fact, to invite Hitchcock to stay in Munich to direct a second Anglo-German film, and he promptly announced that there would be three further projects waiting when he returned to England in early 1926. Hitchcock was delighted and he rushed to tell Alma, who wired her parents that she, too, would be staying on in Munich.

The production of the second Anglo-German venture, *The Mountain Eagle,* in the fall of 1925, was memorable only because it gave Hitchcock an opportunity to acquaint himself more intimately with the Tyrol: the film itself (the story of a crazy love scandal among the hillbillies of Kentucky) was a ridiculous assignment. During a break in the shooting, toward the end of October, the director suffered a frightening and protracted bout of nausea as they were returning from Obergurgl, in the Ötztaler Alps. From his childhood Hitchcock had a terror of vomiting, and when he experienced the dreaded waves of nausea it was, he later concluded, a reaction to a kind of social claustrophobia as much as to gastronomic indulgence; in this case, he felt that, surrounded by people who spoke no English, he was oppressed, unable to make his wants known, unable to assert himself. Thus the disturbed stomach, as he understood it, had a purely emotional etiology. Contrariwise, he could never remember becoming ill because of mere overeating.

In January 1926 the English cast and crew returned to London, Hitchcock to his mother in Leytonstone and Alma to her family in Twickenham. From opposite ends of the city they would meet, sometimes twice weekly, to attend the new American movies and discuss technique over coffee afterward. Only 5 percent of the films commercially screened in London were native British products at this time, and ambitious directors knew they would have to understand American method and content in order to assure the success of their own work.

During the late winter months, the couple's discussions and moviegoing were curtailed for a time, since Alma had more work than her fiancé — she sometimes undertook the editing and script preparations for three and four films at once for Balcon. Hitchcock, however, was waiting for the producer to announce a starting date for the next promised picture. For several weeks, when Alma was detained at the studio, he wrote her long letters — mostly, she remembered, about films, although there must have been some mention of their future together. But then the deliveries stopped, and Hitchcock began to bring them in person to the Reville home in Sandycombe Road. He could not, he said, endure the suspense of waiting for the day's delay, and if he spoke to Alma on the telephone in the evening he wanted to know for certain that she had read the day's letter beforehand.

With Alma — and apparently only with Alma — he began to lose some of the natural diffidence that he had inherited at home. Shyness often masquerades a quirky, hypersensitive pride, an unwillingness to risk rejection or to appear foolish, and in Hitchcock's case shyness took the form, early on, of a Buddha-like deadpan with people he did not know well. Alma was brisk — sometimes even brusque, as when she delivered herself of an instant judgment on someone's ability or personality — and her outspokenness, as well as her willingness to assume all sorts of social responsibilities, commanded Hitchcock's admiration. She was full of good advice about his future.

Toward the end of March, Balcon held a screening of *The Pleasure Garden* for the press and for theater exhibitors. ''A powerful and interesting story,'' wrote an anonymous reviewer in the *Bioscope* for March 25.

This has been well adapted to the screen, and admirable acting and masterly production all combine to make this a film of outstanding merit. The story is clearly and logically constructed, the sub-titling is concise and to the point, and the dramatic interest is held to the last minute. The scenes during Patsy's honeymoon on Lake Como, photographed by Baron Ventimiglia, present enchanting pictures and assist the dramatic appeal of the story. As Alfred Hitchcock's first production, this promises well for future efforts.

The distribution company for Balcon, however — headed by the unpleasant financier C. M. Woolf — thought the film would confuse and upset audiences, with such strange shots as overhead views of a spiral staircase, odd angles and shadows, high contrasts in lighting, and low-angle shots of chorines' legs as they descended to stage level. They may have things like this in German films, Woolf snapped, but English audiences were not accustomed to them. He was right on both counts: from the Germans Hitchcock had learned a good deal about creating atmosphere with light and shadow and with striking camera angles; British moviegoers, however, were accustomed to the rather more simple views presented by American melodrama and by the static, brightly lit drawing-room comedies and romances served up by British studios.

Balcon was persuaded that circulating *The Pleasure Garden* would endanger bookings for several of his other movies, already successful releases at the time, and so the negative and prints of Hitchcock's first complete film were banished to the studio storeroom. Not long afterward, critic Cedric Belfrage wrote in the *Picturegoer* that this was a surprising move, since "Hitchcock has such a complete grasp of all the different branches of film technique that he is able to take far more control of his production than the average director of four times his experience. The fact is that he has crammed twenty years of experience into five years of practise, while his youth is a tremendous asset towards freshness of treatment." But Woolf was adamant. *The Pleasure Garden* would not receive his backing or distribution.

For two full weeks after his announcement, Hitchcock's letters and calls to Alma stopped altogether. She was quite busy, in demand in several capacities at the studio, and the films on which she was working now were released within days of the completion of final photography. There was talk at Islington about Alma's future as a scriptwriter and even as a director, and this, added to Hitchcock's own bitter disappointment, was for a time too much for him to endure. When he was not with his mother, whose strength consoled him greatly, he took long, solitary lunches in the West End — after which he took the underground back to Leytonstone for a long, quiet dinner with Mrs. Hitchcock.

But then, in late April, Balcon told Hitchcock that he had a literary property ready for screen adaptation, and that Eliot Stannard was ready to meet the director for story conferences. Balcon had chosen a popular 1913 mystery novel, *The Lodger,* by Marie Adelaide Lowndes, sister of Hilaire Belloc. Mrs. Belloc Lowndes, as she preferred to be known, had realized her greatest success with this story based on the notorious crimes committed by Jack the Ripper in East London; Balcon thought Hitchcock's strong sense of character and narrative could balance the mystery aspects of the story, and that "A Story of the London Fog," as it was subtitled, would justify any eerie visual touches Hitchcock had learned from the Germans.

Stannard did not need much time to complete the treatment and dialogue, and at the beginning of May Balcon was surprised to hear that they were ready to start shooting. The script had been broken down into separate shots, and these shots had been sketched by Hitchcock and an illustrator; the set designs, furnishings, and props were all noted on paper; the art directors had only to do what was indicated. The film was, in a way, completely assembled on paper before a roll of stock had been exposed. Although Balcon had some reservations about a point or two of clarity in the story, he admired the economy and thorough preparation; at once he signed two of the most popular British stars for the leads, and a supporting cast well known to theatergoers. With that done, he left for America to sell films and hire Hollywood stars.

Principal photography on the film began the first week of May at the Islington studios. Ivor Novello, the Welsh-born, Oxford-educated matinee idol who had been an author and actor since 1916 and in films since 1919 (and who was perhaps best known as the composer of "Keep the Home Fires Burning") was engaged to play the role of the nameless lodger* — and because of his enormous popularity a change in the script was demanded at once. Whether Woolf took action again, or whether this was required by Balcon, cannot be determined. What is certain, however, is that Hitchcock could not conclude the film on the ambiguous note he had hoped, with the lodger going off into the night and his innocence or guilt never clearly resolved. "They wouldn't let Novello even be considered as a villain," Hitchcock said. "The publicity angle carried the day, and we had to change the script to show that without a doubt he was innocent. So I just never even showed the real murderer." Hitchcock resented the imposition, but he was powerless to make an executive decision.

For the role of Daisy Bunting, the mannequin and daughter of the household to which Novello comes, the actress June Tripp was hired. She preferred to be billed without her family name, and as June she had appeared in a handful of minor, wholly forgettable films in the early 1920s. (In 1929 she married Lord Inverclyde and, except for a few brief stage appearances in the early 1930s, retired professionally. Her fame rests on her performance in *The Lodger,* although in private life, as Lady Inverclyde, she had an active career in English society.)

Hitchcock was in his element in the grimy Islington studio, although he felt awkward working near his former superior Graham Cutts, the star director whose career, owing in part to his increasingly sad private life, was continuing to founder. Cutts referred to Hitchcock as "that boy on the set"; and the ease with which Hitchcock worked, and the cooperation he got from his crew, did nothing to stem Cutts's resentment — a resentment that sprang, no doubt, from a quite accurate suspicion that his own star would soon be eclipsed by Hitchcock's. Perhaps partly because of Cutts's hostility toward youthful success, Hitchcock tried to give his chubby-boy face an appearance of maturity by growing a mustache. Alma sustained it for about a month, and with a word from her it was removed.

At work, however, there was nothing intimidated about his manner.

---

* Many writers and some printed credits refer to the lodger as a character named Jonathan Drew, but this designation is nowhere to be found in the film.

His designs for *The Lodger* were meticulously executed, and soon every corner of the studio floor bore the stamp of Bloomsbury, where the story was set. A three-sided house was constructed, with narrow walls and low ceilings in the exact dimensions of a middle-class home. The difficulties of lighting such a set were considerable, but with Ventimiglia's genial patience and Hitchcock's knowledge of how the Germans had moved cameras up and down a staircase (suspended, if necessary, from tracking or scaffolding overhead), the complex and sinuously evocative shots were all achieved with surprising economy.

By the end of May shooting was more than half finished. Hitchcock's confidence grew daily, and he was at ease with his cast. Visitors to the set included Mrs. Belloc Lowndes herself, whose friend Novello found Hitchcock a delight — if occasionally a prankster. Actor-writer Rodney Ackland, asking why Hitchcock was taking so much care to photograph Novello with a flowerpot placed strategically on a shelf behind him, was told: "It was just too tempting, I couldn't resist it. Anyway, with that profile, why should Ivor mind having a flower-pot on his head?" Matinee idol or not, the darkly handsome and effeminate Novello was never, on or off the set, especially shy about his homosexual life. Fascinated by this boldness, and intrigued by what he at first thought a shocking life-style, Hitchcock took full cinematic advantage of the actor's good nature. The director had to have his little joke.

Novello would, as it turned out, be only the first of many Hitchcock actors whose private lives were, if not controversial, at least unconventional. Although Hitchcock himself coveted the image of the bourgeois gentleman throughout his life, the truth is that he equally coveted the knowledge that might have come from a more rebellious — or at least adventurous — exploration of the possibilities of life's alternatives. "Some people might be surprised by this," said an actress who knew him well, "but Hitchcock was always quite comfortable with homosexual or bisexual people. He always told his actors that they really had to be part masculine and part feminine in order to get inside any other character. Subjectivity, he felt, and feeling, transcended gender."

As for the actress June, Hitchcock's major concern was in the proper lighting for her blond wig and the proper photography for her descent down a staircase in the role of a model wearing the season's fashions. As Daisy, she followed Virginia Valli as a brunette actress changed into a blond by Hitchcock; many would have the same experience later.*

*In addition to his obvious personal preference for fair-haired heroines, Hitchcock may have been aware that in late-nineteenth-century culture, a serious emotional nature was typified by brunettes in art. Blonds in fiction were ordinarily naive or frivolous. In Eliot's *Middlemarch*, for example (1871–1872), noble, self-sacrificing, dark-haired Dorothea is contrasted with the shallow, selfish, pale blond Rosamond.

*The Lodger* was completed by early July, at a cost of twelve thousand pounds, and Balcon was nervously hopeful about the result. Cutts, who had often dropped in to watch the shooting, spread the rumors about the incomprehensibility of the film that accounted for Balcon's nervousness; the hope was needed because of the studio's precarious financial situation. To help alleviate that situation, Balcon had recently formed Piccadilly Pictures as the official production unit for Gainsborough Studios. For Piccadilly's distribution, the W. and F. Distribution Company was again engaged, with Woolf as chairman — now legally more involved with Balcon's company — and with Balcon himself as managing director of business operations and the American actor Carlyle Blackwell as executive in charge of production.

During August *The Lodger* was, according to the custom of the time, being tinted in the laboratory; grays and browns and greens were added to subtly complement the tenebrous lighting of the interiors and exteriors the director had so painstakingly lit with his cameraman. It was one of the loveliest, most temperate summers in English history, and Hitchcock and Alma celebrated their birthdays with picnic lunches on the thirteenth and fourteenth, in anticipation of the first screenings of *The Lodger,* which had been set for early September.

But Graham Cutts's displeasure was reaching a more fervent heat that season, and when Balcon returned from America he was met with a storm of protest from the senior director, whose opinion still carried considerable influence. "He had been perfectly happy with Hitch the young handyman and as his assistant director," Balcon wrote.

Hitch could not understand what he had done to offend Cutts and I had to explain to him that he had done nothing wrong; it was only that Cutts was jealous. Hitch was rising too fast for Cutts's taste and he resented him as a rival director in the same studio. . . . Cutts began to tell anybody who would listen that we had a disaster on our hands. Unfortunately, one person who listened to him was C. M. Woolf, who, of course, had the say as to distribution.

Hitchcock suspected that there was once again trouble brewing behind the executive doors. On the day of the screening for Woolf, the Piccadilly crew, and potential exhibitors, Hitchcock was nowhere to be found. He went to Twickenham to fetch Alma (who was on a brief vacation), then took her for hours on a walk around central London: across the Thames, up the Strand, through the West End — it was, she remembered, an aimless walk that continued until late afternoon. Finally, Hitchcock turned away and said, "They've seen it all by now and had a chance to hash it over. Let's go back."

When they walked into the studio, they knew at once that the worst had happened. "Your picture is so dreadful," Woolf said calmly, "that we're just going to put it on the shelf and forget about it."

Balcon was keenly embarrassed for his young director. He was also embarrassed financially, since the film's cost of twelve thousand pounds was a great deal of money, and this now seemed a complete waste. To aggravate matters, both *The Pleasure Garden* and *The Mountain Eagle* were also being held up, since Woolf considered them also unmarketable. But Balcon felt he had to follow the successful release of Novello's *The Rat* with another film featuring the same star. At this point, however, unless Balcon could come up with an idea to salvage *The Lodger*, it was entirely possible that Alfred Hitchcock's film career would be summarily concluded.

Balcon in fact did come up with an idea, and, as it turned out, it was an idea that made history. He canceled the early general trade show, to which the press would have been invited, and announced a postponement until late September. Then he called director Adrian Brunel, a founding member of London's Film Society who was also under contract to him, and asked whether a young Cambridge graduate named Ivor Montagu was still translating titles and reediting foreign films in Brunel's cramped offices behind Shaftesbury Avenue in the heart of Soho.

Balcon had heard about Montagu: He was an intellectual who had studied zoology, he was the son of the eminent banker Lord Swaythling, and he had been brought up in splendor in a house in Kensington. Montagu was, in 1926, just twenty-two, but he had been associated for some time with left-wing politics. Also a founding member of the Film Society, he was regarded as its token intellectual as well as a political and social spokesman (he founded the film technicians' union in London). Although it was always Montagu's dream to be a first-rate director, his talents were not in that area. But his critical faculties were immediately recognizable to the *Times* of London, which sent him to Germany in early 1925 to cover the growth of the film industry there. One of the results of his trip, quite naturally, was a new appreciation of German technique; he also struck friendships with luminaries like Elisabeth Bergner and Emil Jannings.

The day after Woolf's plain negation, Balcon and Montagu discussed *The Lodger* over a luncheon of mashed potatoes and fried onions, at Monaco's in Piccadilly Circus, and Montagu was anxious to see what could be done. Balcon screened it for him, and Montagu was hugely impressed. He found the narrative compelling, the design innovative, and the compositions of the images haunting. He at once suggested some paring down of the title cards and some minor reshooting of a few unclear scenes. He also wanted to bring in E. McKnight Kauffer, the American poster artist who revolutionized British design and who was then living in London, to draw sinister title-backgrounds that would highlight the film's triangular structural and thematic design (the triangle was not only the shape of the notepaper left by the murderer but also a symbol of the film's three-way love contest).

Hitchcock was summoned, and Montagu found him at first a somewhat resentful young man, unshakable in his confidence about his own technical judgment. But Montagu concurred that Hitchcock's technical judgment was indeed virtually impeccable, and when he assured the director that what the film needed was *improving* on its already exceptionally artistic qualities — *not* removing them to make the picture banal — Hitchcock realized that Montagu was no Cutts or Woolf, that he seemed to appreciate his special gifts, and that Montagu's suggestions could save his career along with his trio of films. The troublesome scenes were reshot, the number of title cards was reduced from over three hundred to about eighty, and McKnight Kauffer's designs were inserted at strategic points. Just before the press screening, Hitchcock admitted that what he thought was a good film had indeed been improved. The relationship with Montagu was — for the moment — quite cordial.

Balcon made no secret of his gratitude to Montagu at the studio: he would be brought in as supervising editor of the next two Hitchcock films at Gainsborough. For decades after, Montagu retained a cordial respect for Hitchcock. But in *his* many lengthy discussions about *The Lodger,* Hitchcock never mentioned — much less credited — Montagu ("A few months later they decided to take another look at the picture and to make some changes. I agreed to make about two"). It was the first clear example of an ungenerous streak in Hitchcock's nature. Afraid that sharing some credit with a collaborator might diminish his own stature, he cherished the illusion that every element of a success was his own. Confident in his technical ability (and even in the thematic balance) of his first English film, he would remember it as a success only if he could remember it as entirely his own. In any case, the press rhapsodized. The *Bioscope* proclaimed, on September 16, 1926, "It is possible that this film is the finest British production ever made."

The film's popularity might well have had other social roots. The war of 1914–1918 brought the ultimate challenge to nineteenth-century absolutes and transformed the social and economic structure of Great Britain. The world had literally exploded in violence and death, and these realities filled everyone's consciousness daily. Psychological stress, the transient nature of this world, the precarious order of civilization, the sudden eruption of madness in local crimes — these burst in on a world of rapidly advancing technology at the same time as the most dramatic means of entertainment was reaching millions weekly. And in *The Lodger* Hitchcock depicted these social concerns perhaps better than anyone up to that time. Technically, the film reflected the German influence; generically, it responded to the British predilection for crime fiction. With its subtheme of a jealous detective's error, which very nearly causes the death of the innocent lodger, the film tries to reorder an incoherent world confused about the allocation of guilt and innocence. Social conflicts are thus dramatized as personal dilemmas.

In the liberties it takes with the original source, the film everywhere reveals the sensibility of the director. The sense of common London life is conveyed in the easy bourgeois attitudes of the Bunting family, and in the certain ignorant awe in which the lodger is held at the finale. The family is straight out of Hitchcock's own; mother is the dominant influence, overseeing and commenting on the courting between the young people, who always visit chaperoned, and always in the family quarters. And Hitchcock insists on mother's Catholicism: there is a crucifix standing on her night table, photographed clearly in two separate shots. From his own East End experience, Hitchcock also knew that a lodger has no place in the ordinary life of the family, that he was a shadowy background figure "whose comings and goings," according to two historians, "were nobody's business but his own. His generic nickname is unforgettable however. He was the Artful Dodger. It was a rhyme, and a joke on all the jokes about the lodger as seducer."

Equally revealing is the way in which Hitchcock apparently identifies with both the lodger and the detective. "I'm keen on golden hair myself, same as the lodger is," announces the detective, and it is jealousy that destroys their relationship and nearly kills the innocent man. In one of the boldest scenes in silent film, the detective promises to put a ring on Daisy's finger when he has put a noose around the murderer's neck — and he promptly claps a set of handcuffs on Daisy, actualizing the picture on the lodger's wall of a blond woman in bondage, tied to a stake for torture. "Psychologically, of course, the idea of the handcuffs has deeper implications," Hitchcock acknowledged. "It's somewhere in the area of fetishism, and it has a sexual connotation. When I visited the Vice Museum in Paris, I noticed there was considerable evidence of sexual aberrations through restraint."

But Hitchcock's interest in *The Lodger* is not in the sociopathology of the crime — much less in the identity of the actual criminal. He dwells rather on the *effect* of crime on ordinary people — on the detective's suspicion, but also on Daisy's willingness to believe in the innocence of her lodger precisely because of his smooth good looks, which are always lit to contrast with the blandness of the detective's. And Hitchcock is perhaps most of all interested in the effect of the crimes on the lodger himself, who is driven to track the murderer and kill him in revenge for the death of his own sister. Guilt and innocence do indeed inhabit the same country, for the lodger is spiritually guilty of a murder he is as yet innocent of actually committing.

On still another level, the lodger resembles a filmmaker — and a smitten one, at that: oblivious to everyone around him, he is absorbed with Daisy's grand entrance as a mannequin. She is a simple girl who is to be studied and then, once watched and judged, outfitted with ornate additions to her personal wardrobe. The desire to unclothe and clothe, to estimate and to make over, to see and not to see, is focused in a bathroom scene, when the steam of Daisy's bathwater slowly rises to cover her nakedness as she disrobes. The lodger's hand is shown tentatively turning the knob outside, as if he will disturb her privacy. Then the camera cuts to her legs in the water, as if from her point of view. As the film progresses, the camera moves more boldly to close in on the intimacy, and the last shot is a tight close-up on the pair of kissing lips.

The whole film has a delicate poise between this kind of repulsion and attraction, between paranoia (the murderer is on the prowl) and laughter at that paranoia (people in the street, and in the chorus girls' dressing room, frighten each other for fun and for the sense of relief). There is an underlying fear of the little things of everyday life, which are seen as menacing — beyond the fear that the distracted, neurasthenic lodger may be a murderer (which is, after all, just exactly what he wants to be).

And the ending is pure Hitchcock, with its disturbing association between sex and death. The film opens with the blinking lights of a theater marquee: TONIGHT — GOLDEN CURLS. There follows the story of the murder of young blond women. And at the end, as the blond Daisy and her new lover embrace, the same sign blinks in the background. A joke, to be sure — but a joke that associates murder with the "love night" of Daisy and the lodger, and with their future. The link between bondage and pleasure, between handcuffs and sexual teasing, has come to its logical term: for the first time, Hitchcock has revealed his psychological attraction to the association between sex and murder, between ecstasy and death.

The success of the trade show of *The Lodger* enabled Balcon to schedule a trade show for *The Mountain Eagle,* which the influential *Bioscope* on October 7 said had "an air of unreality. . . . Director Alfred Hitchcock has not been particularly well served by his author, in spite of skillful, and at times brilliant direction." The mixed critical reaction did nothing to temper the enthusiasm for *The Lodger,* however, which everyone in London was eager to see; they would, it turned out, have to wait until January 1927 for *The Pleasure Garden,* February for *The Lodger,* and May for *The Mountain Eagle,* for the theaters were ordinarily booked several months in advance.

But word about *The Lodger* was out well in advance of the first public screening, and before he fulfilled his contract with Balcon for two more films, Hitchcock was approached by John Maxwell, executive head of British International Pictures. Would Hitchcock be interested in signing a multipicture deal with the rival studio, at the princely sum of thirteen thousand pounds a year, more than three times what he was making at Gainsborough? Hitchcock signed at once, and it must have been with considerable relief that Cutts could encounter Hitchcock at the Islington studio and think of him as a threat that would soon be removed. Balcon, of course, was disappointed, but he took the move in good grace and wished Hitchcock well.

Plans were not yet firm for the remaining Gainsborough films, however, and late autumn 1926 seemed a good time to arrange for the wedding. During September, October, and November, Alma Reville concluded the course of instruction required for her conversion to Roman Catholicism, an event that seems to have originated with the insistence of Hitchcock's mother. With Alma duly rebaptized in the Church of Rome, the final arrangements could be set, and the ceremony took place on Thursday morning, December 2. Quietly, almost secretively, a few family members gathered in a dark, ornate side chapel of the Brompton Oratory, Knightsbridge. The Reverend J. J. Bevan, a resident priest at this, one of London's grandly proud Roman parishes, presided. William Hitchcock, large and barrel-chested and awkward, stood best man for his younger brother, and Eva Reville attended her sister. The marriage certificate identifies the "condition" of Alfred Joseph Hitchcock as bachelor, his profession that of film director; Alma Lucy Reville is identified, oddly, as without occupation.

Immediately following the brief service, the wedding party bundled off in taxis to the empty flat Hitchcock had leased at 153 Cromwell Road. Champagne flowed, cakes were served, and the groom reigned proudly as a boisterously genial host. To the attendants and friends the newlyweds might have seemed an amusing conjunction. Hitchcock still looked younger than his twenty-seven years, but was growing heavier by the month, and at five-feet-eight was clearly too short to support almost two hundred pounds with much comfort or grace. Beside him stood his birdlike bride, not even five feet tall, and weighing well under a hundred. There was no doubt in anyone's mind, however, that the bride and groom respected and admired each other's talent, and that a strong bond united them.

Lively and clever, Alma Reville had been one of the few film editors credited on screen in the cinema of the 1920s, along with Ivor Montagu, Emile de Ruelle, and Angus MacPhail (who each would subsequently work with Hitchcock on several films). They were all, at various times, given writing credit as well for the contributions they offered their respective directors, and Michael Balcon was not alone in his belief that Alma might have a significant career as a director herself. Until 1929 she would occasionally write scripts for other filmmakers; after that she worked solely with Hitchcock.

"I was never terribly ambitious," she said years later, and in fact for the next half-century her energies would be geared to the encouragement and protection of her husband. Those who worked with them would observe that they were "really like brother and sister, but in business matters quiet little Alma could be a scrappy little watchdog," and that she was "much shrewder about people than Hitchcock, and a lot tougher. Their relationship was that of working partners." According to Elsie Randolph, one of Hitchcock's favorite feature players and long-term social acquaintance of the couple, Alma was "a co-writer, a cook, a hausfrau — I doubt it was a grand passion. And to tell the truth, she bossed him."

From this time forward, Alma was the ultimate arbiter of the coherent story for a Hitchcock film, and her opinion of the final cut was always required by her husband: she was the last to see a film before its distribution, the last to express an opinion on a difficult scene or a point of narrative, and her advice was always carefully considered if not always followed. The highest praise Hitchcock could offer was: "Alma really liked that last scene you wrote" — a testimony that not only delivered him from the burden of complimenting a writer, but also revealed his estimation of her critical judgment.

The evening of the wedding they took the boat train to France. Stopping in Paris en route to their honeymoon in Switzerland, they met Nita Naldi and her elderly gentleman friend, and on one night fell back to their hotel so roaringly drunk that Alma decided, next morning, never to repeat the experience. To this promise she adhered with almost religious fervor. Hitchcock made no such promise — and that, as it would turn out, was an unwise decision.

Saint Moritz — the resort where millionaires entertain at ski lodges and live in deluxe hotels year round — was Hitchcock's first choice for his experience of the good life, and to this place he and Alma returned, whenever they could, for the observance of their wedding anniversary. Six thousand feet up in the broad Engadine Valley where the river Inn begins, Saint Moritz was, then as now, best approached by train from Zurich. Beautiful as the journey from Paris was, the last two-hour stretch surpassed everything. From Chur they took the twenty-year-old Rhaetian Railway, with its long tunnel near the Albula Pass and more than one hundred other tunnels and bridges delighting Hitchcock the rail enthusiast.

The Palace Hotel provided just what the name promised for the awed English couple — a hotel on a palatial scale, grander than anything they had ever seen. The lobby still retains the dimensions of a small French cathedral, complete with a Raphael Madonna coolly presiding over the ubiquitous prodigality. The two hundred miles of ski and bobsled and toboggan runs in the vicinity engaged the honeymooners' attention only as spectators; never given to sport (much less to anything involving even the slightest risk), Hitchcock contented himself with sleigh rides, watched the skaters, and laughed at the game of golf on ice that had been one of Saint Moritz's curiosities for almost a century.

Here they lived like royalty. Hitchcock decided that, with an enormous salary coming from Maxwell in 1927, there was no need to reserve the savings earned from the Balcon films. He gratified their every whim on the trip, virtually each one being gastronomic. They sipped hot cocoa and munched pastries at local confiseries, took in floor shows and chorales at the casino, and ordered wines from the cellars of the most expensive restaurants in town. In 1926 there was no cinema in Saint Moritz, and their meals were prolonged so that they often had little time between lunch and tea, and so that tea usually became the predinner cocktail hour. Hitchcock was eager to try the specialties of the canton, and so ordered *bündnerfleisch* — the smoked, dried, and thinly sliced beef — which he washed down with generous quantities of Swiss white and Italian red wines.

They did manage, on one gray afternoon, to talk over an idea for a film to be set in Saint Moritz: it must have something to do with a war, Hitchcock thought, or with a dangerous gang of thieves, for what could be more upsettingly inappropriate in this sedate, elegant atmosphere? They submerged the idea in cakes and ales, but quietly — almost ob-

sessively — Hitchcock turned the images in his head like chips in a
kaleidoscope. Eight years later, the designs would be clarified and
brought to the screen in *The Man Who Knew Too much*.

The newlyweds returned to Cromwell Road for a quiet Christmas and
a new year that began auspiciously. On January 24, 1927, *The Pleasure
Garden* was finally released, and Hitchcock was proclaimed "a young
man with a master mind" by the senior critic of the London press.
Balcon and his associates at Islington scarcely had time to offer their
congratulations (or to lament Hitchcock's imminent departure to a rival
studio) when a greater triumph occurred: three weeks later, on February
14, *The Lodger* opened and the name Hitchcock was heard all over
London.
   It was the first time in British film history that the director received
an even greater press than his stars. Crowds formed queues from noon
to midnight, and one quick-eyed critic identified an unbilled member of
the cast. Wasn't that Hitchcock himself, with his back to the camera,
in the newspaper office at film's beginning? And didn't he take a curtain
call at the climax, wedged among the crowd, watching the lodger's
rescue? It was the first time Hitchcock had had himself filmed, as a kind
of visual signature, and the cameo role would become standard procedure for the next fifty years. The movie craftsman would in time be
hailed as an artist of the cinema, but he never lost his showman's instinct. From the publicity-conscious Dickens, whose habits for self-
exposure were widely known, Hitchcock learned something more than
storytelling techniques.
   To critics of his flair for publicity he always explained that if he made
himself publicly known as a director — and this he could do only by
getting mention in the press in connection with his directing — this
would be the way to do what he wanted. Any production company would
be glad to have the attraction of his name. Before long, when distributors issued questionnaires to movie-theater audiences and asked them to
name English film directors, the only name that appeared more than
once or twice was Hitchcock's, and his was counted in the thousands
by the tabulators.
   For his last two films at Gainsborough, Hitchcock and his scenarist,
Eliot Stannard, were assigned the task of adapting plays. "In the twenties we were to a great extent mentally 'stage-bound,' " Balcon wrote.
"We looked to the theatre for much of our screen material and our early
films would certainly now be called 'stagey.' . . . We followed trends
and did not try to make them. It was doubly a mistake to lean on stage
plays because we were making *silent* films, so the plays were deprived

of their very essence, the words! . . . Our policy did not always pay off.''

The first adaptation was an attempt to cash in on the Hitchcock-Novello combination, and it was a patchy melodrama based on a series of sketches by Novello and Constance Collier, who together wrote under the pseudonym David LeStrange. *Downhill* is the story of an innocent young man (a type Novello relished) who takes the blame for a school friend accused of fathering an illegitimate child. Expelled from school and home, he follows a path ''downhill,'' enduring various experiences around the world and even confronting his own weaknesses until he is finally restored to the family's respect.

Stannard completed the script in February, and just before filming began in March the director added the opening title card; the film the audience was about to see was a tale of ''two schoolboys who made a pact of loyalty — and one kept it at a price.'' What intrigued Hitchcock, and what he developed as the film's motif, was the theme of the exploitation of loyalties — an idea that would be deepened in *Shadow of a Doubt, Notorious, Strangers on a Train, Vertigo, North by Northwest,* and *Frenzy.* Friendships, in Hitchcock's works, are dangerous precisely because they risk betrayal: intimacy bears the terrible burden of responsibility.

During the editing, Hitchcock instructed the lab technicians to tint a pale green the scenes of Novello's delirium when his health fails. He remembered, from his earlier playgoing, the green stage-lights for the appearance of ghosts and for the world of fantasy, and he now employed a primitive monochrome — instead of the conventional blurring at the edges — to suggest a hallucinatory state of mind.

At home, the Hitchcocks settled in earnest, and by winter's end the rooms were crowded with the chintz-covered, overstuffed furniture of the period and with the freestanding, fringe-shaded lamps and flocked wallpaper that were equally popular. But visitors were few that year: Hitchcock turned out four films and Alma served as assistant, as script girl and editor, on even more. Their budget permitted frequent patronizing of fine restaurants, but even at the more expensive places, like Simpson's, Hitchcock's tastes were not adventurous — steak and mashed potatoes, a rack of lamb with parsnips, grilled Dover sole.

Alma noted his preferences, learned the personality of the annoyingly variable, ancient oven at home, and on weekends, before they went off to the theater, served generous portions of his favorite dishes. Most often they dined alone — very rarely would an actor or colleague be invited — and they discussed special points of the films they were preparing or the wines they were sampling. Every month after their return

from the Saint Moritz honeymoon, a case of *Apfelwein* arrived as he
had ordered, and he looked forward to the dark, sweet cider for which
he had developed a weakness. On the rare occasion there was a visitor
at teatime, strong drink was served instead; Rodney Ackland recalled
that "white ladies" were then Hitchcock's specialty — "they knocked
one out more quickly and unfailingly than anything."

Part of the Hitchcocks' social reticence undoubtedly stemmed from
his discomfort with the world of glamour and elegance, charm and fashion — a world he found attractive and terrifying at the same time. The
simple Cockney upbringing, the sheltered life of Leytonstone, and the
twenty-six years of life with Mother combined with a certain social diffidence and placed an inevitable distance between himself and the handsome folk of film and theater. Ivor Novello, June, Robin Irvine, Isabel
Jeans — the quartet of leading players in his first two London pictures
consisted of two matinee idols and two wonderfully lovely women. In
*Downhill,* Novello looked sportier than in *The Lodger,* and in the same
film Robin Irvine's smooth, almost adolescent, open features, in his
performance as the school friend, set a number of hearts momentarily
off beat. Isabel Jeans's blond and deliciously saucy attitude undercut her
natural hauteur with a style quite different from June's unshaded charm.

These were popular and attractive and socially desirable performers,
while Alfred Hitchcock — celebrity though he might be — must have
been aware that his fame and riches did not alter his somewhat pouty
expression and expanding heft. He counted on Alma for a professional
encouragement that went beyond mere studio obligations, and he looked
to her for advice that was tempered with devotion. In this he was not
disappointed. For her part, she kept a tidy home, supervised a maid
they knew only as Gladys, corrected discontinuous elements in the scripts
for her husband's new films, and was even more chary of an augmented
social life than he — not because she shared his social discomfort or
his physical shyness, but because she doubted whether Alfred Hitchcock's talents were really appreciated by those who worked with him.
She was proud of her husband, but she was also becoming possessive,
and she discouraged a more active life outside.

Balcon had arranged for his distributors to release *The Mountain Eagle* on May 23, 1927. No one was really terribly surprised that the
London moviegoing public responded with less than wild enthusiasm
for a melodrama about Kentucky hillbillies. The film disappeared quickly
from the urban circuit. Not long afterward, the negative and all existing
copies disappeared altogether, and since then not a single print is known
to have survived (a fact that Hitchcock always insisted was entirely as

it should be). But the same week — perhaps anticipating a cool reception for *The Mountain Eagle* — Balcon was ready with a press screening of *Downhill*, which one influential trade paper called "another personal success" for the director, praising clever pictorial touches. "The story is a distinctly weak one, and only expert handling and imaginative production finally made it interesting." And for the benefit of interested exhibitors, *Bioscope* remarked that "the selling angle is the name of Hitchcock."

By this time, he and Stannard were putting the finishing touches to the last of the films for Balcon — a photoplay of Noël Coward's acerbic social drama *Easy Virtue*. Coward's thirteenth play, it had first been staged in New York in December 1925, and in London the following June, where it had had considerable success. The story of a woman (Isabel Jeans, with curled hair and curling lips) whose second marriage is destroyed by a narrow society's contempt for her tragic past, *Easy Virtue* was an angry indictment of social hypocrisies. At the end of the play, the woman simply leaves her second husband (played in the film with suitable spinelessness by Robin Irvine) and his intolerant family, and she steals away into the night as a party continues. Of the man's character she simply says, "My husband fell short of any ideal I ever had." But Hitchcock insisted on changing the story, emphasizing instead the woman's ostracism and betrayal by her in-laws, and the destructive effects of a scandal-hungry press. Balcon was not at all sure this was a proper deflection of the play's dramatic energy, but he gave Hitchcock the latitude he wanted.

Ivor Montagu, who had been a creative consultant and editor on *Downhill*, was asked to stay on for *Easy Virtue*, but this led to a temporary rupture in their relationship, due to a disagreement in the shooting method of a minor scene, which Hitchcock said nobody would mind in any case. And indeed very few people minded the scene — or the entire picture, for that matter, which was a financial failure. For all the witty and inventive visuals, "he had not then found his particular métier," as Balcon gently put it, conveniently omitting the fact that the project was an assignment.

The disappointing reception accorded to *Easy Virtue* when it was released later that year was more than just a setback for Balcon's studio or the local exhibitors. Since the end of 1924, the number of films produced in Britain had declined, and by mid-summer 1927 the industry was at its lowest ebb. Hitchcock's early successes had been a barometer of hope, but the bad news about *Easy Virtue*, his imminent transfer to British International, and the rumors of disaster in the industry hastened the passage of a curious yet understandable new law. The film business was on the road to extinction, the London Council observed, and the so-called Cinematograph Films Act of 1927 was designed to reinject the necessary economic health. Film exhibitors and distributors now had to fulfill an annually increasing quota of British features; no longer could theater owners simply book endless series of the more popular American films. Under the law, then, there began the production of a rash of low-budget, low-quality "quota quickies," ground out with great haste so that a proportionate number of the more lucrative foreign pictures could also be screened.

Some producers tried to have it both ways: if the law prevented them from importing too many foreign films, then they would import the foreign directors and stars and make the pictures at home. For a short time, London was crowded with imported talent at work on "English" pictures. Among the actors were Tallulah Bankhead, Monty Banks, Carl Brisson, Mady Christians, Lili Damita, Lya De Putti, Pauline Frederick, Dorothy Gish, Lars Hanson, Antonio Moreno, Nita Naldi, Anny Ondra, Will Rogers, Nadia Sibirskaia, Blanche Sweet, Alice Terry, and Anna May Wong. Directors included Monty Banks, E. A. Dupont, Henrik Galeen, Rex Ingram, Lupu Pick, and Tim Whelan. Among the art directors who arrived were O. F. Werndorff and Alfred Junge, and important cameramen like Karl Freund, Charles Rosher, and Werner Brandes also worked briefly in England.

But this immigration did not guarantee that the resulting products would be very much better than the quota quickies. Speed, reliance on stage adaptations, and a glut of British farce and British drawing-room comedy and unimaginative British melodrama still prevailed. H. G. Wells was one of the first men of letters to express public regret over the Cinematograph Films Act: quantity was replacing English quality, he complained. And when the law was being written and debated, George Bernard Shaw said, "My contempt for it deprives me of speech." But they and their friends at the Film Society went unheeded.

In an attempt to counter the trend with pictures of quality, the biggest company in English film history was gradually being formed at Borehamwood, later known for a time as Elstree, on a plot of twenty-seven acres in Hertfordshire. In March 1926 it was called M.E. Productions, and it was administered by John Maxwell, a Glasgow solicitor who had entered the industry as an exhibitor in 1912, slowly acquired a small circuit of theaters, and then became chairman of Wardour Films in 1923. In March 1927 he took over British National Pictures (the English branch — begun by J. D. Williams — of America's First National Picture Corporation, which would, back in America, be absorbed into Warner Brothers). Maxwell at once announced the existence of a new combine: British International Pictures. Hitchcock's arrival in 1927 was a giant step in Maxwell's continuing series of acquisitions and mergers.

British International was not, however, as nourishing of artists as Michael Balcon had been. Balcon was an artist's businessman; Maxwell was a businessman's businessman, a Scottish-English version of the high-powered Hollywood mogul. For his production chief at the studio, Maxwell hired Walter Mycroft, a former critic who established a school of scriptwriters at BIP. Mycroft's cinematic sensibilities were rather too academic and literary (and occasionally bizarre), and he seems to have been just what Maxwell wanted and what Hitchcock would resent: autocratic and quite content to be pretentious.

Whereas Hitchcock's relationship with Balcon had been cordially professional — advantageous to both but not especially warm in terms of friendship — the relationship with Maxwell was coolly efficient. Everyone knew that Hitchcock was now the highest paid director in England, and his arrival at BIP aroused considerable speculation as to how much rein Maxwell and Mycroft would allow him. At Islington he had distinguished himself with a thriller after showing that he could handle the more traditional melodramatics of *The Pleasure Garden* and *The Mountain Eagle,* and then he demonstrated a keen cleverness and stylistic innovation with the broad theatrics of *Downhill* and *Easy Virtue*. Preoccupied with its fervent attempts at executive reorganization, BIP had not come up with a first project for Hitchcock, and so Maxwell recommended to Mycroft that he allow him a free hand for his first film.

The result could not have been more surprising: a story about prize-fighters. Hitchcock submitted for approval an original story and screenplay he had put together at home during two hot weeks in July. (Some suggestions were offered by the faithful Eliot Stannard, and Hitchcock saw that he got some compensation.) He had had good luck with the subtheme of the romantic triangle in *The Lodger* and *Downhill,* and now he dealt with it directly in a bittersweet story of two boxers (played by Carl Brisson and Ian Hunter) in love with the same woman (Lillian Hall Davis).

"I think the thing, strangely enough, that fascinated me about boxing in those days was the English audience that would go all dressed up in black tie to sit around the ring," Hitchcock remarked. And in the film, which began shooting in late August, he stressed just such odd and ironic juxtapositions, simultaneously showing his fascination for the grotesque. The wedding of Nellie and One-Round Jack is attended by their friends from the fairground: Siamese twins fight about which side of the church to take seats on; the fat lady enters somewhat gingerly; the giant strolls in with the midget, and so on. His interest in freaks and freakishness, his increasing reliance on purely cinematic devices (blurred images, distorted montages), and his maintenance of the thematic and structural ambiguity of the title (boxing ring and wedding ring) all recall Hitchcock's exposure to the German school of filmmaking. And the masculine women who were passing characters in *The Pleasure Garden, The Lodger, Downhill,* and *Easy Virtue* now come into full light; the theatrical setting is now a crazy sideshow populated by a gallery of strange types. In *The Ring* (which certainly shows the influence of various German films), the recently married director portrays marriage as a series of "rounds" or "cycles" that comprise a long struggle. At film's end, One-Round Jack regains the loyalty of his wife, who has dallied with his champion opponent, but the circular structure of the story and the succession of round objects that act as markers suggest that long, hard efforts will be required in the couple's future.

*The Ring* was Hitchcock's first original screenplay, and the executives at BIP were astonished at its careful symmetry, its economy of story-telling means, and its psychological sophistication. And since it was a silent film, Hitchcock was able to display what was always his strongest talent: his ability to use strictly visual means to tell the story.* Filming was completed by the end of the summer, and when *The Ring* was screened for the press on the last day of September, Hitchcock was already at work on a firm assignment from Mycroft.

Meantime, however, Alma had contractual obligations to fulfill at Islington, and she began work on the screenplay for *The Constant Nymph* with the author of the novel and its dramatized version, Margaret Kennedy. This film was a great success for Alma and for its director, Adrian Brunel. Ivor Novello starred, with supporting performances from Mary Clare (later to work for Hitchcock), Mabel Poulton, and Benita Hume (who in *Easy Virtue* had played the eavesdropping switchboard operator whose facial expressions, in the film's most famous scene, tell the audience the outcome of a marriage proposal).

On the first of October, the trade papers were raving about *The Ring* ("This is the most magnificent British film ever made," gushed one critic), and Hitchcock undertook in appropriate high spirits the direction of his next assignment: another adapted play — the rustic and hilarious and touching comedy *The Farmer's Wife,* based on Eden Phillpotts's

---

*With the advent of sound, he would have — often none too gladly — to depend on writers. For Alfred Hitchcock, putting images into words was a terrible chore; polishing dialogue was tolerable — creating it was an almost impossible task.

great hit. While filming in Devon and Surrey, he came to appreciate the
back roads and sleepy villages, and to learn the flavor of British country
life. The simplicity and the lack of ''roaring twenties'' fashion appealed
to him, and when he returned to London in mid-October he suggested
to Alma that they buy a country house to use as a weekend retreat.
They narrowed their choice to the area near Guildford, in Surrey, an
hour's drive and as quiet as a movie, Hitchcock remarked — although
the papers were full of the news from America about ''talkies.'' In two
weeks, he finished studio work on *The Farmer's Wife,* with the last
close-up shots of Lillian Hall Davis and Jameson Thomas and Gordon
Harker, his leading players.

In November Hitchcock took another step in his campaign for personal publicity, quite apart from what BIP provided him. He wrote an
open letter to the *London Evening News* in answer to some questions
put to him verbally by a reporter. In it, he acknowledged his admiration
for American methods, referred obliquely to the difficulty of directing
certain stage actors on a film set, and made it clear that he intended, in
time, to exert control over every aspect of his films and to minimize the
collaborative nature of his craft.

''The Americans have left us very few stories to tell,'' he wrote.

But there is no reason why we should not tell stories of *English* boys who leave
the village and make good in the big city — why rural drama should not be found
and filmed among the mountains of Wales and the moors of Yorkshire. Our
history — national and imperial — provides a wonderful storehouse of film
drama. And there is the sea, our particular heritage: not only the Navy but the
great business of the mercantile marine should have a place on our screens.

Perhaps the immediate opportunity lies in more careful and more intelligent
treatment of film stories. The American film directors under their commercially
minded employers have learnt a good deal about studio lighting, action photographs, and telling a story plainly and smoothly in moving pictures. They have
learnt, as it were, to put the nouns, verbs, and adjectives of the film language
together.

But even if we conceive the film going no further as an art, it is obvious that
what we must strive for at once is the way to use these film nouns and verbs
as cunningly as do the great novelist and the great dramatist, to achieve certain
moods and effects on an audience. . . . How many people, I wonder, realise
that we *do* aim at moods in our films? We call it ''tempo,'' and by paying
careful attention to the speed with which we act our little plays we do attempt
to guide the observing minds into the right mood.

A light-hearted comedy played slowly may produce the sense of impending
doom, just as a too brightly acted drama might never give an atmosphere of

tragedy. . . . I had to film a little scene in *The Farmer's Wife* six times the other day because the players took it too slowly to fit in with the mood of the picture.

Film directors live with their pictures while they are being made. They are their babies just as much as an author's novel is the offspring of his imagination. And that seems to make it all the more certain that when moving pictures are really artistic they will be created entirely by one man.

There is no written record of BIP's reaction to this outspoken letter from a contracted director whose job was to film the story and actors packaged by studio executives. But behind Walter Mycroft's immediate announcement of Hitchcock's next two assignments — a story by Mycroft himself and an adaptation of a popular but dreary antiromantic novel — there was an attempt to control the director, to let him know without doubt who was in charge and where the "artistic decisions" really lay.

Studio executives, filmmakers, and audiences around the world knew that 1927 had been a landmark year. In America, Buster Keaton and Harold Lloyd were creating their best pictures, and others at work in Hollywood were Frank Capra, Josef von Sternberg, F. W. Murnau, Victor Seastrom, Ernst Lubitsch, C. B. De Mille, Paul Leni, Erich von Stroheim, Robert Flaherty, and Charles Chaplin. It was also the year that Jolson first spoke from the screen.

In Germany, Fritz Lang and G. W. Pabst were making enormously creative advances in the film, while in France René Clair was developing into a major talent and Abel Gance had just premiered his epic *Napoléon*. In Russia, V. I. Pudovkin applied his theories on film to actual production. England, meanwhile, was coping with a foolish and self-destructive quota system, and Alfred Hitchcock was trying to cope with the disappointing choices made for him by Mycroft.

In early December, the Hitchcocks returned to Saint Moritz, where they celebrated their first wedding anniversary and where Hitchcock renewed his order for monthly shipments of apple wine. Back home for Christmas, he designed something far more elaborate than a mere greeting card, something that in fact advertised himself more than it did the season. "It was made up on a square piece of wood," he explained, "and the wood was cut into jigsaw pieces and put into little linen bags with a label and sent out. They didn't know what the hell they were putting together until the outline came out." And the outline finally pieced together by the curious recipients turned out to be the original sketch of Hitchcock's eight-stroke profile caricature. As he drew it in later years, the figure, like its creator, gained bulk and lost the thin wave of hair, but it was always — like his cameo appearances — unmistakably Hitchcock.

On Christmas Eve he gave Alma a lamb's-wool coat, and at New Year's she gave him the news that by midyear he would be a father.

# Five

1928–1934

"In the beginning, the idea pleased him," recalled an actress who knew Hitchcook very well in later years. "But then, as little Alma grew larger and larger with child, he began to hate her appearance. He resented her — looked on her as misshapen and ugly, and the pregnancy disgusted him."

In early 1928 Alfred Hitchcock pitched himself more and more feverishly into his work and into the task of buying a country house. But he was not only nervous about the pregnancy and repelled by Alma's appearance (she was, after all, becoming distended, bloated — beginning, perhaps he thought, to resemble himself). He was also anxious about a stasis in his career: BIP had announced a disappointing pair of films for him, ideas that engaged his interest not at all. And if his interest was not engaged, his talent, he knew, could not be applied at full tilt, and this would mean a loss of power *in* the films — which would inevitably diminish his bargaining abilities for more power (and thus for more monetary compensation) in the production of future films.

Except for *Blackmail* and the surprisingly autobiographical *Rich and Strange,* Hitchcock's films at BIP — from 1927 to 1932 — do not reveal the passion and intensity associated with his later British films and most of his American films. No one knew better than he that, right from the first paragraph of the treatment, a film idea needs control — an overarching vision of what the final product should be. It would be more than twenty years before he could exert real producer's control, but he knew it when he finally had it; meantime, his early work seems today successful to the point that his touch — or at least his major contribution — is everywhere evident: in the structure and content of the screenplay (and even in the shaping of the dialogue); in the development of plot and theme and images; in the selection of cast and setting; in the style of lighting and the placement and movement of the camera; in the moods created, sustained, and shifted; in the subtle manipulation of an audience's fears and desires; in the economy and wit of the narrative; in the pacing; and in the rhythms of the film's final cutting.

This control over his work — inextricably bound up with his stature in the industry, and with his financial rewards — was not the simple desire of a tyrannical ego to manage everything and everyone as much as he could, although that tendency grew in him in later years and would cause much unhappiness. It was — for Hitchcock as for any artist — in fact justified by a profound inner conviction that he did indeed know better than others what would work in the formulation and expression of an idea. In this regard, it must have been acutely frustrating for him to have to depend so much on others (on studio colleagues, crew, actors, technicians, advertising men) for the realization of his fantasy. A composer determines every note for instruments and voices; a novelist chooses the exact placement of words and the beginnings and endings of sentences and paragraphs; the painter selects colors; the dancer enlivens gesture; the stage actor modifies pauses and rhythms of expression. But the filmmaker must depend on an almost infinite number of variables and an unpredictable array of talents to collaborate with him in the fulfillment of his dream-idea — if in fact he has a dream *or* an idea, and is not simply a contracted member of a company (as are the majority of film directors).

It is this collaborative aspect of filmmaking that is most often forgotten by the most ardent defenders of the so-called auteur theory. In the film schools, in the editorial offices of film journals, and at film festivals there are those devoted to film who would see the touch of the *director* in every moment of each of his (or her) films. The logical result of this somewhat shortsighted approach is that, once a director has made more than one picture, there will be, somewhere, an imaginative film student or a critic looking to make a discovery who will insist that the work of a particular director reveals such and such a personal vision; that a recognizable cohesive rendering of landscape or actors or setting is perceptible, and that a consistent vision emerges from a study of his work (usually canonized at once by being called an *oeuvre* — probably because the filmmaker is an *auteur*). This is, of course, to give most directors much more credit than they deserve, and to give even less to those artisans who contributed to the actual making of the film.

Before it is possible to assert a strong authorial control over a film or a body of work, some hard research is necessary. There must be painstaking study of production files, studio memoranda, and daily call sheets to determine just who was responsible for particular contributions. Likewise, a thorough examination of the stages of the screenplay's development, and of *other* screenplays by the same writer, is called for, to distinguish the contributions of the scenarist. If a particular production designer or art director worked on the film, and if that designer has left files, they, too — like the records of the director's meetings with cinematographers — must be carefully researched. And if a Selznick or a Thalberg or a Goldwyn or a Zanuck has produced the picture, then there was surely a strong controlling hand from the front office, always tempering creative impulses with practical, fiscal reins.

It is important to emphasize these outside influences, for although few directors in fact achieved the degree of gradual authorial control that Hitchcock did in his later years, it is possible for the admirer of his films to make the mistake of assigning a consistent vision to his early work. This not only ignores the creative contributions of others but also asks simple entertainments to bear the burden of a poorly informed prejudice. It raises to the level of high art those early *assignments* — projects not of Hitchcock's choosing — over which he had very little control in the early stages and none at all in the final cutting, and which are only markers of time in his career.

And yet precisely because of his background as an art director, designer, writer, and script supervisor, and because of the important education he gained by observing the German craftsmen, Hitchcock *did* know — perhaps better than anyone before or since — just how to do what he wanted to do in the medium of film. Throughout his career he depended on good stories and the script collaboration of good storytellers. But when it came to the *means* for telling those stories, few in the business ever knew as well as he what to do. And as he grew older, as techniques became more sophisticated, as his feelings about human life and human relationships began to settle — and as he acquired greater production control — a consistent vision, with insistent demons, indeed became observable.

But in 1928 Hitchcock was still far from the realization of his professional ambitions, far even from a recognition of what the prevailing spirit of his stories would be. He could, however, exert considerable creative control in his personal life if not in his films — control over the situations and people he directed in his notorious practical jokes. Many of these pranks were inflicted in a spirit of rebellious, lower-middle-class fun, and certainly derived from the Cockney tendency to deflate pomposity. Other incidents, however, were tinted in crueler colors.

About this time at BIP there was assigned to Hitchcock a property assistant who overdressed for his duties. When he was asked why he sported hand-tailored suits, expensive shirts, and cashmere sweaters to move props and furniture, the man replied that the habit stemmed from his wartime experiences in the Royal Navy, when a crisp appearance was always called for. The mention of the Royal Navy was all Hitchcock needed. At the end of filming on a gloomy afternoon, he invited the assistant to accompany him on a Thames excursion. But Hitchcock arranged for a boat whose only deck was uncovered, and he was delighted when a cloudburst reduced the man's wardrobe to a rumpled mess and his appearance to something out of low farce. On another occasion some years later, a camera operator boasted repeatedly about his elaborate all-electric kitchen. After a week of this talk, the man arrived home one evening to find two tons of coal delivered to his front door. The receipt was marked paid by A. Hitchcock.

Incidents like these were almost moral lessons for the pompous, and no one was hurt. Other Hitchcockian mischief, however, inflicted some real inconvenience or embarrassment on the victims for no apparent reason. A featured actress received four hundred smoked herring for a birthday present and had the unpleasant task of deciding how to dispose of what was left after two days of living with an all-pervasive odor. After shooting *The Farmer's Wife,* Hitchcock gave a reception for the cast and crew — about forty people in all. But the supper was served in the smallest room of a West End restaurant, where Hitchcock brought in aspiring actors as waiters — one to each guest — and instructed them to serve with appalling rudeness and incivility.

"The best practical joke I ever played," he insisted for years after, "was at a London hotel, where I gave a dinner party for Gertrude Lawrence. I always thought blue was such a pretty color, but none of the food we eat is blue. So at this party, all the food was blue. I had the soup dyed blue, the trout, the peaches, the ice cream." How would the guests react? How far would manners and propriety take them? It was perhaps to test them psychologically, to see their response, that Hitchcock did what he did.

On another occasion, the famous actor Sir Gerald du Maurier, with whom Hitchcock had struck up a cordial acquaintance, returned to his dressing room after a successful opening night to find not flowers or a congratulatory telegram, but a horse waiting in the cramped quarters. It must have cost Hitchcock a considerable sum, du Maurier guessed — but it must have been worth every shilling to be remembered as the donor of so bizarre and unforgettable a memento.

Not long after this horseplay, Sir Gerald was invited to Cromwell Road. It was to be a costume party, Hitchcock told him, and he was to wear something wonderfully colorful. At the appointed hour, du Maurier arrived, done up in heavy greasepaint and a wacky Scotsman's kilt. Hitchcock ushered him in to meet the other guests, each of whom had been summoned to a black-tie supper and was appropriately attired. Sir Gerald, mortified, fled; Hitchcock shrugged for the remaining guests and wondered aloud if their old friend had not been perhaps working too hard. And at Christmas that year, as gifts to crew members who lived in small flats, Hitchcock sent enormous and expensive — but hardly practical — pieces of furniture, each of which he knew would have to be returned.

"He never stopped playing jokes on people," Alma recalled, "and now and then I got a little apprehensive." And well she might have, for there were times he went too far and a cruder and crueler streak was evident.

Hitchcock kept a special set of cushions for a sofa in their home, and these he used for guests who were especially shy or fastidious or well mannered: when the victim sat, the cushion made rude and loud noises and Hitchcock looked shocked over the guest's inability to restrain flatulence in public. And at least once he sent flowers and candy and ardent, anonymous love notes to a woman who shared a popular radio show with her husband, to whom she was quite happily married. "I wanted to see what this would do to the husband," Hitchcock explained. "At one point she ran after the driver who'd brought a gift, to try and find out [who the sender was]. And finally the husband said, on the air one day, 'I can't go on with the show, she's run out into the street.' So I had the pleasure of breaking up that show."

Equally unkind was one incident that most witnesses preferred to forget. During a shooting that especially bored him, Hitchcock was "more engrossed in thinking up wicked practical jokes to play on the more vulnerable artists or on his main butt, a property man," according to Rodney Ackland. Hitchcock bet the property man a week's salary that he would be too frightened to spend a whole night chained to a camera in a deserted and darkened studio. The chap heartily agreed to the wager, and at the end of the assigned day, Hitchcock himself clasped the handcuffs and pocketed the key — but not before he offered a generous beaker of brandy, "the better to ensure a quick and deep sleep." The man thanked him for his thoughtfulness and drank the brandy, and everyone withdrew. When they arrived on the set next morning, they found the poor man angry, weeping, exhausted, and humiliated. Hitchcock had laced the brandy with the strongest available laxative, and the victim had, unavoidably, soiled himself and a wide area around his feet and the camera.

It seems difficult to regard at least some of these gestures as anything other than nasty and demeaning. And the handcuffs episode recalls Hitchcock's own statement about the pleasure of bondage and discipline. The injudicious moment of playful bondage in *The Lodger* became, on at least one occasion, a lived reality.

How is one to understand such actions, which typify so much of Hitchcock's time in Britain? Were they compensations for an inner storm of boredom, rebellion, and resentment? Were they a way of making others look as ridiculous as he felt himself to appear, and as uncomfortable? Were they indeed devised as a means of controlling people, catching them off guard and reducing them to helpless embarrassment?

To make others feel childish and dependent — this seemed to be part of his goal. He apparently considered most people a threat: they were better-looking, more intelligent, better educated, more socially acceptable than himself, and by reducing them to a sudden discomfort perhaps he felt he was bringing them to the level on which he always lived. By thus subjugating those he resented (for whatever reason, and on whatever level of consciousness), by submitting them to varying degrees of humiliation and danger, he was not only controlling them, he was in fact exteriorizing his own deepest fears — fears that would later be exteriorized chiefly on the screen, where he could subject vast numbers of people to crisis and dread.

The jokes may also have grown out of his own constant dread of accident — a dread he tried to banish professionally by preparing for every aspect of his films with increasing meticulousness (thus his filmmaking method in fact became a way of taking a stand against chaos). It was as if, early on, he could by playing the prankster prevent the eruption against himself of the terrible or the dehumanizing: his high jinks would pawn off the dreadful on others, and by a kind of sympathetic magic he went scot-free. The surprise attacks, the schemes that allowed him to watch other people experience discomfort, were calculated, carefully controlled antisocial gestures. They were in effect the smaller analogues of the appearance of chaos in a world gone suddenly mad — the chaotic world that Hitchcock was in lifelong fear of and that, in his mature work, he inflicted on his characters and (with safer results) on his viewers.

In this regard, one can consider the terrifying eruption of danger in the everyday lives of ordinary people: Bob and Jill Lawrence in the original version of *The Man Who Knew Too Much*, Richard Hannay in *The 39 Steps*, Robert Tisdall in *Young and Innocent*, Barry Kane in *Saboteur*, Guy Haines in *Strangers on a Train*, L. B. Jeffries in *Rear Window*, John Robie in *To Catch a Thief*, Ben and Jo McKenna in the remake of *The Man Who Knew Too Much,* Roger Thornhill in *North by Northwest,* and, ultimately, all human society in *The Birds.* Hitchcock's films, full of both suspense and surprise, were indeed supremely aestheticized practical jokes, providing millions of people — and the director — with a psychological cathartic.

Any social resentments the young filmmaker harbored at this time could not have been helped by the ridiculous story Walter Mycroft prepared as the basis for Hitchcock's next film. During February 1928, Mycroft strode into Hitchcock's office and said that since everyone enjoyed champagne — and Hitchcock was clearly no exception — why not make a film about it? Hitchcock remembered the disappointing task:

My thought was . . . why don't we do one about a little girl who works at Reims in the cellars and always watches the train go off carrying the champagne. And then she eventually gravitated to the city and became a kind of whore and was put through the mill and eventually went back to her job, and then every time she saw champagne go out she knew, "Well, that's going to cause some trouble for somebody." That was scrapped. . . . So we ended up with a hodge-podge of a story that was written as we went through the film and I thought it was dreadful.

The writing as they went along was closely monitored by Mycroft, who saw to it that the film became a vehicle for BIP's comic flapper, Betty Balfour, in the role of an irresponsible but irrepressible daughter of a wealthy man who sets out to teach her a lesson. Hitchcock found Mycroft's script so banal and tedious that, he told an interviewer, he took it home at night and put it between the pages of *Whittaker's Almanac* "to see if it would have absorbed something interesting by morning."

When they came to the actual filming, Hitchcock was severely depressed — even though he had just negotiated for the purchase of his beloved country house — and it was one of the rare times in his life that he became enraged on the set and shouted at his crew. His wrath was somewhat inordinately aroused by a standard procedure of the time: crowd scenes were filled with the same extras, from film to film — people under contract to the studio. Their dress and hair were simply changed for each picture, and they were photographed in such a way that only the sharpest eye could identify them. But Hitchcock would have in *Champagne* none of the extras who had been photographed in *The Farmer's Wife.* (Perhaps he thought it was the only token gesture of originality and freshness he could bring to the enterprise.)

"New faces!" he shouted at Frank Mills, his assistant director, who complied by scouring clubs and cabarets all over London and by going through boxes of photographs in the offices of players' agents. The search for new faces necessitated several days' delay, which seems to have been just what Hitchcock wanted — a break that could be charged to the cost of the picture. When the final product was finally served to the press late in the summer of 1928, it was found to be "champagne that had been left in the rain all night," despite the "silly but staunch femininity nicely brought out by Betty Balfour in her new flapper role."

Hitchcock could not have cared less.

Alma, meanwhile, continued to work for Balcon, and was putting finishing touches to an equally forgettable film, *The First Born,* directed by and starring the Hitchcocks' old acquaintance Miles Mander. This assignment's only advantage was that she met Mander's young co-star, a former schoolteacher who had recently entered films under the name Madeleine Carroll. Alma mentioned to Hitchcock that Carroll had not only great charm and presence, but good diction too, and that they should keep her in mind for some future sound film.

Throughout the spring, Alma tried to banish Hitchcock's sour disposition. She even convinced him to have family members over for an occasional dinner, although Hitchcock was finally so uncordial to his brother William and William's wife Lil that they stopped visiting to avoid the unpleasantness. William Hitchcock had taken over the management of the family business, which was soon to be sold as part of a large London combine. The news of this operation interested the younger brother not at all. And their sister Nellie was busy with her own family, far from central London, with the result that there was at last little contact between the various family households. Charles Bennett, the actor and playwright whose career would soon be involved with Hitchcock's, remembered going to Cromwell Road about this time and hearing Hitchcock express some resentment about his brother because the man was "large, prosperous and dull."

Other visitors fared better than relatives did. The writer James Hilton came several times and found the dinner extraordinary and the atmosphere in the home impeccable. Anna Lee, whom Bennett had discovered and who was making rapid strides as a young actress, was also a frequent visitor. "Hitchcock himself," she remembered, "was nicer to children in those days than he was to adults."

Later that year, George Bernard Shaw dined at the flat. By this time the Hitchcocks had purchased a complete set of Shaw's work, and the author sat down before dinner and autographed all thirty-one rare editions, signing them "To Alma, who married Alfred Hitchcock." (They also had every first edition of H. G. Wells and James M. Barrie.)

Hitchcock was enormously proud of having guests like Hilton, Shaw, and John Galsworthy in his home, and later, somewhat characteristically, he most of all remembered them as admirers of his work. "Oh yes," he would say casually, "I knew Galsworthy and Shaw. The young Hitchcock had many devotees and I was taken up like that, and they tell me that Shaw always used to look out for my new films. I remember one time I met Shaw I made a slip. I mentioned *Antony and Cleopatra,* and he said, 'Oh no, that's the other fellow.' . . . I knew John Buchan quite well. Especially after *The 39 Steps.* He was gracious enough to say how I'd improved on his book."

These guests invariably complimented Alma on her talents as cook and housekeeper. "I set about trying to create a home that would match Hitchcock's own serenity," Alma insisted with unconscious irony. "On the housekeeping side this meant that our home had to be as orderly and tidy as one of Hitch's film sets. That part was easy because Hitch is neat almost to the point of obsession. In his own words he's an 'ashtray emptier,' and he never washed his hands without using two or three towels to wipe dry the basin and faucets." In time, she could have dropped the qualifying "almost," for as his inner life grew more obsessive, he would expend more energy trying to give others an impression of absolute order and tidiness.

The only ray of cheer in the season was the acquisition of the country house. The one they settled on was in the small village of Shamley Green, about four miles south of Guildford. Half a mile off the main road, set back from Stroud Lane, was an estate called Winter's Grace, and they bought it at once for the then considerable price of £2,500. It was a Tudor house of white stucco and timber, with leaded windows, almost a dozen rooms, space for entertaining guests, and an impressive cathedral ceiling in a main living/dining area. Extensive rear gardens, a strip of land stretching back to an adjacent farm, and a picturesque brook completed a property of great charm — and of great luxury.

It was a grand country house, intended for the affluent and their circle, set in a prime area of Surrey to which members of Parliament retreated, along with members of the Mayfair social set and some successful theater folk. In the fields nearby were cows and horses, raised for sale, breeding, and sport by the local gentry, and beneath the gray, windswept skies the crying of rooks and crows was the only sound heard. The quiet refreshed Hitchcock each weekend after the bustle of London. More guests were brought down to Winter's Grace as Hitchcock supervised alterations to the house and gardens, and soon he installed a fully equipped screening room and a new, modernized kitchen. (Eventually he also purchased a smaller adjacent house, and moved his mother to it after he departed for America in 1939. The main house, which would have been impractical for an elderly lady living alone, he sold at an enormous profit.)

At Shamley Green, just thirty miles southwest of London and convenient for guests, some of the Hitchcocks' happiest hours were passed, and for their soon-to-be-born child it would in time provide an exceptionally pleasant atmosphere. Almost at once, and not only because of Alma's pregnancy, Hitchcock engaged a local woman, Mary Condon, for domestic chores. Alma was not the only one to observe the calming effect Shamley Green had on Hitchcock; Miss Condon preserved a memory of his personality that was quite different from the recollections of those who observed his attitude in London. "You could not wish to meet a nicer gentleman and a very good Catholic too," she said. "Every Sunday he would be at Mass at St. John's Seminary at Wonersh, near Guildford." Such religious observance (up to the late 1930s, in any case) was for the sake of Mother, when she visited, and for their daughter, who was raised to observe the rituals of Roman Catholicism in church, school, and home with a devotion and consistency that her parents really never had.

The daughter was born Saturday, July 7, 1928, in the bedroom at 153 Cromwell Road. By the time of the delivery, when the midwife emerged to inform the father, he was nowhere to be found. The tension in the apartment had closed around him, and he had bolted out the door and disappeared until late afternoon. When he returned, Alma was sleeping and their newborn infant was howling. Hitchcock sat awkwardly near the tiny, red child, afraid to touch her in spite of the nurse's promptings. When Alma awoke toward midnight, he held out a sapphire-and-gold bracelet he had purchased in Bond Street.

"I'd been wanting to get you a nice bracelet for some time," he said quietly. And then he admitted that he had felt terribly guilty about deserting her, and that the gift was a peace offering. "I know I shouldn't have left you, but you seemed to be getting along all right, while I was getting weaker and fainter every minute."

"But you didn't have to go out," Alma replied. "I wasn't really feeling bad at all."

"I know *you* weren't, my dear," Hitchcock said blandly. "But consider *my* suffering. I nearly died of the suspense."

The child was christened Patricia Alma, and the birth certificate, officially filed after the baptism on August 30, was signed by "Alfred Joseph Hitchcock — Film Director."

Within two weeks, both parents were back at work. Alma had been commissioned to write the script for Henrik Galeen's film *After the Verdict,* based on the novel by Robert Hichens (whose work would figure again in the Hitchcocks' life almost twenty·years later), and this was the last film she ever worked on that was not directed by her husband. At the same time, Hitchcock left for Cornwall, which was to double for the Isle of Man in his next assignment, *The Manxman,* based by Stannard (quite faithfully) on Hall Caine's somber romantic novel. The film is best remembered for Jack Cox's shimmeringly beautiful location photography, for an anxious sense of love betrayed, and for the uncharacteristically morbid and unhappy ending. By the time the film was completed, Hitchcock was not the only person disappointed with the results: John Maxwell was so chagrined that he put the film on the shelf and immediately spoke to Hitchcock about another project he had ready.* It is not hard to imagine the director listening to Maxwell but thinking of C. M. Woolf and wondering if the delayed release of a difficult film would be a pattern in his career. For every success, there seemed two setbacks.

But what Maxwell had in mind would make history. In 1928 Charles Bennett's *Blackmail* was an extraordinary theater hit. At once, Maxwell, with Hitchcock in mind for direction, bought the film rights. By November everyone was ready to proceed. Hitchcock, working alone at home on the screenplay, had finished in a matter of days a version that is even darker than Bennett's original.

By February 1929, Hitchcock had received final approval on his script from BIP, and he had settled on a cast: for the role of Alice, Hitchcock chose the leading lady of *The Manxman* — Anny Ondra, a blond Polish-born actress who was working successfully in British silent films; John Longden was signed to play her detective boyfriend; Donald Calthrop was to be the blackmailer on whom they try to fix responsibility for the girl's killing of a would-be seducer; and Cyril Ritchard, then a popular musical-comedy star, was hired to play the ardent artist who is stabbed. By the beginning of April the silent film was virtually complete and ready for final editing — and then something happened that changed the course of the British film industry and of Alfred Hitchcock's career.

Maxwell called Hitchcock to his office and announced that he had set

---

*When *The Manxman* was released the following year, however, audiences loved it, and the *Bioscope* (January 23, 1929) called it a film of "remarkable power and gripping interest."

up a temporary sound studio with some RCA equipment imported from America. The system was not terribly sophisticated, he said, and it was impossible to add post-dubbing, but there it was — sound! For most of the unequipped theaters they would proceed to distribute the silent version of *Blackmail,* but if it could be worked out, some sequences would be reshot, and Britain's first sound film could be released in at least a few updated London theaters later that year.

Hitchcock's accounts of what then happened varied wildly over the decades. But a careful study of the original silent version (still preserved in the archives of the British Film Institute) with the more commonly known (and still available) sound version readily reveals the truth of the situation. Hitchcock completely reshot only a few scenes, with live music and offstage sound effects — most notably, he had Cyril Ritchard accompany himself at the piano while singing a Cowardesque song during the seduction sequence; and he altered Anny Ondra's bedroom scene at home to include a noisy caged bird that sets her (and the audience) quite on edge. But a major problem remained: Anny Ondra's thick foreign accent was entirely inappropriate for the role of the daughter of a Chelsea shopkeeper. For moments of dialogue, Ondra's accent would prove fatal. Nevertheless, a voice test was arranged, and the film of it survives in the vaults of the British Film Institute:

HITCHCOCK: Now, Miss Ondra, we are going to do a sound test. Isn't that what you wanted? Now come right over here.
ONDRA: I don't know what to say. I'm so nervous!
HITCHCOCK: Have you been a good girl?
ONDRA [*laughing*]: Oh, no!
HITCHCOCK: No? Have you slept with men?
ONDRA: No!
HITCHCOCK: *No?*
ONDRA: Oh, Hitch, you make me embarrassed! [*She giggles uncontrollably.*]
HITCHCOCK: Now come right over here, Miss Ondra, and stand still in your place, or it won't come out right — as the girl said to the soldier.

At this point, Anny Ondra collapses in embarrassed laughter at Hitchcock's risqué joke, and Hitchcock, with a triumphant grin, turns to face the camera and calls ''Cut!''

Listening to the playback (and to the comments from the front office), Ondra had to admit — even from these few words — that her accent was indeed not right. But what to do? It would be far too expensive to reshoot every scene with a new actress, even if there could be found a kind and equitable way of dismissing Ondra from the film. No one wanted to do that anyway: everyone in the British film industry, Hitchcock included, liked Anny Ondra — even Graham Cutts, for whom she had appeared, before *The Manxman,* in a film called *God's Clay.*

Hitchcock came up with the answer. He asked BIP to engage the aspiring young actress Joan Barry to stand just off-camera, speaking Ondra's lines of dialogue into a microphone as the actress mouthed them. This was as good a resolution as could be found, but it had two drawbacks. For one thing, Joan Barry's diction was just what a Cockney girl's would not be: refined, studied, slow, and somewhat self-consciously "arty." And the other problem was the inevitable series of awkward pauses in the scenes they reshot with the two women. Viewers can sense the actors obeying off-camera cues; or at least something, everyone notices, is not quite right in the timing.

But this was the best that could be done under the financial circumstances, and the awkwardness does not diminish the astonishing technical advances that Hitchcock made in *Blackmail,* using the most primitive sound equipment. To this day he is justly famous for the scene (added to the sound version) in the girl's home after the killing of the artist. No one is aware of her involvement, and the family is at the breakfast table. A woman from the neighborhood enters and starts chattering away about the recent murder.

"What an awful way to kill a man," she whines. "With a *knife!* Now a good stiff whack over the 'ead with a brick is one thing —there's something *British* about *that!* But a *knife?* No, *knives* is not right! . . . Now mind you, a *knife* is a difficult thing to handle. Not just any *knife* will do . . . a *knife* . . . and with a *knife* . . . And if you come to Chelsea you mustn't bring a *knife!*" As she rambles, the camera moves to Ondra's traumatized face. And at this point Hitchcock imaginatively exploited the possibilities of sound by distorting the neighbor's voice: the audience hears only the subjective impression of what the girl hears, as all the words blur together until only the word *knife* stabs out at her and at them from the soundtrack. Then her father asks her to cut some bread, and she distractedly grasps a bread knife, which then — just as the neighbor says "knife" one last, loud time —seems to leap from Ondra's hands and fly to the floor. (" 'Ere! You might've *cut* someone with that!" scolds the father, in one of the screenplay's moments of tragicomic whimsy.)

This is one of the most discussed scenes in the history of the early sound film, and rightly so. Not content simply to record dialogue, Hitchcock experimented with it to create and sustain in his audience the same dissociation a character feels. It is precisely this element that Hitchcock so masterfully controls by turning the cinematic screws.

"I don't remember any particular feeling that it was an historical occasion," recalled John Longden.

Alfred Hitchcock, however, was beginning to see possibilities in the new medium, and at once began to introduce effects which were ahead of the times. One might say he provided a prototype for the sound-film treatment of drama as René Clair did for the musicals with *Le Million*. . . . I personally preferred the moment when the blackmailer entered the heroine's shop at a time of great menace, and the ring of the shop-door bell was lengthened and magnified like a note of doom.

The sound apparatus itself, according to Longden, was rather primitive; he remembered the large box about two feet square hanging over his head, and Hitchcock calling instructions to talk up into a microphone dangling from it.

This, besides tending to a crick in the neck, hardly contributed to a smooth portrayal of my part. . . . The other memory is of a scene in which I, as a detective, had to walk nonchalantly round a room searching for evidence. As the sequence had to be tense, Hitch did not want to add music, so he suggested that I should whistle some tune. At this time *The Singing Fool,* the first big American talkie success [in England], was all the rage, so Hitch told me to whistle "Sonny Boy," from that picture. This cheeky gesture seems to me the most typical "Hitchcock touch" of them all.

The early movie stage equipped for recording looked and sounded crude and dreadful. The cranking cameras still made a terrific grinding noise, and so the camera itself, for *Blackmail,* had to be installed in a soundproof box. One unfortunate result of this (besides a certain discomfort for the camera operator) was that for a time, until a silencer was developed, the camera lost its mobility, and the effect of a "filmed play," with a certain regrettable lack of motion and life, was revived with a vengeance.

On one memorable day, however, the crew and cast of *Blackmail* were surprised by a special unannounced guest. Elizabeth, Duchess of York, came to see what the shooting of a sound film was like. (She was later King George VI's Queen; then, with the accession of their daughter Elizabeth II, she became Elizabeth the Queen Mother.) The Duchess of York was a movie fan, it turned out, and she was fascinated by the film set. Hitchcock must have been pleased, but he did not lose his professional calm.

"I remember taking her into one of those camera booths," he said, "and it was an awful crush, since they were very tiny." And then he did something very bold indeed. There had been, from the time of Victoria, an unwritten rule that female members of the immediate royal family not be seen in public without gloves and a hat — the distinctive signs of gentility. Since she was daughter-in-law of the king, this of course applied to Elizabeth. But Hitchcock would have his iconoclastic way: "I made her take her hat off and wear earphones. I just simply said, 'Ma'am, I'll hold your hat while you wear these earphones.' And I did and she did and that was that." It is doubtful that anyone else, under whatever pretext, ever so blithely decoiffed a member of the royal family.

When *Blackmail* was screened for the press at the end of June (and released for the general public in late November), there was even more excitement than had attended the premiere of *The Lodger*. Writing in *Close Up,* Hugh Castle, who registered enthusiasm for a film about as often as Halley's comet appeared, wrote that he knew it must have been the most magnificent British movie ever made because two weeks had passed without anyone proclaiming it a "greatest ever" and the pronouncement was therefore about ten days overdue. His account is worth reprinting in part, as much for its mordantly funny description of the fashionable press screening of the time as for his begrudging and uncharacteristic admission that Hitchcock had indeed done something admirable.

Even the poor critic received an invitation to refreshments afterwards. That, of course, constitutes the all-in-all of the English trade show. . . . There was the usual jam, of course. . . . The best seats were filled by friends of the men who trimmed the spotlights, maiden-aunts of the supers who appeared in the artistically-focussed backgrounds, or travellers for the firm who hoped to reap a fortune from the bookings of the masterpiece.

There was a hush in the air. . . . The audience adjusted their ties for the more serious dish awaiting them. General managers and company promoters were observed to fidget, small-part players were getting excited, assistant cameramen were ready, elbow advanced, to point out their own particular close-up to their admiring relatives. . . . When it was all over the Press crowded to the Lounge, which looked like the Battle of Hohenlinden. In the background were the waitresses, like the Isar, rolling rapidly. . . . Flash-light photographers did their stuff, the Elstree stars obtained a due meed of publicity for waiting up half the night, the men who once walked on in a picture made fifteen years ago wrought havoc around the refreshments, and the ladies who supplied the loungers in our cabaret sequences grabbed the sandwiches. A dozen critics looked at their watches and grabbed taxicabs.

But Castle had to admit that Hitchcock and *Blackmail* deserved praise.

It must be said . . . that, considering that he was toying with a medium about which he knew nothing . . . he has made a good job of it. *Blackmail* is perhaps the most intelligent mixture of sound and silence we have yet seen. . . . It is Hitchcock's comeback. While seeing it, you can hardly believe that it was made by the man who gave us *Champagne* or *The Manxman*. . . . Hitchcock succeeds in wedding sound with silence.

Hitchcock knew intimately the setting of the story — this was responsible for the success of the film where the two previous efforts had disappointed. With a story set in his own London — not at the turn of the century in the quiet countryside, nor on a still-primitive island — he showed his easy, inventive, and witty familiarity. The scenes in the shop and family quarters, complete with the drop-in neighbor, are right out of Hitchcock's own childhood, when mealtimes in The High Road were often interrupted by a friend or customer who expected (and got) the family's attention.

*Blackmail* is also memorable for Hitchcock's first extended and clearly recognizable cameo appearance. As Anny Ondra and John Longden ride distractedly in the underground, a small boy leans over to another traveler, Hitchcock, who is trying to read a book. The brat pokes Hitchcock's hat down over his brow, then squirms away. Hitchcock pokes him back, then cowers in fear when the boy comes back to bait him again. The scene is Hitchcock's, the film is Hitchcock's.

Everyone connected with *Blackmail,* in fact, had a huge success — except Anny Ondra. At once, her career in the English cinema was over. She returned to Germany, where she divorced filmmaker Karel Lamač, married the prizefighter Max Schmeling, and retired to a small town near Hamburg. At Christmas in 1930 she sent Hitchcock and Alma a card and wrote on it of her new happiness. Hitchcock sent back his seasonal greeting that year, a card he had commissioned of a circus family (strongman, bareback rider, clowns, trapeze dancers, and the audience enrapt, with one man using binoculars — all against a black cyclorama). "Alfred, Alma and Pat Hitchcock wish you a happy Christmas" read the printed green sentiment inside, and to it Hitchcock added simply, "A boxer!"

"Hitchy," she wrote back at once, "I'm so *happy* here!"

Pleased with the success of *Blackmail* and eager to imitate the exploitation of sound that made American pictures so popular, Maxwell and Mycroft at once put together a musical revue. It was aptly titled *Elstree Calling,* and into it they put everyone connected with the studio.

The result was something of a mixed pudding, designed as an advertisement for BIP, with every contracted director forced to contribute a sketch or two. Hitchcock supervised Gordon Harker in one or two sequences, but no one remembered the director being around for the shooting more than six or seven hours, and Hitchcock could never recall anything about his presence on it.

He was equally unenthusiastic about the next job Maxwell had for him — apparently it was indeed going to be two steps back for each one forward. His assignment was to film Sean O'Casey's play *Juno and the Paycock* with the famous Abbey Theatre Players of Dublin. This he completed in a most perfunctory manner by early winter 1929/1930, and although the film was favorably received, Hitchcock was always right to call it uncinematic. He and Alma simply could not muster enthusiasm in writing their screenplay for the talky melodrama, and the ending, as Andrew Sarris rightly pointed out, "was sentimentalized simply by concluding with Juno in her grief rather than with the Paycock in his cups." Hitchcock,' also rightly, always remained embarrassed by the good notices the photoplay received when it was originally released.

Although *Blackmail* had shown Hitchcock and BIP to best advantage, the British film industry — quota system or no — was still in trouble, for most of the same reasons. Hollywood could still afford to pay screen actors more, and most British performers preferred the stage. In addition, Great Britain did not have the climate of the American film industry, or its economic or social advantages; in England the pictures were always considered mere entertainment for the working classes — smart people went to the theater. Nor were there the German, Soviet, and American advances in technique. The essentially conservative nature of the arts in England effectively prevented the winds of aesthetic change from reaching the island. "Great Britain," as English historian Rachael Low succinctly wrote, "was only on the fringe of these movements. It is in keeping with the general picture that the great revolutionary of stage design in Britain before the war, Edward Gordon Craig, had found little understanding in his own country and left it to live abroad." She could have written almost exactly the same words about Alfred Hitchcock a little later in his life.

The response to *Blackmail* inevitably led to a score of interviews by journalists and radio reporters, and in 1930 Hitchcock realized that if his goal of keeping his name before the public was essential to his freedom, then he had better engage a publicist. In fact he did more than hire someone to represent him: he formed a small company, Hitchcock Baker Productions, Limited, which had the sole task of advertising to the press the newsworthiness of Alfred Hitchcock, producer-director.

Into this enterprise he invested a substantial sum of money annually until his departure for America. The result was not only increased exposure and the creation of an image for Hitchcock as a perennial news event — it also provided him with a shelter against the heavy taxation of his gross earnings.

Throughout his life, Hitchcock liked to give his associates and the public the impression that he neither knew very much nor quite cared about the financial rewards accruing from his work. Somehow it always seemed that others were negotiating on his behalf, that he never involved himself, and that he did not sully his artistic task with the issue of lucre. The reality was quite different. When he formed Hitchcock Baker, he also engaged a tax and financial adviser, J. G. Saunders, who counseled him weekly about his earnings, investments, and the factors that would insure that the bulk of his income would not be forfeited to the support of His Majesty's government.

Hitchcock also let it be known at work and among acquaintances that his business manager handled all his financial affairs, and that he had arranged for himself to be issued only a small weekly allowance. So much was true. His London manager did indeed give him an allowance of ten pounds of pocket money a week in the 1930s. But Hitchcock got around this by regularly dining at a restaurant where he had a charge account. He got the manager of the restaurant to charge him twice the cost of his meal and to give him the change in cash. And then if he ran out of cash before week's end, he simply borrowed money from someone at the studio — which he always had to be reminded to repay. Once, when a technician at BIP begged him for repayment of three pounds, Hitchcock sent the unwieldy equivalent in a leather sack: 2,880 farthings.

One of the conundrums of Hitchcock's personality was a strange amalgam of frugality and flamboyance. Stopping in Cornwall while shooting *The Manxman,* he once engaged an innkeeper in a bitter argument over the price charged for his room. The difference between what he had been told and what he was being charged was less than a shilling — and of course BIP paid in any case. But once he had won the argument, Hitchcock summoned a messenger to send up huge quantities of expensive champagne for everyone in the cast and crew, and he led them to believe that the cost came from his own pocket, not from the production budget.

On the other hand, although he and Alma certainly could have afforded to relocate from Cromwell Road to Regent's Park or Mayfair or Kensington, they kept their modest two-bedroom flat and never replaced any of the original furnishings or carpets, much of which became nearly threadbare between 1926 and 1939. The place was always spotlessly clean, but — unlike their luxurious country house in Surrey — it had an air of shabby gentility that belied the family fortunes. At the same time, Hitchcock would not think twice about ordering tailor-made blue silk pajamas with a matching silk dressing gown — an outfit he liked to wear when ushering in writers.

Whenever he could, Hitchcock preferred to work at home rather than at a studio. In his own quarters, he felt free of the prying — or at least the supervisory gaze — of executives, and his preference for working on a treatment or script at home later carried over to his work in America. Scriptwriters who rang at Cromwell Road were frequently greeted by the director in his favorite pajamas and dressing gown, no matter the hour; the informality put most of them at ease, although some found that it somehow slowed down the beginning of the working session. They were always chatting about this new film, or gossiping about that studio personality, or sipping tea. In the mid-1930s, Charles Bennett departed on more than one occasion wondering if in fact he and Hitchcock had ever got any serious work done. Later, reviewing his notes, he found that somehow they had — and that it was good work, too.

One of Hitchcock's guiding principles in working sessions with his writers was that pushing too hard for a scene or a crucial bit of dialogue would make it clearly artificial. If, on the other hand, a relaxed atmosphere — perhaps with a bit of lunch or a cocktail — was established, the story would, surprisingly often, emerge at its own pace, and from the inner logic that had suggested the basic idea in the first place. This attitude became the rule for Hitchcock's script work, and there is a certain amusing irony about the image of an overweight Cockney padding about his London flat in a dressing gown and discussing, over steak and kidney pie and a beaker of gin or brandy, the most dreadful international intrigues, or ways of kidnapping children, or how to sabotage national monuments. Everything that met the eye suggested a bourgeois English businessman, a decorous husband and father. But the talk was right out of Poe and Saki and de Sade and the most grisly cases recently tried at Old Bailey.

Sean O'Casey had visited Hitchcock on the set of *Juno and the Paycock,* and a mutual respect at once sprang up. In fact they discussed an idea for a second film, to be written by O'Casey and directed by Hitchcock. They agreed it might be interesting to set a story in Hyde Park, where a variety of incidents would happen to a variety of people in the course of a single day. Hitchcock somehow managed to interest Walter Mycroft in the project, and O'Casey went to work. But the collaboration ended mysteriously over a misunderstanding (the details of which are unclear), and Hitchcock — as so often — broke off the relationship. (O'Casey finished a treatment on his own and eventually turned it into a play, *Within the Gates.*)

While O'Casey was writing, Hitchcock and Alma were busy adapting Clemence Dane and Helen Simpson's *Enter Sir John,* which became one of the director's rare whodunits, eventually called *Murder!* The script work in fact proceeded none too smoothly, and by the time the major actors (Norah Baring, Miles Mander, Esme Percy, and Herbert Marshall, in one of his earliest screen roles) were scheduled to step before the cameras, the dialogue had not been finished. This obviously would have been no great catastrophe in the days of silent film, but now it was a cause for concern. Facing trouble, Hitchcock allowed his cast, for almost a week, to improvise their lines; the result, as he admitted, was an arrhythmic patter that lacked spontaneity. This was the last time he ever experimented with spur-of-the-moment dialogue, although not the last time he was fascinated by sound as a malleable special effect.

*Murder!* is a rarity in the Hitchcock catalog. It is a not very engaging story of a producer-director-actor (Marshall) who, while serving on a jury, is stung by his certainty that a woman indicted for murder is innocent and decides to stalk the real killer. She is an aspiring actress (played by Norah Baring), and this sets up a professional interest on his part that becomes an emotional involvement by the final curtain — and it is indeed a curtain, for the happy ending unites the acquitted actress and the amateur sleuth (the juror) on stage as well as in life.

Two of Hitchcock's concerns are apparent beneath the film's turgid melodramatics. There is, first of all, the confusion between "playing" and "doing." The man of the theater sets up a play in his own quarters and prevails on the suspected villain to read for a part that will betray his guilt. The more Marshall talks of the distinction between art and life, the more that distinction breaks down, and finally everyone in the story who is accustomed to playacting roles must take on a real-life role in order to discover who is innocent and who is guilty. (Hitchcock would later explore the same motif in *Stage Fright.*)

The other aspect of the film that Hitchcock emphasizes is the sexual ambiguity of the villain (played by Esme Percy). It is not only in the villain's circus act, in which he dresses as a woman, that the story tilts to reveal a fascination with sexual specialism — the man plays regular stage roles in drag, as well. But the character, Handel Fane — played as a delicate, swooning homosexual — is too much for the film's languor to bear. Hitchcock's camera is finally more interested in probing the byways of unconventional sexual behavior than in exploring the paths of a murder mystery. And in fact the byways are muddied in this case: transvestism is considered an emblem of homosexuality, and homosexuality is somehow associated with "racial impurity" — the villain, it turns out, was driven to murder by the disclosure that he is a "half-caste," by which was meant part-Negro or part-Indian (and perhaps illegitimate as well). This outdated social outlook does not help the picture to overcome the technical flaws that also make it appear a quaint antique to modern audiences.

But it is always fascinating, in the last analysis, to consider Hitchcock's experimental soundtrack for *Murder!* He wanted for one scene the effect of a man's inner meditation as he stood shaving before a mirror, listening to the radio as an orchestra played a passage from *Tristan und Isolde*. How to accomplish this without post-dubbing, which was not yet possible? Simple, Hitchcock told his crew. Marshall first read his speech into a wire recorder, which was then placed beneath the washbasin on the set. Then a thirty-piece live orchestra was arranged behind the wall and ordered to play the selection from Wagner; as the camera rolled, the wire recorder (out of camera range) was snapped on, and the live microphone picked up the recorded voice and the actual music while the mute actor simply stared at his own reflection. If the content is finally tedious, the method never was.

As so often with early sound films, a second, foreign-language version of *Murder!* was directed by Hitchcock at the same time, the better to insure a Continental sale and audience for the picture. Distributors in Germany were interested, and before the German cast arrived in London, Hitchcock went to Berlin to discuss the translation of the script.

"The Germans suggested many changes," Hitchcock recalled.

I objected that if the two scripts were too much different I would end up making two pictures instead of one and we would lose the economic advantage of simultaneous shooting.

That was a mistake. The English and the German versions could not be so closely paralleled because of differences in customs and language. I ran into terrible obstacles in the German version when I came to direct the picture. Although I spoke German, I didn't know the cadences of speech, and I was lost on the set. The actors sounded colloquial to me, but I really couldn't understand what they were saying.

The hero of the German version was a well-known actor, Alfred Abel. I had problems with Abel because he would not do certain things he felt were beneath his dignity. . . . I had him wear a tweed suit for his visit to the girl in jail. I figured that would be natural in the course of his sleuthing.

"I don't visit a girl in these clothes," Abel insisted. He demanded to be dressed in a black coat and striped trousers. There was no arguing with him.

Abel also refused to do a comic scene in which the hero in the English version lodges in a boardinghouse infested with rambunctious children who pile all over his bed as he is served morning tea by the beleaguered landlady (Una O'Connor). It had been one of the best scenes in the completed version, in which Herbert Marshall conveyed a world-weariness and slightly pompous charm that would serve him and Ernst Lubitsch so well two years later in *Trouble in Paradise*. But Abel would hear nothing of the scene.

"You can't do this to such a man!"

Hitchcock replied that the "whole point of comedy is to reduce dignity."

"Not for the Germans," Abel replied.

Continuing the trend toward producing filmed plays, BIP assigned Hitchcock to adapt and direct John Galsworthy's social diatribe *The Skin Game,* which he prepared and photographed in late 1930 and early 1931. Although shorter than an hour and a half in its final form, *The Skin Game,* about a battle between the landed gentry and the nouveau riche, seems to last half a day. Endlessly talky, it reveals a Hitchcock detached from his project.

To save himself from boredom, he rehearsed his actors much more than he filmed them, and Rodney Ackland remembered that Hitchcock "always gave much more vivid performances showing his actors what to do than they ever achieved themselves." One scene he did not act out himself for their benefit was the attempted suicide of a young woman in a garden pool. For the first of several times in his career, he enjoyed watching while his assistants repeatedly tossed an actress into water; this time it was Phyllis Konstam who was hurled into the stage-set lily pond no less than ten times for retakes.

The annual winter holiday at Christmas was substantially extended in 1931, as Hitchcock took his wife and three-and-a-half-year-old daughter on a round-the-world trip. The stopping places included Africa, where they looked up one of Hitchcock's aunts, only to find that the poor woman, now widowed, had fallen on hard times and, quite apart from medical care she required, could barely support herself and her son. Quietly, almost anonymously, Hitchcock regulated her finances, arranged for doctors, and departed as unheralded as he had arrived. Afterward, he never alluded to this kindness (perhaps because in fact he almost never spoke of his family).

The prolonged trip took the Hitchcocks across the Atlantic to the Caribbean and finally home. They arrived refreshed, and with an original idea for a new film. It was to be about a London couple who suddenly receive money from a wealthy relation and decide on a trip around the world that tests not only their loyalty to each other but also the depth of their perceptions and their gratitude for the simple realities of everyday life. They told John Maxwell about it, and he showed some interest. But he also said Mycroft had another project scheduled first — a thriller about a house of thieves, a stolen necklace, a girl and her detective boyfriend, and a breakneck race involving a train, pursuing autos, and a waiting ferryboat. It was to be a filmed version of Joseph Jefferson Farjeon's play *Number Seventeen,* and Hitchcock was furious at having to take it on, for it was a bundle of clichés.

Assigned as Hitchcock's writer was Rodney Ackland, who had scored a huge success in the theater recently, and with whom Hitchcock had hoped to do a film version of John Van Druten's *London Wall* — a project that was perversely handed over to another BIP director, one who *wanted* to do *Number Seventeen.* Ackland remembered Hitchcock's directorial revenge for being commanded to do yet another film that bored him.

He had hit upon a new and fascinating plan for teasing the bosses. He would make *Number Seventeen* as a burlesque of all the thrillers of which it was a pretty good sample — and do it so subtly that nobody at Elstree would realize the subject was being guyed. Not that Hitch had anything against *Number Seventeen* as a thriller [Ackland was mistaken about this] — but he didn't want to make a thriller: he wanted to make *London Wall.*

Alma and I thought Hitch's idea simply splendid. . . . The script was evolved between the three of us during a series of hilarious conferences at the Hitchcock home, the atmosphere of which was considerably more stimulating than that of the studio.

As the heroines of thrillers were invariably dumb, the leading lady of *Number Seventeen,* Hitch decided, must be literally dumb — must never utter a word from beginning to end of the picture. As the climax of a thriller was invariably a chase (generally between a car and a train, at this period), *Number Seventeen*'s climax must be a chase-to-end-all-chases — its details so preposterous that excitement would give way to gales of laughter. It was on these lines and in this spirit that we conceived and wrote the script.

But their satirical intention misfired. The film was shot so swiftly and edited so matter-of-factly that the whole sly point was lost. As intended, the studio executives failed to catch on to the subtle spirit of fun, but the public was baffled as well. Studying the picture today, one can easily see why people were confused and disappointed. The satire is too unfocused to be engaging, and the first portion of the film — when .

Hitchcock usually establishes audience identification — is simply so full of atmosphere and so empty of plot or character that it is hard to care.

There was some delay in beginning work on the next film, about the traveling couple, perhaps because Hitchcock asked for some reediting of *Number Seventeen* (which was not released until after that next film, *Rich and Strange,* had had its own disappointing reception; at that point, Maxwell decided that he might just as well be hung for unleashing an old dog as for setting loose a puppy). In the meantime, the Hitchcocks expanded their social life a bit, and on several occasions members of the technical crews from BIP were invited to come by Cromwell Road for a drink. Sometimes, after the liquor had flowed freely, Hitchcock could be persuaded to do his party piece, "The Whistling Sailor." He would leave the sitting room and return moments later, naked to the waist — a sight that, considering his almost three hundred pounds, must in itself have been in the realm of the comic-grotesque. On his chest and belly he had painted, with his wife's makeup, an enormous sailor's face, its lips rounded into an *O* as though whistling. Hitchcock himself then began to whistle a tune, at the same time wobbling and shaking his enormous paunch, and the big face below his own seemed not only to whistle but to dance a strangely exotic tango for the assembled guests' amusement.

One evening was even more memorable. Hitchcock was encouraged to do himself up in drag, and on this project he spent hours of preparation — sewing sheets, refining the makeup, making a wig. He even somehow allowed the party performance to be captured on film; one of the technicians had been forewarned of the night's special attraction and arrived with the necessary equipment. Carefully guarded for decades after, the offbeat home movie was not shown to anyone but two or three close colleagues. Although the film's existence has been repeatedly denied, it was in fact shown in Hitchcock's private screening room at Universal Studios in 1976 — but no one now seems certain whether it survived the dismantling of his office after his death.

While shooting *Number Seventeen,* Hitchcock began to interview actors for *Rich and Strange,* which he and Alma were gleefully writing in the evenings. (The credits mention an "idea by Dale Collins," but it is impossible to identify him or his particular contribution.) Because Hitchcock was not keen on using Joan Barry, who was one of the few blonds at BIP available that season, he called in alternate performers. Anna Lee came for a discussion, which began oddly, she thought, with Hitchcock's inquiry as to her religious preference. He finally accepted Joan Barry for the female lead, although he could not succeed in erasing the pauses in her speech that eventually took on the length of Homeric caesuras.

But the hiring of one of the supporting actresses for *Rich and Strange* proved particularly fortuitous. Elsie Randolph had made her first appearance on the London stage in 1919, in *The Girl for the Boy,* and from that time forward she was one of London's most popular musical and comedy stars. Best known for her joyous partnership in a number of shows with Jack Buchanan, she was invited to meet Hitchcock while he was preparing the train crash for *Number Seventeen.* For the first part of their interview he spoke about the complicated miniatures and model trains they were using for the sequences of the concluding chase and crash. Over tea and cakes, Hitchcock then described the techniques and invited her to watch a few scenes being photographed. "Since this [*Rich and Strange*] will be your first film," he said, "you'd better watch this." And it was indeed, she remembered, an education in filmmaking.

When she returned to his office another day to discuss the new film, Hitchcock described her role: that of an old maid — the typical I-don't-know, the bore on the ship's cruise — slightly pathetic but more often a dreadful nuisance. Randolph relished the description and the comic possibilities, but Hitchcock was not sure her demure and bright charm, and her natural attractiveness, could be sufficiently altered.

"How do you feel about this part? Do you think you understand this eccentric character?"

Without hesitating, Elsie Randolph snatched up a pair of thick glasses left on Hitchcock's desk by an assistant, put them on, pulled her hair back behind her ears, and said in a piping falsetto, "Oh, well, sir, I've just had my lunch of lark's tongue on toast, and I feel anything is possible!" Hitchcock at once loved her humor, signed her for the role (unofficially, he called the character simply Elsie), and soon afterward invited the actress and her mother for the first of several weekends at Winter's Grace.

But their cordial relationship was no insurance Elsie Randolph would not be the butt of one of the director's practical jokes. Having been told that she not only detested but was sickened by smoky rooms and that she fervently avoided cigarette smokers, Hitchcock (himself a smoker) one day pointed to a fake telephone call-box on the set and asked, "Elsie, would you mind stepping into this for a moment to act out a call? We might add an extra scene for you at this point."

She obliged, and once the door was closed a great cloud of smoke (triggered by the special-effects technicians) suddenly surrounded her. Near collapse, she fled from the set, only to be told later that Hitchcock had put no film in the camera, that no such scene was ever planned, and that the incident was only his little joke. She decided to ignore the incident, and returned to the set as if nothing more than luncheon had intervened. Immediately, they moved on, without discussion, to the next scene. "He was a darling," she said respectfully years later, "but a darling with a sadistic sense of humor." Hitchcock never forgot Elsie Randolph's resilience and good nature, and she was invited to appear in another Hitchcock film (*Frenzy*) forty years later; she agreed — and there was no exploitation of her patience the second time around.

"At Shamley Green, he lived simply but grandly," she remembered, "and he was certainly very generous to me and to my mother when we were houseguests. There was a strange formality about the country house. Pat had to sit at her own little table in the kitchen while the adults dined in grand style, and her father insisted that she curtsy and be very proper with the guests. For all that, she seemed a happy, delightful child, and I loved to look after her." Randolph — like other houseguests — never met Hitchcock's mother on any of these weekends at Winter's Grace, although the widowed Mrs. Hitchcock must have been spending time there. And she never knew (until informed in 1981) that Alfred Hitchcock had a brother and a sister.

As it turned out, *Rich and Strange* was a commercial failure. This greatly hurt Hitchcock, who ever after retained a special fondness for the film and lamented the fact that it went unappreciated. It is one of his most openly autobiographical films, but as in all the others that directly reflect his firsthand experience, it is hard to decipher without some kind of biographical Rosetta stone. The couple of the picture, Fred and Emily Hill — even the names suggest Alfred and Alma Hitchcock — are clearly devoted to each other, but, like the Hitchcocks, are clearly bored with their current lot at the moment they embark on a long cruise. The husband (played by music-hall actor Henry Kendall) likes to take pictures, and is terrified of the nausea that afflicts him at sea; the wife (Joan Barry) patiently sustains his moods — which alternate between devoted good humor and a spoiled, spiky crankiness — and his obsessions (especially his shipboard flirtation with a vamp-eyed middle-European princess — played by Betty Amann — who turns out to be a common adventuress).

The Hills visit Paris, and their adventures mirror the Hitchcocks': they are shocked at the scantily clad chorus at the Folies-Bergère; they are ill equipped to counter the sexual innuendos of strangers; they weave their way back to their hotel room after a night of alcoholic indulgence. (The Paris sequences are a compilation of the Hitchcock honeymoon and the time spent in Germany; the remainder of the film is apparently drawn from the Hitchcocks' recent trip around the world and from the daily stuff of the Hitchcock family life.)

Such clues, scattered throughout the film, provide the tip-off that *Rich and Strange* was, perhaps not intentionally, a kind of open diary or a photo album based on the Hitchcock marriage. There is no doubt that Fred and Emily Hill endure in the film because they have special appreciation for one another's personalities. But there is also the sense that no one except Emily would ever have Fred — which is finally the reason for her polite rejection of a dashing commander's attention: she has the conviction that Fred needs her, and she is quite right. At that very moment, Fred is yielding to the skin-deep charms of a woman who turns out to be simply playing a role.

This theme of the willing, self-deluded man who falls under the spell of an enchanting, manipulative woman reappears in a good deal of Hitchcock's later work and is the most profound indication of his urges (if not the actual truth of his relationships) that he left in his work.

In a final parallel with the Hitchcocks, the Hills of *Rich and Strange* enjoy sudden material blessings but return at the end to their decidedly middle-class, semidetached house, to resume their more secure, less dangerously romantic, and inevitably bickering daily life. A peculiar exception to all of Hitchcock's other work, the film is full of bittersweet resonances about the compromises of marriage and the sense of awe felt at a baby's birth. It also has a pervading sense of spiritual malaise that is emblemized by the recurrent motif of nausea — from Fred's early confinement for seasickness, to the vomiting when the Hills learn that their silent Oriental rescuers have fed them a meal consisting of a dead cat, to the final wave of nausea that passes over Fred's face in the last minute of the film. *Rich and Strange* certainly lives up to its title (which was drawn from *The Tempest* by Shakespeare). A mystified London critic proclaimed: "If you are interested in Hitchcock's work" — and, he might have added, in his life — "you should see this picture. But don't expect another *Blackmail* or *Murder!*"

But if it was rich as an encoded autobiography, the film was too strange for BIP's taste, and it quickly became clear that the association between the studio and its star director was coming to a close. As his last venture, Hitchcock was asked to produce and direct a film of H. A. Vachell's play *The Case of Lady Camber* — to be called, with undeserved provocation, *Lord Camber's Ladies*. Gertrude Lawrence (soon to be subjected to the improbable blue dinner) was to co-star with Gerald du Maurier (soon to be invited to the phantom costume party).

Hitchcock, however, was by this time in a haze of disappointment and depression, and without a clear idea of what, if any, future he had in film. He handed over the scripting and direction duties to Benn W. Levy, with whom he enjoyed a friendly relationship until the film went into production. Levy then thought Hitchcock ill tempered and meddlesome — and neither for the first nor the last time there was in Hitchcock's life a sudden and prolonged rupture in communication.

Confused and professionally adrift in 1933, and aware of vague reports of political troubles in Europe, the Hitchcocks curtailed their travel outside England, retreated more often to the quiet of Winter's Grace, and spent several months investigating a proper school for Patricia. She was a bright, witty, extroverted child, and her parents were anxious to provide her with a good education. In England as later in America, she was sent to fine schools, and she did not surprise the theatergoing Hitchcocks when, early on, she announced that she intended to pursue a career as an actress.

During that year, Hitchcock signed a short-term contract with Alexander Korda, who announced that the first picture to be directed by Hitchcock under this arrangement would be something called *Wings over the Jungle*. But Korda, who was just embarking on his outstanding career in the British film industry, could provide neither the cast, the crew, nor the money for the project, and so Hitchcock was released from the obligation. An offer was then made by independent producer Tom Arnold for Hitchcock to film the musical play *Waltzes from Vienna,* which had had a long run in 1931 and 1932. Arnold signed up the workless Hitchcock (who seems to have been intrigued by the notion of a musical film), and engaged Jessie Matthews — at the time England's most popular musical star — and Esmond Knight, who had created in the West End the play's Johann Strauss the younger.

The enterprise was a desperate one from the start, and it justified Hitchcock's later statement that this was the lowest ebb in his career. Filming was done at the facilities of Gaumont-British, which, after a major reorganization of the company, were now located at Lime Grove Studios, Shepherd's Bush, London. "It was a musical without much music," Hitchcock said, "and it really wasn't my sort of thing." But he put on a good face about it — for a while, anyway — and he seemed to enjoy the period costumes and the theatricality of this poor man's operetta, scheduled to be filmed on a poor man's budget. Journalists visiting the set found the director affable, bright, and given to noonday steaks and lemonade — but also a man who jealously guarded his privacy. In fact, recalled Charles Bennett, Hitchcock had bought an expensive car at the time, and he had the windows blacked up and permanently fastened shut. Privacy became, for a while, an obsession.

Only for a while, however: during the shooting of *Waltzes from Vienna,* Hitchcock spoke to the *Daily Herald* of his future plans, and he indicated that he had not the slightest intention of moving on to Hollywood. "My policy is to make pictures right here — popular pictures which anybody can understand. But without being highbrow, I believe in making them in such a way that they will appeal to the most intelligent people as well. . . . In Hollywood, it's as if the inmates had taken over the asylum."

Still conscious of publicity, Hitchcock agreed to an extended and serious conversation with Stephen Watts, which was eventually published under the title "Alfred Hitchcock on Music in Films." In it, Hitchcock proposed several interesting ideas about the effect of music, sound, and silence on the overall emotional design of a film. Unfortunately, these ideas were not sufficiently integrated into *Waltzes from Vienna,* but there is no doubt that Hitchcock knew whereof he spoke. The remarks are a blueprint for his own productions in America.

When the cameras were rolling, however, no one seemed happy. In her autobiography, Jessie Matthews crystallized the whole experience in one telling sentence: "Alfred Hitchcock directed this one." That was all she had to say in her memoirs about the production of *Waltzes from Vienna.* The comment is a triumph of cool understatement, for Hitchcock and his star did not work congenially. Hitchcock seems to have been irritated by the preeminence accorded to this highly paid, influential star. He reduced her role, moved the camera away from her when he could, interrupted her rehearsals and her takes with an unending litany of corrections, and set the woman on the verge of nervous collapse.

"He was then just an imperious young man who knew nothing about musicals," Matthews later added. "I felt unnerved when he tried to get me to adopt a mincing operetta style. He was out of his depth and he showed that he knew it by ordering me around. . . . I thought the film was perfectly dreadful."

Esmond Knight also found that Hitchcock's reputation for calm, peace, and orderliness on the set was at variance with his attitude during the filming in this case. Knight thought that the film should have been much more lively and amusing, and he attributed its troubles to Hitchcock's crude sarcasm with his cast and to his practical jokes. The sour attitude and the pranks were once again the reflection of a rootless and disturbed creative life within — although Hitchcock always denied that he succumbed to anger, concern, or depression at this time.

"Jessie was not happy under Hitch," Knight recalled, "for he was inclined to indulge in a practice common to many film directors of taking the mickey out of an actor during rehearsal — a stage at which any actor is extremely vulnerable. He used to call me the 'Quota Queen,' and send me up mercilessly. He treated Fay Compton [who played a countess] in exactly the same way. The result was that we never gave of our best during a take, because we were always anticipating some ghastly practical joke to be played on us during the scene — which was very often done, I may say."

By the time *Waltzes from Vienna* was only half finished, Hitchcock had tired of it and had realized his mistake in undertaking a costume musical. After an exhausting day's work in a hot studio where one hundred extras were assembled, he announced: "I hate this sort of stuff. Melodrama is the only thing I can do."

News of this outburst reached Michael Balcon, who was now executive in charge of production for Gaumont-British, and whose offices were not far off. He went over next morning to visit his old colleague, and asked what was next on his agenda, who had engaged him. Hitchcock replied that he was free-lance, and that he still hoped to make a film of an idea he had spun with Charles Bennett during his last weeks at BIP, where Bennett, too, had been chafing. They were trying to do a treatment based on some old Bulldog Drummond stories, Hitchcock said, and they had hoped to do something called *Bulldog Drummond's Baby* or *The Return of Bulldog Drummond* — perhaps with Gerald du Maurier, who would recreate his stage role of the famous crook-catching hero of the stories by Sapper. Balcon seemed to ignite an old spark in Hitchcock, who talked for hours about scenes of suspense and intrigue. That was all Balcon needed, and he posed a suggestion. Since Hitchcock was not obligated to any producer or studio, why not rejoin him, and come over to Gaumont-British with Bennett *and* Bulldog Drummond?

Hitchcock shrugged cannily. "I don't know. . . . We tried to sell the idea to Maxwell, but he didn't like it."

"*I* do," said Balcon.

"There's just one problem. Maxwell owns the film rights to the character of Bulldog Drummond."

Balcon leaned over and whispered with a smile: "Then buy the rights, and I'll buy them from you."

Hitchcock soon had his own reasons — financial and artistic — to smile. He raced back to John Maxwell, bought the rights for £250, and went back to Balcon — to whom he sold them at once for £500. As a late spring warmed London in 1934, Hitchcock and Bennett signed a five-picture contract with Balcon and Gaumont-British and moved into offices at Shepherd's Bush. Balcon congratulated them on their move, and they congratulated themselves on what they suspected would become an important and famous partnership. They were more than justified in this suspicion.

# Six

---

## 1934–1936

THE story conferences for what would be Hitchcock's earlier version of *The Man Who Knew Too Much* were a joy for everyone involved. Balcon never interfered, according to Ivor Montagu, who had been invited back to Gaumont-British to serve as associate producer on the Hitchcock films. Hitchcock supervised script sessions from the center of the sitting room at Cromwell Road, comfortably installed on a velvet Renaissance throne and usually, at this point, in black silk pajamas. "It was indeed pleasant to work with Hitchcock then," Charles Bennett remembered, "although he had a monstrous ego that matched his appetite."

The picture's scenario, a good deal of which had been prepared at Elstree, was given final shape during April and May 1934. Bennett and Montagu would join Hitchcock, Alma, and often Angus MacPhail (who was supervisor and editor of screenplays for the studio) at the Hitchcock home in midmorning and the group would rummage through ideas.

Of his work patterns Hitchcock himself remarked: "Certain writers want to work every hour of the day. They're very facile. I'm not that way. I want to say, 'Let's lay off for several hours, let's play.' And then we get down to it again." And the playing was the reason he initiated the bus trips or boat rides that aborted many an afternoon work session. Refreshed, the team would return next morning with new ideas, a revived sense of humor, and the feeling that being paid for work like this was quite a coup in 1934.

And above and over the collaboration that went into the script, the voice and the tone and the themes were always Hitchcock's. The dialogue, written by Edwin Greenwood, A. R. Rawlinson, and Emlyn Williams, was subject to Hitchcock's approval and even his emendations.

Filming *The Man Who Knew Too Much* required nine-and-a-half weeks, from May 29 to August 2. What went before the cameras was a story that became the outline for a number of later Hitchcock films. Edna Best and Leslie Banks portray parents on holiday in Saint Moritz with their daughter (played by Nova Pilbeam). They are present at the murder of a friend (Pierre Fresnay) who turns out to be a British agent, and who, just as he dies, involves the couple by passing on the information that an assassination plot (masterminded by Peter Lorre) is about to be enacted in London. To keep the parents quiet, the plotters kidnap their child. Back in London, however, the mother — an expert shooter, as is revealed in the film's opening moments — foils the assassination attempt during a concert at Albert Hall, then rescues her daughter from the kidnappers, who are overcome in a shoot-out with the authorities.

This was in fact the story that had germinated in Hitchcock's fancy during his honeymoon trip at Saint Moritz; the daughter, the kidnapping, the details of international intrigue were all filled in later, but he retained what had originally struck him as picturesque and dramatic: the luxury resort, the upper-class characters, the disruption by sinister agents that forms the emotional center of the story, and the use of time itself as the arbiter. The principal photography proceeded smoothly, and Hitchcock was in great humor, his practical jokes for a while more benign and his attitude on the set confident and efficient.

Peter Lorre, who had become internationally famous as the child-murderer in Fritz Lang's *M* in 1931 (and who had subsequently fled the Nazi regime), was Hitchcock's logical choice for the curiously well-mannered kidnapper of a young girl, and Balcon was agreeable to hiring him. Lorre and Hitchcock shared an unconventional sense of fun, and often when a camera shot was ready the crew could find them huddled together in a corner, where they were trading the latest dirty stories. For a time, they also tried to outdo one another in the art of the practical joke. When Lorre one day complained loudly that a suit he owned had been ruined in the studio, Hitchcock admonished that he was behaving childishly; within the week, Lorre received an identical, brand-new suit at his home, tailored by an expensive shop — but the suit was cut in infant-size. By 1937, when Lorre departed for a long stay in Hollywood, they were still at it: Hitchcock (adapting an old ploy) sent a note of good wishes and a dray horse to Lorre's flat, and Lorre retaliated by sending three hundred singing canaries to Cromwell Road at three in the morning.

The editing and scoring of the movie were completed by the end of September (the music could by this time be added after filming), and everyone connected with the picture considered it a triumph. It was, indeed, masterfully conceived. Following the brightness of the snowy slopes in the opening title design that announces the Saint Moritz setting, *The Man Who Knew Too Much* becomes progressively darker, moving to cramped London interiors before ending with the clever, deliberate, parallel reversal of the beginning: a deadly sloping roof at night.

But there were problems. The Board of British Film Censors objected that the scenario ended with London's police in a shoot-out. Hitchcock's scene called to mind the famous Sidney Street siege at the turn of the century, during which London's traditionally unarmed bobbies called in the army and engaged in gunfire to stop a gang of anarchists. That confrontation, which Hitchcock and the censors clearly remembered, was a ploy inspired by the infamous Peter the Painter, an East End terrorist who was clearly the model for Lorre's character. (Winston Churchill, who was Home Secretary at the time, had to make the difficult decision to send in artillery reinforcements.) But despite its historical origins, the censors would not hear of the scene: showing the police with guns would tarnish the image of London's finest, they insisted. Hitchcock could film the scene only if the army brought the guns, not the police. Hitchcock agreed, and approval was given. What he filmed, though, was a scene in which the beleaguered policemen commandeer the goods at a local gunsmith — just before a shot of an arriving van (army reinforcements?) is crudely intercut. The pace of the final editing and the excitement generated by the finale would, Hitchcock knew, distract the censors as well as please the audience.

Another problem was more distressing — and it had a familiar ring. C. M. Woolf was still in the executive branch of Gaumont-British. By this time he was single-handedly in control of film distribution for the entire company, and whenever Balcon set sail for America on other film business, Woolf was left in charge of the studio. He screened *The Man Who Knew Too Much* and decided, as he had with Hitchcock's films before, that it was utter nonsense. He would bring in Maurice Elvey to reshoot it, although nothing would be done until Balcon returned.

Hitchcock was beside himself, for he and Bennett had already begun work on their next script. "Charles, it's all over with, we're through," Hitchcock cried in an unusually frantic telephone call to Bennett at his home in Belgravia. "Let's not even go ahead with *The 39 Steps*, because they'll never finance it. There's nothing I can do."

But there was something Ivor Montagu could do. He went to Woolf and reminded him that Balcon had expected Hitchcock's first picture with Gaumont-British to reestablish Hitchcock's — and the studio's — prestige, and he suggested that on the production chief's return there should have been at least a week's public screening to show for the

money they had spent on the *The Man Who Knew Too Much*. Woolf
relented, but warned that they had a disaster on their hands. To save
the company complete embarrassment, he released Hitchcock's film as
the second half of a double bill at the London cinemas.

"This is glorious melodrama," raved the *Kinematograph Weekly* on
December 13, 1934. "It is artless fiction, staged on a spectacular scale.
. . . Alfred Hitchcock has obviously learnt by past experience that real
money lies only in mass appeal, and with this wise thought in his mind
he has given us a picture of first-class melodrama."

"We'll see what the others have to say," Woolf snarled when this
early notice was brought to him. And see he did, as public enthusiasm
and popular critical response began to equal the film-tradesmen's acclaim. *"The Man Who Knew Too Much* has great thrills, human interest, good work by a sterling cast, and excellent production qualities,"
read a typical review. Hitchcock and Bennett had nothing to fear from
C. M. Woolf from this point on, and to celebrate Christmas and their
success they took their families to Saint Moritz. The Bennetts took to
the ski slopes by day (Pat and, at least once, Alma went along too),
while Hitchcock waved farewell from the balcony of their connecting
suite, then prepared the outline for evening discussion of the next project, and had drinks waiting on their return.

Since he and Bennett had succeeded with the motif of political terrorism and international espionage, Hitchcock insisted that they keep these
ingredients in mind in their treatment of John Buchan's famous novel
*The Thirty-Nine Steps*. They both admired Buchan's sense of the sudden
eruption of terror in the life of an ordinary man on the run from the
police, whose help he needs. But Bennett was of the opinion that, for
all its breathless pacing, the book was devoid of character, humor, and
any potential for audience involvement. "I thought the Buchan novel
was terrible, but it had possibilities — the double chase, for example,"
Bennett said. And Hitchcock agreed.

To remedy the weaknesses of the material, they decided to exploit
two aspects of the contemporary scene: the ominous news reports filter-
ing through Switzerland, and the audience's consequent desire for comic-
romantic elements. Vague rumors about Hitler and the rise of fanaticism
were circulating, and as political arguments filled the dining room of
the hotel, Hitchcock and Bennett knew that the confusion and misty fear
were valuable material for channeling into a film. And at this point they
not only revived a strong "non-point" of *The Man Who Knew Too
Much* — they canonized it. Just as it was never made clear exactly who
was up to the assassination attempt in that earlier film, or exactly what

international issue was at stake, a similar murkiness must be created now.

Angus MacPhail was the one who established the term *MacGuffin* for the deliberately mysterious plot objective — the non-point — which they need not choose until the rest of the story was completely planned. This term Hitchcock quickly adopted, and, of course, he used it to the end of his career. The term, according to MacPhail, derived from an anec- dote he told about two men traveling to Scotland on a train from Lon- don. In the luggage rack overhead was an oddly wrapped parcel.

"What have you there?" asked one of the men.
"Oh, that's a MacGuffin," replied his companion.
"What's a MacGuffin?"
"It's a device for trapping lions in the Scottish Highlands."
"But there aren't any lions in the Scottish Highlands!"
"Well, then, I guess that's no MacGuffin!"

The point is that a MacGuffin is neither relevant, important, nor, finally, any of one's business. It simply gets the story going. In the case of *The 39 Steps*, the MacGuffin is a secret formula — the specifications for a line of fighter planes. But it is to *prevent* the secret from being known — rather than to reveal it — that the adventure-chase is precip- itated; thus the formula, which at first seems crucial, is immediately reduced in significance. Soon after the story begins, the issue fades to- tally in importance for both the characters and the audience.

This red-herring element worked so successfully in the film that after fifty years it refuses to show its age. By avoiding the specific, the film addresses the universality of political intrigue and depravity. In Buch- an's novel, the thirty-nine steps of the title actually lead to a nest of spies, which Hannay, the reluctant hero, finally uncovers. But in Hitch- cock's film, "the thirty-nine steps" is simply the designation for an organization of spies; the dominant issue is one of trust between the leading man and woman — an issue that is reinforced throughout the story by contrasting sets of couples (the Scotsman and his wife, the inn- keeper and his wife, Professor Jordan and his wife).

By the end of the winter holiday, the detailed treatment was finished. In a letter to Balcon, Hitchcock insisted that Alma receive credit on the film for "continuity" and that a salary be budgeted for her. This some- what surprised Bennett, since Alma was not part of their writing con- ferences: she hovered pleasantly and saw to their needs, but for most of the time at Saint Moritz she and Bennett's wife Faith, with six-and-a- half-year-old Patricia between them, took long sleigh rides and wrote cards back home. Alma's credit, Bennett later found out, was simply

Hitchcock's method of increasing his own salary. There is no doubt that she brought a special set of skills to her counsel and advice on the specifics of each film, but this counsel and advice was given in the ordinary manner of a helpmate's suggestions. It was in fact Hitchcock and Bennett, working alone, who invented the theater setting for the opening and closing of *The 39 Steps,* as well as (for romantic interest) the blond, who has no parallel in the novel. Annabella Smith (played by Lucie Mannheim), the hapless brunette spy who first involves the hero and is rewarded by being murdered, was also created, as a balance for the character Pamela.

Back in London, Balcon allowed Hitchcock and Bennett to engage dramatist Ian Hay to write the dialogue for *The 39 Steps,* and in a matter of days it was finished and ready for final executive approval. Photography began on January 11, 1935, the final members of the cast having been chosen in a remarkably timed series of meetings. Robert Donat, whom Hitchcock had much admired when he doubled as father and son in the third staged revival of *Mary Rose* in 1930, was now neatly mustached, and he warmed to his role, a chance at romantic comedy. He had signed even before he knew the identity of his co-star. For a time there was talk of that role going to Jane Baxter, but she had to fulfill an obligation to go on stage with the play *Drake.* Anna Lee was also close to being signed.

And then, on January 9, Madeleine Carroll agreed to take the part. Balcon had gone to America to bring her back especially for this project, but she initially expressed such reservations that he said he would put her in another film if she insisted. Alma, who had met Carroll back in 1928, was particularly delighted when she finally accepted the role, for she had hoped from the start that Carroll would one day be a Hitchcock heroine. University graduate, former schoolteacher, trained in silent pictures, and then one of England's and America's most glamorous film stars, Madeleine Carroll was luminous on the screen.

But Hitchcock knew there might be problems, and he immediately arranged a meeting — ostensibly to discuss wardrobe, but in fact to see what Carroll's attitude was. He feared she was going to act the spoiled celebrity, unwilling to take his direction and to submit herself to the uncomfortable demands he planned to make on her. Handing her the script, he asked her to read a few lines, under pretext of wanting her opinion on the idiom of a certain scene. "Madeleine Carroll suddenly became another person," Hitchcock recalled. "She played in a kind of mesmeric trance. I asked what had become of the gay person I'd met at our first interview. She said, 'But I thought I had to act.' I told her for

God's sake be yourself.'' He had chosen her, he said, because of a
natural quality that was just right for the role.

What he *meant* was that he found her elegance and cool beauty charged
with sex appeal. ''I've never been very keen on women who hang their
sex round their neck like baubles,'' he later explained.

I think it should be discovered. . . . I suppose the first blond who was a real
Hitchcock type was Madeleine Carroll. The English woman or the North German or the Swedish can look like a schoolmarm, but boy, when they get going
these women are quite astonishing. . . .

It's more interesting to discover the sex in a woman than it is to have it
thrown at you, like a Marilyn Monroe or those types. To me they are rather
vulgar and obvious. I think it's much more interesting in the course of the
storytelling to discover the sex. . . . Anything could happen to you with a
woman like that in the back of a taxi.

Carroll left Hitchcock's office uncertain what the first day's filming
would hold, and the woman who followed her in to see the director that
morning — another blond, and just as handsome — had uncertainties
of her own.

Hitchcock had placed an advertisement in the London newspapers.
He needed a personal secretary who could also read scripts, synopsize
them, and handle a great number of details connected with film preparation and production. Over a hundred applicants had come to his office;
all were turned away even before he tested their secretarial skills. But
the woman who passed Madeleine Carroll in the outer office was engaged for the position at once.

Born and raised in Guildford, where her father was managing director
of the *Surrey Advertiser*, Joan Mary Harrison had intended to become a
journalist. Her parents, encouraging her to something better, sent her to
Oxford and to the Sorbonne, where she studied classical and English
literature. Then twenty-four, Harrison's china-blue eyes flashed with
purpose and intelligence. Hitchcock asked her to report next morning to
the set, where she would begin her duties with an instant education in
the technical paperwork connected with the cinema. Her gradual advancement under Hitchcock's tutelage, from secretary in 1935 to continuity assistant in 1936, from script consultant by 1937 to dialogue writer
by 1938 and scenarist by 1939, was certainly warranted by her quick
mind and her sense of organization — qualities that were demanded of
a close Hitchcock aide.

In time it seemed to a number of Hitchcock's associates in England
and America that he harbored unreciprocated feelings toward Joan Har-

rison that went deeper, beyond those of appreciation for a loyal employee. And so her sensibilities had to be tested early, and her reserve — like that of so many initially unsuspecting blonds — had to be broken down. Within a month of her arrival at Hitchcock's office, she was called in while Bennett and he were discussing the story to follow *The 39 Steps*. On the desk was a copy of James Joyce's *Ulysses,* which Hitchcock casually picked up and opened to a marked page. And then, as calmly as if he were reading a news story, he read the notorious toilet scene to his embarrassed secretary, who could not, Bennett remembered, repress her discomfort nor determine why Hitchcock was subjecting her to this odd initiation into the unconventional "new literature."

As of the first day of shooting, Donat and Carroll had not met, and Dickie Beville, Hitchcock's unit manager, was concerned that the first scene scheduled would prove awkward. It was the start of a sequence in which the couple, handcuffed to each other by the spies, manage to escape and flee across the Scottish countryside. Hitchcock had, in fact, decided to exploit the situation. Precisely at eight-thirty that morning, he introduced his two leading players, explained the sequence, and snapped a pair of handcuffs on to their wrists. He then led them through a rehearsal on the sound stage, over the dummy bridge and fences, until he was told that some technical matter needed his attention and he advised them that they could take a rest. But he then told them that he had somehow mislaid the key to the handcuffs, and he vanished until late afternoon while his assistants photographed several insert shots and members of the crew dealt with the problem of sixty-two Scottish sheep (actually imported from Hertfordshire) that were nibbling the bracken and heather carefully arranged on the set for atmosphere.

By teatime, Hitchcock had suddenly found the key (which, Donat later discovered, had been carefully deposited with a studio guard as soon as the manacles were fastened). The actors, of course, were tired, angry, disheveled, uncomfortable, and acutely embarrassed. But Hitchcock was delighted when the rest of the cast and crew found out about his little trick and were shocked. He wanted to know how many people were discussing the manner in which the humiliated couple had coped with details of a decidedly personal nature. "There was no better technician in the business," recalled Jack Whitehead, second-unit cameraman on the film, "but when it came to personal relations, there was certainly a streak of the sadist in him."

"What interests me," Hitchcock said later, "is the drama of being handcuffed. There's a special terror, a sort of 'thing' about being tied up, haven't you noticed? The classic line when somebody in a melodrama is about to be handcuffed goes, 'Oh no, not that, please!' And the answer: 'We must — this is a serious case.' In *The 39 Steps,* of course, it was fundamental." And fundamental not only as an ironic device foreshadowing an ultimately romantic bond, one might add. As in *The Lodger* (and Hitchcock's earlier "bet" with the luckless technician), his own private obsessions were being worked out on the set as in the film.

Ivor Montagu agreed with Bennett that Hitchcock's behavior was at the least unconventional, but it took thirty years for him to break his silence, and even then he was characteristically generous: "It had long been my conviction . . . sustained by working with Hitchcock, that a good director must have something of the sadist in him. I do not necessarily mean to a pathological degree, but that his looking at things and telling characters to do this, undergo that, is necessarily akin to dominating them, ordering them about." Even Montagu's delicate diction, refined sensibility, and reluctance to betray the man he considered the master of the cinema do not entirely cover his awareness that there might, indeed, have been something pathological — something that was, at this time, still kept in check against a monstrous unleashing of its full potential to destroy someone's spirit; eventually, it would lead Hitchcock to endanger life.

To the other players, Hitchcock showed an aloof professionalism that kept them alert. Peggy Ashcroft, whom Hitchcock had also admired on the stage, had been given the small but deeply affecting role of the Scottish crofter's wife, and during the first take of her scene with Donat she was infected by his giggling over some acting gestures they had considered. For the second, and the third, and then the fourth take, the pair ruined the dialogue with their irrepressible laughter as soon as they glanced at each other. Hitchcock, striding to the center of the set, looked at them coolly, then walked to the side and smashed the bulb of a studio lamp with his fist. The shock of the explosion, the noise and the smoke, alarmed the crew and sobered the actors, and the episode (so tautly rendered on film) was photographed perfectly without interruption.

For the remainder of the shooting, until March 18, most of the studio details were managed by Beville and Joan Harrison. "Dickie Beville was a handsome and charming young man, totally devoted to his new bride," according to Charles Bennett. "And I think Hitchcock resented him." At least one incident witnesses that impression. Hitchcock had been in the habit of driving Beville back to central London after the day's shooting, and as they were heading home one Friday evening the assistant was surprised to find that Hitchcock had turned in the opposite direction and that they were speeding down the road toward Surrey.

"But I have theater tickets for tonight!" Beville protested anxiously. "I'm to meet my wife in less than an hour! Where are you taking me?"

"Oh, you'll be there on time," Hitchcock said calmly, and he turned the conversation to the following week's filming schedule. Darkness soon covered their route, and an hour later, stepping from the car, Beville found himself in the quiet but completely unexpected hospitality of Shamley Green. Alma had already arrived, with another (female) houseguest, and the reluctant Beville was forced to accept the director's honorarium: a weekend in the country. "Looks like it's going to be a dirty night, old man," Hitchcock said as thunder rolled across the fields of Surrey. "You'll have to suffer our ministrations."

To retaliate for the forced stay, Beville the next week presented Hitchcock with a terrible concoction — old brandy laced with the same potent laxative he had been told Hitchcock once gave another worker.

"You'll adore it, Hitch," Beville announced. "It's a very old reserve." But after a week passed without any comment from the director, Beville asked if he had had a chance to sample it.

"I didn't want to mention it," Hitchcock said earnestly, "but my mother is sick and when the doctor prescribed brandy, we gave her some of yours. I'm afraid she's going to die."

Stricken with guilt and remorse, Beville sent a large floral arrangement and an offer of help to the patient's flat in Kensington. Two days later he was told that the flowers had been accepted by a neighbor until the return of the hearty Mrs. Hitchcock from a holiday with her cousin in Essex. In her note of gratitude, she said she could not imagine why Mr. Beville would perform such a lovely, generous gesture, and that she was certainly very grateful indeed.

On Thursday, June 6, a premiere showing of *The 39 Steps* was held for the press and the trade at The New Gallery Theatre. At a banquet following the screening were John Buchan (then Lord Tweedsmuir, soon to be governor general of Canada), Sir Philip Cunliffe-Lister, Sir John Simon, Mark Ostrer (one of the brothers who controlled Gaumont-British), and other dignitaries. In front of the head table, at which the Hitchcocks sat with Michael Balcon and his wife, was a floral arrangement that spelled out the film's title. The evening worked its way to the introduction of the director, but when called upon to speak, he simply rose, bowed, and sat again.

"We would have liked a few words from Hitchcock," complained one journalist, "but he could afford to play the part of 'the Buddha of British films,' and let his work speak for itself." The industry's notices were extravagant, as the work indeed spoke for itself: "It's brilliantly directed by Alfred Hitchcock in the naturalistic manner he has made his own," raved one trade periodical; and another observed, "Each detail, even each word, appears to have been fully considered and dove-tailed so perfectly."

What most impressed those at the first screening was the film's richness of psychological detail and the resonant humor. Just as the character played by Madeleine Carroll supported the theme of trust and heightened the sense of tension, so had the character played by Godfrey Tearle supported that theme by inversion while also intensifying the suspense. For Professor Jordan, the seemingly respectable country gentleman and head of a household, admired by his neighbors as much as by the local police authorities, is in fact an anti-British spy — the man with the tip of a finger missing, the man against whom the hero had been warned. Perhaps the character with the most ambiguous moral stance, he is at once a devoted husband and father and a man who harbors dark secrets that prevent him from disclosing his real identity. "I'm a respectable citizen, Mr. Hannay," he protests when he is found out. "What would happen if it became known that I'm not what I seem?" This character stands in for Hitchcock, and gives expression to his fear of a bad reputation; the public image, the persona so carefully constructed, is to be taken as the reality, even when the reality is quite different.

And there is another sense in which Hitchcock reveals himself in *The 39 Steps* — in the character of Mr. Memory. From his earliest days at the music halls, Hitchcock remembered the famous vaudeville performer Mr. Datas. "He always concluded his act by having a stooge ask when Good Friday fell on a Tuesday," Hitchcock recalled years later. "He would then answer that a horse called Good Friday fell in a particular race on Tuesday, June 2, 1874." Mr. Memory, another of Hitchcock's personal additions to the script, is also like Hitchcock himself — the man forced to remember every detail, compelled to give himself up as part of the show, to make his little appearance. He is in a way the obverse of the Professor (with whom he is linked as an accessory in the conspiracy), for whereas the Professor takes care *not* to reveal his treachery and hides behind the mask of public respectability, Mr. Memory (impeccably played by Wylie Watson) is the star entertainer, the man with the deadly secret neatly in his head, the man whose unavoidable death is presented as pathetic and even a little heroic because he cannot avoid answering the dreaded question.

Hitchcock and Bennett had already worked on the treatment of the next film while *The 39 Steps* was being shot, and the new production began the last week of October. Based on short stories of espionage by Somerset Maugham (specifically, selections from the Ashenden cycle) and on Campbell Dixon's theatrical version of one of them, *Secret Agent* turned out to be not only the third in a series of spy films, but also Hitchcock's most overtly moral fable up to that point; he and Bennett used political and romantic intrigue as a fulcrum on which to counterpoise the evolution of a double moral dilemma.* John Gielgud, Hitchcock supposed, would be just right for the reluctant spy — Gielgud acted a highly acclaimed *Hamlet* — and he accepted Hitchcock's offer when the part was described to him as that of a modern-day Hamlet, a man forced to make a number of difficult decisions.

"I found filming terribly exhausting," Gielgud wrote in his memoirs. "I had to get up very early in the morning and was always fidgeting to get away by five or six for the evening performance, so I grew to dislike working for the cinema. Of course, I was paid more money than in the theatre, but I had a feeling that no one thought I was sufficiently good-looking to be very successful. . . . I did not have much confidence in my talent as a film actor and I thought when I saw the film that I was rather poor."

But Gielgud's problem on *Secret Agent* was really neither his schedule (he was playing in *Romeo and Juliet* nightly, with Laurence Olivier, Peggy Ashcroft, and Edith Evans) nor his performance. As the shooting progressed, Hitchcock in fact lost interest in the character Gielgud was portraying. The camera favored the film's leading lady: once again, it was Madeleine Carroll, from whom Hitchcock could scarcely remove his gaze — and in the film she is photographed as stunningly and directed as lovingly as Marlene Dietrich ever was by Josef von Sternberg. To further complicate the problem, Peter Lorre, whom Hitchcock had invited back for the role of the bloodthirsty, amoral assassin, was by this time a pathetic morphine addict. When he was not stealing the scenes in which he appeared (by means of unexpected and unrehearsed bits of acting business), he vanished into the corners of the studio to satisfy his habit. (This explains the film's atypically large number of mismatched shots, and odd jumps — the generally quirky, arrhythmic quality of the scenes in which Lorre appears.)

"Alfred Hitchcock," Gielgud admitted at the time, "has often made me feel like a jelly and I have been nearly sick with nervousness."

*The dialogue was again written by the prolific Ian Hay, and some polishing was contributed by novelist, playwright, and scenarist Jesse Lasky, Jr.

Hitchcock in turn spoke to the press about Gielgud: "His stage experience is no use to him here. I've had to make him rub out everything
and start blank." And though the director plainly adored Carroll, he felt
he had to maintain the advantage over her: "Nothing gives me more
pleasure than to knock the lady-likeness out. . . . That is why I deliberately deprived Madeleine Carroll of her dignity and glamour in *The
39 Steps*. I have done exactly the same thing with her in *Secret Agent* —
in which the first shot of her you see is with her face covered with cold
cream!"

The smaller roles were as curiously and carefully cast as the leads.
Robert Young, who had come to England at Balcon's invitation to make
two films for Gaumont-British, was playing against his type as the attractive, exploitive, and murderous enemy spy. Hitchcock hired Florence Kahn, wife of Max Beerbohm, for the role of the sad and displaced
German wife. "It was her first picture," Hitchcock said years later.
"Not only had she never been to a film studio before, she had never in
her life even seen a movie! I saw her do *Peer Gynt* at the Old Vic and
I thought she'd be just right. In fact she turned out to be a very odd
woman indeed." For the role of her husband, the wrong man who is
killed, Hitchcock brought back Percy Marmont (the dashing commander
of *Rich and Strange*).

Some idea of the unconventional atmosphere that prevailed during
shooting is suggested by the scene involving Carroll, Young, and a Swiss
coachman, played by the famous French actor Michel Saint-Denis. The
whole brief scene was invented extemporaneously when Saint-Denis
visited his old friend Gielgud on the set. No one was quite sure where
the scene would be inserted in the finished film, and although this kind
of inventiveness was always foreign to the Hitchcock method, he had
so lost interest in the picture that any interruption was welcome.

The only aspect of *Secret Agent* that appealed to him — or so he
said — was Madeleine Carroll, whom he rather often upset with his
own confusion. One moment she was being coiffed and directed with
unimaginable loving care, the next moment she was the off-camera victim of a rude practical joke, perhaps to keep her from trading on the
beguiling beauty Hitchcock saw and was rendering on film. Before he
had met Madeleine Carroll, he had set down what he called "rough-
and-ready rules" as to the ideal screen beauty. Apparently she met the
qualifications, and although they would change somewhat with the passing of years, there would occasionally emerge a woman to measure
up — at least for a time. "The eyes should be far apart," he had written, "the face oval or round rather than long, and the way the hair

grows round the forehead is important. The features must not be too decided, and the screen demands a certain animation and sparkle of movement, which is the opposite of self-consciousness.''

Hitchcock's contradictory treatment of Madeleine Carroll — devoted at one moment, almost cruel the next — was the first flowering of a habit that marked his dealings with several leading ladies later. The simultaneous attraction and repulsion, the almost idolatrous gaze of his camera and the concomitant compulsion to reveal some truer human wrinkles, is perhaps the single marker of the spiritual climate of his most mature films, and it was in real life the emotionally schizoid pattern that caused him and his actors, both male and female, considerable pain during the term of their work with him. By 1935, Hitchcock was at his heaviest yet — much over three hundred pounds — and his lumbering discomfort, the awkwardness with which he moved among his cast, must have augmented his feelings of social ineptitude. His neatness and authority ameliorated only slightly the sight of a grotesquely obese man. And his sudden lapses into an attitude of mysterious silence, his imagination of a rebuff, and his inability to thank or to praise were all swiftly characterizing him as an enigmatic, unpredictable presence. Even those who had known him longest were finding it increasingly difficult to understand him. Alfred Hitchcock was becoming a frightening, disarticulate man well before he was forty.

It is in fact this sudden shift to an inner perspective — from the playful extroversion of *The Man Who Knew Too Much* and *The 39 Steps* — that marks the interior value of suspense in *Secret Agent* and *Sabotage,* the film that followed at once. It is, in these films, what happens *inside* the characters that matters. The spying agents, the prime movers of the thrillers, are themselves men of divided heart and intentions; the characters rendered by Gielgud, and by Oscar Homolka and John Loder in *Sabotage,* are themselves ambassadors of Hitchcock's own confused and divided inner loyalties. The theme of both films — the shifts of moral intent — emblemized a struggle within Hitchcock himself, who at this time became more closely involved in the day-to-day preparation of the treatment than ever before. His involvement was in direct proportion to the extent of his own inner disarray. "I liked *Secret Agent* quite a bit," he said later, belying his attitude at the time of production. "I'm sorry it wasn't more of a success."

Partly to distance himself from the disappointment of *Secret Agent,* partly because he liked Saint Moritz, and partly because he was increasingly uncomfortable in London, Hitchcock took Montagu and Bennett with him on an extended holiday in Switzerland after the completion of the editing of *Secret Agent*. It was then the third week of January 1936, which coincided with the death of King George V and the accession of the unhappy Edward VIII. The three men of the cinema had received Balcon's approval to work on an adaptation of Joseph Conrad's novel *The Secret Agent*, which, for obvious reasons, would have a new title: *Sabotage* was the final choice.

Hitchcock and Bennett flew to Basle, where Montagu joined them, and they drove on to a mountain resort near the Jungfrau, where Hitchcock indulged his taste for the cheap Swiss cider. They then stopped at Saint Moritz and worked on the treatment.

Back in London, the dialogue was finished rapidly, by Ian Hay and Helen Simpson, before the end of February. But Hitchcock refused to start filming until the delivery of the new batch of cider he had ordered from Switzerland. And when it arrived, he delayed still further because he had not received the new personal stationery he had designed for his office. All was at last in readiness and to his liking by late April.

Admirers of Conrad were to be greatly shocked by the changes, but the final screen version incarnated the novel's darkness of spirit if not its richness of character. The retarded child Stevie, almost a mystic visionary in the novel, became simply an innocent victim of tragic circumstances in the film; the detective-inspector of the novel became a disguised greengrocer who (and here there is a return to the moral concern of *Blackmail*) exploits his function as a policeman to press his love for a beleaguered married woman; the socialists and anarchists of the novel became vaguely motivated foreign agents; the sleazy tobacconist-magazine shop of the novel became a cinema that houses a saboteur; and the pervasive sense of doom that Conrad attributes to a cycle of "madness or despair . . . an impenetrable mystery" was captured by a tragic gloom and a claustrophobic hopelessness that hang over the whole atmosphere of the picture.

A particular passage in the Conrad novel (it is spoken by the assistant commissioner) typifies the spirit of Hitchcock's films *Secret Agent* and *Sabotage*, and it is worth citing, because it may have struck Hitchcock and Bennett as the very heart of those films; in any case, it expresses the spirit that animates their work.

In principle, I should lay it down that the existence of secret agents should not be tolerated, as tending to augment the positive dangers of the evil against which they are used. That the spy will fabricate his information is a commonplace. But in the sphere of political and revolutionary action, relying partly on

violence, the professional spy has every facility to fabricate the very facts
themselves, and will spread the double evil of emulation in one direction, and
of panic, hasty legislation, unreflecting hate, on the other. However, this is an
imperfect world. . . .

As *Secret Agent* had opened with a false, staged death and ended with
multiple deaths, so *Sabotage* opens with a false death, this one rendered
in a movie-within-the-movie, and it ends with multiple deaths as the
theater in the story is itself exploded. The ironic and metaphoric use of
the cinema house is brilliantly conceived in *Sabotage,* and it is in fact
the first of several times when Hitchcock chose the medium in which
he worked as a correlative for deadly illusion. In one particularly telling
moment, the greengrocer-detective is taken back to the family quarters
that are behind the movie screen, and in fact he walks to the reverse
side of the screen — while a film is being projected — and climbs
through a small window to eavesdrop on the meeting of spies. The film-
within-the-film, of course, is commenting ironically on the action all the
while.

Hitchcock must have chosen Conrad's novel because he shared several of its concerns: the banality of evil, the transference or assumption
of guilt, the disaffection and unsteadiness in human relationships, the
duplicity inherent in the enterprise of espionage and the enterprise of
tracking down the spies. He never discussed this amalgam of concerns
with his cast, but those who read the basic literary source caught the
kindred spirit.

The production was set to begin in May, and a team of actors seemed
settled. Earlier, upon returning from a trip to America, Balcon had announced in the press: "I discovered while in Hollywood that Miss Sylvia Sidney was available for one picture in England. . . . I should have
been a fool if I had let slip the opportunity of signing up such a brilliant
actress. We are looking for a story to suit her now. When we have
found it, Alfred Hitchcock will direct the picture." The picture was to
be *Sabotage*.

On Friday, May 15, Sidney arrived in London and at once went into
conference with Balcon and Hitchcock to discuss script, wardrobe, and
her leading man, about whom there had just emerged some doubt. Robert Donat, whom Alexander Korda had originally agreed to loan out for
the production, had fallen ill and was confined to a nursing home with
severe asthma. Barely able to breathe, Donat was in danger of death for
a while. (Hitchcock sent him a message inquiring just what the trouble
was, and Donat replied with characteristic calm that he was having trouble with his sense of smell. Hitchcock promptly sent, via taxi, sixty pair

of kippers.) Eventually, because of Donat's prolonged illness, Balcon and Hitchcock had to settle on John Loder, about whom no one was very enthusiastic. With the arrival of Oscar Homolka and young stage actor Desmond Tester, the cast was ready to begin.

The same week, *Secret Agent* was being screened for the first time, and the press continued its love affair with Hitchcock's movies. "A worthy companion picture to its august and very successful predecessor *The 39 Steps,*" announced the *Kinematograph Weekly*. "The story unfolds through the psychological reactions of the leading characters. . . . It has intelligent dialogue, good humor, heart interest." Encouraged by this, Hitchcock spent a whole week's salary entertaining the London press in grand fashion at his favorite restaurant, Simpson's in the Strand. (It was also, the press would discover, the setting for an important scene in the new film.) When they asked the title of the latest production, Hitchcock was momentarily at a loss: *Sabotage* had not yet been decided on; there had been some talk of *I Married a Murderer,* but he had wisely rejected that. So he simply replied that it was to be called *The Hidden Power* — probably a pun on the opening incident, in which an electrical power plant is sabotaged by a man whose dangerous power is hidden (quite literally) in the cinema. In any event, the press picked it up and erroneously announced *The Hidden Power* as the title of the new Hitchcock picture.

At the same time, critic C. A. Lejeune wrote a brief comment on Hitchcock's working method and personality.

He loves music, mystery and melodrama. He loves to imagine all the people he knows in melodramatic situations. He gloats over the idea of an aeroplane dropping live bombs on the Aldershot Tattoo. Like the children in *The Brushwood Boy,* he "sets light to populous cities to see how they would burn."

On the set he's a sadist. He revels in spiritual de-bagging. Nothing delights him more than to take a film star with a good opinion of himself, work him until he sweats, and then publicly can the sequence. His language is fierce, and his humour rarely drawing-room. He respects nobody's feelings; but everybody respects him.

Hitch's genius is for draughtsmanship. He is an instinctive visualiser. His film scripts are minor works of art, every shot blocked on the margin of the page in rough design. When a script is finished, he loses interest in the picture. He would rather get on with the next job.

It was C. A. Lejeune who later objected to the cruel death of the boy in *Sabotage* — a death not only faithful to the Conrad novel, but also necessitated by the predominant theme of the spread of chaos and the awful suffering of the innocent through the action of revolutionaries and terrorists. Hitchcock, always careful to please the most powerful critics, readily — and wrongly — agreed with Miss Lejeune's postmortem and, feeling the alienation of an important critic, regretted the sequence ever after.

A crisis was soon brewing at Gaumont-British — between Hitchcock and Ivor Montagu. The issue must have seemed petty to those involved in the production: the director and his associate disagreed over the construction of a tram line for the climactic scene in which a bomb goes off in Piccadilly Circus. Hitchcock, as usual, insisted on accuracy of detail, no matter the cost to his producer. Montagu, on the other hand, argued that the content of the scene was so tense that the audience would not notice whether the details of the set were precise or not. Neither would quarrel openly, so Montagu asked the appropriate Ostrer brother to release him from the production; Montagu saw Alfred Hitchcock only once again before the director's death.

That the stubbornness of both men in fact ruptured their creative collaboration was perhaps inevitable: Montagu was first of all a social and political activist, and only secondarily a movie professional. Hitchcock, on the other hand, would sacrifice anyone, pay any price, when he was convinced of the rightness of his viewpoint. Ironically, in the end, a simplified set was in fact used.

The Ostrer brothers — one of whom did release Montagu from his duties — were in fact the financial power behind the entire Gaumont-British combine, and at the conclusion of *Sabotage* they blithely announced that for financial reasons the studio would be shut down and that Gaumont-British would be simply a distributing company henceforth. Hundreds were at once fired, Balcon among them; he went over to London's branch of MGM. Hitchcock was now free for work with another independent producer, and he signed a two-picture contract with Gainsborough, which as an independent production company could still rent space at Lime Grove.

By mid-autumn, Hitchcock and Bennett had made their customary trip to Switzerland and had prepared a treatment based on a recently published novel, *A Shilling for Candles,* by Josephine Tey. They returned to London for the annual dinner of the Institute of Amateur Cinematographers, held at the Mayfair Hotel on November 3. Lord William Tyrrell, Britain's film censor, was guest of honor, the Duke of Sutherland presided, and the Hitchcocks were seated between Charles Laughton and his wife Elsa Lanchester; facing them across the banquet table were the Balcons, Marlene Dietrich, Douglas Fairbanks, Jr., Ann Harding, Victor Saville, Conrad Veidt, and Erich Pommer.

"How would you like to do a film with *us?*" Laughton asked, leaning over to Hitchcock between sips of brandy.

" 'Us'?" Hitchcock asked. "Who's 'us'?"

"That fellow over there," Laughton replied, pointing at Erich Pommer. "Haven't you two met before?"

They had, of course — and soon they met again and agreed to collaborate the following year, if that could be negotiated.

Before departing London for the winter holiday, Hitchcock supervised the allotment of the annual Christmas gifts. The list was considerably longer than it had ever been — most of the recipients were studio executives, favorite journalists and critics, some theater people, and those who had worked in his films. "Some of the gifts were quite lavish in those days," Bennett remembered. "But one had the impression he gave gifts to please himself in the giving, and to look generous. There was nothing personal about it. It was really all quite automatic and calculated, and the rest of the time he was not especially kind or thoughtful about the people to whom he gave gifts at holiday time. I think he gave gifts because it would help him."

On the morning of December 10, 1936, the Hitchcocks left with Pat and with Joan Harrison for a belated anniversary holiday in Europe. They reached Paris before they knew about Edward VIII's abdication speech that evening. The same day, the influential trade paper *Kinematograph Weekly* termed *Sabotage* a "perfectly framed" picture, and word was received that the film would be banned in Brazil because it was considered an incitement to terrorism and a threat to public order.

# Seven

1937–1939

In the spring of 1937 the new script, with dialogue by Charles Bennett, Edwin Greenwood, Anthony Armstrong, and Gerald Savory, was complete and Hitchcock was ready to cast what was now called *Young and Innocent*. But Bennett soon accepted an offer from Hollywood and left to join Universal Pictures, where he began a long and distinguished career as writer and sometime director, and now Hitchcock began to depend more and more on Joan Harrison, not only for production preparation and personal assistance, but also for rewriting thorny sections of the script. Alma was credited once again for continuity on the film, but this seems to have been a formality to justify additional payments to the family, although she did continue to offer considerable advice privately.

From late March to the beginning of May the filming proceeded at the large Pinewood Studios, after the first few days at Lime Grove were interrupted by major corporate changes involving the takeover of sound stages and laboratory space. The relocation enabled Hitchcock to achieve some of the most spectacular camera effects of his career up till then.

The leading couple were portrayed by Derrick de Marney and Nova Pilbeam. At the film's release de Marney wrote: "Hitchcock's eyes on the set are generally closed. He's been known to take cat-naps even during shooting. Nova Pilbeam was acting with me in her first romantic role. Hitchcock rushed us through one scene at express train tempo. When we had finished, Hitchcock, who had appeared to be snoozing contentedly, opened his eyes with difficulty and consulted his watch. 'Too slow,' he murmured. 'I had that scene marked for thirty seconds and it took you fifty seconds. We'll have to retake.' Hitch was using a stop-watch!''

De Marney also remembered that Hitchcock had a sharp tongue, much

to the distress of his actors: his aim was, de Marney thought, to strip
the actors of their poses, to force them to reveal their natural selves,
their unguarded selves — "and he finds he can do this best by infuri-
ating them." But Hitchcock was curiously tender and patient with Nova
Pilbeam, who had played the kidnapped daughter in *The Man Who Knew
Too Much* and who now, at eighteen, was acting her first adult role.
"Word got round that Old Hitch was turning soft until he himself explained," de Marney continued. "He was afraid that Nova, in self-
defense against his merciless ribbing, might adopt an air of false sophistication. So he was deferential to her, both on and off the lot."
This, however, was the exception; apart from Nova Pilbeam, "he spared
no one."

*Young and Innocent* reflects none of this tension or innuendo, however. It is a film of singular mildness and benevolence and charm.
Hitchcock repeated the basic structure of *The 39 Steps,* omitting the
element of espionage. The Derrick de Marney character is thought guilty
of the murder of an actress who had given him money. He escapes from
the police, and with the initially reluctant but then quite willing assistance of the local constable's daughter (Nova Pilbeam), they track the
real murderer, a jazz drummer with a nervous tic that makes his eyes
twitch. Hitchcock completely altered the Josephine Tey novel: the young
couple of the book become the film's major figures, the detective of the
novel is reduced to a minor character, the sidetracks of the book's plot —
its satire on actors, on a rather suspicious community of monks, and on
a host of subsidiary characters — are all virtually removed, and the film
develops its own major concerns that have no antecedent in Tey's
overwritten and unthrilling thriller.

The first shot is a tight close-up of a woman's face. She is a brunette,
and she is shouting at a man who accuses her of cavorting with "boys."
By the final moment of the picture, the situation is reversed: a blond,
smiling in tight close-up, is safely positioned between her father and her
"boy," cleared at last of the false charges. Between these two shots is
the gentlest of comic melodramas about youth and innocence — and at
the structural center of the film, Hitchcock placed a children's birthday
party, highlighted by a game of blindman's buff.

"The party," Hitchcock said years later, "was designed as a deliberate symbol — in fact it was the clue to the whole film, but no one got
it at the time, and in the American-release prints the sequence was omitted because they thought it slowed down the pace of the picture!" In
that sequence, the adults' wearing of children's party hats while the
children assume adult roles is one of the two major clues to Hitchcock's
meaning; the other is the game of blindman's buff itself. Its sense of

"fumbling in darkness," combined with an arrant playfulness, points to Hitchcock's larger concern, the reason why he called the party "a deliberate symbol."

In *Young and Innocent* he carried forward the images and theme of *seeing* that had involved him so deeply in *Sabotage,* where the business of characters screening and watching and reacting to film is itself the correlative for another kind of perception: inner sight and moral valuation. References to impaired vision abound in *Young and Innocent:* to escape the crowded courtroom, the hero filches the solicitor's spectacles; the murderer's eyes twitch uncontrollably; the children delight in tying up Auntie for a game of blindman's buff; at lunch young boys talk of the escaped suspect dying of starvation in the countryside "with rooks pecking at his eyes." These and a score of other references would later be deepened by Hitchcock in *The Birds,* which picks up and develops the game of blindman's buff at a children's birthday party as well as the motif of birds pecking at eyes both dead and living (the discovery of the body on the shore at the opening of *Young and Innocent* is interrupted by a shot of approaching scavenger gulls). In *The Birds* these images serve as markers in a tragedy of human misperceptions; in *Young and Innocent* they are casual hyphens linking characters in a common human situation.

What seems to have engaged Hitchcock's sense of playfulness even more in *Young and Innocent* is the motif of playacting and disguise. The hero dons eyeglasses to shield his identity. A tramp disguises himself as a dandy in order to help smoke out the criminal. A villain is disguised in blackface to play in a band. The murder victim is an actress. The innocent man on the run is a screenwriter, and Hitchcock makes one of his most hilarious cameos — as a photographer, holding a tiny camera in front of his huge frame and trying, vainly, to get a snapshot of the commotion outside the courthouse. Everyone deals in creating illusion.

But although this film generally treats its themes with a meringue lightness, two moments were obviously designed with such extraordinary care and executed on such a grand scale that they, too, are tip-offs that reveal the director's more serious concerns. Taking refuge from the police in an abandoned mine-shaft, the leading couple are almost lost when the floor of the cave collapses. By using Pinewood's largest stage and by building the floor of his set fifteen feet off the ground, Hitchcock was able to photograph a car poised before its crash below as Nova Pilbeam struggles to reach Derrick de Marney's outstretched hand, their faces filling the screen in anguish as their fingertips reach out. This is almost exactly the setup of the final clinging played out by Eva Marie Saint and Cary Grant in Hitchcock's *North by Northwest*, made two decades later; here, as there, the circumstance epitomizes two underlying concerns of the film (which originate from the fiber of Hitchcock's own spirit): the acute sense of crisis, danger, and accident at the heart of everyday life, and fear about the risk of emotional involvement.

The other tip-off is the justly famous single crane shot, from a vast overview of a crowded ballroom to a tight shot of the twitching eyes of the drummer. Two days of rehearsal with a vast crowd and England's largest crane were needed as the camera swooped 145 feet, with the operator constantly refocusing until his lens stopped a mere four inches from the actor's face. The shot is not just a technical tour de force; it is fraught with thematic significance as well. The bandleader sings: "It isn't a riddle, it's not a puzzle, but who's the man that you seldom think of when you think of a band? . . . When it comes to doing tricks with a pair of hickory sticks, I'm right here to tell you, mister, no one can like the drummer man!" As he continues to sing that the man "we're thinking of" is the drummer man, the camera slowly cranes down and seeks out the drummer, whose nervous tic gives him away. Thus in *Young and Innocent*, for the first time, Hitchcock makes the camera (a device with which he made his own ritual appearance in the picture) the revealing gazer. The ballroom take is the single longest objective shot of the film, and it establishes the camera itself as the ultimate seeker and seer, as it would be later in both *Rear Window* and *Psycho*.

But if the technique of *Young and Innocent* is deliberately bold and full of adult concerns, the scenario is remarkable for its gentleness. The film is full of embarrassed gestures of affection. Boys reach out toward their sister with inchoate, repressed tenderness, and like the hero, they, too, are tentative and shy about touching her arm or clasping her hand. Affections are not fully understood by anyone; innocence tempers youth with a quaint awkwardness. But the small touches are freighted with feeling all the same. There are an unusual number of quick insert shots of handclasps and questioning gazes that are full of hope and affection, and a wonderful mildness that is given freer play than in any of Hitchcock's films up to this point.

Notably devoid of violence or bloodshed, free of sexual innuendo or gamy motivation, set in the quiet English countryside that resembles Hitchcock's beloved Surrey, and suffused with a glowing appreciation for youthful buoyance, the film lingers on the glances of the young, and it is just this that reveals most of all the longing and the suppressed tenderness within Hitchcock himself. The handsome young hero is a screenwriter who masquerades at Auntie's party as an advertising copy-

writer (which Hitchcock had himself been), and who says his name is
"Beachcroft," the name of the cross street at The High Road where
Hitchcock was born and spent his own youth. There is a further link
with his past in the odd imbalance in the constable's family: there are a
(presumably widowed) father, an older daughter who acts as surrogate
mother to younger siblings, and a household that reflects in these and
other details a reverse image of Hitchcock's own family during his
childhood.

At the end of the spring term, the Hitchcocks went down to Sussex,
where Patricia had been enrolled in boarding school. Although she was
not yet nine years old, her flair for dramatics was already evident, and
as part of the end-of-term activities she took part in an elaborately
mounted production of a school play. Her performance reached the attention of Alexander Korda, who took advantage of the child's innocent
notoriety to poke gentle fun at her father, whose brief contract with him
had not been so productive. He sent her a note praising her performance
in the school play ("The King Who Had Nothing to Learn") and offering her a film contract if she were free to work with him.

These were the happiest years for the Hitchcock family. Alma devoted herself to her daughter, visiting school frequently and on weekends taking her to Shamley Green, where Hitchcock joined them late
Friday evening. Everyone who knew him during the middle and late
1930s afterward insisted that Hitchcock was a proud and doting father.
The parents' apparently rigorous vigilance over Patricia's manners was
not unduly harsh, nor was it indeed atypical of polite English family
life. And the girl was a credit to her parents. Clever, outspoken, and
polite, she was her father's best audience for his puns and little domestic
imitations of actors and visitors. Further evidence of the closeness of
the family at this time is provided by the fact that on virtually every trip
outside of school term, the child was welcomed into the adult circle,
which now regularly included Joan Harrison as traveling companion.

There are conflicts as to the exact date, but it seems to have been in
June 1937 that Hitchcock took Alma, Pat, Joan Harrison, and his mother
on an excursion to Italy. Alma spent several days bedridden with viral
influenza, but Hitchcock and his mother, always hardier folk, fared better. Mrs. Hitchcock was anxious to visit the famous Blue Grotto at
Capri, but when she saw the small and somewhat primitive schooner
that she would have to board at Naples, she required considerable coaxing from her embarrassed son before submitting to what she considered
dangerous and undignified means of transport. The rest of the trip was
uneventful, but it remained in everyone's mind as one of the pleasantest

times in a family life that would not always be crowded with pleasant times.

Upon returning to London, Hitchcock was not at all pleased by the situation at Gainsborough, the offspring filmmaking unit that, under Edward Black's supervision, continued in spite of the official demise of Gaumont-British as a production company.* He found things even more chaotic than when he left for his holiday in Italy. *Young and Innocent* had still to be edited, and there was some talk of delaying its release until the studio finances could be regulated. In fact it was not released until February 1938, but this seems to have been more the result of Hitchcock's imminent departure on yet another journey than it was an indication of studio indifference to the picture itself.

The trip this time was to America. Although at the studio he protested that it was simply an extension of the family vacation before Pat returned to school, those who knew him suspected that the intention was also to consider the possibility of an American contract. Charles Bennett had negotiated a very satisfactory arrangement, and other writers, directors, and actors were reporting vastly superior working conditions and compensations for their talents. But Hitchcock told an inquiring press that this late summer trip was simply another holiday.

American producers had of course directed inquiries to Hitchcock, but he simply had not replied. He still had one more picture to make under his two-film deal with Edward Black and Gainsborough, although by summer 1937 he had no idea what that project might be. There was also the Laughton-Pommer offer, which might turn out to be rewarding artistically as well as financially.

Not having visited the United States, the Hitchcocks had no idea what their reaction to America might be. Their life in England, after all, was quite luxurious. As undisputed prince of the British directors, he had more control than any other filmmaker in his country's history. He was also in great social demand, and his Surrey home never wanted for grateful guests. He wined, dined, and cajoled the press, who found him a fascinatingly sybaritic enigma, a man in clear control of his professional destiny and able to direct interviewers with as much subtle intimidation as he directed his cast and crew. There was, in the final analysis, no compelling personal reason to consider leaving England at this time. But there was a commercial reason: the British film industry was at its lowest ebb since the mid-1920s. Perhaps it was indeed just a holiday in New York that he intended. But it is hard not to imagine other consid-

*Although produced by Gainsborough, the film was distributed as ''A Gaumont-British Picture.''

erations as well, since he instructed his publicist to inform the New York press of his imminent arrival.

On August 22 the three Hitchcocks and Joan Harrison arrived in New York aboard the *Queen Mary*. He lost no time in sounding out the spirit of the city. "The thing that astonished me more than anything else when I arrived in New York and attended the theatre that first evening were the fans. There was a large crowd of them outside the theatre. One of them even had an eight-by-ten glossy photograph of me to sign. There were film buffs even then!"

The New York newspapers noted Hitchcock's arrival, observing dryly that his size made him unmistakable in a crowd; and at once there began an exchange of telegrams that would make American cultural history.

Katherine Brown, New York representative for Hollywood producer David O. Selznick, dashed off a wire asking whether she should meet with Hitchcock to discuss his future plans. Selznick's cabled reply, dated August 23, was unequivocal:

> I AM DEFINITELY INTERESTED IN HITCHCOCK AS DIRECTOR AND THINK IT MIGHT BE WISE FOR YOU TO MEET AND CHAT WITH HIM. IN PARTICULAR I WOULD LIKE TO GET A CLEAR PICTURE AS TO WHO IF ANYONE IS REPRESENTING HIM AND WHAT HE HAS IN MIND IN THE WAY OF SALARY; ALSO, WHETHER HE IS DEALING WITH MGM.

Selznick, already at thirty-five one of the great powers in Hollywood, was widely known for his successful achievements in film. Until 1923 he had worked with his father's company, and he thereafter successively became a producer at MGM, RKO, Paramount, and, once again, at MGM, where in 1933 his father-in-law, Louis B. Mayer, gave him the position of vice-president and executive in charge of production. By 1936 he had produced some of Hollywood's most famous films, notably *King Kong, Dinner at Eight, David Copperfield, Anna Karenina,* and *A Tale of Two Cities*. In that year, with financial backing from the Whitney family, he founded Selznick International Pictures, a move that was designed not only to establish his own film empire, but also to facilitate his notoriously intimate involvement with every aspect of his productions (tens of thousands of memos and cables, dictated at every stage of his films, are the most eloquent testimony to his creative zeal).

Selznick was always checking up on the other Hollywood studios. He knew, for example, that Metro-Goldwyn-Mayer had made an initial offer for Hitchcock's services. (MGM in fact had proposed that Hitchcock remain in London, where he would receive $150,000 to make four pictures in two years, plus a $15,000 bonus for completing them on time

and within budget.) While Selznick's Los Angeles and New York offices exchanged cables, the Hitchcock entourage, comfortably installed
in connecting suites at the Saint Regis Hotel, alternated newspaper interviews with forays to the theater and the most famous restaurants.

On August 26 they were the center of attention when they dined at
the 21 Club. "It looks like a prison from the outside," Hitchcock said
as they approached the famous black iron gates. A few moments of
coaxing from Alma and Joan were needed before he agreed to keep their
reservation. "Where are we going — to a prison? I don't want to go to
jail!" The look of panic on his face might have been feigned, but everyone thought the association he had made somewhat odd. Inside, he was
given a tour of the club's old speakeasy facilities, and they all climbed
the stairs behind the false walls, up to hidden, soundproofed rooms once
used for drinking. Back in the main dining room, H. Allen Smith, who
was becoming one of the most famous humorists and journalists in
America, joined them for dinner and conducted the first official newspaper interview Hitchcock gave in the United States.

America was famous for steak and ice cream, Hitchcock told Smith,
and so he had enjoyed plenty of both since his arrival. He admitted
ordering vanilla ice cream for breakfast with a dash of brandy poured
over it, and he said his luncheon and dinner so far had not varied: a
double-thick steak at each meal. Smith thought Hitchcock was exagger-
ating, but when everyone ordered coffee at the end of the meal, Hitchcock shocked the newsman by ordering a second steak to follow his
dessert of an ice-cream parfait. The second steak he followed with still
another serving of ice cream, and when Hitchcock summoned the waiter,
the diners thought at last they would be leaving. But moments later the
21 Club hummed with the gossip: Alfred Hitchcock had ordered a third
steak, and with it, so as not to delay his companions, his third helping
of ice cream.

At last he seemed to finish, with a gulp of strong tea. "Lord!" Hitchcock said with a great sigh as he fingered the teacup. Smith thought he
was commenting on the gargantuan meal. Instead, Hitchcock reflected
aloud on the china cup, his mind perhaps bending back to his perverse
habit of throwing teacups over his shoulder in the London studios. "How
I'd love to shatter this cup. Fling it on the floor. Smash it in a million
pieces. I can't explain it, but breaking things makes me feel fine."

But the director restrained himself, and Smith turned the conversation
to Hitchcock's appetite. With a final swallow of brandy, Hitchcock remarked with uncharacteristic honesty: "I find contentment from food.
It's a mental process rather than a physical. There is as much anticipation in confronting good food as there is in going on a holiday, or seeing

a good show. There are two kinds of eating — eating to sustain and eating for pleasure. I eat for pleasure.'' When this remark appeared in print, Hitchcock regretted it, for it led to the custom of journalistic inquiries about his diet — which he promptly discouraged by sidestepping further comment. His last public statement for many years on his eating habits was given four days later to a reporter from Brooklyn: ''I first started to put on weight when I took to drink,'' he said after Alma, Joan, and Pat slipped away for a shopping trip to Rockefeller Center. And Hitchcock quickly learned how the personal habits of the famous are set down in print to satisfy the curiosity of the public.

After this, he learned to cultivate the admiration of the press in the United States and to direct the conversation according to specific points he had in mind. He also learned to dine moderately — in public, at any rate. Luncheon and dinner companions for years afterward were amazed that a man who ate so temperately could attain a weight ranging from 225 to over 300 pounds. What they might have rightly suspected was that he became more of a secret eater, indulging his appetites the way he developed his film fantasies — privately, in the quiet evening hours and in the retreat of his own room.

The Hitchcocks' American holiday proceeded with considerable public fanfare. The night after the dinner at the 21 Club, Hitchcock was interviewed on the New York radio program ''Gertrude of Hollywood,'' where he overwhelmed his questioner with comparative facts and figures about the English and American film industries. Next morning, leaving their daughter in Joan Harrison's care, Hitchcock and Alma left alone for a two-day trip to Saratoga Springs, New York. ''There it all was,'' he said afterward. ''Houses with verandahs. And rocking chairs. Actually rocking chairs, with people rocking in them. I pointed them out to my wife and we stood and looked at them. If we have rocking chairs in England it is only as curiosities. But here you have them in real life as well as in the movies.'' These bits of Americana impressed him, as did the rhythms of American dialect, and he carefully placed them all under the bell jar of his prodigious memory, where they later provided him with the signs of an easy familiarity that characterize his best American films.

While the Hitchcocks toured New York State and took Pat and Joan with them for another two-day excursion — this time to the nation's capital — the New York offices of the major studios were busy trying to learn who was offering what to Hitchcock. At RKO, producer Pandro S. Berman received a letter from his New York associate Lillie Messinger: She had met with Hitchcock one afternoon, and he was interested in coming to Hollywood to make a mystery film called *The Saint in*

*New York*. But she suggested that Hitchcock and RKO consider as his first project something called *A Puzzle for Fools*. The extant correspondence in the RKO archives stops at this point in the Hitchcock negotiations. Apparently Berman did not pursue the matter, perhaps because, somewhat prematurely, David Selznick encouraged the rumor that *he* was actually far along in a negotiation for Hitchcock's services. At this time, of course, Selznick and Hitchcock had neither met nor corresponded. But the Hitchcocks had accepted an invitation from Katherine Brown to spend several days at her country home in Amagansett, Long Island. There, with her husband James Barrett and daughter Laurinda (who found Patricia a genial playmate), the families had beach picnics as Kay Brown pursued more fully the negotiating of a Selznick contract.

On September 4, with the matter then closer to a resolution, the visitors departed for London aboard the S.S. *Georgic*, having made a quick visit the day before to a police lineup in lower Manhattan. Hitchcock was fascinated by the technicalities involved in arrest, booking, and interrogation. Alma endured this unusual tourist side-trip as she endured his practical jokes and risqué stories: with some embarrassment and an attitude of bemused impatience. "Oh, Hitch!" she would sigh with a look of motherly indulgence, and she would shake her head two or three times. "Oh, Hitch!"

Back at the cramped studios in Islington (where Gainsborough could rent space more cheaply than at Pinewood), Hitchcock quickly completed the editing of *Young and Innocent,* and he and Alma looked for a property to conclude the two-film deal with Edward Black. To their chagrin, they found nothing suitable, and by October Hitchcock found himself in the position of appearing in his producer's office, asking if there might be a script already prepared, a project someone else had been forced to abandon. This egregious exception to the director's usual method was just what Black needed to hear. He knew of the Laughton-Pommer-Hitchcock agreement, and he had heard about the Hollywood proposals. He also knew that a filmmaker working for him with less than full enthusiasm would be a great risk. Yes, he replied, he had a story carefully prepared for the screen that had been abandoned the previous year. Hitchcock could read the script at once. This odd set of circumstances, wildly atypical of Alfred Hitchcock's normal approach to a film, was the climate for the production of his most famous English picture, *The Lady Vanishes*.

Hitchcock always insisted that it was he who had found two young writers, Frank Launder and Sidney Gilliat, to put the screenplay together for him from *The Wheel Spins*, a 1936 novel by Ethel Lina White.

Launder's and Gilliat's senses of humor, he said, corresponded very closely to his own, and together the pair turned out what he considered one of his best scripts ever.

But Hitchcock's version is very far from the truth of the matter.

In May 1936 Frank Launder had suggested that Gainsborough buy the rights to White's novel. "In my contract with Gainsborough," Launder remembered, "there was a clause negotiated by my manager, Christopher Mann, that I should be given the right to write one script a year, and I wanted this to be it. But I had a re-write to do on a film about to go into production, so Sidney was engaged to write a treatment. I then joined him and we wrote the screenplay together."

The director assigned to the film was Roy William Neill, an American working in England. When the script was finished, in August 1936, a crew was sent to Yugoslavia under Fred Gunn, an assistant director, to shoot summer exteriors. But when Gunn fractured his ankle in an accident, the investigating police found the screenplay and, according to custom, insisted on approving the foreigners' impressions of their country.

At once the crew was deported, probably because the first pages of the script seemed inflammatory and dangerous: they indicated a swift cut from a shot of strutting soldiers to one of waddling geese. (Gilliat had asked Gunn to remove these pages before the authorities in Belgrade could find them, but somehow they remained in place during the trip.) When the crew arrived back in London, reports of the minor political unpleasantness, of the injured assistant, and of the diminished enthusiasm of the American director led to the film's cancellation. Edward Black was understandably disappointed, since a substantial cash advance had been invested on the production.

When Hitchcock read the script in October 1937, he at once abandoned the disappointing projects he had considered with writer Michael Hogan, made one or two minor suggestions to Launder and Gilliat about the opening and concluding reels of the film, and said *The Lady Vanishes* could be filmed in a month.

"You never knew quite what Hitch was thinking," Launder recalled, "because he always played his cards close to his chest. He told us he did not care for the opening and thought the last reel could be made more exciting. Sidney worked on the revisions at [Hitchcock's] home in Cromwell Road. The difference between the new opening we wrote and the one in the original script was that the pace was faster. And the last reel was certainly more exciting, with more twists and turns after we had worked on it."

With those few revisions, the script was ready; an examination of the original 1936 version reveals how little was in fact changed by Hitchcock. It was still quite clearly the story of a young woman who, while on holiday in "Brandrika" (a mythic locale near the Balkans), meets a charming old spinster. They both depart for London aboard the Orient Express, but the old lady mysteriously disappears. Everyone denies having seen her, and the heroine turns for help to a young man. At first even he does not believe her — especially when a doctor who is aboard explains that the missing lady is a figment of the imagination, the result of a disorienting blow to the head. Suspicions are aroused, however, when the young couple meet a nun curiously outfitted with high-heeled shoes. The old lady is at last found, and it turns out that she is a spy trying to smuggle a secret back to London — a secret encoded in a folk tune. Several other passengers, including the doctor, are part of an enemy spy ring pursuing her, but she escapes and is finally happily reunited with the young couple back in London.

"I think this is the only case of Hitchcock ever taking over a script completed for another director," Sidney Gilliat said. "I remember him driving me round and round Leicester Square and pointing across at the Empire Theatre and saying, 'That's the first time I've had my name in lights above the title.' The adaptation and screenplay of *The Lady Vanishes* were not written by or for Hitchcock at all."

Casting was completed quickly once Dame May Whitty accepted the key role of the spinster-spy. For the part of the young girl, Hitchcock happily accepted Margaret Lockwood, who was already under contract at Gainsborough. "I was a great fan of Ethel Lina White's books," she remembered.

They were usually about an unfortunate girl on some kind of journey who found herself in trouble. When I heard that Edward Black was at last going to produce the picture, and that Hitchcock was to direct, I of course hoped to play the part. But then two newspapers reported that other actresses had been signed — Lilli Palmer and Nova Pilbeam. But Hitchcock asked for a test on me, and he told me my worries were over. We finished the entire film in five weeks in late autumn 1937, in that cramped and uncomfortable studio at Islington. I suppose what surprised me most of all about Hitchcock was how little he directed us. I had done a number of films for Carol Reed, and he was quite meticulous by contrast. Hitchcock, however, didn't seem to direct us at all. He was a dozing, nodding Buddha with an enigmatic smile on his face.

But Hitchcock's apparent unconcern and his minimal direction of his cast did not mean he was unaware of the ordinary business on the set. "Alma was there quite a bit," according to Margaret Lockwood, "often with Pat, who charmed everyone within listening distance. Alma and

Hitchcock would confer on the details of a certain shot or a line of dialogue. But his habits didn't change very much for his family. He never altered one custom, the idiosyncrasy, during morning and afternoon tea break, of throwing the crockery over his shoulder and smashing it on the floor with airy nonchalance." (Of this habit Hitchcock later explained: "Good for the nerves. Relieves the tension. Much better than scolding the players." And, one might add, a sure way to attract everyone's attention for a return to business after a short break.)

For the male lead, it was at last possible for Edward Black to persuade Michael Redgrave to make his film debut. "I had just done three plays in repertory with John Gielgud's company," Redgrave said decades later. "At the time *The Lady Vanishes* was going into production I had just opened in *The Three Sisters*. I was very reluctant to accept this film offer, but Gielgud, who had already worked for Hitchcock, said he thought it would be a good experience for me, and Gainsborough said I could do the test with my wife, Rachel Kempson." But Redgrave, tired and disinterested, could not summon much enthusiasm for the film.

They offered me a very handsome contract, but I didn't even want to do that one picture. To be honest, I suppose I was something of an intellectual snob at the time, and film acting here in England was not regarded very highly. No serious actor or actress concentrated on film work or appeared very often before the cameras. I think Hitchcock sensed that I preferred the stage, and so he decided to cut me down to size. The first day of shooting he came over to me and said, "You know, don't you, that Robert Donat wanted to play this role in the worst way." I suppose it was meant to make me feel a little unwelcome, but it didn't — I really wasn't trying very hard anyway.

It was precisely Redgrave's casual approach that Hitchcock liked at once and that suited perfectly the role of the young leading man. The director appreciated what he later called Redgrave's "throwaway technique," which gave his speech a natural, slightly glib, and totally unselfconscious tone.

"He wasn't really an actor's director," Redgrave said of Hitchcock.

Maggie Lockwood is right when she says that. And everyone knew that his reputation here in England was more for preparation and technique than for working with his cast. The film didn't depend on any single performance, and strangely enough this put us all at our ease. In fact his own nonchalance made it rather easy for us. He knew where he wanted to put his camera, he knew what mood he wanted to effect. He had the whole thing visualized ahead of time, and once we got to the set, it could all be done very quickly and painlessly.

The filming was completed by early December, and Black was sufficiently delighted with Hitchcock's economy that he honored the director and cast with a party. Mary Clare, who had played the role of Auntie in *Young and Innocent,* was also in the cast of *The Lady Vanishes* (she played the intimidating, black-swathed baroness), and this time it was she who was singled out as the object of one of Hitchcock's rude practical jokes. He found that she was not a drinker of alcohol and politely offered her a concoction he had personally prepared. Thinking it was a fruit drink, she drank heartily — and was soon quite hopelessly drunk. Michael Redgrave was not the only one present who thought that "this was not a very kind thing to do," as he put it.

Hitchcock, however, was evidently feeling confident about his unique success among British filmmakers. Although by the end of November MGM had finally declined to bid for a contract, John Hay ("Jock") Whitney, chairman of the board of Selznick International, joined Kay Brown in London, and they dined with Hitchcock at the Connaught Grille. The evening was quite cordial, but on December 1 Whitney cabled Selznick from London. He had just seen *Young and Innocent* at a private screening and felt that a warning was in order: SAW NEW HITCHCOCK. ESTABLISHES NEW LOW FOR BOTH PILBEAM AND HIMSELF. PLEASE SEE IT BEFORE FURTHER NEGOTIATION. GOODBYE. JOCK.

Selznick replied the next day: CABLE FROM LONDON RECEIVED. I HAVE HELD UP ALL NEGOTIATIONS. HELLO.

But Kay Brown, on December 18, sent Selznick a different opinion about *Young and Innocent:* REGRET DO NOT AGREE WITH JOCK.

In fact the negotiations between Selznick and Hitchcock would not have advanced were it not for the acute critical sensibility of Kay Brown. From her first meeting with Hitchcock in New York until signatures were fixed on contracts in the summer of 1938, she was at every stage the firm, guiding hand that vigilantly guarded not only the interests of her employer but also those of Hitchcock. It is no exaggeration to say that Alfred Hitchcock might never have come to America — and he certainly would not have started with Selznick — had it not been for her delicate and astute negotiations. Not long after this, Selznick entrusted her with another artist he was about to put under contract, and Kay Brown became the close friend and personal representative of the actress Ingrid Bergman. Kay Brown's career — and that of her daughter, Laurinda Barrett — would intersect with Hitchcock's at still other important crossroads later (and so, of course, would Bergman's).

By January 1938, *The Lady Vanishes* was edited and the scoring and titles were very nearly complete. Erich Pommer and Charles Laughton were not at all certain what project they would assign Hitchcock, who had by this time signed a handsome contract with them, but the press was so insistent for some news that on January 18 they announced that their jointly owned Mayflower Productions would produce Alfred Hitchcock's next picture, something called *Empty World,* with Nova Pilbeam. (The project never developed beyond this announcement.) Meanwhile Kay Brown and Jock Whitney had returned to New York for meetings with Selznick about the terms of a Hitchcock contract. They detailed their personal impressions of the British director, as did Jenia Reissar, Selznick's permanent representative in London, who had the benefit of sustained firsthand experience in dealing with him.

Hitchcock had told the Selznick people, none too subtly, that he had read the galley proofs of a soon-to-be published novel by Daphne du Maurier, the daughter of his old acquaintance Sir Gerald du Maurier. The book, scheduled for publication that summer, was called *Rebecca.* Hitchcock's personal entrée would be of value in purchasing the screen rights, and in fact he wanted to make it his own property, clearly hoping that either Mayflower Productions or some other company would back him. But novelist du Maurier's agent was asking a greater price than Hitchcock could pay. Upon Kay Brown's recommendation — she had already molded film history by directing her employer's attention to Margaret Mitchell's novel *Gone With the Wind* — David Selznick read the galleys. On January 9, 1938, he sent Hitchcock a telegram. The message is typical of Selznick. Hot with enthusiasm over an exciting project, he had leaped into the deepest waters of presumption: although he had yet to obtain guarantees either for Hitchcock's services or for the screen rights to *Rebecca,* he had already spoken to several actors in Hollywood, told them the story line, and gauged their interest.

REGRET HAVE TO INFORM YOU [RONALD] COLMAN SO FEARFUL ABOUT MURDER ANGLE AND ALSO ABOUT POSSIBILITY OF PICTURE EMERGING AS WOMAN-STARRING VEHICLE THAT HE WILL NOT DO IT UNLESS HE SEES TREATMENT. . . . CAN SIGN LESLIE HOWARD FOR IT. . . . BILL POWELL HAS BEEN ABSOLUTELY WILD ABOUT ROLE AND ANXIOUS TO DO IT, BUT I TURNED HIM DOWN ON EXPECTATION OF GETTING COLMAN. . . . WISH YOU WOULD DICTATE REPLY IMMEDIATELY UPON RECEIPT OF THIS, GIVING ME YOUR REACTIONS.

Hitchcock had no idea how to respond. Officially he still had no agent, although Sidney Bernstein — the owner of the Granada theater chain and a man with whom Hitchcock had enjoyed friendly relations since the days of the London Film Society — continued to oversee benevolently when Hitchcock received an offer. As so often when he was unsure as to the proper course of action, Hitchcock did nothing, and there is no record of a reply to Selznick's precipitous cable.

But by March things had progressed rapidly, owing mostly to Selznick's insistence and clear intention to get Hitchcock to America and under contract. Selznick and his wife — the former Irene Mayer, whose father, Louis B. Mayer, was once his employer — had seen *Young and Innocent* by this time, and they agreed with Kay Brown: it was a splendid film. Viewing the movie himself resolved any doubts Selznick might have had. He kept the telegrams arriving at Cromwell Road in a constant stream of professional courting. He would, he wrote at one point, be very interested in a picture like *The Man Who Knew Too Much,* and he was sure he could sign Ronald Colman to star in a remake of it. (Selznick was rather taken with the idea of remakes: Ingrid Bergman's first picture for him, *Intermezzo,* was an American version of one of her last Swedish films before she emigrated.)

But then there was a sudden temporary rupture in communication, and both Selznick and Hitchcock thought any chance of a contract between them was lost forever. On March 12 excerpts from an interview with Hitchcock appeared in print: he spoke not only about his current work, but also about how he would handle stars — and how eventually he hoped to control every aspect of his own films by becoming his own producer.

Hollywood? I've only discussed this with David Selznick so far. The matter is still in the air. But if I do go to Hollywood, I'd only work for Selznick. . . .

The point about the star-system is that it enables you to exaggerate from a story point of view. And the stars do bring the audiences into the cinemas. A star's name is like a clarion call and brings in the time factor when, for instance, a film is shown and you want people to come and see it on definite days. A film without stars would have to wait to be appreciated. . . .

As for the film director himself, he will become obsolete unless his status and power expand to that of the producer.

The published interview was forwarded to Selznick by Jenia Reissar, and Selznick's dismay is understandable. He thought Hitchcock's potential employment was virtually certain, lacking only the detail of a formal contract. He also presumed that, as studio head, the decision on casting, and the controlling hand behind the production, would, as usual, be his alone. But Hitchcock said the deal with Selznick was "still in the air," and he clearly had ideas of his own about whose film it would be. So Selznick's cables, with their buoyant praise of Hitchcock's work and their spirited tossing of suggestions for their first film, stopped.

Hitchcock was disappointed, and he wanted Selznick to know it. But he also wanted Selznick to think he was much demanded by other producers. Accordingly, he wrote to Al Margolies, the publicity man he had engaged to represent his interests, and said that he was sorry no firm offer had been made yet by Selznick, that Gaumont-British was ready to renegotiate, and that Alexander Korda had also approached him again. There is no doubt about his real hope, however, for he instructed Margolies to tell Kay Brown that he was terribly disappointed that the Selznick deal had not worked out.

The letter had the desired effect: Selznick, assured once again of Hitchcock's serious interest, authorized Kay Brown to resume final contract negotiations. On May 4 Selznick cabled L. C. Ham, the London representative for a Hollywood-based talent agency headed by Frank Joyce and David's older brother Myron. Hitchcock had by now engaged the Selznick-Joyce agency to represent him, certain that it could not hurt to have David's own brother working on his behalf. Hitchcock and his friend Sidney Bernstein would still confer privately and seek London counsel whenever it seemed advisable, but Myron Selznick — who had a good relation with Hitchcock ever since coproducing *The Passionate Adventure* at Islington — could surely be relied on to link producer and director in a happy professional union.

In his telegram to Ham, Selznick asked if Hitchcock was free to come to California in mid-August to direct a film version of *The Titanic,* based on the novel by Wilson Mizner and Carl Harbraugh. He also wanted Hitchcock to start working on a treatment at once — if this was agreeable and if they could come to final contractual terms — and he asked him to suggest appropriate scriptwriters. Selznick wanted to waste no time, since he foresaw major changes in the story as it stood: it was a somewhat turgid romance about a mob leader redeemed through the love of a good woman he meets on board the doomed ocean liner.

This time Hitchcock was quick to reply. To further ingratiate himself with Selznick, he wrote that here was a curious coincidence, indeed: he had had the same idea — a film about the Titanic disaster! In fact there is no evidence that he had ever really entertained such a notion. All memoranda from Kay Brown and Jenia Reissar confirm that Hitchcock still had Joan Harrison in close contact with Daphne du Maurier's agent to see if at least an option price on *Rebecca* was within his range; he never doubted that the novel was destined for commercial success and

that he could turn it into a first-rate modern British neo-Gothic thriller.
And on the contrary, Hitchcock privately thought that Selznick's proposed film about the sinking of the ocean liner was hopeless from the
start.

"I remember thinking that the only way to make it cinematic would
be to start the opening credits on a tight close-up of a huge rivet on the
side of the ship," he said. "The camera would then dolly back as the
credits roll — slowly, very slowly — and two hours later the audience
would at last see the whole ship in long shot and I would flash the words
*The End*. Nothing else really struck me as very interesting." As late as
July 9, 1938 — just days before the final contract between Hitchcock
and Selznick was signed — the announcement was made that Hitchcock's first production for the Selznick studio would be *The Titanic*,
scheduled to begin in January 1939, although the only statements Hitchcock made throughout the spring and summer were increasingly jaundiced about this picture. "Oh, yes," he told a New York reporter, "I've
had experience with icebergs. Don't forget, I directed Madeleine Carroll!"

Meanwhile, Erich Pommer and Charles Laughton, caught up in the
frenzy surrounding the imminent publication of *Rebecca* and intoxicated
by the rumors about screen rights, snatched up the option to film the
author's previous novel and hopped on the crowded du Maurier–
Hitchcock bandwagon with the announcement that Sidney Gilliat would
work with Joan Harrison on a screen treatment of *Jamaica Inn*, the du
Maurier novel that had appeared in 1936.

This project interested Hitchcock even less than the story of the Titanic. It was a melodrama about nineteenth-century thieves and smugglers on the Cornish coast, with a Brontësque heroine caught, typically,
between loyalty to her family and love for a lawman in disguise. Laughton would star as the demented ringleader of the shipwreckers; and the
capacious soundstages at Elstree would be used for the huge sets and
water tanks — for there would be spectacular scenes of shipwrecks and
storms at sea. But the plans for the lavish costume piece failed to rouse
Hitchcock's enthusiasm. Besides, his sights were fixed ever more im-
patiently on America. To expedite the Selznick contract, he decided to
make his first trip to Los Angeles at once. He left Joan Harrison in
charge of the *Jamaica Inn* script and his daughter, and he and Alma left
London on Wednesday, June 1, traveling first class on the *Queen Mary*
once again.

From shipboard, Hitchcock surprised Kay Brown with a cable. They
would arrive on Monday, June 6, and they would be grateful if she
would meet them. This she gladly did, and escorted them, at Hitch-

cock's request, to the same suite of rooms they had previously taken at
the Saint Regis Hotel. Wednesday morning, leaving most of their luggage behind, they boarded a train for California. Upon their arrival,
Myron Selznick dispatched a driver to deliver the weary couple to the
Beverly Wilshire Hotel. Late the following week, after motor trips to
Palm Springs (which Alma loved for its warm, dry climate) and to the
wine country in northern California (which Hitchcock loved for its lush
vineyards and its proximity to the Old World charm of San Francisco),
it was time for business.

Hitchcock was conducted to Myron Selznick's offices, where his
agents, in an attempt to impress him with their other clients, introduced
him to Ernst Lubitsch, Frank Capra, Rosalind Russell, and Carole Lombard. He reminisced with Myron about the days of *The Passionate Adventure,* in which the role of the ingenue was played by Marjorie Daw,
who later married Myron. And Hitchcock's hosts told him about the
various British artists who had settled quite happily in California: Nigel
Bruce, Ronald Colman, Madeleine Carroll, and others.

But they need not have tried so hard to persuade him. Alma, who
resented the almost impregnable class structure of Great Britain, and
Hitchcock himself, who recognized the dangerous overexpansion and
resulting slump in the English film industry, were both quietly eager to
relocate to America. In 1937, the year he directed *Young and Innocent*
and *The Lady Vanishes,* more than two hundred features were made in
England, yet the studios were deeply in debt because of enormous waste
and inefficiency. The bankruptcies and studio closings, the precarious
world economy, and the darkly uncertain political situation in Europe
all affected English filmmaking directly, and in 1938 fewer than one
hundred films were made, and an even smaller number released. These
sad facts — coupled with the distasteful assignment that still had to be
endured back in London, plus the lure of California's obviously more
elaborate, more commercially successful, more creative film industry —
were all the Hitchcocks needed to make their decision.

But they chose not to appear overeager. RKO, Hitchcock told Myron
Selznick, had approached him with an offer, as had Samuel Goldwyn.
An hour later, Myron had got RKO on the telephone and asked for a
$60,000 contract for sixteen weeks of work in 1939. This the studio
declined, which seemed to disappoint the agent not at all. He figured he
could do better by putting together a contract between his brother David
and Hitchcock; but Myron, who at thirty-nine was already in failing
health that would lead to his premature death six years later, did not
reckon with the tough stance David would take on the Hitchcock deal.
Goldwyn, for his part, did not even make a firm offer.

While the Hitchcocks resumed their tour of the West Coast, the Selznick brothers came to an agreement, and on Saturday, July 2, at a luncheon at the Beverly Wilshire, Myron announced to the press that Selznick International Pictures was ready to offer Alfred Hitchcock a one-picture, twenty-week contract at $2,500 per week — $50,000 for a film to be made in 1939 after the completion of *Jamaica Inn*. Hitchcock had insisted that provision be made for Joan Harrison, and indeed a contract had also been secured in her behalf: as special assistant she would receive a total of $2,500 for the same period (a salary of $125 per week). Myron was particularly proud of this part of the bargain, for it was unusual to bring an assistant along on the professional coattails of an immigrant director. Finally, any provision for Alma's services as writer or continuity adviser would be negotiated separately.

At last Hitchcock met David O. Selznick, and the meeting was cordial: afterward only the final drafting of contracts and the disposition of visa applications remained. The Hitchcocks returned to New York. "We were on the *Super-Chief,*" he remembered, "and a man introduced himself to me. He was Jack Cohn, head of Columbia Pictures in New York and the brother of Harry Cohn. He sat down, had a drink with us, and asked if I knew any of his products — Ann Harding films, and so forth. He named three films and I said I didn't see any of them. And then he asked, 'Well, don't you ever see movies?' I answered no, not very often. He then said, 'If you don't see movies, where do you get your ideas from?' "*

By Monday, July 11, the Hitchcocks were back in New York at the Saint Regis. That night they dined with Kay Brown, for there were now one or two items he wanted clarified in the contract. From her office at 230 Park Avenue the negotiations were concluded in telegrams with Selznick, while Hitchcock remained calm and confident. On Tuesday, July 12, he consented to be interviewed by film critic Otis Ferguson, and he held forth on "The Making of a Melodrama," referring obliquely to "an avid Hollywood producer" with whom he was negotiating.† When Hitchcock returned to the hotel, there was a message from Kay

---

*In fact Hitchcock saw a great number of films, especially for casting purposes. But he always declined to discuss, or to show any interest in, any work other than his own, and he boasted throughout his life that he had never visited another director's set — in clear contradiction of his own memories of Murnau. Late in life, he occasionally admitted admiration for some of Luis Buñuel's films.

† He also said that short stories were one of the best sources of film material. "The O. Henry stories with the plot and ending which are not the conventional formula stuff, and the Poe thrillers, the horrific stories, would fit admirably into such a program, and I for one should like to see the results." And well he would, in time: the Hitchcock television programs, two decades later, incarnated this format.

Brown. The contracts were being rushed to New York and would be ready for his signature on Thursday.

On July 14, 1938, he read the final legal papers, wrote *Alfred J. Hitchcock* in a firm hand, left Kay Brown's office at once, and whisked Alma to a waiting taxi. They boarded the S.S. *Normandie* that same day for the return to London and arrived at Cromwell Road the following Wednesday, July 20, eager to get *Jamaica Inn* over and done with.

For his part, David Selznick had not decided whether Hitchcock's first assignment would be *The Titanic* or *Rebecca,* and the contract had left the matter open. His indecision stemmed partly from a desire to see how Hitchcock would handle the spectacular, watery special effects of *Jamaica Inn.* And he was not at all sure which of the two projects would turn up the most effective script.

By early September, Selznick's telegrams to Hitchcock (now sent through Myron's London office) indicated that he planned *Rebecca* only as a backup picture in case there was a problem with *The Titanic,* "which I sincerely hope will not occur." But his expectations apparently collided with his hopes, for he was at the same time confiding to Jock Whitney that he preferred Loretta Young as the leading lady for *Rebecca,* and on the matter of the script his first choice was Ben Hecht, one of Hollywood's most prolific and gifted screenwriters. Hitchcock countered the proposal of Hecht with his preference for a strong emotional writer.

Apart from the telegrams, however, Selznick's New York and London offices were instructed to find out Hitchcock's intentions about *Rebecca.* Jenia Reissar wrote to Kay Brown that private meetings were continuing between Joan Harrison and Daphne du Maurier, meetings undertaken on the pretext of discussing historical detail for the script of *Jamaica Inn.* "Joan Harrison is Hitchcock's mouthpiece," Reissar wrote Selznick. "Hitchcock would have bought [the rights to *Rebecca*] himself if he knew definitely that some company was interested in it and would let him make it. I think Hitchcock wants to make that picture, and by buying it he would have liked to ensure that he would in fact direct it himself."

Meanwhile, Daphne du Maurier let it be known that she was not at all pleased with the screen preparation of *Jamaica Inn* that was about to go before the cameras. She required considerable convincing from Selznick and his London representatives that a Hollywood version of *Rebecca* would be far more faithful to the spirit of the novel, and when people pointed out to her Selznick's fidelity with *David Copperfield* and *Anna Karenina* (and the unprecedented care that was going into the preparation of *Gone With the Wind*), she felt more confident. On August 5, *Rebecca* was published in London, and four weeks later du Maurier sold the screen rights to Selznick for $50,000.

*Jamaica Inn* was filmed from the first of September until mid-October in an atmosphere Hitchcock tried to forget for the rest of his life. "I was associated with two extremely difficult men, Erich Pommer and Charles Laughton," he commented later. Laughton's petulant ego, his habit of stopping rehearsals or even the filming for hours while he brooded over the right gesture, the proper stance or walk, and the correct "inner feeling" of a scene, transformed Hitchcock's disaffection into undiluted anger. The only way to prevent a complete disruption of communication between the director and the star was for Hitchcock to indulge his own fantasies at key points in the narrative; thus he instigated the appalling exaggeration of a sadistic scene in which the deranged Laughton, protesting how much he is in love with Maureen O'Hara, binds and gags her.

"I am primarily interested," Hitchcock said at the time, "in the Jekyll-Hyde mentality of the squire." It was this Jekyll-Hyde counterpoint, openly acknowledged for the first time, that informed the bulk of his work later on (especially the quartet of films about the doubling or splitting of the personality — *Shadow of a Doubt, Strangers on a Train, Psycho,* and *Frenzy*). In fact such moments in *Jamaica Inn,* showing Hitchcock's real interests and obsessions, were the only ones filmed with any passion. The schizoid relationship between Laughton and O'Hara in the picture recalls Hitchcock's treatment of Madeleine Carroll during the filming of *The 39 Steps* and *Secret Agent;* and it emblemized the increasingly obsessive Jekyll-Hyde mentality in Hitchcock himself, a man who, like Laughton in the film, was capable of generosity toward relatives and servants, and of a savage obsession with beautiful women from whom he felt forever isolated.

After its October debut in London, *The Lady Vanishes* became at once the most popular British film up to that time, while in America it confirmed Hitchcock's reputation as the single greatest foreign filmmaker. The American critics and public, anxiously awaiting Hitchcock's arrival in 1939, were wild with enthusiasm. The picture was the event of New York's Christmas season: the *New York Times* called it the best picture of the year, a judgment echoed by members of the New York Film Critics Circle, who later gave it their highest award.

*Jamaica Inn,* however, disappointed everyone when it opened (fortunately, not until after Hitchcock had begun *Rebecca*). "Penny dreadful," sniffed London's *Film Weekly*, ordinarily single-minded in its devotion to Hitchcock. "The makers of the film seem less at pains to make our hair stand on end than to prove to us that they can fake a shipwreck as well as Hollywood.'' And the New York critics were equally confused. "It will not be remembered as a Hitchcock picture,'' wrote Frank S. Nugent, "but as a Charles Laughton picture.'' Howard Barnes, about to become the great Hitchcock champion in the popular press, wrote even more angrily in the *New York Herald Tribune* that the picture was "singularly dull and uninspired. Charles Laughton has an almost contemptuous disregard for the medium and is always content to give a show rather than to integrate the emotional and psychological factors which add up to a genuinely fine performance. Here he has given a show, and it is not a good one. . . . . *Jamaica Inn* is a mannered and highly lackadaisical melodrama.'' Other reactions were as low and dispirited as the reactions to *The Lady Vanishes* were brimful with delight.

The Hitchcocks' last months in England were spent making the necessary departure plans and visiting family. Perhaps trying to forget his sorrows over *Jamaica Inn,* however, Hitchcock was drinking more seriously and more often, and for the first time he was missing appointments. One evening he even confused the arrangements for dinner — as a telegram to Elsie Randolph (dated October 7, 1938) reveals. She was appearing in *Room for Two* at the Comedy Theatre, London, and Hitchcock was to meet her at the stage door after the show; from there they would go out to eat. She waited until midnight and then finally went home, thinking it was she who had mixed up the date. But the next morning Hitchcock's message was delivered, detailing both his wanderings and the effects of copious consumption of alcohol. Full of toilet humor worthy of a British schoolboy, the message included outrageous puns about "passing" the theater and "passing" the gin he had drunk.

By December, Selznick expected that Hitchcock and Joan Harrison were well along with a first treatment of *Rebecca,* and he wanted to settle on the choice of a writer. But Hitchcock replied that he did not want to make that selection until the treatment was finished, since it would be impossible until then to determine the exact tone of the necessary dialogue. Writing the screenplay would be especially difficult, Hitchcock added, because of the novel's first-person narrative. Hitchcock said that the task simply could not be rushed, and Selznick caught the implication: Hitchcock had his own pace, and he must be given more freedom than other directors to indulge it. In a Christmas greeting, Selznick avoided any reference to Hitchcock's work schedule — and well he might have, since he was more concerned at that point about reports that Hitchcock's obesity had resulted in borderline diabetes. He wished his new director good health in 1939, and issued a friendly warning about his nutritional habits.

The resentment Hitchcock had felt over being forced to direct *Jamaica Inn* was symptomatic of his uneven involvement in the British film world. The years with Balcon — up to 1927, and again from 1934 through 1936 — had been much the happiest time of his work in England. But they had alternated with less satisfying enterprises. For most of his time at British International, he had chafed under the supervision of John Maxwell and Walter Mycroft, and his only refuge had been in the technical challenges of early sound film.

But the prevailing difficulty of Alfred Hitchcock's English period lay with the British temperament itself. The elitists in cultural and academic circles were hostile to the idea that cinema could be an art form, and they were consistently condescending to British filmmakers. The industry, it was thought, was populated by middle-class workers who catered to lower-class audiences. "If you examine the history of the cinema," Hitchcock reflected later,

you will see that the art of filmmaking was often held in contempt by the intellectuals. That must have been true in France, and it was even truer of the British. No well-bred English person would be seen going into a cinema; it simply wasn't done. You see, England is strongly class-conscious. . . . The general attitude in Britain is an insular one. Outside of England, there is a much more universal concept of life, which one gets by talking with people and even by the manner in which they tell a story. British humor is quite superficial and also it's rather limited.

Even before her husband, Alma Reville Hitchcock recognized that he would never be fully appreciated on home territory. Snobbery deprived the British film of the status accorded only to exotic German productions. In earlier times, on the other hand, poetry, painting, and music had been a vital part of the daily life of ordinary men, but by the first third of the twentieth century (as Bertrand Russell was pointing out), only sport captured that attention and devotion.

"The truth is," agreed the editors of an influential cinema journal, "that the average attitude of England and the English to art is so wholly nonchalant and clownish that it is quite useless to expect any art to indigenously flower there. Isolated instances may here and there crop up, but *really* the Englishman can only be roused to enthusiasm on the football field." And Rachael Low, the most thorough chronicler of the British film industry, put the matter succinctly: "It was as if, in order to prove what good sports they were, the more cultivated critics would put their standards in abeyance for an American film: but for a British one of similar quality they would insist on gravely measuring it by the very highest standards and finding it wanting."

It was this philistinism, this inverse snobbery, that led the English to treat Alfred Hitchcock's work as decent entertainment but certainly nothing more. Lionized he might be, and financially rewarded. He was a gifted storyteller, the majority agreed, but an *artist . . .* ? Obsessed as the critics were with the consciously arty alternation of light and shadow, silence and speech and *montage* (the magic word from the Russo-French school), they could not see beneath the surface in Hitchcock's entertainments. "The fact is," wrote Arthur Vesselo in 1936, after considering *Sabotage,*

that there is only one maker of crime films in this country who deserves the name. Anyone may guess who he is — Alfred Hitchcock. . . . Hitchcock is our native Fritz Lang, and in many ways a true disciple of the master. Like him he displays an intuitive appreciation of the significance — almost mystical at times in its bizarre excitements — which we can be made to attach to the shadowy underworld of criminality, violence and monstrous disaster. Like him, too, he is a superb craftsman, with an eye not merely for the unusual but for the emotionally effective. His technique is that of contrast, balancing the normal against the abnormal, slowness against speed, sound against silence, humour against terror, in such a way that our perceptions are heightened whether or not we understand his technical means. . . . But often the sum-total of a Hitchcock film is a sense of disappointment, based in the realisation that the film's intellectual substance is too slight to hold it together.

And so, while the British brethren praised obvious technique, Hitchcock was quietly developing the tradition of an emotionally compelling narrative by carefully planning a series of shots that drew the audience into the story and then deeper, into frequently ambiguous psychological responses. Unconcerned with "intellectual substance," he allowed themes to emerge naturally from the seriousness of the storytelling method, an ethos of art espoused by none other than Henry James, to mention only one twentieth-century artist. Had Hitchcock been German or Russian or French, he would certainly have been estimated more highly. But he was a fat, unglamorous young man from Essex who worked in humdrum Islington and at Elstree, totally absorbed in his work. It was unthinkable that he be considered an artist. His film stories, after all, were specifically and recognizably English, whether photographed in the Surrey countryside, on the Cornish coast, or in the alleys of Bayswater.

But if an artist is one who uses a particular medium to express something of his own vision, one who exercises his own creative imagination and understanding in the selection and employment of specific means at his disposal, then Alfred Hitchcock — who had demonstrated from the start a strongly intuitive grasp of the possibilities of film — could quite accurately be called an artist. He was also consistently inventive. "Like most artists," wrote Rachael Low, "his conscious objective was not to express himself, an object which, like happiness, is rarely attained by direct pursuit, but to express something to others." He was indeed an exceptionally creative artist in spite of the stuffy British response — exceptional as Bertrand Russell spoke of the exceptional man: one having "a quality of energy and personal initiative, of independence of mind, and of imaginative vision."

It was only natural, therefore, that Alfred Hitchcock responded favorably, at last, to the American enthusiasm for his work. He was disgusted by the professional snobbery of Great Britain, dismayed at its lack of technical facilities and photographic inventiveness, and disappointed in the restrictions placed upon him by unimaginative studios. David Selznick was offering him, Hitchcock thought, everything he needed: facilities and freedom and finances. He would, in America, be able to tell greater stories on a greater scale. And for Alma, there was at last the chance for her husband to receive the recognition he deserved. These were not unreasonable hopes, but they would soon be revealed as unrealistic expectations.

In February 1939 the Hitchcocks sold Winter's Grace at Shamley Green, gave up the lease on 153 Cromwell Road, and prepared to depart London. Hitchcock spent several days with his mother in Kensington while Alma supervised the packing and shipping of their possessions. London's late winter suddenly turned sharply colder and depressing, and the Hitchcocks were eager for the side trip to Florida they had planned to precede their arrival in Los Angeles.

On the first of March, a quiet, overcast day, the *Queen Mary* left Southampton with six people in the Hitchcock suites. The cook and the maid — infallible signs that the family was arriving in America as a prosperous and polite unit — were two efficient, undemanding women, unsure about relocating to a strange continent. But they were comforted and amused by Pat, who found the whole enterprise gloriously exciting. Her parents remained quiet shipboard guests, Hitchcock huge and lumbering in the first-class lounge when not privately indulging an almost constant appetite. Alma, who could not even be seen if she happened to be walking behind him, wrote to those she had left behind and to those she would soon be seeing again in New York. From the beginning, there seems to have been no doubt in her mind that the United States would be her new permanent home; she supplied by her own certainty the measure that was lacking in her husband.

Meantime, Joan Harrison, their friend and personal assistant (if not their confidante — for this they never really seemed to have) maintained an elegant, reserved patience and devoted herself to the family needs and to daily work on the script for *Rebecca*. Completing this almost stereotypical picture of the well-to-do British family were two small dogs — the dark spaniel, Edward IX (so named following the abdication of the previous king), and the white Sealyham, Mr. Jenkins. Indeed, the Hitchcock entourage resembled a Constable grouping, or a curious conglomerate of figures from an early van Eyck portrait. Yet there was also something faintly fantastic, almost Hogarthian about them, too — something a little raw, untried, and ingenuous beneath the surface gentility. And with this admixture they were quite rightly suited for the contradictions of Hollywood.

William Hitchcock and his son Alfred, in front of the family business (about 1906)

Alfred J. Hitchcock, 1924

National Film Archive/Stills Library

Directing *The Mountain Eagle* in Munich (1925), with assistant Alma Reville

Alfred and Alma Hitchcock (center), about 1930, at home in Cromwell Road, with production secretary

Producer Michael Balcon

The first day's shooting of *The 39 Steps* (1935), with the handcuffed
Madeleine Carroll and Robert Donat

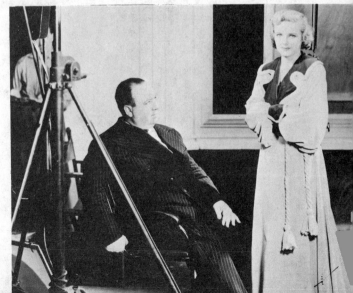

With Madeleine Carroll
on the set of *Secret Agent*
in 1935

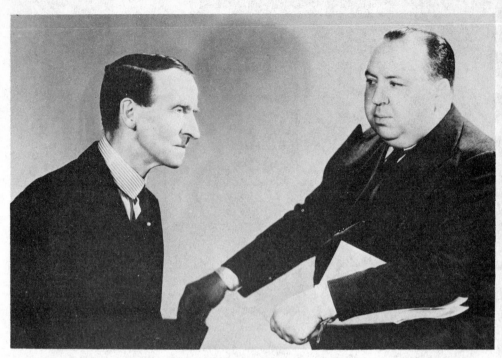

ABOVE: With John Buchan, 1937. BELOW: With script assistant Lydia Schiller and star Joan Fontaine, on the set of *Rebecca*, 1939

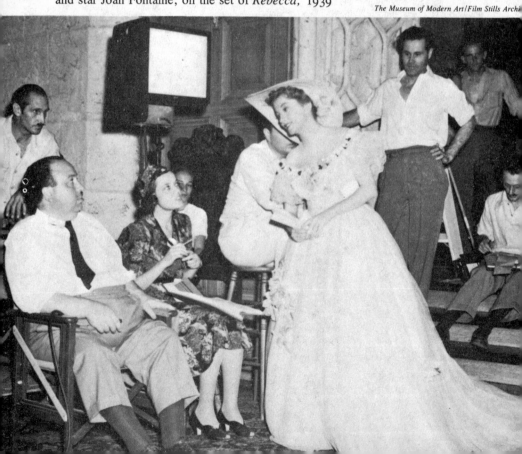

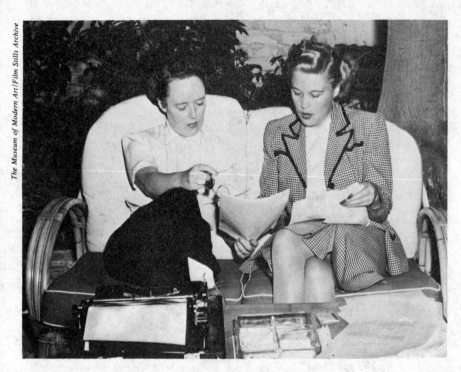

Alma Reville Hitchcock and Joan Harrison, preparing script
revisions for *Suspicion,* 1941

With daughter Patricia
nd actor Robert Cummings
at Universal Studios,
1942

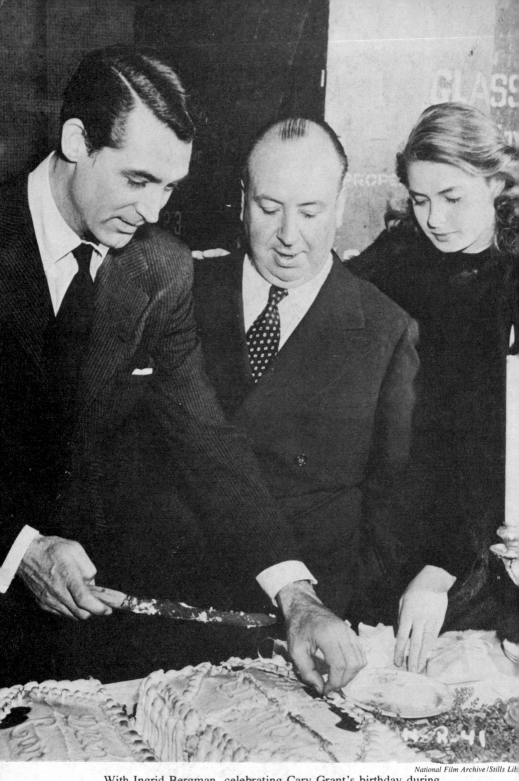

With Ingrid Bergman, celebrating Cary Grant's birthday during
the production of *Notorious*, 1946

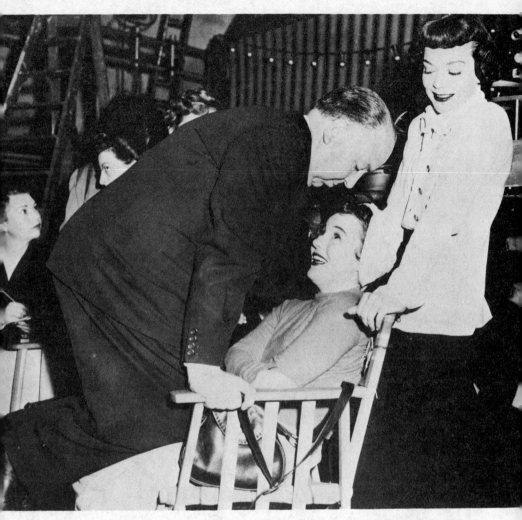

With Patricia (seated) and leading lady Jane Wyman, on the London set of *Stage Fright*, 1949

At Santa Cruz, 1951

Alma, 1952

# Eight

1939–1940

THEY seemed in no hurry to arrive in Los Angeles after Kay Brown confirmed the news: Selznick was absorbed with his mammoth production of *Gone With the Wind,* and he had not decided Hitchcock's first directing assignment. Their agreement had specified no starting date, and the director was not to be paid until his first day at the studio. With this hiatus Hitchcock thought it would be reasonable for the family to see something of America first.

For the first several days they did not get very far from New York. On March 6, Hitchcock accepted from the Yale Drama School an invitation to deliver a guest lecture on the making of melodrama and the creation of suspense — a speech that left the students somewhat confused since he took for granted their knowledge of several terms peculiar to the cinema. But the Yale audience was impressed with his knowledge of the history of British theater: they had expected Hitchcock to be like several other moviemakers they had recently heard, who were rather badly informed about stagecraft. But there was Hitchcock, talking about Shaw and Mrs. Patrick Campbell, Sardou and Sybil Thorndike, Barrie and Fay Compton. He avoided, during a question period, issues he felt less familiar with, and he often referred the questioner to specific scenes in his own films as examples of the construction of suspense and of emotional complexity through strictly visual means.

Back in New York, there were more interviews, arranged through Selznick's New York office and conducted at the Saint Regis, which was now Hitchcock's favorite New York stopping place, or at the 21 Club, now his favorite New York dining place. On March 15 he was attended by four members of the New York press at dinner, and they gave him no rest until he came up with a list of his ten favorite films —

some of which are still familiar to moviegoers, others of which seem to
have been included by him simply because they popped into his mind:
*Saturday Night, The Isle of Lost Ships, Scaramouche, Forbidden Fruit,
Sentimental Tommy, The Enchanted Cottage, Variety, The Last Command, I Am a Fugitive from a Chain Gang, The Gold Rush.*

To Hitchcock's amusement, the press accompanied him everywhere — right to Pennsylvania Station, where the Hitchcocks boarded
the *Florida Special* for Palm Beach. When she awoke to see palm trees
and orange groves, Pat thought they had arrived in California, but their
maid, who already missed everything English and found the Florida air
and climate strange and uncomfortable, cried and said they were a million miles from home and nobody would ever find them. She was not
much encouraged by beach outings, nor by the red face that stared back
from the mirror after a day of the strong Florida sun.

By the end of March they had slipped quietly into Los Angeles, and
Alma was relieved that there was no army of journalists at Union Station to greet them. Instead, they were met by Marjorie and Myron Selznick and their daughter Joan, who was close to Pat's age and who
undertook to explain the geography of the city to her new playmate.
Riding to the apartment Myron had rented for them, Hitchcock asked
about the starting date for his first film. To his surprise, he was told that
David now had the idea that Hitchcock would direct *Intermezzo,* which
would be the first American film for Ingrid Bergman, the young Swedish actress David had just signed to an exclusive contract. Hitchcock
replied, somewhat anxiously, that their script for *Rebecca* was well
along, and Myron countered that it would undoubtedly be produced at
some time, his brother just did not know when.

The three-bedroom apartment on the upper level at the Wilshire Palms
Apartments, 10331 Wilshire Boulevard, was lavishly furnished and ide-
ally located. Its living and dining rooms overlooked the boulevard, directly south of which, and a short ride away, was the Selznick studio in
Culver City. The rear bedrooms opened out over the requisite California
pool, and the sun shimmered off ubiquitous white appointments —
carpeting, draperies, chairs, walls. Everything was white. Pat said she
was reminded of a Swiss snowstorm, but Alma said it would be a long
time before they saw snow and that that was fine with her. (Joan Harrison's apartment, on the ground floor of the same building, was deco-
rated in pastels, and this they soon found more congenial for prolonged
script sessions.) Myron at once helped Hitchcock stock the living room's
wet bar, and on their first shopping excursion the next day they met
several of their neighbors at the Wilshire Palms, among them Franchot

Tone, whose marriage to Joan Crawford had just terminated, and one of the Ritz Brothers.

"We had indifferent luck with our group," Hitchcock wrote later. "The maid got homesick and returned to England; the cook left us. . . . With only cookbooks for a script, [Alma] memorized and executed my dishes to such perfection that there's been no need since to hire more than an understudy for the role." But since Alma sat in on most of the working sessions for *Rebecca,* an understudy was in fact required several evenings weekly, and they were more or less permanently joined by a solidly loyal German woman with a flair for sauces, custards, and pastries. In the first ten weeks, Hitchcock added another twenty-five pounds to his already outsize girth, and a dark suit, for cosmetic camouflage, soon became his ordinary costume.

The first weekend in Los Angeles, Hitchcock took Alma and Pat to Sun Valley, Idaho, which, he had been told, resembled their beloved Saint Moritz. They arrived in time for the last of the winter season's sports events, and from their suite at the Sun Valley Lodge they looked out on the skiers racing down Bald Mountain, in one direction, and Dollar Mountain, in the other. It was here that Hitchcock met, one Saturday evening, Ernest Hemingway, who had come back from the Spanish Civil War and was finishing his novel *For Whom the Bell Tolls.* Hemingway had seen most of Hitchcock's pictures and liked their sassy, offbeat humor. He said that his new novel would make a good film, but Hitchcock, who thought he was fishing for an offer to collaborate, said he did not understand politics. Four years later, when he saw how successful the novel was as a film, Hitchcock would offer Hemingway a chance to work on a major script.

Back in Los Angeles, the interviewers arrived daily, and Hitchcock took to longer and longer script sessions, the better to keep them waiting and sustain the image of a prodigious worker. The truth was that he would sit for an hour or two with Joan, spinning outrageous scenes that had no counterpart in the novel, and then ask her to add dialogue while he slipped out for a drive in the tiny Austin he had bought. For the rest of his days Hitchcock would firmly maintain that he had never driven a car in his life, for fear of being stopped by a dreaded officer of the law. But from 1939 to 1941, when he went to work at Universal Studios, he frequently drove himself around the neighborhood, delivered Pat to the Marymount School on Sunset Boulevard, and took the family to Sunday worship. Eventually his professional status, and the difficulty of situating himself comfortably behind a steering wheel, led him to engage a driver, and for virtually the entire second half of his life special care was taken in choosing men for this discreet position.

In their social life, the Hitchcocks preferred the few people they had met on their previous visit, and for the most part they avoided the English colony that had settled as a group unto itself in Hollywood. Alma was not at all eager to reinvolve herself with Britons, and Hitchcock had to agree that their countrymen did seem to overdo the posture they maintained. Instead of the stuffy English gentlefolk, they invited Carole Lombard — who was at this time also represented by Myron Selznick — to dine with them, and soon she brought her new husband, who was acting in *Gone With the Wind*. She and Clark Gable were easy companions, raucous and unaffected, and Hitchcock especially liked Carole's risqué humor, which contrasted with her magnificent fair beauty. He quickly found that he preferred people like the Gables to the rather tight little British community in Benedict Canyon.

"C. Aubrey Smith headed that contingent," he said later. "I think there were some British writers included in their number, but it was primarily actors of the stature of Clive Brook, Conway Tearle and Ronald Colman, though it was probably Colman who succeeded in breaking it up. I think they had their own cricket team. And I shall always remember the weather vane atop Smith's house up on Mulholland. It consisted of three stumps and a cricket bat that swivelled in the wind."

One visit was enough for him and Alma. They kept their social contacts to a few people from the Selznick studio, and to couples like the Gables, who appreciated a bad pun, a good bottle of liquor, and the kind of jokes that could be told only after Pat was put to bed and the cook retired for the evening. Otherwise, on the subject of the general population, Hitchcock was straightforward: "Los Angeles? The place itself is all right, but it isn't easy to understand the people."

Their excursions to the local restaurants took them to David and Maude Chasen's in Beverly Hills, where Thursday dinners became as sacred a ritual as Sunday mass at Good Shepherd Church (a place, Hitchcock agreed with fellow parishioner Rosalind Russell, that really should have been called "Our Lady of the Cadillacs"). Soon, the Hitchcocks' booth at Chasen's in fact became more hallowed a sanctuary than Good Shepherd, and one was more certain to find Alfred Hitchcock there on Thursdays than in a church pew on Sundays. This, to be sure, tells us as much about California preaching as it does about the cooking at Chasen's, for he was not, after all, a man who suffered mediocrity patiently. From the Chasens he learned about the preparation of American meals and American cocktails, and soon he had rented storage space at the Los Angeles Smoking and Curing Company, where he kept abundant supplies of the English bacon and Dover sole that he was having sent to California several times each month. This, it became clear, was his single most obvious extravagance — not the desire for a lavish Los Angeles movie-star palace.

"What I want is a *home,*" he said at the time, "not a movie set with a heating plant added. All I need is a snug little house with a good kitchen, and the devil with a swimming pool. First thing the real estate agents start talking about is the pool. Then they discuss the tennis court. Finally they get around to talking about the barbecue arrangements in back of the rose garden. They never do talk about the house. Maybe they're ashamed of it."

House-hunting was one of the few diversions that seemed to keep Hitchcock awake during the first slow months in California. David Selznick, still busy with his Southern epic, had not asked to see the *Rebecca* script yet. Hitchcock drove around town, shopped with Alma, and did a prodigious amount of dining and dozing — often combining the latter two activities.

One evening Dan Winkler, a Selznick executive, took Hitchcock to a notoriously bold floor show in West Hollywood, where the chorus girls ended their final number wearing little more than the musical notes that accompanied them. "Hitch," Winkler reported to Selznick the following Monday, "slept." At a more respectable and private gathering, Hitchcock was introduced to Thomas Mann, who had also arrived from Europe and was being much honored in California. Mann engaged Hitchcock in a discussion of the relationship between fiction and film. "Hitch," Mann later told his son Klaus, "slept." Another evening, the Hitchcocks invited the Gables and Loretta Young to dine with them at Chasen's. "Before the salad was served," Alma remembered, "Hitch slept." This characteristic might have reminded some companions of the Fat Boy in Dickens's *Pickwick Papers,* who could fall asleep at the drop of any voice. At one dinner party Alma shook her husband awake after everyone else had departed. "Wouldn't it be rude to leave so early?" he asked, not aware that more than a few minutes had elapsed since their arrival.

It would be easy to attribute this social somnolence to a perverse and vulgar demonstration of boredom, but there were other, more probable reasons for it. Hitchcock was an early riser, he was hugely overweight, he exercised only his mind (and that, all day, at full speed, as he considered scenario ideas, read, or made script corrections), he dined often and on rich foods, and he could not, for all his insistence, tolerate alcohol well. When he was not clearly the center of everyone's attention, it took very little wine to detach him, to the point of a snoring slumber, from company.

On Monday, April 10, 1939, Hitchcock officially went on the payroll at Selznick International Pictures, and from that date he appeared daily at a small office — usually with Alma and always with Joan Harrison — to work on what he thought would be the final script for *Rebecca*. Only a few days before, David Selznick had at last made up his mind to make this Hitchcock's first film (he assigned Gregory Ratoff to direct Ingrid Bergman and Leslie Howard in *Intermezzo*). Selznick, already overworked and exhausted, looked older than his thirty-seven years. He worked at everything with a proprietary zeal unmatched in the history of Hollywood, and he made it clear at once that *Rebecca* would receive his constant attention, even though there was still a good deal of work left on *Gone With the Wind*.

Hitchcock told Selznick that there was a first draft almost complete, that in London he had had all the help he could get from the writer Michael Hogan, and that Joan Harrison was now working on the script. Selznick told Hitchcock that Lillian Hellman wanted to make some contribution to the early part of the dialogue (particularly to the scenes involving the brashly formidable American dowager, Mrs. Van Hopper), but Hitchcock doubted that Hellman's peculiar Southern sensibility was right for his needs, and Selznick did not force the issue. A man named Martin Buckley was brought in for a few days, but he was replaced by Philip MacDonald, whom Selznick agreed to over his own recommendations — names that included, among others, Charles Brackett, Delmer Daves, Sam and Bella Spewak, S. N. Behrman, and St. John Ervine. It was clear from the start that Selznick was allowing Hitchcock considerably more latitude in preparing a film than he allowed any other contracted director, and this consideration made the producer-director relationship, for the time being, quite cordial.

MacDonald worked from a ninety-page outline Hitchcock, Alma, and Joan had prepared. The dialogue and action were described in unusually fine detail, in prose narrative form, and all that seemed necessary were the changes from indirect to direct discourse, some transitional scenes, and a heightening of tension. Instead of the typical Hollywood film treatment (which contained about fifty scene descriptions in fewer pages), Hitchcock had set down several hundred scenes, each with precise specifications for the dialogue, action, and camera placement. This was how he had prepared his English films, and he foresaw no reason to alter his carefully thought out, economical, and visually arresting approach. Balcon, Black, and even Maxwell had not much interfered with this method, and Hitchcock did not expect interference from Selznick. This was his biggest and most unfortunate presumption. When he submitted the screenplay of *Rebecca* the first week of June, he expected swift approval and the announcement of a shooting date in July. What he got, on June 13, was a thick envelope containing a lengthy document in which Selznick (who described himself in the first sentence as "shocked and disappointed beyond words") detailed why he was rejecting virtually the entire composition.

Arriving at the studio that morning, Hitchcock opened the package to read one of the legendary Selznick memos, this one dated June 12. "It was so long," Hitchcock said in 1969, "that I've just now finished reading it. I think it'd make a very good film. I'd call it *The Longest Story Ever Told.*" Selznick had disapproved of Hitchcock's handling of the du Maurier novel from first page to last. Hitchcock had begun his script with a scene in which a cigar-smoking Maxim de Winter, sailing to the Riviera, causes his fellow passengers to become violently nauseous. "I think the scenes of seasickness are cheap beyond words, and old-fashioned in the bargain," Selznick commented about this and about a repetition of the vomiting aboard a smaller boat later (scenes that apparently reflected the director's fearful memories of motion sickness); and he had equally strong words about the humor Hitchcock had used to punctuate — and, Selznick thought, weaken — an essentially somber Gothic melodrama. "We bought *Rebecca,* and we intend to make *Rebecca,*" Selznick insisted, "not a distorted and vulgarized version of a provenly successful work."

The successful work was the popular tale of a shy young girl, paid companion to a blowsy American matron, who meets the dashing and handsome widower Maxim de Winter and is whisked off to marriage and to Manderley, his estate in the English countryside. There she is tormented by the housekeeper, who nourishes a fanatical devotion to the first Mrs. de Winter — Rebecca — a woman who, it turns out, was a wicked creature and not the wonderful wife to whom the new bride thought she compared unfavorably.

"David insisted," according to Hitchcock, "that we should follow the book exactly. He decided that with so many readers who had their own favorite scenes, they'd be disappointed if they weren't included in the film." And it was not only that Hitchcock had discarded what Selznick thought was the heart and soul of the book: he had also sacrificed character for facile humor, and he had failed to draw any convincing support for the personalities of Mrs. Danvers (the housekeeper), Maxim, or the nameless second Mrs. de Winter (whom Hitchcock had called, perhaps with puckish humor, Daphne in his script, thus making the poor girl "Daphne de Winter" — an obvious allusion). Selznick also lamented the vulgarization of the secondary characters and Hitchcock's odd creation, in the style of Brontë, of a lunatic grandmother in a tower of Manderley. "It is my regretful conclusion," Selznick wrote at the end of a depressing but cogently argued litany of complaints, "that we should immediately start on a new treatment, probably with a new writing setup."

One of the few elements of the novel left unaltered in Hitchcock's treatment was, by an odd quirk of Hollywood history, the screenplay's single most troublesome aspect — one that, at the last, had to be changed. The Motion Picture Production Code (an outgrowth of the so-called Hays Office, under the vigilance of Will Hays) would not allow Maxim de Winter to emerge, as he does in the novel, unpunished for the murder of his first wife — a crime, in any case, for which he feels no guilt because of her consummately wicked character. It would be necessary, the Hays Office insisted, to attribute Rebecca's death to an accident, or to otherwise alter the situation so that the happy ending, when Maxim and his new wife face a brighter future, did not depend on the cavalier dismissal of a capital offense.

It was this thorny bit of narrative that led Selznick to engage Robert E. Sherwood to help with the last part of the script. (Comparisons of the original and final scenarios confirm the statement of Charles Bennett, who was in close contact with Selznick and Hitchcock at the time, that the screenplay "is ninety percent the work of Michael Hogan, although some rewrites were done by Joan. Very little, at the end, was contributed by the one who is most famous and therefore most credited, Sherwood.")

Robert E. Sherwood brought to his task, however minimal, the perfect amalgam of experience. He was an American playwright (author, most notably, of *The Petrified Forest, Tovarich,* and *Waterloo Bridge*); he had written screenplays in England, and so had an ear for British diction (as he had demonstrated in *The Scarlet Pimpernel, The Ghost Goes West,* and *The Divorce of Lady X*); and he had recently and successfully adapted two of his own plays to the screen (*Idiot's Delight* and *Abe Lincoln in Illinois*). He was the man, Selznick thought, to solve the censorship problem — for censorship, Selznick protested to Jock Whitney, was the greatest inhibitor of screen artistry: "We need at last to have something like the freedom that newspapers and magazines and book publishers and the legitimate stage have. . . . Instead, this shortsighted industry allows itself to be strangled by this insane, inane and outmoded Code.''

Hitchcock, of course, had no choice but to accept the demands of the Hays Office, as well as those pouring forth from the Selznick office. ''I was a minor figure in a vast film industry made up of entrepreneurs who headed the studios,'' he wrote. Even so, up to that point,

the rules were broken a little in my case. I was permitted to participate in the preparation of the script. This was considerate and flattering, except for one thing — the hours. I had a dim recollection of trying to keep awake at three a.m. in the producer's summer house, while attempting to construct a script with the help of the famous playwright Robert Sherwood. Naturally Selznick dominated the scene — pacing up and down, apparently oblivious to those around him who were nodding off — and he did not even notice that the long, lanky Mr. Sherwood, having imbibed somewhat, was trying unsuccessfully to sail a small boat in the swimming pool. By dawn, of course, nothing much had been accomplished, but that was the producer's way.

Typically, Hitchcock drew an image of himself as the quiet, sober professional, surrounded by somewhat childish or inebriated colleagues. It is certainly true that Selznick was a driven, compulsive worker who insisted on being deeply and personally involved in every aspect of his productions. But it is also true that at this point in his career he was a man with as accurate a sense as Hitchcock of what would make an artistic and commercially rewarding motion picture, and he was a man who combined intelligence and business sense with that rare, indefinable, and much maligned quailty, good taste (which in him was never priggish). As for Sherwood, he had been hastily signed for what everyone knew was clean-up work, and, like Hitchcock, he resented Selznick's unorthodox working hours as the script approached completion at summer's end. But everyone was being handsomely compensated, and Selznick was generous with food and drink and accommodations, those fringe benefits that have always been taken for granted in Hollywood.

Hitchcock, however, was not an easy man to work with unless he was in complete command of the situation and felt that no one was trying to infringe on either his control or his ''authorial voice.'' Of this period, Selznick's advertising and publicity director, Whitney Bolton, remembered: ''I will not pretend that Mr. Hitchcock always was the most consistently amiable of human creatures, nor will I evade that he delighted in needling those around him. He needled stars, staff, press agents, any and all. . . . He had a way of speaking that commands attention, and if he didn't get it he tended to fret a little.'' In Selznick's concise diction, ''Hitchcock was not a man to go camping with.''

While the script was revised, the problem of casting continued. David Niven was among those being considered for the role of Maxim, but Hitchcock said Niven was "entirely too shallow." He had other objections to actors like William Powell, and Selznick (who could, of course, have hired any players he wanted) was eager to find actors with whom Hitchcock really wanted to work; this would assure greater care during rehearsals and a better finished product. Finally a name emerged that the director found agreeable.

Laurence Olivier, who had had instant popularity when his previous film, William Wyler's *Wuthering Heights,* opened in May, was by mid-June delighting Broadway audiences in Behrman's *No Time for Comedy*. He accepted Selznick's offer to return to Hollywood, hoping with his bride-to-be, Vivien Leigh, that she would go from *Gone With the Wind* to the female lead in *Rebecca,* for which Selznick promised she would be considered. At once Selznick let it be known from coast to coast that in casting the heroine of his new film he intended to conduct another highly publicized search and elaborate screen-testing, just as he had in casting Leigh as Scarlett O'Hara in *Gone With the Wind*.

Filling the supporting roles was easier. From the British colony in Hollywood Selznick signed C. Aubrey Smith, Leo G. Carroll, Nigel Bruce, Reginald Denny, and Melville Cooper. For the role of the intimidating housekeeper Mrs. Danvers, he had first wanted Alla Nazimova or Flora Robson. But Kay Brown, as so often, came up with the perfect actress: Judith Anderson. (In the completed film, the scenes in which the housekeeper and the new mistress of Manderley confront each other are among the most dramatic moments. "Although Hitchcock is full of kind impulses," wrote one reporter at the time, "he is never happier than when seeing someone writhe. The sadistic cruelty which Mrs. Danvers manifests towards the second Mrs. de Winter is precisely the sort of thing which brings the roses to Mr. Hitchcock's rather extensive cheeks.")

And for the role of Mrs. Van Hopper, the vulgar American dowager who employs the heroine, the leading candidates were Lucile Watson, Laura Hope Crews, Mary Boland, Alice Brady, and Cora Witherspoon. But one evening the Hitchcocks went to the Pasadena Playhouse, where they were impressed by the performance of a Texas lawyer who preferred acting. Her name was Florence Bates, and Hitchcock recommended her to Selznick, who at once hired her for the role of Mrs. Van Hopper.

Meantime, they looked for the right leading lady. Between May and August more than a score of actresses were rehearsed, dressed and put before the camera, photographed, and argued over by Selznick, Hitchcock, and two other directors whose advice Selznick valued, George Cukor and John Cromwell. By August 19 the choice had been narrowed to Anne Baxter, Margaret Sullavan, Olivia de Havilland, and Joan Fontaine.* The consensus was that Anne Baxter was, at sixteen, too young, although Hitchcock told Selznick that Joan Harrison and Alma preferred her to Joan Fontaine, whom they pronounced "too coy and simpering to a degree that is intolerable . . . and Margaret Sullavan is far ahead of either." Selznick, however, rejected Sullavan as incredible for a role that demanded that extreme passivity be credible and sympathetic. Olivia de Havilland was reluctant to compete with her sister Joan Fontaine for the role, especially since she herself had just played a major role in *Gone With the Wind* and her sister's acting jobs had not, up to that time, been so important or successful.

Toward the end of August, Hitchcock finally joined Cromwell, Cukor, and Selznick in the opinion that Joan Fontaine was the best candidate. The most recent of her several tests had been on July 26, and Selznick asked her to do another. She politely replied that she would be honored to play the role, but she simply would not submit to another test; besides, she was to marry Brian Aherne on Saturday, August 19, and then depart on her honeymoon.

This apparently struck panic into everyone concerned, for the picture was ready to start shooting, the rest of the cast was waiting, the schedule had been drawn up, and Selznick wanted to waste no more time. He was also concerned that his English actors might, if the European war spread, abandon the picture and return home for the inevitable fighting (which would, he said, put them all "in a fine pickle if they walked out in the middle — not so much of a pickle as Poland, I grant you, but still a pickle"). The day after her wedding, Joan Fontaine received a telegram informing her that she would play the part and advising that Selznick would be grateful if she would curtail her honeymoon and return on Labor Day for final wardrobe fittings and the start of principal photography.

Things then happened quickly. On September 7 Selznick's office accepted the final revisions of the script, and the next day the cameras started rolling. But it had been a bad week for the world, and the concern showed on the faces of everyone gathered on the set. On Septem-

---

*Among those who tested in the role, in addition to a somewhat frantic Vivien Leigh, were Jean Muir, Lucille Fairbanks, Heather Angel, Frances Reid, Katharine Bard, Rene Ray, Nova Pilbeam (to whom Hitchcock, for some inexplicable reason, was bitterly opposed), Sylvia Weld, Julie Haydon, Dorothy Hyson, Ellen Drew, Pauline Moore, Louise Campbell, Fay Helm, Anita Louise, Mary Kay Dodson, Loretta Young, Augusta Dabney, Frances Dee, Joan Tetzel, Agnes Fraser, Virginia Gilmore, Helen Terry, Margaret Lang, Maevis Raeburn, Miriam Patty, and Jacqueline Templeton.

ber 1, Germany had invaded Poland; two days later, England had declared war on Germany; and by September 8, when filming began, there were fears that London would very soon be heavily bombed. Hitchcock was sick with fright for his family back home, and this — every bit as much as his trepidation about the lavish production, coupled with the inexperience of the leading lady and the distracted anxiety of the mostly English cast — contributed to his uncharacteristically slow progress the first few weeks.

By the end of September, the film was alarmingly behind schedule, which meant that the cost (which Selznick had hoped to keep to about $800,000) was sure to reach $1 million. Selznick was nevertheless irritated by Hitchcock's economical method of shooting, and his irritation grew to outright anger. Whereas Hitchcock had usually delighted producers with his already famous technique of "cutting in the camera" (that is, by shooting only those camera angles that would be used in the final edited picture), Selznick realized that this method afforded him little chance as producer to make his own creative alterations later. This, of course, was exactly what Hitchcock intended, as it was exactly what Selznick wanted to avoid — the disposition, into Hitchcock's hands, of virtual control over the film before it reached the editor.

"It was no secret," according to John Houseman, who was soon to be a creative consultant for Selznick, "that all had not been roses between Hitchcock and David during the making of *Rebecca*, to which Hitchcock had attempted to apply the very personal creative methods that had made him world-famous. These methods were profoundly repulsive to David O. Selznick, who belonged to the school of the well-made, producer-controlled, strictly-adhered-to shooting script and who, besides, was determined on this, Hitchcock's first American picture, to assert his producer's position of power."

Another important reason for the delays was the special care Hitchcock felt was necessary to elicit a convincing portrayal from Joan Fontaine. Not yet twenty-two, she was visibly anxious about this major role. In addition, she and Florence Bates were the only American actors, and Laurence Olivier made no secret of his disappointment that he was playing opposite her and not Vivien Leigh.

"One thing in my favor was that I was comparatively unknown," Fontaine recalled. "Hitchcock used to call me into his office and we'd sit and talk about everything in the world. I think he felt a bit uncomfortable with all those established stage actors. I think that there was also a social thing there — Hitchcock's origins were within the sound of Bow bells, so he didn't get around much socially. And I'm sure he never intended to. He preferred to entertain at home, where he could be lord of the manor.''

Very soon, her willingness to submit to Hitchcock's mentorship encouraged him (for the first but not the most dramatic time in his American career) to exercise over a leading lady a kind of moral tyranny that had been impossible in England, where he had worked with established, independent, and tough-minded stars like Madeleine Carroll and Sylvia Sidney. But here was a young, timid bride whose training had not suited her to the grandeur of a Selznick-Hitchcock production. She was glad for the guidance, but it took some time before she realized that in fact Hitchcock wanted the guidance to go further.

"He seemed to want total possession of me," she remembered.

He wasn't convivial, and he didn't arrange for us all to lunch together or to sit down for a chat. He was a Svengali. He controlled me totally. He took me aside and whispered, "Now kid, you go in there and you do this and that.'' And then he would say, "Do you know what so-and-so said about you today? Do you know that Olivier doesn't want you in this role? Well, never you mind. You just listen to me.'' Now some of what he told me might have been true, but of course it also made me feel absolutely miserable all the time. To be honest, he was divisive with us. He wanted total control over me, and he seemed to relish the cast not liking one another, actor for actor, by the end of the film. Now of course this helped my performance, since I was supposed to be terrified of everyone, and it gave a lot of tension to my scenes. It kept him in command, and it was part of the upheaval he wanted. He kept me off balance, much to his own delight. He would constantly tell me that no one thought I was any good except himself, and that nobody really liked me and nobody would say anything good about me except himself.

Despite the control he exercised over his leading lady, Hitchcock was growing anxious during these weeks. He began, quite soon into the shooting, to chafe under Selznick's meddling — even though everyone assured him that Selznick was in fact interfering in the daily details far less than he did with any of his other productions, and that he was providing Hitchcock with much more freedom than he afforded other directors. "This is turning out to be a Selznick picture," Hitchcock observed, quite rightly, in late September. That would probably mean (as everyone knew it would for *Gone With the Wind*) a great commercial success — but Hitchcock was, after all, on a weekly salary. That he was not benefiting artistically annoyed him more, however, than the prospect of inequitable compensation.

Single-minded, stubborn, and usually brilliant when it came to his method of filming, Hitchcock found himself in the unprecedented and unhappy position of having to cope with an equally single-minded, equally stubborn, and often equally brilliant producer. Their relationship required enormous patience and the display of frequent gentlemanly compromise, of which each was capable, but which both parties offered with increasing reluctance. Selznick was expansive, sometimes explosive, emotionally volatile — but people knew where they were in the hierarchy of his affection and estimation. Hitchcock, on the other hand, was secretive and emotionally subdued, and he affected a reserved and serious manner, the better to keep his cast and crew alert for his moods and demands.

In addition, there was the matter of Hitchcock's worry for his family in England, his anxiety over what Selznick's future plans for him might be, the lurking threats to his health precipitated by his epicurean lifestyle, and an increasingly tense atmosphere at home.

Pat was happily enrolled at the Marymount School, and she had no difficulty adjusting to California life or making new friends. Alma was happy to have quit England, and her only reason for wanting to return was to bring to America her mother and her sister Eva. The considerable monies Alma and Hitchcock were able to bring with them from London, and the Selznick salary he was receiving weekly, enabled them to live more than comfortably, and very soon they were traveling with real-estate agents to look at houses in Bel-Air, the fashionable private area north of Sunset Boulevard. When they mentioned this to Carole Lombard at dinner one evening, she leaped up and hugged her host. Would he like to rent her furnished house for a year or two, since she was moving to Gable's ranch in Encino?

The next day they all drove to 609 Saint Cloud Road, and by the middle of October the Hitchcocks had left Wilshire Palms. The house was simple and snug, as Hitchcock wished, not at all like the grand mansions that lined Sunset Boulevard, and the furniture showed the effects of Hollywood parties. Alma was delighted to be in a house, and the added space enabled Pat to invite friends more often. The Hitchcocks' cook went along with them, and not wanting to lose her now that they planned on entertaining more frequently, Hitchcock made her a gift of his roadster. He then bought himself (or more accurately bought Alma, who was now doing the family driving) a shiny new Cadillac.

But the relocation did not lessen a quiet tension that had set in — a strain that derived not primarily from the uncertainties of the war or the vagaries of Selznick's option on Hitchcock's contract. The fact was that Alma's direct, day-to-day involvement with her husband's work had gradually diminished as Joan Harrison's had increased. The women remained on extremely friendly terms, but everyone who knew the Hitchcocks could clearly see that he appreciated more about Joan than her talent and undivided attention to his creative needs. Quite simply, he adored her. Although she was always careful to show that, for her part, everything was strictly business, she could not have avoided noticing that Hitchcock's feelings for her were more than professional, more than paternal. He was too unsure of himself emotionally (and probably too sure of what her response might be, or might not be) to make a precipitous, vulgar overture. And it would be many years before he would ever seriously consider activating strong feelings for any woman other than Alma — with whom, by his own admission, his relationship had already become strictly chaste.

And so he nursed his unarticulated longings in a kind of silent, gray romantic gloom that hung over the family like the mists over Manderley. "There are only two women I ever could have married," he confided to Charles Bennett one evening, "Alma, whom I did, and Joan, whom I didn't." By the end of the year, his doctor weighed him in at 365 pounds. It takes no training in psychiatry or medicine to see that there could have been a physical disaster at any moment, a collapse that would have been attributable to outrageous overindulgence and a life that was frustrated at work, anxious at home, full of concern for a family abroad, and tense with conflict between a sense of duty to England and a desire to remain in Hollywood and find a project that could morally and socially justify not returning to the homeland.

Most poignant of all, however, was Hitchcock's hopeless romantic dream, his yearning for Harrison, with whom intimacy was not possible. At forty — and regularly, for the rest of his life — Alfred Hitchcock joined history's long list of aching, unrequited lovers who drew energy and inspiration for their work precisely from the fact that they were indeed unrequited. When this pattern repeated itself, his work became richer, more universal in scope, more overtly tender. Film would not only be a refuge and expression of his deepest longings, it would be the forum through which he would probe into the reality behind the longing, the dread of isolation behind the dream. But for now, there was only the diffusion of grief, without the creative freedom to transmute that grief into art.

The opportunity for Hitchcock to do a film that would justify his stay in America, however, came rather sooner than he expected. Selznick announced that independent producer Walter Wanger wanted to borrow Hitchcock's services for a film. This provided Selznick with a ready-made solution to several problems: the details involving the completion, release, advertising, and promotion of both *Gone With the Wind* and *Rebecca,* which would require his constant attention; his polite but knotty relationship with Hitchcock; Selznick's need to raise cash quickly to cover taxes, film expenses, the cost of studio operations, and his mounting personal debts accrued while gambling; and, according to those who knew him best, his fear that with two monumental productions in progress simultaneously he was, at thirty-seven, burning himself out of energies and ideas.

And so on Thursday, September 21, Hitchcock accepted an invitation to lunch with Walter Wanger. The talk was lively, and they parted in a state of high excitement. Back at the studio, no one had any idea that Hitchcock's buoyant manner had anything to do with an imminent shift in his career or that he had found a film idea that would validate his staying in Hollywood. At the same time, back at *his* office, Wanger was almost crying with joy. He telephoned Selznick at once, and by Tuesday a letter of agreement was ready for Wanger's signature. That same day, Hitchcock's speed in shooting scenes of *Rebecca* increased dramatically.

Walter Wanger — born Walter Feuchtwanger — came from a wealthy family in San Francisco, where he was born in 1894. His cosmopolitan, sophisticated, and liberal attitude derived not only from an alert and encouraging family life, but also from studies at Dartmouth, Heidelberg, and Oxford. In his early twenties he was a New York theatrical agent, and during World War I he served as an aviator and then worked in intelligence and handled publicity for the American embassy in Rome, where he produced a film about the allied war effort. "I was impressed by the force and power of film," he said of this experience. "That's when I made up my mind that this was going to be my niche."

Assigned to work at the Paris Peace Conference, Wanger's liberal sensibilities deepened, and while pursuing a peacetime career as a theatrical and screen producer in London and New York, he never lost his optimism that under his influence film could change the course of human events. "Believing in motion pictures as an international force, I really wanted to see our work become a respected calling. I thought it was almost as important as the State Department." Between 1923 and 1939, he produced films for Paramount, Columbia, and MGM before becoming an independent producer for United Artists, and during those years he was reponsible for such films as *The Cocoanuts* (starring the Marx Brothers); *The Bitter Tea of General Yen; Queen Christina; Stagecoach; You Only Live Once;* and *Blockade.* The last two mentioned were notable for their controversial social and political topics, but commercial pressures from the studios usually forced Wanger into less provocative and more popular enterprises.

In 1936 Wanger had purchased for $10,000 the screen rights to *Personal History*, the memoirs of foreign correspondent Vincent Sheean; but screenwriter John Howard Lawson, who was under contract to Wanger, could not fashion a timely and dramatically compelling script, and the project was for a time abandoned. By 1938 several other writers (Budd Schulberg and Harold Clurman among them) had reworked the screenplay, setting the story in Nazi Germany and adding material about the Spanish Civil War and new political crises in Europe. Wanger then signed William Dieterle to direct. But the Bank of America refused to finance a film that might muddy the waters of American neutrality.

Wanger's own feeling of urgency about the world situation became compellingly acute, however, and the same week *Rebecca* began filming, the press announced that he had raised the money on his own. Inspired by the invasion of Poland to proceed without bank financing, he hired John Lay and John Meehan, two writers from *The March of Time* news series, hoping that they could fashion a new screenplay that would attract Claudette Colbert and Charles Boyer as leading players. By this time, Wanger had spent over $140,000 for script work. He planned to put *Personal History* before the cameras by November 20, to release it on Washington's Birthday, and to keep the budget at $750,000. As it turned out, the final cost would be over $1.5 million; the film would not begin shooting until March (after still more trials with the script, and without Colbert and Boyer); the release would not be until late August 1940; and the title would eventually be *Foreign Correspondent* — directed by Alfred Hitchcock.

Selznick had waited to arrange the Wanger-Hitchcock luncheon until after Hitchcock's return from interviewing actors in New York. He preferred to give Hitchcock the impression that the two producers had not discussed the loan-out of his services and that the idea was strictly Wanger's. But on the same day Wanger and Hitchcock lunched, Daniel T. O'Shea, secretary of Selznick International Pictures, was dictating the final draft of the contractual letter that Wanger's legates signed the following week. Prophetic instincts, it seems, proved justified in all quarters.

The agreement, dated September 26, 1939, was typical of many Hollywood exchanges of talent at the time; it provided that Alfred Hitchcock would be loaned to Walter Wanger "to assist and collaborate in the writing, adaptation, script, dialogue and continuity of, and to direct, the photoplay now entitled *Personal History*." The rather one-sided major conditions suggest the extent not only of Selznick's power but also

of Wanger's willingness to accede at once and to risk so much to ac-
quire Hitchcock's services for a film project that had given him, so far,
nothing but trouble. The contract specified that Hitchcock would work
for Wanger immediately after the completion of *Rebecca;* that Selznick
could recall Hitchcock for retakes even after he had begun working for
Wanger; that Hitchcock's name would appear in press announcements
and advertising with the remark that the arrangement was by courtesy
of David O. Selznick; that Selznick would not be held responsible if
Hitchcock failed to provide expected services; and that, if Wanger paid
Hitchcock any bonus, equivalent sums would be paid to Selznick. Most
significantly, Wanger would have to pay to David Selznick — in
advance — the equivalent of $5,000 weekly for a minimum of twelve
weeks. And from this $60,000 sum, Hitchcock was paid — weekly, by
Selznick, according to the terms of *their* contract — only $2,500. The
100 percent profit was Selznick's, but it was little compared to what he
would negotiate for himself later.

Monday, November 27, was Hitchcock's first day with Wanger, but
there was little to occupy him: the latest of Wanger's contracted writers
was still hidden away, trying in vain to come up with a screenplay.
"The script is now being written by one of the leading scenarists in our
industry — John Meehan," Wanger told a meeting of United Artists
stockholders on December 5. "Meehan has a profound understanding
of deep, human emotions and of ambitious young people. . . . We can
rely on Meehan to give us something powerful, unusual, human and
popular." Proclamations like this to stockholders in Hollywood film
companies are common enough — praise for the craftsman of a work
in progress, and a tone of conviction about the future. In this case,
however, the producer might have meant his remarks more to encourage
Meehan than to excite the assembled shareholders, for there was not,
even by Christmas, a page of script that Hitchcock could shoot.

Wanger than began to panic, although he himself was largely to blame
for his predicament. There had been many, many changes in the treatment (and there would be many, many more) because he insisted on an
almost impossible timeliness, an up-to-the-minute revising of the film
melodrama to jibe with the international headlines. Hitler's entrance into
Austria, England's declaration of war on Germany after the invasion of
Poland, the capitulation of Holland, Denmark, Belgium — these were
events past and yet to come that he at various times wanted reflected in
the screenplay, and this passion for topicality rendered most of the work
antique by the time it had returned from the typist.

The approach of the holidays and the enforced idleness caused Hitchcock considerable anxiety. He expected each morning to hear news of a bombing of London, and because direct communications between America and England were frequently disrupted and unreliable even at the best of times, he could not be sure how the daily uncertainties and the constant threat of danger affected his mother. Alma, on the other hand, simply wrote to her mother and sister and informed them that she would come to London as soon as she was allowed and bring them back to America. Her mother-in-law, however, was more stubborn. Mrs. Reville might be willing to pack up and relocate, but Mrs. Hitchcock had no intention of leaving Britain. She had been through a war twenty-five years earlier and survived that, and she would survive again. Coming to America was not even an open question.

At the same time, Hitchcock's countrymen were leaving California in sufficient numbers and returning for service of one sort or another. At age forty and weighing 365 pounds, active military duty was not an issue in any case. But how long could he remain in America if there was not a film in production? There was no doubt he could serve the cause of British propaganda and the British ideal by making films with a pro-British spirit and a British cast in America — others were doing as much, at the direct request of Churchill himself. But there was no fixed starting date, and the idea for such a film remained as unclear as the international situation. At Saint Cloud Road, he and Alma took an early draft of Wanger's script and began to work. Joan Harrison joined them daily, but all they seemed to produce was a series of sketches — some amusing, some bizarre — about a reporter's narrow escapes amid European turmoil. There was no focus to what they were doing.

For their daughter's sake, the Hitchcocks tried to make the first Christmas in America as festive as possible. There was a tree, and Alma invited the Gables for Christmas punch. Clark had just returned from the Atlanta premiere of *Gone With the Wind,* and Carole entertained the small gathering with outrageous imitations of the film's Southern gentry.

Gift-giving in Hollywood, as in so many business communities, is very much a political activity. Many feelings wait anxiously to be hurt, the better to have a good story for the next party; others draw up gift lists resembling copies of the telephone directory, the better to promote goodwill toward men, if not peace on earth. Wanger sent Hitchcock an opulent, ten-dollar box of fancy candies, and to Joan Harrison he delivered the same and a basket of liquor. From Hitchcock he received, with a mixture of amusement and annoyance, a sack of potatoes.

No one greeted 1940 optimistically, but after the holiday, Hitchcock realized that sitting at home with Alma and Joan was getting them nowhere. He thought that if he had Wanger engage a cast, things might move along; necessity would be the mother of invention. On January 4 Selznick had a call from his friend Wanger. If Selznick would loan Joan Fontaine for the lead in *Personal History,* Wanger and Hitchcock were ready to offer the leading roles to her and her husband Brian Aherne. A week later Wanger got his answer: the Ahernes were going on tour in *The Beaux' Stratagem.* Having promised Fontaine time to do a play, Selznick was going to wait, hoping to loan her out at a higher price after the opening of *Rebecca.*

But there was another reason for Selznick's refusal to help cast Wanger's film from his own list of players: he was angry. Wanger, to keep Hitchcock occupied and to get some work in return for the salary he was paying, had called the director in to the studio the first week of January to supervise retakes on Wanger's film *The House Across the Bay.* This was clearly outside the terms of their agreement. At the same time, Hitchcock had called Daniel O'Shea to ask if Selznick was receiving extra payment from Wanger for Hitchcock's work on this picture. If so, Hitchcock said, this was even more unfair than the 100 percent profit Selznick was already making off his services; Hitchcock wanted part of the revenue for his unexpected work. He was told the truth: no extra monies were being paid. For his part, Selznick felt a keen proprietary interest in Hitchcock's present and future, for he was certain that Hitchcock's fame in America was largely attributable to his own efforts as producer. In a letter to Frank Capra he wrote:

I suggest that you give particular attention to the case of Alfred Hitchcock, and decide for yourself whether any studio in your knowledge, in the entire history of the business, had ever given the publicity build-up to a director that I have given to Alfred Hitchcock, and the proof of this build-up is that whereas his agent could not get bids for him at the time I signed him, he is now in tremendous demand, despite the fact that his first picture since that time has not even been seen . . . and is not yet edited!

Anxious to keep Wanger in line with the contract, and equally eager to follow *Gone With the Wind* with the finished Hitchcock film, Selznick at once summoned Hitchcock back to Culver City for a week of retakes on *Rebecca.* By the first week of February, however, Hitchcock was back with Wanger, and after a fruitless meeting in which they pored over the collection of scripts that were gathering dust, Hitchcock asked Wanger to let the director's most valuable colleague from the English days come in to help salvage the script.

Charles Bennett was available, and he signed on to work for four weeks at $1,000 per week. He and Hitchcock, with Joan Harrison helping in the rearrangement of scenes and continuity, closeted themselves for eight hours daily the entire month of February. They began with little more than the Sheean title and the book's setting in Holland, but they agreed that the ingredients for success must be the ingredients of the most popular film they had done together, *The 39 Steps*. They went back to John Buchan's novel, extracted several chase scenes, and even found the inspiration for what became some of the new film's most famous elements — an innocent-looking mill as the cover for a nest of spies, and a secret landing place for enemy aircraft. But the new story was set in Holland. "We'll have the hero see a windmill turning against the wind," Hitchcock announced. "He'll know that's some kind of enemy signal."

With their old energies sparked, they were able to create lively and amusing scenes with astonishing rapidity. Their script for *Personal History* was not, as Wanger expected, developing as a piece of anti-Nazi, antiwar propaganda at all, but as a picaresque story, a romantic melodrama with considerable comic tone, about a somewhat dim-witted American journalist sent to cover the European situation in August 1939. He discovers an enemy plot to assassinate a Dutch diplomat, and falls in love with the daughter of an English pacifist, only to find that her father is the chief enemy spy.

And so the burden of a year of tension began to lift from Hitchcock's spirit — tension from a trip halfway round the world, from the relocation to a radically different culture and climate, from anxieties about Hollywood success and his domain within the Selznick empire, and perhaps even tension he felt as a result of his self-imposed isolation from the English movie community in America. For indeed, there was something special about that February. For a while, at least, it was the old, comfortable trio from London. It was as if they had all moved backward in time and were once again working together at Shepherd's Bush under Mick Balcon's liberal supervision. They knew they were going to compose a script about international espionage and world conflagration, but Hitchcock's own attitude that month was anything but anxious and tense. When they had temporary difficulty with the plot, they would make the American equivalent of their earlier sudden jaunts from London to Saint Moritz: they drove down, in Hitchcock's new Cadillac, to Palm Springs. They reminisced about lunch at Simpson's and daytrips on a Thames riverboat, about Switzerland and its apple wine, about Ivor Montagu and Sylvia Sidney, about weekends in Surrey, about the problems with Peter Lorre and the pleasures of *Young and Innocent*.

The only thing to disturb the atmosphere of clubby nostalgia was the inevitable and in this case swift realization that time had not, after all, been reversed. Their deepest feelings had changed about work and about ·

each other. Bennett had easily settled into California life and would soon direct as well as write. Joan Harrison was beginning to want a career of her own as a producer. They were too sharp a team to misinterpret this temporary reunion, to see it as the facile happy resolution in some mediocre Hollywood melodrama: that was a plot device they would never have appreciated, much less constructed.

It was the films themselves that had, in England, provided the reins of reality, for they had revealed the spiky edges of Hitchcock's view of human relations; their characters endured the collision of desire against duty that anguished his own soul. In a place and time wild with uncertainty, Alma and Joan and Bennett could be certain only that Hitchcock's confident control and his dark, detached vision would shape this new work, too. They had only to wait, only to listen.

*Personal History,* Hitchcock decided with Wanger's approval, would be even more lavish than *Rebecca,* with spectacular sets in dozens of diverse settings, and dramatic sequences approaching and even surpassing the scale of a De Mille epic. Wanger, who had arranged for the film to be made at the independently owned studios of Samuel Goldwyn, had promised him a freer hand than Selznick had allowed and had even said Hitchcock could have, within reason, the cast and crew of his choice. At once the director was determined to do something grand, something memorable that would compare favorably with any Selznick production.

The script was nearly complete by March 1. Bennett then had another commitment, and James Hilton, who had written the scripts for Garbo's *Camille,* and whose novels *Goodbye, Mr. Chips* and *Lost Horizon* had been turned into successful films, was brought in for a week (at a fee of $1,750) to polish the dialogue. At the same time, Hitchcock asked for and obtained the brilliant production designer William Cameron Menzies, who on February 29 had won the Academy Award for his work on *Gone With the Wind.* He met with Hitchcock and Rudolph Maté and began to prepare sketches. Maté was the ideal cinematographer. Born in Poland and raised in Hungary, he had worked for the great European filmmakers before emigrating to America. He had been responsible for, among other notable achievements, the photography of Carl Dreyer's *Passion of Joan of Arc* and *Vampyr,* of Fritz Lang's *Liliom* and, in Hollywood, of Wanger's productions of *Blockade* and *Trade Winds.*

The typical Hollywood script of the 1930s and 1940s contained forty or fifty master scenes, each of which had dialogue and action for one group of characters in one place — very like a theatrical script. The film director then worked out each scene as he went along, filming several long shots (or "cover shots") and repeated takes of each scene from different angles, in order to allow maximum freedom of choice and alteration in the editing stage later. But Hitchcock's finished script for *Personal History* had hundreds of scenes, each with precise specifications as to grouping, action, and camera position. On each page of the script, Hitchcock had designed a small panel representing the screen, with the figures, backgrounds, and actors carefully placed so that each movement was a small tableau quite by itself.

This work was supervised by art director Alexander Golitzen, who met daily with Hitchcock, Menzies, and Maté to discuss Hitchcock's unprecedented demands for almost one hundred three-sided sets, ranging from a massive city square in Amsterdam, to a three-tiered interior of a windmill, to the cabins of an airliner that crashes into the sea. For each of hundreds of scenes, detailed blueprints were drawn up, and from them, floor plans and detailed lists of props were assembled. Because the film was budgeted at $35,000 per day, no time could be wasted once filming began.

In advance of the first day's shooting, the director and his chief assistants met with more than a score of artists and supervised the work of 558 carpenters, electricians, plumbers, and property men, plus engineers and a wide variety of technicians. This enormous crew was astounded at Hitchcock's intimate knowledge of every technical aspect of film — although the property and wardrobe supervisors wondered how they would keep the sets and costumes clean for the windmill sequence: Hitchcock had ordered one hundred birds. The scene (photographed during the first week of shooting in mid-March) already seemed complicated enough, with the mill's huge interlocking wheels and narrow staircases, not to mention the heavy and dangerous construction cranes for carrying the camera and its operator up and around the walls and actors.

While Wanger, Hitchcock, and Joan Harrison were completing casting, Alma was preparing to leave for England to fetch her mother and sister. Eager to capitalize on her trip, Selznick asked if she would be willing to stay an extra week, meet his London staff, and greet the press for interviews before the English release of *Rebecca*. She agreed when Selznick sent over an extraordinarily generous check for $5,000 to cover all her traveling expenses and those of her family.

Unlike Selznick, Wanger was content to leave Hitchcock alone at his work. Hitchcock had not felt this kind of trust since his days with Michael Balcon. Wanger allowed him final cast approval, as well as control over production design, camera requirements, and even, almost to the very end, the final cut. But there were two problems the film faced all though the shooting (which lasted from March 18 until May 29): Wanger's insistence on adjusting the picture to the daily news headlines, and the burden inherent in the unprecedented number of lavish, expensive, and gigantic sets, both exterior and interior.

During filming, several important events marked the spread of the war in Europe, and with the announcement of each, Wanger called Hitchcock to ask if there was some way the news could be integrated into the scenario. On April 9 Germany invaded Norway and Denmark, and then, on May 10, Belgium and Holland; on May 14 the Dutch surrendered, followed, on May 28, by the Belgians; the fall of Paris was predicted, and that occurred on June 10, while Hitchcock was busy with retakes and first editing. Yes, he replied most often to the producer's inquiries, it would be possible to make some minor adjustments . . . and then, as usual, he went his own way; and Wanger, dropping in to see the rushes of a day's shooting, would naively congratulate Hitchcock on the timeliness of the script, while Hitchcock kept a straight face. The finished film (except for the last minute) has about as much to do with the politics of the war as *Tosca* has to do with Napoleon's campaign in Italy: the historical setting provides a distant background for a personal story of adventure, love, and betrayal.

Wanger was especially excited about Hitchcock's handling of the grand sets, which included a 600-by-125-foot mock-up of Waterloo Station (crowded with five hundred extras in tailored English summer clothes and used for but a few seconds of film time); the detailed facsimile of the Amsterdam public square (on a ten-acre set that cost $200,000 and, because the action was designed to occur in a rainstorm, necessitated the diversion of the Colorado River and the construction of an elaborate sewer system); the interior and exterior of an airplane with four motors, a 120-foot wingspread, and an 84-foot fuselage (which alone cost $160,000, and which was, for the crash into the sea, suspended by wires in an enormous studio tank in which actors floundered while hidden blades churned the waters of the "ocean"); and the 80-foot windmill, with its vast intermeshing mechanism.

Hitchcock's cast served him well, although he later insisted: "I would have liked to have bigger star names. . . . I went to Gary Cooper with it, but because it was a thriller, he turned it down. . . . I always ended up with the next best — in this instance, with Joel McCrea. Many years later Gary Cooper said to me, 'That was a mistake. I should have done it.' " Laraine Day, young and dark-haired, acted with an easy warmth and a natural, professional timing that contributed to what remains one of the most underrated characterizations in the body of Hitchcock's work, but the filmmaker showed little interest in directing her or developing her role. When he was satisfied with the camera setups, in fact, he usually dozed during a long take — especially if the shooting occurred after lunch.

"Hitchcock," Joel McCrea remembered, "had a habit of drinking a pint of champagne at lunch. After lunch one day, there was a long scene with me just standing there and talking. When the scene was over I expected to hear 'Cut!' and I looked over and there was Hitchcock snoring with his lips sticking out. He had fallen asleep. So I said, 'Cut!' and he woke up and said, 'Was it any good?' I said, 'The best in the picture!' and he said, 'Print it!' "

But later in the filming the director paid McCrea more attention: during the watery scenes in the large studio tank, Hitchcock ordered several retakes of the shots in which McCrea and George Sanders dive from an airplane wing. When McCrea protested that this was an expensive waste of so many suits from the wardrobe department, he (like Peter Lorre years earlier) received a new outfit from Hitchcock — in child's size.

Only one among the cast received the director's quiet admiration: Albert Basserman. Probably the greatest classical actor in prewar Germany, Basserman was forced, with his Jewish wife, to flee the Nazis in 1933. His friend Ernst Lubitsch persuaded him to accept a small part in *Dr. Ehrlich's Magic Bullet* in 1939; and in *Foreign Correspondent* (as *Personal History* was retitled on April 8), his second American film, his performance as the Dutch diplomat was delivered with great dignity at the age of seventy-three. As for Robert Benchley, who played the tippling journalist in London, Hitchcock was delighted to have him write his own dialogue, which capitalized on the public's familiarity with Benchley's elegant, self-parodied sarcasm.

At the same time, one of the most charming and overt personal touches found its way into Hitchcock's script additions to *Foreign Correspondent:* the proposal of marriage aboard ship during a North Sea storm. The scene between McCrea and Day is very like Hitchcock's proposal to Alma fifteen years earlier, and the disarmingly forthright, cliché-free dialogue could have come right from them:

MC CREA: I'm in love with you and I want to marry you.

DAY: I'm in love with *you,* and I want to marry *you.*

MC CREA: Hmmm . . . That cuts down our love scene quite a bit, doesn't it? . . . How do you think your father will feel?

DAY: I think father will be delighted.

While Hitchcock was at work for Wanger on *Foreign Correspondent,* Selznick was discussing various possibilities for lending him out once again. Hal Wallis, then in charge of production at Warner Brothers, was the first to try to deal with Selznick: it was his plan to have Hitchcock direct *The Constant Nymph* with Laurence Olivier and Vivien Leigh. In addition, there was talk of Hitchcock going to Universal to direct Margaret Sullavan in *Back Street;* or to MGM, for *A Woman's Face,* with Joan Crawford, and *Escape,* with Norma Shearer.

Meanwhile, Selznick held fast to the terms of his renewable option on Hitchcock's services, and on June 24 a new contract was signed: Hitchcock would receive $2,750 per week (a raise of $250) and there would be a $15,000 bonus if two pictures were completed in one year. On the day of signing, Selznick told Hitchcock that he might very well decide to produce a remake of *The Lodger* (the rights to which had been purchased by Hitchcock himself).* Selznick's idea was to cast Jean Gabin and either Joan Fontaine or Ingrid Bergman. Hitchcock was indifferent except to the proposal of Bergman, and Selznick dropped the idea almost at once. Three days later, he reached an agreement with Harry E. Edington, executive producer at RKO Radio Studios: Hitchcock would be sent to RKO for a year to direct two pictures, beginning in September 1940.

It is not entirely surprising that Hitchcock again agreed to a renewal of the Selznick deal. First of all, the option right originally negotiated by Selznick remained in legal force: Hitchcock was in effect bound for a minimum of five pictures, five years service, or both (although, had he really desired, Hitchcock could have been freed from this obligation). But it was also clear that Selznick, uncertain that he could maintain the high standards of *Gone With the Wind* and *Rebecca,* was becoming dependent on lending out his stars and directors as he was himself going into a kind of producer's hibernation during the war. This meant that Hitchcock would be working for other producers and studios in any case — and if others would be as cordial and as liberal as Wanger, Hitchock was effectively his own producer. "I was lucky," he reflected, "because I was always being loaned out to other studios and I was always my own boss." Although Selznick was making great amounts of money by selling him to other studios, and although this caused Hitchock understandable irritation, the prospect of creative freedom attracted him as much as financial compensation.

With *Foreign Correspondent* almost ready to premiere, Hitchcock de-

---

*Although after *Rebecca* Selznick lent Hitchcock to other studios without interruption until 1944, he occasionally flirted with ideas for another Hitchcock picture at his own studio even before *Spellbound*. Under consideration at various times, in addition to *The Lodger,* were remakes of *The Man Who Knew Too Much* and *The 39 Steps,* as well as *A Bill of Divorcement, The Woman in White, Little Men, Tom Brown's School Days, Bird of Paradise, Symphony of Six Million, What Price Hollywood,* and *The Lost Squadron.*

cided, now that Alma had returned and settled her mother and sister in California, to make a quick trip to his own mother, simultaneously hoping and fearing that she would accept a similar invitation to immigrate. On June 27 he stopped in New York to meet with RKO executives and add stipulations to his contract: Joan Harrison, who was along on the trip, would assist him in any RKO film, and he would have his new secretary, Carol Stevens, on the payroll as well. At the same time it was agreed that his first project for RKO would be a film based on Francis Iles's novel *Before the Fact*. It turned out, however, to be the second.

In England, Hitchcock found his mother as indomitable and stubborn as ever, although he was saddened to see how, in less than a year and a half, she had developed ailments and seemed to have aged dramatically. She was seventy-seven, and her slowness alarmed him. She flatly refused to consider relocating to America. "Travel," she insisted, "is a nasty business." She did agree, however, to give up her London flat and move down to the cottage he had retained in Shamley Green, adjacent to Winter's Grace. If there were to be air strikes against England, she would certainly be safer there. And he was glad when his brother William agreed to move to Guildford to be near their mother.

Hitchcock and Joan then visited her mother, made the rounds of London theaters and bookshops, and returned to Hollywood on July 3, just days before the first bombs fell on England.

It was in fact that dark turn in the fortunes of the English people that was curiously predicted by the conclusion of *Foreign Correspondent*. As it had been originally written, the last scene was to have shown McCrea and Sanders en route to America after their airplane had been shot down by a German ship.

MC CREA: The German government will have to answer for this.

SANDERS: Documents will undoubtedly be found, old boy, proving that it is a British trawler disguised as a German battleship, and the whole thing has been organized by the pirate, Churchill, to drag America into the war.

But Hitchcock returned from England with the news that everyone was speaking about an imminent bombing. Wanger heard of this and, true to form, wanted to change the ending of the film. Theater bookings were scheduled for mid–August, however, and Hitchcock was due at RKO. What could be done?

Hitchcock told Wanger that the only solution was Ben Hecht — playwright, novelist, and probably Hollywood's quickest screenwriter — the man most responsible for saving producers' problem films. Most of the seventy motion pictures for which he received credit (most notably *De-*

sign for Living, Twentieth Century, Crime Without Passion, Viva Villa!, Barbary Coast, Nothing Sacred, Gunga Din, Wuthering Heights) were written in less than three weeks, and on more than fifty others he worked without screen credit but for handsome compensation — up to $125,000 for each (among them Back Street, Queen Christina, The Hurricane, and Gone With the Wind, which, according to some historians, he virtually saved single-handedly).

In one day, after a meeting with Wanger and Hitchcock, Hecht turned in a revised ending, and McCrea, Day, and a few extras were summoned for the filming of the new conclusion. There was no doubt that it was a hastily added scene, dramatically unjustified, out of character and out of line with everything that had preceded. The film as it had been constructed occurred over a two-week period, from August 20 to September 3, 1939, the day England declared war on Germany. The new ending leaped to the now imminently anticipated future, with the bombing of London raging outside a radio studio and McCrea at the microphone:

Hello, America! I've been watching a part of the world being blown to pieces. A part of the world as nice as Vermont and Ohio, Virginia, California and Illinois, lies ripped up and bleeding like a steer in a slaughter house. And I've seen things that make the history of the savages look like Pollyanna legend. . . .
[Bombs are heard outside and the electricity is cut off.]
I can't read the rest of the speech I have because all the lights have gone out, so I'll just have to talk off the cuff. All that noise you hear isn't static. It's death coming to London. Yes, they're coming here now. You can hear the bombs falling on the streets and in the homes. Don't tune me out! Hang on — this is a big story, and you're part of it. It's too late now to do anything except stand in the dark and let them come. It feels as if the lights are all out everywhere — except in America.
[The American national anthem is heard in the background from this point through the final roll of credits, at which point it surges up in a mighty chorus.]
Keep those lights burning! Cover them with steel, ring them with guns! Build a canopy of battleships and bombing planes around them. Hello, America! Hang onto your lights! They're the only lights left in the world!

Like Charles Chaplin's impassioned plea at the end of The Great Dictator (made the same year), Foreign Correspondent breaks the rules of dramatic logic and structure to make its political and social point. But the ending does not urge American entry into the war: it urges military readiness and vigilance against the forces of war, and in fact Wanger, Hecht, and Hitchcock were careful to observe the Production

Code's insistence that Germany not be specified, and that American war activity not be encouraged. Defense and vigilance, however, were other matters, and the ending begged for these. *Foreign Correspondent*'s last scene, filmed on July 5, 1940, was a tragic example of art predicting life: the first German bombs fell on England just five days later.

The news worsened on Hitchcock's forty-first birthday. He awoke the morning of August 13 to hear that the Battle of Britain had begun in earnest, and that there was a terrible air war over England. Initial attempts to contact his family were fruitless, as all communications into England were disrupted. For the next several days he was in a quiet state of terror and did not leave the house. Publicity people from the Wanger offices and the Hollywood press corps were eager for interviews regarding *Foreign Correspondent,* however, and he finally had to break his nervous isolation. But he did not rest, nor was he an easy companion at home or with his colleagues until at last he found out that his mother was quite safe, and that Surrey was, so far, intact.

In addition, his anxiety was aggravated by the criticism that began to come from England. The British press and a significant portion of the film and theater community unleashed a storm of protest against Hitchcock, Victor Saville, and others of their countrymen who were safely employed in America while Britain fought off the Nazi menace in a terrifying air war. Word of the jubilant New York premiere of *Foreign Correspondent* (on Tuesday, August 27, at the reopened and refurbished Rivoli Theater) was little consolation for Hitchcock: two days earlier, Michael Balcon's angry remarks about him had appeared in London, and on Monday they were reprinted in America.

Hitchcock's former employer had called him a deserter along with all "who prefer to remain in Hollywood instead of returning home to aid their country's war efforts." Hitchcock, in fact, was the only one he referred to in particular: "I had a plump young junior technician in my studios whom I promoted from department to department. Today he is one of our most famous directors and he is in Hollywood while we who are left behind short-handed are trying to harness the films to our great national effort."

Angry and hurt, Hitchcock struck back.

Balcon's view is colored by his own personal experiences with Hollywood, which have invariably wound up unfortunately for Balcon. He's a permanent Donald Duck. We have all placed ourselves at the disposal of our government. By what authority does this man take this attitude? I can only regard it as his personal feeling. The British government has only to call upon me for my services. The manner in which I am helping my country is not Mr. Balcon's

business and has nothing to do with patriotic ideals. Mr. Balcon apparently
hates Hollywood. I can only put his remarks down as personal jealousy. How
else could he be so unintelligent?

In fact there was little Hitchcock could have done even if he had
caught the first available flight back to London. He was ineligible for
active military service, and any good he could do for the British cause
as a propagandist or craftsman was better done in America, where film
studios were still busy. In addition, Balcon was unaware, or chose to
ignore, the open secret of Churchill's support of British filmmakers in
America: Hollywood's product was one of the most effective weapons
of propaganda in galvanizing America's sympathies toward England.

At the same time, Hitchcock had other professional concerns that made
him irritable. He appeared on the radio as co-host of a special program
about immigrant directors, and he remarked openly that he needed the
compensation he would receive from the broadcast "because of extraordinary relocation expenses" he had incurred in Los Angeles. He also
said there was a possibility he would return to London to make a film
about General James Wolfe, the British hero of Quebec. This he probably mentioned for Selznick's benefit, for he knew that the last-minute
decision to lend him to RKO for the next two films indicated the likely
prospect of similar future decisions — decisions that would prevent
Hitchcock from planning for specific projects in advance and deprive
him of the opportunity to carefully prepare his scripts.

Hitchcock also let it be known around Hollywood that he felt he should
share not only the credit but some of the cash profits Selznick was making on the sudden stardom of Joan Fontaine. Selznick was furious.
"Hitchcock had better not make himself ridiculous by any such statements," Selznick wrote in a memo to Daniel O'Shea,

in view of the fact that too many people saw the Fontaine tests for *Rebecca*
many, many weeks before Hitchcock ever arrived in Hollywood [a "fact" not
consistent with the truth, as Hitchcock, if not O'Shea, certainly would have
known] . . . that our option agreements with Fontaine were signed long before
Hitchcock arrived in Hollywood . . . that many of the people who saw [screen
tests made by director John Cromwell] to this day think that she was better
under Cromwell than under Hitchcock . . . and finally that, carrying out
Hitchcock's idea to a logical conclusion, we should assume that Hitchcock is
sending a weekly check to Micky Balcon, who developed Hitch!

By the beginning of September, *Foreign Correspondent* was receiving enthusiastic notices and gratifying box-office receipts around the
country. Hitchcock returned from its Canadian premiere and at once

began shooting the first film under the RKO deal. *Before the Fact* was postponed, for it looked to be a difficult script project. Instead, Hitchcock began a picture that, for the rest of his life, he said he never wanted to make — claiming that he had undertaken it simply as a favor to his friend Carole Lombard (who had just gone over to RKO also) and that he had no feeling for its genre, the screwball comedy (of which it was one of the last popular examples).

The RKO archives tell a different story, however. It was true that he wanted very much to work with Lombard. But it is also true that he was wild about this particular idea. "I want to direct a typical American comedy about typical Americans," he said the first week of shooting. And he was even more enthusiastic than Lombard was about the original story and screenplay by Norman Krasna that had been bought by the studio in November 1939. It concerned a married couple, very devoted but given to endless fighting, who discover after many years that, owing to a geographical technicality, their marriage had not been legal. The ultrathin story line followed them through a stereotypical plot: husband loses, fights for, and wins back snappy, proud wife.

Krasna had submitted the script without a title (although he had contracted for a treatment under the name *No for an Answer*), and by the time Lombard had read and agreed to do it, the property had been variously called *Who Was That Lady I Seen You With?*, *And So to Wed*, *Here We Go Again!*, *The Lady Said No!*, *Some Call It Love*, *Two of a Kind*, *That Was My Wife!*, *Return Engagement*, *Temporarily Yours*, *Dangerous but Passable*, and *Slightly Married* — all rather sophomoric variations on the typical marital-comedy titles of the time. Finally the studio decided on *Mr. and Mrs. Smith*, and on Hitchcock as director because Lombard and he begged to do it.

When Lombard and Hitchcock could not secure Cary Grant to play opposite her, they considered virtually every leading man in Hollywood, from Fredric March to George Brent; just a week before shooting, a contract was signed with the amiable Robert Montgomery, who was to receive $110,000 for eight weeks' work — $40,000 more than Hitchcock received for more than twice that time.

Filming began on September 5 and continued until November 2. Selznick had his staff keep in constant contact with Harry Edington, and Daniel O'Shea reported that "Hitchcock has been bearing down on the cost of *Mr. and Mrs. Smith* in order to demonstrate to the world after *Rebecca* and *Foreign Correspondent* that he is not only a great director but a reasonably priced one."

During production, Carole Lombard, well aware of Hitchcock's reputation on the set, was full of practical jokes herself. Responding to the rumor that he referred to actors as cattle, she set up a corral on the stage the first day of shooting and brought in three heifers, which stomped and mooed, bearing on neck tags the names of the three principal actors. She also kept up a running political gag with Montgomery. As the November presidential election approached, she increased her enthusiastic support of Franklin Roosevelt while Montgomery continued to endorse Wendell Willkie. After Montgomery had parked his car in the lot each morning, Lombard sneaked out and pasted Roosevelt stickers to the fenders; Montgomery painstakingly removed them each night, and she cheerfully reapplied a new batch the next day. They never mentioned what they both knew, nor did it spoil the friendly atmosphere of their work together.

A comparison of Norman Krasna's completed screenplay with the final film reveals the interesting details added at Hitchcock's explicit demand; as always, they are markers of motifs in his personal life. During filming, he and Alma made plans to resume celebrating their December 2 wedding anniversary with a holiday to Saint Moritz, a custom that had been interrupted for the previous several years. The trip seems to have been something of a peace offering from Hitchcock to his wife, who had had very little to do on the first three American films — and although she appeared to her acquaintances quite happy to be running the house, spending time with Pat, and reading novels for potential screenplay material, there was no doubt that she was, as one actress said, decidedly second to Joan Harrison in Hitchcock's professional lineup.

But he assured Alma that they would return to Saint Moritz for the first two weeks of December, and in fact he memorialized that promise in his alterations to the final scenes of *Mr. and Mrs. Smith,* in which Robert Montgomery, feigning unconsciousness, mumbles not once but four times: "We'll go away the first two weeks in December . . . Playing in the snow, we'll have a lot of fun . . . The first two weeks in December, we'll go away to that ski resort . . . yes, the first two weeks in December." Earlier in the script, Hitchcock added a pointed reference to the setting of his own marriage proposal — a proposal whose consequences seem to have been very much on his mind in 1940. "Remember how sick you were on that night boat?" Montgomery asks Lombard, and the dialogue recalls Alma's condition the night of her husband's shipboard proposal fifteen years earlier.

More perversely, Hitchcock also created the odd scene in which Gene Raymond, Lucile Watson, and Philip Merivale retreat to an office bathroom for a private discussion. Their conversation is made difficult by a noisy flushing toilet on the floor above. Hitchcock had been warned by

RKO that the Hollywood Production Code was quite strict about the sight and sound of the toilet, believing that device too indelicate for the American screen. But Hitchcock took the risk, and the sound editor had only to distort the noise so that it could be heard as banging steam-pipes. The filmmaker would take his vengeance twenty years later when in *Psycho,* he pushed his iconoclastic, schoolboy perversity to its bath-room limit by photographing in some detail the action and sound of a toilet. (And at least once in his later life, he presented friends with what he considered the ultimate in refinement and luxury — a noiseless toilet for their guest bathroom.)

But most personally in *Mr. and Mrs. Smith* (and perhaps most sub-consciously so) is the first occurrence in a Hitchcock film of an appar-ently idle remark that would be inserted into subsequent films with an obsessive insistence. Justifying the drinking of a beakerful of brandy, Lombard says to Raymond: "This isn't alcohol — it's medicine. It kills the germs. All in one gulp, now!" In a dozen films, from *Mr. and Mrs. Smith* to *Vertigo* (where James Stewart, urging a glass of brandy, says to Kim Novak, "Here, Judy, drink this straight down — it's just like medicine"), the dialogue is punctuated with the classic validating ex-cuse that Hitchcock's off-screen companions heard so often: "It isn't alcohol, it's like medicine!" And in one gulp, a Hitchcock cocktail disappeared. As everyone knew who lunched or dined with him, espe-cially in the privacy of his home, he preferred this medicine to any other.

Despite Hitchcock's intentions, the trip to Saint Moritz had to be postponed to another year: European travel was not advisable that De-cember. But Selznick, knowing the Hitchcocks' disappointment and as capable as anyone of a sudden generous impulse, invited them to an-other anniversary celebration — a party in Atlanta to mark the first birthday of *Gone With the Wind.* Since the proceeds from this event were marked for the British War Relief Fund, Hitchcock would be a most appropriate guest. Besides, Selznick might have reasoned, his presence could not hurt the publicity campaign the producer was waging in anticipation of the upcoming Academy Awards: *Rebecca* had been nominated in no less than eleven categories. But this anniversary fete was spoiled too — by bad weather, which grounded the Hitchcocks' plane in Louisville and prevented their arrival for the Atlanta festivities. They returned to Saint Cloud Road weary from a fruitless trip and wor-ried about the health of Alma's mother, who had just settled in Holly-wood when she was taken suddenly and desperately ill.

The Hitchcocks' only holiday consolation that year was the report on an East Coast sneak preview of *Mr. and Mrs. Smith:* on December 30, an audience in New Rochelle, New York, rated it — along with *Rebecca* and *Foreign Correspondent* — one of the best films of the year (a judgment not shared by later generations of moviegoers). When it opened at Radio City Music Hall on January 20, 1941, it brightened a dreary winter, sold out the first nine days, and sealed the American audience's love affair with Hitchcock and his sense of humor. "The striking thing about this film," commented *Look* magazine, "is that Hitchcock has employed the same strategy that marks his blood-chilling melodramas. . . . Here again are his unmistakable touches — the same casual approach, the same pell-mell finish, the same corner-of-the-eye viewpoint, the same direction by indirection. The net effect is the same, too: another Alfred Hitchcock hit."

But before long, the joy would begin to go sour. There would soon be deaths on both sides of the family. Some were expected and merciful; at least one was shocking and mysterious. But none of them, as they might have feared, was due to the spreading war.

# Nine

---

## 1941–1944

ENGLISH novelist Anthony Berkeley Cox, who in 1932 had written *Before the Fact* (under the pseudonym Francis Iles), had sold all rights to the book to RKO three years later. When Hitchcock discussed film projects with Harry Edington in June 1940, he at once selected it. It was a bizarre story of a woman so fanatically in love with her husband that she lives with the knowledge that he is an embezzler, a philanderer, and then a murderer. Finally, she discovers that he is planning to kill her, and at the same time she finds she is pregnant. Feeling that her husband "must not reproduce himself," she leaves a suicide note, then calmly drinks the poisoned milk he offers her, and dies. Hitchcock not only liked the weird psychological angle about obsession and death, he also felt the English setting would justify an English cast — a film, in other words, that would keep the British home fires burning in America.

RKO had tried to produce a film version since 1935. Emlyn Williams was originally asked to do a script, and Louis Hayward was to play the charming villain. In 1939 RKO approached Robert Montgomery and Geraldine Fitzgerald; but then Olivier wanted to do it, and newcomer Maureen O'Hara was to play opposite him. In May 1940, while Hitchcock was finishing *Foreign Correspondent*, the trade papers reported RKO's misgivings about casting Olivier as a murderer, and when Hitchcock spoke to Edington in June, he said that he, Alma, and Joan would revise the story by making the husband's deeds the fictions in the mind of a neurotically suspicious woman.

It is important to emphasize this single point, because Hitchcock always insisted that the situation was quite different: he wanted, he said for years afterward, to follow the novel faithfully. But this idea did not occur to him at the time, for it cannot be found in the first treatment he submitted to RKO, and it is contradicted by memos in which he stated emphatically that he wanted to make a film about a woman's fantasy life. By December 1940 he and Alma and Joan had done what they could with the scenario (having consulted, among other drafts, one submitted by Nathanael West just before his death that month), and Hitchcock asked that RKO engage playwright and screenwriter Samson Raphaelson to collaborate.

The choice of Raphaelson might seem odd for a British story, since Raphaelson was an American who had to that time been best known for his play *The Jazz Singer* (which became the first American sound feature in 1927) and for several successful scripts written for and with Ernst Lubitsch. He himself observed: "Hitchcock's material was never very close to mine. I was more comfortable with Lubitsch's style and tone." But he accepted the invitation to work with Hitchcock, and there was great cordiality and mutual respect during the weeks of work from late December to early March. On their own, however, Alma and Joan were adding scenes to Hitchcock's specifications. By late March the scenario was hopelessly tangled, a mixture of mood and style and motivation that could never sort itself out on film. "Perhaps this explains," Raphaelson said, "why the picture has less of the Hitchcock insignia than any of his pictures — there is no distinguishing scene of the kind for which he's famous, no carousel or national monument or brilliant set piece."

The production, a far less lavish film than either *Rebecca* or *Foreign Correspondent* (and shot entirely in the studio), took longer to film than either of those great spectacles. Shooting began on February 10, 1941, and dragged on until July 24. Joan Fontaine, whom Hitchcock and RKO borrowed from Selznick, was somewhat more confident after she received good notices for *Rebecca,* but there was not a very warm working relationship between her and Cary Grant, who was signed to play the irresponsible husband. Contributing even more to the daily problems was a sudden shift in Hitchcock's mood. He had greatly enjoyed making *Mr. and Mrs. Smith,* and he expected, with Fontaine and Grant, to whip up an elegant psychological thriller. But what began in earnest optimism quickly turned sour.

First there was the problem of the film's title. At the time it was customary for studios to engage George Gallup to poll the nation's moviegoers on their responses to proposed titles. He reported that *Before the Fact* had a lukewarm reaction. Hitchcock's first choice was *Fright,* RKO's was *Suspicious Lady,* and soon Gallup was testing fifty other titles.* Hitchcock felt that the lack of a definite title gave the production an atmosphere of the haphazard and a lack of focus — attitudes he shunned at all cost and energy. In spite of his annoyed appeals, the studio refused to decide. A few days before the film's release in November, the executives finally agreed on a name Hitchcock had clung to since early summer: *Suspicion,* which he picked up from the second paragraph of the novel ("Suspicion is a tenuous thing, so impalpable that the exact moment of its birth is not easy to determine . . . .").

Also, Hitchcock's own suspicion that the cast and crew were disenchanted was aggravated by his discovery that his cameraman, Harry Stradling (who had worked for him on *Jamaica Inn* and *Mr. and Mrs. Smith*), had been asked by RKO to photograph a second film at the same time. Never able to sustain signs of divided loyalties or energies, Hitchcock stormed into Harry Edington's office and threatened to stop directing unless he could be guaranteed Stradling's single-minded attention to storyboard sketches and set designs. "I have a raving maniac on my hands with Hitchcock!" Edington wrote in a memo. After a week, Stradling was taken off the second project and turned over to a still-pouting Hitchcock.

But the problems continued to multiply. No one had any clear idea how the picture would end. Not only was this completely foreign to Hitchcock's method, it also threw the actors into complete confusion, for no scene or line of dialogue had a sure purpose. For the first time in years, Hitchcock fell ill, and shooting was canceled for more than a week. He returned exhausted and depressed, and Joan Fontaine began to complain about his disinterest in her and the picture. "Hitchcock does not appear to be giving as close attention to this picture as he should be," one of Edington's staff reported, "and we have good cause to worry about the quality of this production. As a matter of fact, Joan Fontaine has indicated that Hitchcock has not been so exacting on his requirements for her as he was in *Rebecca*." The turmoil then caused Joan Fontaine several bouts of indisposition, and things were so bleak that by April 18 there was talk of canceling the film altogether.

All during this time Alma and Joan worked feverishly on various endings. One possibility was for Cary Grant, in a sudden gesture of uncharacteristic heroism, to join the Royal Air Force to atone for his thievery. This resolution, rightly abandoned, had him dying in an attitude of penance and patriotism, and avoided the problem of a final murder or suicide. By early May the studio realized that in order to recoup

---

*Among the most amusing possibilities were *Search for Tomorrow, Sable Wings, Last Lover, Men Make Poor Husbands, Romantic Scapegrace, Love in Irons, Girl in the Vise.*

the substantial and unexpected costs expended so far RKO would have to release the film quickly and widely — preferably before the summer.

But Hitchcock demanded more time — and a good thing, too, for by the middle of July there was still no ending for the film. They hoped, at one late point, to surmount the censor's objection to the pregnant wife's deliberate suicide by adding a scene in which Fontaine had illicit meetings with another man (suicide was occasionally permitted by the Production Code as the tactic of a sinner). But as it often is, the power of the sneak preview was considerable: when the still-untitled film was screened in Pasadena with this ending and the audience laughed, Hitchcock and his cast had to shoot still more footage. Alma and Joan devised a new ending, but the variants were so numerous by this time that no one was quite sure what kind of story they were telling. The final decision was to reveal that Fontaine's suspicion was based on her own neurosis and that Grant was innocent of everything except foolishness and fiscal irresponsibility.

On August 19 the scoring and dubbing were at last complete, and a November release date was set. Everyone was nervous, and Hitchcock was ready to disclaim the picture.

To everyone's surprise, however, audiences loved the film, although critics were divided by the revelation that everything was the wife's fantasy and that the husband was little more than a spendthrift. "This is a far finer film than *Rebecca,*" wrote Howard Barnes in the *Herald Tribune* on November 21. "The climax is altogether acceptable. . . . Hitchcock has made another brilliant film in *Suspicion.*" But over at the *New York Times,* Bosley Crowther was not so enthusiastic. "The ending is not up to Mr. Hitchcock's usual style. . . . Still, he has managed to bring through a tense and exciting tale, a psychological thriller which is packed with lively suspense." The public's love affair with Joan Fontaine continued undiminished, and for this performance she later received the Academy Award as best actress.

All this time, David Selznick was keeping careful watch over the director and star he had lent out, aware that the success of their work at RKO greatly affected their future drawing power with him. In January he was so disturbed by Joan Fontaine's radio performance in *Waterloo Bridge* that he drafted a letter to Hitchcock. She had adopted an English accent for the role, and Selznick complained that it sounded ridiculously forced; if she tried to maintain it with Hitchcock, it would badly affect their film.

"You will be criticized for not having stopped it," he wrote, "and Joan's career will be materially damaged. I am therefore writing you quite selfishly, but with the conviction that it is in your interests too.'' But Daniel O'Shea prevailed on Selznick to discuss the actress's accent and tone in person with Hitchcock, and not to send the letter: Hitchcock was sure to show it to Fontaine, he said, since he was well known to delight in fanning resentments.

Selznick, of course, continued to be protective about Hitchcock, and he took every opportunity to remind people that the director was under exclusive contract to David O. Selznick. When together, the men enjoyed a cordial relationship, regularly exchanging gifts and praise and good wishes. But Selznick knew he had to keep close watch on Hitchcock's working habits when they were apart. As *Suspicion* moved toward completion, Selznick was eager to start Hitchcock's next project, for he was paying him weekly. He lined up John Houseman, who had worked with Orson Welles and the Mercury Theater from 1937 through the production of *Citizen Kane,* to work on a film idea for Hitchcock. ''I think we ought to get Hitchcock started on his next story before he starts on whatever vacation you may be giving him,'' Selznick wrote to O'Shea. ''In this way work can proceed on the story while he is still on vacation. . . . Would you please organize it with Hitchcock and with Houseman as soon as Hitchcock finishes at RKO?''*

After the loan-outs to Wanger and RKO, Selznick seriously considered bringing Hitchcock back to his own studio to direct. *Three Faces East, The White Feather, The Song of the Dragon, The Man in Half Moon Street,* and *The Woman in White* were properties he considered for Hitchcock and Ingrid Bergman, but John Houseman was keen on teaming them in a film of Stefan Zweig's *Letter from an Unknown Woman.* Selznick, acting on the astute advice of Kay Brown, replied that this was not Hitchcock's kind of material. (Houseman later produced the film himself, hiring his friend Joan Fontaine to star and Max Ophuls to direct.) Val Lewton, also on Selznick's staff at the time, was given the task of trying to package Charles Boyer and *Les Misérables* for Hitchcock to direct, and Mary Pickford and *The Bat.* For his part, Lewton — who was not trying to be amusing — thought Hitchcock could be put to good use directing *Treasure Island.* He was not keen on Hitchcock as a storyteller: ''I think the Hitchcock-type of story fundamentally wrong, and that we need something better and more substantial than the old-fashioned chase pictures which he turns out when left to his own devices.''

---

*Selznick was not so proprietary about Hitchcock that he could not help a good cause, however. He readily agreed to a request that Hitchcock direct a few sequences of a short nonprofit film in support of the Anglo-American volunteer charities. No further information about this project has survived.

The most interesting idea under serious consideration in the spring of
1941 was an original story Hitchcock told Selznick at dinner one evening. It was, Selznick noted, ''a very interesting, if rather erotic story
that he thought would be wonderful for Ingrid Bergman, and that I think
he would like to direct. He says Joan Harrison has the whole story
which is based on the true account of a couple that were kidnapped by
brigands. The young wife of a military attaché or something of the sort,
and a close male friend, after being kidnapped, were chained together
by Chinese brigands for six months. I can understand the appeal of this
to Hitchcock.'' At the same time, Selznick, Hitchcock, Harrison, Kay
Brown and others thought about remaking *The Lodger* and *The Man
Who Knew Too Much,* and Gaumont-British realized a hefty profit by
selling Selznick the rights.

In June Selznick exercised the option on Hitchcock's contract for a
third year, and Hitchcock agreed to make one picture over a twenty-
week period at a salary now increased to $3,000 per week. Since 1939
Hitchcock had received from Selznick a total of $354,375 in salary and
bonuses. This was no small compensation for a little over two years of
work, but when Hitchcock learned of certain other payments that were
being made, he was not impressed with his own: Selznick had cleared
$130,000 for the Wanger and RKO loan-outs; Cary Grant was paid
$112,500 for *Suspicion,* and Joan Fontaine $69,750. When he considered the efforts expended, he found remarkable imbalances. Players
were getting as much as $15,000 per week while he was paid $2,750.
It seemed unfair, and it was.

The issue of fairness might also have occurred to Hitchcock in February, when the Academy Awards for the films of 1940 were presented.
Over *The Grapes of Wrath, The Great Dictator, The Long Voyage Home,
The Philadelphia Story, Our Town,* and *Foreign Correspondent,* the
best-picture award went to *Rebecca* — which meant that Selznick, as
producer, was the recipient. (George Barnes was also honored for best
cinematography on the same film.) That year, the Academy began the
practice of sealed envelopes and great secrecy, and the nominated directors had to parade up to the stage of the Biltmore Hotel for the announcement of the winner. Those who were present — Hitchcock,
George Cukor, Sam Wood, and William Wyler — tried to betray as
little discomfort as possible. The envelope was opened by Frank Capra,
and the best-director award went to the only absentee: John Ford.

Hitchcock insisted, for the rest of his life, that he felt no disappointment over never receiving the Academy's award for best direction (despite his five nominations). ''What do I want with another doorstop?''

he liked to ask. But his closest associates knew that the snub by Hollywood rankled him — as would become clear in 1968, when, in his sev-
enties, Hitchcock was presented a special Oscar.

Selznick was concerned with fairness too, however, and he felt cheated
when Hitchcock began to take frequent trips to places far from Culver
City to discuss making short films for the British Library of Information. "Don't you think," he asked an aide, "we really ought to try to
delineate clearly, once and for all, just how much time Hitchcock is
going to spend on British government matters? . . . I see no reason
why we should pay a man $3,000 weekly and let him spend as much
time on British government matters as he and the authorities wish. . . .
He hops off to New York or Canada every few weeks, staying away
two or three days at a time, and it costs us $500 per day."

The truth of the matter — which Selznick quickly discovered — was
that Hitchcock was doing more than contributing his talent to British
propaganda films. He was also deepening his old acquaintance with Sidney Bernstein, now the British Library's supervisor, with whom he hoped
to form a production company to make films in London and Hollywood
after the war. They began to spin ideas during the summer of 1941,
while Selznick, Houseman, and the finale of *Suspicion* waited. By September, Selznick was justifiably angry: "It seems to me that we ought
to get Hitch working at the studio as the best means of controlling him.
He has good offices, a secretary . . . the writer is at the studio, Houseman is at the studio. . . . It is ridiculous that a man who is getting his
salary should not have to report for a full day's work at the place where
he is employed."

This division of Hitchcock's attention caused the first serious rift with
the otherwise tolerant Selznick, who by this time was paying Houseman
and Joan Harrison to work on a treatment of a Hitchcock idea about
fifth columnists sabotaging American defense plants. Originally called
*U.S.* and then *Sabotage,* the property was finally registered as *Saboteur*
in a vain attempt to avoid confusion with the director's 1936 British
film. Between August 20 (as the finishing touches were being put to
*Suspicion*) and the end of October, Hitchcock worked intermittently on
treatment and script with the young writer Peter Viertel (son of the
director Berthold Viertel and his actress-screenwriter wife Salka).

For a while, Selznick hoped to produce the film himself, and to sign
Gene Kelly for the leading role, but as the delays mounted it became
clear that Kelly would not be available (MGM signed him to a long-
term contract), and Selznick quickly lost interest. By late September
Selznick had suppressed his resentment long enough, and a confronta-

tion with Hitchcock seemed inevitable. Instead, he dictated an eleven-page letter — which he intended Daniel O'Shea to send to Hitchcock over his own signature — detailing the sore points.

First, Hitchcock had asked for a bonus at the outset of working on the script for *Saboteur,* since he knew Selznick was bound to lend him out to another studio at another huge profit. When he was denied the bonus — and additional monies that he asked be paid to Joan Harrison, to entice her to remain at his side — he stormed out of the studio, went home, and refused to work for a day. Selznick replied (through O'Shea) that this appalling outburst was an outrage, that Hitchcock was being paid $500 per day to stay in his office and work on the screenplay, and that Joan Harrison, "by your own statements, does little more than take down your own ideas. . . . I think it is high time that you took stock, and realized how increasingly difficult it is becoming for us to meet your growing reputation for slowness and for extrava-gance."

Then there was the matter of Hitchcock's loud complaints about his regular salary. "Actually," Selznick countered, "your agents ham-mered out of us a salary very much larger than you had been offered by all other studios in town, over a long period of time, with no takers; and executives at other studios laughed at us when they learned what we had agreed to give you, in view of what they apparently were certain they could have secured you for. Furthermore," he continued, referring to Hitchcock's 1938 American visit,

you personally made a visit over to see if you could better our proposition, saw other studios, spent a great deal of time in town investigating the possibil-ities, and when you tried to get additional money from us over and above our high offer, we told you frankly and bluntly that we would not consider paying you any more. . . . You came to us by your own selection, and with your eyes open, and presumably were delighted with your deal. I might observe that the wisdom of your decision has become apparent, even though your memory may be rather short. . . . Nor would it, in my opinion, be inappropriate to point out to you how fortunate you were in your assignments, particularly *Rebecca.*

The letter — a sharp and virtually impregnable setting-forth of the facts — was never sent. O'Shea wisely preferred to talk over the issues personally with Hitchcock and Myron Selznick, and thus to avoid antag-onizing an already edgy director.

By November, Selznick had decided to sell *Saboteur* to another stu-dio, as Hitchcock knew he would. Darryl F. Zanuck, at 20th Century-

Fox, was interested, but only if Henry Fonda and Gene Tierney could be signed for the leads. Selznick was more eager to negotiate a deal for Orson Welles to produce the picture at RKO. Welles, he thought, "would leap at the chance to have Hitchcock working under him, and this would appeal to Welles's vanity." Welles, however, whose creative relationship with Houseman on *Citizen Kane* had not ended very cordially, declined to discuss a Hitchcock-Houseman script, and on November 7 Selznick concluded a deal with Frank Lloyd, who would produce *Saboteur* at Universal Studios. Lloyd agreed to pay Selznick $130,000 and 10 percent of the gross receipts for Hitchcock and his script.

John Houseman has provided a vivid reminiscence of the autumn writing period.

I was instructed to use my British background, as well as my cultivation and charm, to establish good personal relationships with Hitch and to cajole and encourage him into conceiving and preparing an "original" screenplay. . . . I had heard of him as a fat man given to scabrous jokes — a gourmet and an ostentatious connoisseur of fine wines. What I was unprepared for was a man of exaggeratedly delicate sensibilities, marked by a harsh Catholic education and the scars from a social system against which he was in perpetual revolt and which had left him suspicious and vulnerable, alternately docile and defiant. He was an entertaining and knowledgable companion. . . . But his passion was for his work, which he approached with an intelligence and an almost scientific clarity to which I was unaccustomed in the theatre. . . . He came up with a notion for a picaresque spy story — a U.S. version of *The Thirty-Nine Steps* — with a transcontinental chase that moved from coast to coast and ended inside the hand of the Statue of Liberty. . . . Working with Hitch really meant listening to him talk — anecdotes, situations, characters, revelations and reversals, which he would think up at night and try out on us during the day and . . . the surviving elements were finally strung together into some sort of story in accordance with carefully calculated and elaborately plotted rhythms.

But Hitchcock's emotional rhythms were anything but carefully controlled. While Houseman derived enormous enjoyment from Hitchcock's daily performances of the scenes he had invented on his own — from watching the director lumber before his writers and act out little vignettes from what he thought were his best scenes — Hitchcock himself, according to Houseman, felt "rather like a pimp . . . divided between humiliation over these performances and the pleasure he always felt at trying out his gimmicks on a new audience." And Houseman knew that Hitchcock was furious at the idea that all his effort would in the end profit Selznick more than anyone: "This grievance over what he quite rightly regarded as the exploitation of his talent became so deep that it finally affected the quality of the picture.''

Further complicating Hitchcock's annoyance, during the final script preparation Joan Harrison at last felt that she had had enough apprenticeship under her famous employer, and she decided to strike out on her own. Over the next decade she wrote or produced a number of independent pictures, and then returned to produce Hitchcock's television shows for several years. He always insisted that he did not blame her for wanting her independence, but in fact there were many years of no contact at all between them. Indeed, he never understood why anyone would ever wish to leave off working with him, for whatever professional or personal reason. He would simply announce to someone he felt he could trust, "Next we're going to do . . ." or "When you get started on . . ." — it never occurred to him to inquire whether someone had other plans, or other hopes. Working for Hitchcock was, he considered, reward enough in itself; one could simply not hope to advance any further.

Houseman was right: the quality of *Saboteur* was inferior. When the film was finally produced, early in 1942, that assessment was confirmed. Robert Cummings, Priscilla Lane, and Otto Kruger were neither strong nor eccentric enough to be Hitchcock types, and in spite of the little punctuations of perverse humor by Dorothy Parker (the second Algonquin wit, after Benchley, to be summoned to spice the dialogue of a Hitchcock picture), the film turned out to be an undistinguished series of synthetic and unrelated incidents. Frank Lloyd, after paying so much for Hitchcock and the script, had little cash left for proper values in design and art direction, and the finished film has a cheap, underdesigned look. The single moment of Hitchcockian power and dread is the swooning, vertiginous fall of the saboteur from Miss Liberty's hand in the film's last moment.

Apart from that remarkable trick effect (a traveling matte shot), the film is a plodding recapitulation: the handcuffs and the escaping couple are drawn from *The 39 Steps* (and Cummings's escape from a mansion's storeroom by setting a fire is based on Hannay's escape from a storeroom by blowing it up with dynamite — a scene in the novel that Hitchcock had not used in his film version); the sudden appearance of a circus troupe recalls the odd assortment of freaks in *The Ring* and *Murder!*, and reflects the director's ongoing fascination with grotesques; the theater audience laughing at murder on the movie screen while murder surrounds them repeats a motif of *Sabotage;* the revolver pointed from behind a curtain with only one person aware of it is drawn from *The Man Who Knew Too Much;* and once again (like Godfrey Tearle in *The*

*39 Steps*), an elegant villain protests, "I'm a respectable citizen, I'm widely known . . .''

As had happened with *Suspicion,* the enthusiastic notices that greeted the opening of *Saboteur* surprised everyone at the studio — especially after a delicate situation involved Hitchcock in a contretemps with the United States government. During the final editing in April, he decided to add actual newsreel footage to the episode involving the saboteur's bombing of a battleship in the Brooklyn Navy Yard. Hitchcock selected a few shots of the crippled S.S. *Normandie,* France's legendary liner which had been taken over by the American government and officially renamed the U.S.S. *Lafayette* before burning in a suspicious fire at a Manhattan pier on February 9; the next morning it lay floating on its side, having listed under the weight of tons of water poured to extinguish the blaze.

"I cut to the hulk of the *Normandie,*" Hitchcock said. "I cut back to a closeup of the saboteur, who, after staring at the wreck, turns around with a slightly smug smile on his face. The Navy raised hell with Universal about these shots because I implied that the *Normandie* had been sabotaged, which was a reflection on their lack of vigilance in guarding it." The shots remained in the film despite the Navy's objection, however — perhaps because an investigation into the possibility of sabotage in fact was undertaken at once.

During the early weeks of production on the film, Alma left Los Angeles for New York to oversee Pat's Broadway debut. Their daughter had shown a consistent interest in drama and was about to begin her professional life on the stage at the age of thirteen. Auriol Lee, the actress who had played the novelist in Hitchcock's *Suspicion,* was best known for her stage direction of six plays by John Van Druten. At the time she met Pat Hitchcock, Lee was looking for a child to play the lead in Van Druten's new play, *Solitaire,* scheduled to open in New York under her direction early in 1942. Pat read for her and for the author in June 1941, was signed at once, and began to prepare for Broadway. In July Auriol Lee finished her role in Hitchcock's film and set off for a cross-country auto trip to New York to resume her theatrical career. She never arrived. Auriol Lee, who had been such a warm and encouraging mentor, was killed in an auto accident outside Kansas City. When Pat finally came to New York to begin rehearsals for the play, it was under the direction of Dudley Digges.

"I'm not looking forward to the first night," Pat said after the dress rehearsal. "I think I'll be nervous. But one good thing — my father won't be in the audience. He's making a picture in Hollywood." *Solitaire,* with Pat playing opposite Victor Kilian, was a comedy-drama

about a poor little rich girl and a middle-aged hobo. Critics found it
frail and uninspired, and audiences, as Samuel Goldwyn once said in
another context, stayed away in droves. It closed after twenty-three performances at the Plymouth Theater, and Pat returned with Alma to Saint
Cloud Road. Her father, involved in filming *Saboteur,* never saw her in
the play.

But they were not long at Saint Cloud Road. In the spring of 1942
the Hitchcocks began to look for their own home — or, more accurately, Alma began to look while her husband listened, in the evenings,
to the results of her house-hunting. By late spring she had found an
elegant little colonial; Hitchcock paid the asking price of $40,000 and
they relocated. The house was at 10957 Bellagio Road, just the other
side of the golf course from Saint Cloud, nestled behind cool and protecting trees.

Within days, Pat's bedroom was covered from floor to ceiling with
photographs of her favorite movie stars: Cary Grant, Bob Hope, Bette
Davis, Bing Crosby, Clark Gable, Gene Autry, Frederic March, Humphrey Bogart. Wrapped around the modest story-and-a-half house was a
lush confusion of green planting and several wonderfully gnarled trees.
The white-painted brick and gray-brown shingles, small-paned windows, dormers, and deep-set porches gave a variety of texture that reminded them of Winter's Grace at Shamley Green.

The spacious dining room with paneled walls, where they at once
started offering small dinner parties, overlooked the garden. The kitchen,
however, was undistinguished, and it took twenty years for Hitchcock
to complete its redesign. By that time, the rest of the house boasted
Aubusson carpets, several valuable paintings, a copy of a chair from the
Bank of England, two chairs covered in needlepoint designs made by
Alma, and — in an odd departure from Hitchcock's ordinarily impeccable taste in furnishings — stainless-steel flatware inspired by airline
silver he had admired. In the master bedroom, multiple table lamps
threw soft lighting on the A-frame ceiling, the larger-than-king-size bed,
two club chairs, and a fireplace. The house, with neither swimming pool
nor screening room, was not the conventional Hollywood residence, but
Hitchcock had at last got his "snug little house." He was also apparently bitten by the house-buying bug, for soon afterward he purchased
a second home, farther north and even more secluded.

But the move from Saint Cloud to Bellagio Road was motivated by
more than a simple desire to be a homeowner rather than a renter. It
was also necessitated by a tragedy.

While Alma was attending Pat's New York debut, Hitchcock and the world were stunned by the news: Carole Lombard had been killed in an airplane crash while returning from a War Bond tour of the West. The Hitchcocks' vibrant friend and benevolent landlady was only thirty-three, and Hitchcock's confusion and anger over her death aggravated the problems of shooting *Saboteur*. Although their professional relationship had been limited and their social one was by no means intimate, Hitchcock had grown to relish her surprising combination of ladylike elegance and verbal vulgarity.

Carole had also endeared herself to Hitchcock with the sense of the macabre she shared with him and her husband Clark. One evening in 1941, the Hitchcocks invited the Gables to Saint Cloud, and during dinner Hitchcock mentioned the South American and Australian natives' custom of headshrinking. Gable said he owned a shrunken head, and Carole added that they had thrown the dreadful thing into a ravine in Coldwater Canyon one evening, but after they arrived home they regretted their disrespect and went back to fetch it. Carole then took the head, and she and her gardener built a tiny coffin and buried it — in what was now Hitchcock's garden!

Hitchcock's eyes widened at the news that his own backyard was a cemetery for a shrunken head, and they proceeded to concoct a wildly improbable publicity stunt. Full of delight, they planned the details of a midnight exhumation party, to be attended by all of the press and a gathering of celebrities. After supper, everyone would be handed shovels and pickaxes and the disinterment would begin. But the eerie event never occurred. By a tragic twist of fate, the only graveyard activity that winter was Carole's burial. At once Hitchcock decided to look for a new home, and soon they were at Bellagio Road. The shrunken head was exhumed only in his art — in two gratuitous moments of shock-effect in *Under Capricorn,* made seven years later in England.

In the spring of 1942, while the prints of *Saboteur* were being shipped and the critics' verdicts awaited, Selznick was anxious for Hitchcock to begin his next project — and Hitchcock was just as eager to get over the disappointment of *Saboteur*. Jack Skirball, who had been Frank Lloyd's associate at Universal, was willing to pay Selznick's price of $150,000 for eighteen weeks of Hitchcock's services (Hitchcock would receive about a third, thus making Selznick a richer if still inactive producer).

On April 13 Margaret McDonell, one of Selznick's story editors, invited Hitchcock to lunch and suggested several ideas. Patrick Hamilton's play *Angel Street* had been turned into a film script called *Gaslight,* and she thought it would be just right for him. But he turned down the costume melodrama in spite of its thriller aspects, insisting that he had learned his lesson about period pieces from *Jamaica Inn*. The only other idea that interested him was something she had remembered called *The Ventriloquist*.

For several days after this lunch, Hitchcock worked alone on a treatment of this curious idea: A ventriloquist commits bigamy, murders his first wife and, haunted by his crime, confuses reality with paranoic delusion. As his second wife comes to warn him that the police are in pursuit, he mistakes her for his first wife, and in his fear falls over a cliff to his death. "Hitchcock really likes this!" Mrs. McDonell reported to Selznick next day. But Selznick thought it was entirely too bizarre, and while Hitchcock tried to write up a treatment he was told the idea had been rejected. Echoes of the concept and its alchemy of guilt, fear, and illusion would later occur in the final scene of *Vertigo*.

When Selznick rejected the idea, Hitchcock at once left town for several days — officially to supervise some technical problems with the musical scoring of *Saboteur* in New York. He also went to Washington, to assure the capital's press corps that the film would be perfect for a War Bond rally. When he returned to Hollywood, Margaret McDonell suggested doing a film of John Buchan's novel *Greenmantle,* with Ingrid Bergman, Cary Grant, and Herbert Marshall, or Buchan's *No Other Tiger,* a story of jewel theft. ("Hitch enthused particularly," Mrs. McDonell reported, "about the climax where the beautiful dancer is found hanging from the chandelier.")

But the idea they finally settled on was generated by her husband, writer Gordon McDonell. He and Hitchcock discussed it over lunch at the Brown Derby on May 5; the next day Hitchcock took the idea to Jack Skirball; and on May 7 (the day *Saboteur* premiered at Radio City Music Hall), the Skirball-Selznick contract was finalized. Hitchcock was firmly committed to direct a film called *Uncle Charlie,* McDonell's story of a homicidal maniac who takes refuge from the police with his sister's family, but who is gradually found out by his favorite niece. After his accidental death, the niece keeps the secret of her beloved uncle's dreadful identity.

To work on a script in May and June, Hitchcock asked for Thornton Wilder, whose sense of small-town American life in his play *Our Town* he had greatly admired. (Hitchcock's insistence on an established American writer reflected his growing desire to develop as American a flavor to his work as possible, and to separate himself from the Englishness to which he felt obligated in his films until America was forced into the war. At this point he severed almost all contact with the faithful Charles Bennett, who had collaborated so well from 1934 to 1940.) The weeks with Wilder were among the most cordial in Hitchcock's career, and although the Pulitzer Prize winner did little more than help scout locations and work on a prose treatment, he and Hitchcock shared similar curiosities about the details of small-town life.

But just as they were about to turn their notes and prose summaries of sequences into a script, Wilder went off to the army. And just as Hitchcock began to work on the script alone, something happened that entirely altered its content, theme, and purpose: he began to receive frequent and worried letters and cables from England, informing him that his mother had suddenly developed a series of complicated conditions that put her in very poor health. There were kidney problems and intestinal obstructions. William Hitchcock let his brother know that he was alarmed — especially because their mother refused to enter a hospital and would take only what care she could get at home, in the cottage in Shamley Green.

Hitchcock, of course, was on a strictly controlled schedule under Skirball and Universal — a schedule doubly rigid because of the Selznick information that Hitchcock had had the habit of going to New York or Canada for his own purposes. In addition, it was not easy to book air travel to England in the summer of 1942 — and a boat trip, even for the best of reasons, would simply require too much time.

And so he remained in California, a decision no one faulted him for but that cost him considerable personal anguish. To a few associates he even began to confide memories of his childhood, of his parents, of life in Leytonstone. At this point, for the first time in his life, the usually secretive Hitchcock poured his soul into the first spiritually autobiographical film of his career. The final script (dated August 10, with dialogue by short-story writer Sally Benson, Alma, and Hitchcock) is his response to personal crisis. The picture he finally called *Shadow of a Doubt* would become a handbook of all the literary and cultural influences on his own life, and it would be as near as he would ever get to wearing his private heart on his public and professional sleeve. Perhaps that is why the film was always one of Hitchcock's own favorites. But few people in his cast or crew guessed the depth of his personal anguish or crisis at the time — or the extent of his self-disclosure.

Casting was completed in July and locations prepared in the peaceful California community of Santa Rosa. From Selznick's roster, Hitchcock took Joseph Cotten, whom he wanted for the handsome, sociopathic uncle who strangles rich widows; and from Samuel Goldwyn he borrowed Teresa Wright. She had received Oscar nominations for her first three films — *The Little Foxes, Mrs. Miniver,* and *Pride of the Yankees* — and had won for *Mrs. Miniver.* Her Broadway career had begun as understudy to Dorothy McGuire in the production of *Our Town,* and it is likely that from the start Thornton Wilder himself suggested her to Hitchcock for the role of the niece who undergoes a moral education.

"He did such homework before he began the picture," Teresa Wright recalled.

He saw the film completely in his mind before we began — it's as if he had a little projection room in his head. When he told me the story the first time we met in his office in June 1942, we could have been sitting in a theater seeing a finished film. So during the shooting he made us feel very relaxed. His direction never came across as instruction. We felt we could trust him, and he gave us guidance and a sense of freedom. He was very calm, as if we were just making a contribution to something that had been completely foreseen. No one plans a film as completely as he did, and no one saw it as clearly as he did from the very start. Other directors usually let it happen while they're making it, but with him everything could be more serene, and more enjoyable.

We were the first film company to work in Santa Rosa, and everyone there got involved in one way or another. Edna May Wonacott, who played the younger sister, was the daughter of a Santa Rosa grocer [Hitchcock picked her himself after visiting the man's shop and comparing it to his own father's] and the local policeman carefully coached the actor-policeman. Everyone was wonderful to us, even when our nighttime shooting interrupted their quiet routine.

She remembered, too, the endless series of word games and puns Hitchcock used to keep his cast and crew entertained. On location, he began to assemble a list of the ideal production company: a leading lady named Dolly Shot; a man named Ward Robe; a villain called Mike Shadow; a German spy known as Herr Dresser; a character designated as Mae Kupp; a cameraman, Otto Focus; a child actress called Fay Doubt; a ballerina, Mme. Panover; the director would be Manny Takes, the cutter Eddie Tor, the designer Art Director, and the electrician Xavier Arcs.

To further distract himself from the troublesome family news, from the situation of the war, from the fate of England, from his own feeling of isolation, Hitchcock set himself the challenge of scrupulous fidelity to the details of Americana. Originally he had hoped to film the interiors at the actual house in Santa Rosa used for the exterior shots, but space problems made this impossible. The technical difficulties then became a series of hurdles to surmount: lengthy traveling shots at night; the lighting-up of four city blocks; the careful arrangement of crowds and traffic; the arrival of a train at the local station, belching smoke blacker and more demonic than usual, to Hitchcock's precise specifications. And the problems and patterns of sound equally intrigued him. "He used sound like no one else I've ever known," Teresa Wright said.

If any other director asked an actor to put down a teacup, it would be only that. But with Hitch it was done for a reason. If an actor was strumming his fingers it wasn't just an idle strumming, it had a beat, a musical pattern to it — it was like a sound refrain. Whether someone was walking or rustling a paper or tearing an envelope or whistling, whether it was a flutter of birds or an outside sound, it was carefully orchestrated by him. He really scored the sound effects the way a musician writes for instruments.

Hitchcock likewise respected Teresa Wright, especially her thorough preparation and quiet professionalism, and their mutual admiration lasted until his death.

Hitchcock's relations with the other members of this cast were equally genial. "I was ushered into his office," remembered Hume Cronyn, who played the role of the meek, mother-dominated neighbor, "and Hitch asked me if I had ever been in northern California. I said no, and he told me what marvelous country it is, with miles and miles of vineyards. 'When the day's work is done, we go out to the vineyards and squeeze the grapes through our hair,' he said. I suggested that this sounded more like a part for him than for me. All I could see was Hitchcock as Bacchus."

Cronyn made his film debut in *Shadow of a Doubt,* and after acting again in Hitchcock's next film, he later collaborated on the treatments for two of the director's pictures. He and his wife Jessica Tandy, who would join the long list of Hitchcock actors twenty years later, became frequent visitors to the Hitchcocks' homes for many years. The same camaraderie prevailed with Joseph Cotten, whom Hitchcock told to go and pick his own wardrobe for the role of the suave villain. "He said I should dress as if I were a rich man going to a resort for a vacation," Cotten recalled. "No director was ever easier to work with." For the kindly but imperceptive parents, the gifted stage-and-screen actors Patricia Collinge and Henry Travers were perfectly cast.

For all Hitchcock's private worries, the location photography in Santa Rosa proceeded with a holiday atmosphere. One weekend in August, the Hitchcocks concluded negotiations for their second home, in Scotts Valley near Santa Cruz. Built in the prevalent California-Spanish style, it was a white plaster house with arched doorways, a red-tiled roof, and great charm, surrounded by huge redwood trees, some as wide as fifteen feet in circumference. Set in seclusion on a sixteen-hundred-foot elevation, amid two hundred acres of gorgeous countryside overlooking Monterey Bay, it became the family's weekend retreat for twenty-five years. Often they brought the cook up from Bel-Air, and the first change Hitchcock made was to install dining banquettes in a combined kitchen/dining area.

But the grim news continued to come from England all during the summer. Mrs. Hitchcock developed an intestinal abscess, slipped in and out of coma, and was receiving daily visits from a physician. Her youngest son told no outsiders of this increasingly bad news but his fervent involvement in polishing and repolishing — and personalizing — the script continued at unprecedented pitch. Pat went up to Santa Rosa for her summer holiday and won over the cast and crew with her quick wit and superb imitations of her father, while Alma peered over the script girl's shoulder and casually checked details of continuity. The social highlight of the summer was the celebration of Hitchcock's forty-third birthday, which he turned into a press event. He created some suspense after dinner by holding up a long carving knife, drawing it toward his neck, and, with a broad smile, threatening to slit his own throat. For a moment no one moved, and then, without a word, he sat down and ordered brandy for everyone. It is hard not to wonder if this unusually macabre display was at least partly due to the strain of work and family news, to a guilty awareness of his own comfort and safety while his mother, now in rapid decline, languished in war-torn England.

The company arrived back in Hollywood for the studio work in mid-September, and the dreaded news arrived soon thereafter. Hitchcock was informed of his mother's death within hours of the event, the morning of Saturday, September 26. She was in her seventy-ninth year, and the day was her fifty-fifth wedding anniversary. She expired quietly, in the presence of her son William and Dr. F. W. Gordon, who stated the cause of death as acute pyelonephritis, an abdominal fistula, and an intestinal perforation. The last week had been extremely unpleasant, Hitchcock was told, but his mother had insisted on staying at the cottage. It is this single event, anticipated by months of anxiety and followed by months of quiet sorrow, that transformed the entire enterprise of *Shadow of a Doubt* into a network of personal references. And the film is as much a key to the complexities of his inner life, and of his guilt, as it is a network of meanings illuminating his relationships to his family, to his own divided self, and to the divided culture from which he had emigrated.

First, Uncle Charlie, the character played by Joseph Cotten, is a man with whom Hitchcock clearly identified: the script describes him as "awfully neat and fussy," as Hitchcock himself was proud to be. In his childhood, Uncle Charlie had an accident exactly modeled on the one in Hitchcock's childhood that left him with a barely perceptible scar on his chin. The description in the film is a description of the young Hitchcock: "Such a quiet boy, always reading," says his sister. "I always said Papa never should have bought you that bicycle. You didn't know how to handle it. He took it right out onto the icy road and skidded into a streetcar. We thought he was going to die. He was laid up so long. And then when he was getting well there was no holding him. It was just as though all the rest he had was too much and he'd had to get into mischief to blow off steam." The speech, one of the few ever actually written by Hitchcock, was drawn directly from his own life experience.

The elegant villain's sentiments — a momentary nostalgia for the past and a contempt for the present — were the director's, too, each word written by him weeks after Wilder left the project: "I keep remembering those things — all the old things. . . . Everybody was sweet and pretty then, the whole world. A wonderful world. Not like the world today. Not like the world now. It was great to be young then."

But if Hitchcock drew on his own experience and feelings to associate himself with the elegant strangler (strangulation is always the Hitchcock villain's preferred method of killing), he also identifies with the character played by Hume Cronyn, who is obsessed with committing murder in fantasy and lives with a sick and demanding mother who is never seen. There is still more of Hitchcock in the father of the family: he refuses to drive the family car, is a regular reader of *"Unsolved Mysteries,"* and is somewhat sexless and desiccated, totally overwhelmed by the arrival of the "bad blood" of the family.

The mother of the house, the villain's sister, was named by Hitchcock for his own mother, Emma, at the first scripting session. She has an amusing habit that characterized Mrs. Hitchcock from the early days in Leytonstone: "Mama, you don't have to shout," corrects the younger daughter as her mother shouts into the telephone. "Really, Papa, you'd think Mama had never seen a phone. She makes no allowance for science. She thinks she has to cover the distance by sheer lung power!" The character of Emma, written while Emma Hitchcock was in her final illness, is the last benevolent rendering of a mother figure in Hitchcock's films, and her antecedent is Hitchcock's own mother. His confused feelings, his guilt, the clash of love and of resentment, were unleashed by her death, and the portrait is limned more darkly in later films, beginning with the possessive and tyrannical mother of *Notorious.*

There is something of Hitchcock in the younger children, too. The baby of the family is a boy keen on problems of arithmetic and of logic, always interrupting theoretical conversations with challenges to the grown-ups. And the younger girl is, like him, a voracious reader of the romantic classics (*Ivanhoe* — whole sections of which Hitchcock knew by heart — is specified); she is intuitive about the evil uncle, afraid of stories that will give her bad dreams, and she boasts, after stepping on sidewalk cracks, "I broke my mother's back three times!"

But it is the two Charlies — uncle and niece with the same name — who are a spiritual summary of the light and dark sides of Hitchcock's own adult nature, which is represented by the monstrousness of the uncle and the innocence of the girl, who is virginal, inexperienced, trusting, and who is contrasted with her uncle. Unaware of his crimes, she says prophetically: "I'm glad that mother named me after you and that she thinks we're both alike. I think we are too. I know it . . . We're not just an uncle and a niece. It's something else. I know you. I know that you don't tell people a lot of things. I don't either. I have a feeling that inside you somewhere there's something nobody knows about . . . something secret and wonderful. I'll find it out . . . We're sort of like twins, don't you see? We have to know." Her words are followed at once by the "espousal scene," in which a ring is slipped on her finger, sealing the union between the two Charlies. "When I try to think of how I feel," says Teresa Wright as Charlie, "I always come back to Uncle Charlie."

The awful link between the two, as types, is made explicit in the words written for Joseph Cotten by Hitchcock, and uttered in the infernal, smoke-filled bar:

We're old friends, Charlie. More than that. We're like twins. You said so yourself . . . You think you know something, don't you? You think you're the clever little girl who knows something. There's so much you don't know. So much. What do you know, really? You're just an ordinary little girl living in an ordinary little town. You wake up every morning of your life and you know perfectly well that there's nothing in the world to trouble you. You go through your ordinary little day and at night you sleep your untroubled, ordinary little sleep filled with peaceful stupid dreams. And I brought you nightmares. Or did I? Or was it a silly inexpert little lie? You live in a dream, you're a sleepwalker, blind! How do you know what the world is like? Do you know the world is a foul sty? Do you know if you ripped the fronts off houses you'd find swine? The world's a hell! What does it matter what happens in it?

These two characters represent, then, the dual drives within Hitchcock himself, drives that created a tension he sought to resolve in the death of Uncle Charlie and the note of sad hope at the end: "He thought the world was a horrible place," Teresa Wright reflects. "He couldn't have been very happy, ever. He didn't trust people. He seemed to hate them. He hated the whole world. He said that people like us had no idea what the world was really like.'' And the detective (played by MacDonald Carey) replies, ''It's not quite as bad as that. But sometimes it needs a lot of watching. It seems to go crazy every now and then. Like your Uncle Charlie.''

Alfred Hitchcock was living with inner demons of lust and possessiveness, of romantic, dark fantasies about killing, and of unfulfilled sexual daydreams. He could be crude and cruel and tyrannical with his cast and mercurial and unpredictable with his colleagues. Like Uncle Charlie, he coveted the good life and above all the respectability of a good name; he hoped to settle permanently in Los Angeles and in Santa Cruz, just as Uncle Charlie hoped to remain permanently in Santa Rosa, and, believing he would, deposited $40,000 — the amount Hitchcock had just paid for the house on Bellagio Road — in a Santa Rosa bank. Like the gift-giver Uncle Charlie, Hitchcock was capable of the sudden, inexplicable act of kindness — the gift of a car to his cook, the financial support of a relative, the sudden sending of cases of wine to a former colleague, a letter to help someone in need of work.

The structural element at work in *Shadow of a Doubt* that expresses this division in Hitchcock's spirit is the almost infinite accumulation of doubles: the two Charlies; two detectives in the East pursuing Uncle Charlie, then two in the West; two criminals sought; two women with eyeglasses; two dinner sequences; two amateur sleuths engaged in two conversations about killing; two young children; two older siblings; two railway-station sequences; two sequences outside a church; two doctors; two double brandies served at the ''Till Two'' bar by a waitress who has worked there for two weeks; two attempts to kill the girl before the final scene; two scenes in a garage, one a declaration of love and one an attempt at murder — and so on, almost past counting.

The duality is established by Hitchcock's camera as well, from the opening moments when it introduces the uncle and niece in parallel viewpoints: the larger view of their respective cities, then the exteriors of the houses, then the windows, then a slow dolly shot to each, lying fully clothed on a bed until interrupted by a conversation about money. And there is of course the linking device of the waltz from *The Merry Widow*, the tune that leaps precognitively from head to head between the two.

This motif of the double had been an important convention in late Victorian stories, and it is to that era — Hitchcock's own — that the inserted dissolves of the waltzing couples in *Shadow of a Doubt* point.

The double had been taught to Hitchcock in school, and it was reinforced in his moral education and in his leisure reading. It is central, for example, to Robert Louis Stevenson's *The Strange Case of Dr. Jekyll and Mr. Hyde* (1886), and to Oscar Wilde's *The Picture of Dorian Gray* (1891) — popular works during Hitchcock's adolescent years, and works he had read several times before beginning his film career. The resurgent Gothicism in late Victorian literature and the suddenly abundant stories of dual personality were the modes for exploring the dark underside of human nature, an exploration that led inevitably to the work of Sigmund Freud at the very end of the Victorian era.

Like Stevenson and his story of Jekyll and Hyde — the autobiographical elements of which were first pointed out by G. K. Chesteron in a 1927 biography — Hitchcock's *Shadow of a Doubt* and three later films about the doubled or split personality (*Strangers on a Train, Psycho,* and *Frenzy*) reveal their creator's essentially puritan traits. Good and evil are sharply distinguished but exchangeable; the disclosure of human failings taints the cherished sense of propriety; fastidiousness is the trait of one who (as Chesterton said of Stevenson and one can say of Hitchcock) "knew the worst too young; not necessarily in his own act or by his own fault, but by the nature of a system which saw no difference between the worst and the moderately bad." Both Stevenson and Hitchcock endured puritanical repressions; both conjured up images of the late puritan-Victorian wasteland that was inhospitable to maintaining an honorable public life and a happy private one at the same time. And both Stevenson and Hitchcock depended on their wives for frequent collaboration and constant support.

Hitchcock's private style and, opposed to it, his calculated bourgeois exterior, were signs of an inner division. He considered all life unmanageable, and his obsessive neatness (like his careful preparation of a film) was a way of taking a stand against the chaos he believed was always at the ready, to be fended off with whatever wit and structure one could muster. Social life he thought to be a giant hypocrisy. He carried the burden of disguise as all his suave villains do, and the attempt at elegance concealed the boyish secret, the second, hidden, imagined life. The paradox of Alfred Hitchcock was that his delight in his craft could never be liberated from a terrible and terrifying heritage of desire and its concomitant guilt.

That he should have played out this inner dilemma in the characters, plot, and theme of *Shadow of a Doubt* is not surprising. As he wrote and directed it, his mother was dying, his homeland was in crisis, his professional life was not yet under his control, and Joan Harrison had left him to pursue her own career. On a deeper level, there was the

sudden convergence of all the inconsistent drives within him. He was a
profoundly Victorian Catholic, a rigid moralist, who ate and drank too
much. He was a classical filmmaker and a manipulator of effects who
loved a technical challenge. He was a childlike romantic living in an
isolated, chilly gloom. Meticulous at work, he was cavalier and reckless
about his health. Proper in public, he was inclined, if there was no
microphone present, to outrageous toilet humor. He was the soul of
gentility for the press, but he secretly reveled in the ugly, and coolly
presented it for his audience's consideration.

Familiar with the demonic and the dreadful, in the throes of his personal gloom, he created, in *Shadow of a Doubt,* a dramatic illustration
of the psychological reality that C. G. Jung called "the shadow" in all
of us and that Robert Louis Stevenson proposed beneath the niceties of
rhyme:

> *I have a little shadow that goes in and out with me,*
> *And what can be the use of him is more than I can see.*
> *He is very, very like me from the heels up to the head;*
> *And I see him jump before me, when I jump into my bed.*

Alfred Hitchcock was, in fact, both Charlies, a walking illustration
of Montaigne's observation, "We are double in ourselves, so that we
believe what we disbelieve and cannot rid ourselves of what we
condemn."

With *Shadow of a Doubt* ready for a winter release, Hitchcock turned
at once to a project that had engaged him for some time: the technical
challenge of filming a story in the smallest possible acting space, con-
centrating on facial close-ups and dramatic intensity and on deriving
more from character and situation than from plot development. Selznick
had arranged for him to go over to 20th Century–Fox for his next two
pictures, under a forty-week contract that would pay Selznick $300,000
and Hitchcock less than half that. In November and December the idea
for the first film, about survivors adrift in a lifeboat, was discussed at
the Fox offices; A. J. Cronin was first considered for screenwriter (because Hitchcock's second picture at Fox was to have been Cronin's *The
Keys of the Kingdom*), but Hitchcock pursued Ernest Hemingway.*

Hemingway was then in Cuba, and on December 30, 1942, Hitch-

---

*The agreement between Selznick and Fox stipulated that the second picture was to begin before
the end of 1943; this clause annoyed Hitchcock, since it meant that his salary would not be increased — which is perhaps why he was in no apparent hurry to get on with the script or shooting
of the first film. As a result of his foot-dragging, the second film for Fox was never made.

cock sent him a lengthy telegram outlining the story, which began with the mid-Atlantic torpedoing of a freighter carrying a mixed group of passengers; the whole film was to be set in the lifeboat in which they take refuge with a shipwrecked Nazi officer. Hitchcock was willing to go to Miami to meet Hemingway for further discussion, but in January the disappointing reply came from Cuba: Hemingway, grateful for the invitation, declined because of other writing projects. Hitchcock and Kenneth Macgowan, producer of the film for Fox, resumed the search for a screenwriter for the film, which was at once called *Lifeboat*. At the same time, Hitchcock, eager to collaborate with another popular and serious writer like Thornton Wilder, convinced Macgowan to engage John Steinbeck to work on a prose treatment of his story.

The single distraction from work came from England. Hitchcock's brother William (who had been present at their father's death in 1914 and their mother's in 1942) was then in his early fifties. During the weeks after Mrs. Hitchcock's death, there had been no further word from the family. Then, on January 4, in his home on Warren Road, Guildford, William Hitchcock died under mysterious circumstances. The coroner insisted on an inquest and six days later a verdict was returned. The report notes, with quiet discretion, that the cause of death was "congestive cardiac failure probably contributed to by the taking of paraldehyde, thus aggravating the cardiac failure and precipitating death. Paraldehyde was self-administered."

Of this older brother very little is known. William and Alfred were never very close, and their meetings in adult life were infrequent. William had taken over the family business after their father's death and had supervised the absorption of the several Hitchcock shops into a larger English corporation — Mac Fisheries — in the 1930s. Alfred Hitchcock's customary silence about his family became an obsessive reticence after his brother's apparent suicide, and some of the filmmaker's associates felt there was nagging and gnawing guilt festering in the soul of the younger brother, who had been absent during the accumulation of family sorrow. He had played no substantial role in the war effort, a fact the British press frequently recalled; now he had not been present at or after the deaths of his mother and brother.

What is certain about Hitchcock's feelings at this time, however, is that the family deaths focused his own constant terror of sudden tragedy. One morning in January, wheezing and straining in his effort to tie his shoes, he knew he had to do something about his obesity. "I weighed just under three hundred pounds," he said later. "My ankles hung over my socks. My back ached." He decided at once to lose a hundred pounds and he set for himself an ascetic regime of black coffee for breakfast and lunch, a small steak and salad for dinner, and no alcohol. (By contrast, an ordinary dinner prior to the diet consisted of relishes, a roast chicken, a small boiled ham, potatoes, two vegetables, bread, a bottle of wine, salad, dessert, and the beloved brandy that appears, like his own cameo, in fifty-one of his fifty-three films. His lifelong craving for ice cream was usually satisfied later in the evening.)

By the end of 1943 Hitchcock had dropped a third of his weight; the scale registered just over two hundred pounds, and photos taken before and after were printed in a mock-up newspaper for his ritual appearance in *Lifeboat*. During the diet he visited a doctor weekly to have his vital signs monitored, and this habit continued for the rest of his life. The diet, however — as with most weight-losers — was difficult to maintain; given the mercurial changes in his weight for the next four decades, his longevity was astonishing.

Most of Hitchcock's associates congratulated him on the weight loss, but Selznick knew of a concomitant danger: "I am sincerely and seriously worried about Hitch's fabulous loss of weight," he wrote in May. "I do hope he has a physician, as otherwise we are liable to get a shock one morning about a heart attack or something of the sort." Up to this time, Selznick had been paying huge sums to insure Hitchcock for each picture. But by the end of 1943, although his weight had dropped, the Occidental Insurance Company of Los Angeles refused Selznick's application to insure the health or life of his star director.

Hitchcock's heart, a medical examination found, was enlarged 16 percent and he had a severe abdominal rupture. If the hernia was corrected, the company advised, a policy could be drawn up. Hitchcock refused the operation and took to wearing a restraining truss until corrective surgery in 1957. It must be counted another puzzling contradiction that the man who lived in abject terror of accident or sudden death spent so many busy years with an easily remediable condition that could have become life-threatening at any moment.

The difficulties of realizing a script for *Lifeboat* were considerable. John Steinbeck, who thought that Hitchcock's obsession with a single set inhibited the drama, left the project after sketching a few scenes and a prose summary. MacKinlay Kantor was then brought in, but Hitchcock was disappointed with him and asked Macgowan to let him go. Finally Jo Swerling, who had crafted several scripts for other directors, worked on the screenplay until mid-July; but just before shooting began that month, Hitchcock, working alone at home, rewrote all the dialogue himself. He then asked Ben Hecht to read the script and to make some suggestions about the final scenes, as Hecht had done for *Foreign Correspondent*.

Although the entire action of *Lifeboat* was strictly confined to a floating raft in a large studio tank (with rear-projection of sea and sky), the circumstances of filming were neither simple nor comfortable. "We were always falling in and out of the water," recalled Hume Cronyn, whom Hitchcock invited to join the cast. "We were covered with crude oil, and when we finished a scene there might be an hour waiting for a new camera setup. We would climb down, go to our dressing rooms and change to dry clothes, then go back to the raft and start over again."

In addition, Hitchcock ordered the construction of enormous wind fans and water-spraying machines, and he subjected his performers to several days of shooting a storm (in this regard, the entire film may be seen as a variation or sequel to the finale of *Foreign Correspondent*, but in this case the traitor is still aboard and at the helm of a life raft). During these difficult scenes, several of the actors inevitably fell ill with chills and fever — Tallulah Bankhead more than once. "I was black and blue from the downpours and the lurchings," she wrote in her memoirs. "Thanks to the heat, the lights, the fake fog, and submersions followed by rapid dryings-out, I came up with pneumonia early in November."

"She stood up to being doused by 5,400 gallons of water," Hitchcock said later, "and she got a round of applause from the stagehands." But the applause, other members of the company later insisted, was inspired not so much by her bravery as by another kind of display. Trouper though she was, Bankhead raised eyebrows in Hollywood as elsewhere, and Hitchcock relished her bawdiness as much as he admired her professionalism. "Tallulah was something of an exhibitionist," Hume Cronyn said,

and somewhere along the way she got tired of wearing underwear. We all had to climb up a ladder to get into the tank of the boat, and there she was — no underwear, and exposed for all the set to see.

One day a lady from *Good Housekeeping* or *The Ladies Home Journal* visited the set, and she was outraged. She went off to the front office and raised absolute hell about Bankhead — that it was a disgrace and that obviously all the stories she had heard about Hollywood were true. As a result there was a big fuss, and the head of publicity at Fox had to come down to the unit manager on the picture and say, "Now look, this has got to stop. You get Miss Bankhead to wear some underclothing or else we close the set. And if you close the set it's a damn nuisance, because we won't get any publicity for the picture."

The poor unit manager was about as glad to tell Tallulah this as he would have been to go into a cage of starving lions. So he went to Hitch and asked him to speak to her. But Hitch simply replied: "I've always tried to be very careful of getting involved in departmental disputes. And in a case like this it's hard to decide where the responsibility lies. You might consider this is a matter for the wardrobe department, or perhaps for the makeup people — or perhaps it's even for hairdressing!" And that was the beginning and end of his involvement with that.

"The whole point about Tallulah," Hitchcock reflected later, "was that she had no inhibitions. Now some people can take this, others can't." Hitchcock could, and he reveled in her antics. On the last day of shooting in November, he presented her with a white Sealyham puppy: it had, he announced, already been named Hitchcock. Later, he told the press that Tallulah had given a "Bancock performance" — a display of her own talent and nature, somewhat softened by his direction.

Another player — young Mary Anderson, whom the studio was preparing for an important career — did not impress the director so much. She was eager to please him and his cameraman, however, and she wanted to learn about details like profile photography.

"Mr. Hitchcock, what do you think is my best side?" she asked, taking a seat near his director's chair.

"My dear," he answered without looking at her, "you're sitting on it."

When *Lifeboat* was released in 1944, a storm of controversy broke at once. "Unless we had seen it with our own eyes," Bosley Crowther wrote (echoing the angry sentiments of Dorothy Thompson, who gave it "ten days to get out of town"),

we would never in the world have believed that a film could have been made which sold out democratic ideals and elevated the Nazi superman. Mr. Hitchcock and Mr. Steinbeck failed to grasp just what they had wrought. They certainly had no intention of elevating the superman ideal. . . . But we have a sneaking suspicion that the Nazis, with some cutting here and there, could turn *Lifeboat* into a whiplash against the "decadent democracies." And it is questionable whether such a picture, with such a theme, is judicious at this time.

Macgowan, Hitchcock, Bankhead, and everyone else connected with the film were astonished, for its central thesis was quite clear to them: the cause of democracy was doomed unless the Allies summoned their courage, united their various strengths and talents, disregarded their national differences, and abandoned petty disagreements. As played by Walter Slezak, the Nazi captain was correctly seen as intelligent, perceptive, patient, and single-minded, and it was this amalgam of qualities that the film urged on the motley crew of American survivors and the disjointed Allies.

More disturbing to critic Crowther, however — and to audiences outside a few major cities — was the clear common humanity shared by the wily Nazi and his American companions on the raft. If the German officer could be selfish, conniving, and murderous, so could the others: together (with the exception of the black man aboard) they savagely beat the Nazi and dump him overboard. When another Nazi climbs aboard after a second U-boat is torpedoed nearby, one of the Americans urges, "Exterminate him! Exterminate them all!" — an unambiguous reference to the universality of killer impulses that was perhaps too much for an audience in 1944.

If *Lifeboat* made a plea, in fact, it was one for a unity and idealism that would have to be achieved amid the conditions of personal loss — conditions with which Hitchcock himself was recently familiar. Bankhead loses her camera, her typewriter, her fur coat, and her diamond bracelet ("Little by little, I'm being divested of all my worldly possessions!"); a young mother loses her baby, a sailor his leg. And the entire population of the lifeboat loses a sense of direction and of superiority. All the loss and the fear are felt amid the silence of the sea: Hitchcock insisted there be no musical soundtrack. The sense of being adrift — with no background but the infinite ocean, no escape but the waters that beckon to destruction and annihilation (the only real freedom) — gives the film a strange, hallucinatory texture, the sensation of floating in an endless nightmare with no sure harbor.

During the completion of *Lifeboat*, David Selznick agreed to Hitchcock's request — supported by one from Sidney Bernstein — that he be permitted to return briefly to London. Hitchcock was not happy to give up the relative security of life in California, but he felt that he should make some gesture of contributing his talents to the war effort. At that time there was a troupe of French actors taking refuge in London — the Molière Players — and Bernstein suggested that Hitchcock direct them in two short films supporting the French Resistance and the Allied cause. On Sunday, December 5, Hitchcock left for twelve weeks in England.

Everyone was uneasy about the trip — he most of all. There were family matters for him to settle, and memorial visits to the graves of his mother and brother. There was the shock of seeing parts of London destroyed, the theaters closed, the film studios mostly abandoned. Without Alma, who stayed behind in Los Angeles to nurse her own mother (who died shortly thereafter), Hitchcock was lonely and depressed in England, and the preparations for the two French films were a somber and distracted enterprise.

But Sidney Bernstein, ever the encouraging colleague, had something to cheer him: Bernstein was anxious to pursue the idea they had often discussed casually, the formation of a production company to make films alternately in London and California after the war. Rightly, Selznick suspected that the invitation to work on propaganda films for the Ministry of Information was subordinate to these plans for the future. "I hope," Selznick cabled his English representative Jenia Reissar, "that one of the motives behind bringing Mr. Hitchcock back to England is not a desire to negotiate a private deal with him for the future."

Hitchcock was eager to form a company with Bernstein. Although Alma had applied for American citizenship immediately upon resettling in the United States, Hitchcock himself was in no great hurry to do so. He had fashioned a lucrative career for himself in America, and he had escaped the enormous British tax bite the same way he had escaped the London bombings; but there was still a lingering desire to do something for England, to contribute time and talent, and Bernstein's proposal would enable him to have the best of both worlds. He could, under the suggested scheme, be his own producer, pick his own subjects, aid the postwar British economy, reestablish ties with old colleagues and old haunts — and at the same time he could also have the grander comforts and compensations of Hollywood. A deal with Bernstein, who owned and operated the Granada theater chain in England, would enable Hitchcock to divide his time and his energies between two countries, each of which, for different reasons, claimed his loyalties.

In London, Hitchcock settled into a suite at Claridge's, and while writer Angus MacPhail and an assistant worked on stories to be rendered into French dialogue, he entertained at long luncheons. To Alexander Korda and Vivien Leigh, who were also at Claridge's that month, he told the stories of the two short films he would make at the Welwyn Studios with a French cast and crew. (The production company was called Phoenix Films, probably a reference to the hope that France, like the mythic bird after its death, would rise after the war.)

The first, *Bon Voyage,* was a twenty-five-minute melodrama about the shifting moralities of the French Resistance, and Hitchcock very rightly worried whether, with a murder committed by one of the characters who was supposed to be a hero, it would ever be shown in France. It never was — nor was the second film, *Aventure Malgache,* a thirty-one-minute story, told in flashback, suggesting that a group of French actors in exile was animated by the same spirit as those in the underground on home soil. As it turned out, the films were made quickly (both were shot between January 20 and February 25) and shipped out to a disappointed French distributor, who shelved them at once. No one was much interested in providing them with subtitles and releasing them in England (they ostensibly celebrated the *French,* after all), and most prints disappeared.*

But there was another project that had Hitchcock's attention. Aware of Selznick's desire to make a picture about the healing possibilities of psychotherapy, Hitchcock had looked for an appropriate literary property to buy. He was eager to avoid controversial topics and he intended, for once, to beat Selznick at his own game by purchasing the film option on an adaptable novel and reselling the rights to the outwitted producer. Before he left for London, Hitchcock had read just such a property: *The House of Dr. Edwardes* — a bizarre tale of witchcraft, satanic cults, psychopathology, murder, and mistaken identities, set in a Swiss asylum. Originally published in 1927 in London, and in America the following year, the copyright to the novel — written by John Leslie Palmer and Hilary Aidan St. George Saunders under the collective pseudonym Francis Beeding — had reverted to the authors in 1939.

Hitchcock proceeded to convince Selznick that the odd novel could be substantially reworked to become a thriller in which psychoanalysis solved a mystery. Selznick, who was in fact himself consulting a psychotherapist at the time, was wildly enthusiastic: "I'd like to stress," he wrote to his story editor Margaret McDonell, "that I'm almost desperately anxious to do this psychological or psychiatric story with Hitch."

The first thing Hitchcock did upon arriving in London, therefore, was to buy all the remaining film and performance rights to the novel (his successful gambit was coincidentally facilitated by the death of one of the authors). As soon as Angus MacPhail had completed the treatments for the two French pictures, Hitchcock put him to work on a treatment for *The House of Dr. Edwardes.* But by the end of February, very little had been written.

Selznick, who had finally decided it was time to bring Hitchcock back to his own studio for a production, was ready to buy the rights from the director and begin filming as soon as Hitchcock returned to America. The producer at first wanted Joseph Cotten, Dorothy McGuire, and Paul Lukas in the leading roles eventually played by Gregory Peck, Ingrid Bergman, and Leo G. Carroll. He busily made plans and awaited news of the script. What he could not know was that time spent in London, the French films, the empty cottage at Shamley Green, and deep lone-

---

*The British Film Institute has retained a copy of each.

liness had combined to depress Hitchcock beyond his abilities for effective script work. Nevertheless, Hitchcock cabled Alma (for Selznick's benefit) that *The House of Dr. Edwardes* was shaping up, and that he looked forward to her contributions to it. MacPhail's treatment, he added, was finished.*

In March Hitchcock returned to New York from London, checked into the Saint Regis Hotel, and cabled Selznick that he would like to do the script with Ben Hecht, who was living in Nyack, New York.

At once Hitchcock and Hecht set to work. They visited the Hartford Retreat in Connecticut and met with its chief of staff; then they toured other mental hospitals in Connecticut and in New York's Westchester County before moving on to the psychiatric wards at Bellevue Hospital in New York City. Hecht, working from a detailed outline Hitchcock put together in two nights, then sat down and began to produce almost twenty pages of script a day. Officially, Selznick was Hecht's superior, but Selznick was in Culver City and Hitchcock was at his elbow in the East, and by the end of April a script was complete.

The Hitchcock-Hecht collaboration was a fruitful one. The two men shared an interest in the darker passages of the human mind. (Hecht was also in analysis at the time, and he and Selznick often compared the experience). While Hecht kept Hitchcock on course in developing a coherent plot, Hitchcock introduced Hecht to the idea of the terrifying possibilities of everyday life, which often contains small traumas that affect the spirit and can affect drama. "Hitchcock taught Hecht to be a cynic without even the conviction of his own cynicism," as one of Hecht's chroniclers has stated. Hecht found Hitchcock genial enough — "the gentlemanly Alfred Hitchcock," he wrote in his autobiography, "gave off plot turns like a Roman candle." But he also noticed that Hitchcock was putting more of his own soul into their work than he expected; at this time, Hecht wrote succinctly, Hitchcock was "beaming amid his nightmares."

The finished script, which initially had only some of the love interest augmented by Selznick later, concerns an amnestic psychiatrist who is wrongly accused of the murder of the doctor whose position he has assumed at an asylum. Through the patience and love of another analyst — and as they become romantically involved — the mystery is solved and the real killer (the former chief of the asylum) is unmasked.

---

*The existence of the Hitchcock-MacPhail treatment is doubtful, since as late as the following autumn Selznick was complaining: "I am quite upset over my inability to get hold of a copy of the treatment which Hitchcock brought back from England . . . . , for which he was paid a very substantial amount of money."

For all the twists and turns of the story, Hitchcock's recent experience comes through. There is a sense of brooding guilt in *Spellbound* — the name finally suggested by one of Selznick's secretaries — and a sense of the legacy of family neurosis, the imprint of an adult's distance from childhood memories long buried under an avalanche of fearful repression. From the turgid grotesqueries of the Beeding novel, Hitchcock (with Hecht) fashioned a story about the multiple layers of guilt he himself felt so deeply. "I'm haunted," says Gregory Peck (as the hero) wistfully, "but I can't see by what."

The story's two stories of guilt were Hitchcock's own, irrepressible at last: one man (Norman Lloyd, as the obsessed Garmes, who finally attempts suicide) believes his negligence was responsible for his *father's* death; another (Peck) believes his negligence was responsible for his *brother's* death. But the kindly analyst (Ingrid Bergman) responds to these demons that haunted Hitchcock: "People often feel guilt over something they never did. It usually goes back to their childhood. The child often wishes something terrible would happen to someone, and if something *does* happen to that person, the child believes he has caused it. And he grows up with a guilt complex over a sin that was only a child's bad dream."

Those words, by Hitchcock himself, address the admixture of resentment and guilt that characterized his relationship with his own father (as Peck's cry — "Unlock the doors! You can't keep people in cells!" — may recall Hitchcock's childhood memory of being locked, by his father, in a prison cell). And in the oddly inappropriate use, by an analyst, of the word *sin,* the hand of the Victorian-Catholic moralist is revealed; Hitchcock's concept of sin was never that of English liberalism, which identified it with bad manners or poor judgment. The sin was fantasized, was in his mind — and so the "sins" of the characters in *Spellbound* are cleared up, resolved, forgiven, by being declared imaginary.

After *Shadow of a Doubt,* with its dark exploration of the underside of human nature — and of the underside of his own jolly social exterior — Hitchcock created, in *Spellbound,* a sense of fevered guilt and tortured romanticism that follows from that earlier exploration. *Spellbound* is the first film in which he dealt with guilt incapacitating the reach toward love, and in every film to come he would affirm this mutual, tragic connection. In Hitchcock's emerging world, lover and beloved never find liberation from the shackles of their past, can never rise from the chains of resentment and remorse. His work became a more acute spiritual autobiography with every film — an autobiography based on outer experiences that transmuted themselves into tortured, guilt-ridden fantasies.

From love and loss — whether on a romantic or a family level — work was the only refuge, and the pattern is described by Michael Chekhov as the grandfatherly analyst in *Spellbound:* "It is very sad to love and lose somebody. But in a while you will forget. You will take up the threads of your life where you left off not so long ago. And you will work hard. There's lots of happiness in working hard. Maybe the most.'' After his various losses, this was what Hitchcock himself had found to be true.

"I won't do this movie,'' Ingrid Bergman said at first, "because I don't believe the love story.'' But her objections were overridden by Selznick. (After dropping the idea of Dorothy McGuire, he had also abandoned hopes of wooing Greta Garbo back to the screen for the role of the cool psychiatrist who, somewhat improbably, combines therapy with love.) Bergman was surprised and delighted, however, that Hitchcock did not suffer Selznick's meddling quite as gladly as the cast expected. "When Selznick came down to the set,'' she remembered,

the camera suddenly stopped, and Hitchcock said the cameraman couldn't get it going again. "I don't know what's wrong with it,'' he would say. "They're working on it, they're working on it.'' And finally Selznick would leave, and miraculously the camera would start rolling again. It was his way of dealing with interference, and although I think Selznick finally guessed that it was a ruse, he said nothing. I think Hitchcock was one of the few directors who could really stand up to him. Selznick then left him alone after that. They were two strong men, but I think they had great respect for each other.

According to Gregory Peck, "Selznick believed in treating his actors like little tin gods, but he was a little hard on directors. Hitchcock, I think, learned to take it all in stride.''

The cast found Hitchcock calmly efficient but cool during the shooting of *Spellbound*. The joking, the little conferences, the wines at lunch, the stream of puns — all these earlier characteristics of his manner on the set were absent, along with even the milder forms of his notorious practical jokes. It was as if he had left his sense of humor in England, back with the rubble of war and his family's graves. There was a strange detachment in his manner — a distance that kept everyone quiet and alert and obedient. "He would sit patiently,'' Ingrid Bergman recalled,

and he would listen to my objections that I couldn't move behind a certain table, for instance, or that a gesture on a certain line was awkward. And then when I was finished complaining to him and I thought I'd won him over to my point of view he would say very sweetly, "Fake it!'' This advice was a great help to me later, when other directors wanted something difficult and I thought no, it was impossible. Then I would remember Hitchcock saying to me, "Fake it!"

But he didn't mingle with us on the set. He would be polite, but if people got noisy he knew how to get silence. He would lower his voice almost to a whisper so no one could hear him. And gradually everyone would have to keep quiet. It was a kind of intimidation tactic, perhaps. Of course we had all heard about his feeling that actors are cattle, and we expected something worse.

To irritate us, he would say, "Well, all my fun is over now that you actors are here." Because all his fun had been in the preparation, the writing, the camera setups, the fantasy of his mind, he regarded us as intruders to his fantasy. But he was always very controlled. He never lost his temper or screamed at anyone. And yet he always got what he wanted.

Gregory Peck, who had just made a stunning film debut and was one of Selznick's brightest young stars, agreed that Hitchcock was somewhat detached and distant.

He really didn't give us very much direction, although I was so inexperienced I felt I needed a good deal of direction. In answer to my questions about mood or expression, he would simply say that I was to drain my face of all expression and he would photograph me. I wanted more than that; the business was so new to me. But if he didn't give much direction, he did give me a case of wine when he found out I was a novice about wine. He was more than willing to improve my education in that regard. . . . But I had the feeling that something ailed him, and I could never understand what it might be.

Photography lasted from Monday, July 10, to Friday, October 13, and at the conclusion Hitchcock, much to Selznick's annoyance, decided to exercise his option for the twelve-week vacation his contract allowed. (On August 31, he had signed a new agreement with Selznick, more than doubling his salary, retroactively, to $7,500 weekly, or a total of $150,000 for the twenty weeks work on *Spellbound*.) Selznick was not simply irritated because the star director's vacation meant an interruption: he was well aware that Hitchcock was off to London to continue negotiations with Sidney Bernstein. The moviemakers' world is a small one, and Selznick learned that the two Englishmen were about to announce the formation of Transatlantic Pictures, to make films in England and America when Hitchcock's contract with Selznick finally expired. Hitchcock and Bernstein were intent on making a color film — color films were becoming increasingly popular following the success of Technicolor in such films as *Gone With the Wind* — and they hoped to cast Ingrid Bergman, who, Hitchcock felt, could be won away from Selznick at the right moment.

Another reason for Selznick's irritation was that the postproduction on *Spellbound* presented major problems — mostly involving the complicated dream sequences for which Selznick, at Hitchcock's request, had hired Salvador Dalí. "Selznick thought I wanted Dali only for publicity purposes," Hitchcock said.

That wasn't true. I felt that if I was going to have dream sequences, they should be vivid. I didn't think we should resort to the old-fashioned blurry effect they got by putting Vaseline around the lens. What I really wanted to do, and they wouldn't do it because of the expense, was to have the dream sequences shot on the back lot in the bright sunshine. . . . But I used Dali for his draftsmanship. I wanted to convey the dreams with great visual sharpness and clarity, sharper than the film itself. . . . Chirico [Giorgio de Chirico, the Italian painter] has the same quality, the long shadows, the infinity of distance, and the converging lines of perspective.

And so the eccentric Dalí had arrived in Hollywood, amid much fanfare. He spent most of September and early October working with Hitchcock' on the content of the dreams, and produced more than a hundred sketches and five oil paintings for the set designer to execute. The translation to film of the symbolic dreams, entirely the product of Hitchcock's imagination, was accomplished by trick-photographer Rex Wimpy.

But Dalí's bizarre surrealist ideas (some of which had derived from *Un Chien Andalou* and *L'Age d'Or,* the films he had designed in Paris with Luis Buñel in the late 1920s) went to extremes, and even Hitchcock had to admit that Selznick was right: the dream sequence as designed and first filmed went on too long and became too complicated.*

By the time Hitchcock left for London, the photography of the dream sequences was still incomplete, which further annoyed Selznick. He first tried to engage Josef von Sternberg to direct them, but settled for William Cameron Menzies, who filmed the rooftop miniatures, the gambling-house dream, and the cutting of the eye-studded draperies. At Menzies's own request (because he thought the entire episode unappealing), he was uncredited on the film, and when the press and the public swooned over the final effect and made the film a commercial success, Hitchcock gladly took the credit for himself.

The music for *Spellbound* was also a problem. As early as September 11, Hitchcock sent Selznick a "spot musical score," which listed the

---

*Ingrid Bergman felt, however, that the original dream sequence as shot was more effective: "It was much longer and more interesting. It was really something to put in a museum. The final film did not include this complicated footage, in which I became a plaster statue in the man's dream (which meant we shot the film backward, with me breaking out of it). There were so many wonderful things in it, but they decided to cut it all down to a minute or two instead of the twenty-minute sequence we worked so hard on. It was such a pity. It could have been really sensational."

spots or places in the script he thought music should be heard. Selznick's first recommendation was Bernard Herrmann, a New York conductor whose music for Orson Welles's *Citizen Kane* and *The Magnificent Ambersons* quickly raised him to the first rank of Hollywood composers. Someone else suggested Leopold Stokowski, who had worked with Walt Disney on *Fantasia*. "I'm not too keen about the Stokowski idea," Selznick wrote in a staff memo, "because as I understand it, on the last job he did he drove everyone out of their minds as regards time and expense. I still can't see anyone to compare with Herrmann." But Herrmann was unavailable, and Selznick signed Miklos Rozsa, whose lush score won the Academy Award and established the theremin as the standard musical instrument of cinematic psychosis.

As his departure for London approached, Hitchcock's spirits improved, and he warmed to several social events. He and Alma hosted a wedding reception following the marriage of actress Anna Lee to director Robert Stevenson. "I gave Anna Lee away twice," he announced to a guest crowd that included Ingrid Bergman and Joan Fontaine, "— once when I didn't cast her in *Foreign Correspondent,* and today when I gave her away to her groom." And then he regaled the guests with an uproarious monologue in which he suggested that the entire marriage ceremony was really a string of movie titles. "I wonder who the writer and producer will be for next year's movie hits," he asked. "Who would like to appear in *To Have and To Hold . . . In Sickness and In Health . . . Until Death Do Us Part . . . For Richer, For Poorer . . . For Better, For Worse?*" and he came up with appropriate casts for this series of melodramas, romances, and screwball comedies.

On October 15, two days after Romanoff's catered an end-of-shooting party on the set of *Spellbound,* Hitchcock left for England. He just missed seeing his daughter Patricia's second Broadway appearance — in *Violet,* Whitfield Cook's theatrical rearrangement of a collection of stories. Playing an obstreperous brat who sets out to untangle the love life of her much-married father, Pat filled the title role at New York's Belasco Theater for a dreary twenty-three performances (the same-length run she had in *Solitaire*) before poor attendance closed what one critic called "a depressingly synthetic comedy." But the vivacious Pat, now sixteen, was undaunted and looked forward even more earnestly to a serious career in the theater.

In London, meanwhile, Hitchcock met with Sidney Bernstein to draw up plans for their new corporation. He was also scheduled to meet with Eric Ambler, whom Selznick was considering as scriptwriter for their next production; but there is no record of any conference. Fifteen years later, however, Ambler would meet Hitchcock under different circumstances: when Ambler and Joan Harrison announced their wedding date.

The return from England, in time for Christmas, was met by news from Selznick's offices: there was so much confidence about the forthcoming success of *Spellbound,* with its winning Hitchcock-Hecht-Bergman team, that Selznick was ready to proceed with a story Hitchcock had wanted to do for some time. It turned out to be not only Hitchcock's most beguiling romance, but also one of his most alarmingly personal films — full of repressed passion, desire and danger, and the conflicts of duty.

"We're just bundles of inhibitions" was a line he had written for Ingrid Bergman in *Spellbound.* Now he was on the verge of creating a new script — again for Bergman, for whom his feelings were becoming more complicated — and he turned to a consideration of how those inhibitions might affect a love-smitten, repressed romantic. The new work would have the patina of espionage melodrama, but that was just an excuse — his now legendary MacGuffin, or plot pretext, for a more subtle self-disclosure. No character and no performance, until James Stewart in *Rear Window* and *Vertigo,* would come closer to Hitchcock's self-understanding than — of all people — Cary Grant in *Notorious.*

# Ten

---

## 1945–1949

"I HAD a long lunch with Hitchcock last Friday," Margaret McDonell had reported in a memo to David Selznick on Monday, August 7, 1944. "He is very anxious to do a story about confidence tricks on a grand scale, in which Ingrid Bergman, whom he wants very much, could play the woman who is carefully trained and coached into a gigantic confidence trick which might involve her marrying some man. . . . He would rather like a diplomatic stake and the background of Washington towards the end of the war — possibly Argentina as the foreign power. . . . The training of such a woman would be as elaborate as the training of a Mata Hari."

The idea of rehearsing and transforming a woman so that she takes another social identity is central to the films of Alfred Hitchcock, as it was central to his approach to women who acted for him. In the treatment of *Secret Agent* he had at first put greater emphasis on the selling into espionage work of the Madeleine Carroll character, a step that would inevitably lead to romantic or at least sexual compromise. And later, in *Vertigo* most of all, this motif of making over a woman according to a fantasy would be explored in all its demonic depth. The demonism would flash forth in real life, during the twilight of Hitchcock's career, in his attempt not only to coach and to train, but also to control and to compromise an actress for whom he had carefully created a screen persona.

But that outcome was the culmination of an idea that was forming earlier. On September 15, 1944, Hitchcock dined at Chasen's with William Dozier, a producer for RKO, and outlined the story of a woman sold for political purposes into sexual enslavement. (*Who Is My Love?* was the title he then had in mind.) Dozier agreed that it could be a compelling movie, and soon he and Selznick were discussing the possibility of a sale to RKO — a package deal that would repeat the Hitch-cock-Hecht-Bergman collaboration. But at this time Selznick was not at all sure he would sell the package rather than do the film himself: the basic idea, it turned out, had originated with him, but in more tepid tones than Hitchcock had described. Selznick had read a two-part short story, "The Song of the Dragon" by John Taintor Foote, in the November 12 and 19, 1921, issues of the *Saturday Evening Post*, and he had kept them in his file of unproduced stories for years before finally passing them on to Hitchcock during the filming of *Spellbound*.

By the time Hitchcock returned from England at Christmas in 1944, he had an outline ready, and he soon received approval from Selznick to contact Hecht in Nyack. For three weeks they closeted themselves in Hecht's cluttered workroom and hammered out the major scenes of the first draft, which Hitchcock rewrote each night back at the Saint Regis. Soon firmly entitled *Notorious*, the story concerned a loose-moraled woman, daughter of a Nazi spy, who is impressed into service at the end of the war as part of the United States government's efforts to outwit a group of Nazis living in Brazil. Although in love with the American agent who engages her for the task, she agrees to go so far as to marry an old acquaintance who heads the German spy ring. She is then discovered by her husband, who, with the help of his tyrannical mother, slowly poisons her. Near death, she is rescued by the American agent she still loves.*

The Hecht-Hitchcock collaboration proceeded smoothly, primarily because Hecht cared little how much Hitchcock rewrote. "The merger of Hitchcock and Hecht as a director-writer team," reported Frank Nugent at the time,

was, like most Hollywood collaborations, a sort of shotgun marriage, the shotgun being held in this instance by producer David O. Selznick. Mr. Selznick never has played Cupid so well. Even their story conferences were idyllic. Mr. Hecht would stride about or drape himself over chair or couch, or sprawl artistically on the floor. Mr. Hitchcock, a 192-pound Buddha (reduced from 295) would sit primly on a straight-back chair, his hands clasped across his midriff, his round button eyes gleaming. They would talk from nine to six; Mr. Hecht would sneak off with his typewriter for two or three days; then they would have another conference. The dove of peace lost not a pinfeather in the process. They did not even play jokes on each other.†

---

*The poisoned drink, denied to Hitchcock as an element in *Suspicion* and actualized harmlessly in *Spellbound*, is at last fully exploited in *Notorious*.

†Certain memos in the RKO and Selznick archives suggest that, just before filming began, Clifford Odets was paid to do some minor script revisions, but there is no evidence of any contribution incorporated into the final shooting script, and no record of correspondence or payment survives.

"The whole film was really designed as a love story," Hitchcock said many years later.

I wanted to make this film about a man who forces a woman to go to bed with another man because it's his professional duty. The politics of the thing didn't much interest me, but I realized we had to have a reason for the Germans to be in Brazil. We thought of jewel mining, precious minerals, that sort of thing, and then one day I said to Hecht, "What about uranium?" and he shrugged and said he didn't think it mattered, that one MacGuffin was as good as another if we were really putting together a love story.

By the end of March we were back in Los Angeles and Selznick read what we'd put together. By this time I'd decided on the uranium angle — uranium hidden in wine bottles seemed like a good idea — and he called me in and said, "What's all this about uranium in wine bottles?" And I said that uranium, as far as I knew, was an unstable element, just like the world, and that everybody knew it was rare. It seemed to me that ever since Rutherford split an atom of it and released a lot of energy, that someone, someday, would make a bomb out of it. And with all the talk in 1945 of some devastating secret weapon we were supposed to be developing, my angle sounded topical. Selznick thought the whole thing was somewhat harebrained. I insisted that even Hecht had agreed with me — it didn't really matter, we were telling a love story.

The business of the uranium remained a considerable source of publicity for Hitchcock to the end of his life. To François Truffaut, to this writer, and to many others, he always insisted that he had chosen the device of uranium ore in Nazi experiments quite coincidentally, far in advance of the detonation of the atomic bomb in Japan in August 1945. He maintained that he and Hecht clarified the script's parenthetical reference to uranium after visiting Dr. Robert A. Millikan at the California Institute of Technology in May or June, and that this visit created enough nervousness on the part of Millikan and the Federal Bureau of Investigation that — as Hitchcock told it — the director was himself placed under surveillance during the shooting of the film. He always emphasized, in every discussion of *Notorious,* that he was virtually a prophet, having thought of the uranium angle in 1944, a year before Hiroshima.

But Hitchcock's calculated image of himself as a prophet does not coincide with the truth; inspired by his sense of publicity, he told a better story than the facts reveal. By the time *Notorious* actually began filming, in October 1945, Hitchcock had made yet another trip to London (from late June to late July, to meet again with Sidney Bernstein), and he had returned to Los Angeles for final script work in September — after the bombings of Japan, and after he had spent several weeks in New York testing actors, among whom were several famous German refugees he finally cast in the film. On the basis of news from these German contacts, and from the accounts that flooded the world press after the surrender of Germany (in May) and of Japan (in August), Hitchcock and Hecht refined the last addenda to their script just before the first day of production.

In May Selznick had received a letter from the FBI warning that any film depicting American intelligence officers would have to have State Department approval before export of the film would be permitted. This was communicated at once to Hitchcock, with the advice that the MacGuffin of spies and intelligence activities should remain just that — a MacGuffin, entirely subordinate to the romance that Hitchcock had always wanted to emphasize in any case.

It was this letter to Selznick (unfortunately not preserved in the Selznick archives, but mentioned in a memorandum from him to Daniel O'Shea, dated May 21) that probably later inspired Hitchcock to talk about his being under government "surveillance." FBI files reveal no such personal scrutiny. And in fact the filming of *Notorious* could not have proceeded as smoothly as it did that autumn and winter under such tense conditions (especially with a largely non-American cast). The extremely sensitive Hitchcock, more frightened than ever of authorities who might question his intentions (his wife, after all, had become a citizen and he had not), would surely have been emotionally incapable of directing a picture under the oppressive and suspicious circumstances an FBI investigation would create. All the evidence suggests that in truth the uranium was included after the fact, and that Hitchcock heard of the existence of Nazi refugees in South America from the German, Jewish, and anti-Nazi refugees he had come to know in New York and Los Angeles.*

In any event, Selznick grew cooler by the day, and during April he ordered that joint script sessions be held at his home (as he had done on *Rebecca*). Hitchcock knew what this meant, and he was not eager for these conferences. Selznick ordinarily called the working sessions for late in the evening, and eleven o'clock was a typical beginning time. Earlier Hitchcock and Hecht would dine at Romanoff's, to clear some thorny sections of the script and pool their defenses about what Hitchcock thought was a first-rate script. As the appointed time approached, Hecht would prepare to depart for Selznick's house, but Hitchcock predicted that it mattered little if they were late, since Selznick would pace

* Salka Viertel's *The Kindness of Strangers* (New York: Holt, Rinehart & Winston, 1969) is a lively account of this refugee community.

and shuffle and not settle down to serious consideration until three in the morning. Several nights were passed just as he said, to his profound annoyance.

Hitchcock spent late summer and early autumn at New York theaters. By September Selznick, deeply involved in the production of the epic *Duel in the Sun,* had sold the entire *Notorious* package to RKO for $800,000 and 50 percent of the profits, and Dozier and Hitchcock had assumed the producer's responsibilities. Ingrid Bergman and Cary Grant had been contracted for the leading roles, and to them Hitchcock added the distinguished German actor-director Reinhold Schuenzel, dancer-mime Ivan Triesault, and the versatile Louis Calhern. Dozier selected Claude Rains for the sympathetic villain — Hitchcock had oddly wanted the epicene Clifton Webb — and when Ethel Barrymore rejected the role of the villain's mother, RKO suggested Mildred Natwick. But the role of the spidery, tyrannical Nazi matron demanded a stronger, older presence. Schuenzel proposed one of the great actresses of prewar Germany: Leopoldine Konstantin. She had acted with Max Reinhardt's Deutsches Theater from 1908 to 1937, and had made an American tour in 1911/1912. Her role in *Notorious* turned out to be her only American screen performance (she was so unknown in Hollywood that RKO negotiated a paltry salary), but it was also one of the unforgettable portraits in Hitchcock's films.

Principal photography lasted from October 1945 to February 1946. The Hitchcocks' social life had been virtually nonexistent while the director was engaged in publicity activities. In July, for her daughter's seventeenth birthday — and before Pat departed for Marymount College in Tarrytown, New York — Alma gave a dinner party in her honor; Hitchcock ordered two dozen bottles of a perfume that had been specially created and named for *Spellbound* and had them distributed to his daughter's dinner guests. Alma, in the autumn, continued as the ideal hostess and companion, accompanying her husband to several radio shows on which he made publicity appearances — not to publicize his films, but to publicize himself. In the earlier part of the year he was on Milton Berle's radio program in New York (for which he was paid $2,000 — half what he had asked); and later, contestants tried to guess his identity on *Which Is Which?* But the biographical data he submitted was so vague that he stumped the stars and won $1,000.

In November *Spellbound* opened throughout the country, and within weeks was on its way to earning eight times its cost during its initial release. Critics were as enthusiastic as the public; and when the Academy Award nominations were announced, the picture was in competition for best picture, best direction, best performance by an actor in a supporting role (Michael Chekhov), best cinematography, best special effects, and best musical score (it won only in the last category).

Also within weeks, a new lease was given on the popularity of psychotherapy. Such was the power of film in pretelevision 1945, when almost 70 percent of the American people attended movies at least once weekly. In several major cities therapists placed advertisements for their services — and were quickly reprimanded by their colleagues and by professional societies. And in at least one case a fraud associated himself with Hitchcock's film: in Los Angeles, someone calling himself Bernard Gindes bought space in the classified section of the telephone book, proclaimed himself as a psychiatric adviser on *Spellbound,* and announced that he was accepting clients. Selznick's offices at once investigated the man, whose listed address proved false. Days later, Mr. Gindes could not be found.*

Soon tensions between the Hitchcocks grew. His several trips to England, the deaths of their mothers, the increasing alienation of Alma from the production of the films, and Hitchcock's obvious fascination for Ingrid Bergman conspired to sharpen the normally quiet undercurrent of resentment that crosscut their need and dependence on one another. Those who attended the small dinner parties at Bellagio Road at the time (the guests included Ingrid Bergman and her husband Dr. Petter Lindstrom; Cary Grant, recently divorced from heiress Barbara Hutton; Teresa Wright and her husband; and Anne Baxter and her husband-to-be John Hodiak) were always sure of an elegant dinner with the right wines and the right appointments, and dancing afterward.

But visitors noticed that there was a chill in the air when they came upon the Hitchcocks alone. With dinner guests they were models of mutual respect, even playing to one another's culinary caprices. But more than one daytime visitor, ushered to the living room to await Hitchcock's arrival, heard voices raised in angry recrimination in the upstairs bedroom. They were like children with each other at times like this, and for a day or two after these spats, Hitchcock acted like a punished schoolboy — pouting, moody, and glumly attentive to the small, active woman who was his creative counselor and his motherly muse, prodding and encouraging and correcting him in private, but always appropriately quiet and subsidiary in public.

But Hitchcock's sense of duty at home and at work clashed with a long-suppressed sexual life he neither understood nor fully wanted ("Food is usually the substitute for sex," he said years later). And that

---

* In fact the only psychiatric adviser to the film was Selznick's own therapist at the time, Dr. May E. Romm, who is listed among the credits.

clash, resonating within him, was at last heard — with merely the lightest fictive veil — in *Notorious,* in the dialogue Hitchcock completely revised in the first days of shooting.

*Notorious* is in fact Alfred Hitchcock's first attempt — at the age of forty-six — to bring his talents to the creation of a serious love story, and its story of two men in love with Ingrid Bergman could only have been made at this stage of his life. The death of his mother, the deeply maternal relationship to his wife, the seeming suicide of his brother, the unrealized and misshapen, adolescent romantic impulses of a lovesick middle-aged director toward an unapproachable goddess — all released a flood of conflicting feelings that made *Notorious* not only possible but necessary — the artistic rendition of an inner life that might have exploded if denied expression. Hitchcock's work on this picture became, as it was on no project up to this time, a way of dealing with the conflict between private desire and public duty, between passion and pretense.

These life-motifs are represented by the characters played by Grant and Rains, who externalize the two sides of Hitchcock himself. Grant, as an emotionally constricted man who never smiles and who admits, "I've always been scared of women," is full of unspent passion for Bergman, but he can neither articulate his love nor respond to her desire for him. Instead, he prefers to believe that she is an unregenerate tramp. Rains, on the other hand, is the outspoken lover, aware that other men are more handsome, yet jealous of Bergman, who finds him repulsive. "You always affected me like a tonic," he tells her. . . . . "I knew that if I saw you again I'd feel what I used to for you — the same hunger. You're so lovely, my dear."

The conflicts press against Bergman, who accepts the role of sexual blackmailer in a sad attempt to win approval from the man she really loves. But the world she enters is so laced with deception that all the true feelings become blurred. The truth of passion — as when Grant kisses Bergman outside the wine cellar — is used as if it were a lie, to throw the pursuing Rains off the trail of their real purpose. That moment, in fact, is the stencil for all the deceptive glances and small talk of the film.

If the different attitudes of the two men mark the conflict between the desire for both a passionate and a dutiful life in Hitchcock himself, that conflict was further complicated by an adolescent confusion between food and sex, expressed in the three-minute balcony kissing scene in which Grant and Bergman nibble at each other's lips and ears and neck while talking about the evening meal. The origin of this scene — devised by Hitchcock in an attempt to circumvent the Hollywood restric-

tion about prolonged kissing — shows the odd connection Hitchcock
made between conversation, action, and intention. The kissing, he insisted, gave the public

the great privilege of embracing Cary Grant and Ingrid Bergman together. It
was a kind of temporary *ménage à trois*. . . . I felt that they should remain in
an embrace and that we should join them. So when they got to the phone the
camera followed them, never leaving the close-up all the way, right over to the
door — all in one continuous shot. . . . The idea came to me many, many
years ago when I was on a train going from Boulogne to Paris. There's a big,
old, red brick factory, and at one end of the factory was this huge, high brick
wall. There were two little figures at the bottom of the wall — a boy and a
girl. The boy was urinating against the wall, but the girl had hold of his arm
and she never let go. She'd look down at what he was doing, and then look
around at the scenery, and down again to see how far he'd got on. And that
was what gave me the idea. She couldn't let go. Romance must not be interrupted, even by urinating. . . . [Grant and Bergman] told me they felt very
awkward in that scene in *Notorious*. But I told them not to worry, it would
look great on film, and that's all that mattered. It's one of my most famous
scenes.*

This was certainly a curious memory to have affected Hitchcock so
deeply over the years, and an even stranger one to connect with the
ardent passions of *Notorious*. But the juvenile and sometimes pathological association between matters of bedroom and matters of toilet (suggested as early as the tearing of the bathroom tissue while talking of
marriage in *Secret Agent*) would become even more confused in his later
films, and in his later life.

The finished film reveals the confusions of desire and duty, love,
food, sex, and elimination; it is also representative of a sharp new assessment of the mother-son relationship. How this operates in *Shadow
of a Doubt* has been explored earlier. There, Hitchcock's own dying
mother was alluded to in the unseen and ill Mrs. Hawkins, of whom
characters speak with concern three times. In *Spellbound*, after his visit
to England to deal with the last of his mother's things, Hitchcock reflected himself in the remarks of the police investigator (Art Baker),
who, resentful of his mother's demands, justifies Hitchcock's remaining
in America during his own mother's final illness: "She's still complaining, and feels I ought to get transferred. I asked if she thought I should
sacrifice a chance of promotion for her. And the boss made some crack

---

*Ben Hecht visited the set the day the balcony kissing scene was shot, and recognizing that it
was one of Hitchcock's many additions, said: "I don't get all this talk about chicken!"

about me being a momma's boy.'' The character exists only for the sake of this statement about his mother. But in *Notorious* the role of the mother is at last fully introduced and examined. No longer relegated to mere conversation, she appears here as a major character for the first time in an Alfred Hitchcock picture, and all at once — as later, through *Psycho, The Birds,* and *Marnie* — Hitchcock began to make the mother figure a personal repository of his anger, guilt, resentment, and a sad yearning.

As the two men of the film stand in for two aspects of Hitchcock's desires (the passionate and the repressed), the two women (Ingrid Bergman and Leopoldine Konstantin) fuse and confuse the roles of wife and mother. At the two critical moments in his relationship with Bergman, Rains goes to his mother's bedroom — once to announce his marriage and berate his mother's jealousy, later to ask for her help when he discovers his wife's treachery. The detail is drawn from Hitchcock's own life: his long custom, during the years he lived in Leytonstone, of reporting to his mother while standing at the foot of her bed each evening. Both Bergman and Konstantin are called "Madame" in the film, the term used by Hitchcock to refer to Alma all during their life together.*
And Ingrid Bergman is given one of Alma's legendary characteristics, drawn from the scene of Hitchcock's marriage proposal: "I don't care for boats,'' she says while being poisoned. "I always get seasick.'' There are also multiple references to Bergman as Grant's "momma,'' and to the situation between Rains and Konstantin, which resembles more a marriage than a filial relationship.

This confusion of mother-love and erotic love — brilliantly suggested by the merging shadows of mother and son as seen from the drugged Bergman's point of view — is not peculiar to Hitchcock, of course; it has often enough been the catalyst for famous literary and artistic transmutations. What is so poignant about its manifestation in Hitchcock's life at this time, and in this film, is that both kinds of love were in fact limited to longing and fantasy and unfulfilled expectations. Hitchcock had not seen his own mother in the last three and a half years of her life, and he was far from her when she died; his wife, by his own atypically candid admission, lived with him in a chaste companionship; and his most beautiful, most lovingly photographed leading ladies were never more than idealized figurines.

Most revealing, the character of Claude Rains, infatuated (like Hitchcock) with Bergman, found his rival not in Grant but in his mother-as-jealous-wife.

---

*According to those who worked with him as far back as the 1930s, he always referred to Alma in this manner. The custom endured, in conversation and in his infrequent letters, until his death.

RAINS: Mother, is it necessary for you to address Alicia as Miss Huberman?
I do wish you'd be a little more cordial to her.

KONSTANTIN: Really? I thought I was behaving very well. Has she been
complaining about me? [*He shakes his head.*] I am grateful.

RAINS: You might smile at her.

KONSTANTIN: Wouldn't it be a little too much if we both grinned at her like
idiots?

RAINS: Please, Mother, I want to enjoy myself.

KONSTANTIN: Is it so boring to sit with me alone?

RAINS [*in an exasperated mutter*]: Not at all, not at all.

It is tempting to see this as a reflection of Hitchcock's earlier conversations with his own mother, but although the words were added by
Hitchcock himself, one cannot know just how close is the parallel. It
does, however, represent the kind of verbal exchange Alma and Hitchcock could have had in private when one of his leading ladies became
an object of his fantasy — as did Ingrid Bergman.* For the rest of his
life, Hitchcock told an elaborate story — a fiction fresh, at the time,
from the workshop of his own fervid imagination — of Ingrid Bergman's hysterical refusal to leave his bedroom after a dinner party at
Bellagio Road until he agreed to make love to her. Given the circumstances — the presence of the actress's ever-vigilant husband and of
Alma and other guests — and given the discretion, kindness, and, most
of all, the rather different tastes of Ingrid Bergman, the account is certainly apocryphal.

Hitchcock's memory of this period in his life is consistent with a level
of fantasy and of sexual longing so deep that he identified with a surrogate, the character played by Cary Grant. He saw himself as a lover
only in fantasy, and if in the story he circulated about his leading lady
he was not the lover in fact, it had to be only because, for him, the
moment was not yet right. And it also had to be because the guilt over
Alma would have been too great — as would the fear of her (Hitchcock
chronicler John Russell Taylor noted that "there are those who claim
that Alma is the only person he is really frightened of").

*Notorious* may be best remembered by film students for its startling
direction — the single descending elevator shot, from a vast overview
of party guests to a tight close-up of a key in Bergman's hand; the long
kissing scene; the rhythmic intercutting of the final descent by the four-
some along the grand staircase — but less academic moviegoers respond to its obsessive, tainted romanticism. Hitchcock ironically locates

---

*It must be emphasized that although Bergman's private life was in considerable turmoil at the
time, there is nothing to suggest that she herself ever encouraged Hitchcock's attention.

and inverts faithfulness, trust, and patriotism in the sustained motif of drinking: in the opening drunken party ("The important drinking hasn't started yet," Bergman announces), which leads to the morning-after hangover ("Drink it!" Grant orders, indicating the fruit juice; "Drink all of it!''); in the alcoholic drinks taken as refuge from rejection at the outdoor café and the Rio apartment; in the several cups of poisoned coffee; in the MacGuffin of the uranium ore in the wine bottles. All the drinking is valueless and finally dangerous.

Hitchcock himself finalized the careful structure of the film; the first six scenes are completely reversed by the last six, and the major acts of the narrative are marked by three progressively darker and more intimate kisses. And within that structure he drew together his tortured longings and conflicting desires — the dark, death-haunted fears of love and loving, the yearning to atone, the family resentments, the lost aspirations and the keen hope of renewal — and combined them in a speech he wrote for Bergman. On the airplane to Rio, Grant informs her of the suicide of her traitor father (appropriately accomplished, as with the Nazi leaders at the end of the war, by poison capsule), and the camera holds to the suddenly empty, memory-swept desert of her pale features as she speaks:

"I don't know why I should feel so bad. When he told me a few years ago what he was, everything went to pot. I didn't care what happened to me. But now I remember how nice he once was. How nice we both were. Very nice. It's a very curious feeling — as if something had happened to me and not to him. You see, I don't have to hate him anymore. Or myself."

These painful words and the distant gaze of a beautiful, weary woman gave form to a new collision in Alfred Hitchcock's life: between a desire for freedom from the past and for an end to self-reproach, on the one hand, and a residue of bittersweet memories and filial, surrogate guilt on the other. Enhanced by the actress's superbly poignant delivery, few words in any Hitchcock film are fuller with intimate meaning.

Unfortunately, Hitchcock's internal clash of desires was exacerbated by the rekindling of a professional clash of wills, for David O. Selznick at once sought to rescue a foundering career — and a fragile nervous state — by bringing Hitchcock back for one more picture before the expiration of their contract. In the months preceding, Selznick had been sending frequent memoranda to Hitchcock and to William Dozier, tossing off ideas for Hitchcock's next picture for sale to RKO. Among the possibilities were *The Lost Weekend, The Spiral Staircase* (then called

*Some Must Watch*), *Love Letters, Murders in the Rue Morgue, The Turn of the Screw* (to star Joan Fontaine), and *The Devil's Disciple*. Finally, however, Selznick decided to bring Hitchcock back to his own company for a picture under his own supervision.

Since 1933, the year it was published, Robert Hichens's novel *The Paradine Case* had been a pet project for Selznick. At that time he had planned to produce it at MGM, with John and Lionel Barrymore and Diana Wynyard in leading roles. By 1936 he hoped to interest Greta Garbo in it, but she found too distasteful the story of an elegant slut who exploits the passions of a respectable lawyer who is to defend her from a charge of murdering her blind husband. By 1940 Hedy Lamarr and Leslie Howard had been mentioned, Ronald Colman (whom Hitchcock much preferred) having turned down the role of the defense attorney. Now, with Hitchcock back from RKO in early 1946, Selznick wanted to go ahead with a production of *The Paradine Case*. Gregory Peck was assigned the male lead.

From the start the project was in disarray, and it engaged no one's interest very passionately. That it was finished at all was little short of miraculous, for it was certainly a lame-duck enterprise, a work assigned to a departing director by his increasingly neurotic and unselfconfident producer. Selznick's worried and worrisome attitude and Hitchcock's disgust with the content and method that were forced upon him conspired to produce an uneasy atmosphere from which Hitchcock could scarcely wait to extricate himself.

During March, Selznick permitted Hitchcock and the production assistant, Barbara Keon, to work at Bellagio Road, but Selznick very quickly found that little work was being done on the assigned treatment. "The Hitchcock unit," he complained to Daniel O'Shea, "has become a country club, with Miss Keon as a charter member." The Hitchcocks and the disfavored Miss Keon were in fact, until May, passing weekends in Santa Cruz, where considerable attention was given to Hitchcock's plans for his independent production with Sidney Bernstein. Hollywood is a small world, after all, and it took no time for Selznick to discover at one Sunday dinner party, from Ingrid Bergman herself, that Hitchcock and Bernstein were indeed planning their first film, and that she would very likely play the lead in it.

She was not, however, speaking too freely, for on April 11, 1946, the *Daily Film Renter* of London reported that the two Englishmen had formed Transatlantic Pictures to produce films alternately in London and Hollywood, and that the first production (which in the end turned out to be the second) would star Miss Bergman in an adaptation of Helen

Simpson's novel *Under Capricorn.** Simultaneously, it was announced that Hitchcock would also direct for Transatlantic a modern version of *Hamlet* — a project that must certainly have caused consternation among those who thought that serious dramatic art was inconsistent with Hitchcock's presumably pedestrian and commercial concerns.

Victor Peers, who had been production manager with Hitchcock a decade earlier, was engaged to discharge similar duties at the London offices of Transatlantic (located at 36 Golden Square, the corporate headquarters of Granada, Bernstein's theater chain); and when the company was registered in America, Peers was listed as vice-president, Bernstein took the chief position, and Hitchcock (for financial reasons) was named as secretary of the corporation. By the time production began on Transatlantic's film, Warner Brothers had bid successfully for exclusive rights to distribute the company's films in America, and the Bankers Trust Company of New York had agreed to finance its first two ventures up to the sum of $5 million.

While Bernstein and Britain anxiously awaited Hitchcock's scheduled return to London in the late spring of 1946 to consider other films and directors for the fledgling company, Selznick's slow burn flashed into a furious conflagration; Hitchcock's disinterest in *The Paradine Case* was now an open secret, in spite of Selznick's somewhat reckless allotment of a lavish budget that would eventually reach $4 million. He agreed to have an old acquaintance of Hitchcock's — former physician O. H. Mavor, who wrote under the name James Bridie — come to America to work on the treatment of the film, but when Bridie arrived in New York on May 5, Hitchcock simply turned over to him a sheaf of notes and at once departed for London. Bridie rummaged around New York for a fortnight and then, feeling unhelped and unhelpful, cabled Selznick that he was withdrawing from the project and returning to London. He sent along at the same time a prose treatment with some dialogue — an outline of the Paradine perfidy but with no trial, no courtroom drama, none of the brooding romanticism that Selznick had desired.

Meanwhile, Hitchcock went first to Nice, searching, on Selznick's behalf, for a French actress to play Mrs. Paradine in case the negotiations to hire the Italian actress Alida Valli should fail. (They did not, but at that time it was not at all clear that she would be allowed a visa,

---

*Hitchcock knew Simpson socially and professionally. She was coauthor, with Clemence Dane (pseudonym of Winifred Ashton) of *Enter Sir John,* which had been the literary basis of *Murder!*. Simpson had also collaborated on the dialogue for *Sabotage,* and Hitchcock had suggested her friend Dane as a writer for *Rebecca.* The performance rights to *Under Capricorn,* therefore, were available at a reasonable fee.

since there seemed to have been some involvement between her husband and the Italian Fascist government during the war.)* By mid-May, after stopping to attend the war-delayed Paris premiere of *Spellbound,* Hitchcock arrived in London to scout locations in and outside the city for background plates to be used for the new film, and to study the exact measurements of the Old Bailey court for its eventual reconstruction at RKO, where *The Paradine Case* would be filmed under Selznick's constant supervision.

Hitchcock and his unit manager Fred Ahern also photographed the exteriors and charge rooms of the Bow Street magistracy, cells and cell corridors, and the solicitors' rooms at Holloway Prison. They found the right house in Portland Place to be used for the exterior of the leading man's home; and they traveled out to Cumberland to find an estate appropriate for the Paradine country house, finally settling (it was Selznick's only pleasure up to this point) on an estate that could have doubled for *Rebecca*'s Manderley. This research and second-unit photography occupied almost two months — or so Selznick was told. In fact Hitchcock spent a fair portion of the time with Sidney Bernstein, engaging a staff for their company and planning financial contingencies.

Selznick, meantime, was frantic to have a script ready when Hitchcock returned, and he tried, alternately, to hire S. N. Behrman, Samson Raphaelson, Philip Barry, and Elmer Rice to work with him. All were unavailable, however, and on July 11 Selznick, who had met with Alma several times to find out what Hitchcock had had in mind for certain sections of the story, wrote to his assistant: "Clearly there is no one that is entitled to screen credit but myself. Giving Alma credit is giving her considerably more than she is actually entitled to, even though she was a contributor to the early scripts, which were thrown out, and was helpful editorially in conferences."

Selznick's memos at this time waver between a warm generosity and a kind of frightened stinginess. Still another indication of the producer's growing emotional crisis that year was his uncharacteristic inability to make major creative decisions. Among the titles he "firmly fixed" at various times from 1946 through 1947 were *Mrs. Paradine Takes the Stand, The Lie, Heartbreak, The Grand Passion, A Question of Life and Death, A Woman of Experience, The Dark Hour, A Crime of Passion, This Is No Ordinary Woman, Guilty?, The Indelible Stain, Guilty!, The Woman Who Did the Killing, Hanging Is Easy, The Accused, Bewildered, The Green-Eyed Monster,* and *Woman and Wife.* He decided

---

*Back in Hollywood, Selznick and his staff were negotiating with the agents of actresses who might substitute for Valli. Among those seriously considered were Joan Crawford, Vivien Leigh, and, apparently to no one's amusement, Ginger Rogers.

on *The Paradine Case* only hours before the film was sent for its world premiere at the Bruin Theater in Westwood Village on December 31, 1947 — a fact revealed in the film's hastily inserted plain title design, which was crudely at variance with the prevailing Gothic lettering of the rest and which remains on all extant prints to this day.

By August Hitchcock had returned, picked up the script as Selznick had doctored it, and gone at once to Santa Cruz to work on the storyboard and set and camera designs. By this time Selznick was trying to reestablish peace with Bridie (Hitchcock had met with him briefly in London), and Bridie had sent on some additional dialogue.

Hitchcock's dissatisfaction with the Selznick empire, which was diminishing in effectiveness and prestige and efficiency, was no doubt aggravated by certain physical discomforts he complained about at the time, although they remain mysterious and unverifiable. Almost at once, hypochondria seized him with a vengeance, and from Santa Cruz to Selznick's offices and back again he would often mutter, to anyone who might listen or to himself, "Something is wrong, something is very wrong." Alma chauffeured him to a small platoon of physicians, who could find only the hernia and the fluctuating obesity — little more — to explain the patient's bouts of withdrawal and his attacks of sudden, inexplicable anxiety.

His only refuge was in the technical challenges he set for himself — four cameras would simultaneously film the courtroom scenes so that the emotional exchanges between the actors could be maintained in simultaneous takes. His humor improved somewhat for two weeks in December 1946, when he and Alma went to work on the script with Ben Hecht at his California home, in Oceanside. (For eight days of doctoring the script, Hecht received $10,000 and the promise that he would not be credited for his work on a screenplay he felt was deeply flawed; all that remains of his contribution to the film is Gregory Peck's final monologue in the court, which contains the character's breakdown and apology.) Hitchcock also spoke with Hecht about scripts for Transatlantic, and this of course angered Selznick, who still hoped to retain both of them for future motion pictures.

Hecht, Hitchcock, and Selznick had myriad difficulties agreeing on plot and character development before the producer himself took over the writing single-handed when filming began. In addition, Joseph I. Breen, administrator of the Motion Picture Production Code spawned under Will Hays, was bearing down on what he thought unseemly elements in the script. As various drafts were submitted for the required approval, Breen stampeded along a warpath of puritanical objections:

the design of the prison cell must not include a toilet; indelicate and profane words and phrases must be omitted — such as "Good God!" and "Good Lord!" and "Oh Lord!" and "God knows"; the word *smut* must be stricken from the dialogue; and the phrase *disorderly house,* referring to a sloppy home, must be omitted since it might be taken to mean a house of prostitution. "Finally," Breen wrote in a long letter, "in the scene in the bathroom it would be advisable to omit any showing of Gregory Peck in the bath, even by suggestion, in order to avoid showing a man and a woman in the bathroom at the same time" — even if fully clothed.

It is not hard to understand the rush of liberty, which often became license, that prevailed in Hollywood once this lunatic brand of censorship at last disappeared. Against the code, and Breen as its guardian, Hitchcock would have to battle several more times in his career — a major victory being won in Hollywood's single most iconoclastic image, which no one thought Hitchcock would be able to realize: the sight and sound of the flushing toilet in *Psycho* thirteen years later. As that water flowed, it took away, along with Janet Leigh's notebook page of financial figuring, years of unhealthy and extreme censorship.

After almost a year of trouble with the script, the cameras at last began to roll on December 19, 1946, even though the participation of Alida Valli in the role of Mrs. Paradine was still not certain. The first thing Hitchcock wanted was to anglicize Gregory Peck's appearance and manner with a mustache, but Ann Harris, from Selznick's London office, reported that barristers are always clean-shaven, and that all photos of judges and barristers bore this out. They had to settle for graying his dark hair, although the tribulations of making the film could have accomplished that without makeup.

Selznick, now in a panic about the script, decided to rewrite it completely — on a day-to-day basis — and to send down fresh dialogue to the set each morning just as the actors were ready to step before the camera. "This, of course, drove Hitchcock to distraction," Gregory Peck remembered.

It was so foreign to his method of working. Selznick was totally disorganized but essentially a lovable man, while Hitchcock, whose manner was not quite so lovable, was totally organized. This created an unavoidable tension between them, and it clearly affected Hitchcock's attitude during production. He seemed really bored with the whole thing, and often we would look over to his chair after a take and he would be — or pretended to be — asleep. Something was troubling him even more than during *Spellbound,* I think. He was never sadistic or cruel or openly unkind to anyone on the film, but he was obviously suffering terribly about something during the shooting of *The Paradine Case.*

Because he confided in almost no one throughout his eighty years, it is impossible to pinpoint with absolute certainty the source of Hitchcock's anxiety at this time. But the context in which the making of this last Selznick film occurred suggests several causes.

First, there was the imminent shift in his career, to becoming his own producer — a shift he had long desired but that must have given him some concern, for he would now have to demonstrate (as, eventually, he could not) that he could economize without loss of quality. In several memos, Selznick predicted that Hitchcock's attitude toward production costs and efficiency would alter when he became his own producer, and no prophecy could have been more accurate.

Second, Hitchcock seems to have had at this time a growing awareness of the swift passage of time, and of the fact of aging, and this became manifest in the increasing frequency of little psychosomatic illnesses and more numerous visits to his physicians. Small aches and pains grew, in his mind, to be symptoms of major ailments that never could be diagnosed. His weight again began to creep up, although not yet (as it would by 1950) to the outrageous level of a decade earlier. But at this time food and drink once more became a refuge from several pressures — as they do for many like Hitchcock who are nervous or lonely or driven by fierce demons of creativity to produce in volume, as if against the onrush of time. Also, the indulgences at table were linked to a paradoxical revulsion and contempt for the physical in general, and for his own body in particular.

Finally, as if it were the focus for his anguish, there was the temporary departure from Hollywood of Ingrid Bergman, who was in New York performing Maxwell Anderson's *Joan of Lorraine*. In *Spellbound* and *Notorious* they had been a perfect team, he molding her character and screen persona with loving detail, she attentive to every nuance, illuminating every scene with her rare combination of inner poise and outer control. When *Notorious* opened in August, critics and audiences were transported, and many noticed that rarely in the history of film had an actress been so delicately, adoringly photographed as she was in the film's final bedroom scene.

Playing a woman sick unto death, Bergman was rendered in shadow and half-light, in all her strong fragility; Hitchcock arranged the scene in such a way that there is a radiant tenderness about her, almost a halo of enveloping desire. The camera draws so close to her that Cary Grant, who has come to rescue her in a fairy-tale moment (the beloved snatched from death), is very nearly blocked out and is not followed by the camera, which comes simply to worship the actress. It is easy in film to distinguish aesthetic distance, a simple celebration of another's pres-

ence, from a deep emotional involvement: the former attitude characterized D. W. Griffith's approach to Lillian Gish, and F. W. Murnau's
approach to Janet Gaynor; the latter characterized Josef von Sternberg's
approach to Marlene Dietrich, and Hitchcock's to Ingrid Bergman.

And so the shooting of *The Paradine Case* proceeded in a haze of
gloomy confusion, with Hitchcock both anxious and distracted. For a
time he seems to have taken solace in his direction of Ann Todd, who,
like Alida Valli, was appearing in an American film for the first time.
In 1930 Hitchcock had seen her in *Honour's Easy* at Saint Martin's
Theatre, London. "In the right part she would do extremely well," he
told an interviewer from the *Daily Mail* at that time, pointing out her
cool-blond detachment combined with extraordinary photogenic features
that, he knew at once, could reveal mysteriously attractive passions
beneath.

"He takes the trouble to study his actors quite apart from what they
are playing," Ann Todd recalled, "and so is able to bring hidden things
out from them. He always realized how nervous I was and used to wait
for the silence before 'Action' and then tell a naughty, sometimes
shocking story that either galvanized me into action or collapsed me into
giggles; either way it removed the tension." But on at least one occasion he took a more physical approach to her. Preparing for one scene,
she was especially nervous and was reclining on a bed, wearing an
elegant dressing gown as her costume. "Hitchcock took a flying leap
and jumped on me, shouting 'Relax!' For a moment I thought he might
have broken my bones."

Todd, too, was aware of the conflict between Hitchcock and Selznick
at the time. "I think power helped Hitchcock," she said.

Perhaps it compensated him for his feeling that he was ugly. But his power
clashed with Selznick's. Hitch prepared an elaborate five-minute take in the
film — up a staircase, into a room, with me and Greg Peck talking all the
while. We rehearsed it with all its complications, then shot it about thirty
times to get it exactly right. But then Selznick heard about it, and came down
to the set, demanding that the whole thing be done in the ordinary way, in
short takes and intercuts. 'We're not doing a theater piece!' [Selznick] cried.
And that was that. Of course Hitchcock had to give in; he knew who he could
bully, but he also knew who he had to obey.

The tensions Hitchcock felt at this time were expressed with unusual
harshness in an interview he gave to a reporter from India. As so often,
his anger was directed not at circumstances, but at the actors on whom
he depended to realize his inner vision; the curious element here is that

*The Paradine Case* was not at all his vision or script, but Selznick's. Hitchcock's resentments, however, remained deep:

Actors! I hate the sight of them! Actors are cattle — actresses, too. I tell them I hate the sight of them and they love it, the exhibitionists! Any profession that calls for a man to have to use paint and powder on his face in order to earn a living gives me evil thoughts. Think of it: little bits of powder, little bits of paint on the face of adult men and women so they can pay the rent. My own daughter Patricia made her Broadway debut recently. I sometimes shudder when I think of a daughter of mine doing that.

If his cast noticed that spirit, none of them let it affect their work or their estimation of his cool professionalism. Valli, who returned to Europe later after a short American career, managed the role of the treacherous Mrs. Paradine with a glacial beauty and astonishing control of her first foreign-language part, and Hitchcock had to admit a begrudging admiration for her when the picture was complete. Ann Todd, also a stranger in Hollywood, was taken under Alma's wing and invited for a weekend in Santa Cruz. Escorted on a tour of the house, she was astonished at the great supplies of food, drink, and dry goods that the house held: "Stacks and stacks of everything — piles and piles of lavatory paper, in surprising abundance in closets and cupboards. And we had just been through the Battle of Britain, when everything was in such short supply back home in London. I was really rather shocked at the surplus of everything, just everything. They were very kind to me and looked after me with great care. But the surplus of supplies!"

During filming, Selznick grew angrier. "Hitch has slowed down unaccountably," he fumed. "I know that he is passing the buck to everybody. . . . We must face the fact that Hitch is out of hand." Before photography was finished, Selznick had dictated over four hundred memos based on his intense daily involvement in the production — from writing the final script to checking costumes to looking at the rushes each morning.

By the time filming was completed (on May 7, 1947), Selznick and Hitchcock — each trying, with uneven success, to cope with his own inner demons and creative doubts — were at their lowest emotional ebbs. For over a year, Selznick had been trying to get Hitchcock to sign a new long-term contract (for five pictures, at $100,000 per picture), but his efforts were unrewarded. "I'm getting the run-around," he complained just before the news of Transatlantic was released; and when that news was finally confirmed, Selznick's memos, which alternated giddy elation with almost unbearable anxiety, were outspoken:

I am getting increasingly depressed. . . . I am on the verge of collapse and
not thinking clearly, and am having under these conditions to try to patch up
and rewrite the Hitchcock script. . . . The extent to which we have been paying for the preparation of *Under Capricorn* or whatever is Sidney Bernstein's
future production program is perhaps demonstrated by the fact that it suited
Hitchcock's purpose better to be drawing our salary to prepare a picture for
himself, Bernstein and Bergman.

In order to qualify for the Academy Award nominations, Selznick
rushed *The Paradine Case* to a premiere on New Year's Eve, in advance of its scheduled opening at Radio City Music Hall a week later.
The reactions could not have been more personally hurtful to Selznick,
who must have imagined Hitchcock gloating. "Slick and garrulous,"
complained one critic; another said that there was "scant lack of artistry
in *The Paradine Case*," but that there was "merely too much David O.
Selznick. . . . *The Paradine Case* could have been cut to good effect
with a meat-axe, but the Hitchcock touch is there." And the day after
the New York premiere, as if on cue, Selznick had to deal with Hitchcock's complaint that he was not paid the stipulated extra pay for a day
of retakes. Hitchcock insisted that his per diem postproduction fee of
$1,000 be sent at once.

Even before the holiday, Hitchcock (much to Selznick's horror) had
begun working on the script for his first independent film. It was originally to be *Under Capricorn,* but Ingrid Bergman, still on assignment
to finish two films after her Broadway appearance, was unavailable. So
Hitchcock and Bernstein decided to wait and to attempt in the interim a
swift film version of Patrick Hamilton's 1929 play *Rope,* which had
impressed them in its West End premiere. It would, Hitchcock thought,
provide him with the chance to produce quickly, economically, and in
a daring new way: in uninterrupted ten-minute takes, and so that the
eighty-minute action of the play, which is synchronous with real time,
would also be presented in just eighty minutes of film time.

The deliberate, self-imposed restrictions of place had fascinated
Hitchcock in *Lifeboat,* but a certain languor resulted from several long
periods of constant dialogue without action or cutting — without the
insertion and rearrangement of separate pieces of film to establish point
of view, to gather emotional momentum, and to sustain audience interest and involvement. This restricted method, carried to its ultimate logical extreme in the uninterrupted ten-minute takes of *Rope,* turned out
to be an intriguing failure. There is simply no tension, no point of view,

no generation of feeling —although this derives as much from theme as from method.

The film's technical challenge, however, was exactly what Hitchcock seemed to want. He had not renewed the Selznick contract precisely because he thought that the dramaturgy of *The Paradine Case* was creaky and uninvolving — and it was filmed in black and white, too, at a time when more big-budget productions, those destined for splashier publicity campaigns and for wider distribution, were made in color. *Rope,* he decided, would show everyone how modern he could be. It would be Hitchcock's first film made in the Technicolor process, with a camera roving constantly from actor to actor, from room to room in a Manhattan penthouse. Even its story would be shocking, and to that end he insisted that the play's delicacy be discarded and that its singularly repellent narrative be injected with gruesome humor.

In late autumn of 1947, Hitchcock invited Hume Cronyn to work on a prose adaptation of the play. The story — about homosexual lovers who murder a friend for the intellectual experience of it, then hide the body in an antique chest from whose closed lid they serve a buffet supper to the dead man's family and friends — was substantially preserved, but the ethical dilemma had to be solved rather homiletically at the end. As a result, a deadly erotic tension vanished amid shrubberies of technique.

"He was very revolutionary in the way he approached *Rope,*" Hume Cronyn said.

It was written to be shot in those tremendously long takes, and I think he found that fascinating — he was always intrigued by the innovative. But I think that sometimes this led him astray where the narrative was concerned. He became so fascinated with the images that sometimes the direct line of the story got lost and there would be some awkwardness in the dramatic construction.

Our conversations during the treatment stage — while we were writing the scene summaries, before the dialogue was added — were very detailed about characters. When we came up against a block and our discussions became very heated and intense, he would stop suddenly and tell a story that had nothing to do with the work at hand. At first I was almost outraged and then I discovered that he did this intentionally. He mistrusted working under pressure, and he would say, "We're pressing, we're pressing, we're working too hard. Relax — it will come." And of course it finally did.

By early December (with Selznick fidgeting over the final cut of *The Paradine Case*), the treatment was finished and Cronyn was anxious to write the dialogue with Hitchcock. "I always wanted to do the dialogue after I'd finished the treatment, and so he let me work on it. Then I brought him what I'd done and he said very quietly, 'Yes, that's very nice.' And then he got in another writer, a playwright.'' The playwright was Arthur Laurents, whose 1945 work *Home of the Brave* was then being scripted for film production by Stanley Kramer.

"Hitchcock knew exactly what he was dealing with in this story," according to Laurents.

I arrived in Los Angeles and was put to work at once. Sidney Bernstein was something of an amateur at film production, but he was a fine gentleman and he supported both Hitchcock and myself enthusiastically. The first thing Bernstein told me was that every line of *Rope* had to be a pure gem; after all, it was their first coproduction.

When I had finished the first draft, just before Christmas, I left for New York for a holiday. When I returned to do the rewrites, I found that Hitchcock had reinserted some of the original play into the text, and that he had made other adjustments.

The collaboration between Hitchcock and Laurents was productive and pleasant. Laurents, not yet thirty, was made a member of the Hitchcock family, often taken to lunch at Romanoff's and invited for Christmas to the house in Scotts Valley, Santa Cruz. He remembered a curious alternation between relaxed merriment and a kind of vague tension.

Away from Hollywood, severed at last from the restrictions of Selznick's supervision but committed to the responsibility of his own production, Hitchcock's respite from work sometimes seemed uncongenial. The imminent technical problems of *Rope,* with walls and furniture whisked away as the camera ceaselessly and silently moved, engaged Hitchcock's ingenuity on paper in the late preparation stages. But this challenge seemed an escape from some pervasive unhappiness — just as his recreational drinking was becoming more and more an escape, and more and more self-indulgent. Alma was obviously concerned, and on several occasions angry arguments about this carried from the master bedroom through the house in strident, embarrassing echoes.

The central characters of the story were presented none too subtly. According to Laurents:

We never discussed the homosexual element of the script, but Hitchcock knew what he wanted to be able to get away with. He was as intrigued by the varieties of sexual life and conduct as he was by the varieties of movie-making methods — in fact, he was like a child who's just discovered sex and thinks it's all very naughty. It was obvious to anyone who worked with him that he had a strong sense of sin, and that whether he was a regular churchgoer or not, his Victorian Catholic background still affected him deeply. He might have been indirect in dealing with sexual things in his films, but he had a strong instinct for them. He thought everyone was doing something physical and nasty behind every closed door — except himself: he withdrew, he wouldn't be part of it.

By the time the set on the rented sound stage was ready at Warner Brothers, the casting problems had been settled. For the role of the smug, antisocial, misanthropic former schoolmaster of the two murderers, Hitchcock had hoped to sign Cary Grant. RKO, however, had exclusive rights to his services at the time, and so Hitchcock offered the role to James Stewart. This was inspired casting-against-type, for Stewart had returned from the war an Air Force hero and had reestablished his film career as the platonic form of middle-American hero in Frank Capra's *It's a Wonderful Life*. The role in *Rope* had to be slightly softened for him, and his $300,000 salary raised Hitchcock's budget to almost $1.5 million. But the relationship between director and actor was so mutually respectful and friendly that Stewart would later be invited back for the leading roles in three Hitchcock masterworks. For the passive, nervy pianist, Hitchcock cast Farley Granger, whom he had seen in a preview of Nicholas Ray's *They Live by Night;* and the clearly sociopathic, dominant partner, which Hitchcock had hoped Montgomery Clift would play, was eventually given to John Dall. Clift, whose film career was just under way, dreaded a role that could perhaps raise eyebrows.

If the script and its resolution lacked tension — and even the reliable Ben Hecht could do little more than tighten up the last scene — then at least the circumstances of filming provided suspense abundantly, for work on the soundstage was an unalloyed horror. On Monday, January 12, 1948, the cast was assembled for discussions, a first reading, and final wardrobe fittings; the next day, they rehearsed for thirteen hours and stumbled away unsure that they were doing a film and not a play. Until late the following week they rehearsed each gesture and movement, with the filmless camera weaving around and after them and finding its cue marks on the floor, often missing a table and bumping a prop man.

"Every movement of the camera and the actors was worked out first in sessions with a blackboard like football skull practice," Hitchcock explained.

Even the floor was marked and plotted with numbered circles for the 25 to 30 camera moves in each ten-minute reel. Whole walls of the apartment had to slide away to allow the camera to follow the actors through narrow doors, then swing back noiselessly to show a solid room. Even the furniture was "wild."

Tables and chairs had to be pulled away by prop men, then set in place again
by the time the camera returned to its original position, since the camera was
on a special crane, not on tracks, and designed to roll through everything like
a juggernaut.

But the most magical of all the devices was the cyclorama — an exact miniature reproduction of nearly 35 miles of New York skyline lighted by 8000
incandescent bulbs and 200 neon signs requiring 150 transformers.

Hitchcock's demands for this background quickly exasperated the
electricians and photographer Joseph Valentine, whose earlier work on
*Shadow of a Doubt* had seemed simple by comparison. The technical
demands were completely appalling, in fact: Hitchcock insisted on the
gradual fading of daylight to night-sky, without the camera stopping,
which meant that the lighting grids had to be precisely executed. "Each
miniature building in the distance was wired separately for globes
ranging from 25 to 150 watts in the tiny windows of the skyscraper-
miniature," according to the director, "and 26,000 feet of wire carried
126,000 watts of electricity for the window illumination."

The first filming began at last on January 22, and the first ten-minute
reel was finally and successfully completed on the third take. Other
reels — all in a single shot instead of the usual dozens or even hundreds
of separate shots — had to be made six, ten, or even fifteen times in a
day. Even if a whole scene was nearly finished, it could be and was
often ruined by an actor's missed line, a table bumped, a wrong cue.
"The really important thing being rehearsed here is the camera, not the
actors!" complained James Stewart once.

"He couldn't sleep nights because of the picture," Hitchcock remarked. "It was the bewildering technique that made him worry."

But it was not only the visual technique that had everyone anxious.
"It was hard to see how the picture was going to work," Stewart explained. "We had a lot of rehearsal, but the noise of the moving walls
was a problem, and so we had to do the whole thing over again for
sound, with just microphones, like a radio play. The dialogue track was
then added later." Stewart, who admired Hitchcock's courage, also realized that *Rope* was, in the final analysis, uncinematic. "I think he
realized later that giving up the device of the cut was giving up the tool
for pacing, for impact. It was worth trying — nobody but Hitch would
have tried it. But it really didn't work."*

*No less a famous visitor than Noël Coward was much impressed by Hitchcock's bold tech-
nique. His diary entry for January 29, 1948, includes: "Went out to Warner's to see Hitchcock
directing *Rope*. . . . Really very exciting, a whole reel taken in one go without resetting lights.
. . . It cannot be applied to all pictures, but from the writer's point of view it is wonderful."

During the fifteen rehearsal days and twenty-one days of filming (the production was concluded on Saturday, February 21), Hitchcock maintained an attitude of contagious control on the set, and somehow his actors managed to acquit themselves without yielding to the awkwardness and inconvenience of an unprecedented (and, since then, unrepeated) technique for the filming of an entire motion picture. More often than before — perhaps because he knew how difficult a task it was for them — Hitchcock invited his cast and crew to supper parties at Bellagio Road. As Farley Granger remembered, a kind of Old World, English ambience prevailed at these gatherings, although after the wine had flowed sufficiently there might be dancing, or, when the women left the men alone over brandy and cigars, Hitchcock would encourage a round of dirty stories. There was always a ratio of bathroom jokes included, at Hitchcock's urging.

The soirees also included celebrities not associated with *Rope*. Robert Cummings and his wife were often invited, and Cary Grant, and Ingrid Bergman and her husband Dr. Petter Lindstrom (their "domestic harmony," she herself related in her autobiography, "had not improved"). During this period — and perhaps precisely because of the confusions of Ingrid Bergman's emotional life at the time — Hitchcock grew more possessive of the star who would soon go with him to England for one more film before she made a dramatic change in her life and career. With Ingrid Bergman in the Hitchcock group, he often became moody and withdrawn, although she never noticed this. Her own lively and generous spirit contributed much to parties, and she seems always to have been unaware of Hitchcock's severe (if controlled) infatuation for her.

Certainly this infatuation was never articulated, much less activated, and this makes even more touching the image of one of Hollywood's most admired immigrant stars affecting a graceful gaiety when her personal life was so unhappy; and the corresponding image of one of Hollywood's most admired immigrant directors, affecting a watchful distance as he fixed a sad, rapturous gaze on her. "Ah, yes," Hitchcock had Joan Chandler say in *Rope*, "Ingrid Bergman! She's the *Virgo* type — I think she's just lovely!"

Though Hitchcock's manner during these gatherings was often somewhat melancholy, and though he was harboring a secret passion he was powerless to confront, there was nothing concealed or hesitant about *Rope*. In Hitchcock's previous films, murders had always taken place decorously, offscreen. The killing here (which is not shown at all in Patrick Hamilton's play) occurs in hideous close-up in the first minute

of the film. And the strangling of the young man is soon a source of
savagely unfunny jokes: referring to the rigors of murderer Granger's
piano practice, unknowing characters casually utter ironic phrases like
"Knock 'em dead!" and "These hands will bring you great fame!" and
"I could strangle you!" and "You've been playing a foul trick!"

The final impression left by the film (which Hitchcock later withdrew
from circulation, preferring that it not be shown) is not one of admiration for a difficult technique. Nor is it one of admiration for the drama
of a cool contest of wills over the issue of sterile Nietzschean bookish-
ness, earnest though that subtext might be. This first film entirely under
Hitchcock's control as producer is in fact his coldest work; its obsessive
methodology never conceals its misanthropy. When it was released in
August 1948 — to mixed reviews and a lukewarm public response —
there was some talk about the single set, but no one paid much attention
to the ten-minute takes. Several social and educational associations across
America, however, condemned *Rope* as undesirable and dangerous, and
a few European theaters who were then booking films from Warner
Brothers asked for substitutes. In Zurich, irate theater-owners begged
for prints of *Life With Father* to calm their angry patrons.

With *Rope* completed, Hitchcock lost no time in setting to work,
again with Hume Cronyn, on the treatment of his next film. It was to
be based on Helen Simpson's 1937 novel *Under Capricorn*. In 1944
Margaret McDonell had sent Hitchcock a copy of the novel and of an
unpublished dramatic version by Margaret Linden and John Colton, and
it was McDonell who suggested that its gloomy amalgam of shared guilt,
renounced passion, and rather masochistic fidelities (all in a story set in
Australia in 1831) would appeal to Hitchcock, who had so well understood the spirit of nineteenth-century romanticism.

Hitchcock bought the dramatic rights in 1945 (for the token price of
one dollar) and managed to interest Ingrid Bergman in the property; but
in order to assure greater control than Selznick was affording him at the
time, he decided to wait until he and Bernstein had their new company
afloat. At last, after completing *Rope* while they waited for Bergman to
finish stage and screen obligations in 1947 and early 1948, they decided
to go to England to film *Under Capricorn*.

Hitchcock insisted to the end of his life that he made the film to
please Ingrid Bergman. "I was looking for a subject that suited her,
rather than myself." But this brooding, morbid melodrama about the
extremes of marital fidelity — even to the point of retaining a spouse's
murderous secret and assuming guilt — really suited Hitchcock more

than it ever did Ingrid Bergman, notwithstanding the fact that it was a costume drama. "The thing about it I resented," he said years later, "was that I could never feel comfortable in those costume dramas. I couldn't understand the characters, how they bought a loaf of bread or went to the bathroom." Apart from this, however, the enveloping sense of guilt; the spirit of remorse, of the need for confession before punishment exacts a terrible price; the contrasts of characters who alternately save and kill (Michael Wilding as opposed to Margaret Leighton, who respectively play characters who sacrifice for love and betray for love) — all these simply graft onto a period melodrama several mainstream Hitchcockian concerns.

And so, after four years of waiting, Hitchcock and Cronyn began to work on the treatment, mostly on weekends at Santa Cruz. Hitchcock's attitude seemed one of anxious anticipation combined with high enthusiasm. "At Santa Cruz," Cronyn remembered, "usually the weekend was more than one's digestion and capacity could stand. He was the perfect host, of course, and he took a marvelous, malicious delight in seeing his guests fall apart with all those vintage wines and liquor he'd force." And similarly, into the treatment — as into *Suspicion* and *Spellbound* and *Notorious* (and even a detail he got Sidney Gilliat to add to *The Lady Vanishes* and one he had Selznick add to *The Paradine Case*) — Hitchcock managed to insert with equally marvelous, malicious delight, the motif of the drugged drink.

Before the end of March the treatment was finished, and Hitchcock gave it to Arthur Laurents. "Now, Arthur, we're going to do *Under Capricorn*," he announced, never thinking his offer would be rejected. But Laurents was unexcited by the story and respectfully declined the invitation — a rejection the director took as a personal affront. At once Hitchcock cabled James Bridie in Glasgow, then Sidney Bernstein in London, and on Saturday, March 27, he left alone for England on the *Queen Elizabeth*. Until the end of June he worked at various times with Bridie, Peter Ustinov, and Marjorie Bowen on the problems of developing a coherent narrative out of the novel and the play, and by the time Transatlantic Pictures was ready to present a budget to Bankers Trust of New York for the loan to make the film, the amount requested had soared to $2.5 million.

After a brief return to Los Angeles to settle matters regarding distribution and to collect his family, Hitchcock returned to London and to the Elstree Studios for the filming of *Under Capricorn*. Patricia had become even more serious about her training for the theater, and her father gave her the opportunity now to study at the Royal Academy of

Dramatic Art. While her parents checked into a suite at the Savoy, she went to stay with cousins in Golders Green, and to attend classes in Gower Street.

Hitchcock's return to London for his first feature film production in a decade was greeted with alarming chilliness; his absence during the war still angered many in English cultural and social life. The British press noted the arrival of star director and star actress only in brief news items, and the few journals to publish substantial articles or interviews were none too warm in their assessment of his career since he had left England.

Hitchcock intended to film *Under Capricorn,* as he had *Rope,* in ten-minute takes and in color. The color of this new film turned out a great success; the ten-minute takes had mostly to be abandoned, although there are several shots that run six or eight minutes. But the most disturbing problem was the strain that the production — exacerbated by the complications in the leading lady's private life — was putting on the Hitchcock-Bergman friendship. "He got such pleasure out of doing those camera tricks," she reflected in an interview years later,

and of course the continuous shots and the moving camera were very hard on everybody. We rehearsed for days, and then at last we would put on makeup and have a try at a reel. We would have perhaps six minutes just fine and then suddenly something would go wrong and the whole reel would have to begin again. Hitch just insisted.

Then the propmen and the business of all that moving furniture while the camera was rolling — it just drove us crazy! There were walls flying up into the rafters as we walked by, all the lights were movable, a chair for an actor to sit on would appear just off-camera the minute before the move. What a nightmare! The whole floor was filled with numbers and everybody had to be on the cued number at the right moment or the shot was ruined. It's the only time I ever cried on the set.

I think he did this to prove to himself that he could. It was a challenge only to himself, to show the movie industry that he could figure out and accomplish something so difficult — so much technique, so much to show off. But he was determined, and the whole thing became very, very difficult.

And of course the audience couldn't care less. If he had cut to close-ups and several interrupting cuts in a sequence they would have been just as happy. They didn't need to see a camera rolling uphill, going under tables, all around the actors in this murderously difficult fashion!

Hitchcock remembered the agony Bergman felt then, and her reaction to the problems imposed by his unorthodox method. "She got into a terrible state — just told me off. And I did what I always do when people start to argue. I just turned away and went home. Later they told me she was still hysterical twenty minutes later. She didn't even know that I'd left. Next day she said, 'Okay, Hitch — we'll do it your way.' I told her, 'It's not my way, Ingrid — it's the *right* way!' ''

A respectful calm then prevailed, helped considerably by a young Englishwoman Hitchcock engaged as continuity director for the film. Peggy Singer had had a solid grounding in every aspect of script preparation, and her talent and devoted support of Hitchcock smoothed many of the production problems on *Under Capricorn*. She also worked on Hitchcock's next film, but then she was employed by other producers until 1957, by which time she had married the gifted Canadian film editor Douglas Robertson. Peggy Robertson came back to Hitchcock as his script supervisor and personal assistant on *Vertigo,* and her creative energies and tireless loyalty were crucial from that time to the end of his career.

By the end of September, things on the set had improved somewhat, and the always conscientious Bergman, ever the alert and honest professional, had to admit that there was really some merit in Hitchcock's maddening method, and that her uninterrupted ten-minute confession scene looked quite fine in the finished film. Later in her career, she said, ''everybody made such a fuss and I even received the [1974] Academy Award for *Murder on the Orient Express* because I did a long speech in one take. Well, that really wasn't so new, was it? I had done that for Hitch back in 1948!''

Just before *Under Capricorn* was completed, however, something happened that forever changed the lives of several people involved in the film. Ingrid Bergman finally met Roberto Rossellini, whose work she had so much admired. Her meeting with the Italian filmmaker was historic, for there began a professional and personal relationship that scandalized millions and led to the couple's brutal ostracism when they deserted their spouses to work together as artists and to live together as lovers. Bergman's departure deeply wounded Alfred Hitchcock. "He resented her going off with Rossellini,'' according to Arthur Laurents, ''and his resentment wasn't just because he adored Bergman. It was because she was leaving him for another director.'' It was another of those actions that he took as a deep personal slight. Leaving Hitchcock to work for someone else or turning down an offer to work with him was almost unforgivable.

After fifty-five shooting days, the filming of *Under Capricorn*'s interiors was completed and Hitchcock returned with Alma to Los Angeles. (He timed his entrance and departure from Great Britain so that, by carefully following certain technicalities, he avoided paying taxes.) The

English weather having made it impossible, as usual, to film exteriors, there remained some final scenes to be done in Hollywood at the Warner Brothers ranch; and for the Government House at Sydney, Hitchcock used the pillared front of Canoga Park High School. These details occupied him the first two weeks of November, and then the film was finished. Warners, however, which was handling the distribution, scheduled the release for the following September.

Although Hitchcock was now ready to proceed with Bernstein on a film version of yet another play to follow *Rope* and *Under Capricorn* (this time, an old French melodrama), Transatlantic Pictures had realized no earnings on its first two projects, so that third venture had to be postponed. Instead, for some reason that remains unclear, Hitchcock wanted to return to London for his next film, regardless of whether it would be a Bernstein coproduction. Perhaps this was simply because London was the setting of the novel Hitchcock had chosen as his source: Selwyn Jepson's *Man Running*, which he had read earlier that year (it had first appeared serialized in *Collier's* in 1947) and which had been published to good notices in America as *Outrun the Constable*. Perhaps it was because he had first assigned the screenplay to James Bridie, and Bridie disdained travel to America. Perhaps also it was because he felt the theater setting should be filmed on location in the London he knew so well, and because in the story as he envisioned it there would be a supporting cast of zanies that only English repertory actors could bring to life.

Whatever the reason, it certainly was not any kind attitude on the part of the British press or film community that encouraged Hitchcock to return. He may, however, have wanted to prove himself in home territory once again, with a film vastly different from *Under Capricorn*. In addition, in his own childish way, he simply liked hotel living. The gratification of his (mostly gastronomic) whims at any hour, the well-appointed high teas, the service, the slightly crusty dignities that had once annoyed the Cockney in him — all were now welcome and, indeed, demanded amenities. At the Savoy, at Claridge's, at the Connaught, and in the polite drawing rooms of Mayfair and Kensington to which his status now readily admitted him, Hitchcock held a small court. He was still, after all — and determinedly — a British subject, even if his wife and daughter had taken American citizenship.

There is no record of business meetings with old colleagues or any attempt to reestablish earlier associations, but several people who saw the director briefly in 1949 during the making of what was eventually called *Stage Fright* had the impression that he would very much have liked to unite Hollywood technology with English respectability and

manners; there was a sense that after the war — even though (and perhaps in a strange way because) his family had dwindled to only a surviving sister and several distant relations to whom he was never close —
Hitchcock could have been quite comfortable alternately making films
in London and Hollywood. He could, as he said, plan extended holiday
trips in the intervals.

Hitchcock's lifelong love of travel and his increasing tendency to
multiply vacations whenever possible seem to have derived from something deeper than just a desire to get away from the pressures of studio
production, or from the routine of a shooting schedule and an almost
invariable life at home. Just as during the years at Gaumont-British he
used any excuse to whisk a writer to Saint Moritz for work on a scenario, so, once the war was over, and until his first bout of serious illness
in 1957, he created for himself opportunities to produce films and to
shoot them in places that necessitated considerable traveling.

From 1949 to 1956 he made important parts of his films in New
York, Washington, D.C., Connecticut, Quebec, the French Riviera,
Vermont, Morocco, and London; he led press jaunts from Indonesia to
Australia to Japan to Rome; and he did location scouting in Africa for
a project that was finally abandoned. In each of these places, he was
never too proud to play the tourist, although he usually had his meals
flown in from Paris, New York, or London. In each of these places he
also tirelessly conducted rapid-fire publicity conferences about himself
and his work. Publicists and agents, he always felt, could do just so
much; most of the job of promotion was up to him, and the success of
that promotion depended on his presence. To that end, he combined
business with pleasure, and over a period of almost eight years he cir-
cled the globe several times annually.

His agents, of course, were delighted with this habit. By the late
1940s he had, after the death of Myron Selznick, become firmly established as one of the major clients of MCA (once the Music Corporation
of America), the world's largest talent agency. He was looked after by
Leland Hayward (briefly) and Taft Schreiber before being represented
exclusively by a former Cleveland movie-usher named Lew Wasserman,
whose judgment and advice also guided Bette Davis, Jean Arthur, Errol
Flynn, James Stewart, and Frank Sinatra, among others. President of
MCA since 1946, Wasserman had by this time developed an affectionate respect for Hitchcock, and he saw to it for many years that the
friendliness of their business dealings never impinged on the borders of
that respect. For his part, Hitchcock appreciated the vigilance Wasserman exercised and among the gifts regularly exchanged, Hitchcock presented the agent with a Bernard Buffet portrait of the recipient. In Lew

Wasserman, Hitchcock found the right guide for his interests and success, and Wasserman played an increasingly important part in the director's late career.

From December 1948 to March 1949, Hitchcock and Alma worked at home on a treatment and script of *Stage Fright,* and they invited Whitfield Cook to write the dialogue with them. He had been the author of Pat's second Broadway play and was a frequent and generous host to her and her parents when they came to the East Coast. At the same time, James Bridie said that he would polish several scenes when Hitchcock finally went to England for filming.

By January they had fallen into a fairly predictable routine. Cook arrived at Bellagio Road at ten o'clock in the morning; they worked until one, and after a ninety-minute break for luncheon they resumed work until six. The finished scenario, which contained some additions by Ranald MacDougall, was 113 pages long and looked like a typical Hitchcock shooting script: every word of dialogue was annotated with a corresponding camera movement and the dimensions for each shot. Satisfied with this meticulous preparation — which meant, for Hitchcock, that the film was really finished and he was ready to proceed with a new project — the director then took a wire recorder and dictated a list of "things I must have" — all the technical apparatus, sets, unusual costumes and props, special effects — and after a secretary transcribed that list, he sent it to the London studio.

"Find me a piece of land jutting into the sea, with a road running along it," he added later in a call to his British art director. "There must be a lonely house and a jetty, and anchored off the jetty a schooner." Location scouts were dispatched to the coastline of England, and the right place was found. Ultimately, as they might have expected, the weather blocked their plans, and elaborate matte paintings and miniatures had to do for the final effect; the entire film, except for one or two background plates, was photographed on the largest of Elstree's stages.

Since the production was to be financed and distributed by Warner Brothers, with whom Hitchcock had signed a multipicture deal that gave him unprecedented freedom in his choice of material, cast, and writers, Hitchcock knew that *Stage Fright,* the first film under that contract, would have to show the kind of profit *Rope* and *Under Capricorn* were not showing. To guarantee this, he requested and got for the leading role the actress who had just received the Oscar for best performance that year: Jane Wyman — who was, as it turned out, happy to accept an invitation to travel, since she had just been through a divorce from actor Ronald Reagan. To play the enigmatic older actress, Marlene Dietrich was signed. She had recently won new admirers in Billy Wilder's film *A Foreign Affair,* and an addition to her family had the press proclaiming her the world's most glamorous grandmother. Hitchcock's film would prove them right.

Before he arrived in England that May to complete the casting, Hitchcock drew over three hundred pencil sketches for the film and turned them over to his cameraman. He also arranged with Sir Kenneth Barnes to use the rehearsal theater of the Royal Academy of Dramatic Art in Gower Street. By June the cast was complete (other roles were played by Michael Wilding, Alastair Sim, Richard Todd, Sybil Thorndike, Kay Walsh, Joyce Grenfell, and Miles Malleson), and Hitchcock's shooting schedule set Monday, June 13, as the first day of filming. His biggest scenes included a rainstorm at a theatrical garden party — to be photographed from above, over a blanket of black umbrellas (the scene nearly duplicates one in *Foreign Correspondent*) — and some elaborate camera work in which Richard Todd is followed without a cut (a la *Rope* and *Under Capricorn*) from a street to the second floor of a house — as off-camera the doors and walls flew up to the rafters and a giant machine transported camera and operator up and around a vast staircase.

*Stage Fright* concerns a young drama student who plays a real-life role to clear a man of a murder charge. She finds, however, that he is indeed guilty, but in the process her affections are transferred to the police inspector on the case. Underneath a somewhat sprawling story is a wonderfully realized comic treatment on the nature of role-playing in real life. The opening of the film is a pointer in the right direction, in fact: credits dissolve against a rising theatrical safety curtain, and the scene behind the curtain is not a stage setting but actual London; when the curtain is fully risen, the viewer is in the action of the story. At once, then, the distinctions between theatrical life and street life (and, in what follows, between art and life itself) begin to blur. As the story unfolds, everyone assumes false identities, everyone plays a role. Appearances slip and slide, and nothing is certain in a world marked by costumes and matinees and benefit garden parties and the lies of false friends.

Hitchcock was inspired by a typical Englishman's love of theater and show-people, and by a fascination with the blandishments of the actor's life, which he had observed at close quarters from his youth. Pat's request to stay on for an extended term at the Royal Academy that year might well have further encouraged his gentle jibes at apprentice actresses. In a benevolent gesture not undiluted with a certain sarcasm, he gave her a small role in *Stage Fright* as one of Jane Wyman's friends —

and somewhat ungraciously, he named her character Chubby Bannister (a girl, he said, you could always lean on). For Jane Wyman, Hitchcock had little attention, and her remarks about working with him were forever after much kinder than his.

With Marlene Dietrich, on the other hand, there was a cautious respect. "Marlene was a professional star — she was also a professional cameraman, art director, editor, costume designer, hairdresser, makeup woman, composer, producer, and director." She was, moreover, the only actress ever allowed substantial creative freedom on his set. She would appear early each morning and, as members of the crew recalled, proceed to instruct cinematographer Wilkie Cooper on the proper lighting for herself. Astounded, the crew brought the matter to Hitchcock — and they were even more astounded when he ordered them to do her bidding. From her seven films with Josef von Sternberg, which had established her as the essence of the femme fatale, she had accumulated an expert knowledge of light and shadow and angle; Hitchcock not only gave her a free hand designing her image in this film but also gave her free rein in selecting her wardrobe and jewelry.

By the beginning of September, production of *Stage Fright* was complete and the three Hitchcocks were ready to leave England. Alma, as always, was the most eager to depart. There was some talk about returning to London at Christmastime to direct another picture, but the misfortunes of Transatlantic Pictures grew more and more apparent, and soon the Hitchcock-Bernstein venture was part of their respective histories. Arriving in California, Hitchcock found himself — for the first time in years — professionally inactive. And as always, that caused him almost as much anxiety as the sight of a policeman.

# Eleven

---

## 1950 – 1955

For the first time in more than a decade, there was no project to occupy him, nothing waiting to be adapted, no major actress or writer engaged for a new story. Jack Warner had extended the distribution agreement for the now quietly defunct Transatlantic Pictures, and Hitchcock at least had a multipicture deal with that studio under which he would act as his own producer and have a free hand in his choice of material.

But little good that freedom did him in late 1949 and early 1950, when he was alternately depressed over his professional inactivity and cheerfully confident that a film idea would presently arise. He began to take an interest in the cultivation of the vast acreage he owned in northern California, and he consulted vintners and horticulturists, who advised him on raising grapes appropriate to the soil and climate of Santa Cruz. In two seasons there was a healthy crop, from which he realized a healthy income.

By 1950 Alfred Hitchcock had amassed considerable wealth, international fame, substantial Hollywood bargaining power, two homes, land, stocks, and some Texas cattle and oil interests. But he had still not achieved the kind of success as producer-director he had hoped for, and this gnawed at him. During this time he affected the image of a part-time gentleman farmer and part-time producer, but in fact he was mostly a full-time wanderer, traveling from Bel-Air to Scotts Valley and back, lunching at Romanoff's or the Brown Derby, dining at Chasen's or Perino's or at home alone with Alma, or with at most a few colleagues who expressed to one another concern about his drinking.

"A very dry martini," he would say to his guests, "is simply two parts gin to one short glance at a bottle of vermouth." After a cocktail

hour-and-a-half on such occasions, he would impress the diners with
Dover sole he had ordered flown over, or a lobster soufflé from Maxim's that had just arrived on an air transport from Paris. Without a film
to be the repository of his creative energies, Hitchcock reverted to the
patterns of eating and drinking he had tried to curb during more active
periods. The pounds lost returned quickly and, as is typical in such
cases, he soon weighed more than before.

Early in the spring of 1950 *Stage Fright* opened — to generally unenthusiastic notices; it would take several decades before the film was
properly gauged — and Hitchcock told the inquiring press that it would
be the last of his comic thrillers. He said he planned a four-part horror
fantasy, to include Michael Arlen's "The Gentleman from America"
and Lord Dunsany's grisly story of murder and cannibalism "Two Bottles of Relish." While in New York on a publicity trip, he gave an
afternoon acting clinic for students at the Theatre Guild and dined with
the judges of the student auditions, Leo G. Carroll, Leslie Banks, Cedric Hardwicke, and Sidney Blackmer. Back in Los Angeles, he continued to add the requisite press activities to what became a regular forum:
the more rarefied atmosphere of the lecture hall. On April 12 he spoke
at the University of California at Los Angeles after showing clips from
the new film. Thus began a tradition of student previews, alternately at
that campus or at the University of Southern California — colloquia that
he seemed to enjoy (or at least exploited) for the next twenty-five years.

Hitchcock's good humor at the UCLA student gathering that April
evening might have flowed from the fact that he had just read a certain
recently published novel. He at once instructed his agents to negotiate
terms for the film rights, warning them not to mention his name, for
that would raise the price. On April 20 they concluded a deal for the
rights to Patricia Highsmith's first book, *Strangers on a Train,* for
which — to his delight and her annoyance — he paid only $7,500.

It is easy to understand what attracted Hitchcock to the story of two
men who meet accidentally and whose lives become linked when one
of them, an alcoholic, psychopathic playboy, suggests to the other, a
handsome young architect, that they commit murder for each other. What
struck Hitchcock was the possibility for carrying forward one of his
favorite themes, the exchange of guilt (already explored in *Shadow of a
Doubt, Notorious, Rope, Under Capricorn,* and *Stage Fright*), and of
adding to it a treatment of the coexistence of good and evil within a
single relationship and within the shared personalities of the two
strangers. What excited him even more was the idea of rendering this
theme dramatically in the film's *form* — a series of doubles or pairs, as
in *Shadow of a Doubt* eight years earlier.

The most reflective passages of Highsmith's novel could have been
taken from a Hitchcock diary (had there been one):

But love and hate, he thought now, good and evil, lived side by side in the
human heart, and not merely in differing proportions in one man and the next,
but all good and all evil. One had merely to look for a little of either to find it
all, and one had merely to scratch the surface. All things had opposites close
by, every decision a reason against it, every animal an animal that destroys it.
. . . Nothing could be without its opposite that was bound up with it. . . .
Each was what the other had not chosen to be, the cast-off self, what he thought
he hated but perhaps in reality loved . . . there was that duality permeating
nature. . . . Two people in each person. There's also a person exactly the
opposite of you, like the unseen part of you, somewhere in the world, and he
waits in ambush.

At last Hitchcock had found a story and a sensibility ready for his
own special handling, a story that spoke to his own inner experience of
division. This, after the disappointing reception given to *The Paradine
Case, Rope, Under Capricorn,* and *Stage Fright,* would reestablish him
as a master storyteller in the area of the psychological suspense thriller.
He again contracted Whitfield Cook, and by the end of June they had
hammered out a sixty-five-page treatment in which they tightened the
story; limited the setting to the East Coast corridor of Washington-
Arlington-Long Island; contrasted the twilight world of the anarchic
madman with the broad daylight of politics, government, and professional tennis; and indicated an unprecedented series of shots that would
formally signify the association between the two apparently opposite
men and the moral worlds they represented.

But while he and Cook were reconstructing Highsmith's somewhat
breathlessly florid melodrama, Hitchcock could not find a first-rate writer
willing to undertake a screenplay assignment. "I remember when I was
working on *Strangers on a Train,*" he said, "I couldn't find anyone to
work on it with me. They all felt my first draft was so flat and factual
that they couldn't see one iota of quality in it. Yet the whole film was
there visually."

The treatment was first submitted to Dashiell Hammett, whose mystery novels *The Maltese Falcon, The Glass Key,* and *The Thin Man* had
been brought to the screen in the thirties and forties, and whose status
as one of the originators of the so-called hard-boiled detective fiction
made him just the right screen writer, Hitchcock thought, to give voice
to the psychological and physical brutalities of *Strangers on a Train.*
But the meetings with Hammett were unaccountably sabotaged, apparently through nothing more mysterious than a secretary's carelessness.

By the first week of July the story editor at Warner Brothers, Finlay McDermid, had welcomed to the enterprise — at a salary of $2,500 per week — the formidable Raymond Chandler. Chandler's novels *The Big Sleep, Lady in the Lake,* and *Farewell, My Lovely* had been translated to film, and he had himself written the screenplays for *Double Indemnity, The Unseen,* and *The Blue Dahlia.* Hitchcock met him only once, very briefly, before Chandler took the treatment, the novel, a ream of paper, and a secretary to his home in La Jolla.

Because Chandler's contract allowed him to work at home, Hitchcock had to travel for their conferences. Chandler hated these "god-awful jabber sessions which seem to be an inevitable although painful part of the picture business," and he particularly disliked Hitchcock's visits and interference. According to his biographer, Chandler became foul-tempered, uncooperative, and insulting. "One day, while waiting at the front door of the house for Hitchcock to get out of his limousine, Chandler remarked to his secretary: 'Look at that fat bastard trying to get out of his car!' The secretary warned him that he could be heard. 'What do I care?' replied Chandler."

What really irritated Chandler was what often irritated writers before and since: Hitchcock's insistence that the script adhere to his visual requirements. "The thing that amuses me about Hitchcock," Chandler wrote to his British editor, "is the way he directs a film in his head before he knows what the story is. . . . He has a strong feeling for stage business and mood and background, not so much for the guts of the business. I guess that's why some of his pictures lose their grip on logic and turn into wild chases. Well, it's not the worst way to make a picture. . . . But he is as nice as can be to argue with."

And argue they did — not because their sensibilities were so different, but because indeed they were surprisingly similar; the tension generated between them derived not from a confrontation between complementary talents, but from a smoldering suspicion that each knew the other's soul rather more fully than either desired. "Our collaboration was not very happy," Hitchcock recalled later. "After a while I had to give up working with him. Sometimes when we were trying to get the idea for a scene, I would offer him a suggestion. Instead of giving it some thought, he would remark to me, very discontentedly, 'If you can go it alone, why the hell do you need me?' He refused to work with me as director."

In midsummer Chandler completed a first draft that he thought remained faithful to Hitchcock's intentions; it had the crazed playboy apprehended for the murder of the architect's wife, committed to an asylum, and last seen writhing in a straightjacket. Hitchcock, who had returned from location scouting in New York, Connecticut, and Washington, dictated the elements he wanted altered, met with his art directors and designers, and departed again in a state of high excitement for Forest Hills, where he photographed the Davis Cup matches between America and Australia, intending to use these long shots for the film's suspenseful tennis game. Chandler, meanwhile, was complaining to his agent, Ray Stark, that Hitchcock was "full of little suggestions and ideas which have a cramping effect on a writer's initiative. You are in a position of a fighter who can't get set because he is continuously being kept off balance by short jabs." Nevertheless, Chandler went ahead with the requested revisions.

By the end of September, Hitchcock had returned to Hollywood, where he read Chandler's second draft and immediately told Finlay McDermid that a new writer was needed. At the same time, unaware of Hitchcock's disapproval, Chandler was shifting positions and complaining that his work on the second draft was made difficult because of Hitchcock's absence. "Are you aware," Chandler wrote to McDermid,

that this screenplay was written without one single consultation with Mr. Hitchcock? . . . Not even a phone call. Not one word of criticism or appreciation. Silence. Blank silence then and since. You are much too clever a man to believe that any writer will do his best in conditions like this. There are always things that need to be discussed. There are always places where a writer goes wrong, not being himself a master of the camera. There are always difficult little points which require the meeting of minds, the accommodation of points of view. I had none of this. I find it rather strange. I find it rather ruthless. I find it almost incomparably rude.

McDermid, by this time, was as confused as Hitchcock. First Chandler had complained of too much interference in his work; now he complained of insufficient collaboration. "These veerings of temperament," as Chandler's biographer suggested, "generally expressed in a superficially calm and even lawyerly way in his correspondence, were natural for a writer who invested a great deal of feeling in whatever he did or said. They were the source of his strength as a novelist, allowing him to make imaginative leaps into the minds of his characters. But they were a nuisance when it came down to a cooperative venture like making a movie."

Chandler's script was less coherent than ever, and on Tuesday, September 26, in a final effort to salvage a production the studio almost canceled, Hitchcock dismissed him from the film. At Hitchcock's suggestion Czenzi Ormonde, one of Ben Hecht's assistants, was hired to rework the dialogue with Barbara Keon, whom Hitchcock knew from the Selznick studio.

"Hitchcock succeeded in removing almost every trace of my writing from it," Chandler commented when he received a copy of the final script months later. That estimation is dead accurate, as a comparison of his work with the finished film reveals. Those devoted to Chandler, who usually credit the success of *Strangers on a Train* to him and only minimally praise Hitchcock for the dark rhythms of the film, do not take into account that the final script is entirely the work of Czenzi Ormonde (with some help from her mentor Hecht), Barbara Keon, and Alma Hitchcock, who, under her husband's supervision, wrote the dialogue, scene divisions, and sequence specifications between September 28 and October 16.

On Tuesday, October 17, Hitchcock left for New York, his casting completed. Jack Warner assigned to Ruth Roman, one of his contract players, the role of the senator's daughter. From MGM Hitchcock got Robert Walker, whom he wanted, against type, as the elegant psychopath. Walker had been the prototype of the charming American boy-next-door in films like *The Clock, Since You Went Away,* and *See Here, Private Hargrove,* but by 1950 his life was in serious emotional and physical disarray, and this would be his last complete film: the final shots of *My Son John* the following year were taken, after his death, from the final shots of *Strangers on a Train.* For his role with Hitchcock, the two worked out an elaborate series of subtle gestures with which they hoped to bypass the censor's rumblings about the subtheme of a homosexual courtship.

When Hitchcock could not sign William Holden for the role of the tennis pro who aspired to Washington society, he brought back Farley Granger, who had played in *Rope.* Pat Hitchcock had a call from her agent, who advised that there was a plum of a role she might like in her father's new film — that of the spunky Barbara Morton, whose physical resemblance to the murdered woman very nearly precipitates a doubling of the first crime. Formally, as if she were a stranger, Hitchcock interviewed his daughter for the role, did a screen test, and agreed she might be right. She was more than right, as it turned out: she provided the perfect semicomic counterpoint to the studied seriousness of the other players.

"We never discussed *Strangers on a Train* at home," Pat told an interviewer at the time. "On the set he gives me direction as well as criticism. I might as well be Jane Jones instead of Patricia Hitchcock." This attitude seems to have been calculated by her father to avoid any charges of preferential treatment, and until late in the shooting schedule his refusal to treat his daughter differently won both of them the respect of their colleagues.

From October 20 to 25, the location scenes were shot at Pennsylvania Station in New York City, at the Danbury, Connecticut, railroad stop (used for the film's mythic Metcalf), and at various locations in the nation's capital. By the last of the month the cast and crew had returned to Los Angeles — where Hitchcock found that deer had come down from the hills and destroyed the vegetable garden behind his house. Thenceforth the garden was planted only with flowers.

On the set, Hitchcock — keen with enthusiasm over the structure of the film — drove himself and his actors with unusual zeal until the film was complete, just before Christmas. He was at the studio at seven each morning, and often worked until nine in the evening. An amusement park was constructed according to his exact specifications in the Los Angeles suburb of Chatsworth, at the ranch belonging to director Rowland V. Lee, although the tunnel of love at a Canoga Park fairground was used in addition.

Considerable nighttime shooting was necessary, and Farley Granger remembered that Hitchcock therefore had made detailed drawings, which were carefully inserted in the script book.

Sometimes he would look unhappy as we were shooting, and I would go over and ask him if something was wrong. "Oh, I'm so bored," he would say. And he *was* bored. He had figured out everything in advance, and now he was just hoping that he would get half of it on film.

Some of us were invited to his house for dinner, and there he liked to bring up a topic for discussion, listen to our remarks, and then comment. He was a director at dinner, and he seemed as emotionally detached there as he was on the set.

Granger also recalled that Hitchcock's disinterest in Ruth Roman and the role she played led him to be outspokenly critical and harsh with her, as he had been with Edith Evanson on the set of *Rope*. "He had to have one person in each film he could harass."

One night Hitchcock had a special kind of harassment planned for another player in the film: his own daughter. In an unusual report, the publicity department at Warner Brothers prepared a press release that described an incident involving Pat, who had begged for a ride on the Ferris wheel. When she reached the topmost point of the ride, Hitchcock ordered the machine stopped and all lights extinguished. With the area in total darkness, he left to direct another scene in a far corner of the park while she became hysterical with fear. An hour passed before he ordered the carriage lowered and his trembling daughter released.*

The rest of the cast found various ways to pass the time between setups at the fairground and at the Southgate tennis courts, where local pro Jack Cushingham coached Granger and acted the part of his opponent in scenes that were shot in ninety-seven degree heat. This discomfort Hitchcock endured without removing his jacket, although everyone knew his weight made the work even more burdensome under the circumstances. He nevertheless continued to direct the smallest details on the film and now seemed compulsively involved. He personally selected an orange peel, a chewing-gum wrapper, wet leaves, and a bit of crumpled paper that were used for sewer debris in a scene in which Walker strains to reach a dropped cigarette lighter. And he ordered satin bedsheets so that no lint would appear on the dinner jacket Walker wore in one unusual scene.

Equal care was taken with the most dramatic moments, and Hitchcock engaged his cinematographer in long conferences about them. Robert Burks, who had been a special-effects photographer at Warners, began with *Strangers on a Train* the major collaboration of his career: it was he who shot all of Alfred Hitchcock's feature films (with the exception of *Psycho*) from 1950 to 1964. "You never have any trouble with him as long as you know your job and do it," Burks recalled. "Hitchcock insists on perfection. He has no patience with mediocrity on the set or at a dinner table. There can be no compromise in his work, his food or his wines."

Perhaps the most memorable sequence in *Strangers on a Train* is the climactic fight on a berserk carousel, a segment whose design reveals Hitchcock's mathematical, optical, and engineering skills. Hitchcock once described the intricacies.

This was a most complicated sequence. For rear projection shooting there was a screen and behind it an enormous projector throwing an image on the screen. On the studio floor there was a narrow white line right in line with the projector lens and the lens of the camera had to be right on that white line. The camera was not photographing the screen and what was on it, it was photographing the light in certain colors; therefore the camera lens had to be level and in line with the projector lens. Many of the shots on the merry-go-round were low camera setups. Therefore you can imagine the problem. The projector had to be put up on a high platform, pointing down, and the screen had to be

---

*Warner Brothers press release #HO 9–1251, Nov. 30, 1950, Warner Brothers production archives, Doheny Library, University of Southern California, Los Angeles.

exactly at right angles to the level-line from the lens. All the shots took nearly half a day to line up for each setup. We had to change the projector every time the angle changed.

The final effect of this sequence is terrifyingly vivid. As Walker and Granger fight, the carousel, whirling at breakneck speed, nearly throws them off. When the carousel breaks down, there is a massive explosion, screams are heard, bodies and machines fly about. To realize this, Hitchcock took a toy carousel and photographed it blown up by a small charge of explosives. This piece of film he then enlarged and projected on a vast screen, positioning actors around and in front of it so that the effect is one of a mob of bystanders into which plaster horses and passengers are hurled in deadly chaos. It is one of the moments in Hitchcock's work that continues to bring gasps from every audience and applause from cinema students.

But the enduring value of *Strangers on a Train* is not in the technical achievement, admirable though that is. An obsessively structured film — as chilly and tough in its situation as *Young and Innocent* and *Stage Fright* were warm and *Notorious* full of passionate longing — *Strangers on a Train* reveals an artist determined to reestablish himself after a period of disappointment with work and relationships. Hitchcock had set forth feelings about family and women in *Shadow of a Doubt* and *Notorious,* and he had explored the vagaries of sexual congress, emotional tyrannies, and the dangers of neurotic self-abnegation in *Rope* and *Under Capricorn.* Now there was an intensive exposition of a deeper split within himself.

The controlling idea of *Shadow of a Doubt* had been the motif of the double, which expressed a personal inner tension that flourished around the time of Hitchcock's separation from family and country. Now, in *Strangers on a Train,* the deeper roots of that tension were explored. As in the earlier film, the form of the film is its meaning: doubles and pairs, accumulated and intercut in an almost endless series, mediate the theme. ("Isn't it a fascinating design?" Hitchcock liked to ask proudly. "You could study it forever.")

There are, at the outset, two pairs of feet and two sets of train rails that cross twice. Walker and Granger meet when their crossed feet accidentally touch under a table. Walker orders a pair of double drinks. Later the two men are related by a crosscutting of words and gestures: one asks the time and the other, miles away, looks at his wristwatch; one says in anger, "I could strangle her!" and the other, far distant, makes a choking gesture; and so forth.

There are two respectable and influential fathers, two women with eyeglasses, and two women at a party who delight in thinking up ways of committing the perfect crime. There are two sets of two detectives in two cities, two little boys at the two trips to the fairground, two old men at the carousel, two boyfriends accompanying the woman about to be murdered, and two Hitchcocks in the film. The director, who at first had wanted to make his cameo in the Mellon Library or as a passenger on the train, finally decided to appear with the double of his own large form — carrying a double bass fiddle.

All this doubling — which has no precedent in the novel — was quite deliberately added by Hitchcock, and is the key element in the film's structure. (In this regard, he also gave the homosexual angle a wider reference, making it serve the theme of two aspects of a single personality.) Walker is Granger's "shadow," activating what Granger wants, bringing out the dark underside of Granger's potentially murderous desires.

Furthermore, while the two Charlies in *Shadow of a Doubt* located two moral realities within a single family, *Strangers on a Train* locates those double realities in separate social and political arenas that Hitchcock overlaps. Walker inhabits the world of darkness, marked by the shadows that crisscross his face, the gothic gloominess of his Arlington mansion, and the boat — *Pluto* — that he takes to commit murder and that relates him to the god and household of the dead; he is the counterpart of Granger, who inhabits the world of light, represented by bright, open-air tennis games, light-colored attire, and formal Washington dinner parties. And Walker is photographed in one visually stunning shot as a malignant stain on the purity of the white-marble Jefferson Memorial, as a blot on the order of things.

The series of doubles, which Hitchcock dictated in rapid and inspired profusion to Czenzi Ormonde and Barbara Keon during the last days of script preparation, finally serves to associate the world of light, order, and vitality with the world of darkness, chaos, lunacy, and death. These two worlds were not mutually exclusive for Hitchcock, as his own memories and desires reminded him daily. Generous with his daughter, whom he encouraged and supported throughout her London studies, he could also be callously inconsiderate of her feelings and fears. Thoroughly devoted to Alma and a slave to her estimation of his work, he could ignore her for weeks and fall into a romantic fixation over an actress. Filled with longing for human contact and for companionship, he never had the gift of sustaining much contact and could never really support the responsibilities of friendship. Fascinated with the techniques of conventional and unconventional sex, he recoiled from physical and emotional intimacy like a child before a dark and frightening forest, retreating instead into a private world of fantasies, which were exposed in his films and sometimes in impolite conversation. The extremes of conduct — the unleashing of anarchic impulses while pursuing a stereotypical image of public respectability — characterized his own state of soul just as they characterized Walker and Granger in the film.

In Highsmith's novel, there is no cyclorama of Washington order and politics and social convention; and the fairground setting, which in the book is simply a melodramatic setting for the murder, became in the film a major symbol of a contrasting domain. From Jonson's *Bartholomew Fair*, from Thackeray's *Vanity Fair*, from Bunyan's *Pilgrim's Progress*, from Goethe's *Faust*, and from *The Cabinet of Dr. Caligari*, Hitchcock drew the tradition of the fairground as the place where the demented aspects of life are concentrated and expressed, where all the Dionysian riots and year-long repressions are set free. This is the place — as it had been more gently in *The Ring, Murder!, Saboteur*, and *Stage Fright* — where the underlying grotesquerie is enjoyed, where Walker travels to a murderous underworld and unleashes demonic forces. And at the finale, the fairground is the place where the cycle of lunacy is broken, the whirling carousel destroyed so that normality may be restored. Walker's presence has set the orbit out of control; order must be reestablished.*

The theme of the double was available to Hitchcock from the literary traditions that were familiar to him. From E. T. A. Hoffmann's first novel, *The Devil's Elixirs*, and his tale "The Doubles" he took the device of the doppelgänger. "I imagine my ego," Hoffmann wrote, "as being viewed through a lens: all the forms which move around me are egos; and whatever they do, or leave undone, vexes me." The statement is virtually an epigraph for *Strangers on a Train*.

From Heinrich Heine's *Ratcliff*, which he had read several times during the Selznick years, Hitchcock knew the dramatic value of describing two persons drawn together by fate, by love, and by murderous impulses. From "William Wilson," by Edgar Allan Poe, he had taken the same motif, as he had from Dostoevski's tale "The Double." Stevenson's *The Strange Case of Dr. Jekyll and Mr. Hyde* he knew intimately, not to mention H. G. Wells's "Love and Mr. Lewisham," Kipling's "At the End of the Passage," and Wilde's *The Picture of Dorian Gray*. Guy de Maupassant had dealt quite frankly with his own psychic dilemmas in "The Horla" and "Peter and John," and there were numerous

---

*Both the killer and his victim are associated with broken circles — burst balloons, crazy carousels, broken gongs, shattered eyeglasses, and bitter fights at a record shop — images of order disrupted, harmony destroyed.

examples in the tales of Hans Christian Andersen and Alfred de Musset.

In the Romantic and Victorian precedents, the double always reflected strong inner conflict, a conflict between the fear of involvement with life and the concomitant fear of noninvolvement, stagnation, and death, a conflict between the reach toward wholeness and the danger of disintegration. Intimate with these sources, Hitchcock could make the double — in *Shadow of a Doubt* and *Strangers on a Train,* as later in *Psycho* and *Frenzy* — the messenger of death. He required no training in psychology to be aware of this common creative currency and its attendant imagery: it was one of the few recurring motifs in the art and literature of his time, and inevitably the cinema, *his* cinema, capitalized on the forms and patterns of this device.

Hitchcock and all the aforementioned artists were kindred spirits. Many of them shared his personal traits and afflictions: compulsiveness, mercurialness, a fixation on alternately indulging in and avoiding food and alcohol, a fiercely romantic fantasy life, a fear of insanity, a sense of personal greatness, an irrational fear of sudden death, hypochondria, and claustrophobia (which in the case of Poe took extreme form as a terror of being buried alive). A tendency to isolated brooding and a horror of accident and chaos marked all these men and their fictional protagonists — and from Poe to Stevenson to Hitchcock there was a further link: the fascination with death as an almost magical way of evading it. The literature Hitchcock read thus merged, in *Strangers on a Train,* with the fears and lineaments and demons of his own soul — with the elements, unarticulated in real life but dimly perceived, that were expressed through his films and occasionally unleashed in cruel jokes, outrageously scatological comments, and, most poignantly, a systematic withdrawal from all forms of the human sharing he so desired.

All of this artistry comes together in a single moment of the film, in the one shot that reveals Hitchcock's greatest care and originality: the murder scene. Robert Walker, having pursued Laura Elliott to the amusement-park island, flicks open her cigarette lighter. Her face, filling the frame as she looks directly into the camera, is suddenly blocked as Walker steps into the frame and his hands grip her throat. Her eyeglasses fall to the ground and then, in one of the most unexpected, most aesthetically justified moments in film, the camera observes the strangling and the final collapse of the woman as a huge reflection in one of the eyeglass lenses, the shadowy distortion marking at once something gruesome and infernal, a moment wrenched from a terrible nightmare.

To achieve this startling hallucinatory effect, Hitchcock supervised the construction of an enormous distorting lens, then photographed his two actors reflected in it at a ninety-degree angle. Like such later Hitchcock sequences as the shower murder in *Psycho,* the final attack in *The Birds,* the collapse of the dying Cuban woman in *Topaz* and the rape-strangulation in *Frenzy,* this brief moment, the extraordinary care he took in planning and filming it, and the strange visual effect he produced, vindicate François Truffaut's observation that Hitchcock filmed scenes of murder as if they were love scenes, and love scenes as if they were murder scenes. In the oddly appealing visual originality there is a stark fusion of the grotesque and the beautiful, a merger celebrated in aesthetic theory by Baudelaire, Joyce, Cocteau, and others. The aestheticizing of the horror somehow enables the audience to contemplate more fully its reality; instead of turning away from Hitchcock's image, repulsed, the viewer gazes, and so is forced to assess feelings, reactions, and moral judgments about the acts themselves.

There can be no doubt that for Alfred Hitchcock there was a special fascination in planning and filming the most outrageous human deed in unforgettable and visually arresting ways, the better to impress his audience with the almost chimerical nature of the act of murder. But it is also true (and nowhere more true than in this particular murder scene and in the party scene, where Walker demonstrates the convenience of quiet strangling as a perfect way of killing) that Hitchcock saw something beautiful, something desirable in the act of murder itself — something of wishful dream as much as dreaded nightmare.

Throughout his life, Hitchcock was singularly intrigued by the act of strangling, and from the earliest days to the end of his life that fascination revealed itself seriously on film and jokingly in life. The act of murder by strangling is described or implied in *The Lodger, Secret Agent, Young and Innocent, Shadow of a Doubt, Notorious, Stage Fright,* the later version of *The Man Who Knew Too Much, Vertigo,* and *North by Northwest.* It is visually detailed in *The Lady Vanishes, Jamaica Inn, Rope, Strangers on a Train, Dial "M" for Murder, Rear Window, Torn Curtain,* and *Frenzy.* In *Strangers on a Train,* Hitchcock announced the motif from the beginning: in Walker's necktie — Hitchcock himself designed its strangling lobster claws — and in the advertisements, for which he had himself photographed inserting the letter *L* into the word STRANG[L]ERS. He delighted in showing friends in social situations "how to strangle a woman with only one hand," and he loved posing as a strangler (as the photographs in this book suggest). A famous photo sequence by Philippe Halsman shows Hitchcock doing various things to a bust of his daughter. The final gesture: strangling her.

With principal photography on *Strangers on a Train* completed by Christmas 1950, Hitchcock and Alma left for a holiday at Santa Cruz, where he negotiated the first sale of his grape crop. On March 5 of the following year the preview was held at the Huntington Park Theater and Alma, Jack Warner, Whitfield Cook, and Barbara Keon were in the Hitchcock party. Raymond Chandler and Czenzi Ormonde sent perfunctory notes expressing regret that other commitments prevented their attendance, and no one was more surprised than they were when the Screen Directors Guild awarded the film a prize.

At the end of March, Alma and Pat sailed from New York for a two-month trip through Europe.* Hitchcock, pleased with the advance publicity and studio excitement over the new film, wanted to settle on another story at once, and he did not join his family until May 18, by which time they had arrived in Rome. From there, they motored together through Germany, Holland, Norway, and Sweden before sailing back, on June 12, to New York. All that is known of this unusually long and private family holiday is that Hitchcock read widely, and in vain, to find a literary source for a new film, and that, crossing the Atlantic, Pat met a young American businessman she would eventually marry.

*Strangers on a Train* was scheduled for national release in a dozen American cities from the end of June through early July, and Hitchcock flew to all of them to create publicity. With her usual goodwill and good humor, Pat agreed to a demanding schedule of press activities on behalf of the film too, representing her father for the New York premiere on July 3 that marked the reopening of the old Strand as the newly refurbished Warner theater.

Meantime, audience reaction was pouring into Jack Warner's office. In Massachusetts, Wisconsin, Ohio, Maryland, and Michigan several social and church groups and a number of individuals resented the explicit murder and the implicit sexual specialism — although Warner was consoled by favorable reports from Oregon, Kansas, Illinois, Virginia, and Canada. But the general box office receipts soon told the true story: *Strangers on a Train* was a success, and Hitchcock was pronounced at the top of his form as master of the dark, melodramatic suspense thriller. By year's end the CBS Theatre had presented a radio version with Ruth Roman, Ray Milland, and Frank Lovejoy, and it was such a hit that the play was broadcast again — with Dana Andrews, Robert Cummings, and Virginia Mayo — some three years later.

Hitchcock's infusion of technical wizardry into a narrative about psychopathology had apparently sounded the deepest creative and personal springs he had tapped since *Notorious,* but for the time being Hitchcock

*The trip followed Pat's last attempt at a Broadway career — in the short run of *The High Ground,* in February 1951.

once again found himself thwarted, without a project to write and produce. The family vacation had done little to allay a growing nervousness that he would be unable to maintain his new success. For the first time, he revealed to the press his restiveness about finding a story with dramatic impact.

"Where can you get movie stories that are better than today's headlines?" he asked in July. "Government officials turn crooked, planes go 1500 miles an hour, the world waits for days to learn whether a war will end, diplomats disappear. How can you top that for drama and suspense? I thought I'd stop everything with a picture called *Mother, Are You a Spy?* Or maybe I'll have the King of England running a Communist cell in Buckingham Palace." Then he told of an idea that would require almost a decade of refinement before providing the inspiration for one of his most famous films. Describing a scene in which people chase each other all over the faces of Mount Rushmore, he said: "I want to have one scene of a man hanging onto Lincoln's eyebrows. That's all the picture I have so far."

For a few weeks it seemed that Hitchcock might direct *The Wages of Fear,* about a crew of men with a cargo of dangerous explosives. But the negotiations with the author and publisher failed under the burden of Parisian bureaucracy and the story was sold to director Henri-Georges Clouzot.

The fall and winter of 1951 was a period of almost ghostly calm in Hitchcock's life. Socially, he and Alma very nearly dropped out of sight, and many of their occasional dinner companions wrongly supposed they had resumed traveling or had retreated permanently to Santa Cruz. But Hitchcock was at Bellagio Road, in a quiet panic. He read novels, biographies, and plays, but nothing struck his fancy, and no original idea developed.

Pat provided the only distraction of the season. During the European holiday she had met and was subsequently courted by a New England businessman, and in September the *New York Times* announced the engagement of Patricia Alma Hitchcock to Joseph E. O'Connell. Grandnephew of the late cardinal archbishop of Boston, he was at the time treasurer of the Thomas Dalby Corporation of Watertown, Massachusetts. They were married at Saint Patrick's Cathedral, New York, in January 1952.

"Alma and I were relieved, in a way, when our daughter decided that being a mother of sticky-fingered children required all her creative attention," Hitchcock said later in reference to Pat's marriage and theatrical career. (On April 17, 1953, Hitchcock's first granddaughter, Mary

O'Connell, was born; Teresa followed on July 2, 1954, and Kathleen on February 27, 1959.) He was not the first father to suspect — rather unfairly, in this case — that his little girl was marrying beneath her station. His attempts to lure his son-in-law into the film industry were met unenthusiastically, and with Pat's new and independent life a strained distance often characterized her father's attitude to her. Alma, however, remained a loyal friend to her daughter.

At the same time, Hitchcock himself needed Alma's support and attention more than ever, for Jack Warner was anxious to take up his option for Hitchcock's next picture. On January 3, 1949, Warner and Hitchcock had signed a contract for Hitchcock to produce and direct four pictures over a period of six-and-a-half years, for a total compensation of $999,000.* A generous clause also allowed Hitchcock to alternate the Warner films with productions at other studios, and it was undoubtedly this unusual term (which Hitchcock never took advantage of), as well as Jack Warner's uncharacteristic patience with the director's indecisiveness at this time, that encouraged Hitchcock to offer, in a letter dated February 7, 1952, to direct an extra picture without salary at the end of the contract. (This promise he fulfilled, returning to Warners in the midst of his later tenure at Paramount to direct The Wrong Man in 1956.)

By February 1952, after the excitement of Pat's marriage and her own silver wedding anniversary, Alma was finally able to give full attention to the problem of her husband's professional inactivity, and in fact she relished the prospect of more involvement; except for The Paradine Case and Stage Fright, her contributions had been merely peripheral for the past decade. Hitchcock was now almost sick with anxiety over the creative stasis in his life. Word of this circulated in Hollywood, and soon David Selznick — who was himself in a painful state of inactivity — wrote to Hitchcock suggesting that they do a film together (perhaps Murders in the Rue Morgue) starring Jennifer Jones, who was now his wife. Hitchcock was apparently so appalled at the idea of regression to what he considered Selznick servitude that, despite his desperate circumstances, he did not even reply. Shortly thereafter, as if on cue, Alma came up with the logical idea.

Nos Deux Consciences was a play written in 1902 by Paul Anthelme (the nom de plume of Paul Bourde). By 1947 a nephew of the playwright had inherited the rights and sold them to writer-agent Louis Verneuil, who for $15,000 drew up a one-hundred-page treatment, wrote a first screenplay, and transferred these manuscripts and all rights to

* The films turned out to be Stage Fright, Strangers on a Train, I Confess, and Dial "M" for Murder.

Hitchcock and Transatlantic Pictures. When Transatlantic was dissolved, the rights were sold to Warners, with the understanding that eventually Hitchcock would try to fashion a film from the treatment he and Alma subsequently wrote in 1948. Since then, three more drafts (the respective work of William Rose, Leslie Storm, and Paul Vincent Carroll) had been submitted to Hitchcock, who had all but abandoned the project when his own company failed.

At once Alma dug out the earlier drafts and the old notes from her conversations with Hitchcock about the story, and she suggested that the time was ripe for them to tackle to project again in earnest. At first he thought that this was sheer desperation, but then he read the drafts and the malaise lifted. His renewed enthusiasm is not difficult to understand. Raised in the traditions of Roman Catholicism, Hitchcock was fascinated by the plot premise: that a priest cannot reveal the identity of a murderer who, within the seal of ritual confession, has disclosed his crime, and that this law of silence must be kept even if the priest himself is ultimately charged with the crime.

But there was more than a cultural interest motivating Hitchcock — there was a personal one, too. In *Strangers on a Train* he had dealt fiercely with the universality of guilt by exploring its transference from character to character, and now, in what came to be called *I Confess*, he was ready to associate himself more intimately with that broader-based feeling. *Strangers on a Train* already had touched something crucial in his deeply rooted Victorian-Catholic sense: the need for confession. As a schoolboy Hitchcock had marched to the confessional booth each week while the English Jesuits gloomily reminded him and his peers of their sinfulness and their need for repentance and absolution. And the impulse to confess one's guilt to someone else had already figured in the emotional climaxes of Hitchcock's films — in *Foreign Correspondent*, where Herbert Marshall asks forgiveness of Laraine Day, and especially in *Under Capricorn*, where Ingrid Bergman delivers a ten-minute confession to Michael Wilding. Moreover, in an affecting way, *I Confess* is Hitchcock's testimony to his wife of twenty-five years, and it is perhaps the film that finally deals most directly with her place in his life.

As soon as they had reworked the treatment, in February, Hitchcock took Alma to scout locations in Quebec, where the story was to be filmed — a city rich in traditions of French Catholicism and abundant with religious iconography, priestly garb, and images of the crucified Christ. But they did not proceed directly. After flying to New York, they hired a limousine and were driven for a visit to the Pennsylvania farm where Samson Raphaelson and his wife Dorshka then lived. They arrived the afternoon of Washington's Birthday, amid a fierce snow-storm, and after some difficulty negotiating the walk along an icy path, the Hitchcocks were welcomed by their former colleague.

Dorshka Raphaelson had banked the house with forsythias she had coaxed into bloom, her husband tended a roaring fire, and the smell of grilled lamb chops (known to be a Hitchcock favorite) drifted from the kitchen. There were wine and warmth and memories of collaboration on *Suspicion* a decade earlier. Finally, Hitchcock summarized the story of his new film and asked his host if he would like to write the screen-play for *I Confess*. But Raphaelson did not especially like the material, and he replied politely that he had other commitments for the next sev-eral months.

By the beginning of March the Hitchcocks had seen every quarter of Quebec and had listed the places they thought most photogenic: the lavish Château Frontenac hotel; the Parliament building and the Hall of Justice; the Lévis ferry; the docks at Wolfe's Cove; the sloping, narrow streets of the old section; and a variety of churches, including the ornate Saint Jean-Baptiste and Saint Zéphyrin.

But they still needed a writer, and at Alma's suggestion they headed for New York and the theater, where they met William Archibald, whose stage version of Henry James's *The Turn of the Screw* had been a suc-cess in 1950. Archibald agreed at once to collaborate. Since the story's antagonist was a German refugee, a frightened sacristan who murdered when he was caught stealing, Hitchcock wanted someone who could handle the character's special fears and speech patterns. After seeing George Tabori's new play *Flight into Egypt* — about the plight of Eu-ropean refugees — he brought the dramatist back to Los Angeles and, when Archibald's draft arrived in late April, set Tabori to work on re-vising the dialogue. By this time, the original play (already much changed in all the treatments) was virtually unrecognizable.

There was more difficulty than they anticipated. The main charac-ter — a man whose war experience led him from human romance with an ardent girl to the divine romance of priestly commitment — was not vivid, and Hitchcock was afraid that unless they had an actor who evoked sympathy, the priest would remain slightly wooden and martyrlike. Through May and June, Hitchcock and Barbara Keon discussed casting and prepared the scene breakdown, while Alma drew up lists of special production requirements. Each evening she listened as Hitchcock read the detailed summary of sequences polished that day.

What her reaction might have been cannot be known, for the Hitch-cocks' privacy was as sacred as the church confessional where the story began. But what was emerging, and what could not have escaped Alma's notice, was a subplot more haunted and guilt-ridden than that involving the principal characters. *I Confess* was still the story of the alien sacristan who kills a man and then confesses his sin to his wife and to the priest who has employed him. But in typical Hitchcockian fashion the guilt he acknowledges has a more complex field, for the murdered man was blackmailing the priest's former (and now married) girlfriend.

Effectively, the sacristan has killed for another, and the multiple confessions of the film — confessions of guilt, of love, of past silence, and of passion repressed — are balanced on this central character. Like Hitchcock, the frightened, secretive refugee is a man haunted by displacement, by guilt over the betrayal of trust, and by remorse for the pain he has caused his wife — who is named, significantly and boldly, *Alma*. (In the play, and in all earlier drafts of the screenplay, she is called Madame Bressaude.)

"I wanted to pray," the sacristan protests to the priest in the opening speech, written by Hitchcock himself, "but no one can help me. I have abused your kindness. You gave my wife and me a home, a job, even your friendship . . . It's a wonderful thing, for a refugee, a man without a home . . . You trusted me. . . . I must confess to you, I must tell someone. I want to make a confession."

Hitchcock's identification with this character becomes clearer later, when the sacristan's fear of police capture leads him to kill his wife. "I thought of the police. I'm always afraid of the police. . . . Where is my Alma? I loved her. It made me cry to see her work so hard." In almost the identical words, Hitchcock spoke, in later years, of the assistance Alma gave him throughout his life, and at no time more loyally and more substantially than in 1952.

By the first of July, Montgomery Clift had been signed by Hitchcock for the role of the priest. Talented, handsome, and one of the most popular screen actors of that day, Clift was at the same time an unhappy and troubled man, moody and neurotically dependent on both alcohol and on his acting coach Mira Rostova. "There are some actors I've felt uncomfortable with," Hitchcock recalled, "and working with Montgomery Clift was difficult because he was a method actor and a neurotic as well."

On July 24 Clift joined Hitchcock in Jack Warner's office to meet the leading lady. Anita Björk had just been hailed by critics in Europe and America for her performance in Alf Sjöberg's screen version of *Miss Julie*. But she arrived in Hollywood with an illegitimate child and lover, and Warner, with the angry public reaction to Ingrid Bergman's personal life still fresh in his mind, insisted that the actress be at once dismissed. With only two weeks until the start of location shooting in Quebec, they had to find an available star replacement. Hitchcock's choice was another major actress of the day — a blond, and one he felt confident with — Anne Baxter.

The granddaughter of Frank Lloyd Wright, she had been educated privately, had appeared on Broadway at the age of thirteen, and at sixteen had been considered for the leading role in *Rebecca*. "Back in 1939, I was precocious but not sophisticated," she remembered. Hitchcock had been very kind with her then, and they had met socially many times since. She was not only an Oscar winner in 1946 and a nominee for *All About Eve* in 1950, she was also Mrs. John Hodiak, and the Hitchcocks often invited them to dine in the years after *Lifeboat*.

When Baxter arrived to begin makeup and wardrobe tests for *I Confess*, she found that Hitchcock was "very quiet, and he kept his hands in repose, but he commanded a great deal of respect with his mesmeric eyes. He had an extraordinary stillness, but then he could move with sudden speed — it was like lightning masqueraded in a Buddha's casing. There was a terrific duality about him, and he would do anything to avoid people overreacting to him." Later, when it came to the actual filming, she found that he did not care so much that the *actors* acted — he wanted *the camera* to act.

But the first thing he ordered for Anne Baxter was that her blond hair be colored even more blond. "He was very particular about wardrobe and hair. I felt I wasn't as pretty as he wanted a woman to be in his films, and as he wanted me to be. There was a lot of Pygmalion in him, and he was proud of how he transformed actresses. When I arrived, everything happened so fast that they didn't design a new wardrobe for me; they altered Anita Björk's clothes. Naturally, I was a little overwrought about the haste, but he simply said, 'Anne, it's only a movie!' " She recalled thinking he was right, but that feelings and careers were also at stake.

On August 21 the first scene was filmed in Quebec, and the same day — already off the production schedule — Hitchcock arranged for the faithful Barbara Keon to be signed as a writer to work with him on several difficult scenes as they proceeded. (A large and businesslike woman, Barbara Keon never elicited from Hitchcock the emotional response other secretaries or assistants, unwittingly, did.) The cast and crew were accommodated at the comfortable Château Elysée hotel, while Hitchcock, Keon, and Alma resided at the palatial Château Frontenac.

Immediately, problems arose, owing largely to the erratic Montgomery Clift. Karl Malden, who was playing the role of the detective, had befriended Clift in earlier days when they were both stage actors in

New York. Malden agreed with Anne Baxter that there was considerable tension on the set of *I Confess*. "It had to do with Mira Rostova," he said. "Monty depended on her, kept a distance from Hitchcock and from the rest of us to go over his lines with her, insisted on her approval before a scene could be shot. Naturally this created a deep division and tension."

The tension carried over into the shooting of the church scenes. "Mira stood behind a pillar," according to Anne Baxter, "and Hitchcock was of course normally very calm, but he got furious because Monty would glance over for her approval on a particular take, or for her reaction to the way he read a line. Hitchcock never confronted Monty directly, because that was never his way. He got to him through Karl Malden, whom Monty trusted and listened to."

There was, however, another, more insidious problem than Clift's relationship with his coach: his drinking, which threw a cover of embarrassment and inconvenience over the entire production. Anne Baxter remembered that their scenes together were exceptionally difficult because of this, and that Hitchcock could not or would not deal with the matter firmly on his own authority. "Poor Monty was drinking so heavily, virtually all the time," she said.

He was so confused and removed from what was going on around him that his eyes wouldn't focus. We had to do an important dialogue on the Lévis ferry, and I was to look longingly at him while baring my soul. To do that, I needed something, some response from him. But there was nothing, just a blank and distant gaze, and I had to imagine a look on his face. He was so disturbed and unhappy, but Hitchcock never talked to him. He had the assistant director, Don Page, handle everything.

Hitchcock, for his part, did not like Clift's method acting any more than his dependence on drink and dialogue coach. He found annoying the star's introspective approach to the requirements of a role and his tacit refusal to cooperate on the set. But at the same time, Hitchcock was fascinated by Clift's private life. He considered the actor something of an exotic, for Clift was one of a long line of professionals who led a bohemian and sexually ambivalent life. According to biographer Patricia Bosworth, Clift never wholly integrated his homosexuality into his life, and there was a deep guilt he tried to cover with great amounts of liquor (among other means of escape).

Hitchcock was no stranger to inner torment and guilt himself, but his drinking was still under control and did not interfere significantly with his work. He found Clift's conduct difficult but psychologically intriguing. Having just dealt with the subtheme of a homosexual courtship in

*Strangers on a Train,* Hitchcock saw in Clift yet another actor, like those in some of his other films, who led openly homosexual or bisexual lives — some of them perhaps because in the entertainment world unconventional expression was considered somewhat chic and daring, others because it was simply for them honest and natural and they chose to live their lives neither falsely nor fearfully. In England, Hitchcock had been almost wide-eyed over the discovery of the variations on sexual conduct, and his discoveries about actors like Ivor Novello, Henry Kendall, Charles Laughton, and others were now repeated in the cases of Montgomery Clift and the German actor O. E. Hasse, who was playing the killer-sacristan. Hitchcock was not openly contemptuous, nor was he uneasy about their sexual conduct. He simply found the two men endlessly interesting.

Before they left Quebec to film the interiors in Hollywood, an odd thing happened that further strained communication during production. On a beautiful Sunday, Anne Baxter suggested to Alma that they take advantage of a free afternoon and drive out to enjoy the Canadian countryside. Hitchcock was in conference with his camera crew in preparation for the next day's work, and Alma, who had established a warm relationship with the actress, readily accepted. But they would have to return by dinnertime, Alma said, since she always dined with Hitchcock, who could not bear to eat alone. That, Baxter replied, would not be a problem; they would allow sufficient time for the return trip.

There was indeed a problem, however. Unusually heavy traffic snarled the roadway back to the city, and Alma, who tried to cover her anxiety, was obviously in a panic as the dinner hour approached. By the time they arrived at the hotel, she was over an hour late. Anne Baxter remembered the tiny Mrs. Hitchcock almost running through the lobby and across the dining room to where her husband sat, in angry isolation, glaring at the two women. "There he was, sitting like Jove, furious at us. Alma tried to lighten the tone, but he would not be placated. I saw then how totally dependent he was on her. He needed her to be with him at the dinner hour, and she hadn't been there. And she had been strangely terrified too, as if she thought something dreadful would happen to him without her. He didn't forgive me for that dinner delay for a long time. Our relationship was strained from that time on."

Alma, who had become once again with *I Confess* Hitchcock's most supportive collaborator, was not only his occasional muse, a force behind the creative throne — she was also his surrogate mother, a force behind his emotional throne. "Alma was Hitchcock's stabilizer," according to Karl Malden. "He could balance everything off her, for she was his literary mind. She knew when the dialogue was right, when the

speech rhythms were right.'' Malden, Baxter, and other associates recognized that Alma knew how dependent Hitchcock was on her, and they
noticed that she rather liked that dependence.

On October 2 the last three weeks of studio work began, and Hitchcock, in an expansive mood after Jack Warner told him how pleased he
was with the production, gave a dinner that weekend at Bellagio Road
for his cast. Perversely — and typically — he forced extravagant quantities of drink on Montgomery Clift (who had, of course, brought Mira
Rostova as his companion for the evening). The discomfort of the other
guests increased as they watched Hitchcock enjoy Clift's swiftly diminishing sobriety, the systematic unraveling of his manner and coherence.

Finally, after the actor had consumed a great deal of both liquor and
wine, Hitchcock poured him a full beaker of brandy and dared him to
drink it in a single quick gulp. Anne Baxter and Karl Malden watched,
motionless with horror, as the glass changed hands. Clift drank, and a
moment later fell to the floor, face down, in a perilous alcoholic stupor.
For a moment everyone stood more terrified than embarrassed. Then the
host's dog, Philip of Magnesia (successor to Edward IX), bounded over
and sniffed the body. Karl Malden and his wife Mona sprang to the
moment, lifted Clift, and drove the unconscious actor home.

There was no celebration when the picture was completed at the end
of the month, and for a long while Hitchcock saw no one connected
with it — except, of course, Alma, with whom it had begun, and whose
single-minded attention is everywhere indicated in the gentle strength
of Dolly Haas, who played Alma, the murderer's wife in *I Confess*.

For their twenty-sixth wedding anniversary, the Hitchcocks traveled
to Saint Moritz, where they stayed quietly at the Palace Hotel until after
Christmas 1952. While *I Confess* was in preproduction, Hitchcock had
agreed to do, as his fourth and final film for Jack Warner, an adaptation
of David Duncan's novel *The Bramble Bush*. But now, on the winter
holiday, he and Alma could not develop a satisfactory treatment, and
he cabled Warner that he might first direct a story by Francis Iles about
a mild country physician who murders his wife (Iles had provided the
literary basis for *Suspicion*). He thought this tale of crime would make
a good vehicle for someone with Alec Guinness's quietly mysterious
manner. But word from England informed them that the actor was not
available for at least a year. The Hitchcocks returned to Bel-Air with no
hint of what to do next, and as usual the interlude — which would be
welcomed by many artists and even necessary for some after an intense
period of work — threw him into a distracted aridity.

In mid-February of 1953 *I Confess* opened to lukewarm reviews. The

consensus over the next several weeks was summed up in the words of
a critic who wrote that "the whetted knife of Hitchcock's direction blunts
itself again and again on a ponderous, equivocal situation." The *Los
Angeles Times* interviewed the director about his next production, and
again he mentioned *The Bramble Bush,* saying that the story was in an
embryonic state. Soon he dropped that property, however, and began
poring over recent plays in an effort to find something he could film.

The play he settled on was Frederick Knott's melodrama *Dial "M"
for Murder,* which had opened in London and New York, respectively,
in June and October 1952. When the studio began to negotiate for the
screen rights for Hitchcock, they learned that Alexander Korda had purchased them for a modest £1,000. The news that Warner and Hitchcock
were interested was amusing to Korda, who had never managed to lure
the director to his studio — and it was profitable news as well, for he
asked and got £30,000 to transfer the screen rights.

In May and June things happened quickly, as they often did once
Hitchcock had a story. Frederick Knott arrived from London to make
some suggestions; Hitchcock signed (for the role of the inspector) John
Williams, who had acted in *The Paradine Case* and whom he had seen
in the New York stage version of *Dial "M" for Murder;* Ray Milland
agreed to play the charming villain; and Jack Warner announced that
the production would be one of the studio's three-dimensional films.

One of Hollywood's gimmicks — inspired by the panic reaction to
drastically decreased movie attendance in the early 1950s after television invaded the American home — the three-dimensional movie
flashed in 1952 and sputtered out within two years. The process did not
interest Hitchcock, who recognized it for what it was — essentially
anticinematic, with its constant reminder to the audience that they were
"out there" and not drawn, visually and emotionally, "into" the story,
its action, and its mood. At this point, the director's only desire was to
get through with the filming as quickly and as unceremoniously as possible. All he needed was the right leading lady to bring some glamour
and life to the picture.

The right leading lady — and according to Hitchcock, the most cooperative actress he ever directed — came along in the person of blond
Grace Kelly. She had appeared, pleasantly but not very effectively, in
two black-and-white films by other directors, but Hitchcock saw a test
she had done in New York and then a preview of John Ford's *Mo-
gambo.* At once he settled on her. "I was delighted to accept this one-
picture deal," she recalled, "because most movie offers meant signing
a seven-year exclusive contract with a studio, which I wanted to avoid."
She ultimately starred in three of Hitchcock's pictures — one of the

happiest associations in Hollywood history — before abandoning her film career to marry Prince Rainier III of Monaco.

Principal photography was accomplished between July 30 and September 25. Although only a single, stage-bound set was used during the filming, half of the shooting was given over to elaborate rehearsals necessitated by the difficulties of the tricky process. "Hitchcock was terribly encumbered and frustrated by having to do the picture in 3-D," his leading lady remembered.

But Hollywood had been hit by television in a bad way, and Warner Brothers had even been closed for about five months. This was the first picture being shot there after this time, and there we were, just a small group of us, rattling around in a big studio.

The camera was the size of a room, and one day someone said to him on the set, "Well, Hitch, is that your dressing room?" The machine was so gigantic, and Hitchcock had a terrible time. He wanted to remain very faithful to the play, cutting away from the main room only when absolutely necessary, but with this camera it was like having to go into a boxing ring with your hands tied. But he was so extraordinary. I never saw him lose his patience — he never became angry. I would get furious for him, when I saw the frustrations and the things he wanted to do and the technicians said, "Oh no, with the camera we can't do this and we can't do that."

We all knew at the time that it would never be shown in 3-D. We knew it was a dying fad and the film would be released in a normal flat version, but this was what Mr. Warner wanted.

Since the technique deprived Hitchcock of his usual freedom with camera placement and angle, he instead devoted himself heartily to the wardrobe for his star. "I was very nervous when I first met him, but he was very dear with me," she remembered.

We talked about the clothes. Except for the red lace dress, everything was bought off the rack. He wanted to go from a bright and colorful wardrobe to a drab and depressing one as the woman's fortunes changed.

Then he wanted to make a fancy velvet robe for me. He said he wanted the effect of light and shadow on velvet for the murder scene at the desk. I was very unhappy about it, and I told him I didn't think it was right for the part. He said he wanted a particular effect, but I said, "I don't think that this woman is going to put on this great fancy robe if she is getting up in the middle of the night to answer a ringing phone and there's nobody in the apartment!"

And he said, "Well, what would *you* do? What would *you* put on to answer the phone?" I said I wouldn't put on anything at all, that I'd just get up and go to the phone in my nightgown. And he admitted that was better, and that's the way it was done.

When we saw the rushes of the scene, he was nice enough to say I was right, and after this I had his confidence as far as wardrobe was concerned. He gave me a great deal of liberty in what I would wear in the next two pictures for him, and when he brought in Edith Head to design the clothes, she and I worked together wonderfully well.

For the opening credit sequence, Hitchcock, trying to find something — anything — a little bit different to relieve the tedium of the production, wanted to fill the screen with a close-up of a hand dialing a telephone exchange that begins with M. But the stereoscopic color camera could not get clear focus for such a large image in close-up, and to satisfy Hitchcock's insistence on proper perspective, a giant telephone dial and an enormous wooden finger had to be built. He personally selected the set dressings, ordering two prints by Rosa Bonheur for the walls, and Wedgwood and Staffordshire figurines for the mantel.

The difficulties of shooting the murder scene caused Hitchcock considerable anxiety, and during the week of rehearsals and multiple takes for the attempted strangulation of the heroine and the stabbing with scissors of the hired killer, Hitchcock lost almost twenty pounds. "This is nicely done," he said after one take, "but there wasn't enough gleam to the scissors, and a murder without gleaming scissors is like asparagus without the hollandaise sauce — tasteless."

But hollandaise sauce was evidently one of the items excised from his meals, for by September 30 — partly because he was exhausted from the demands of the film and partly because he wanted to look better for the publicity photos with his lovely new star — his weight had dropped 40 pounds, to 219. The weekly Thursday dinner at Chasen's was temporarily given up, and Alma or the cook nightly prepared a small steak or some of his Dover sole. Evenings and weekends at Bellagio Road were exercises in asceticism for Hitchcock, and every Monday morning a physician monitored his vital signs on the movie set.

"All through the making of *Dial 'M' for Murder*," according to the leading lady,

the only reason he could remain calm was because he was already preparing his next picture, *Rear Window*.* He sat and talked to me about it all the time, even before we had discussed my being in it. He was very enthusiastic as he described all the details of a fabulous set while we were waiting for the camera to be pushed around. He talked to me about the people who would be seen in other apartments opposite the rear window, and their little stories, and how

---

*In the summer of 1953, Lew Wasserman arranged for Hitchcock to sign a multipicture deal with Paramount Pictures. The agreement called for Hitchcock to produce and direct and eventually own all rights to five films (they turned out to be *Rear Window, The Trouble with Harry, The Man Who Knew Too Much, Vertigo,* and *Psycho*) and for Paramount to produce and own four; but the studio got only one in the last category, *To Catch a Thief.*

they would emerge as characters and what would be revealed. I could see him thinking all the time, and when he had a moment alone he would go off and discuss the building of that fantastic set. That was really his delight.

But at the same time, Hitchcock was delighting in trying to shock his new actress. "One time he turned to me," she recalled, "when he had been telling Ray Milland some very raw kinds of things, and he said, 'Are you shocked, Miss Kelly?' I said, 'No, I went to a girl's convent school, Mr. Hitchcock, I heard all those things when I was thirteen.' And of course he loved that sort of answer."

And he was also, it seems, delighting in the strange details of the violent attack. "We took nearly a week to shoot that whole little sequence," she said years later. The finished scene, like other scenes of violence in Hitchcock's work, has clear references to sexual struggle; with its separate inserted shots of the actress's legs pushing against her oncoming attacker, and in the frenzied ambiguity of the strangling, it reveals a care delineated even more vividly in his later, longer murder scenes.

There had been no mention of Grace Kelly acting in the new Hitchcock picture, and she had not been offered a script to read. She was surprised, therefore, back in New York in October of 1953, when she received a call from her agent with the news that Hitchcock expected her for wardrobe fittings for *Rear Window*. At the same time, she was offered the role eventually played by Eva Marie Saint in Elia Kazan's *On the Waterfront*. That picture, which was to be made in New York, suited her plans better than the necessity of returning to Los Angeles; forced to make a swift decision within an afternoon, however, she decided to go back to Hitchcock after she read the new script. Based on a 1942 short story by William Irish (pseudonym of Cornell Woolrich), the screenplay Hitchcock had commissioned from writer John Michael Hayes made something quite different of "Rear Window."

"Hitchcock was searching about for a studio and a commercial property," Hayes remembered. "He had not done too well at Warner Brothers, and he was really having difficulty finding a studio to accept him. We had the same agents at MCA, and they thought that my radio background in comedy and suspense might make me acceptable to him. He already owned the Woolrich short story, and they suggested I work with him on it." After some preliminary meetings, at which Hayes impressed Hitchcock with his detailed knowledge of *Shadow of a Doubt,* the writer went off to draft the treatment for *Rear Window* — a task he accomplished so skillfully that James Stewart agreed to star (and to accept a percentage of the film's profit instead of a salary) on the basis of that alone. Then Hitchcock put Hayes to work on the screenplay.

We met infrequently while I was writing the script, but afterwards we sat down and broke it down shot for shot, and he showed me how to do some things much better. The stamp of Hitchcock's genius is on every frame of the finished film, but the impression that he did every bit of it alone is utter nonsense. I did what every other writer did for him — I wrote! But to read Hitchcock's interviews, it's possible to get the impression that *he* wrote the script, developed the characters, provided the motivation.

I knew that he liked the script when he told me that Alma liked it — that was the only way he could offer a compliment. He also said that since my salary was so low (I was paid only fifteen thousand dollars for writing the treatment and script and revisions of *Rear Window*), he thought I deserved a bonus. But then he said we ought to wait and see if it would look as good on film as it did on paper.

After it was edited we screened it and he said we would have to wait and see if the critics liked it. When the critics liked it he said we would have to wait and see if the public liked it. By that time I realized that he kept putting me off because he wanted me to do his next picture at the same salary.

Later, when we disagreed on some points in the next film, he said, "Don't get me angry or you won't get the bonus for *Rear Window*," and I just said, "Hitch, please don't ever mention that imaginary bonus again." He didn't, and I never got it.

Very quickly, by November, Hitchcock engaged the remaining actors for his film. James Stewart would serve as Hitchcock's chair-bound alter ego, a photographer whose mobility is limited by a hip-to-toe plaster cast. Stewart is clearly a Hitchcock surrogate in *Rear Window*. The character's wheelchair resembles a director's chair; with a long lens he spies on his neighbors (seen through the rectangular "screens" of their open windows); he gives them names and imagines little stories about their lives. Also like Hitchcock, he watches and admires as a woman models a dress and a nightgown for him. She is a creature who arouses delight, but with whom, as the script insists, intimacy is threatening; looking and admiring is enough. In this regard, Hitchcock instructed composer Franz Waxman to add the motif-song "To See You Is To Love You" to the score. That romantic involvement is perceived as intimidating is also indicated by the screenplay's association of Stewart with Raymond Burr (the wife-murderer): Stewart is a traveling photographer, Burr a traveling salesman, and each is pressured by emotional demands from an attractive blond.

In every aspect of the production, Hitchcock was assisted by Herbert Coleman, who was to become over the next several years one of his

most creative collaborators. Hitchcock had been introduced to him on
the set of *Dial "M" for Murder* by Ray Milland; by that time, Coleman
had been with Paramount for over thirty years, and had risen from script
clerk to become a gifted and trusted assistant director and creative consultant. At the time they met, Coleman had been honored recently by
the Directors Guild of America for his work as assistant to William
Wyler on *Roman Holiday,* and Hitchcock knew at once that he would
be a congenial addition to a kind of unofficial team he was engaging.
Editor George Tomasini and costume designer Edith Head at this point
also joined regular cinematographer Robert Burks, camera operator
Leonard South, and several technicians as members of the ongoing
Hitchcock crew who came to know exactly what the director wanted
and how to give it to him. And for four consecutive films, bonus or
not, John Michael Hayes was Hitchcock's scenarist.

The major concern before and during production was the enormous
and elaborate set, whose construction Hitchcock supervised. *"Rear
Window* is set in James Stewart's Greenwich Village apartment,"
Hitchcock told the press. "But in order for him to observe his neighbors
we had to build a set containing thirty-one other apartments he sees
from his window. An ostensibly one-room set turned out to be almost
the biggest one ever made at Paramount. . . . We had twelve of those
apartments completely furnished. We never could have gotten them
properly lit in a real location."

The film was engaging Hitchcock's enthusiasm in a far different way
from his previous productions: the technical challenges were, for a
change, hugely satisfying instead of intensely frustrating. Unlike the
convoluted mechanics he had devised for *Rope* and *Under Capricorn,*
and unlike the unwieldy 3-D process that was forced upon him, the
elaborate studio set for this picture impressed and delighted participants
and visitors; Hitchcock's mood lightened, his energy increased, and his
ideas became at once deeper and more clearly communicated than ever
before. "About this time I felt that my batteries were really fully
charged," he recalled proudly. "The whole production of *Rear Window*
went so very smoothly," according to James Stewart. "The set and
every part of the film were so well designed, and he felt so comfortable
with everyone associated with it, that we all felt confident about its
success." And no wonder: Hitchcock had a cooperative crew, a polished cast, full support — without interference — from Paramount's
front office. And most of all he had a charming leading lady whose
talent and career and public image he was going to mold, lovingly and
insistently, according to his own design.

With her cool, elegant beauty, her suggestion of inner passion, her

flashes of congenial wit — and her willing submission to his mentorship — Grace Kelly was the answer to his professional fancy and personal fantasy. He imagined for a time that there would never be a need
to have any other actress, and there was even talk of reviving his old
dream, a film of Barrie's delicate, mystical romance *Mary Rose*.

At once, Hitchcock took his careful construction of Grace Kelly's
image further than he had in *Dial "M" for Murder*. Edith Head recalled
that he was extremely clinical in his preparation of the clothes the actress would wear. "Every costume was indicated when he sent me the
finished script," she said. "There was a reason for every color, every
style, and he was absolutely certain about everything he settled on. For
one scene, he saw her in pale green, for another in white chiffon, for
another in gold. He was really putting a dream together in the studio."
One of the many elements linking Grace Kelly's character to the other
women in the film (who are seen in neighbors' windows) is the pale
green suit, which is carried forward in the brilliant green outfit worn by
"Miss Lonelyhearts" later. "This," Hitchcock agreed "added a great
deal."

And his attention to detail went as far as Grace Kelly's shoes. Herbert
Coleman recalled that on the first day of shooting *Rear Window* Hitchcock spent an entire half-hour directing a close-up insert shot of the
actress's shoes — a shot he never used in the finished film. When, at
lunch, Coleman asked the reason for this, Hitchcock replied blandly,
"Haven't you heard of the shoe fetish?" At the time, Coleman took the
answer for a perverse joke, but later he and Hitchcock's audiences would
see examples of the director's curious interest in, among other films,
*Vertigo* (when James Stewart insists on a specific pair of properly sexy
shoes for Kim Novak — shoes that are shown several times in close-
up) and *Marnie* (when Tippi Hedren's legs, with high riding boots, are
twisted against an open safe in a grotesque parody of sexual writhing);
and *Shadow of a Doubt* (in which the final struggle between Teresa
Wright and Joseph Cotten on the train is almost completely described
in terms of shoes and legs) had used a similar image earlier.

"At the rehearsal for the scene in *Rear Window* in which I wore a
sheer nightgown," Princess Grace remembered,

Hitchcock called for Edith Head. He came over to her and said, "Look, the
bosom is not right. We're going to have to put something in there." He was
very sweet about it; he didn't want to upset me, so he spoke quietly to Edith.
And then everything had to stop. The assistant director was going crazy trying
to keep everything under control.

We went into my dressing room and Edith said, ''Mr. Hitchcock is worried because there's a false pleat here. He wants me to put in falsies.''

''Well,'' I said, ''you can't put falsies in this, it's going to show — and I'm not going to wear them.'' And she said, ''What are we going to do?'' So we quickly took it up here, made some adjustments there, and I just did what I could and stood as straight as possible — without falsies.

When I walked out onto the set Hitchcock looked at me and at Edith and said, ''See what a difference they make?''

At the beginning of 1954, the executives at Paramount suggested to Hitchcock that he make a film of David Dodge's novel *To Catch a Thief,* the rights to which the studio had owned since the book's publication several years before. The story was set on the Riviera, and since Hitchcock relished the chance to travel, to combine pleasure with business, he turned the project over to John Michael Hayes. ''When he found I'd never been to the south of France,'' said Hayes, ''he arranged for me and my wife to go, at studio expense, so that I could research the locales. The trip was, of course, very welcome, and by the time I returned I had a good idea of what to do with the novel.''

The delay was appropriate in any case. Hitchcock wanted to cast, in her most alluring role in Technicolor, the glamorous Grace Kelly, with whom — as everyone understood — he was clearly enchanted. Opposite her would be the suave and ageless Cary Grant; at fifty, he was entirely acceptable as leading man for the actress, who was half his age. But she was committed to three other films first, and Hitchcock had to wait — but not for long, since in those economical and more efficient days the three films were completed between January and early May 1954.

Meantime, Hitchcock and Hayes worked on the script. ''On *To Catch a Thief* he got involved in the script work every day, which had not been true of *Rear Window,*'' the writer remembered. ''The work was a pleasure for most of the time. What made us a good team was that he had such brilliant technique and knowledge of the visual, and ego and conviction; and I think I was able to bring him a warmth of characterization.'' This is an entirely accurate assessment. In the quartet of films scripted by John Michael Hayes, there is a credibility and an emotional wholeness, a heart and a humor to the characters that other Hitchcock films — like *Strangers on a Train* and *I Confess* before, and others after — conspicuously lack.

By late April the script was finalized, and Hitchcock allowed that Hayes did a remarkably fine job. The cuts Hitchcock made minimized most of the secondary characters and emphasized the already daring dialogue. *To Catch a Thief* is noteworthy for its verbal and visual sexual puns and double entendres, and it was in fact one of the films of the fifties that pushed further the limits of adult humor. Grace Kelly's wordlessly bold kiss, square on the lips of the astonished Cary Grant (with whom she is not yet on a first-name basis) was of course inspired by Hitchcock's repeated anecdote about the cool blond who attacks a man in the back of a taxi, but the dialogue later goes even further.

GRANT: What do you expect to get out of being so nice to me?
KELLY: Probably a lot more than you're willing to offer.
GRANT: Jewelry — you never wear any.
KELLY: I don't like cold things touching my skin.
GRANT: Why don't you invent some *hot* diamonds?
KELLY: I'd rather spend my money on more tangible excitement.
GRANT: Tell me, what do you get a thrill out of most?
KELLY: I'm still looking for that one. . . .
GRANT: What you need is something I have neither the time nor the inclination to give you — two weeks with a good man at Niagara Falls.
KELLY [*later, at a picnic lunch*]: I've never caught a jewel thief before. It's so stimulating! [*Offering him the cold chicken*] Do you want a leg or a breast?
GRANT: You make the choice.
KELLY: Tell me, how long has it been?
GRANT: Since what?
KELLY: Since you were in America last.

In the next sequence, Kelly invites Grant to her hotel suite for an intimate dinner and a good view of the fireworks, seen in the background over the horizon throughout the following exchange.

KELLY: If you really want to see fireworks, it's better with the lights off. I have a feeling that tonight you're going to see one of the Riviera's most fascinating sights. [*In her strapless, low evening gown she moves closer to him.*] I'm talking about the fireworks, of course.
GRANT: May I have a brandy? May I fix you one?
KELLY: Some nights a person doesn't need to drink. . . .
GRANT: . . . I have about the same interest in jewelry that I have in politics, horse racing, modern poetry and women who need weird excitement. None.
KELLY [*as she sits seductively on the divan, her diamond-and-platinum necklace glittering above the bodice of her white strapless gown*]: Give up — admit who you are. Even in this light I can tell where your eyes are looking. [*Closeup on her chest and necklace and generous décolletage.*] Look — hold them — diamonds! The only thing in the world you can't resist. Then tell me you don't know what I'm talking about. [*The fireworks shoot intensely, seen in clear focus between them in the background. She kisses his fingers one by one, then places his hand underneath the necklace. Cut to close-up of raging fireworks.*] Ever had a better offer in your whole life? One with everything!

GRANT: I've never had a crazier one. [*Cut to vast fireworks.*]

KELLY: Just as long as you're satisfied! [*Fireworks again.*]

GRANT: You know just as well as I do this necklace is imitation.

KELLY: Well *I'm* not! [*They kiss; cut to fireworks, then back to the passion-ate, long kiss, then back to the final frenzy of fireworks to the end of the scene.*]

That there was no public or industry outcry about these details in 1955, when the film was released, remains something of a mystery it-self, for films with less obvious innuendo ran into considerable difficulty with Hollywood bluenoses and religious censors.

To expedite the location shooting of the film in the south of France, Hitchcock in May dispatched a crew headed by Herbert Coleman to photograph the auto chases and several important background scenes that could be filmed without the stars. Meanwhile, the director went to London to publicize *Dial "M" for Murder*. The press, however, was more interested in his weight loss, which by now was over one hundred pounds. "It's been murder getting down to this weight," he com-plained, "sheer masochism. For months it's been one meal a day — a lamb chop and a few beans. And not a drop to drink." But the energy that resulted from this regimen was prodigious indeed, and after several days he was off to the Riviera. The leading quartet — Kelly and Grant, joined by Jessie Royce Landis and the dependable John Williams — arrived in late May, and everyone stayed happily at the Carlton Hotel in Cannes.

The month of June was a memorably happy one for everyone in-volved in the location shooting on and near the Riviera. The French critic André Bazin, one of the most influential theorists of postwar Eu-rope and co-founder of the famous periodical *Cahiers du Cinéma*, vis-ited Hitchcock during the shooting of the flower-mart sequence in Nice. The meeting was cordial, if more guarded than most of Hitchcock's encounters with critics — not because they had an interpreter, but be-cause Bazin was intimidated neither by Hitchcock's fame nor by his calculated direction of the interview.

In print, Bazin had made quite plain his belief that within certain limitations Hitchcock was a technician and story teller of considerable distinction, but he could not go so far as others in bestowing the mantle of genius on him. Their encounter, documented in a famous essay that appeared several months later in *Cahiers du Cinéma*, began the critical debate over Hitchcock as serious artist that has prevailed internationally. One of the proximate results was that the French directors Eric Rohmer and Claude Chabrol joined forces and started writing the first extended critical appreciation of his films (a 1957 work more important for its provocative and seminal suggestions than for any sustained depth or factual accuracy).

With Bazin, Rohmer, and Chabrol, there was sounded in the community of critics and filmmakers the call to take sides about the value of Alfred Hitchcock's work. By the time of Bazin's death, in 1958, the critical bibliography had begun in earnest. Hitchcock always displayed a cool disinterest in serious critical commentary on his work, and for the most part this was sincere. But toward the end of his career, when he was much less active, praise from critics and academics provided a degree of consolation against the general indifference Hollywood always offered.

Hitchcock discussed his appreciation of Gallic art and gastronomy with the French crew of *To Catch a Thief,* but he was somewhat less enthusiastic about what he considered an excess of manners among the French, and this provided him with numerous opportunities to continue his tradition of puncturing pretense. René Blancard, the noted French actor who appeared in the film, presented himself on the set with what his director thought was a certain unnecessary hauteur.

"Good morning, Monsieur Blancard," Hitchcock said. "Did you sleep well?"

"Yes, thank you," replied the actor in heavily accented English.

"And with whom, Monsieur?" The French crew was even more amused than their American colleagues, and the filming proceeded with no outsize vanity.

The company returned to Hollywood in early July for the studio shooting, and Hitchcock, not entirely satisfied with what remained a rambling, rather formless comic thriller, tried to tighten up the final scenes.* But as Edith Head remembered, he had his heart set on an elaborately vulgar costume-ball sequence for the finale, the sole purpose of which was to show off his leading lady in a shimmering gold gown. The sequence, which Hitchcock tried to present as a satiric exercise, occupied the cast and crew for over a week in August, and they were still doing retakes on his birthday — Friday the thirteenth — when everyone on the set interrupted work to honor the director with champagne and an enormous birthday cake. He was delighted and touched, and said he was surprised — and for a moment there were more eyes winking on the set than arc lights flickering overhead, for whenever he

---

*John Michael Hayes recalled that, during the filming of the final rooftop sequence, Hitchcock summoned him up to the high scaffolding. "Look at them all down there," the director said to his writer. "They think we're discussing something important or profound. But I only wanted to find out whether you're as frightened of heights as I am."

was shooting a film on August 13, it was tacitly understood that the day would be appropriately marked; the wound would have been deep and irreparable if the occasion had been ignored.

Soon after, the film was concluded and Grace Kelly rushed to her next assignment. Neither she nor Hitchcock was sure whether they would work together again; after two more films directed by others, in fact, she relocated permanently to the Riviera in 1956, as Princess of Monaco. In later years she and Hitchcock visited occasionally, and she retained vivid and warm memories of their collaboration. "I learned a tremendous amount about motion-picture-making," she said later. "He gave me a great deal of confidence in myself."

The release of *Rear Window* in August 1954 helped to maintain Hitchcock's own self-confidence. The world premiere engagement at New York's Rivoli Theater was a benefit for the American-Korean Foundation, which was formed to provide emotional and material relief after the conflict in Asia. The opening night (August 4) saw a mob scene that rivaled the old days of Hollywood, before the movie industry had been threatened by the popularity of television. With his customary good grace, David Selznick sent Hitchcock a message of congratulations, calling the film "a brilliant display of motion picture craftsmanship"; and this time Hitchcock replied, writing that Selznick's was the note he would most treasure. The reply was signed "Love, Hitch."

There was no creative diminuendo for Hitchcock, no holiday after completing *To Catch a Thief,* and no doubt about his next project. He had read J. Trevor Story's short comic-grotesque novel *The Trouble with Harry* in 1950, when it was first published in England and America, and even before he arrived in France to shoot *To Catch a Thief,* he had given it to John Michael Hayes to adapt. By the time of the birthday party, the script was very near completion, and there was only the matter of putting the horse back in front of the cart by buying the production rights. Hitchcock instructed Herman Citron, one of his agents at MCA, to negotiate a purchase — and to do so, as usual, without using the Hitchcock name.

Story and his publisher were somewhat disenchanted to learn the identity of the buyer after they had agreed to a price of $11,000. They went through with the deal, however, since they had long before given up any thought of Hollywood interest. An evaluator at Paramount had reported four years earlier that the novel was "an engagingly uninhibited little story written in a highly amusing style," but that the humor was "too fragile and whimsical and the story too fanciful for transposition to the screen. Although the characters are presented as real people they belong to a slightly fey world and the plot itself is much too tenuous for a screen comedy. Not recommended.''

With the instant success of *Rear Window* and the anticipated success of the colorful *To Catch a Thief* (which was later judged so gorgeous that it won an Academy Award for Robert Burks's cinematography), Paramount was willing to let Hitchcock have his way.* The studio approved his $1-million budget, and at the end of August Hitchcock sent Herbert Coleman to New York to find an actress among the theater's new faces.

The story by Story piqued Hitchcock's humor. In *Rear Window* the director had dealt (at some distance) with the problem of a corpse's disposal, and he had decided on a solution far more gruesome than the one in Cornell Woolrich's tale: Hitchcock's murderer dismembers his wife's body and parcels out the limbs to various sections of the city. (As Hitchcock acknowledged, this recalled the infamous Mahon case in England.) In *The Trouble with Harry,* Hitchcock relished dealing with a similar problem, but now in a sly comic tone — although in the finished film the comedy is securely linked to a sense of the grotesque anchored by the typically Hitchcockian association between death and sex.

Quickly, casting proceeded. Herbert Coleman and his wife Mary Belle arrived in New York, and their daughter Judy convinced them to take her to see the new musical *The Pajama Game.* Coleman was so impressed by the leading lady that he went backstage, introduced himself as a representative of Alfred Hitchcock and Paramount Pictures, and asked to meet her. Only then did he realize that the woman in question was not Carol Haney, who was billed in the program, but an understudy who in movie-script fashion had risen to sudden fame by replacing the ailing star. The lucky and talented actress, then just twenty and with a pixieish vigor, was Shirley MacLaine. The next day Coleman was in Paramount's New York office, arranging a test for Hitchcock's and the studio's approval. Everyone was more than pleased.

By mid-September Hitchcock had swept through New York, complementing his cast with the noted actress Mildred Dunnock, John Forsythe, Mildred Natwick, and, in his fourth role for Hitchcock since 1931, the amiable, seventy-nine-year-old Edmund Gwenn. The company proceeded quickly to Vermont, since, as Mildred Dunnock remembered,

---

* According to John Michael Hayes, ''Bob Burks gave Hitch marvelous ideas and he also had a very tense time with Hitch. He worked long hours and by the end of every picture was emotionally worn out. He was a painstaking craftsman and contributed greatly to every picture during those years.''

Hitchcock was anxious to photograph the autumn landscape colors in full glory; the fall foliage was, he told her, the real reason for insisting on the actual locations for a film that could otherwise have easily been shot in the Paramount studios.

But there were such heavy rainstorms in October that much of the carefully planned exterior photography in East Craftsbury was canceled and the director and his cast had to use the "cover set" — an interior set, ready in case of inclement weather, that had been built in a school gymnasium in Morrisville. Even this was difficult, however, for the gym had a tin roof, and the continued heavy rainfall prevented recording synchronous sound (the dialogue had to be rerecorded in Hollywood later). At the same time, the all-important leaves were falling in the storms. Hitchcock, dining with his cast at the Lodge at Smugglers Notch, above Stowe, took a stoic attitude and once again said that after all, it was only a movie, adding that the countryside would outlast them all, and the motion picture, too.

The remark was almost a tragic prophecy, for the next day an 850-pound color camera, mounted on a crane, crashed to the floor of the gymnasium, grazing Hitchcock's shoulder as he leaned forward to call directions to his players. A few bright hours intervened, and some background shots were photographed; these were later artificially added to scenes shot in Hollywood (the actors were filmed before a screen in the studio on which the outdoor shots were projected from the rear). By the time the skies finally cleared, the company, already behind schedule, had to depart for California. A few crew members remained behind, gathering fallen leaves that were eventually attached, one by one, to plaster trees inside the Paramount studio.

The return to Hollywood in November was marked by one important and happy turn of events amid a flurry of scheduling problems and some abrasion between Hitchcock and Shirley MacLaine. After trying in vain to secure Bernard Herrmann for earlier films, Hitchcock was at last able to sign him to compose what turned out to be a jauntily quirky score for *The Trouble with Harry* — and for the next nine years there flourished a brilliant collaboration. That it should have been so successful is perhaps surprising, for each of these men was stubborn, often intractable, not given to the patient endurance of complaints from temperamental associates or subordinates or studio bosses. But beyond their proud and gifted personalities lay common bonds: Hitchcock and Herrmann shared a dark, tragic sense of life, a brooding view of human relationships, and a compulsion to explore aesthetically the private world of the romantic fantasy. Herrmann's first musical score for Hitchcock helped to lighten the tone of a basically static, stage-bound film — and the director was delighted that the music never intruded upon the sound of the body being dragged over dry ground, the "little noiseless noise among the leaves" that recalled Keats and, now, Hitchcock.

With four films completed in seventeen months — an extraordinary accomplishment under any circumstances, even for a much younger director — Hitchcock took Alma to Saint Moritz for their anniversary and for Christmas. In January they went to Paris for the dubbing of the French actors' voices in *To Catch a Thief*, and at the Joinville studios Hitchcock met a twenty-three-year-old film reporter who came for an interview. But the nervous young man was soaked to the skin after a fall into an icy pond nearby, and the appointment had to be rescheduled. The name of the disheveled admirer was François Truffaut.

# Twelve

1955–1959

E VEN before the Hitchcocks arrived home, John Michael Hayes had started work on his next assignment. Hitchcock's agents had purchased from David O. Selznick the rights to *The Man Who Knew Too Much*, a film the director had for a long time wanted to refine and remake. During the Selznick period, Hitchcock and John Houseman had considered reworking the story to give it an American setting, but they could not endow the characters with much life; the political angle in the story, as Hitchcock remembered, kept cluttering the narrative.* But now, with the gifted and prolific Hayes as his collaborator, and after fifteen years of familiarity with American life and manners, Hitchcock felt ready to transform his melodrama into a story of a family nearly destroyed by international terrorism, kidnapping, an assassination plot — and by its own nonchalant temperament. Politically prophetic, psychologically mature, and emotionally whole, the story that Hitchcock envisioned had to be written, he insisted, with first-rate dialogue.

In mid-January, after the return to Bel-Air, Hitchcock and Hayes worked out a seventy-page treatment for the picture — setting the story in Marrakesh and London — gave it a structure, and planned the arrangement of scenes. Hayes then began to write the screenplay, with astonishing speed and skill. At the same time, Hitchcock and Alma prolonged their winter holiday, spent more time with their two young

---

*In a memorandum dated December 30, 1941, John Houseman reported to Selznick on a projected remake. The new version was to begin in Sun Valley, Idaho (instead of the original setting in Switzerland), move to a South American setting and a carnival background, then return to New York. The center of the plot was a scheme to kill the president of Brazil in order to jeopardize American relations. A gala at the Metropolitan Opera was to replace the climax at the Albert Hall and the hideout of the spies would be in a Victorian mansion in Fort Lee, just across the Hudson River in New Jersey.

granddaughters, and retreated to Santa Cruz. Alma now felt easier about giving presents to her grandchildren. Earlier, when the Hitchcocks were in Vermont for *The Trouble with Harry,* she and Mary Belle Coleman had visited a country store, where Alma had wanted to buy two rocking chairs for Pat's daughters; she hesitated and finally did not make the purchase, however, for Hitchcock had warned her about giving the grandchildren too much attention. They would be spoiled soon enough, he warned — although he did not specify what would be the cause of the spoiling. But now, at least for a time, Hitchcock seemed more at ease with gift-giving — in fact, he seemed more at ease with all of life, with his family, and with his work.

Also at this time, Hitchcock signed a lucrative contract with Richard E. Decker, a Florida businessman who decided to try his hand at publishing an Alfred Hitchcock mystery magazine. "I simply sold him the right to use my name," Hitchcock said. "It was like the Fred Astaire dance studios — I had nothing to do with the operation of it at all" (except, of course, to endorse the checks that regularly arrived).* For a while, Pat Hitchcock O'Connell's name appeared on the masthead as "associate editor"; her father had arranged for a small income to be diverted to her.

But the tidy compensation for the use of his name and image on various publications would be far exceeded by the terms of an imminent deal that forever altered Hitchcock's fortune and further established his fame. During early 1955, Lew Wasserman and his colleagues at MCA met several times with Hitchcock, with television executives, and potential sponsors. If the Hitchcock name meant profits at theater box offices, why not try to reach the audience at home too? With this reasoning, negotiations took place for a series of television melodramas called *Alfred Hitchcock Presents.*

Meantime, Hitchcock played the host more often and more genially at Santa Cruz, and the interlude was one of the most content in his life. Although he did not win the Academy Award, Hitchcock was pleased when nominated as best director of the year, for *Rear Window.*

"The Mystery Writers of America gave me the Edgar Award for best mystery writing for that film," according to John Michael Hayes,

and I thought Hitch would be delighted. But he didn't come for the ceremony, and when I brought the little ceramic statuette into his office, he pushed it back

---

*Hitchcock also began receiving fees and a share of the royalties on anthologies of stories "edited by Alfred Hitchcock," but in the case of these too, he was paid simply for the use of his name; the introductions over his signatures were invariably ghostwritten by uncredited editors.

to me and said, "You know, they make toilet bowls from the same material."
I felt that he resented my receiving an award when he didn't.

A few weeks later, I wrote a piece for the *New York Times* on working with
Hitch. It was quite benevolent and praised his films — but he called me in and
said, as he tore up the article, "Young man, you are hired to write for me and
Paramount, not for the *New York Times*."

Confused and resentful of the condescending treatment, Hayes went
back to work on the script for *The Man Who Knew Too Much* while the
Paramount offices, throughout February and March, were busy with set
and costume design, casting decisions, scheduling studio and location
space, and the thousands of details necessary to produce an expensive
motion picture.

Hitchcock realized at once that he would have to have a top-notch art
director for the film, which would be photographed in North Africa and
London as well as in the Hollywood studio, and he asked Robert Burks
to recommend the best man at Paramount. Thus it was that Henry Bumstead, who was at the time working with Michael Curtiz on *The Vaga-
bond King*, was brought in — to Hitchcock's ultimate delight, for Bumstead's production designs for *The Man Who Knew Too Much*, *Vertigo*,
*Topaz*, and *Family Plot* are magnificent contributions to the visual artistry of Alfred Hitchcock's films.* At the same time, a young woman
named Suzanne Gauthier, who was doing clerical work in the art department at Paramount, was recommended to Hitchcock as a bright,
loyal, and discreet assistant, and she later became — and remained until
the end of his career — Hitchcock's private secretary.

Amid the press of activities, Hitchcock was able to secure James
Stewart for the leading role in the film. "I remember that he used to
resent having to have actors speak in films," Stewart said. "Whenever
he had a chance, he liked to cut down the dialogue. For him, the visual
was the major element in film."

Shortly after Stewart arrived at Hitchcock's office, in mid-April, it
was announced that Hitchcock was going to swear American citizenship. The decision had taken years, but now at last he was ready to
follow Alma, who had pledged allegiance to the United States a decade
earlier. Hitchcock surprised his associates by asking the authorities if it
would be possible for the judge to come to the studio to administer the
oath to him there, since he wanted to lose no work time; but Coleman
and Bumstead replied that this was not appropriate, and although Hitch-

---

*It was standard Hollywood procedure that the supervisor of the studio art department — in this
case, Hal Pereira — also be credited on major films. According to Bumstead, however, this credit
was indeed only nominal, and Hitchcock worked closely only with him and not with Pereira.

cock protested that he should not have to appear at the Los Angeles County Court with a crowd of common immigrants, he reluctantly interrupted his schedule.

Bumstead drove him to the ceremony, and on Wednesday, April 20, 1955, Alfred Joseph Hitchcock became a citizen of the United States of America. Back at the studio, champagne and cake were served, toasts were offered — and Hitchcock, with undiluted irony, announced that on Saturday he was leaving for his mother country to decide on the locations for *The Man Who Knew Too Much* and to engage the right foreign players for key supporting roles.

But apparently it was not only his sense of irony and timing that was undiluted: his puckish desire to shock was also manifest that same day. Henry Bumstead, as seriously professional a colleague as Hitchcock could have wanted on his staff, was summoned to the director's office and put in a situation that recalled the days of Dickie Beville. Hitchcock called in his secretary and asked, as if it were as natural as a request for coffee, "Dolores, how would you like to screw Henry Bumstead?" The poor woman was as astonished and embarrassed as the art director, but before either of them could recover or reply, Hitchcock simply continued the business of the day, as if he had said nothing at all.

The business of the day, as it turned out, concluded with his first meeting with an actress he had long wanted to direct. "In 1951, Hitchcock and I met accidentally at a party," Doris Day remembered. "Neither of us had a reputation for being partygoers, and I think we were both surprised to meet in that setting." She was even more surprised when he complimented her on her performance in a film called *Storm Warning,* and he said he hoped that sometime she would do a picture with him. In 1955 the time came, and although she had never before left America and still found the idea of air travel unnerving, she took her husband's advice and accepted the chance to work with Hitchcock and Stewart, who was now a sharer in the profits on the Hitchcock films as well as a dependable star.

"The first time I saw Hitchcock on *The Man Who Knew Too Much,*" Day said, "I was with Edith Head, talking about my costumes. Hitchcock came in, wanting to see the sketches and discuss them. On that day he threw some of them out and was very precise about exactly what he wanted for my wardrobe." But if the precise care for her screen appearance recalled his earlier approaches to Ingrid Bergman and Grace Kelly, nothing in his personal manner or attitude to Doris Day indicated anything other than cool cordiality. And this would eventually cause her considerable anguish — not because she expected a particularly profound friendship, but because he seemed remote and uncaring.

Soon the schedule called for Hitchcock to leave for London, although the script was far from complete. "Hitchcock was not with me during the writing of the screenplay for *The Man Who Knew Too Much,* as he had been on *To Catch a Thief,*" according to Hayes. "We had done the detailed treatment, but shooting time came very quickly and they all had to leave for London and Africa. So they all departed with only the first few scenes ready. I continued to write eight or ten pages a day from Hollywood, and they were flown over by courier to them. Then I went to London and wrote as pages were delivered to the set. It was really done on the rush."

But rush or no, the script as rendered by Hitchcock on film was turning out to be a masterpiece. Bernard Miles, founding director of the Mermaid Theatre and an actor Hitchcock admired, was cast in the original Peter Lorre role (now revised and even more complex), and Brenda de Banzie agreed to play the character's wife, one of the most emotionally fascinating personalities in any Hitchcock film.

"Hitchcock knew Cockney rhyming slang and backward slang and all the best risqué stories from the East End," Miles remembered.

We traded jokes and reminisced about film studios of earlier days, and I found him quiet, persuasive, and rather easygoing. At the same time he was an invincible Cockney who never wavered a millimeter toward an American accent, although he had been more than fifteen years in California. And he never dressed like an American moviemaker.

He cultivated a kind of old-style British ordinariness in his manner and speech and appearance. But this was something of a very clever mask on his part, because I think he knew he couldn't come on strong with people, or use an aggressive tone — it just wasn't his personality to be that way. He always seemed more concerned with technical matters than with the actors, and he gave us all the impression that this was a leisurely enterprise, and that he was just along for the ride.

I remember James Stewart telling me, "We're in the hands of an expert here. You can lean on him. Just do everything he tells you, and the whole thing will be okay." I took his advice, and it was a very genial experience — probably because Hitchcock and I shared a kind of secret knowledge about British humor and slang. But he certainly did not annoy his cast with excessive attention.

It was precisely that casual approach to his actors — an approach that came dangerously close to complete neglect of them — that led to the leading lady's unhappiness. "My husband and I and Jimmy and [his wife] Gloria Stewart arrived in Marrakesh several weeks after London," Doris Day remembered, and the poverty and malnutrition there upset me even more than being so far from home. I loved Mr. Hitchcock's humor, and of course he was polite in every way, although I don't think he could understand why I wasn't keen on the native food. He was very generous and lavish at the hotel dining room, ordering food from Paris and London, and insisting on the right wines for each course — but when we were shooting the exterior scenes in Africa I began to become very upset.

He never said anything to me, before or during or after a scene, and so I thought I was displeasing him, and I was crushed. We simply shot the scenes, and that was that. Everything was very civilized and polite and businesslike, but I was convinced that I must have been the worst actress he'd ever had — he just never said anything to me, and I had the impression that he felt saddled with an actress he didn't want.

I told my husband it was obvious I should try to get out of the picture before we did most of the interiors back in California, and finally I had to arrange a personal meeting with Mr. Hitchcock. I told him I knew I wasn't pleasing him, and that if he wanted to replace me with someone else, he could.

He was astonished! He said it was quite the reverse, that he thought I was just doing everything right — and that if I hadn't been doing everything right he would have told me.* Then he said he was more frightened — of life, of rejection, of relationships — than anyone. He told me he was afraid to walk across the Paramount lot to the commissary because he was so afraid of people. I remember feeling so sorry for him when he told me this, and from that point I felt more relaxed about working for him.

Doris Day's performance, in fact, is flawless — particularly in the scenes involving the kidnap of the son, which are certainly one of the clearest examples of controlled hysteria recorded on film. The scene in which James Stewart sedates Day before breaking the news of their son's kidnapping is a wonderfully etched portrait of a woman under emotional siege. She and Stewart rehearsed the scene alone, and when Hitchcock arrived she was able to give him a perfect performance in one take. The mother of a young son of her own at the time, she interiorized the woman's emotions so deeply that the result did not seem calculated or intellectualized. "What happened to me in that scene seemed very real," she said. "I actually experienced the feeling that I was losing my little son to a kidnapper. I was living that ordeal."

At the same time, Stewart, in his third role for Hitchcock, was surprised neither at Hitchcock's low-key approach to actors nor at Doris Day's first-rate performance. "In the beginning," he said, "it certainly threw Doris for a loop. Doris surprised a lot of people with her acting

---

*After filming *Rear Window*, actress Thelma Ritter remarked to a friend: "If Hitchcock liked what you did, he said nothing. If he didn't, he looked like he was going to throw up."

in *The Man Who Knew Too Much,* but she didn't surprise Hitch, who
knew what to expect from her. A singer's talent for phrasing, the ability
to put heart in a piece of music, is not too far removed from acting, in
which the aim is to give life and believability to what's on paper.''

And another important member of the cast, Reggie Nalder (who played
the assassin), recalled Hitchcock's calm and detached manner from start
to finish. A Viennese dancer and stage actor, Nalder was acting in his
first American film thanks to Hitchcock, who advised him during the
scene at the Albert Hall in which he gazes at the man he is to kill,
"Look lovingly at him, as if you're glancing at a beautiful woman."

In its final realization on screen, the climactic scene in the Albert
Hall — one of the great sequences in Hitchcock's work — is full of
tension and anxiety as the point of view shifts from that of Doris Day
to that of Nalder to that of the viewer to that of the cymbalist whose
crucial clash is meant to cover the sound of the fatal bullet. The moral
issue is finally as clear as the suspense: will Doris Day cry out, risking
her son's life to save a man she does not know? Or will she remain
silent, witnessing the man's death but perhaps saving her son? This is
where the suspense lies — not first in the external order, but in the
realm of mind and will and emotion, where the conflict always lay for
Hitchcock, as for his protagonists.

In the preface to the second edition of her novel *Wise Blood,* Flannery
O'Connor wrote of the dilemma of the internal order: "Free will does
not mean one will, but many wills conflicting in one man. Freedom
cannot be conceived simply. It is a mystery, and one which a novel,
even a comic novel, can only be asked to deepen." That is exactly the
scope of the moral tension in Hitchcock's seriocomic film *The Man Who
Knew Too Much*: many wills conflict in one person. And Doris Day's
scream, which interrupts the harmony and order of the concert, is the
inevitable result of the clash of external and internal forces.

One need not know much about the politics of the story — and Hitchcock tells nothing in this regard — because the real concern is the feelings of the characters, whose complexity was so well articulated in John
Michael Hayes's script.* The motif of singing finds its meaning in the

---

*The characters of this second version are in every way superior to those of the first, in which
Lorre's strange companion (Cicely Oates) is simply present and never becomes a character in her
own right. Neither she nor Lorre have any of the wholeness of Bernard Miles or Brenda de Banzie.
Likewise, the child in the first version (Nova Pilbeam) is simply an excuse for a kidnapping; in
the second, the child (Christopher Olsen) is from beginning to end a link between the parents, the
sign alternately of their distance from and their drawing toward one another. Where the dialogue
insists that his father "knows too much," the child always answers questions by saying, "I guess
so." For a fuller examination of the structure of this extraordinary film, see Donald Spoto, *The
Art of Alfred Hitchcock,* pp. 267–281.

scream at the concert and is perfectly balanced by Brenda de Banzie's scream at the embassy moments later as Doris Day gives an impromptu recital. Now the mother (Day) is the musician, singing and forcing the clash of wills in the *surrogate* mother (de Banzie), who acts compassionately by screaming and releasing the child. Doris Day is the woman forced to give up her career as singer because of her husband's career as physician; thus her scream at the Albert Hall becomes a song — the cry of anguish, the cry to be saved, to be reborn. A concert becomes literally an act of *concertantes,* "those struggling" to decide in favor of life.

But if the finished film was a great achievement by all concerned, the relationships between the collaborators were quickly turning sour. "After four films with Hitchcock," John Michael Hayes said,

I felt I deserved a salary increase. I felt I had given him good scripts and done more than competent work — and the critics and audiences thought so too. But Hitchcock was very lean when it came to money, and he always put off the subject of a raise. After four films I had been paid only a total of $75,000 — before taxes — which was not very much compensation even in those days. I had a family, and frankly that salary spread over more than three years was barely enough to support us.

But it wasn't only — or even primarily — the issue of money. Hitchcock had brought in his old friend Angus MacPhail as a technical adviser on *The Man Who Knew Too Much* while we were shooting in London. MacPhail had been with British intelligence, and Hitchcock thought he could contribute something to the business about the Arab and French spies. But poor Angus MacPhail was a dying alcoholic, and all he could do was sit there, shaking with his disease.*

I think that Hitchcock might have been trying to do MacPhail a favor by giving him work, since they had known each other years earlier. But the man really did no work on the script, so that when I got back to Hollywood and Paramount gave me the news that Hitchcock was insisting on having MacPhail's name appear on the screenplay credit with mine, I was shocked.

Hitchcock told me that MacPhail's name would stay on it, and I said I would submit the matter to arbitration with the Writers Guild. He told me that if I did that he would never speak to me again, and that I would never work with him again. But to me this was a matter of principle, and even of my career, which Hitchcock was not at all anxious about. The Guild did settle the matter: they read the drafts of the screenplay and considered all the notes and memoranda, and they decided that it was indeed entirely all my work — and MacPhail's

---

*"It was very sad," Herbert Coleman agreed. "Often we just had to cart him off from his apartment to a hospital. He wasn't capable of much."

name came off. And then I knew my days with Alfred Hitchcock were numbered.

Finally, as if he knew it would be impossible for the screenwriter, Hitchcock clinched the severance of their collaboration by asking Hayes to go to Warner Brothers with him to do a film without taking a salary.

Hitchcock had agreed to do a film for them for only a percentage of the profit, with no salary, and he felt I should do the same. He said I owed it to him, because he had made me famous, taken me out of obscurity and made me a film writer. But I couldn't afford to work without pay — and on a project I tried to discourage him from undertaking.

Well, he didn't take my advice too kindly. It was really very sad. I had worked hard for low wages. We were forming ideas for other pictures. Then he wanted me to work without pay, and to stay on as his faithful and subordinate "young man." But I couldn't make a decent living working with him. I couldn't work as a subordinate any longer. He kept saying, "You will do exactly as I say," and I felt that was unreasonable.

For years I puzzled over the end of our relationship. I learned so much from working with Hitch, so much about every aspect of film construction, about cinematography and story planning. In spite of his idiosyncrasies, I enjoyed the experience, and I felt it was very sad when it ended so bitterly and so unhappily. I felt it could have gone on, that we could have done six or ten or a dozen more films together. I thought we were an effective team, but then he was telling other people that he had got out of me all he could, and that I wasn't following orders — which was certainly true in a way, since I had my family and my career to think about. For a long, long time I felt sad that he wanted to end the collaboration.

By the end of July 1955 the filming of *The Man Who Knew Too Much* was complete, and on August 4 *To Catch a Thief* opened nationally. Moviegoers lined up to gaze at the glamorous pictures of Grace Kelly and Cary Grant, even if the critics were divided. "Quite often," wrote one typical negative reviewer, "you can look beyond the actors and enjoy the view without missing anything important." At the same time, the *Hollywood Reporter* felt that Hitchcock had made more mistakes in the first five minutes of *To Catch a Thief* than in all his pictures before. This comment, according to John Michael Hayes, sent Hitchcock to bed for three days, prostrate with grief and anxiety.

He recovered as soon as he decided to take another long trip, however. The journeys to Africa and England for *The Man Who Knew Too Much* had been convenient excursions, opportunities to mix pleasure with business, and for his next project he hoped to continue his globe-trotting; the following year, in fact, he would scout locations in South Africa for an espionage thriller. But at the moment, in late August, he went ahead with his promise to Jack Warner, and he brought Angus MacPhail to California, and then to New York, to work with him on the new film.

As it happened, Warner Brothers owned the film rights to a treatment of a true story that coincided perfectly with Hitchcock's view of the world as a place where innocence and guilt are confused, and where the thin membrane of ordered civilization is stretched over a world of social chaos and metaphysical uncertainty. On January 14, 1953, a New York musician named Christopher Emmanuel Balestrero was arrested and charged with robbery. He was innocent, but before he was cleared (when the real thief struck again and confessed), he suffered through the double nightmare of imprisonment and his wife's mental collapse. Herbert Brean detailed this bizarre and sad story in "A Case of Identity," which appeared in *Life* magazine in June 1953, and at the same time he sold to Warners a screen treatment.*

What intrigued Hitchcock was not only the confusion of innocence and guilt and the opportunities to film at last the details of arrest, indictment, and imprisonment he had seen in New York years earlier: there was also, he told Maxwell Anderson (whom he asked Warner to hire to work with him and MacPhail), enormous emotional potential in the situation of the wife's breakdown — an element that had been added, late in the writing, to the script of *The Man Who Knew Too Much*. Hitchcock said he would stress an innocent man's terror and his wife's trauma, the loss of mental health and stability in a family not on vacation (as in the previous film) but in familiar neighborhood settings. In the new film he would again detail the threat to a household and to sanity, but not in an exotic foreign locale, amid international assassination plots and mysterious governments; instead, the disorder and the madness would enter the living room. From this film on, mental trauma over confused identities marks all the Hitchcock pictures.

It seems, then, that a sudden shift occurred in Hitchcock's emotional interest and aesthetic concern, from the fundamentally warm and comic tones provided by John Michael Hayes's scripts for *Rear Window, To Catch a Thief, The Trouble with Harry,* and *The Man Who Knew Too Much* to the obsessive fear of lost identity in the films now to come — *The Wrong Man, Vertigo, North by Northwest, Psycho, The Birds,* and *Marnie.* Yet in fact this was not a sudden shift, but a return to his

---

*The Identified Man,* a television version written by Adrian Spies, was seen on *Robert Montgomery Presents* in December 1953. The part of Balestrero was played by Robert Ellenstein, who later — as a quiet hit-man — kidnapped Cary Grant in *North by Northwest.*

profoundest concerns — not an aberration, but the resumption of his basic gravity.

Following the dark and haunted entrance into the world of the double in *Shadow of a Doubt* and *Strangers on a Train,* and after the exploration of personalized guilt in *I Confess,* there had been the arid period ending with *Dial "M" for Murder.* The Paramount contract and the collaboration with the brilliant and energetic Hayes gave Hitchcock the opportunity to escape, for a time — to make a simple effort at financial success and wide popular acceptance in a series of colorful films that dealt with the demonic only obliquely and at a great emotional distance. The quartet of Hitchcock-Hayes films, with their witty characters, offered a breathing space, a respite amid the typically brooding, insecure, and fearful romanticism and the intuition of a severe division in human nature that characterize all his other films from *Shadow of a Doubt* to the later masterworks. The departure of Hayes from Hitchcock's life, the temporary return to Warner Brothers, and a television program he saw all conjoined to put him in touch with the darker and deeper caverns of his own spirit.

The television program he happened to watch one early summer evening in 1955 was a dramatic episode on *Pepsi-Cola Playhouse,* but it was not the drama that intrigued him — it was the leading lady, a fine-featured blond named Vera Miles. Even in the grainy, unsubtly lit monochrome of early television, Hitchcock recognized a remarkable face and presence that could, with very little transformation, appear strikingly reminiscent of Ingrid Bergman or Grace Kelly. He had to see her again, and a major development in his career gave him the chance.

For some months, Lew Wasserman had repeatedly urged Hitchcock to agree to begin a television series. His feature films were drawing several millions; television could draw tens of millions. At that time, suspense melodramas appeared frequently on *Kraft Television Theatre, Philco TV Playhouse, Studio One, Ford Theatre, Armstrong Circle Theatre, The U.S. Steel Hour, Climax,* and other dramatic series, and a number of programs since 1949 had already been devoted exclusively to the suspense genre (*Lights Out, Suspense, The Web, Danger,* and *The Clock*). Hitchcock could, his advisers insisted, quickly establish himself as the master of the home screen. This would be, Wasserman stressed, the logical extension of his cameo appearances in his films. He need not interrupt his feature production plans, of course: executive producers could be hired to oversee the selection of scripts and directors for his approval, and Hitchcock could even direct a handful of the short teleplays annually, using his favorite stars.

Most persuasive of all, however, was the fact that they could arrange a most lucrative deal for him. They knew that television — with expanded networks, more channels, increased broadcast time, and ever-growing numbers of commercial sponsors eager to advertise their products — was waiting for new programs every season. In a matter of weeks, arrangements were finalized between the Columbia Broadcasting System and Bristol-Myers to offer a weekly half-hour series, *Alfred Hitchcock Presents*. For only peripheral involvement, Hitchcock would receive one of the best contracts in entertainment history: $129,000 per show, and all rights of sale and rebroadcast would revert to him after first airing. For his television company's name, Hitchcock chose Shamley Productions, in memory of his English country house.

To act as executive producer, Joan Harrison was brought back to the growing Hitchcock empire. She had produced a few reasonably successful pictures (among them a classic *film noir* by Robert Siodmak, *Phantom Lady*), and she knew the Hitchcock touch well enough to assure that the TV material would be rightly handled. "It was Hitchcock's way of paying her for her earlier loyalty," according to one writer, "but as time went on she became rather proprietary about Hitchcock — she wanted people to know she had a certain power and control over his affairs. And in this regard she rather resembled Alma."

Actor Norman Lloyd, who had moved from Orson Welles's Mercury Theatre to *Saboteur* and *Spellbound* and into television direction himself, was engaged as associate producer and occasional director. Lloyd and Harrison shared complete responsibility for the television programs. Hitchcock "contributes nothing except script supervision," Harrison said flatly during the series, adding that she did the hiring of writers and directors, "but his mind is like a threshing machine, chomping out ideas as we walk, and at meals, ideas every minute." Hitchcock confirmed his tangential involvement: "Miss Harrison does the casting, yes, and Norman Lloyd. I try to put out fatherly words of advice without trying to usurp their position."

According to Lloyd, Hitchcock demanded that "the work be done at the highest possible level of execution." Lloyd compared him to Churchill — "ruthless, but tender. . . . You feel it. And you can take it or leave it." He and Joan Harrison took it — and so did the American audience, who at once watched in such numbers that from 1955 to 1960 *Alfred Hitchcock Presents* was rated annually as one of the most popular programs ever broadcast.*

*The show, in the original half-hour format, moved to the NBC network from September 1960 to September 1962, at which time it was expanded to *The Alfred Hitchcock Hour* and returned to CBS until the fall of 1964. From 1963 to 1965, Norman Lloyd was executive producer, replacing Joan Harrison, who had by this time married novelist/screenwriter Eric Ambler. The final season, which concluded in the autumn of 1965, was presented by NBC.

There is no doubt that the polished scripts, direction, and casting contributed greatly to the program's popularity, but there is also no doubt that its success was sealed by Hitchcock's presence and by his regular appearance. To the syncopated measures of Gounod's "Funeral March of a Marionette," the camera photographed Hitchcock in silhouette as he stepped into the life-size outline of the caricature he had drawn of himself. (Hitchcock was inspired to use the theme music after hearing it in F. W. Murnau's *Sunrise* [1927]; Murnau had stipulated that it be the musical background for the sequence involving the young couple and a photographer.) He then framed the week's story with comic, acerbic comments that astounded and amused his listeners. James B. Allardice, a sometime playwright (*At War with the Army,* 1949), was hired to write the memorable prologues and epilogues delivered by Hitchcock.

"When I first started," Allardice said, "I was told that Mr. Hitchcock did not wear a wrist watch, did not wear rings and did not like eggs. This advice has never bothered me. Hitchcock is very objective toward death. Dead bodies are not necessarily sacred to him." As evidence of this, Hitchcock screened *The Trouble with Harry* for Allardice and told him this was the kind of offbeat humor he wanted to introduce to television. And he wanted to bring his audience in on a great private joke, the way he brought them in on private jokes and information withheld from the characters in his films. He wanted to risk something unheard of in those days: to mock the sponsors of the program.

"Remember the old saying, 'A knock is as good as a boost,' " Hitchcock said. "My guess is that the sponsor enjoys my lack of obsequiousness, but in the beginning they had difficulty in getting used to my approach and they took umbrage at my less worshipful remarks. However, the moment they became aware of the commercial effects of my belittling — they took a look at their sales charts — they stopped questioning the propriety of my cracks. But there's no getting around it, I did take getting used to. The tradition is that the sponsor must be coddled. In such an atmosphere I was a novelty."

The humor at once drew the audience into a friendly conspiracy against the commercial interruptions. "I hope to offset any tendency toward the macabre with humor," Hitchcock explained, "a typically English form of humor. It's of a piece with such jokes as the one about the man who was being led to the gallows to be hanged. He looked at the trapdoor, which was flimsily constructed, and he asked in some alarm, 'I say, is that thing safe?' "

And so, one or two days a week, Hitchcock was driven to the Revue Television Studios, on the Universal Pictures lot, where he filmed the prologues and epilogues for ten or a dozen upcoming programs. His plain, deadpan delivery and detached attitude was a brilliantly constructed counterpoise to what the audience heard him say and sometimes — surprisingly, given the unphysical Hitchcock — saw.

· HITCHCOCK [*sitting and reading a paperback book*]: Oh, good evening. I'm reading a mystery story. I find it helps me take my mind off my work. This one is very interesting, but of course it will never replace a hardcover book — it makes a very poor doorstop. . . . In each of our stories we try to teach a little lesson or point a little moral — things like Mother taught: Walk softly and carry a big stick. . . . Strike first, ask questions after — that sort of thing. Tonight's story begins in just a moment, after the sponsor's message, which, like ours, also tries to teach a lesson or point a little moral.

· HITCHCOCK [*standing near a torture rack*]: Good evening. This is called a rack. It is a type of medieval chaise longue. The victim lies down and his limbs are fastened to these rollers at each end. The body is then stretched to and past the breaking point. They were quite droll in those days.

· HITCHCOCK [*alone, facing the camera*]: Good evening. When I was a young man, I had an uncle who frequently took me out to dinner. He always accompanied these dinners with minutely detailed stories about himself. But I listened — because he was paying for the dinner. I don't know why I am reminded of this, but we are about to have one of our commercials.

· HITCHCOCK [*at the end of a program*]: You needn'g sit there staring. We're not going to show you any more. In fact, I'm not even going to tell you what happened. Television audiences are becoming entirely too dependent.

· HITCHCOCK [*shown tied to railroad tracks*]: Good evening, fellow tourists. I think this proves that in some ways the airplane can never replace the train.

· HITCHCOCK [*at Christmastime, bricking up Santa Claus in a fireplace*]: Good evening. . . . He's not a bad chap, but his taste in ties is terrible.

Herbert Coleman put the matter succinctly: "Hitch's delivery was priceless, but he couldn't have succeeded as a popular presence or delivered those comments without the talent of Jim Allardice, one of the best writers he ever had."

Though his television appearances were accompanied by amusing monologues, Hitchcock privately had no illusion about the artistic limitations of the medium. "In three days' shooting," he said, "there can be no question of comparable quality. Television just can't match the scope of pictures." Years afterward he reflected: "You can't be fancy on television. You have limited money and a few minutes and you cannot go one half-minute over."

It was for his television series that Hitchcock first selected Vera Miles, intending her to be the star of the premiere of *Alfred Hitchcock Presents* on October 2. Within days of her appearance on *Pepsi-Cola Playhouse* she was contracted to a five-year, three-picture arrangement beginning

January 2, 1956. At the age of twenty-six, the former beauty queen was now in line to be what everyone was led to expect — Hitchcock's new Grace Kelly. To guarantee that her image would not be modified by any but his own careful plans, her contract required that her services be exclusively for Hitchcock and specified that she was never to appear in advertisements for swimsuits or lingerie nor in any "unladylike or unseemly" commercial. At the same time, the director informed Miles that her first film appearance for him would be in the role of the hapless Rose Balestrero, the wife who suffers a breadown in *The Wrong Man*. She would play opposite Henry Fonda, whom he knew from the start was the one to convey the sense of moral outrage felt but unarticulated by Christopher Balestrero.

"The first thing I did when I put Vera Miles under contract," Hitchcock recalled, "was to have Edith Head design a complete wardrobe, not just for the picture but for general wear so she wouldn't go around in slacks looking like a Van Nuys housewife." The personal wardrobe, carefully supervised, was perhaps the single most important element in refashioning the actress's image.

"When he signed Vera Miles," according to Edith Head, "he asked me to study her. 'She's an extraordinarily good actress, but she doesn't dress in a way that gives her the distinction her acting warrants,' he said. 'She's not outstanding because she uses too much color. She's swamped by color. I think the reason I was so impressed with her to begin with was that I saw her in black and white on television.' So we reduced Vera to black and white photography."

For his first directed teleplay (the program with Vera Miles was made second but broadcast first), Hitchcock chose to film a radio drama. He had heard Joseph Cotten narrate the disturbing tale of an emotionally paralyzed businessman, contemptuous of any display of feeling, who, in a Dantean twist of retributive fate, is physically paralyzed in an auto accident and thought dead. He is brought to the morgue in a state of coma vigil — eyes open and unblinking, hearing and comprehension intact, body immobile except for an unobserved fingertip — and he is given up for dead. A single teardrop, however, signals the coroner that he is alive.

In the tradition of "The Premature Burial" by Edgar Allan Poe and the classic stories of retribution, *Breakdown* was a significant first choice, for it summarized the motifs of sudden punishment and the terror of enclosure, immobility, and madness that would characterize Hitchcock's imminent features *The Wrong Man, Vertigo,* and *Psycho.* The final shot — of Cotten's blank stare, a premature death-mask staring out at the viewer — is from this time forward Hitchcock's preferred image, and with it he seems to have given expression to the deepest terror in his soul, a terror that went as far back as the story of his own brief childhood enclosure in a prison cell (a boyhood story, as production designer Robert Boyle said, "that probably never actually happened. . . . Hitch told it so often, and it was convenient for the press, that he probably came to believe it himself").

The stare of madness, the gaze of one immobilized within the prison of his own flesh or sin or emotional constriction, concludes nine of the twenty dramas Hitchcock directed for television — *Breakdown, Revenge, The Case of Mr. Pelham, Wet Saturday, Four O'Clock, Lamb to the Slaughter, Dip in the Pool, Banquo's Chair,* and *The Crystal Trench* — as well as, of course, his feature *Psycho.* \* In *Breakdown,* tears for which Cotten had criticized an employee ("Can you imagine that? He was crying? A man should exert some control over his emotions!") become the only sign of the character's life and sole means of survival ("Look!" cries the doctor. "Those are tears! He's alive!") as he stares blankly.

Within a week of *Breakdown,* Hitchcock brought in Vera Miles and directed her in *Revenge,* in which she plays a role that is in fact a curtain raiser for her performance in *The Wrong Man* and that locates one of Hitchcock's favorite images of woman: the doll-like beauty, rendered powerless by delusion or romantic fixation or sexual trauma, who at once invites and then entraps and makes guilty a man who is drawn to her. Here, she is a woman recently released from an asylum, whose husband returns from work to be told that she has been attacked by a stranger. They later depart for a short vacation (no clues having been found), and from their car she sees a man and cries, "That's him! That's the one who did it!" The enraged husband follows the stranger and kills him. Resuming their journey later, she points to yet another man and cries, "There he is! That's the man!"

Paramount Pictures, meanwhile, had arranged for the world premiere of *The Trouble with Harry* to be held in Barre, Vermont, on Friday, September 30. The city was humming with activity when Hitchcock and Shirley MacLaine arrived for a lobster dinner at the civic auditorium,

---

\*Cf. the women of *The Wrong Man* (the mad stare of Vera Miles), *Vertigo* (the affectless gaze of Kim Novak as a woman obsessed with the past), and *Marnie* (the traumatized gaze of Tippi Hedren as she is stripped and then ravished by Sean Connery). Wide stares also characterize a dead woman in *Psycho* (Janet Leigh's wide eye, open and stilled after her fall to her death in the shower), a woman in severe shock in *The Birds* (after Tippi Hedren is attacked by a flock of birds), a woman shot to death by her lover in *Topaz* (Karin Dor's head snaps back and she gazes up at a high camera as she slips to the floor), and a woman strangled in *Frenzy* (the last shot of Barbara Leigh-Hunt, her eyes open in death, her tongue grotesquely thrust forward).

but Hitchcock sat in quiet splendor, refusing the shellfish since it was one of the foods unknown at home in Leytonstone. Governor Joseph Johnson, over Hitchcock's shoulder, extolled the Vermont apple cider, the Vermont-style lobster, the Vermont potato chips, Vermont harvest salad, Vermont rolls and Vermont butter, Vermont apple pie and Vermont cheddar cheese, and coffee with Vermont cream that the menu chauvinistically proclaimed.

As quickly as he could, Hitchcock returned to Los Angeles (just hours after the event, in fact). His television series had its debut two days later, Alma was planning for their trip to Europe later that month, and Maxwell Anderson had sent a first draft of *The Wrong Man* for Hitchcock's approval. But most of all, Hitchcock told his closest colleagues, Vera Miles was waiting for him. The truth is that she was cultivating the attention of the man she would soon marry, actor Gordon Scott — a relationship Hitchcock soon discovered and deeply resented.

Immediately after the broadcast of *Revenge,* Hitchcock brought in the mild, plain-faced Tom Ewell (fresh from the successful play and film *The Seven-Year Itch*), whom he directed in *The Case of Mr. Pelham,* which is perhaps the single most typically Hitchcockian television program. Ewell's character — like Poe's frightened but crafty William Wilson — believes that his rigorously ordered and carefully planned life is being disrupted by an exact double. In an attempt to upset the similarity, Ewell affects a style considerably different from what his friends expect, and at the conclusion the real Ewell is rejected (precisely on the basis of the different personality) and the double is accepted because of his likeness to what everyone expects. The episode ends with the real Ewell being taken away to an asylum in an image directly recalling the 1919 expressionist classic that had so impressed Hitchcock, Robert Wiene's *The Cabinet of Dr. Caligari.* Rarely seen anywhere after its premiere on December 4, 1955, *The Case of Mr. Pelham* fuses the established Hitchcock theme of the double with the terror of madness and enclosure as the inevitable result of the loss of security.

When Hitchcock finished this short teleplay, he was suddenly exhausted and unaccountably depressed. No one could quite understand the reasons for this sudden change in mood. The television series had become an instant success, he was at the top of his profession in income and popularity, and he had even found a leading lady he intended to mold into a new star. But it was perhaps the intense, if brief, experience of *The Case of Mr. Pelham,* following so soon after his reentrance into the dark world via *Breakdown* and *Revenge,* that took a toll on him. Unable to confide in his family, unwilling to talk intimately with acquaintances, and essentially friendless, he apparently never considered the possibility of counseling to help explore the array of fears and feelings that he kept hidden.

Instead, Hitchcock tried to escape the gloom by taking a trip. In mid-October, as *The Trouble with Harry* opened amid a flurry of confused reactions, he and Alma left for France, Germany, and Italy to supervise the foreign-language dubbing of that film. "We never know what happens to our pictures abroad," he told a reporter from *Variety,* "and now it's a question of finding out. I want to make sure that the man who does the dubbing knows English. . . . There's no point in changing dialogue and losing the joke."

But most of the necessary precautions had been taken by Paramount's foreign offices, and there was little technical work for him to do when he arrived in each city. The trip, once again, was a vacation — he simply could not admit that he wanted or needed a vacation; the pretext of business was the cover for escape and pleasure. "He consistently optioned books whose stories were set in places he wanted to visit," John Michael Hayes recalled. "The stories never got filmed, but the trips were comfortably extended. Everyone was very amused by the elaborate subterfuge."

To further prolong this particular trip — and so that Maxwell Anderson could incorporate the changes Hitchcock requested in *The Wrong Man* script — he and Alma embarked on a tour of Paramount's publicity offices in India, Japan, Thailand, and Hong Kong. For seven weeks, until December, they endured airplane delays, foul weather, uncongenial menus, and the demands for attention by hopeful Asian actors — circumstances that would have irritated any other traveler, but that actually served to distract Hitchcock from his psychological distress. By the time they reached New York, in January 1956, his spirits had lightened and he was ready to inspect the actual locations where the Balestrero story unfolded.

From his favorite fifth-floor suite at the Saint Regis Hotel, Hitchcock immediately called Maxwell Anderson at his Connecticut home and asked if they could meet at once about revisions. What Hitchcock read when Anderson arrived, however, was dialogue even more vague than before, and after a couple of hasty meetings Hitchcock realized that he did not have the best writer for a film that was supposed to adhere meticulously to the historical detail of event, place, and time. Anderson's diction was poetic, almost fanciful, while Hitchcock wanted a sense of earthy realism, urban abrasion, and a judicious avoidance of fantasy.

Hitchcock had originally asked the playwright to collaborate because of his verse play *Winterset,* which dealt with the moral implications of false indictment in the Sacco-Vanzetti case, and because of Anderson's keen sense of grotesque evil in his Broadway adaptation of William March's novel *The Bad Seed* a year earlier. Anderson's delicate play *High Tor*, which mingled ghosts past and present with real people, intrigued Hitchcock, and was the reason he asked him to do a first draft of his next film (*Vertigo*), but *The Wrong Man* was not shaping up as the literalized nightmare Hitchcock wanted. In desperation, he had Herbert Coleman contact Angus MacPhail, who he thought could be counted on if some control were exerted.

And so Hitchcock returned, with Anderson's curiously detached script, to Los Angeles. While a temporarily lucid MacPhail set himself to the task, Hitchcock spent time between January 13 and 16 directing one of his most O. Henry–like teleplays, *Back for Christmas*. John Williams (from *The Paradine Case, Dial "M" for Murder,* and *To Catch a Thief*) played a man who carefully carries out the murder of his wife (Isobel Elsom) and her subsequent interment in their basement. He then calmly leaves for the winter holiday they had planned, only to learn that his wife had arranged, in their absence, to have the basement excavated and a wine cellar installed — she literally comes "back for Christmas," when his capture is implied.

Hitchcock then held meetings with Henry Fonda and Vera Miles, and told them he wanted them to come with him to Florida, where the Balestrero family had relocated after Rose was discharged from the asylum. The meeting with the people for whom the wounds were still sensitive was understandably somewhat awkward, and Hitchcock took his small company for a few days rest in Saint Petersburg.

Angus MacPhail, meanwhile — with Herbert Coleman as guide and guard — flew to New York to visit all the locations of the story: the Stork Club, the Prudential insurance office in the Victor Moore Arcade, and the Balestrero home a block away, on Seventy-fourth Street, Queens. In early February Hitchcock and a few technicians proceeded to New York and the leading couple returned to California to await the call for the start of production.

Hitchcock arranged a meeting with William B. Groat, the judge who tried the Balestrero case, and Judge Groat confirmed the details of the mistrial: on April 21, 1953 (the third day of trial), a juror named Lloyd Espenschied rose from his place and irately asked, "Judge, do we have to listen to all this?" The question, as Herbert Brean wrote, "implied a presupposition of the defendant's guilt by a juror — a violation of his responsibility to refrain from any conclusion until all evidence is in. It gave the defense an opportunity to move for a mistrial." And during this interval, the real culprit was captured while attempting another robbery.

After meeting with Queens District Attorney Frank O'Connor, who as a trial lawyer had defended Balestrero, and with as many as they could find of the original participants in this unsettling human drama, Hitchcock set the start of production for mid-March. While waiting for Vera Miles to arrive, he gave a "Ghost-Haunted House Party," in a rented brownstone on East Eightieth Street, on March 7. Invitations were sent to executives from Warner Brothers' New York office and to the press, and the menu was printed on the reverse of a tombstone-shaped announcement.

"Carte de mort," he had written. "Morbid morgue mussels, suicide suzettes, consommé de cobra, vicious-soise, home-fried homicide, ragout of reptile, charcoal-broiled same-witch-legs, corpse croquettes, barbecued banshee, opium omelette, stuffed stiffs with hard sauce, gibbetted giblets, mobster thermidor, tormented torillas, ghoulish goulash, blind bats en casserole, python pudding, fresh-cut lady fingers, Bloody Marys, Dead Grand-dad, formaldehyde frappe." No one thought the weak puns terribly amusing: the odd association of nauseating items with cannibalism, death, and dismemberment seemed, on the contrary, surprising from a man who was apparently such a proper British gentleman, and who, from all accounts in the press and from television seemed a serious gourmet.

He had, in fact, returned to his old habit of indulging in great quantities of ice cream privately, and although he was abstemious at the table, a condition was beginning in his system that would cause a life-threatening crisis within a year.

On March 8 Hitchcock rushed to Newark airport to meet Vera Miles; Alma remained at the Saint Regis. The actress's makeup tests were held within the week in New York, and Hitchcock took her to Mrs. Balestrero's bargain-basement store to select from the rack clothes similar to those the real Rose had worn. On March 26 the production company moved north to the Edelweiss Farm in Cornwall, New York, to shoot the scenes at the Balestrero's summer resort, and the next day they proceeded to the Greenmont Sanatorium in Ossining and used the actual building in which the poor woman was confined for treatment during her breakdown. From there they returned to New York City, where they filmed in the felony court and in the cells Balestrero had occupied in Manhattan and Queens. By the beginning of April, *The Wrong Man* was just on schedule, and everyone appeared satisfied.

But it was only an appearance. Most of the actors — including Henry Fonda, whose thorough preparation elicited everyone's admiration — were required by Hitchcock for only two hours of work each day. Nei-

ther Fonda nor Anthony Quayle nor Esther Minciotti knew that behind
the scenes, during the other hours of each day of production, an unpleasant scenario was being rehearsed. Vera Miles was being detained
by Hitchcock for eight and nine hours daily, trained and put through the
poignant scenes of her breakdown over and over until she was nearly
sick with exhaustion. The situation began to resemble the control Carl
Dreyer had exerted over Renée (Maria) Falconetti in *The Passion of
Joan of Arc* three decades earlier, although in Hitchcock's case the control was never physically abusive, and in Vera Miles's case the breakdown never crossed from acting to reality, as in the case of the unfortunate Falconetti. Nevertheless, there was the atmosphere of Svengali
and Trilby.

Hitchcock had begun by sending two dozen American Beauty roses
to Miles's dressing room each day, with strangely ardent greetings, which
she destroyed at once. The daily call sheets on *The Wrong Man* in the
Warner Brothers archives indicate that by mid-April the director and his
leading lady were scheduled for long "story conferences" each day, at
Hitchcock's insistence, and that the rest of the cast was not required.
One can infer nothing from this notation except that he wanted privacy
with her — for what discussions shall perhaps never be known; but Vera
Miles was soon in a state of angry resentment.

On April 15 shooting was temporarily halted, and Miles married Gordon Scott, who was in the midst of starring in a quintet of Tarzan films.
From this date to the end of production in Los Angeles in early June,
the private conferences between Hitchcock and Miles were less frequent, and eventually their relationship seemed back on a coolly professional keel. She had found his attentions excessive and unwelcome, his
manner proprietary and suffocating. And all he would tell the press was
"Vera Miles is the girl who is going to replace Grace Kelly." Grace
Kelly had not been the object of such obsessive conduct, however. He
had maintained an altogether gentler and more casual attitude with her
(perhaps because she insisted on maintaining a busy social and professional life *apart* from a Hitchcock set), although it was clear to everyone that Hitchcock idolized her. But he also felt "abandoned" by her
when she left for Prince Rainier and Monaco — as he had felt "abandoned" by Ingrid Bergman. By the time the less established Vera Miles
came along, his manner and mood had toughened.

Meanwhile, Paramount was preparing a gala California premiere for
*The Man Who Knew Too Much* and had agreed to yield the proceeds
from the May 22 event to the University Religious Conferences, a group
that trained students for work in India "with a view to help combat
inroads of Communism in that area." This was a neat idea on the stu-

dio's part at this difficult time in Hollywood, when suspicions about political allegiances cast disturbing atmospheres. Hitchcock joined columnist Hedda Hopper, James Stewart, and Doris Day for an awkward picture-taking session in the theater lobby while the sound system temporarily collapsed. The event grossed $18,000, which seemed to Hitchcock a lot of money to give away.

He was consoled, however, by the box-office receipts for his film. Within a week, *The Man Who Knew Too Much* was already America's most financially successful film of the year, and his agents informed him that *Rear Window* had thus far grossed $10 million — almost five times its cost. For Hitchcock and Stewart, who shared large percentages of the profits, this was good news. It also helped in renegotiating the television contract with CBS and Bristol-Myers, and with the publishers of *Alfred Hitchcock's Mystery Magazine* and the anthologies of stories to which Hitchcock sold his name. At the end of the year, Hitchcock's income for 1956 was over $4 million — on which, thanks to the shelters in land, oil, and cattle arranged by his financial advisers, he paid not a cent of tax. Just a year after taking American citizenship, the apparently diffident Cockney was an evidently affluent Californian. The greater part of these monies was reinvested and some portion put into a remodeling of the kitchens in the two houses. There seems to have been no interest or impulse, then or at any time, to philanthropy or charitable causes.

With *The Wrong Man* completed, Hitchcock, Alma, Robert Burks, Herbert Coleman, and Angus MacPhail left for London. There, from June 19 to 24, Hitchcock met with the Colonial Office to discuss his next film, to be made in central Africa. "It is based on a story by Laurens van der Post called *Flamingo Feather,*" he told a reporter from the *Evening Standard,* "about political intrigues among the natives. First we are going on a tour of Swaziland, Nyasaland and Tanganyika to get some idea of how much the film will cost. We don't expect to visit regions that are too remote. I'd like to direct it from a tall chair at a reasonably comfortable distance."

The story, written in the tradition of the John Buchan espionage thriller, would give Hitchcock a chance to return to the exotic, color-drenched locales similar to those he had used so well in the *The Man Who Knew Too Much*. He also hoped, according to *Newsweek,* to cast Grace Kelly in the lead — an unlikely prospect, since her marriage to Prince Rainier had taken place on April 18 and her permanent retirement from the screen had been taken for granted. Hitchcock chose to treat that royal wedding rather casually, in fact, and he had declined what was perhaps the most desired invitation of the decade.

Instead, he prolonged his trip and added to the traveling company his sister Nellie Ingram — now twice widowed. He planned, as long as they were heading for South Africa, to visit relatives who had long ago settled there. And so they stopped in Swaziland, Kenya, Uganda, and neighboring regions, staying finally in Johannesburg, where Hitchcock and MacPhail met with diplomat-author van der Post. Almost at once they discovered that in addition to story difficulties there was a legal problem regarding the fifty thousand native extras Hitchcock said he needed. Within days the project was abandoned, and the journey became simply a holiday, which is very likely what Hitchcock had wanted all along. MacPhail, in any case, as Herbert Coleman remembered, did not seem capable of any serious work.

Alfred and Nellie Hitchcock called on their father's sister Mrs. Emma Mary Rhodes and her son, their cousin Cecil J. Rhodes, whom they had not seen in over twenty-five years. They spent two days in Durban, reminiscing about Leytonstone and Shamley Green, about England between the wars, and about the scattered remnants of the family; and Ellen Kathleen Hitchcock Lee Ingram, "a small, quiet, graceful little lady," according to Coleman, warmed to the occasion and became an outgoing family hostess.

But Hitchcock did not prolong the family reunion, and on July 24 the group resumed their journey by ship to their next stop: Italy's Lake Como. It was, he told his sister, one of the loveliest spots in the world, and he was anxious for her to enjoy its natural beauty and its luxury. His generosity at this time, it should be noted, was a happy and welcome exception to the customary indifference he showed his sister and, according to one associate, the plain refusal to help her in later financial straits. At this time, anyway, he was certainly more openhanded.

Everyone was relaxed and in good humor during the trip up to that time, and they all remained so until the morning of July 25, when they heard the news of the collision of the liner *Andrea Doria* with the freighter *Stockholm* off the eastern coast of America. There was some anxiety for a time aboard their own ship, and genial reassurance was offered by their captain. Throughout the day Hitchcock and his small band maintained a party atmosphere, the better to banish the irrational demons of anxiety that the disaster might be contagious.

By August 10 they had returned to America — and Nellie to England — and Alma arranged for a house party at Santa Cruz to celebrate their homecoming and their birthdays. Although the Hitchcocks rarely mixed houseguests, a large gathering was planned, with an elaborate weekend of luncheons and dinners featuring Alma's homemade pâté (which her husband consumed in great quantities) and crabmeat from New England (which of course he would not touch), pressed duck and exquisite roasts and fresh Dover sole.

The conversation centered on Hitchcock's favorite things: food, drink, Hollywood gossip, and film — in that order. From the talk, it was clear to everyone that Hitchcock's insistence to the press that the never saw films was patently untrue. He had seen everything — not at public theaters, but at private screening rooms at Paramount and Warner Brothers. The custom lasted through the 1970s, for a visit to Hitchcock's offices at Universal Studios usually involved a chat about a new film he had just ordered sent to his private screening room. His public statements that he did not see films should perhaps be taken to mean that he did not find much he thought memorable — "photographs of people talking are not film," as he liked to put it.

For several weekends that summer, Alma brought up to Santa Cruz their cook from Bellagio Road. The sight of the trio would have seemed slightly ludicrous to bystanders along the route who recognized the inhabitants of the car: the cook sitting in the rear, drawing up the menus and lists of groceries; Hitchcock in the front passenger seat, affecting imperturbability; and Alma, barely seen above the steering wheel she gripped along the inland route to the north.

Hitchcock's confidence in Alma did not, however, extend to what he knew was her estimation of his sporadic drinking. Before lunch at Santa Cruz, he liked to drink a tumblerful of Cointreau — and this, as one guest cannot forget, was consumed in one great swallow, after a furtive glance to see that Alma was out of sight. "He always said he hated the idea of swallowing food or drink, and in fact everything seemed to be taken in one huge gulp," Herbert Coleman recalled. Others witnessed the odd habits of a man who perhaps loved the idea of being sated more than the act of ingestion, which somehow seemed to him indelicate and reminded him of nausea and sexual activity — connections he frequently made to dining companions at inappropriate moments.

Back in Hollywood on August 22, Hitchcock quickly directed another teleplay — Wet Saturday, with another former colleague, Sir Cedric Hardwicke. The story concerned a madwoman (now apparently Hitchcock's stock character) who murders her beau and whose father tries to implicate a neighbor as the villain. That same week, David O. Selznick, trying to raise cash, was concluding a contract to rerelease the Hitchcock films he owned, and for advertising he asked Hitchcock's permission to use the famous sketch that was now known to millions via television. Through Herman Citron, one of his representatives at MCA, Hitchcock replied that the permission was denied. The following year, when Hitchcock wanted to use the Selznick-owned title *Spellbound* for his television series, he had to ask Selznick for permission — which was, as he might have expected, denied.

In October Hitchcock was ready to proceed with plans for his next feature film, to star James Stewart and Vera Miles, and which was then being adapted by Maxwell Anderson from a French novel called *D'Entre Les Morts* by Pierre Boileau and Thomas Narcejac, the authors of *Les Diaboliques*. Although Anderson's work on *The Wrong Man* was largely unsatisfactory, Hitchcock still hoped that the peculiarly poetic mixture of romance, fantasy, and hard realism that characterized his plays could be brought to the transformation of a novel of deception, exploitation, and emotional fixation. But Gloria Stewart requested a postponement of preproduction until after the Christmas holidays so that she and her husband might take a delayed vacation. This Hitchcock agreed to, and very soon it turned out to be a fortunate delay: Anderson submitted, a few days later, a script (rather awkwardly entitled *Darkling I Listen*) that was not only unshootable but also incomprehensible.

While a new writer was sought and the Stewarts took their holiday, Hitchcock began to sketch out hundreds of specifications for scenes of *From Amongst the Dead* (a temporary literal translation he knew Paramount would never approve). "The story called for a sophisticated metropolitan setting," he said, "and of all those in America, San Francisco fits that — especially in terms of the surrounding country and its architecture." The city itself, its landmarks and vertiginous streets and the areas around Santa Cruz, would provide appropriately lush and photogenic settings for a film he saw as wreathed in colorful silences and the mists of time and memory and longing.

The story was not at all clear to him, however. He knew he had to reject not only the novel's unappealing cardboard characters, but also the cheap mechanics of the central action; just how this was to be accomplished in a coherent narrative he did not see. What he did see was a series of *tableaux vivants* — scenes in an old cemetery, in a redwood forest, at a mission church, in an old stable, at a museum. While art director Henry Bumstead worked with a staff and tried to follow the somewhat vague suggestions, Hitchcock distracted himself by directing, between October 18 and 22, his least distinguished teleplay, a pallid variation on *Rear Window* called *Mr. Blanchard's Secret*. In this a sus-

picious observer believes — wrongly, as it turns out — that her neighbor has killed his wife. Nothing happens, either in the story or in the
sensibilities of the audience.

Further distraction was available, for a time at least, in the publicity
for *The Wrong Man,* which Warners decided to release in New York on
December 22, in the fantastic hope that it might qualify for some Academy Award. The critics, however, mistook a cool Kafkaesque nightmare for a Hitchcockian turn at cinema verité, or Italian neorealism,
and the most excitement the film generated occurred on December 27,
when the notorious "Mad Bomber" planted a pipe bomb at the New
York theater that was showing the film. No one was hurt, and Hitchcock's reply to the inquiring press was that the perpetrator (eventually
caught and identified as George Metesky) was "a man with a diabolical
sense of humor." It was indeed the absence of any humor or color or
suspense in the new film that audiences found perplexing.

At the start of 1957, the fifty-seven-year-old Hitchcock began to feel
suddenly and unaccountably weak, complaining to Alma of vague abdominal discomfort. Ignoring some unusual warning signals, however,
he accepted another script from Joan Harrison, and from January 9 to
11 he directed *One More Mile to Go* for the television series. Routinely
photographed, it is remarkable only in its odd presage of scenes from
*Psycho.* Here, David Wayne dispatches his wife and hauls away the
body in his car, only to be stopped by a policeman — the auto lights
have failed, and the officer insists on leading car and driver to a place
where the trunk can be pried open, the trouble remedied and, of course,
the culprit revealed.

But the three days work enervated Hitchcock even further, and on
January 12 he took to his bed. Five days later, in acute distress, he
agreed to meet his physician at Cedars of Lebanon Hospital, and he was
admitted at once and advised to have the long-ignored hernia corrected.
"Dr. [Marcus] Rabwin," Alma said later that day, "does not regard
the operation as serious, but it is essential. Hitchy has had this hernia
for years, but it never caused him any trouble until a few weeks ago,
when he suffered pain. So now he has decided he will have surgery at
once rather than risk having an attack when he is making a picture or a
TV show. He is very confident he will have no difficulty and so are my
daughter and myself. He's very cheerful."

As usual, Alma was his best stand-in press representative, for in fact
Hitchcock was in a barely controllable panic. Added to his own fierce
sense of privacy about his body and an exaggerated Victorian squeamishness about common functions that struck a surprising contrast with

his toilet humor, Hitchcock also had enjoyed extraordinarily good health over the years, and this was his first hospitalization in America.*

"The biggest shock," he told a reporter,

was the indignities to which institutions of healing subject your person. I'm not a squeamish man, but some of the things they do to you in hospitals are no less than obscene. When they came in to prepare me for surgery and tied a label on my wrist with my name on it, I thought, "They must think I'm ready for the morgue." — "It isn't that," they told me, laughingly. "We just don't want you to get mixed up with anyone else and have the wrong operation." That in itself was a thought-provoking notion.

I had colitis, which was painful, and I'd had a hernia for years, and I had done nothing about either. I had those things taken care of. . . . A New York doctor once told me that I'm an adrenal type. That apparently means that I'm all body and only vestigial legs. But since I'm neither a mile runner nor a dancer and my present interest in my body is almost altogether from the waist up, that didn't bother me much.

In ten days he was resting comfortably at home, enjoying the ministrations of Alma, Pat, and his granddaughters, and Herbert Coleman brought daily reports of Hollywood news. Although still under contract to Paramount, the deal allowed him to make films elsewhere, and MCA had made a one-picture deal with MGM. During the convalescence, Hitchcock read a novel by Hammond Innes called *The Wreck of the Mary Deare*, and this was his choice for the film to follow *From Amongst the Dead*.

There was no doubt in his mind about who to get for the writer, either. He had been introduced to Ernest Lehman by Bernard Herrmann, and following a congenial lunch the previous year, Hitchcock had investigated Lehman's impressive credits — expert scripts for *Executive Suite, Sabrina, Somebody Up There Likes Me, The King and I,* and *Sweet Smell of Success.* Lehman was under contract to MGM, and although he was not very enthusiastic after reading the Innes novel, he relished the idea of working with Alfred Hitchcock. "I had met him briefly, on the set of *Rear Window,*" Lehman remembered. "He wasn't yet a legendary figure, a myth, in those days — he was just that much-talked-about, wonderful director who had made *Shadow of a Doubt* and

---

*To a number of actresses, over the years, Hitchcock confided that if he was using a public toilet and another man entered the room, he would quickly raise his legs within the stall "so that no one could tell there was anyone there." For the inveterately Victorian Hitchcock, the quite ordinary business of the human body was fine material for jokes, fine for fantasies — but no one must ever have the impression that such business was part of his real life.

*Strangers on a Train.''* But their meeting to discuss a collaboration had
to await Hitchcock's full recovery.

The convalescence was not helped by the discovery that the new writer
on *From Amongst the Dead* was sending gloomy signals to Hitchcock
through Herbert Coleman. Before his surgery, Hitchcock had agreed to
let Alec Coppel take over the assignment. An Anglo-American stage-
and screenwriter whose services Hitchcock could have quite cheaply,
Coppel had written *The Captain's Paradise* for Alec Guinness in 1952,
and his new play *The Genius and the Goddess* was ready for Broadway.
Hitchcock had been persuaded by Paramount executives that Coppel was
the right man to salvage the picture. They could not have been more
injudicious.

Throughout February, however, Coppel wrote; and the results were
soon perceived as woefully disappointing. Hitchcock was tempted to
abandon the project when he was suddenly overtaken by a more serious
illness. At four o'clock on the morning of March 9, Alma called Herbert
Coleman to come to Bellagio Road at once. Her husband was in great
pain, moaning inconsolably, and she feared a heart attack. It is unclear
why she did not call a physician directly, but Coleman responded to her
plea, rushed to the house, and was shocked to find a jaundiced Hitchcock clutching his chest and begging for help.

They called Lew Wasserman, Dr. Marcus Rabwin, and Dr. Walter
Flieg, and within an hour the patient was back at Cedars of Lebanon,
where the doctors administered tests that at once confirmed their diagnosis. The years of gastronomic richness had at last caught up with him,
and he required surgery to remove a diseased gallbladder and dangerously obstructing gallstones. The operation was performed on March
11. "I suffered two internal hemorrhages," Hitchcock told a columnist
later. "I was told that this often happened to people and not to worry.
So I wasn't alarmed. But they told my wife she had better see a priest."

This time the recuperation, in hospital and at home, took a month,
and Hitchcock brooded about Alec Coppel's unshootable screenplay and
the news that another major delay was inevitable. But most disappointing of all — and the item that produced a great burst of anger — was
that his new Galatea, the woman of whose appearance and image and
career he planned a complete transformation, told him by phone that
she definitely would be unavailable to appear in *From Amongst the Dead*.
"Vera, instead of leaping at the chance of her life, got pregnant!"
Hitchcock cried. "She was going to be a real star with this film, but
she couldn't resist her Tarzan of a husband, Gordon Scott. She should
have taken a jungle pill!"

The resentment at what he considered Vera Miles's impudent ingratitude smoldered forever after. "I nearly had a relapse when she broke the news," he said twenty years later. "It was her third child, and I told her that one child was expected, two was sufficient, but that three was really obscene. She didn't care for this sort of comment." And there he was — without a script or a star, and with the severe dietary and travel restrictions that impeded any of the usual escape mechanisms in times of depression. Alma stretched the frontiers of her culinary imagination and prepared delicacies that seemed rich but were permissible.

In a final attempt to find a writer, Hitchcock called Kay Brown at her New York office. She was now with a major agency, and their social encounters, which had been infrequent over the years, had recently been reestablished on both coasts when Hitchcock had cast her daughter, Laurinda Barrett, in a small role in *The Wrong Man*. Who, he wanted to know in a strained and desperate tone, might Brown suggest to collaborate with him?

When Kay Brown heard that the setting was San Francisco, she at once mentioned playwright Samuel Taylor, who was a native of that city. Best known for his successful Broadway play *Sabrina Fair*, Taylor had worked with director Billy Wilder on the play's screen adaptation (and was, coincidentally, succeeded in that capacity by Ernest Lehman). Samuel Taylor was regarded as a skilled and sensitive craftsman and a generous and patient writer. Within days, he was in Hollywood.

"I arrived and Hitchcock gave me the Coppel script and we began to talk," Taylor recalled.

But I didn't read the French novel it was based on. He didn't want me to. He knew exactly what he wanted to do, and he explained several scenes in meticulous detail. But the story was missing, and really human characters were absent. We began to map out the story move by move, and he saw everything in his mind. What he needed was a writer to help articulate what he saw.

Working with him meant writing with him, and that is not true of most directors. Hitchcock never claimed to be a writer, but actually he did write his screenplays insofar as he visualized every scene in his mind and knew exactly how he wanted it to go. I realized that the characters had to be personalized and humanized, and further developed. He always had the graveyard scene in his mind, for example. But the events leading up to it were completely unclear and unmotivated.

Taylor went off to northern California to scout locations and to absorb the atmosphere of the places Hitchcock had in mind — places that were part of the imagery, but for which Hitchcock could not devise a coherent narrative alone. And this gave the director his opportunity to meet again with Ernest Lehman.

"Hitchcock and I hit it off smoothly from the very start," Lehman said.

I think he sensed that he'd be "safe" with me. He cast those around him very carefully, based on his unconscious readings of their potential behavior — whether they'd be threatening to him, perhaps be the type who could leap up and show anger. I was quiet, respectful, interested, maybe even interesting, and obviously one who would easily fit into the role of "sitting at the feet of the master." It was on the basis of that one luncheon meeting, set up by Benny Herrmann months before, that Hitchcock asked for my writing services when he decided to do *The Wreck of the Mary Deare* at MGM.

Hitchcock had a certain authority that went beyond the record of his proven achievements; his body shape, his manner, his way of speaking somehow gave him an extra measure of power over those within his orbit. The fact that he *was* judgmental, that he did tend to look down on other filmmakers, that his elaborate diction did hint at a superiority of attitude, ironically gave those who worked for him an advantage they may not have been aware of. I, like the writers who had gone before me, worked doubly hard in order *not* to be looked down on by Hitchcock, in order not to be considered inferior.

We writers who worked with him owed him a hidden debt. Even though many of us griped now and then, because this emperor did not have as many garments on his storytelling rack as we had been led to believe by the myth-makers — he was, after all, a director, not a writer — he somehow got writers to do better than they would have done *without* his austere, demanding corporeal presence.

Now, when Hitchcock asked MGM to ask me to write *The Wreck of the Mary Deare,* I was flattered but turned the project down cold. I did not think it was a viable film project, Hitchcock or no Hitchcock. But because he and I were both handled by MCA Artists, and because Edd Henry, who covered MGM for the agency, kept prevailing upon me to at least have lunch with Hitchcock, I finally agreed to do that. And of course after one luncheon, I was so charmed by the man, and so convinced that *he* probably knew how to do the film even if I didn't, that I quickly changed my mind and said yes, and the project was announced officially in the press.

Each day we would meet at Hitchcock's house, and we would spend the day together — supposedly, I thought, to work on the picture. But every time I brought up *The Wreck of the Mary Deare,* I saw looks of anxiety cross his face and he would adeptly change the subject and we would wind up gossiping, and talking of food and wine, and having marvelous lunches together. Now and then, but not often, we'd say a few words about our film project, and I soon realized two important things: Hitchcock had no idea how to do the novel as a picture, and I was even less enthusiastic about its possibilities than when I had first turned it down.

About this time, Samuel Taylor returned from northern California with a script for what would eventually be called *Vertigo*. "Hitchcock seemed pleased," Taylor recalled, "and we agreed on some changes, but I was especially happy when he showed the script to Jimmy Stewart. He burst into Hitch's office at Paramount and said, 'Well, at last these are real people — now we have a movie, now we can go ahead!' We could all tell that this was a very important project for Hitch, and that he was feeling this story very deeply, very personally."

The finished script and film bear everywhere the stamp of Hitchcock's deepest personal feelings — about himself, about his idealized image of woman, about the dangerous borders of emotional fixation, and about death, which is the romantic's ultimate obsession. "At about this time," according to Samuel Taylor, "Hitch began to consult his physician more often. After his recovery from the surgery, he had his blood pressure and pulse checked every week at the studio, and a few years later he was having this done every day." Not yet sixty years old, the sense of irreversible accident that informs so much of Hitchcock's work was now pervading his life. In *The Trouble with Harry*, he had tried to laugh at death and deny burial. But from this new film onward, death is the final arbiter.

Although he had a script, Hitchcock still needed a leading lady, and Lew Wasserman had begun a search of the major studios for a woman to replace Vera Miles. After some persuasion, Hitchcock agreed to Kim Novak, for whose services Wasserman had negotiated with Harry Cohn at Columbia Pictures. By 1957, after half a dozen major roles and careful grooming by Cohn (who planned her as a replacement for Rita Hayworth at Columbia), the uneven screen appearances of Kim Novak did not prevent her from being Hollywood's number-one box-office attraction and one of the highest paid stars in films. In return for her loan-out to Hitchcock, Wasserman agreed to let Cohn have the equally popular James Stewart (whose career Wasserman, at MCA, also managed) for another picture at Columbia with Kim Novak the following year.

The actress had been promised a long vacation that summer, and so the film had to be delayed. Before she departed, however, she met with Edith Head for costume fittings. "She arrived with all kinds of preconceived ideas about what she would wear and how she would and wouldn't look on screen," Edith Head remembered.

She announced that she wouldn't wear a gray suit with her hair dyed blond for the Technicolor camera, since she was afraid she would look vague and washed out. She also said she couldn't possibly wear dark brown pumps, since they would exaggerate what she thought were her rather fleshy calves. Well, I told her to take another look at the script. For the scene in which she was to wear a gray suit and a white scarf with her platinum hair drawn back, Hitchcock had been very specific. He insisted that she was to look as if she just stepped out of the San Francisco fog — a woman of mystery and illusion. Of course eventually when she got to the picture, she did exactly what Hitch wanted.

Herbert Coleman remembered quite clearly Novak's first meeting with Hitchcock: "He wanted me to bring her out to the house before her vacation. To her surprise, he chatted about everything except the film — art, food, travel, wine — all the things he thought she wouldn't know very much about. He succeeded in making her feel like a helpless child, ignorant and untutored, and that's just what he wanted — to break down her resistance. By the end of the afternoon he had her right where he wanted her, docile and obedient and even a little confused."

After she returned from her vacation, there was a final irony. She refused to start work until she had received a check promised her by Harry Cohn — a percentage of the loan-out fee he had won from Wasserman and Paramount; but by the time she had the money and was ready to start, Vera Miles had given birth to her child and was available to do the role. Hitchcock, who had Miles under contract, could have rethought the whole issue. He chose not to do so, however, and with Novak at last ready to work and Hitchcock still angry over Vera Miles's untimely third pregnancy, he set a starting date of mid-September.

From 1957 to the end of his life, Hitchcock was less than generous in his estimation of Kim Novak's work for him. "She was scared stiff and put on a defensive front the first time we met," he told Hedda Hopper. "I had to relax her, give her confidence. . . . It was very hard for me to get what I wanted from her, since Kim's head was full of her own ideas." But there was one good thing about the experience, he confided years later: "At least I got the chance to throw her into the water" — a reference to the scene in which she was to pretend suicide by leaping into San Francisco Bay. He delighted in remembering that he asked for multiple retakes in the studio tank — which involved the forlorn woman's leaping fully clothed into the water, climbing out, changing into a dry outfit, then being forced to jump in again.

A happier addition to this production, however, was the return to Hitchcock's staff of Peggy Singer. She had, since her days as continuity supervisor on *Under Capricorn* and *Stage Fright,* worked for other directors and married film editor Douglas Robertson. Now, as Peggy Robertson, she was reengaged by Hitchcock as script supervisor. Her help was invaluable, and soon she was Hitchcock's personal assistant, providing him with strong support, keen creative suggestions, and relieving him of many of the burdens connected with each production from 1957 to the end of his career. Credited as "Assistant to Mr. Hitchcock" from *The Birds* through *Family Plot,* she was in fact, if not in actual status, his associate producer — much as Herbert Coleman was from 1954 to 1959 (and again in 1968). The unhappy termination of the Hitchcock-Robertson relationship that occurred twenty-two years later could not have been foreseen in 1957 — although it was the kind of break that had numerous precedents in the lives and professions of other Hitchcock associates.

Henry Bumstead resumed, on *Vertigo,* the post of Hitchcock's art director. "Try to use a lot of mirrors," the director told him — and in the picture mirrors do in fact brilliantly serve the motif of the doubled and split image. The mirrors, which would become an even more important prop in *Psycho,* are placed strategically in the flower shop, Podesta Baldocchi; at the department store, Ransohoff's; at Ernie's Restaurant; and most of all, in Novak's hotel room, where she is transformed, for the second time in the film, into an idealized double, a fantasized image.

While he waited for the first day of shooting, Hitchcock — whose energies had returned at full tilt — directed two more teleplays. From July 17 to 19, he completed *The Perfect Crime,* with Vincent Price and James Gregory — a typical Hitchcockian exercise on the exchange of guilt. And from July 29 to August 2 he directed one of three hour-format programs: *Four O'Clock,* with E. G. Marshall as a man who plans to kill his wife but who is trapped with the time bomb meant for her execution. To Cornell Woolrich's contrived story Hitchcock brought the same sense of claustrophobia he gave to *Breakdown,* and a typical shot ends the teleplay: Marshall's face, frozen in a trancelike, almost mummified state.

Also in August, Ernest Lehman came to a decision about *The Wreck of the Mary Deare.*

I arrived at his house one morning and said, "Hitch, I hate to have to say this, but I really don't know how to do this picture. You're going to have to get yourself another writer."

Hitch didn't even blink. "Don't be silly, Ernie," he said. "We get along so well together, we'll simply do something else."

"But what?" I asked.

"We'll talk about it," he said. "We'll come up with something."

And then I asked plaintively, "But what'll we tell MGM?" I was under contract to the studio. They were paying me every week to write *The Wreck of the Mary Deare*.

"We won't tell them anything," said Hitch, smiling.

For weeks and weeks we met every day and talked about food and wines and the town's latest scandals, and now and then we talked about possible movies that both of us might want to do together — and frankly, nothing that Hitch wanted to do appealed to me and I said so. And one day I said, "I want to do a Hitchcock picture to end all Hitchcock pictures, that's the only kind of picture *I* want to do, Hitch." And by that I meant a movie-movie — with glamour, wit, excitement, movement, big scenes, a large canvas, innocent bystander caught up in great derring-do, in the *Hitchcock* manner.

And then one day he said, a little wistfully, "I've always wanted to do a chase sequence across the faces of Mount Rushmore."

Well, that was *great,* and I told him so, and that became the impetus for what was to become, after more than a year of blood, sweat, and story conferences, *North by Northwest.* We moved over to his Paramount office, where he was getting ready to make *Vertigo,* and we talked every day, and I made notes. And we talked and talked, and all I seemed to come up with was that the film was going to start in New York City, and there'd be something happening at the United Nations, and then the film would move in a northwesterly direction to Mount Rushmore in South Dakota and then maybe keep going on to Alaska.

I knew I wanted an innocent man as the protagonist, but I wasn't sure whether he would be a sports announcer or a newspaperman or an advertising executive or a Frank Sinatra–type entertainer, and I didn't know who would be chasing whom or why, other than the fact that it would have something to do with the then very hot Cold War. And an outline started forming in my head and on paper, and Hitch would throw ideas at me and I'd throw ideas at him, and some of them one of us would like and some of them both of us would like — but rarely — and I still hadn't figured out who the innocent protagonist was and what he had gotten himself into.

And one day Hitch told me that a New York newspaperman had once given him an idea, at a cocktail party, that he thought Hitch might use and should feel free to use if he wanted to — an idea about some government agency creating a decoy nonexistent agent to throw some enemies of the government off the trail of a real, existing agent; and Hitchcock and I discussed the possibility that our innocent bystander could be mistaken for the nonexistent decoy, and that would automatically plunge him into our plot line. I immediately told Hitch that this would work for me, and promptly latched on to the decoy device as an important cog in the story wheel.

And while Hitch plunged more deeply into preproduction work on *Vertigo,* I pushed my little plot as far as Grand Central Station. And then one day Hitch said to me, "Don't you think it's time you told MGM we're not doing *The Wreck of the Mary Deare?*"

I was appalled. "Me? *I'm* not going to tell them."

"You mean *I'm* going to have to do your work *for* you?"

"Absolutely," I said.

And he did. He gathered all the MGM executives in a big room, told them it would take me too long to write *Mary Deare,* that we were going to do another picture first — *first!* — which delighted them, because they thought they would now get two Hitchcock pictures. And he spun a vague but beautifully told tale that got only as far as Grand Central Station. Then he looked at his watch, said, "Sorry, gentlemen, I must go now, but you'll see the rest of it at the preview," and left a roomful of dazed but delighted MGM executives and returned to his office at Paramount, where he started *Vertigo.*

And I started to face the grim fact that I had to construct and write a screenplay based on a very thin outline of an opening act and just about nothing else. So naturally, the first thing I did was avoid the typewriter by going on a two-week research trip to New York, the United Nations, Glen Cove, the *20th Century Limited,* Chicago, the Ambassador East Hotel, and Mount Rushmore, which I half climbed before scurrying down to safety.

Hitch was not a writer, but he was enormously helpful to me as the writer. I knew the film had to be scripted expertly and in the style of the unique star that he was, or he simply wouldn't accept it — he was Alfred Hitchcock, after all, and he was the producer and the director of this movie. And if he didn't like what you came up with, you damned well did it over again and did it better. And whenever you got stuck, if you could find him you talked it over with him until he forced you to solve your story problem, or you subtly forced *him* to solve it for you.

From September to December, the long-delayed film based on the Boileau-Narcejac novel and written by Samuel Taylor was shot in northern California and back at the Paramount studios. From the situation that precipitates the story, Hitchcock finally seized on a new title, and although Paramount was chary of the public's acceptance, they agreed to *Vertigo.* The narrative for this, his richest, most obsessive, and least compromising film, fascinated the studio executives.

James Stewart plays "Scottie," a San Francisco lawyer-turned-detective who discovers his acrophobia — a pathological dread of high places — during a rooftop chase in which a police colleague comes to his aid and falls to his death. The acrophobia is manifest in vertigo, a psychosomatic illness that produces dizziness and a sensation of drifting in spinning space — a frightening but also strangely pleasurable sensation. Stewart resigns from the force and is asked by an old schoolmate (played by Tom Helmore) to follow the schoolmate's wife (Kim Novak), who, he says, believes that a long-dead relative has come back to possess her and lead her to a repetition of the ancestor's suicide.

Stewart reluctantly accepts the assignment and trails Novak, eventually saving her when she throws herself into San Francisco Bay. In spite

of his desire to protect her from her illusions, however, he cannot —
because of his fear of heights — climb to her rescue when she hurls
herself from a church tower. Overwhelmed by guilt and the loss of the
woman he had come to love, Stewart suffers a breakdown that even
his friend and former fiancée (Barbara Bel Geddes) is powerless to
alleviate.

After his convalescence, Stewart sees a woman whose striking resemblance to his dead beloved elicits a Pygmalion-like obsession. He follows her and asks for a date — and at this point a flashback reveals that
the woman is the very same one who was apparently the schoolmate's
wife. She was in fact Helmore's mistress, and a participant in a carefully contrived plot to kill the real wife by throwing her from a tower.
Stewart, it turns out, had been set up as a witness to an apparent suicide
that masked a murder. He finally guesses the truth when Novak — after
being completely transformed a second time, by Stewart now, into a
nonexistent image (in clothes, hairstyle, makeup, and manner) — wears
a necklace left over from her costume in the murder's plot. He forces
her back to the church tower, she admits the truth, and accidentally falls
to her death.

Working with James Stewart on *Vertigo* was no problem, for he knew
just what his director wanted and was able, in this dark and romantic
fable, to tap depths in his own abilities that had never been captured on
screen before. "After several years I saw the film again," Stewart said,
"and I thought it was a fine picture. I myself had known fear like that,
and I'd known people paralyzed by fear. It's a very powerful thing to
be almost engulfed by that kind of fear. I didn't realize when I was
preparing the role what an impact it would have, but it's an extraordinary achievement by Hitch. And I could tell it was a very personal film
for him even while he was making it."

And although Hitchcock always insisted that Kim Novak was difficult, she really gave the performance of her career. "What fascinated
me," Hitchcock said, "was the idea that Jimmy Stewart was trying to
turn the girl into someone she once had to play as part of a murder plot
and is later trying not to be — and I'm not sure Kim Novak had the
ability to put this across." But Samuel Taylor, the screenwriter, en-
dorsed the majority opinion: "If we'd had a brilliant actress who really
created two distinctly different people, it would not have been as good.
She seemed so naive in the part, and that was good. She was always
believable. There was no 'art' about it, and that's why it worked so
very well."*

---

*James Stewart agreed: "Kim was wonderful — and it was all Hitch's doing."

Hitchcock's objections to casting, however, are minor considerations in understanding *Vertigo*'s place in his life. This film was his ultimate disclosure of his romantic impulses and of the attraction-repulsion he felt about the object of those impulses: the idealized blond he thought he desired but really believed to be a fraud.

To the final page of the shooting script (dated September 12, 1957), Hitchcock added: "And she is in his arms, pressing tightly against him in desperation, and he holds her tight, and they kiss deeply, passionately. The kiss ends but they remain together, holding together, and Scottie's eyes are tight with pain and the emotion of hating her and hating himself for loving her." The kiss is not quite so deep and passionate in the final edited film, since Hitchcock had already staged the ultimate kissing scene of his career moments earlier in the hotel room.*

His camera had always drawn close to passionate lovers, and in the kissing scenes Hitchcock tried to embrace the lovers himself — creating the effect of what he called "a ménage." In *Notorious* (on the balcony, and later in the rescue scene in Ingrid Bergman's bedroom), in *Strangers on a Train* (the kiss between Farley Granger and Ruth Roman), in *I Confess* (where Montgomery Clift and Anne Baxter are encircled by a moving camera), in *Rear Window* (when Grace Kelly draws near to James Stewart in a double-printed shot that prolongs the kiss in a kind of quivering expectancy), and in *To Catch a Thief* (when Grace Kelly and Cary Grant kiss long and deeply as they recline on a divan), there are cinematic parallels to the effect a viewer feels upon walking around Rodin's famous romantic sculpture *The Kiss,* which was always one of Hitchcock's favored works.

Like that statue, the kiss in Hitchcock's American films is frankly sexual but also has a complex emotional referent; like that statue, too — which was to have been part of a group called *The Gates of Hell* — there is in Hitchcock a sense of imminent frustration and damnation; Rodin's sculpture was inspired by Dante's Paolo and Francesca, the pair who kissed and so were damned.† Hitchcock represented the lovers in *Vertigo* as Rodin had represented the lovers in *The Kiss* — by focusing on the touch of the mouths, with the rest of the bodies lightly touching

---

* "I had the hotel room and all the pieces of the stable made into a circular set," he explained. "Then I had the camera taken right round the whole thing in a 360-degree turn. Then we put that on a screen, and I stood the actors on a small turntable and turned them around. So they went round, and the screen behind them gave the appearance of your going around with them. That was in order to give him the feeling that he was back in that particular spot — the stable."

† The connection between intimacy and damnation was later made explicit in Hitchcock's *Torn Curtain,* where the climactic ballet being danced to Tchaikovsky's *Francesca da Rimini* describes the situation of Paolo and Francesca and illuminates the significance of everything that has happened to the lovers in the film.

and the man's pose deliberately rigid, with the element of hesitation inhibiting the flow of passion. For Hitchcock as for Rodin, love and beauty are, as one art critic wrote of the *The Kiss,* "associated with pain, and with the idea of sphinx-like incommunicability and unattainability." The concretized form of the romantic concepts of unattainability, immolation, and damnation gives *Vertigo,* too, its power to grip the beholder.

In no other film did Hitchcock have so clear a masculine alter ego than James Stewart in this film. The probing questions of a man who wants not only to solve a mystery and to save a woman but also to exert the control that comes from complete knowledge had their counterpart in the protracted, private conferences Hitchcock held with the actresses he most favored — Madeleine Carroll, Joan Fontaine, Ingrid Bergman, Grace Kelly, and Vera Miles — and five years later the tendency would reach its saddest and most destructive expression in an obsession from which he would never recover. "He is suffering," says the doctor about James Stewart in *Vertigo,* "from acute melancholia, together with a guilt complex." The diagnosis was articulated by Hitchcock himself, and it was indeed a self-diagnosis, locating the pain he felt in each decade of his career and describing his own most recent reaction to the disappointment he felt over Vera Miles.

But along with what Hitchcock might have thought were his strongest romantic impulses, there was a hesitancy caused by contrary urges. The belief that any beautiful woman was a deception, a cheat, and a dangerous seduction of spirit and body caused a simultaneous attraction and repulsion in him that created his own spiritual vertigo. The most famous trick shot he devised for the film — the combination of a forward zoom and a reverse tracking shot to achieve the effect of the dizzying elasticity of dimensions — is itself the visual equivalent for the admixture of desire and distance, the longing to fall and the fear of falling, the impulse toward and the revulsion from, that define the somatic and spiritual condition of vertigo.

*Vertigo* is the profoundest treatment Hitchcock could offer of the opposing drives that the film described as spiritually poisonous (as did all the films about the "double"). Here, the clash of opposite impulses derives partly from the cycle of shame, fear, and guilt, and partly from a greater aesthetic awareness that the carefully designed beauty of a film actress is itself illusory. The attraction to and repulsion from this object of deception and desire are clearly indicated in the scenes in which Stewart moves closer to the woman who is to be refashioned for a second time.

STEWART: Will you have dinner with me?

NOVAK: Dinner and what else?

STEWART: Just dinner. [*Later.*] We could just see a lot of each other.

NOVAK: Why? Because I remind you of her? That's not very complimentary. And nothing else?

STEWART: No.

NOVAK: That's not very complimentary either.

STEWART: I just want to be with you as much as I can.

The impulses are sexual and domineering, but the gestures are freighted with fear; the character does precisely what Hitchcock had done with his most beloved actresses.

STEWART [*selecting clothes for Novak*]: No, that's not it — nothing like it.

SALESWOMAN: But you said gray, sir.

STEWART: Now, look — I just want an ordinary, simple gray suit.

NOVAK: I like that one.

STEWART: No, it's not right.

SALESWOMAN: The gentleman seems to know what he wants.

STEWART: . . . I want you to look nice. I know the kind of suit that would look well on you.

NOVAK [*aware of his desire to dress her up the way she looked before, like the woman who is now thought to be dead*]: No, I won't do it!

STEWART: It can't make that much difference to you. . . . Do this for me. [*To the saleswoman.*] Now we'd like to look at a dinner dress — short, black, with long sleeves and a square neck.

SALESWOMAN: My, you certainly do know what you want, sir!

NOVAK [*later*]: Why are you doing this? What good will it do?

STEWART: I don't know. No good, I guess. I don't know. . . . There's something in you. [*He reaches to caress her face but pulls away.*]

NOVAK: You don't even want to touch me.

STEWART: Yes — I do.

NOVAK: Couldn't you like me — just me the way I am? When we first started out it was so good — we had fun. And then you started in on the clothes. All right, I'll wear the darn clothes if you want me to — if you'll just like me.

STEWART [*gazing at her red hair but obviously thinking of the blond he had adored*]: The color of your hair!

NOVAK: Oh, no!

STEWART: Please, it can't matter to you!

NOVAK: If I let you change me, will that do it? If I do what you tell me, will you love me?

STEWART: Yes . . . yes.

NOVAK: All right then, I'll do it. I don't care anymore about me.

Never were romantic exploitation and self-abnegation so clearly articulated in a Hitchcock film, and never was that complexity so confessional as in *Vertigo*. "He made you over, didn't he?" Stewart shouts at
Novak, referring to the killer (Helmore) after discovering the duplicity
in which she was involved. "He made you over just like I made you
over — only better. Not only the clothes and the hair, but the looks and
the manner and the words. And those beautiful phony trances! . . .
And then what did he do? Did he train you? Did he rehearse you? Did
he tell you exactly what to do and what to say? You were a very apt
pupil, weren't you? You were a very apt pupil!"

Throughout his career, Alfred Hitchcock strove to realize his dream
ever more fully. But the dream involved a conflict between brutal sensuality and fastidious refinement, between reality and art. In his stories,
that conflict is the key to the suspense — and especially to the deepest
kind, emotional and romantic suspense. "Suspense," he said that year,

is like a woman. The more left to the imagination, the more the excitement.
. . . The conventional big-bosomed blonde is not mysterious. And what could
be more obvious than the old black velvet and pearls type? The perfect "woman
of mystery" is one who is blonde, subtle and Nordic. . . . Movie titles, like
women, should be easy to remember without being familiar, intriguing but
never obvious, warm yet refreshing, suggest action, not impassiveness, and
finally give a clue without revealing the plot. Although I do not profess to be
an authority on women, I fear that the perfect title, like the perfect woman, is
difficult to find. . . . A woman of mystery is one who also has a certain
maturity and whose actions speak louder than words. Any woman can be one,
if she keeps those two points in mind. She should grow up — and shut up.

The beauty of Hitchcock's most memorable stars is equaled, in fact,
only by their coolness, a quality that has become synonymous with the
Hitchcock woman. None of them has the earthy quality of, for example,
Ava Gardner or Rita Hayworth in the films of the 1940s and 1950s, or
like virtually any of the leading ladies in film after the mid-1960s. Like
Hitchcock's motion pictures, the most carefully calculated feminine per-
sonae — those he devised for Madeleine Carroll, Joan Fontaine, Ingrid
Bergman, Grace Kelly, Vera Miles, Kim Novak, (and later) Eva Marie
Saint, and Tippi Hedren — tease the intelligence and the imagination
before responding to emotion and desire. And with all of them, as with
the protypical Victorian, hair is an ultimate erotic fixation.*

---

*There are curious, lingering shots of a woman's hairstyle (or of the back of her head) in *The
39 Steps, Young and Innocent, The Lady Vanishes, Rebecca, Foreign Correspondent, Mr. and
Mrs. Smith, Saboteur, Shadow of a Doubt, Notorious, The Paradine Case, Stage Fright, Rear
Window, To Catch a Thief, Vertigo, North by Northwest, Psycho, The Birds,* and *Marnie.*

"I was very much intrigued by the basic situation of *Vertigo,*" Hitchcock confided, "— of changing the woman's hair color — because it contained so much analogy to sex. This man changed and dressed up his woman, which seems like the reverse of stripping her naked. But it amounts to the same thing. I really made the film in order to get through to this subtle quality of a man's dreamlike nature." And the man, of course, was really Hitchcock himself. Like James Stewart in *Vertigo,* Hitchcock chose fantasy over reality, and he could not respond to a woman until she was refashioned to correspond with his dream.

Hitchcock's conflicting feelings about women were perhaps the single most dramatic and painful realization of his own experience of a divided personality. On the one hand, Woman was an abstraction, almost a remote goddess in her purity and coolness. But — "in the back of a taxi," as he liked to say — what such a woman might do was really what he *wished* she would do.

In this regard, Hitchcock's preference for women assistants accompanied an equivalent dislike of men. He cultivated actors like Joseph Cotten, Henry Fonda, James Stewart, and Cary Grant for what they could provide him in his films, but there was never the intimacy of friendship, and they knew it; more often (as, for example, with John Gielgud, Michael Redgrave, Laurence Olivier, Gregory Peck, Anthony Perkins, Rod Taylor, Sean Connery, Paul Newman, and Frederick Stafford) he made no attempt to conceal his discomfort and even his resentment of them — most of all because they appeared to possess what he lacked.

Isolated as a child and as an adolescent, virtually closeted with his mother until his marriage at twenty-seven, taught as a student and an apprentice to cultivate the good opinion of others, Hitchcock harbored a lifelong terror of breaking the law and thus being thought a "bad boy." (When asked what he would like on his tombstone, he replied: "This is what we do to bad little boys.") His quiet, observant personality and his retreat behind a mass of restricting obesity made him at once safe from the (mostly imagined) blandishments of women and from competition with other men.

Hitchcock's temperament was very like that of Henry James, who also partook of Victorian puritanism in its American and English variants. As Leon Edel wrote of Henry James, so it was with Alfred Hitchcock: a "spiritual transvestism" — which fascinated the director in its literal and figurative senses — protected a sense of masculine integrity. It was thus true of Hitchcock, as Edel wrote of James, that all his life he harbored "within the house of the [artist's] inner world the spirit of a young adult female, worldly-wise and curious, possessing a treasure

of unassailable virginity and innocence and able to yield to the masculine active world-searching side, . . . an ever-fresh and exquisite vision
of feminine youth and innocence. For this was the androgynous nature
of the creator and the drama of his [art]: innocence and worldliness, the
paradisical America and the cruel and corrupt Europe.'' Just as in Henry
James's fictive world, it was safer in Hitchcock's to be a little girl because little girls endured and grew wiser with experience. The women
are confronted with the moral dilemma, the choice, the drama of action
and imagination.

The Victorian girl, of course, was presumed to be sanguine, sensible,
and gifted — but not at all intellectual or aesthetic or learned. During
the time when this attitude was being modified in the first quarter of the
twentieth century, Alfred Hitchcock was in his formative years as student and young professional. In his films — and in *Vertigo* especially — the woman is shown to be at once victim and victimizer. She
appears cool and remote and aloof, but actually she yearns to express a
raging passion.

Hitchcock's desire to strip naked his female characters psychologically (''Tear them down at the very start,'' he said, ''that's much the
best way'') and to have them tear into him (explicit in his repeated
anecdote about a lascivious woman in the back of a taxi) was at once
his expression of an urge to humanize the screen goddess and a way of
feminizing himself, of complementing his stolid and studied exterior by
dealing — even hurtfully — with the inward, passionate nature he could
not articulate. In *Vertigo* one learns as much about Alfred Hitchcock
from the complex dualities of the Kim Novak character as from the
tormented, doomed lover played by Stewart. And from the opening pro-
logue — the rooftop chase after an unknown person, and the suspension
of Stewart over an abyss — through the turns of the narrative (a series
of ever slower chases after some other unknown) until its final image of
Stewart poised on the brink of eternal loss and madness, Hitchcock made
no concessions.

In Bernard Herrmann's musical score that dream mode is sustained
and the lost world of California's Spanish past is everywhere evoked.
Memories and fragments of forgotten hopes float like lily pads in the
score, which resonates with Herrmann's references to the magic fire
music from *Die Walküre* and to the *''Liebestod''* from *Tristan und
Isolde* (wholly appropriate for the modern tale of two Isoldes). The music and the sound effects are elusive and lonely, fragile and ghostly —
a ship's horn in the fog of San Francisco Bay, whispers and muffled
conversations as background in public places, hollow footsteps on a
cemetery garden path.

And, as so often in Hitchcock, it all leads from obsession to ultimate loss. In *The Trouble with Harry* the major motif is the loss of a good reputation in a puritan New England town; in *The Man Who Knew Too Much,* it is the loss of sophistication and of family security abroad; in *The Wrong Man* it is the loss of innocence and family unity at home; and in the trilogy *Vertigo–North by Northwest–Psycho* it is finally the loss of identity itself. Hitchcock engaged writers to develop the stories and to contribute the dialogue, but the choice of the property was his, and at every stage of the story's development, his approval was always necessary. His collaborators gave him only what he wanted, or only what he would accept, and everything he demanded.

The emotional landscape of *Vertigo,* with its haunted and hopeless pursuit of an empty ideal, is Hitchcock's ultimate statement on the romantic fallacy. In expressing this view, he resembled his countryman Ernest Dowson (1867–1900), a sensitive artist also increasingly given to excessive drinking. Like Hitchcock, Dowson had a horror of disorder. The one romance of Dowson's life, with a London waitress, was probably an invention of his perfervid imagination. Never convinced that he could find real love, he wanted to kill off all its possibilities in advance and lament the loss ever after. All the stories in his collection *Dilemmas* (1895) tell about frustrated love — the failure of a weak man and his melancholy retreat into the solitude of the disturbed romantic — and any of them could have been transmuted into cinematic terms by Hitchcock, whose spirit they share.

In Dowson's most famous poem, "Cynara" (whose true title is *"Non sum qualis eram bonae sub regno Cynarae"*), the impassioned lover cries out for madder music and stronger wine, even as he aches in the shadow of his lost love. As *Vertigo* did later, Dowson treated in the novel *A Comedy of Masks* (which he, too, produced with the help of a collaborator) the contrast between the appearance and reality of personhood as typified in the contrast of mask versus face. This was of course a common currency in Victorian allegory, and the terms augured the masklike, staring face that forms the background for the opening and conclusion of the spiraling credit designs for *Vertigo,* which Hitchcock hired Saul Bass to realize. Both Hitchcock and Dowson were, like the characters played by Stewart and Novak, "wanderers" (the term used in the film script). Both, like Stewart's character, had their deepest conversation in "a whispered *colloque sentimental* with the ghost of an old love," as Arthur Symons said of Dowson.

And the effect of *Vertigo* was no accident. According to Samuel Taylor, "Hitchcock knew exactly what he wanted to do in this film, exactly what he wanted to say, and how it should be seen and told. I gave him the characters and the dialogue he needed and developed the story, but it was from first frame to last his film. There was no moment that he wasn't there. And anyone who saw him during the making of the film could see, as I did, that he felt it very deeply indeed.''

Principal photography on *Vertigo* was completed just before Christmas, and Hitchcock asked Lew Wasserman and his wife to join him and Alma for a Caribbean holiday in Jamaica. Stopping at the Hotel Carillon in Miami Beach, he told Herbert Coleman in a telephone call that Florida's resort hotels seemed to be designed in "Early American Nightmare," a judgment echoed by others before and since. During their vacation, Ernest Lehman sent about seventy pages of what, at this stage, was titled *In a Northwesterly Direction* for Hitchcock's consideration, and the writer received a telegram in short order. Hitchcock was pleased, Alma was delighted, and Lew Wasserman said it was too good for MGM. That was just the encouragement Lehman needed, and even though he had occasional troubles with the sprawling narrative in the early months of 1958, he continued to hammer out an astonishing scenario in his lonely office in the Irving Thalberg Building at MGM.

"I kept trying to quit the project in despair," Lehman said,

but my agent, who was also Hitch's agent, wouldn't let me. He said, "You can't do that, you already quit *Mary Deare*." So back I went to the typewriter and sweated my way out of another corner I had written myself into the day before. And that, for the most part, was the way the picture got written — with the daily conviction that it was impossible to write, that Hitch would never arrive at MGM, and that this was all some horrible game I had to play until I finished it, or got rescued, or maybe the studio got demolished in an earthquake.

A year later, Hitch was shooting the picture. As one scale said to the other as Alfred Hitchcock approached, "Do not take this man lightly." I never did, not after I saw *North by Northwest* on the screen for the first time.

For a while in early 1958 Lehman's script-in-progress bore the working title *Breathless* — which described the story's multiple chases as well as Lehman's feelings after long working sessions. From the start, the project was written with Cary Grant in mind, and this created, for a time, a delicate situation: James Stewart pleaded with Hitchcock for some idea of the script and said he would turn down all other offers for the new picture. "I didn't want to come straight out and tell him we had Grant in mind," Hitchcock revealed later, "so I just told him that we didn't have anything on paper yet. Then one day he called and said he couldn't put Columbia off any longer, that he had to report with

Novak for *Bell, Book and Candle*. I was of course very relieved, and I simply said, 'Well, Jimmy, that's our loss. I guess we'll have to look for someone else.' "

While Lehman worked, a television script came along that Hitchcock could not resist. Roald Dahl had adapted his own story *Lamb to the Slaughter,* about a woman psychologically derailed by the news that her husband wants a divorce. She fetches a leg of lamb from the freezer, clubs him with it, and then cooks the lamb and serves it to the baffled police who come looking for the murder weapon. Hitchcock filmed it in two days, on February 18 and 19, with Barbara Bel Geddes as the distracted murderess; the final shot directly prefigures the final shot of Anthony Perkins in *Psycho* — the broad smile on the face of a lunatic who gazes out at the viewer. *Lamb to the Slaughter* remained Hitchcock's favorite achievement in television, a typical fantasy about the relationship between food and violent death that anticipates *Frenzy.*

"I hate to say it," said Hitchcock, obviously not hating to say it at all, "but I always thought a good red wine put into one's mind the thought of menstrual blood." Remarks like this, meant to shock, usually had the desired effect, and often preceded other comments about human and animal organs. His sense of the grotesque was never more sharp than when he drew odd connections between matters of the table and intimate bodily functions.

About this time, Hitchcock asked Henry Bumstead to come out to Bellagio Road to redesign his study. "I want it to be like Gavin Elster's office in *Vertigo,*" he told the art director, referring to the rich paneling, the deep, comfortable chairs, and the red carpeting and antique appointments. Bumstead, always a cheerful colleague, was somewhat surprised to learn that Hitchcock expected him to provide his time and services without charge — just for the privilege of being able to say that he had redesigned a room in Alfred Hitchcock's home.

What was even more surprising, however, was that when the job was complete, exactly according to Hitchcock's specifications, there was neither a gesture nor word of thanks or appreciation. Alma asked Bumstead if Hitchcock had told him how happy he was, and she was obviously embarrassed at the reply. Next day, Hitchcock called to thank him — and to ask if he would go with them to Santa Cruz to take a look at the iron gates and interior furniture and see what could be done.

In mid-April, Hitchcock's spirits shifted dramatically. He was nominated for (and subsequently won) a Golden Globe Award for the best television series of the year; and he directed one of his wittiest teleplays, another Dahl story, called *Dip in the Pool.* In this short melodrama,

Keenan Wynn, in an attempt to cheat his shipmates out of the pool money they bet on the daily mileage, schemes to be rescued from a fall overboard to delay their trip and win the cash for himself. But he is destroyed by his own plot, for the woman he engages as an accomplice turns out to be a mental patient who is disbelieved when she reports his leap. The final frame shows, once again, the transfixed stare of the madman, bobbing in the water toward his self-actuated death. The O. Henry reversal is consistent with the prevailing mordant wit, and Hitchcock was in high good humor after filming was completed on April 16.

But the next afternoon changed everything. Alma returned from her doctor, who reported that the tests he had ordered to diagnose some apparently minor ailment revealed cervical cancer. She was to enter the hospital the next day for surgery. The Hitchcocks had previously invited Samuel Taylor and his wife Suzanne to dine with them that evening, and the plans went on without alteration. "We had a lovely time, and Alma prepared one of her usual fine dinners," Samuel Taylor recalled. "We had no idea anything was critical until the next day, when we learned that she had been admitted for an operation."

Hitchcock was beside himself with anxiety. While Alma was in surgery, he dined alone at a nearby restaurant, allaying his loneliness with a hearty meal as he had done in childhood, on the night he thought his family had abandoned him. After Alma's recovery, he not only never visited the restaurant again — he refused to go near it. "The restaurant," Alma said, "is indelibly associated with a night of goose pimples. Therefore he wants it blotted out of his life. Hitch has a simple formula for eliminating suspense and strain from his life: everything he does is planned well in advance."

But the possibility of Alma's death, and his own solitude, struck panic into him. Ernest Lehman remembered accompanying Hitchcock to the hospital for several visits with Alma, who seemed less upset and anxious than her husband. Even when she was recuperating at home, Hitchcock was less interested in proceeding with photography on the Lehman script than she was in seeing him get on with it, and she finally found his anxious manner so tiresome that she begged him — and MGM — to move along with the production. She had no intention of prolonging her confinement, and she saw no reason why he should simply mope.

Hitchcock's only consolation during these days seems to have been several meetings with financial advisers, who came to discuss the ingenious arrangements for collecting his salary from MGM. Hitchcock was to receive $250,000 and 10 percent of the gross profit on all earnings over $8 million. So that he would not lose all this in tax, it had been further specified that the flat salary was to be paid at the rate of $75,000 during filming, $75,000 on January 15, 1959, and $50,000 annually on the same date in 1960 and 1961. The 10 percent profit — which turned out to be, over the next twenty years, in excess of $20 million — was to be banked and paid in annual installments beginning in January 1962. For this and other reasons that became clear after 1959, the decade to come would see the accumulation of staggering sums in the Hitchcock coffers. He was realizing, even more than he had hoped, another fantasy: becoming an American millionaire.

And Cary Grant was not doing badly by the terms of his contract, either: he was to be paid an outright salary of $450,000, plus the same profit percentage as Hitchcock, plus an extra $5,000 per day beginning seven weeks after the contract was signed and continuing until the production was complete. The seven weeks, however, came and went before shooting began, and Grant's income turned out to be astronomical.

As filming approached, the other players were easily cast. Leo G. Carroll returned for his sixth role in a Hitchcock picture; Jessie Royce Landis was cast as Grant's mother (although she was almost a year younger than he); and James Mason was given the part of the elegant villain. For the female lead, MGM tried to force Hitchcock to accept Cyd Charisse, but he insisted on Eva Marie Saint.

"I watched every hair on her head," he said about the wardrobe and preproduction tests.

She had two wardrobes made for her, and I discovered when we screened them that the wardrobe designer was dressing her up as a waif — she was dressing the Eva Marie of *On the Waterfront*. . . . I went along to Bergdorf Goodman's myself and sat with her as the mannequins paraded by. I chose the dress for her.* . . . I suggested she be dressed in a basic black suit, . . . a heavy black silk cocktail dress subtly imprinted with wine-red flowers in scenes where she deceives Gary Grant; in a charcoal brown, full-skirted jersey and a burnt orange burlap outfit in the scenes of action. . . . I did the same for Grace Kelly, who was rather mousy in *High Noon*. She blossomed out for me. . . . I took a lot of trouble with Eva Marie Saint, grooming her and making her appear sleek and sophisticated. Next thing, she's in a picture called *Exodus*, looking dissipated. . . . I acted just like a rich man keeping a woman: I supervised the choice of her wardrobe in every detail — just as Stewart did with Novak in *Vertigo*.

But in this case, as Eva Marie Saint and Ernest Lehman confirmed, there was no personal obsession for a cool-blond leading lady. "He did

---

*This Hitchcockian predilection was signaled as early as *The Lodger*, where Ivor Novello does precisely the same thing for the actress June, whom he observes, dresses up in a new wardrobe, and courts.

have great affection for her," Lehman added, "but who didn't?" Saint recalled Hitchcock's detailed supervision of her wardrobe and her role, and what impressed her most was the care he took in selecting a collar of rubies to match the red-on-black gown — a choice that brought to life the identical offer of Joseph Cotten to Ingrid Bergman in *Under Capricorn* ("I was wondering if a bit of jewelry would help — a collar of rubies, maybe?").

A comic thriller about mistaken identity, political depravity, sexual blackmail, and ubiquitous role-playing, *North by Northwest* — the title was finally suggested by MGM's story editor Kenneth MacKenna — is a superbly paced picture that took Hitchcock and his audience all over the country. Filming began on August 27, 1958, in New York, at the exterior of the United Nations, at the Plaza Hotel, at the CIT Building at 650 Madison Avenue, at Grand Central Station, and on the Phipps Estate in Old Westbury, Long Island. (Before departing, Hitchcock quickly directed the teleplay *Poison*. It took a jaundiced view of psychiatry in its story of an alcoholic [James Donald] who insists that he's being attacked by a deadly snake.)

Everywhere he went, Hitchcock was lionized. As a result of his weekly television appearances, he was now a national figure, and he gladly drew his caricature, for autograph seekers, on everything from children's schoolbooks to restaurant menus.

Ernest Lehman remembered one special restaurant occasion.

During location shooting in New York, he took me to dinner at Christ Cella. He'd had a few martinis, and in a rare moment of emotional intimacy, he put his hand on mine and whispered, "Ernie, do you realize what we're doing in this picture? The audience is like a giant organ that you and I are playing. At one moment we play *this* note on them and get *this* reaction, and then we play *that* chord and they react *that* way. And someday we won't even have to make a movie — there'll be electrodes implanted in their brains, and we'll just press different buttons and they'll go 'ooooh' and 'aaaah' and we'll frighten them, and make them laugh. Won't that be wonderful?"

The desire to manipulate an audience's sensibilities to the utmost was, Hitchcock always insisted, the root of his love of cinema. But he also insisted that for him the real challenge and real joy were in the creation of the motion picture *on paper* — the story conferences, the approval of script, the storyboard and camera planning — and that the actual filming was boring and annoying. "His main purpose in life," said Lehman, "may not have been the one that appears to be so obvious — namely, the making of movies. He had to make them, of course, to keep the franchise on his reputation, his fortune, and his life-style. But his greatest pleasure, his true raison d'être, may have been just to feel comfortable, to sit and spin tales and play with ideas, to be at ease, eating, drinking, without anxiety — and making movies, after all, was hard work and produced considerable anxiety in him.''

Be that as it may, the production moved on to Chicago in September, and then to Rapid City and to Mount Rushmore. Hitchcock was still the star of the company everywhere.

But then the United States government stepped in with an objection to the film — not to the brightly cynical attitude the script took toward American intelligence officers, but to the use of Mount Rushmore. A newsman had asked Hitchcock about the climactic chase, and, taking a paper napkin, Hitchcock had drawn the faces of the presidents and had then indicated, with a trail of dots, the course of the scramble over the monument.* The eager journalist kept the napkin and published it in the local newspaper, and by the time the crew arrived at Rapid City a notice had arrived from the Department of the Interior revoking the permit for the use of the monument because of "patent desecration." This news reached the national press at once, and one irate editor suggested that "Mr. Hitchcock go back home to England and draw people scampering on the Queen's face."

"Due to the objection of the government," Hitchcock later explained, "we weren't allowed to have any of the figures on the faces even in the interior studio shots. . . . We were told very definitely that we could only have the figures slide down between the heads of the presidents. They said that after all, this is the shrine of democracy." By the time they returned to Los Angeles for indoor photography (from September 17 to December 17), the Department of the Interior reissued the production company a permit to use mock-ups of the Mount Rushmore faces "on condition that only the shoulder, or below the chin-line" was used in close-up shots involving live actors.

But with the help of Robert Boyle, who had designed the sets for *Saboteur* and *Shadow of a Doubt,* Hitchcock prepared the visual design of the film in such a way that nothing seemed sacrificed. "No director I've worked with knew as much about films as he did," according to Boyle. "A lot of directors I worked with knew a great deal, but they didn't have his technical skill. . . . He was always trying to make the visual statement, and there was no such thing as a throwaway shot.''

---

*Because of the physical impossibility, there was never any question of actually placing the actors on the faces of the mammoth Gutzon Borglum sculpture. The trip to Mount Rushmore was for the sake of some background shots and inserts at the cafeteria. The complicated final chase was filmed entirely at MGM studios.

The last ten minutes of the film comprise one of the most famous set pieces in Hitchcock's career — the realization of a longtime desire. He had at last celebrated the giant, impassive faces.

Although the tone and style of *North by Northwest* is sharply different from the films that preceded and followed it, it has some of the same concerns. After the dark obsession of *Vertigo,* Lehman's script for *North by Northwest* was a refuge for Hitchcock, a temporary respite from his hidden anxieties and his romantic fantasies. But it was also a response to critics who said that in his two previous films he had lost a comic sense.

With *Vertigo* and *North by Northwest,* Hitchcock concluded two quartets of films — four with James Stewart, four with Cary Grant. From *Rope* to *Vertigo,* Stewart was closer to a representation of Hitchcock himself than any presence until Sean Connery's in *Marnie.* Elsewhere one of Hollywood's clearest exponents of the ordinary man as hero, Stewart's image was reshaped by Hitchcock to conform to much in his own psyche. He is in important ways what Alfred Hitchcock *considered himself:* the theorist of murder (in *Rope*); the chair-bound voyeur (in *Rear Window*); the protective but decidedly manipulative husband and father (in *The Man Who Knew Too Much*); the obsessed, guilt-ridden romantic pursuer (in *Vertigo*). These four roles provided James Stewart with the most substantial roles of his career and Hitchcock with an alter ego attractive enough to engage the sympathies of his audience.

Cary Grant, on the other hand, represents what Hitchcock *would like to have been:* the suave, irresponsible playboy (in *Suspicion*); the ultimate savior of a blond he nearly destroys (in *Notorious*); the wrongly accused hero who wins the glamorous Grace Kelly (in *To Catch a Thief*); and finally (in *North by Northwest*) the theatergoing executive whose frantic, perilous journey ends with the blond lifted up from espionage to bed.

January and February 1959 were spent mostly in editing rooms and the scoring studio, as Hitchcock supervised what he termed, in a memorandum to MGM production chief Sol Siegel, "a lot of rough spots, necessary retakes and photographic flaws." He conceded that there might be a number of corrections to make, but said that it would "take an audience to tell us what else to cut." This memo — a full page of troubleshooting, including a request that Siegel see the rough cut and make suggestions of his own — is an important one, because it is so much at variance with what Hitchcock maintained publicly about *North by Northwest* — namely, that the final film is only what he had prepared and that studio pressure had not forced on him a single change.

The truth, according to the legal correspondence and production files, is quite different. Although it was MGM's stated policy "to defer to him even when we had no legal obligation to do so" (as Kenneth MacKenna reminded the New York office), the executives did in fact offer some important points about the final cut, which Hitchcock eventually heeded. In bargaining over these, however, Hitchcock managed one moral victory. After all the trouble with the Department of the Interior and the National Park Service, he wanted to remove a credit acknowledging their cooperation. There had been nothing but trouble and delays and adverse publicity in obtaining all the necessary permissions, and citizen Hitchcock especially resented the authorities' insistence that in the film "the enemies of Democracy are defeated at the Shrine of Democracy itself." That is indeed what happens — but the federal government's bureaucratic guardians of democracy were stripped of cinematic recognition.

During the weeks of final editing and dubbing, on March 25 and 26, Hitchcock took time to direct yet another teleplay — *Banquo's Chair,* a wittily ambiguous ghost story based on a slight tale by Rupert Croft-Cooke. John Williams was enlisted once again, this time to play a retired detective who asks an actress to impersonate the spirit of a murdered woman, thus to trap the conscience of the suspected criminal. The ploy works — except that the spirit turns out to be perhaps genuine.

In April, while a second-unit crew on *North by Northwest* reworked some exterior photography and the suggestive final shot of a train entering a tunnel, Hitchcock took Herbert Coleman, Henry Bumstead, and Samuel Taylor to London. The purpose of the trip was to scout locations and to research courtroom procedures for the next film, to be adapted by Taylor from the novel *No Bail for the Judge,* by Henry Cecil (pseudonym of Henry Cecil Leon, a British judge). The original scenarist was to have been Ernest Lehman, but Lehman had developed misgivings about the project and had withdrawn before starting, even as he continued to revise *North by Northwest.* During the shooting of that film's crop-dusting sequence in Bakersfield, California, Hitchcock, angry at what he considered Lehman's defection, had refused to speak to his writer for four straight days.

The new project, one Hitchcock passionately wanted to realize, was complicated by emotional and personal problems from the very first day. Departing from Los Angeles International Airport, Hitchcock seemed more agitated, more anxiously supervisory of what he considered his "people" than ever before. Quietly jealous of family members who took his associates' attention away from himself, Hitchcock barely noticed the presence of Henry Bumstead's wife, or of their children, or of the Coleman family, who had come to say good-bye. Once a project was underway, there was to be no distraction, no turning back for considerations of home or personal relations. This was a corollary of what he expected of actresses who might also be young wives: it was unthinkable that they would put home or family or pregnancy above their commitment to him. "It was a shame," Herbert Coleman said sadly. "He just didn't know how to relate to people."

Once again, Hitchcock and Taylor had done a great deal of preparation. "The visual story was really completed, shot for shot, when we started to work on the dialogue," the writer remembered. "We were going to make the film in London, and we had to do some research about the courts and the underworld — particularly, the way of life of London's prostitutes." Everyone connected with the project agreed that it was going to be one of the great Hitchcock films — and even before the script was complete, he had his cast: a brief treatment submitted through the stars' agents had convinced Audrey Hepburn, Laurence Harvey, and John Williams that the story was brilliant and that the film could show them all to their best advantage. Regarding Hepburn, Hitchcock told the London press on arriving, "I'm quite prepared to try a cool brunette if I come across one."

The story certainly had its unsavory aspects, but Hitchcock told Taylor they would avoid the sensational. It was the tale of a barrister (Audrey Hepburn) whose father (John Williams) is a judge of capital cases at Old Bailey Court. Walking home one evening, he leaps to prevent a taxi from hitting a dog, but loses his footing, falls, and injures his head. Mistaken for a drunk as he staggers away, he is taken by a prostitute to her home. He awakens in the morning to find her body stretched across his, with a knife in her back. He calls the police, says he remembers very little, but also says that he must have committed the crime.

Taken to prison, he is visited by his barrister daughter, who is convinced of her father's innocence. She goes to his home and surprises a gentleman thief (Laurence Harvey), with whom she strikes a bargain: she will not turn him over to the police if he will help her enter the London underworld of thieves and prostitutes and find the person responsible for the murder. From here, they join forces and exonerate the judge, but not before several twists of the plot involve them in more danger than she expected.

"Now, Sam," Hitchcock said to Taylor one morning after breakfast at Claridge's, "I've arranged for you to interview some ex-prostitutes. It's all been set up over at Paramount's offices here in London." And so it was. "The Paramount office," according to Taylor, was managed by two charming elderly ladies. They went to the police for help and came up with an ex-prostitute who was then working as a secretary in an insurance company. (I remember thinking that I wasn't at all sure she had improved her situation in the world.) So we sat down to talk and she recounted some rather bizarre stories — sexual sadism and masochism and all sorts of strange specialties. And when I went back to Hitch, of course he insisted I tell him everything in great detail. He adores all such stories, since, after all, he had admitted for years that the vice museums in London and Paris and other places totally fascinated him.

As the weather turned warmer, their research and writing continued at an astonishing pace. With Bumstead and Coleman engaged in pre-production designs and research, the whole film was, typically, taking shape on paper, and by the time they returned to Los Angeles in late May every camera angle, every dressed set, every spoken word, and every element of suspense and laughter had been keyed into the script. When this screenplay was delivered to Paramount, an executive wanted to know from Hitchcock what "all that stuff" meant. "These pieces of paper," he replied coolly, "are in the process of becoming what will one day be referred to by you as *our picture.*"

But "our picture" was, almost at once, and in spite of the smooth and detailed preproduction, doomed never to reach the screen. While finishing work on *The Unforgiven* in Mexico, Audrey Hepburn received the final script of *No Bail for the Judge.* "When she read it," according to Herbert Coleman, "that was it — the Hitchcock film was virtually canceled from that minute." Although Hepburn had agreed to do the picture, she objected to the addition of a scene in which she was to be dragged into Hyde Park and raped. Samuel Taylor insisted, years later, that the scene was to be filmed very discreetly; others among Hitchcock's associates, however, remembered that it was planned explicitly enough to cause Audrey Hepburn considerable anxiety.

And it is worthwhile to note that her new film, *The Nun's Story,* opened on June 18, 1959, at Radio City Music Hall and was soon playing to full houses everywhere. It is commonly agreed that the role of Sister Luke was her finest achievement. Robert Anderson's sensitive script and Fred Zinnemann's painstaking direction had provided her with the role of her career — one whose quiet integrity, inner struggle, and anguished sense of purpose she was not at all anxious to undermine by rapidly inverting her public image. Within days of her receipt of the finished Hitchcock script, she requested further time for recuperation at her home in Switzerland, and from there word was sent that she was pregnant and would have to be released from the film.

Hitchcock was in New York when he received the news, and the corridors of the Saint Regis Hotel shook with a rare outburst of anger. Then he was stung by a further slap: *North by Northwest* was to follow *The Nun's Story* at Radio City in mid-July, but after the first few days it was clear that Zinnemann's film — the Hepburn vehicle — would be held over and that Hitchcock's would be delayed at least a month. During meetings with MGM executives in New York, Hitchcock suggested they build up more advance publicity for his film. At the same time, he cabled Paramount that *No Bail for the Judge* was canceled immediately.

"I spent more than $200,000 on *No Bail for the Judge* and then decided against doing it," Hitchcock said later, after refusing to take up the film with another star.* "They said to me, 'But you can't just let all that money go,' and I said, 'If we go on you will lose three million dollars,' and then they asked no further questions." Like Selznick and Warner before, and those at Universal after, the executives at Paramount realized that to hold Hitchcock to a work in which he had lost interest would be to court disaster.

Hitchcock's mood was not lightened by the events of the following months. The image of Audrey Hepburn attended him everywhere. *North by Northwest* was eventually delayed until *The Nun's Story* had been booked in every major American city. Then, at the San Sebastian International Film Festival, the two were in competition for first prize; Hitchcock lost. And at the Venice Film Festival, *The Nun's Story* was the hit of the season and *North by Northwest* was seen only outside of competition. Whenever Hitchcock arrived for publicity and press events, the photograph of Audrey Hepburn, covered chastely from head to toe as a Belgian nun — cool, but neither blond nor brunette, and nothing like a rape victim — gazed calmly from theater marquees, magazines, newspapers, and posters. It is unlikely that the irony amused him.

And so he continued the promotional tour for *North by Northwest* with less than cheerful enthusiasm. On July 1 he was in Chicago, where he was joined by Eva Marie Saint, Leo G. Carroll, and an army of journalists for a glittering, old-fashioned movie premiere, complete with champagne reception, fleets of Mercedes-Benz limousines to transport the guests of honor, and crowds of fans restrained by police barricades.

---

*Samuel Taylor pointed out that there was another complication: recent laws in London exacting harsh penalties against prostitutes for public solicitation. Key moments of their story depended on such importuning and, according to Taylor, were thus rendered implausible by the new ordinances. But this point of plot could have been reworked; and in any case, Herbert Coleman and others always maintained that it was Hitchcock's fury over the loss of Audrey Hepburn that really made him abandon the film.

Since the New York premiere was delayed, Hitchcock decided to return to Hollywood, where he took advantage of his contract with Laurence Harvey. In three days, from July 7 to 9, he filmed the teleplay *Arthur,* in which Harvey (in a variation on Lord Dunsany's "Two Bottles of Relish") grinds up the body of a woman he has strangled and feeds her to his chickens. Brusquely directed, this is the first Hitchcock production with a blunt and angry violence exercised against a female protagonist. In every preceding work for television and theatrical release (with the exception of *Strangers on a Train,* which was remarkably faithful to the novel), the principal woman is treated with a measure of sympathy — most especially in the quartet of feature films that had just preceded. But in *Arthur* — and in the film Hitchcock quickly substituted for *No Bail for the Judge* — there emerged a style that radically departed from everything that had preceded during thirty-five years of filmmaking.

By mid-summer of 1959, Hitchcock had decided on the unexceptional contrivance of a horror thriller as the basis for his next feature: *Psycho,* by Robert Bloch, the author of a number of the stories adapted for his television series (and directed by others). And with this project there occurred an almost instantaneous change in Hitchcock's sensibilities. Of all his films, *Psycho* is the most famous — and the most shocking for audiences both then and later. Its legendary shower murder changed the course of Hollywood history, and although few filmmakers matched its technical virtuosity, many tried to imitate its powerful sensual violence.

To attribute this new violence — aimed almost entirely against women from *Arthur* and *Psycho* onward — to an accumulation of resentment against Vera Miles, Kim Novak, and Audrey Hepburn, among others, would be perhaps simplistic, although it is hard to avoid seeing a connection between Hitchcock's increasingly chilly remarks at the time and the ugly fate to which essentially sympathetic women were subjected in his films from this time forward. All that summer he continued to complain to the press about his leading ladies: Hepburn was no longer "possible," and there was still a problem with Vera Miles, who remained under contract to him. He said she was supposed to have been his great star but had preferred pregnancy: "Then she divorced her husband, Gordon Scott — he's one of the Tarzans, you know — and now she wants me to tell her what she's going to do next. She cost me several hundred thousand dollars. *I* don't know what I'm going to do with her. Movie careers have a rhythm, you know. She broke the rhythm, and it means making a whole new start."

But there was perhaps something else, emerging from a deeper point within him, that pushed Hitchcock's anger to a fuller artistic outlet. "He truly thought that he never got angry," according to Ernest Lehman. "In fact, he told me he didn't believe in anger; it was a foolish, wasteful emotion. But the truth was that there were times when he was seething with anger — all of it carefully repressed." And this was one of those times in his life.

The women in the Hitchcock stories had become increasingly remote but, at the same time, increasingly threatening. The overtly sexual invitations of Laura Elliott in *Strangers on a Train,* visually detailed with surprising explicitness, had invited — almost justified — her strangling by Robert Walker. But from that point on, the anger abated, and the women — as represented by Anne Baxter, Grace Kelly, Vera Miles, and Kim Novak — were revealed to be emotionally challenging but for the most part physically unthreatening. They were the carriers of certain erotic energies that might be illusory and were certainly deceptive, but their coolness was a calculated safeguard — just the way Hitchcock preferred the women and the actresses in his own life. ("I can't stand those women who wear their sex around their neck like baubles — no mystery about them.")

But after that remoteness was revealed to have been (in *Vertigo* and *North by Northwest*) largely Hitchcock's own creation, and not indeed something within the characters themselves, something shifted in his personality from latency to actuality, from resentment of his own unrealized erotic longings to a fierce anger toward those who aroused those unrealizable longings. This was never articulated, of course, and perhaps it was never even acknowledged, but it was clear in the new dark tone his films adopted.

When *North by Northwest* was released nationally, it was praised by the critics and the public as one of Alfred Hitchcock's great films and one of the best films of the year; and ever since it has been rightly considered a classic of the comic-thriller genre. In its style, its wit, its easy glamour, and its encapsulation of the richest Hitchcock images, Ernest Lehman had given the director a story and screenplay that ranks among the sharpest and most mature Hitchcock and Hollywood ever had.

Just when they heard the good news about the film's reception, Hitchcock and Alma left for several weeks at Santa Cruz, where the quiet was disturbed only by an accident on his sixtieth birthday. As a florist was delivering a gift, their beloved Philip of Magnesia bounded in front of the truck and was killed. The Hitchcocks almost at once replaced him with two West Highland white terriers named Geoffrey and Stanley, who subsequently made their screen debut in *The Birds* on their master's leash, and who gave their names to the registered production company for *Marnie*, which was distributed as "A Geoffrey Stanley Production."

Back in Los Angeles, the Hitchcocks accepted, to Anne Baxter's surprise and delight (since such acceptances by the Hitchcocks were rare), an invitation to her home for dinner. "My poodle Petunia adored him," she recalled. "I remember after dinner he sat quietly on the sofa, stroking the dog, digesting the dinner. It was the most peaceful I'd ever seen him. No facade was necessary — no strangers or interviewers were staring at him. It was just we three. Alma knew him and I knew him, and he knew that neither of us, nor the dog, would talk back."

For three days near the end of August Hitchcock directed perhaps the strangest teleplay of his career. Joan Harrison had sent him a selection of properties, and he chose Stirling Silliphant's script based on A. E. W. Mason's short story "The Crystal Trench" — the story of a woman who waits many years for a great thaw to release her husband from imprisonment within a glacier. It was photographed by Hitchcock with a curious emphasis not on the complex feelings of the wife, but on the blank and frozen stare of the husband, who gazes in apparent repose while actually in a timeless twilight of guilt — for a locket he clutches reveals a secret love. The script and the final teleplay suggest an emotional autobiography of Hitchcock himself: the emotionless gaze of the husband resembles the director's own deadpan attitude to camera and viewers each week, and the motif of fidelity and hidden passion has its Hitchcockian counterpart, too, in his relationship with Alma and his yearning for several of his leading ladies.

Joan Harrison had been ready with another suggestion earlier that summer. She had in mind a young writer to adapt Robert Bloch's *Psycho* for Hitchcock. But when the writer delivered a first draft and left for a holiday, Hitchcock knew a complete overhaul was necessary. On the advice of several MCA executives, Hitchcock interviewed Joseph Stefano, a composer and lyricist who had begun his screenwriting career just recently with *The Black Orchid*. The two of them settled in for several weeks of story conferences and Stefano soon discovered the pattern that was familiar to every other writer engaged by Hitchcock. "He loved to sit and gossip," according to the scenarist "and then we would have lunch and somehow get around to talking about the picture. But he left me pretty much on my own after we had discussed the general idea of a scene. He wanted to talk about almost anything else but the job at hand. And I felt that if it was going to be done the way he wanted, I'd have to see his films, so I asked to have a number of them screened for me."

Hitchcock insisted on fidelity to the basic story — although he took Stefano's advice and made the leading characters more sympathetic. *Psycho* remained, in outline, true to the novel. It is the story of a woman who steals $40,000 from her employer and plans a new life with the debt-burdened lover she intends to marry. Stopping at a lonely motel on the way to him, she meets the proprietor, a shy man apparently under the tyranny of a powerful mother. While taking a shower at the motel, the young woman is attacked — by the old mother, it seems — and brutally stabbed to death. After a private detective is also killed as he is searching the house of mother and son, the dead woman's fiancé and sister investigate on their own. Before another act of psychopathic madness occurs, it is discovered that the old lady has been long dead, her identity "kept alive" by the true killer: the deranged son who murdered her and assumed her identity.

Stefano's script took shape quickly and much to Hitchcock's pleasure ("Alma liked your opening scenes very much" was the only way Hitchcock could express his satisfaction and was the single moment of appreciation he offered the writer). Because Hitchcock intended to make the film as cheaply as possible — he wanted to produce a low-budget thriller that was superior to the other low-budget thrillers that flourished that year — Hitchcock decided to use his television crew and studio and to cast the picture as inexpensively as possible.* Anthony Perkins owed Paramount a picture, and he could be signed at a reasonable fee, as could Janet Leigh (who, like Perkins, was eager to work for Hitchcock), John Gavin (another Paramount player), and Vera Miles, who, Hitchcock figured, might just as well be put to work since she was being paid a weekly contract salary in any case.

Hitchcock was always as parsimonious with salary as he was with praise. Aware that people's careers were advanced by simple association with him, he was usually able to negotiate the lowest salaries. His most valuable assistants ordinarily received the minimum permissible. On the other hand, he could show sudden concern for his colleagues' financial benefit — especially if there was an outside source of funds to cover the expense. Ernest Lehman recalled the director's secondhand beneficence.

> One day Hitch told me that he thought MGM should pay me for my original story for *North by Northwest*. I told him I couldn't expect that — after all, I was under weekly contract to the studio. "Then *I'll* ask them," he said. And

---

*\*Psycho* was brought in at a budget of $800,000, and within six months of its release Paramount drafted a check to Alfred Hitchcock in excess of $2 million for his services on the film. Long before his death, that amount was realized more than ten times over.

he did. As a result of his going out on that limb for me, MGM paid me a bonus of $25,000. He certainly didn't have to do that, but he could have these sudden generous urges of the spirit that were quite memorable. I'm sure many people were touched by these surprising, impulsive moves of his.

Nevertheless, Hitchcock's employees ordinarily agreed to accept substandard fees — perhaps out of admiration for their boss, perhaps out of hope for continued work with him. Whatever the motivation, they all knew that actors' salaries, especially those of major stars, infuriated him.

While Stefano completed his script, Hitchcock and Alma departed, in mid-October, for the premieres of *North by Northwest* in England and France. But before they left, Herbert Coleman announced that he was soon to quit Hitchcock's employment — before *Psycho* went before the cameras. "There were two reasons for this," Coleman said. "I didn't much care for the sort of movie that it was shaping up to be. But I also wanted to strike out on my own as a producer and director. After all, I'd been with Hitch for six years and worked closely with him on seven films. I'd learned a great deal, but now I felt I wanted to grow, and to stretch my talents further." To Coleman's surprise, Hitchcock took the news rather badly.

He just couldn't understand me, and he wouldn't even talk to me for weeks afterward. I think he felt he owned me and my family for life. He felt this way about others, too. He just couldn't imagine that we'd want a change in our careers, or the chance to broaden our experience. I said I wanted to remain a friend, but for a while he made that difficult. I don't think Hitch ever really formed any lasting friendships. He was afraid that if he did, he would have to give of himself, and he simply didn't know how to do that in any way except in a movie.

One set of relationships that remained constant, however, involved Hitchcock's agents and financial advisers. At this time MCA's chief officers and Hitchcock's representatives (Jules Stein, Lew Wasserman, Herman Citron, Arthur Park, and Edd Henry) were undertaking the complicated negotiations by which MCA would become a major conglomerate and the parent company of, among other subsidiaries, Universal Pictures. There had always been a strong bond of interdependence between MCA and Hitchcock, and after the famous merger was completed it was also arranged for Hitchcock to leave Paramount Pictures and go over to Universal. There, by exchanging the rights to *Psycho* and to his television programs for corporate stock in 1962, he became MCA's third-largest stockholder.

Government decisions soon compelled MCA to yield its agency activities (because of charges of conflicts of interest), but Herman Citron, Arthur Park, and George Chasin formed a talent agency that, to the time of Hitchcock's death, continued to represent him. With the vigilance of Wasserman at MCA/Universal and with Citron as negotiating agent, Hitchcock was assured of fierce loyalty on both sides, extraordinary contracts, and the accumulation of fabulous wealth for the last two decades of his life.

During the glorious European autumn that year, the Hitchcocks enjoyed a gala welcome in London, then a week in Paris before their return to New York and Los Angeles in mid-October. Arthur Pincus of MGM, arranging the publicity trip, wrote to the studio's Paris office about the conditions of Hitchcock's cooperation with the press:

A suite at the Plaza Athénée is a *sine qua non* of Hitchcock's visit. He puts it quite simply: He will not receive newspaper people in his bedroom, and he will not receive them in a public room of the hotel or anywhere else. It must be in his own suite or no interviews.

His insistence on seeing one interviewer at a time stems from a personal idiosyncrasy. In broad terms it goes something like this: He feels he can be charming and persuasive with one person, but he feels lost and uncommunicative when a group is present. In any case, this is what he wants and this is what he will have to get. With regard to his schedule in Paris, this is what he wants understood.

In a matter of weeks, from late November until early January, Hitchcock directed *Psycho* at the Revue Studios, the television branch at Universal Pictures that Paramount rented for him.* Everything was done in utmost secrecy. The clapper-board and company designation for the film was "Wimpy," the better to throw everyone off the track and discourage reading of the novel that had just appeared.

"I enjoyed making *Psycho,*" Anthony Perkins said. "In fact, I accepted the film before I'd even read the script. [Hitchcock and I] got on very well, and he let me make several changes and suggestions. It was my idea that I should eat candy throughout the film. I thought it would be more interesting if the killer were a compulsive candy-eater." Perkins had no part in the legendary shower sequence, however, for he was in New York that week preparing a Broadway role; Hitchcock used a stand-in for the shadowy figure of the man disguised as the old woman.

"From the start," Joseph Stefano recalled, "Hitchcock had decided

---

*Because he had decided to use the crew of the television series, Hitchcock engaged John L. Russell as cinematographer instead of Robert Burks. The director insisted, however, on his veteran editor George Tomasini.

to use a nude professional model for the shots in which a torso would be glimpsed, so he wouldn't have to cope with a trembling actress." About that central 'sequence, which has evoked more study, elicited more comment, and generated more shot-for-shot analysis from a technical viewpoint than any other in the history of the cinema, Hitchcock always retained a cool attitude. And rightly so, for he delegated the design and the shooting of it to the brilliant artist who had created the title designs for *Vertigo* and *North by Northwest*, and who, eventually, would do so for *Psycho*, too. "I'm going to get Saul Bass to do a storyboard for the shower scene," he told Joseph Stefano when they reached this point in the script, "so we know exactly what we're going to do."

For Janet Leigh, this role and this scene provided the challenge of her career.

He sent me the book before I agreed to do the role, and he told me the small and not very interesting part of Marion Crane would be improved and made more sympathetic. And it was. By the time we were halfway through photography, everyone knew we had a good picture, but no one had any idea it was going to make history.

He told me he hired me because I was an actress. "I'm not going to direct every nuance," he said. "But if you don't come up with what I need, I'll bring it out of you — and if you give too much, I'll tone it down. What you do has to fit into my framework and within my camera angle." I took him quite literally, and I knew my range and intention had to be for him and with him, and we related to one another very respectfully.

The planning of the shower sequence was left up to Saul Bass, and Hitchcock followed his storyboard precisely. Because of this, although we worked on it for almost a week, it went very professionally and very quickly. But it was, of course, very grueling to stand in a shower getting drenched for a week.

As it happened, Hitchcock made two important — and personally revealing — additions to Bass's designs: the quick shot of the knife entering the woman's abdomen (done by a fast-motion reverse shot), and the shot of blood and water running down the drain. "It had been my idea to do it entirely as a bloodless sequence without overt violence," according to Saul Bass, "but he insisted on inserting those two shots." And to the description of the brutal murder in the screenplay — only generally stated by the writer — Hitchcock added to shot 116: "The slashing. An impression of a knife slashing, as if tearing at the very screen, ripping the film." If there is a vicious anger throughout *Psycho*, this is the single moment that spreads that anger before and after it.

But it was not the brutality of this sequence that caused alarm at Paramount: it was the unprecedented shot (and sound) of a toilet being flushed. This, not the scarcely glimpsed, soft-focus nudity in the shower, was the most iconoclastic image in the picture — more influential than Hitchcock's killing off of the leading lady almost halfway through the film. Toilet imagery, as mentioned, and allusions to bodily functions not only surfaced in Hitchcock's humor — they also mark a recurrent, obsessive motif in his films. Everything about *Psycho* was bold; and in Hitchcock's mind, perhaps nothing was so bold as this explicit lavatory detail.*

The technique, the planning, George Tomasini's editing, and Bernard Herrmann's shrieking score for strings gave the shower scene precisely the effect Hitchcock wanted. (Originally he had designed the shower murder to be accompanied only by the cries of the woman and the splashing of the water. Herrmann, however, asked Hitchcock to hear the music he had composed for it, and afterward Hitchcock had to admit that the score significantly improved the scene.)

As part of Hitchcock's desire to direct the audience more than the actors, he insisted that when *Psycho* was released no one be allowed into the theater once the film began. The advertising campaign reflected his desire and marked a new aggressiveness — for he was now making demands on and intimidating his viewers even before they came to see his films. And the tactic extended to the critics as well. "Hitchcock's major sin," reflected Kenneth Tynan some years later, "was to have antagonised the critics before they ever saw the picture. He had urged them by letter not to divulge the ending, and he had announced that nobody would be admitted to the cinema once the film had begun. Thus they went to the press show already huffy and affronted; and what they reviewed was not so much the film itself as the effect of its publicity on their egos."

"I remember the terrible panning we got when *Psycho* opened," Hitchcock said. "It was a critical disaster. One critic called it 'a blot on an honorable career' and a couple of years later he reviewed [Roman] Polanski's *Repulsion* by saying it was 'a psychological thriller in the classic style of Hitchcock's *Psycho*.' My films went from being failures to masterpieces without ever being successes. Perhaps the films are too subtle for critics. They seem to take about a year to sink in." But very quickly the public made the decision, and the profit was enor-

---

*The toilet was a prominent prop in *Secret Agent*, too; and Hitchcock insisted on the euphemistic initials *B.M.* whenever he could (on John Hodiak's chest tattoo in *Lifeboat*, and engraved on a ring in *Shadow of a Doubt*). The toilet is a hiding place in more than fifteen Hitchcock films, and it is often the place where lovemaking is prepared or where spies discover secrets — as, for example, in *Vertigo*, *North by Northwest*, *Marnie*, *Torn Curtain*, and *Topaz*. His adolescent fixation continues right up through *Family Plot*, where the toilet has been modernized into a portable, chemically-controlled contraption.

mous. "I was sufficiently interested in the picture's success to contact Stanford University Research Institute so they could find out why it was such a hit. But when they wanted $75,000 to do the research job, I told them I wasn't *that* curious."

Filmmakers and students and moviegoers have been more curious about this film than any other Hitchcock picture, for in it (with considerable assistance from his creative associates) he formulated a treatment and supervised a scenario infinitely richer than the novel on which it is based, and he created a masterpiece within its genre. *"Psycho* is important," according to Joseph Stefano,

not so much for what it is, but for what it is not. It lacks everything predictable in Hitchcock up to that time. The characters in it were not people he knew or wanted to know — they were not the Cary Grant or Grace Kelly or James Stewart types.

But he had reached a point in his professional life when he was ready for a totally different kind of picture. In his previous films he told things about himself he thought were true, but in *Psycho* he told more about himself, in a deeper sense, than he realized. He had been very concerned about his health, and I think he made the picture at the very time he was grappling with his own mortality. After all, he had been very ill in 1957, and Alma had been very ill in 1958. And then in 1959 along came this murderous film. I think it was the sudden-death aspect that involved him emotionally.*

Beyond such gothic elements as the desolate, remote setting, the forbidding gingerbread house, the dark and stormy night, the confined and demented relative, and the bizarre murders is another gothic element: the secret. Everyone in *Psycho* has a disguise or something to hide — the hidden treasure; the furtive plans of lunchtime lovers at the opening; wedding-day tranquilizers secretly taken by Janet Leigh's co-worker (Pat Hitchcock, in her last role for her father); the cash undeclared for taxes by the possessive father (Frank Albertson); the bottle of whiskey hidden in an employer's desk; the secrets of illicit affairs, stolen cash, concealed identities, and undiscovered murders. With the insistence of a man driven by the press of time, Hitchcock designed a gothic film whose every moment was so carefully interlocked and so organically arranged that the flow of events always seemed inevitable and casual, never forced or artificial. In imposing this stylistic unity, he made Stefano's script consistent with the visual design, the camera movements, the props, and the acting.

---

*To François Truffaut, Hitchcock said: "I think the thing that appealed to me and made me decide to do the picture was the suddenness of the murder in the shower, coming, as it were, out of the blue. That was about all."

But the most significant gothic element — the one Hitchcock had preferred for years and at last had the chance to synthesize within the appropriate genre — was the mirror. From the famous film *The Student of
Prague,* which had so impressed him in his teenage years, he had first
learned of the enormous emotional power of the mirror to convey schizophrenia in a dramatic narrative; and he had followed its increasingly
sophisticated use in *Der Andere, The Cabinet of Dr. Caligari, Secrets
of a Soul, M,* and *The Last Laugh.* In preparing *Vertigo,* Hitchcock had
told art director Henry Bumstead to use mirrors wherever possible, and
he gave the same direction to the crew on *Psycho,* a film in which
mirrors are endlessly accumulated: at the hotel; at the office, where Janet Leigh regards herself in a hand mirror; at her home; in her car; in a
used-car-lot washroom; at the motel counter and in the motel rooms;
and, most tellingly, in the room of the killer's "mother," where the
meaning of the double mirror becomes clear.

The mirror is not only, as in gothicism, a prop suitable for the representation of the split personality — it also marks the need for intro-
spection, as Hitchcock knew from his earlier reading of Tennyson's *The
Lady of Shalott,* Matthew Arnold's *Empedocles,* George Eliot's *Adam
Bede* and *Middlemarch,* and Dickens's *Our Mutual Friend.* Required in
his school years, these works presented to Victorian society the mirror
as an image of self-awareness. To see the world more clearly and to
partially disguise ourselves, insisted these books and Hitchcock's films,
one wears eyeglasses. But for a true glimpse of our divided selves, one
consults a mirror. ("I'll buy you a new mirror," Hitchcock had added
to the script of *Under Capricorn,* "and it'll be your conscience.")

The mirror as a symbol of the fractured personality is complemented
in *Psycho* by the "cutting" imagery: in Saul Bass's title designs, which
tear and split the names; in what Hitchcock called the basic geometry
of the film — the bisecting horizontals and verticals (a motif in part
established by a construction crane that cuts the horizon of Phoenix, by
the bed and bedposts of the hotel, by the standing John Gavin and the
supine Janet Leigh, and, most of all, by the horizontal motel and the
looming, vertical house); and in other suggestions of slashing — a telephone pole that "slices" Leigh's parked car; scythes and rakes suspended over heads in a hardware shop; and the murderer's raised knife.
The cutting imagery establishes a visual design in which conflict in the
viewer extends the conflict within the characters — and this could have
come effortlessly and naturally only from a visual genius intimately familiar with conflict himself.

But Hitchcock's carefully planned imagery and visual geometry do more than provide a neat collective symbol for the split personality. His relentless manipulation of the audience's identification with the characters gives the structure of *Psycho* a moral function: to reveal a split in the desires of the viewer, a split that is manifest in the clash between squeamishness and curiosity that is the essence of the picture.

The viewer's sentiments ride with the camera from simple gazing at Janet Leigh (in the opening scenes, when she is half-dressed) to wondering about her decision to steal (when she is again half-dressed) to wanting her to escape from her employer and a suspicious patrolman. In the same way that the viewer is led to identify emotionally with her plight while this sympathy clashes with one's intellectual rejection of her theft, so is there a conflict later in the viewer attitude Hitchcock creates toward Anthony Perkins. Shocked by the senseless shower killing, one nevertheless admires the thoroughness with which he cleans the bloody bathroom — a fastidiousness that recalls Hitchcock's boast that "when I leave the bathroom, everything is so clean you'd never know anyóne had been in there." Similarly, Hitchcock sets his camera so that after a car containing the corpse momentarily stops sinking into in a swamp, the viewer is relieved when it disappears at last with a septic gurgle. ("When Tony Perkins is disposing of his victim," said Hitchcock, "the audience is terribly alarmed when the car containing the body stops for a moment in the swamp! . . . . This is one of the great mysteries of the psychology of audiences.")

The point of view at the opening of the film in fact establishes this audience identification and attraction/repulsion response. The camera moves through a partially opened window and into a darkened room, finds an empty chair, moves over, and — just like the spectator in the movie theater — "sits" in the chair. The field of vision tilts up, and the first thing seen is a seminude couple, obviously caught in their intimacy; the first response in a viewer, therefore, is one of mixed pleasure and embarrassment, followed by a "clash of wills" that is elicited throughout the film, until a new meaning is revealed in the doctor's final remark, "When the mind houses two personalities, there is always a conflict, a battle." That this conflict should be created and perceived and sustained in the viewer of *Psycho* is a mark of true visual genius. ("You don't get a dissipated viewpoint with Hitchcock," as Janet Leigh said. "You get a very pure approach to each nuance, and to each moment.")

This audience manipulation has, then, an artistic and even a moral function. From first frame to last, the viewer is involved in this film as perhaps in no other film by Alfred Hitchcock. The act of watching *Psy-*

*cho*, in itself, implicates the viewer; and all the gazing involved — by the viewer, by Janet Leigh, by the suspicious patrolman, by Perkins — is shown to be a partial and imperfect seeing, mere watching without real vision or perception. (This is, of course, a classical motif — as old as the blind Oedipus who finally "sees," the blind seer Tiresias — and as modern as the shocking *Un Chien Andalou* by Dalí and Buñuel, for which Hitchcock admitted a deep admiration.) This is why Martin Balsam, the private eye, is stabbed in the eye; and why Vera Miles hits a suspended bare light-bulb, causing it to swing and cast shadows that make the empty eye sockets of the mother's skeleton seem to have darting eyes. Like all the seeing in the film, however, the skull's "gaze" is an empty, illusory, dead stare, recalling most of all the astonishing open stare of Janet Leigh's corpse — the stare that has its origin in her smug stare-smile early in the film, as she drives her car and considers her crime, and that points forward to the mad stare-smile of Perkins at the end, grinning at the triumph of death over life.*

The staring in Hitchcock's *Psycho* (as at the conclusion of so many of his teleplays) is not only morally sightless — it is a prelude to death. Thus, Perkins spies on Janet Leigh as she disrobes for her fatal shower. And to gain access to his concealed peephole, he removes from the wall a painting of Susanna and the elders, the biblical story (in Daniel 13) of a woman overtaken in her bath by voyeurs whose passions were aroused as they spied on her from a secret place as she prepared to bathe. The artistic representation of voyeurism and sexual exploitation is thus replaced, in the world of this film, by the action itself; and the knife murder, therefore, is deliberately recorded as a stylized rape scene, an artistic depiction beginning with close shots of a screaming mouth and a raised knife.

What Hitchcock makes clear, moreover, is the degree to which the audience is implicated in all this. One not only watches Perkins watching — the camera swings round and the viewer stares with him. The watching therefore has the moral function of a supreme irony — as ironic as the final protest of "Mother" from beyond the grave, who (like the chair-bound director and chair-bound viewer) cannot, as the voice says at the end, "do anything but just sit and stare, like one of his stuffed birds. They know I can't move a finger, so I'll just sit here quietly in case they do suspect me. They're probably watching me — well, let them. They'll see what kind of a person I am. I'm not even going to

---

*This motif — the illusory nature of what is seen in life — perhaps illuminates the significance of the haunting zoom shot to the crossed bronzed hands on Mother's vanity table: the illusion of gentle hands crossed in life or in death.

swat that fly! I hope they are watching! They'll see and they'll know, and they'll say, 'Why, she wouldn't even harm a fly!' "

Hitchcock's childhood habit of watching his family, his schoolmates, life itself, from the safety of the sidelines — the habit of a frightened boy who happened to have an artistic sensibility — received its severest assessment in this film, with its integral motif of the morality of the gaze (a theme nowhere suggested in Bloch's novel). In Hitchcock's major films, the moment when the predator becomes the prey is often linked with the moment of gazing: in *Rear Window,* it is when the killer, Raymond Burr, looks back at James Stewart; in *Vertigo,* the audience watches as Stewart twice watches and pursues Kim Novak; in *Psycho,* it is as the viewer moves at last through the rear window and *into* the screen to visually participate in what was only suspected and indirectly observed in *Rear Window* — it is as the killing is realized in all its full horror.

The eye is, in all this, the matrix of identity and guilt. The symbolism is the logical fulfillment of the twitching eyes of the murderer in *Young and Innocent,* the epitome of all the images of vision in Hitchcock's films — images that identify sinful gazing and faulty vision as the symptom of a pervasive guilt. Just as a murder in the animated Disney cartoon *Who Killed Cock Robin?* is made real by the characters in *Sabotage,* the Hitchcock film in which it appears, so the animation of the nightmare sequence in *Vertigo* is actualized by the grim discovery of deception shortly after; and in *Psycho* the painting of corrupt gazing and perverse intentions is transformed into reality by the unleashing of a monstrous, lunatic repression. The dialectic of watching and being watched has, by the end, received its ultimate treatment in *Psycho,* more than in any other film by Alfred Hitchcock.

All of this is expressed by Hitchcock's insistence on changing the killer's hobby from stuffing animals, in the novel, to stuffing only birds. The sexual wordplay is obvious — "stuffing birds" is the hobby of a sexual psychopath — and the gazing eyes of stuffed crows and owls can see nothing. "Owls belong to the night world" as Hitchcock pointed out; "they are watchers, and this appeals to Perkins's masochism. He knows the birds and he knows that they're watching him all the time. He can see his own guilt reflected in their knowing eyes." This explains other avian imagery: the crucial shot of Perkins knocking over a sketch of a bird when (in his "son personality") he discovers the body of Janet Leigh — the last "stuffed bird" is, aptly, a woman named Crane, who came from Phoenix (a city named for the mythic bird that returns from the dead); and why, when Perkins suggested candy, Hitchcock insisted it be candy corn, a confection that resembles the kernels pecked by chickens. (As will become clear, everything about *Psycho* points forward to and aesthetically necessitates Hitchcock's next feature film, *The Birds*.)

For all the study and all the structural analysis that *Psycho* has received, it was for a long time difficult, owing mostly to Hitchcock's obsessive secretiveness, to penetrate the brilliant gothic facade of the film and to see just how much of the director himself is in it. It is perhaps not enough to agree simply with Charles Bennett, who told Hitchcock quite openly that the film's cruelty showed its maker was "a sadistic son of a bitch"; or with the English critic who said it was the work of "a barbaric sophisticate." ("Who knows," Hitchcock replied, "she may be right.") To be sure, the film has a pervasive sense of doom, and even of monstrous and uncontrollable madness, that surpasses anything he had done before; and even the grotesque humor cannot finally mask a sense that Hitchcock describes not only the world of nightmare — which one could dismiss as fantastic and unreal — but the world of everyday, recognizable situations and emotions that are swallowed up in the kingdom of death.

That this picture followed the wounded romanticism of *Vertigo* and the genial cynicism of *North by Northwest* is, however, not so surprising. All three films have as their emotional focus a desperate, duplicitous blond; all three films have at the center a personality that is unknown (the real Madeleine Elster in *Vertigo*) or nonexistent (the fictitious George Kaplan, invented by intelligence agents in *North by Northwest*) or long dead (Mrs. Bates, the killer's mother in *Psycho*). Amid Hitchcock's desperate and desperately controlled emotional life, these films became a triptych of pain and delusion and death, created from the depths of private frustration and longing, without even the balm of deep friendship.

After the departure of Grace Kelly and the anguish of various perceived rejections by Vera Miles and Audrey Hepburn, something hardened in Hitchcock; something closed over his always fragile capacity for warmth. *Vertigo* was a summary of all his own romantic fantasies; it was artistically possible only because some measure of hope continued to survive in him, and because of the sensitive script he was given by Samuel Taylor. The cool adroitness of *North by Northwest*, with Ernest Lehman's spiky wit and a patina of political and personal distrust, did not cover over the fact that it was a bittersweet farewell to glamour and romance. And then there was the disruption of his plans for Audrey Hepburn and *No Bail for the Judge*.

Something new was happening in Hitchcock's movies, something laden with fears he had never fully represented on screen, something that caused the raging, murderous shout of *Psycho*.

*Herbert Coleman*

With Herbert Coleman
in France for the production of
*To Catch a Thief,* 1954

Directing Cary Grant and Grace Kelly
in *To Catch a Thief*

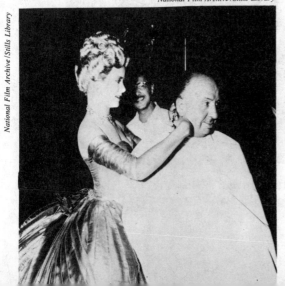

With Grace Kelly, 1954

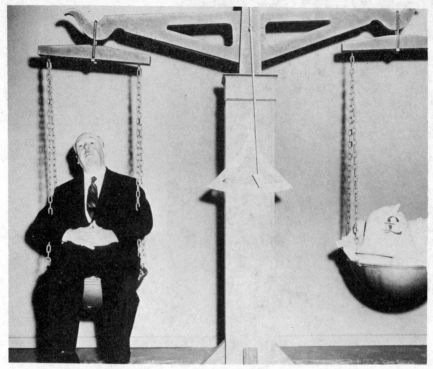

Introducing one of the television programs in 1955

Vera Miles arriving in New York for
filming of *The Wrong Man*, 1956

With actress Mary Scott, on the set of *Mr. Blanchard's Secret,*
a 1956 teleplay

Samuel Taylor

With Ernest Lehman during productio
of *North by Northwest*, 1958

Directing Kim Novak in *Vertigo*, 1957

Directing Janet Leigh in the shower sequence from *Psycho*, 1959

Tippi Hedren during the week-long filming of the final attack in *The Birds*, 1962

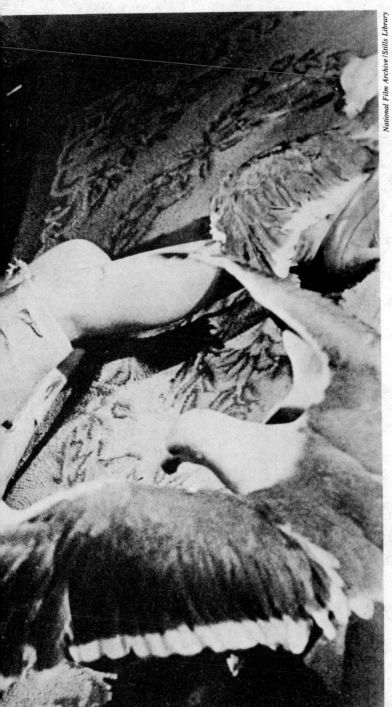

With Tippi Hedren, on the set of *Marnie*, 1963

Showing Suzanne Taylor how to strangle a woman
with one hand — Saint Moritz, 1966

New Year's Eve, 1966, at Saint Moritz with Suzanne and Samuel Taylor, and Alma

Receiving an honorary degree
from Columbia University, New York, 1972

With Alma in London, on the set of *Frenzy*, 1971

Celebrating the conclusion of *Family Plot* in 1975,
with Lew Wasserman (center) and Ernest Lehman

# Thirteen

1960–1964

Aт the beginning of his career, from 1925 through 1938, Alfred Hitchcock directed 23 feature films in England. Then, from 1939 through 1959 — from age forty to sixty — came the most prolific period in his life: 24 feature films, 2 short films, and 15 television shows, an impressive list by any standard of judgment. But then, from 1960 on, there was a drastic reduction in his creative output, and the tally from that year until his death in 1980 was 6 features and 5 television shows.

After *Psycho*, Hitchcock's financial fortune was forever assured, and soon a deal was struck that guaranteed him a creative home-base and the freedom to work essentially without interference. Also, he remained in amazingly good physical health for most of his last twenty years, although his indulgences at the table and the bar were never curbed for long; likewise, until the last few years his powers of reason and concentration were unaffected by any of the factors that might have modified those powers in others.

The reason for the cutback in production, then, must be sought elsewhere. And it was indeed something inside him that changed everything: a sad and ultimately destructive passion, pursued from behind a mask of love and activated with increasing indiscretion. He never recovered from this period. It seemed, forever after, to have killed something in him.

At the beginning of 1960 no one could have foreseen how close he was to disaster. In February he directed, with apparent diffidence, an hour-long teleplay called *Incident at a Corner*, with Vera Miles and George Peppard; Miles was once again cast as a woman who has imagined (or may have imagined) an event that throws several lives into disarray. Apart from this one exercise, however, Hitchcock undertook a prolonged vacation — actually a series of weekends at Santa Cruz — where he read a new novel sent for his consideration. Winston Graham's *Marnie* struck him as full of possibilities for a story of sexual intrigue (an aspect of adult life Hollywood was then beginning to confront more directly), but he put this aside until he could be sure of a leading lady attractive and strong enough for the enigmatic, frigid, compulsive thief.

But then in April, before leaving with Alma for Europe and Asia to attend international openings of *Psycho,* an item in the *Santa Cruz Sentinel* caught his attention and sent him back to the shelf of literary properties he had optioned but that still lay inactive. The paper reported that in La Jolla, California, on one quiet spring evening, over one thousand birds descended through a family's chimney, destroying most of the household goods and grotesquely injuring the housewife when many of them were caught in her hair. Hitchcock was at once reminded of Daphne du Maurier's strange short story "The Birds," published in a 1952 collection whose film option he had purchased. He reread the story, found it strong on atmosphere but weak on plot and character, and could not see a film emerging from it.

The trip took the Hitchcocks to Honolulu, Sydney, Tokyo, Osaka, Hong Kong, Singapore, Rome, Naples (whence they took the hydrofoil for a few days rest on the island of Ischia), and finally to Paris and London. During a short detour en route to Paris, Hitchcock's well-known predilection for wine was rewarded when the mayor of Dijon invested him as a Chevalier du Tastevin at the Burgundy Wine Festival in May. He then wore the ribbons of that fellowship at a banquet at Chez Max in Paris; hundreds cheered him there and at a festival of his films being presented at the Cinémathèque Française. François Truffaut, who had recently become an international celebrity himself after the release of his first feature film, *Les Quatre Cents Coups (The 400 Blows),* sat in rapt admiration, as did Claude Chabrol, who had followed his 1957 publication of a monograph on Hitchcock with four of his own films.

To everyone who was present that warm evening in late May 1960, it was clear that something more than the Parisian spring, the acrid smoke of Gauloises, and the bouquets of burundies was in the air. A devout homage was being offered to Hitchcock, and not just by autograph-seekers, but by the young directors who were splashing up new waves on the shores of film culture. And Hitchcock accepted it. "He loved the adulation," said screenwriter Joseph Stefano, who heard an account of it when Hitchcock returned to Los Angeles. "He loved the attention and the fuss and the fame, and if he didn't understand it, he didn't feel compelled to. It was good for business, and it was good for his ego.''

Robert Boyle, frequently Hitchcock's art director over a period of forty years, agreed. "Hitchcock appreciated other people's appreciation of him, and he did nothing to correct any impressions they might have of his genius. When they compared him to the great Russian filmmakers, he could easily discuss Eisenstein's *Potemkin* or Pudovkin's *Mother* as well as they'' — and this convinced them that he was their leader, the man who showed that the most popular form of entertainment was also a vehicle for the creation of art. And Hitchcock rigorously avoided any discussion of the content of his films. Only the technique interested him, and references to themes or motifs or concerns made him uneasy and inarticulate. But those references could obviously be left to others; he had become, as the *Herald Tribune* international edition proclaimed that week, "the idol of the Gallic avant-garde school.''

Hitchcock used the Paris fete to announce his next two projects — not because he was at all sure they would materialize (or even that he wanted them to), but because the event seemed to warrant news of the future, and neither for the first nor the last time he felt that something was expected of him. There was a French play by Robert Thomas he was going to film at 20th Century–Fox, he said — *Piège pour Un Homme Seul (Trap for a Solitary Man)* — and he delighted his audience by describing the plot, about a woman who returns after a brief and mysterious absence only to be rejected by her husband, who insists that she is not his wife. He also had in mind a story that had appeared in *Reader's Digest* called "Village of the Stars'' — about an airplane ordered to drop an atom bomb. Then countermanding orders come through, but the bomb has already been loosened and must be dropped somewhere. And at this maddening point, Hitchcock smiled and changed the subject.

In London for the premiere of *Psycho* ten days later, he wore the silk ribbons of the "Grand Officier de la Confrérie des Chevaliers du Tastevin'' at every publicity function held at Claridge's, lifting his dangling silver cup like a talisman and instructing reporters more on the fine points of vintage wines than on the plot of *Psycho,* which he declined to discuss.

Back home in early July, Hitchcock met with Ernest Lehman, who had an idea for a picture and had communicated briefly with Hitchcock's assistant Peggy Robertson during the director's absence. Lehman recalled the project's origins:

It all started with an idea I had that it might be exciting to do a whole Hitchcock suspense thriller in Disneyland, a background that the whole world was wanting to see — so why not bring it to the world?

The story would be about a popular entertainer, a jazz pianist, who had been blind from birth, whose sight is miraculously restored with an advanced double-corneal-transplant operation, and when he gets to Disneyland, which is the first place he wants to see, he discovers that he has "the eyes of a murdered man" and is soon on the trail of the killer, who is out to get *him*.

Hitch loved the idea and I fell to work on it immediately, with Jimmy Stewart in mind for the newly sighted adventurer.

While Lehman worked, Hitchcock made a brief reentry into Hollywood social life. David O. Selznick invited him to a party, and it was there, over cocktails, that Hitchcock told him how Audrey Hepburn's refusal to play the rape victim in *No Bail for the Judge* had forced him to abandon the project. Hitchcock was still furious over this, he told Selznick; she had no right to be choosy, he said, since she had failed to demonstrate that she was a star in America — an opinion neither shared by Selznick nor supported by the facts (she had won an Academy Award for *Roman Holiday* and had been nominated for *Sabrina* and *The Nun's Story*).

There was also talk that evening about another Audrey, for just then Hitchcock was directing Audrey Meadows to good effect in a teleplay based on Roald Dahl's *Mrs. Bixby and the Colonel's Coat* — a perfect vehicle for the actress and for Hitchcock. It was the story of a cheating wife whose lover gives her a mink coat. She tries to get the coat home by pawning it and giving the ticket to her dentist husband, saying she found it in the street. The husband returns the next day not with the mink, but with a worthless substitute — about which, of course, the wife can say nothing. On a subsequent visit to her husband's office, she finds his attractive nurse wearing the mink.

During the summer and early autumn, Hitchcock continued to meet irregularly with Lehman on the project tentatively titled *The Blind Man*. "Intriguing as my story idea was, I was running into seemingly insurmountable plot difficulties," Lehman remembered.

Instead of beating my head against the obstacles until I broke them, I started quietly looking for exit doors. Then, one fateful day, Walt Disney, after viewing *Psycho,* announced to the press that he would never even let his children see that film, much less allow its director to shoot a picture in his amusement park. That announcement became one of the straws that broke a writer's back, the other straw being the writer's philosophy that when the story-going got too tough, the tough got going — through the nearest exit.

Later, around Christmastime, I gritted my teeth and, with all kinds of apologies for my ineptitude, told Hitch that I was abandoning the project and moving on to other ventures, which disappointed him immensely. With total justification, he was, in his controlled and highly civilized manner, furious with me, and we exchanged very polite good-byes.

I must say, I wish he, or someone, had locked the doors and told me I couldn't leave because I still think it was a good idea, and with Hitch and me hanging in to the bitter end, I might have licked the screenplay — and with his visual imagination brought to play on the experiences of a blind man seeing the world for the first time, it could have been a memorable film.

This was then, another project that failed to come close to production — the third since Hitchcock had concluded *Psycho,* and the fourth in two years. No one would have been very much surprised if Hitchcock had taken a leisurely approach in trying to find a project to match *Psycho* in commercial appeal, but he felt compelled to keep looking vigorously; the acclaim he was receiving was also encouragement to continue his success. (In January 1961 the Hollywood Foreign Press Association cited him as "the great master of suspense for the international motion picture world.") With nothing readily available, however, he turned up more often at Revue Studios, and during the first week of 1961 he directed *The Horseplayer,* about a priest (Claude Rains) who on the advice of a parishioner and because the church needs a new roof bets church money on a sure win.

Hitchcock's visits to his television staff had another motive, however. He was looking for someone for *Marnie* — some new personality he might be able to hire cheaply, train intensively, and mold into a new star. But none of the actresses seemed right. About this time, he began to relax somewhat in his introductory appearances on the television program — in one he was even seen dragged, kicking and screaming, to a lunatic asylum. One of the crew said of this sort of thing: "It's a ham performance he would never tolerate from an actor in one of his own pictures. The humor is about on the same level as a parlor comedian mincing around in a woman's hat" — which Hitchcock also did for one introduction. "Once he turned up with an arrow sticking through his head and recited 'I shot an arrow in the air, it fell to earth, I know not where.' That's Hitchcock the clown. The Hitchcock I admire is that man sitting in a canvas chair studying the setup for the next scene to be shot. That's Hitchcock the camera."

Most of 1961 was a quiet, lonely year for the Hitchcocks. They spent numerous weekends in northern California, but most of these trips seem to have been planned at the last moment, in the absence of local invitations. Although it might seem that Mr. and Mrs. Alfred Hitchcock would be among the most desired guests in Hollywood, most people were uneasy about having them over. His discrimination about food and wine and cigars was well known, and he could, as Joseph Stefano pointed out, be depressingly petty and superior. "He would criticize people for minor things, as when he told about a young director who'd invited him to dinner. He thought it was outrageous that the butler wrapped an un-chilled wine in a napkin. He could go on endlessly about unimportant matters of etiquette like this, and a lot of people were put off by him."

Still looking for an actress, Hitchcock returned to Revue in July, where he took over from an ailing director the supervision of *Bang! You're Dead* — about a little boy who trots around town unaware that the gun he is pointing at passersby has live bullets left in its chamber. His game of Russian roulette is interrupted just in time by his frantic parents, and the bullet aimed at the family maid pierces a wall instead. The program had little interest for Hitchcock; he would return for only one more effort in television (which was beginning to bore him), and this would be a year later.

Then, as if it were one of the planned surprises of his films, some-thing occurred just after his birthday that settled his schedule for the next year and a half. In the Santa Cruz newspaper he read the story of yet another bird invasion, this one more widespread and more devastat-ing than that of the preceding year. A SEA BIRD INVASION HITS COASTAL HOMES, proclaimed the giant headline, and the violence was unnerving: windows were shattered, streetlamps broken, cars damaged, and pedes-trians nicked and soiled. At once Hitchcock was on the telephone to Joseph Stefano, who was under contract to write three more scripts for him. But when they met to discuss making a film from Daphne du Maurier's "The Birds," Stefano said that frankly he was not enthusias-tic about either birds or the story.

Discussing alternative writers with Alma and with Peggy Robertson, Hitchcock soon realized that since there was no plot or character devel-opment in the short story, he would have to have someone — preferably a novelist — who could provide these qualities; what attracted him to the story was the suddenness and inexplicability of the reversal of nat-ural order — the same qualities that had attracted him to *Psycho*. But he knew there would have to be a story with sympathetic characters. Samuel Taylor and Ernest Lehman had other commitments and, refusing advice, Hitchcock avoided contacting John Michael Hayes.

He turned instead to Evan Hunter, whom he had met briefly while directing *The Crystal Trench*. Among an impressive list of publications (some under the pseudonym Ed McBain), Hunter had contributed to the

Hitchcock mystery magazine, had had one of his short stories adapted
for a Hitchcock program, had himself adapted another writer's story for
the same series, had had two of his novels turned into films, and had
created a television series that was about to begin that season.

In September Hunter arrived at Hitchcock's Paramount offices to begin what would be the long and arduous task of developing *The Birds*.
"Hitchcock told me that he felt he was at the beginning of a golden
period of his career," Hunter said, recalling that Hitchcock had discussed with him the recent success of *Psycho* and the plans then being
formulated for the director's move to Universal Pictures. At the same
time, according to Hunter, Hitchcock's expectation of a "golden period" sounded like a self-imposed challenge. Referring to his five Academy Award nominations for best direction (most recently for *Psycho*),
Hitchcock had said: "Always a bridesmaid, never a bride." When they
began to discuss the project, Hitchcock told Hunter not to worry about
technical problems of birds or bird attacks, since that would be the task
of the art department and the special-effects team. "Our intention, he
told me, was simply to scare the hell out of people. Even more than he
had done in *Psycho*, he said he wanted to arouse intense emotions from
his audience."

Hitchcock's creative collaboration with Evan Hunter — like that with
many others in his life — began smoothly and cordially but ended am-
biguously, with a residue of resentment tempered, on Hunter's part, by
great respect. "He was a very possessive man," according to the writer.
"He virtually monopolized me and my family while we were in Los
Angeles, even though the monopoly was one of kindness. He hosted us
at dinners, took us to the races, made a Halloween visit to our children.
. . . We got on fabulously — for the time being, until the contretemps
over *Marnie*."

Hitchcock's monopoly over the scenarist was a creative and benevolent and generous one that, as Hunter was quick to admit, taught him
an infinity of things about the art of film. But another kind of monopoly,
over another kind of person and talent, was about to occur, and this had
its genesis one morning while Hitchcock and Alma were watching the
NBC network's *Today* show. He saw a commercial featuring an attractive, elegant blond who passed across the screen and smiled, turning
amiably in response to a little boy's wolf-whistle. Ironically, the advertisement was for Sego, a diet drink. But it was not the product that
interested him, it was the blond. That morning, he told his agents to
find out who she was, and that afternoon an appointment was made for
her — not with Hitchcock, whose name was not to be mentioned, but
with an executive at MCA.

The model, named Tippi Hedren, came for her meeting the following day — it would be to discuss television commercials, she thought, since her successful modeling career in New York had led her to relocate to California for that purpose. The next afternoon — Friday, October 13, 1961 — she met for a first interview, and was asked to leave her file of photographs and reel of commercial appearances. Over that weekend, unknown to her, Hitchcock and Alma reviewed the material. His decision was immediate and irreversible; all that had to be determined was the model's reaction to an offer.

On Monday, still thinking that more advertising jobs awaited her, Tippi Hedren was called back to MCA and introduced to still more agents and executives. Her curiosity increased with the number of offices into which she was shown, and finally, on Tuesday, Herman Citron asked if she would accept certain terms for an exclusive, seven-year contract to producer-director Alfred Hitchcock. It was the first time his name had been mentioned, yet a contract and opportunity to join his production company was already being offered to her. She was puzzled, but also flattered — and with the uncertainties of a modeling career, not to mention the responsibilities she faced as the divorced mother of a four-year-old child, she was indeed looking for some kind of secure and guaranteed income.

"It was never my ambition to be an actress, much less a movie star," she said. "I had never thought of myself that way. I was a model, and I had come to Los Angeles not only to try for better work than was available in New York, but also because I wanted my daughter to grow up in a home with a yard and trees and a neighborhood to roam and play in.* In 1961 that seemed possible in Los Angeles, but it was difficult in New York." Her agent had already expressed his concern about the future of her career in modeling — a profession that is ordinarily insecure and short-lived for all but a very few. "And then this offer was just handed to me. It seemed like a fascinating new possibility, but later I thought that I really found it so new and difficult — I'd had no acting experience at all — that I overcompensated by working too hard, by sometimes being too accommodating to the crueler demands of the business of movie-making."

The terms of the contract were certainly modest by any Hollywood standards. She was to receive $500 a week for the first year, with a slight annual increase thereafter pursuant to the escalation clause. That base wage had been her average weekly salary for making television commercials, but of course the commercials had also produced substan-

---

*Her daughter, Melanie Griffith, grew up to become a film and television actress.

tial additional compensation from the residuals for each airing. There would be nothing comparable to these royalties in her film contract, so this meant that she was taking an enormous cut in salary — to $25,000 per year for 1961/1962, and, with the small increment, to $30,000 the following year. This she accepted, however, in the belief that a regular weekly income, guaranteed for up to seven years, was a wiser option than the unpredictable monies of modeling, which could be drastically reduced at any time.

And so, after conferring with her agent, Tippi Hedren was ushered in to meet Alfred Hitchcock. "I thought that all these preliminaries were handled very thoughtfully and very discreetly. Since I was someone with no experience of the film world, they knew that I would be nervous if I'd been introduced to him immediately — that I would have been worried about what to say and what to wear. He wanted them to meet me — and he wanted to meet me — without my feeling any need for special preparation."

At that first meeting, Hitchcock talked to her about everything except commercials and television and movies and show business; typically, he took her on a verbal tour of the world, describing great restaurants in foreign cities, special wines and foods and delicate sauces, travel by plane as compared to travel by boat, and hotels in exotic ports. She too had traveled widely, and she felt able to contribute to the conversation. "I suppose I didn't feel I was being tested or examined by him because I never thought I would be working for him. I had heard that he and Evan Hunter were working on a script, but it never occurred to me that I would have anything to do with it. I imagined that he wanted people like me — models without acting experience — for the television show."

But shortly thereafter it became clear that his plans for her were not so modest. Later that month she was brought in to meet Edith Head, who, just as with Grace Kelly and Vera Miles, was given the task of designing not only a lavish wardrobe for Tippi Hedren's screen tests, but also a complete wardrobe for her personal life. "That part I found surprising — he spent as much money on an outright gift of a personal wardrobe as he did on my year's salary. And there was a string of pearls, too. Later I found out that he thought the string of pearls I wore the day I met him was too large for the afternoon color I was wearing, and he told someone he would do something about it." ("It was really very clear, wasn't it?" Samuel Taylor remarked years later. "He was doing *Vertigo* with Tippi Hedren.")

By early November Hitchcock and Alma had rehearsed with Hedren, at Bellagio Road, for the screen tests, and he brought in Martin Balsam to act as her leading man in three of the most expensively designed trial runs in Hollywood history; Hitchcock rivaled, in fact, anything Selznick had ever attempted for *Gone With the Wind* or *Rebecca*. There were complete sets and costumes ready for the model to do key scenes from *Rebecca* and *Notorious* — trappings that had to be destroyed immediately after because Hitchcock did not own the rights of performance or reproduction. And then, for her color test, he directed her in the picnic scene from *To Catch a Thief* (the scene described on page 350); the erotic wordplay and gradual physical intimacy that had been played out by Grace Kelly and Cary Grant was duplicated shot for shot. "She was wonderful about it all," Martin Balsam recalled. "It was evident that she was very nervous and unsure of herself, but she had studied every line and every move that was asked of her, and she tried very hard to do everything just right, everything Hitch asked of her."

Hitchcock was also a little nervous. Two days before the tests, the dreadful Bel-Air brush fire had destroyed over five hundred of his neighbors' homes. When told on the morning of November 6 that they would have to evacuate the house, the Hitchcocks stored their silver, art, and other valuables in the wine cellar and fled. But their section of Bel-Air was spared. With thousands of others, they had to remain at hotels for several days before being permitted to return home.

As the year ended, Hitchcock returned to his office at Paramount for more conferences with Evan Hunter, and Tippi Hedren was free to devote more time to her daughter and to getting settled in her rented house. Her famous new employer recommended that she gain weight, and one afternoon there were two bushels of potatoes delivered to her doorstep with a written reminder that in sufficient amounts they were rich in calories. Before Hitchcock and Alma went to Saint Moritz for the holidays, instructions were left with his local wine-shop, and on Christmas Eve Tippi Hedren received a case of Dom Perignon. At nine o'clock the next morning she received a telegram, in humorously fractured French, conveying holiday greetings from the Hitchcocks in Switzerland.

As soon as they returned, Hithcock reviewed Hunter's first draft of the screenplay and made copious written comments, scene by scene; a study of these critiques gives the distinct impression that the director was taking more care with the development of this scenario than with any since *Vertigo*. During the last days of January, when his offices were still located at Paramount before the move to Universal, he worked with unusual intensity, asking Hunter why this character did that, and why that situation did not necessitate this reaction. After more work, the script reached its final form, just before shooting began in northern California that March.

*The Birds* was to be the story of a rich San Francisco socialite (Tippi Hedren) who meets a brash young lawyer (Rod Taylor) in a pet shop. Despite the lawyer's abrasive manner, she is attracted to him, and she travels to his weekend home in Bodega Bay to deliver a pair of love-birds he had sought. She learns that he lives with his mother and young sister, and she leaves the lovebirds for the sister as a birthday gift. Returning to town, the socialite is scratched by a swooping sea gull. Later, she accepts an invitation to the lawyer's home for dinner, in spite of his mother's clear disapproval of her. After another ominous indica-tion that something is wrong with the birds in the area, the socialite goes to help at the sister's birthday party the next afternoon — and at that party a flock of gulls attacks the children. Also involved is the local schoolteacher who was once in love with the lawyer.

The violence then increases — a flock of sparrows rushes into the house through the chimney (a scene directly inspired by one of the newspaper reports that Hitchcock had read); a neighboring farmer is pecked to death; an attack sets off a gasoline explosion; and the school-teacher is killed while protecting her students. Finally the leading char-acters become virtual prisoners in the house, and after the socialite is viciously set on by a mass of birds, the others know they must take her to a hospital. During a lull, they leave through a gathering of birds, and the final frames show them slowly driving away before the next savage onslaught.

"The girl represents complacency," Hitchcock said in a rare instance of thematic analysis. "The mother panics because she starts off being so strong, but she is not strong, it is a façade: she has been substituting her son for her husband.* She is the weak character in the story. But the girl shows that people can be strong when they face up to the situa-tion. . . . But as a group they were the victims of Judgment Day. . . . I felt that after *Psycho* people would expect something to top it."

By February 1962 Hitchcock had moved to Universal, and the con-tract for his first films there was signed only days before he settled into the richly appointed complex he would use to the end of his career. There was a large office for him, with handsome furniture and the at-mosphere of a board chairman's suite; a private dining room for enter-taining guests and colleagues; offices for his assistant Peggy Robertson and for Suzanne Gauthier, now his personal secretary; a receptionist's

---

*Anthony Perkins says to Janet Leigh in *Psycho:* "A son is a poor substitute for a lover."

area; a comfortable screening room; and workrooms for art directors and film editors. It was clear from the arrangement of Hitchcock's bungalow that he was there to stay, and that the new home of Alfred J. Hitchcock Productions, Incorporated, located the center of a small but powerful empire in the industry.

When the finishing touches to the script were completed, Hitchcock knew he had to finalize his decisions about casting. But which major actors would submit to the grueling months ahead, the hardship of coping with thousands of birds — and the possible dangers some of the staff suspected but none could accurately foresee? "Evan," Hitchcock said one morning in early February, "there will be no stars in this picture. I'm the star, the birds are the stars — and you're the star." And so it was to be.

Apart from inviting, for the role of the mother, the great stage actress Jessica Tandy, Hitchcock rejected suggestions to put established actors in key roles; that would have increased his budget, already greatly inflated for special effects. Instead of Anne Bancroft as the schoolteacher (Hunter's idea), he cast newcomer Suzanne Pleshette — whom he had seen first on television, as he had Vera Miles and Hedren; for the leading man, he gave Rod Taylor his first major role. And then one afternoon he pointed down the corridor outside his office, to Tippi Hedren, and said, "Look, Evan — there's Melanie Daniels," the leading character of the film. Hunter asked if she had the range for comedy and tragedy that the role demanded, and Hitchcock, still looking at her, simply said, "Evan, trust me."

Three nights later, Tippi Hedren was invited to join the Hitchcocks and the Wassermans for dinner at Chasen's, and at her place was a gift box from Gump's, San Francisco, containing a bird pin in gold with seed pearls. Hedren then knew that she was to do more than television work or supporting roles. But she could have no idea of the traumas ahead.

From the beginning, Hitchcock and his expanded technical crew knew that the problems in *The Birds* would be numerous. Hitchcock met with production designer Robert Boyle, with photographer Robert Burks and film editor George Tomasini, and, it seemed, with almost as many special-effects experts as there were birds in the film. Of the 1,500 shots planned for the film (about twice as many as a normal film, and almost three times as many as Hitchcock ordinarily included), almost 400 were difficult trick and composite shots.* In addition, Ray Berwick trained

---

*A lengthy illustrated study of the special technical achievements of the film was published in *Cinefantastique* 10, no. 2 (fall 1980), pp. 15–35. Several trick shots were also detailed by Robert Boyle in *Film Comment* 14, no. 3 (May–June 1978), pp. 33–35.

hundreds of gulls and crows and ravens to dart at the right moment, to perch, return, and swoop over actors' heads. Mechanical birds were constructed for a few shots involving children. Animation was to be used for many scenes. Trick photography was devised for many sequences, involving a combination of many shots in a single frame, with expert matte paintings by Albert Whitlock. All the resources of the cinema to 1962 were brought to the making of this film, and it was swiftly becoming Hitchcock's most expensive, most technically ambitious, and most rigorously planned.

"The overall design I had for the film from the very beginning," Robert Boyle remembered, "was inspired by Edvard Munch's painting *The Scream* — the sense of bleakness and madness in a kind of wilderness expressing an inner state. It was just what Hitch wanted. He insisted on a subjective approach, so that the audience would emotionally share in the characters' feelings as well as their fears of physical danger. The actors worked almost six months, but the artists and special-effects people and those in the optical department worked on the film for over a year."

Throughout the shooting in northern California, crewmen were scratched and assistants pecked, and finally injections against tetanus were ordered for everyone. The Humane Society, meanwhile, saw to the kindly treatment of the birds, supervising the generous feedings and calling a prompt end to the day's work so as not to overtax them.

In over twenty weeks of shooting (almost eight in northern California, the rest at Universal Pictures), the schedule allowed Tippi Hedren only one day free, since Hitchcock required her constant presence. "He gave me the best education an actor could have. With any other director it would have taken fifteen years, but he had me involved in every part of the film — script completion, wardrobe design, special-effects work, dubbing. It was his film from start to finish, and he wanted me to learn how he put it together."

Before they left for the location shooting, Hitchcock had decided to revive *Marnie,* and Evan Hunter was brought in for work on the treatment and first draft even while they moved north to film *The Birds*. Hunter knew that the story of a compulsive thief with severe sexual problems would need considerable research in the area of abnormal psychology and dream theory, and that great care would have to be taken so that the drama of the story, and its oddly tender possibilities, would not be engulfed by the sensational plot — especially if it was to be, as Hitchcock hoped, the vehicle to mark Grace Kelly's return to the screen. While Hitchcock directed birds and people in March, Hunter began a year's work on a script that would finally be taken away from him.

By March 22, a good deal had happened around Alfred Hitchcock. To begin with, he had decided to slightly embellish Tippi Hedren's first name. A variation on an affectionate Swedish diminutive her father had given her in early childhood, the nickname Tippi had long before unofficially replaced her baptismal name, Nathalie. But henceforth, Hitchcock decreed, in every connection with Alfred Hitchcock and his films, the name was to appear enclosed in single quotation marks: 'Tippi' Hedren. It was the first gentle move of proprietorship.

Then he brought in two members of his crew and asked them to keep careful watch on the activities of Miss Hedren when she left the set — where she went, whom she visited, how she spent her free time. To them such protectiveness seemed necessary only when she was at work, surrounded by birds, but there seemed to be another motive involved. The amateur private eyes kept up their surveillance only a few days, after which they decided that following a woman to a shop or to a telephone or to a luncheonette, where she had gone one afternoon with some of the crew members and local children, seemed neither interesting nor important enough to warrant time away from their other responsibilities.

In addition, Hitchcock — and subsequently the *New York Times,* on March 20 — somewhat prematurely announced that Grace Kelly would indeed play the lead in *Marnie.* London papers picked up the story the next day, after Hitchcock had spoken to Peter Evans of the *Daily Express* somewhat boldly about the Princess's "sex appeal, . . . the finest in the world." The announcement was sufficiently upsetting to the citizens of Monaco to pressure the princess to withdraw from the negotiations, a decision that apparently disappointed her and certainly infuriated Hitchcock.

With this alteration of his expectations, another change was noticeable in his work with Tippi Hedren. He began to take unusual care in the rehearsal and preparation of every shot — directing her "down to the movement of an eye and every turn of my head," she remembered. And he also started to take her aside for longer story conferences about the film, which made her increasingly uncomfortable. On and off the set, he was always staring at her, as she and others vividly recalled.

Hedren felt she could have coped with this for the remaining weeks of shooting, and in fact she received warm support and encouragement from others in the cast. "She was frightened and inexperienced," according to Suzanne Pleshette, "and he very carefully led her every step of the way." Soon, however, matters took a different turn. "He started telling me what I should wear on my own time, what I should be eating, and what friends I should be seeing. He suggested that such and such a person was not good enough for my company, or that someone I might have a social engagement with was not right. And he became angry and hurt if I didn't ask his permission to visit friends in the evening or on a weekend."

Even before the company moved back to Los Angeles later that spring, she was trying to hide her anxiety. She confided to her friends that Hitchcock was making things very clear to her: he felt he had plucked her from obscurity and was making her a major Hollywood star, and that she should be grateful and attentive to his advice and his plans for her. It did not matter to him that she did not much want to be a Hollywood star, or that she would have been quite content with smaller roles or television work. He had chosen her, he was changing and training her, and there should be no argument about it, he said — thousands would have gladly replaced her. And as the weeks passed, she wished someone would.*

"He could be two different men," Hedren said of the last difficult weeks of shooting *The Birds*. "He was a meticulous and sensitive director who gave so much to each scene and who got so much emotion into it — and he was a man who would do anything to get a reaction from me." It was not the first time that, out of earshot of everyone but the woman on camera, he had whispered a wildly obscene or scatological comment just before the film rolled. These comments Hedren chose to ignore. But she had to deal more directly with his attempt to force martinis on her during rehearsal — by flatly refusing them. "I had always heard that his idea was to take a woman — usually a blond — and break her apart, to see her shyness and reserve broken down, but I thought this was only in the plots of his films." Now it was happening to her, and she did not like it.

To a casual visitor on the set, of course, things seemed to be in quiet good order. Hitchcock had instructed his secretary to have things ready each morning: his desk cleared, pencils sharpened and arranged in the pewter mug, logbook opened to the day's shooting schedule and appointments, cigar humidor dusted. Peggy Robertson was on the sound stage when he arrived, seeing that everything was ready for the first setup. Suzanne Gauthier handled minor crises, such as a mislaid case of Montrachet. Unfailingly cheerful and panic-proof, these two women surrounded Hitchcock with protection and dedicated themselves to his perpetual tranquility. To see the arrangement of his office and his film production unit was to have no hint of struggle. As for Hitchcock himself, he kept to his usual orderly and ordered regimen. More obsessively

---

* "I brought her to Hollywood," Hitchcock told an interviewer. "I changed everything about her. Svengali Hitch rides again."

neat than ever, he became a compulsive emptier of ashtrays and used two or three hand-towels to dry the basin and faucets of his office lavatory.

This sense of calm and order was, however, a sharp variation from the spirit of the film's finale. "I always believe in following the advice of the playwright Sardou," Hitchcock remarked. "He said, 'Torture the women!' . . . The trouble today is that we don't torture women enough." The comment might have been intended as puckish perversity — to arouse the curiosity or indignation of his audience, to provoke a reaction. But when it came to shooting the climax of *The Birds,* Hitchcock might well have set out to correct the "trouble" by following Sardou's advice literally, and to a horrifying degree.

The final great attack of the birds was to involve the leading lady herself: she would be caught in a room full of crows and gulls and ravens that would tear at her until she collapsed in a state of shock. Tippi Hedren had been told, before the week's shooting began, that of course mechanical birds would be used for this scene, since anything else would be practically impossible. But when she arrived on the set that Monday morning in June, the assistant director, James Brown, informed her that mechanical birds would not be used, because it had been determined that on film they would look like artificial props.

An hour later, the new approach began. Two men, wearing protective gloves and carrying huge cartons, were carefully positioned — one on each side of the camera, facing the actress, who stood against a wall. The entire set was enclosed in a giant cage and then, as Hedren waved her arms and fought them off, live birds were thrown at her while the cameras rolled. "There was no precedent for anything like this, and no one knew what to expect," she recalled. "All of us thought that it could be done very quickly — and no one hoped so more than I. We thought maybe after one or two takes they'd have the film they'd need." But the shooting continued throughout the day. Birds were hurled at her; frightened, they flew away as she defended herself against the gulls and crows with wild, increasingly honest and unacted gestures of terror. Then the cameras stopped, a new setup was arranged, her clothing was torn slightly and stage blood painted on, the makeup for a scratch was applied by artist Howard Smits, her hair was disarrayed a little more — and the ordeal continued.

And Hitchcock? "He was terribly upset by all of this," according to Tippi Hedren, who remembered that he was so nervous that he could not appear on the set until everything was ready.

"He wanted to shoot it," Evan Hunter said, "but something in him didn't want to shoot it, and everybody could hear how nervous he was."

It was, of course, an even greater trial for Tippi Hedren, and the trial went on into Tuesday — and then into Wednesday. New camera setups, swift shots, more torn costume, more "blood and wounds" applied — and now the occasional real peck from a startled or anxious or ornery bird, for the creatures were by this time not enjoying the work any more than the actress. Cary Grant, making a picture on a nearby stage, dropped in to watch a few takes and praised Hedren's courage, and everyone else who saw what was going on knew that Hitchcock was fortunate. An established actress would never have submitted to this extreme abuse.

"Day after day after day," according to Jessica Tandy,

for an entire week, the poor woman put up with that. She was alone in that caged room, acting, with the birds coming at her, and with costume changes and makeup applications and all the stage blood she couldn't even go to the commissary for lunch. She lived with that hour after hour, and I just don't know how she did it.

It would have been one thing to act it out in only the time it takes on the screen — about a minute or two — but to shoot it over so long a time! If it had been me I would have just hated to go into the studio each morning, and I'm sure she found it all very trying. A lot was on her shoulders, and it must have been an awful strain. I'm terribly glad I didn't have to do it!

Hollywood, to be sure, has a long history of exacting painful trials from professional stuntpeople and even from actors, the better to achieve realism and engage the viewer's astonished attention. Lillian Gish and Richard Barthelmess endured freezing temperatures and real ice floes for climactic scenes of D. W. Griffith's *Way Down East;* Harold Lloyd, who lost a thumb and a finger for the sake of a film, never used doubles for his most dangerous stunts; Buster Keaton often risked death and dismemberment; Lon Chaney caused himself great pain for the makeup and distortions that made him famous — and thousands of actors have fallen from horses, leaped from buildings, and dashed through flames while the cameras turned. A single actor, however, is rarely subjected to trying conditions as repeatedly as was Tippi Hedren in this case.

"The week was perfectly dreadful," she recalled, "really the worst week of my life. Each day I thought — and they told me — just one more hour, just one more shot." But then, on Thursday, as Hitchcock and George Tomasini reviewed the previous day's takes, a new difficulty arose: in those shots in which Tippi Hedren was forced to the floor as the birds dove and pounced over her, the birds had flown away too quickly. "And so on Thursday the wardrobe mistress took me into my dressing room, where elastic bands were tied around my body, with nylon thread that was pulled through tiny holes in my costume. I soon found out what this was for. One leg of each bird was tied to each piece of string, so that when I lay on the floor they couldn't fly away but would bound and perch all over me. This went on for the rest of the day while they tried to get the shots they wanted.''

On Friday, Thursday's ordeal was repeated for close shots and odd angles, and by afternoon the physical and emotional torture — it can hardly be called anything else — had just about taken its toll on Hedren's admirable patience and cooperation. Then one bird became particularly agitated and went for her left eye. A catastrophe was avoided, but a deep gash appeared on her lower lid. At that point she became hysterical and suffered a complete collapse. The set was cleared at once and she was taken home, but a weekend's rest was insufficient; when she came back to work on Monday morning, she was in such a distraught state that she could not be roused from a brief nap in her dressing room. She awoke to find herself under sedation, back at home.

Hitchcock was told by her physician that she could not possibly return for at least a week, and when he replied that she was needed for every shot, the doctor insisted that in her present condition she would not be able to sustain work at all. And so for the first time since Hitchcock's and Joan Fontaine's illness during *Suspicion,* a Hitchcock film was closed down for a week for medical reasons. About this time, Alfred Hitchcock began to say more and more frequently to interviewers (in one context or another): "To paraphrase Oscar Wilde, 'You destroy the thing you love.' "

Eventually the filming was completed quickly and quietly, and without incident, by the first of July. Tippi Hedren was then permitted a vacation, and Hitchcock and his technical crew began the complicated process of editing, designing the tricky composite and matte shots, supervising the animation and perfecting the double-exposed film, directing the artists engaged to hand-paint birds onto several key frames, and meeting with Bernard Herrmann, Remi Gassmann, and Oskar Sala. That trio devised a musicless sound track in which all the bird noises were artifically created on an electronic instrument called the Trautonium (named after Friedrich Trautwein, its inventor); their work gave the sound track its unusual power — every noise and effect was orchestrated, every sound filtered and altered to support the feeling Hitchcock wanted in each scene.

"One of the first things I do," Hitchcock said later, "is make a dubbing script. In other words, I dictate every sound that will be on the sound track other than dialogue or music. And the silences are in the dubbing script too. The only area over which you have no control is the music. But that's inevitable because the musician will say that he must compose it later and not right on the set. You're really helpless in the hands of the musician. The only way out is careful planning.''

Everyone connected with the production had realized that Hitchcock was in an unusual state of emotional upset during *The Birds;* those most closely involved knew that it had to do with his strange fixation on Tippi Hedren, while others thought he was disturbed about the technical difficulties, or that he was simply afraid the picture would not match *Psycho* for emotional power. But the reasons for his distress go deeper — as reflected in *The Birds,* which explores the fragility of human relations and the fear of loss and abandonment. The bird attacks seem in fact to be symbolic manifestations of fragile human relations — or, more accurately, the attacks exteriorize the *failure* of human relations.

Hitchcock had attached yards of brown paper to the walls of his office and had graphed the rising and falling of action in the story. Similar careful study of the episodes in their proper order in the finished film shows that each incident with birds immediately follows a scene describing a character's fear of being alone or abandoned.* Every character in the story has chosen to live in a way that rigorously avoids loneliness while creating, unwittingly, situations of emotional isolation. The leading man and woman, the mother, the schoolteacher, the adults at the café — every personality is defined by a terrible loneliness caused at least in part by emotional isolation and fear of another. The dialogue between Tippi Hedren and Suzanne Pleshette focuses this idea.

HEDREN: There's nothing between Mr. Brenner [*Mitch Brenner, the lawyer*] and me.

PLESHETTE: Isn't there? Well, maybe there isn't. Maybe there's never been anything between Mitch and any girl.

HEDREN: What do you mean? . . .

PLESHETTE: I was seeing a lot of him in San Francisco. Then one weekend he invited me up to meet Lydia [*his mother*].

HEDREN: When was this?

PLESHETTE: Four years ago. After his father died. Of course, things may be different now.

HEDREN: Different?

PLESHETTE: With Lydia. Did she seem a trifle distant?

HEDREN: A trifle.

* Viewers who regard *The Birds* as a traditional narrative with a beginning, middle, and firm conclusion are disappointed with the film's finale (which Hunter originally had developed further before Hitchcock excised it). But *The Birds* is perhaps better appreciated not as a linear narrative, but more as a tragic lyric poem whose episodes are like stanzas that emotionally reinforce a single theme. Federico Fellini has also called the film a poem, affirming that it is his favorite among Hitchcock's works and one of the great films of all time.

PLESHETTE: Perhaps things aren't quite so different. You know, her attitude nearly drove me crazy. When I got back to San Francisco I spent days trying to find out exactly what I'd done to displease her.

HEDREN: What had you done?

PLESHETTE: Nothing. I simply existed. So what's the answer — jealous woman, right? Clinging, possessive mother? Wrong! With all due respect to Oedipus, I don't think that was the case.

HEDREN: Then what was it?

PLESHETTE: Lydia liked me — that's the strange part! Now that I'm no longer a threat we're very good friends.

HEDREN: Why did she object to you?

PLESHETTE: Because she was afraid.

HEDREN: Afraid you'd take Mitch?

PLESHETTE: Afraid I'd give Mitch!

HEDREN: I don't understand.

PLESHETTE: Afraid of any woman who would give Mitch the one thing Lydia can give him — love.

HEDREN: That adds up to a jealous, possessive woman.

PLESHETTE: No, I don't think so. You see, she's not afraid of losing Mitch. She's only afraid of being abandoned.

HEDREN: Didn't Mitch have anything to say about this?

PLESHETTE: I can understand his position. He'd just been through a lot with Lydia after his father died. He didn't want to risk going through it all again.*

It is important to stress, in this regard, that — as with every one of Alfred Hitchcock's films — the script was the work of the screenwriter. But the characters and their situations, and the story and the content of each scene were worked out by writer and director together. In fact, Evan Hunter remembered that an important scene to be filmed was presented to him one morning completely written. "I arrived and was handed the scene between Tippi Hedren and Rod Taylor that takes place on the hill, above the house, during the children's birthday party. I read it and was told it was to be shot that day." Hitchcock himself had written the scene, precisely because it carried forward, from the dialogue just quoted, the theme of abandonment.

HEDREN: You see — Rome — that entire summer I did nothing but — it was very easy to get lost there. So when I came back I thought it was time I began finding something again. [*She then changes the topic to the myna bird*

---

*The passage recalls the words of Claude Rains to Leopoldine Konstantin (playing his mother) in *Notorious:* "You've always been jealous of any woman I've brought into this house!"; and those of the psychiatrist in *Psycho* (regarding Anthony Perkins as the schizophrenic Norman Bates): "His mother was a clinging, demanding woman, and for years the two of them lived as if there was no one else in the world."

*she bought for her prim aunt, who is certain to be shocked by the "new four-*
*letter words" it has picked up from her niece. They discuss this and the con-*
*versation continues.*]

TAYLOR: You need a mother's care, my child!

HEDREN: Not my mother's!

TAYLOR: Oh — I'm sorry.

HEDREN: What have you got to be sorry about? My mother? Don't waste
your time. She ditched us when I was eleven and went off with some hotel
man in the East. You know what a mother's love is!

TAYLOR: Yes, I do.

HEDREN: You mean it's better to be ditched?

TAYLOR: No, I think it's better to be loved. Don't you ever see her?

HEDREN [*turning away to hide her tears*]: I don't know where she is. ·[*Re-
covering her composure.*] Well! Maybe I ought to go join the *other* children.

They then return to the party, where, after an attack of birds, the
viewer is told quite plainly that it is the girl's eleventh birthday — exactly the age when the leading lady was abandoned as a child. As elsewhere, Hitchcock had altered the dialogue so that it would structurally
conform and give meaning to the bird attack that immediately follows.

In another important way, Hitchcock developed the theme of vision
that he had linked to the watching birds of prey in *Psycho.* Over forty
times in *The Birds,* characters say "I see" or "You see" — and most
of these statements were additions Hitchcock made in the second draft.
The words are like a refrain punctuating every stanza of his cinematic
poem, just as every sequence ends with a dissolve of a character staring
out into space. Hitchcock also chose to push to its limit the grotesque-
ness of an earlier image — Mrs. Bates's empty eye sockets in *Psycho,*
an image logically extended here in a triple jump-cut to the pecked-out
sockets of the dead farmer.

Also as in *Psycho,* all the vision images and words about seeing point
to the main character's empty stare — wide and unperceptive — at the
conclusion (that is, in *The Birds,* to the woman's gaze in shock after
she has been attacked at the end of the film; also, the final bird attack
on the leading lady recalls the shower murder in *Psycho*). Moreover,
lashing out and beating at nothing with her arms, Hedren unknowingly
strikes at a man who tries to calm her, her eyes frantic with terror. She
thus becomes the horrifying literal fulfillment of Anthony Perkins's remark in *Psycho:* "We scratch and claw, but only at the air, only at each
other — and for all of it we never budge an inch."

All the bird-related images of watching and spying, and all the corresponding motifs of fear and abandonment were ready to transfer from
*Psycho* (a film steeped in bird imagery), but their artistic currency had

been prepared years earlier, in Hitchcock's school days. Bird-watching and the careful identification of species were a British national pastime and were part of the country gentleman's training he received at Saint Ignatius. And one of the most famous late-Victorian paintings synthesized the connection between birds and unpredictable eruptions of chaos: in Edward Burne-Jones's *Love and the Pilgrim* (painted 1896–1897), Love is a garlanded angel — a giant "lovebird" — with a spear, inviting a dark-robed pilgrim who emerges from a thicket to take the angel's hand and follow. The country journey ahead shows thorns and brambles, and there are numerous small birds in the thicket left behind and a large flock overhead that is prevented from attacking only because of Love's protecting wings. From early medieval times, birds had been representations of ill luck; in late-Victorian art and poetry they became markers of dramatic chaos.

Although *The Birds* has a more open-ended view of life and human relationships than *Psycho,* and although its last moments were deliberately designed not to be seen as "last moments" (Hitchcock ordered that the words *The End* be omitted), the film is punctuated with situations and dialogue clearly based on Hitchcock's own personal background and is, to that extent, rooted in specificity. "He told me that he was terrified of birds," recalled an actor who worked with Hitchcock later. "With this film he came into contact with very few actual birds — he always kept his distance from them." More important than the film as personal exorcism and confrontation of that fear, however, is the fact that in *The Birds* the lawyer and his mother and sister bear a striking resemblance to the Hitchcock household after the death of his father, when Mrs. Hitchcock gradually depended more and more on her son. Hitchcock, too, "went though a lot with [his mother] after his father died," as Suzanne Pleshette says of Rod Taylor, trying to explain why the character (like the director) remained with mother and denied his own social life well into his mature years. Throughout, the character Mitch strangely resembles "Hitch." And several of Hitchcock's legendary practical jokes are also inserted into the script.

In a larger perspective, however, few other films have come as close as *The Birds* to fulfilling what Otto Rank wrote of the art form:

It may perhaps turn out that cinematography, which in numerous ways reminds us of the dream-work, can also express certain psychological facts and relationships — which the writer often is unable to describe with verbal clarity — in such clear and conspicuous imagery that it facilitates our understanding of them. The film attracts our attention all the more readily since we have learned from similar studies that a modern treatment is often successful in reapproaching, intuitively, the real meaning of an ancient theme which has become either unintelligible or misunderstood in its course through tradition. . . .

An obscure but unavoidable feeling takes hold of the spectator and seems to betray that deep human problems are being dealt with here. The uniqueness of cinematography in visibly portraying psychological events [is that it] calls our attention, with exaggerated clarity, to the fact that the interesting and meaningful problems of man's relation to himself — and the fateful disturbance of this relation — find here an imaginative representation.

The "exaggerated clarity" of this apparent science-fiction thriller by Hitchcock indeed expresses "meaningful problems" of human relations. And Hitchcock, using the birds (of art and England and *Psycho*), explored with a demonic ferocity the "fateful disturbance of this relation" — not only in a vaguely comprehensible universe, but within the contours of his own professional and personal life.

It may also be noted that one of the clearest parallels to Hitchcock at this period of his art is Hieronymus Bosch, the Flemish painter who died in the early sixteenth century. Both were craftsmen steeped in personal guilt and the conviction that their own misshapen condition made them outcasts in the world; both perceived life as an effort to avoid the always imminent calamity and accident that were sure to befall the unwary. Both loved mystery stories and the countryside away from the cities of their work, and both found human relations painful and disturbing. A severe moralism characterizes their works, and a personalized, stylized sense of evil is represented by birds. In Bosch's *Garden of Earthly Delights* — as often in Hitchcock's films, from *The Pleasure Garden* through *The Birds* — birds dwarf and tyrannize pathetic human beings; in Bosch's *Temptation of Saint Anthony* the tempting witches cavort in the shape of birds.

An obsession with images of sin and sex and venality, and the motif of trickery and assumed identities also characterizes the mature work of each man; a profound distrust of the world marked Hitchcock's attitude in his films, as it did Bosch's in *The Conjurer* and *The Ship of Fools*. Both artists were held to be competent workers in their time, but until they died comparatively few admitted that they created great art. Seekers after the ideal and moralists in spite of themselves, Bosch and Hitchcock each spoke out of the sadness of his age and the experience of massive evil — and each addressed the terror of human isolation that he perceived within his soul, a terror that provided the strongest clue to the meaning of damnation. And finally, each artist regularly tucked himself into a modest corner of his own work as a signature; Bosch's face and Hitchcock's cameo are more than seals of authorship — they peer as players in their own nightmares.

Although the final editing of *The Birds* lasted from July 1962 to early the following year, Hitchcock's anxious energy in supervising it and pursuing other interests was unabated. Tippi Hedren was, for a time, away from the studio, and he chose at once to pitch himself into the direction of this third hour-long teleplay. *I Saw the Whole Thing,* photographed from July 23 through 27, turned out to be his last effort for television. It is not memorable for its courtroom melodrama, in which a mystery writer (John Forsythe) defends himself against a charge and in doing so reveals that his wife is guilty; rather, it is important because once again Hitchcock thought he had found a new subject for transformation and training — even while the painful feelings and memories about Tippi Hedren were fresh in his mind and still salted his conversation. Cast in a small role for the teleplay was an actress named Claire Griswold, the young wife of novice director Sydney Pollack. During a break in the filming, Hitchcock invited her to a private luncheon, at which he said, "Miss Griswold, you and I are going to do business." Within days, he had signed her to an exclusive seven-year contract.

And so began a repetition of the previous autumn. A personal wardrobe was again designed ("Bring me your body," he told her, "and I will dress it"), and a lavish triad of screen tests was readied — including one long scene from *Anastasia,* for which Cathleen Nesbitt was brought in to play the dowager empress.* Then the quietly erotic love scene from *To Catch a Thief* was rehearsed and meticulously directed. The actress recognized at once what was happening and decided that she did not like it. Hitchcock was asking her to repeat every gesture, every attitude, every intonation of Grace Kelly in that scene. "I was very touched," she said, "by his evident need to re-create Grace Kelly — or whoever it was he wanted to re-create out of the raw material that was me — but I didn't really want to go along with that sort of thing."

Hitchcock was not to be so easily put off, however. While Evan Hunter continued to work on a first draft of *Marnie,* and while Robert Boyle began the task of designing the complicated film and planning for its many locations and exteriors, Hitchcock spent the fall of 1962 supervising wardrobes for Claire Griswold and introducing her to the executives at Universal and MCA. Whenever she mentioned her family or her private life, Hitchcock changed the subject; he did not wish to hear about anything outside her work at the studio with him.

---

*Telling François Truffaut about this test, in Claire Griswold's presence, Hitchcock announced that he thought her performance superior to Ingrid Bergman's in the original film. That judgment, according to Miss Griswold, was embarrassingly inflated and highly subjective: "He wanted to see what he had to see, and that was that."

At this point her uneasiness increased further. She and her husband were invited to dine at Bellagio Road, but Hitchcock barely addressed her husband or took any interest in his career; quite to the contrary, he spoke contemptuously of all other film directors as a group. (Sydney Pollack eventually directed, among other films, *They Shoot Horses, Don't They?; Jeremiah Johnson; The Way We Were; Three Days of the Condor;* and *Tootsie.*) Such occasions were not entirely pleasant, and the Pollacks felt that Hitchcock was creating an odd kind of rivalry: on one hand, Tippi Hedren was being held before Griswold as a competitor for Hitchcock's full attention; and, on the other hand, Claire was being placed in the center of a struggle between the two men. As a young, quite happily married mother, she did not relish the latter role; and whereas Tippi Hedren had been a friend since their early years as New York models, any suggestion of jealousy was repellent. In addition, the star of *The Birds* was not eager to begin work on another Hitchcock assignment, and Claire Griswold harbored no interest in *Marnie* at all.

When Hitchcock finally settled on Tippi Hedren for the lead role, the new trainee realized that she herself would be free for the next year. Griswold discussed this at a luncheon with Peggy Robertson, and explained that since she was not going to be used for a film, she and her husband planned to expand their family. Robertson advised Griswold of Hitchcock's expectation that there would be no appropriate time for such matters within the next seven years — she was expected always to be available, for any role, under any circumstances. Griswold made up her mind at once. Very shortly thereafter, Hitchcock's office was informed that Mr. and Mrs. Sydney Pollack were awaiting the birth of their second child. (There is no evidence that Vera Miles or Audrey Hepburn or Claire Griswold shared advice on the matter of how to avoid a Hitchcock production, but it would have been understandable if the director had become suspicious.) The following year, by mutual consent, the contract between Griswold and Hitchcock was terminated, and she settled, most agreeably, into the private life she always preferred.

Long before *Marnie* began, there were several curious developments. Hitchcock sent to Tippi Hedren's five-year-old daughter a strange and somewhat frightening gift: an elaborate and expensive doll of her mother dressed as the character she played in *The Birds,* complete with miniature green suit and elegant coiffure — but the doll was packaged in a tiny pine box. Then, under pretext of a complicated makeup session, Hitchcock made a life mask of his actress, and for a long time jealously guarded her delicate features, captured forever in perfect repose. Another devotee might have cherished a photograph or a ring or a garment, but Hitchcock had already designed her pictures, jewelry, and wardrobe. The doll and the mask were perhaps almost magical for him — and, with their complex of life and death, possibly totems of a great and necessary pain.

During a long winter holiday, Hedren continued to receive deliveries of short, ardent notes, gifts of wine and delicacies, and news of pre-production on the film. The handwritten messages on Hitchcock's engraved notepaper were the most effusive he had ever written, full of a sometimes shy, childish emotionalism, sometimes strictly businesslike and detached, sometimes embarrassingly passionate — his styles, like his intentions, seemed to clash, and it is unlikely that he was any less confused than the recipient.

At the same time, he was designing a lavish dressing room–trailer for her use, complete with bathroom, a refrigerator-bar (which he stocked with his favorite wines), and personal stationery for her (ordered and printed to match his own exactly). The trailer was finally installed adjacent to his bungalow at the studio, with a ramp leading directly into his private office, so that he could have immediate and unobserved access to her. When production finally began, she quickly learned to invite friends and members of the crew to join her there at the end of the day, to avoid the increasing awkwardness of being alone with him. Ignoring her stated commitment to the man she would soon marry, he crowded her with attention and even began to court her parents, who were invited to a birthday dinner for her in January at his home.

Hitchcock's methods of film preparation with writers and designers have often been described in this book. The contents of preproduction meetings have been gathered from the personal reminiscences of his associates, diaries, and available memoranda and files from studio archives. But in preparing *Marnie* in early 1963, Hitchcock was apparently aware that this was to be a qualitatively different production from any other, and he did something unprecedented: he taped his conversations with writer Evan Hunter and production designer Robert Boyle. The transcripts of those tapes are fascinating, for they reveal the precision with which he foresaw every scene, and they disclose as well the personal touches, the obsessions, and the array of memories, fantasies, and images that contributed to the construction of a surprisingly personal motion picture.

Beginning on February 4, Hitchcock described in exact detail for his two collaborators every shot of the first half of the film, the interior and exterior locations, the props, the spatial relationships between characters — and, in greatest detail, the physical, costumed appearance of the title character. "We go to close-up," he said, "to show her hair blowing in the wind while she's riding the horse — that's a leitmotiv that goes through the film." But at key points in his discussion of the characters of Marnie and Mark, it is clear that he was thinking of Tippi Hedren and Alfred Hitchcock. "When the girl goes out after their first meeting in the office, she may just glance at him — but it doesn't mean anything. The main purpose of this scene is that this man was attracted to her right in that office when he gave the nod to hire her. But she's quite unresponsive — polite, but she doesn't want to get involved or anything like that."

The scene he had envisioned most carefully, however, was that toward which the entire picture moves — and that which eventually led to Hitchcock's break with Evan Hunter. He described the honeymoon cruise of a man who has married a compulsive, frigid thief.

Each of the images must make a statement. . . . Now it's night in this scene. The cabin of the ship has to be a bedroom and a sitting room, a suite — and she's in a negligee. He's in shirt and pants. And he comes over to embrace her now. Now is the moment. And she turns on him and walks away and sits in a far corner of the sitting room.

He comes to the door and says, "What's wrong?"

And in rather bold language she says, "It's animal and the whole business is horrible" — and the language here will be quite outspoken — and he tries to talk her into being sensible about it, but she won't attempt it at all. . . .

And then you get the second night in the cabin. He comes to her and she tries to resist — and then she turns her head away and you follow her head as he forces her down onto the bed, and you know —

Here the tape recorder was disconnected while, as Evan Hunter clearly remembered, Hitchcock described the rape scene. "I didn't want to write that scene for him, and I told Hitchcock so. I thought it would break sympathy for the character of the man, and it's totally unmotivated. But Hitch said he wanted it in the film, and he insisted that at the exact moment of the rape he wanted the camera right on her shocked face." Shortly after this conference, Hunter returned to his home to continue writing the script, and to consider the disturbing demand Hitchcock was making.

Ten days later, for Saint Valentine's Day, Hitchcock sent his star a long, bizarre, and impassioned telegram. After recounting the legends of the two martyrs named Valentine, he added that they were very likely both legends about one person — himself. He then wondered why, as a martyr, he should be singled out by the *Encyclopaedia Britannica* to

symbolize the festival of lovers. He concluded by reminding her of his
martyrdom, which, he added, caused exquisite pain for the martyr "Al-
fredus."

Things were not helped by the imminent publicity tour that Tippi
Hedren had to make with Hitchcock and several executives to promote
the national release of *The Birds* on March 29. Two days before that,
they arrived in New York for a private press screening at the Museum
of Modern Art, and earlier that same day Hitchcock told newsmen that
Tippi Hedren was under exclusive contract to him and that he had absolutely no intention of making her available, on a loan-out, to another
studio. At the same time, he announced that his next picture would be
*Marnie*.

Within days, Hedren left for a celebration of her film debut in her
Minnesota hometown, and Hitchcock returned to Los Angeles, where
he planned an even more elaborate publicity campaign for the premiere
of the picture in London. Two jet-black mynas were to be labeled Alfie
and Tippi and placed in the foyer of the Leicester Square Odeon, he
ordered, and a recording nearby would squawk his clever tag-line, *"The
Birds* is coming!" At the same time, he reported to a visiting London
journalist his satisfaction with his star's performance: "Her reactions in
*The Birds* were subtle, and that was what pleased me about the girl.
You know, she never acted before. . . . She had nothing to unlearn.
. . . I controlled every movement on her face. She did purely cinematic
acting of very fine shadings all the time. She wasn't allowed to do
anything beyond what I gave her. It was my control entirely."

On April 2, Evan Hunter sent Hitchcock a revised draft of *Marnie*,
with two versions of the crucial scene they had discussed, urging Hitchcock to reject the rape scene and to substitute a more reasonable, more
consistent, and less offensive sequence. On April 10, Hitchcock replied
that it was clear the film still needed a great deal of work, that he
himself felt he had gone stale on it, and that he was therefore going to
delay until a fresh mind could be brought to it. Hunter at once sent
word back that he would continue to work with Hitchcock and would
gladly wait until they could both return to it "with fresh minds." The
project had been close to him for over a year, Hunter added, and it had
become very important to him. But Hitchcock was not being candid
with his writer — he was being deliberately ambiguous. On May 1,
Hunter's agent received a call from Peggy Robertson saying that the
writer was dismissed from the picture and was being replaced by another — "a fresh mind." Hitchcock had no intention of delaying a single day. Hunter had held out for his own opinion too long, and this
Alfred Hitchcock could not tolerate.

The new writer was indeed a novice, as Jay Presson Allen called herself, and she arrived in Los Angeles in early May with her husband and daughter, excited about working with the great Hitchcock. "Somehow," she remembered,

he had got hold of an advance script of my first play, *The Prime of Miss Jean Brodie.* I think he wanted a woman's point of view on *Marnie,* and that's why he asked me. He was an extraordinary teacher, although in the first few weeks I wasn't sure we were ever going to get a script done. He wanted to relax, to talk about almost everything else. I think he was tired by this time, and he was disappointed with what had happened to the picture so far. I always felt it was a somewhat fated project, but he was mad for Tippi Hedren, just as he had been obsessed with a series of cold blond actresses before.

Nevertheless, after some preliminary socializing with the Hitchcocks, she and the director settled into the business of reworking the script according to his strict specifications. "Alma was wonderful all during this time," Jay Allen recalled. "She was much shrewder about people than Hitchcock, and a lot tougher. They had a marvelous partnership, a working relationship with all its dynamics and all its tensions."

The work continued that summer of 1963, interrupted only by a Fourth of July house party at Scotts Valley to which Jay Allen and her husband Lewis were invited. They were astonished at the quantity and variety of vintage wines, and soon Hitchcock's new writer and her spouse knew that their inclinations and tastes and capacities were not as rich as their host's. Eventually, after the film was completed, it was in fact Hitchcock's severe drinking, far beyond his limited tolerance, that alienated the Allens altogether. At the same time, she was aware that he was a genius, a mentor in this new aspect of her career as a writer, and that she was absorbing a complete education. But she was also aware that he was mythologizing himself. "It's easier for someone who's shy and repressed to live as a myth," she said. "He didn't do it deliberately, but it was a wonderful defense mechanism."

By September *Marnie* was ready for the cameras, and Tippi Hedren joined her new leading man, Sean Connery, for meetings with Hitchcock and the crew. When the first scenes were filmed, a routine was established. At three-thirty in the afternoon, Hitchcock announced a tea break, at which he would preside and deliver a speech — on the history of the Orient Express, for example, or on his past films; or he would tell tired jokes while members of the cast and crew tried to drift away so that new camera setups could be prepared. Finally, everyone had left, and he would sit alone with the look of a sensitive fat-boy who has run away from the cruelties of his peers, or who has been abandoned by them.

But as shooting continued, it became more and more apparent that the film was turning into a different story from what had been originally planned. "Hitch was a very Edwardian fellow," according to Jay Presson Allen. "He put lids on himself. To work out his repressions, he created a framework — his art. It was his way of legitimizing everything and transforming his feelings and repressions into something creative." And his way of transforming feelings was, in this case, the film *Marnie* itself, which was becoming a strange and driven and distorted parable of the attitude Hitchcock was taking toward Tippi Hedren.

He gave Robert Burks unusual instructions about photographing her face — the camera was to come as close as possible, the lenses were almost to make love to her. For a scene in which she is kissed by Sean Connery the close-up is so tight, the frame filled so fully with pressing lips, that the tone is virtually pornographic. And the rape scene — weird in its incomprehensible mixture of the male character's initial tenderness that at once becomes crude exploitation — caused everyone considerable discomfort. The film was becoming the story of a director's desire for an inaccessible actress who, therefore, became even more an object of fantasy. Visitors and guests were eventually prohibited from the set. At the end of every day, he sent champagne to her dressing room. And by November he was telling her his recurring dream.

"You were in the living room of my house in Santa Cruz, and there was a rainbow, a glow around you. You came right up to me and said, 'Hitch, I love you — I'll always love you,' and we embraced." (He could have been describing the final metamorphosis of Kim Novak in *Vertigo*.) "Don't you understand," he asked in a low voice, "that you're everything I've ever dreamed about? If it weren't for Alma . . ." Tippi Hedren's feelings and intentions, and her own private life, seemed of no concern to him.

"But it was a dream, Hitch," she told him. "Just a dream." And she left her dressing room.

"Hitch was a fantasist," Jay Allen said. "But in Alma there was no fantasy. He would go off and have his fantasy-romances, and Alma dealt with it. She didn't understand it, but she dealt with it." For the women drawn into the attempt to realize the fantasy, however, detachment came far less easily than for Alma.

Soon Hitchcock devised other approaches. That autumn he invited MCA executives to the set to see what he was proudly proclaiming as an Academy Award performance. He announced to everyone that this was his ultimate actress, the one he had waited decades to direct, and that she was giving the finest performance in any of his films. And then he began to speak even more candidly, and to tell more and more people about his feelings for her. They were not surprised at the feelings; they were astounded at his admission of them. All this naturally caused the object of his fancy more and more anxiety, and her only concern was to finish the film without a major confrontation. But he gave her not a moment's rest, and he enlisted allies to find out why she could reject a man so in love.

"We all know about your private life," one nervous executive said to her in a tone suggesting that her reputation might have been other than what it was and that she need not be so unyielding. When she asked what he meant — other than her impending marriage to her agent, which everyone knew was scheduled for after completion of the film — he had to say that he meant nothing.

There was nothing revealed by the graphologist to whom Hitchcock sent a sample of Hedren's handwriting, hoping to receive a report of a duplicitous personality. For months he tried to find reasons for what he finally considered — in his ultimate confusion of actress and role — her frigidity. Frigidity, he reasoned, could have been the only explanation for her rejection of him and his desires. He had become the Sean Connery character of the film, studying patterns of behavior, pressing, pursuing, transforming his interest in zoology and instinctual behavior into a tragic and degrading ultimatum.

Amateur analysts might look at this sad episode and seek easy explanations for Hitchcock's injudicious, unworthy, and unkind conduct. Some might suggest that the events could only have been set in motion by a man in his sixties who had lived a life of severe repression, who by his own admission had lived chastely for over thirty years — that a healthy, active libido, earlier, would have prevented this entire chapter of his life. Others would perhaps describe it as the ultimate fantasy of the ultimate filmmaker, closing the gap between art and life — a case of Hitchcock so involving himself in the realization of his story that the lines demarcating reality became hopelessly blurred. And then there is the response of a social historian, perhaps, or a cynical observer of Hollywood, who might point out that, after all, things have always been this way; seduction is known in every profession and is taken for granted — especially in the performing arts — as an occupational hazard that most people calmly negotiate. None of these responses is sufficient, however — although there is perhaps something true and relevant in each of them.

Everyone knew of Tippi Hedren's pain and anger at this time. Possibly only she clearly saw the look of anguish and frustration and desire that marked Hitchcock's expression each day for months. But only Hitchcock himself knew the depths of his pain, and he never confided this to anyone. Had he wished, he could easily have found women to gratify his sexual desires, but for Alfred Hitchcock — dreamer, fantasist, romantic — it was the pursuit of the dream that mattered. Had he actually touched the closest incarnation of his dream, the moment of physical contact might have been intolerable for him, and he perhaps would have turned as he turned from an argument or from any tense or threatening situation.

In his case, it is not difficult to summon as much compassion for the frustrated lover as for the put-upon beloved — for not only was the passion not shared, but his bewilderment and grief were abnormally deep and long-lasting. Unrequited devotion is at some point an experience in many an adult's life, and is hard enough to endure. But if one *wants* his devotion to remain unrequited, and selects as its recipient an individual clearly and unmistakably unattainable — as, for instance, the wife is to her blackmailing husband in *Marnie* — then the resultant grief and sense of loss moves to a profound level. In the end, time and distance healed the memories for Tippi Hedren. But Hitchcock tended his wounds forever after; his professional and personal decline can be traced to this sorry period more than to any creative crisis.

The crew and the studio personnel, however, continued to act as if there were no severe tension at all. In January, as if it were the most natural thing in the world (as indeed, in a sense, it was), Hitchcock summoned Jay Presson Allen to discuss a first draft for the project he had waited forty years to realize: a film of James Barrie's fragile, preternatural romance *Mary Rose*. His masterpiece, as he foresaw it, had at last found its worthy exponent in Tippi Hedren, and his desire to revive the often abandoned work made eminent sense now. The play's doomed, dreamy, ghost-haunted characters perfectly matched his own ideal; the central action — the changelessness of love and the beloved, the meeting and union of time and memory — conformed to his own spirit.

Hitchcock and Allen talked, the writer produced a first draft within weeks, and Hitchcock sat down, over one weekend, and supplemented it with the most poignant additions he ever made to a submitted script. "If you plan to be bald and fat," Mary Rose says to the man who loves her, "I daresay I shan't mind!" And, later, the words spoken to Mary Rose came from Hitchcock, and from his heart, too: "I was searching for you — or for something you might have been." Finally, to a second draft submitted on Valentine's Day in 1964, he added the narrator's epilogue. "Once more," the camera directions indicate,

the island is seen as we saw it first, a sweetly solitary place, a promising place. And now again, we hear Cameron's voice. "The island. Surely we all know at least one such tempting place, . . . such an island where we may not go. Or if we do dare to visit such an island, we cannot come away again without embarrassment. And it takes more than a bit of searching to find someone who will forgive us that.

"Well, that is it. Let's go back home now. There of course it's raining, as usual. And there's a naughty boy waiting for punishment and an old villager who had the fatal combination of a weak heart and a bad temper. He's waiting to be buried. All the usual, dependable, un-islandly things. You understand."

But the film was never to be, for the gentle mood in its script was not matched on the set of the production in progress.

"I was agonizingly sorry for both of them," Jay Presson Allen said of the final days of the shooting of *Marnie*. "It was an old man's cri de coeur. She had her own life, and everyone was telling her not to make Hitchcock unhappy. But she couldn't help making him unhappy! By the end of the film he was very angry with her." He was, first, upset enough to refuse her permission to accept the Photoplay Award as most promising new actress of the year. *The Tonight Show*, then televised from New York, was to be the forum for presenting the citation, but Hitchcock could not bear her departure even for two days. Telephoning for her, he rejected the award, canceled the appearance, and thus created a long and unfortunate resentment of her by both the magazine and the television program.

And then it happened. In late February Hitchcock finally lost any remnant of dignity and discretion. Alone with Hedren in her trailer after the day's work, he made an overt sexual proposition that she could neither ignore nor answer casually, as she could his previous gestures. There was no precedent in his life for such boldness — as there had been no precedent for the savage bird attack he had forced her to endure. Until that afternoon, she and his staff thought that if the final filming could be carried off without an incident like this, the strain for all of them would rapidly diminish. But he brought the issue to an ugly moment of crisis. She was appalled and shaken, but he persisted and became threatening: they would cancel plans for *Mary Rose;* her income would be reduced so that she would not be able to help her parents; she would be forced to accept small roles in shabby television serials Universal was beginning to market; he would ruin her, make her as notable a mockery as he had a star. These alternatives she could accept; acquiescence she could not.

Forever after that bitter and humiliating afternoon, he refused to address Tippi Hedren personally. He never even uttered her name, referring only to "that girl." His directions on the set were given through assistants, and her questions had to be relayed to him by an equally circuitous route. From that day forth he also lost all interest in *Marnie*. He stopped speaking of an Oscar-winning performance and at once began to belittle Hedren to anyone who would listen. He would still make *Mary Rose,* he said, but with another actress — Claire Griswold, perhaps. (In fact MCA/Universal was as unenthusiastic about *Mary Rose* as they had been about *Marnie*. "Lew Wasserman didn't like *Marnie,"* Jay Allen recalled. "It was made at a time of career crisis for Hitch. And they didn't like the first drafts of *Mary Rose*. They knew it would make him fall back into the Tippi trap.")

Hitchcock seemed to want *Marnie* to fail, in fact, and he no longer took any concern even for the technical details, the special effects, or the careful use of rear projection and artificial sets that, with much hesitation, had been planned for major scenes. He refused the advice of designers and assistants to use alternatives to these inferior, almost makeshift movie means. He ceased to care about anything around him. For years he refused to discuss the glaring technical blunders in the picture, and at last he took refuge in a revised version of the facts that he probably came to believe: "I needed more time for everything, script, sets and so forth. . . . That was a technical mix-up, and something of which I did not approve. We were very pressed for time, or I would have scrapped the whole thing and started over."

For years, a cadre of Hitchcock's admirers (this author among the most defensive of them) concocted tortuous arguments more admirable for their ingenuity than consistent with the facts: to account for the sloppy technique of the film, rationalizations were adduced to demonstrate that these aberrations were deliberate on Hitchcock's part, a conscious reversion to an expressionistic style that used artifice to represent a disordered psyche. But the real reason was simpler and sadder, and those reviewers who were critical, it should be admitted, were right: these moments in *Marnie* are not emotionally disturbing, they are simply visually jarring; they mark not a deliberate use of unconventional means, but are simply unpleasant examples of the director's cavalier disinterest in the final product.

Hitchcock passed the spring of 1964 in a gloomy semi-isolation, emerging from the retreat of home and Alma only to look at a reel or two of *Marnie* and to give the pretense of seeking his next film property. At the same time, his affluence and his investments increased magnificently — and so did his fanatic commitment to routine, as if it were a way of taking a stand against the inner chaos and division. His closet held six identical dark suits (made to order at $300 each), six identical pairs of shoes, ten identical ties, and fifteen identical shirts and pairs of socks. "I am," he told an interviewer that season, "a creature of habit and order." Of the invariable nature of his daily outfit he said: "I think it relates to one's tidiness of mind. I have a very tidy mind and I think life becomes so much less complicated if the clothes are standard and routine."

The revenues from *Psycho* — then up to $14 million — were soon matched by the first months' receipts on *The Birds,* which quickly brought in $11 million. The magazines and story anthologies to which he sold his name also enjoyed a burst of unexpected success, and since he received a percentage of their profit, this increased his income too. The syndication of his television series — soon to end — brought him, it was reported at the time, a profit of $7 million.

"Money *per se* has never been important to me," Hitchcock told a questioner. "Business matters are a mystery to me and I frankly leave all the economic negotiations to others." That money itself was never important was true enough — but what money could buy became more and more important. By this time the expanded and refurbished eat-in kitchen at Bellagio Road had cost more than the original price of the entire house; and the wine cellar below, installed at a cost of $75,000, held vintage wines worth more than twice that amount. Hitchcock had also acquired a Picasso, for he was advised it was a good investment; eventually it was insured with a small collection for over $250,000. He continued to add to the walk-in refrigerator — huge slabs of meat were shipped from distant points, and Jurgensen's of Beverly Hills delivered gourmet delicacies with Kantian regularity. If some appetites were unsatisfied, others were indulged more freely.

When a reporter asked Hitchcock if there was a connection between his business success and his social life, he replied: "I have a couple of real friends — a couple of businessmen." He might have been thinking of Lew Wasserman of MCA, and Herman Citron, his agent.

As for Hitchcock's involvement in business, an alumnus of MCA remarked that he was "one of the shrewdest businessmen in the industry" at that time.

It's true he never involves himself directly in financial negotiations, or in deals for talents or scripts. But this is only because haggling over terms causes strain and stress and, unlike the characters in his productions, he hates having any tension in his life. His negotiator reports back on everything to Hitch, and gets directions from the boss on what terms to make about capital gains, residuals, foreign rights and all that sort of thing. . . . Hitch was one of the first directors, you know, to stop taking a salary from a studio and branch out as an individual entrepreneur so his taxes would be at the corporation level, not the high personal-income level. The man has made millions and he's invested with an eye toward further return with the lowest possible tax bite. He's in real estate and oil wells, he has a big stock portfolio and he's even a partner in owning huge herds of cattle.

In May Hitchcock and Alma left for a month's vacation in Europe, where they stopped in Yugoslavia and Italy, dined in Monaco with the prince and princess, and visited Ingrid Bergman in Paris — where Hitchcock again met François Truffaut, and agreed to enter into a partnership for a book of interviews covering the senior director's career. Still insisting he would someday film *Mary Rose,* he also told the press he would soon begin working on a screenplay of John Buchan's *Three Hostages;* but that, too, was never seriously developed. By the first week of July Hitchcock was going through the motions of promoting *Marnie* in New York, Philadelphia, Washington, Cleveland, and Chicago. He then returned to Bel-Air to await the reaction to the film, and was not seen at the studio for several weeks after the depressing verdict came in.

Whereas reviewers and audiences alike were divided in their reaction to *The Birds,* there was virtual unanimity about *Marnie.* After Hitchcock's long string of successes, they roundly denounced him for this picture. One New York journalist was among the few who liked it; but his judgment (that it had "a human warmth and sympathy that makes it Hitchcock's most appealing film since *Rear Window*" and that it was "an altogether superior film") was not shared. On the contrary, most agreed that it was "pathetically old-fashioned and dismally naive — a major disappointment." Everyone leaped to criticize the film's technical ineptness, and in the same breath said it was dated in its simplistic psychological case-history. With this film, Alfred Hitchcock fell from public grace and severed an abiding relationship he had enjoyed with audiences and their spokesmen in a decade of major films and television shows.

And yet *Marnie,* years later, has an intimate and curious appeal unique in Hitchcock's output. Its lack of structure and its dreamlike, almost hallucinatory texture draw the viewer into an empathy with its lacerated emotions. Unlike any of his works, it is fretted with open pleas for love. "Why don't you love me, Mama?" Marnie asks in an early scene.

"I've always wondered why you don't.'' And at the end, learning the truth of her past, she cries, "You *must* have loved me, Mama — you *must* have loved me!'' Mother (Louise Latham, in a moving portrayal of a misguided soul) replies, "Why, you're the only thing I ever did love — it's just that I was so young. . . .'' The film is laced with lines like these that convey a naked feeling Hitchcock had never allowed in his films before. It was as if the upheaval and yearning in his own heart had demanded an unambiguous expression at last in his work. His deepest need was certainly responsible for the truth of the film's feeling. But so was Tippi Hedren, whose quiet strength, on screen and off, dignified a cheerless story and a pathetic year.

# Fourteen

1964–1972

N o one was surprised to hear that Alfred Hitchcock's winter holiday at the end of 1964 would be prolonged. An almost funereal quiet had settled over his offices at Universal, and visitors to Bellagio Road found him poring over short stories, crime novels, news reports, and even recent plays in search of a new film idea. The executives at MCA/Universal, although respectful and encouraging, were firm: whatever he chose to do, he would have to use "big names" for his cast, and the details of story, script, production values, and design would have to be submitted for their scrutiny. No one on the executive floors of Universal's "black tower" was keen on repeating the disaster of *Marnie*.

Because Hitchcock never spoke in any but the most confident phrases, nothing can be found in public statements at this time to suggest that he had any concern for his status as one of the era's most enduringly successful filmmakers, or that he felt there was any truth to some of the rumblings in the press — that the master had not only lost touch with contemporary audiences, but that things were worse: he had lost his technique and humor. In addition to such negative publicity, his television program was not to be renewed by the network. Always conscious of his image and aware that to a great extent he was dependent on the press to maintain it, Hitchcock could not have been unconcerned by what was going on around him, as newer and bolder television series flashed across the home screen and younger directors and executives moved into offices in the major studios.

He was in his sixty-sixth year, and the atmosphere of awe and legend that surrounded him — and that he had done very much to create and sustain — now revealed its burdensome aspect. His successes had been great and uninterrupted for a decade, but the single critical and popular failure of *Marnie* was enough, in the fickle way of the industry, to lose him considerable loyalty. Among the Oscar-winning films of 1964 were *My Fair Lady* and *Mary Poppins* — certainly no threat to what Hitchcock was doing. But it was also the year of *Dr. Strangelove, Zorba the Greek,* and *Goldfinger.* In addition, foreign films were no longer the special province of an elite; Fellini, Truffaut, and Ingmar Bergman drew large crowds to theaters and had followings on campuses all over America.

Hitchcock, who had for years protested that David Selznick's custom of long-term contracts and lavish productions was prodigal and counterproductive, had repeated the same pattern himself. And if he had recalled, in the early sixties, Selznick's creative stasis after *Rebecca,* it would have been only natural. After *Psycho,* what could he do to extend himself? *The Birds* increased his fortune, but there were complaints about its lack of resolution; what was a startling virtue in the European cinema was apparently a sign of weakness in America.

Earlier, uncertain about a new project, Hitchcock had fallen back on what was a proven type of picture — the result was *Dial "M" for Murder* — and he decided to "fall back" again as he and Alma concluded their winter trip to Saint Moritz and went south to Italy on business. He would take the advice of Universal and return to the comic thriller that had served him so well — and that, everyone felt, he could still monopolize. *Topkapi* was a hit that year — a caper film about a jewel theft. It owed something to Hitchcock's method and treatment, but he could out-Hitchcock the Hitchcock imitators, and that was what he planned.

In Rome, a meeting was arranged with two of the most successful writers of the European postwar cinema. Agenore Incrocci and Furio Scarpelli, who collaborated as Age and Scarpelli, were the Ben Hecht and Charles MacArthur of Italy, and since 1950 they had written a series of light comic films that often featured bumbling small-time crooks. Their best-known satires were the enormously successful films written with director Mario Monicelli, notably *I Soliti Ignoti* (distributed in the United States as *Big Deal on Madonna Street*) and *La Grande Guerra* (*The Great War*). By 1965, they were in their mid-forties and riding the crest of a great wave; they were also part of the new European cinema, which was making every studio in America aware of a style different from the standard Hollywood gloss.

The story Hitchcock discussed with them derived from his fascination with crime, with life in the large luxury hotels he knew so well, and with the possibilities of ethnic humor, which was then newly acceptable. "The central figure in the story is an Italian-American, manager of a New York hotel, who takes in members of the family from Italy,'' Hitchcock explained. "But they're all crooks. It's a sort of Mafia in a big New York hotel — a comedy melodrama. The chef, the chief cashier, housekeeper and the bell-boys will all be members of the same family. They will all be lovable Italians. It will be a murder movie with overtones of comedy.''

Age and Scarpelli began to work on the script, and eventually they came to Universal to discuss the first draft with Hitchcock. But somehow the idea never developed satisfactorily; what kept emerging was a script that more closely resembled something to be filmed by Pietro Germi or Vittorio De Sica — or even their own previous work for Monicelli. The cultural gap was too much for Hitchcock to bridge, and the project never reached an advanced stage. For over a year, however, he continued to speak of it as something he hoped to realize. In the summer of 1965 he tried to interest Marcello Mastroianni in it, with either Sophia Loren or Claudia Cardinale, to capitalize on their successes with Fellini and De Sica. But it was not to be.

Returning to Bel-Air and Universal, Hitchcock's spirits were buoyed by news from the Screen Producers Guild. They planned, on Sunday, March 7, to present him with the twelfth Milestone Award for his "historic contribution to the American motion picture.'' Jack Benny, David Selznick, and Cary Grant were to be among the hosts of the event, and Samuel Goldwyn and Jack Warner promised to attend. The evening demanded substantial preparation, and Hitchcock helped edit a thirty-four-minute compilation of film clips. Awaiting word on the progress of Age and Scarpelli (and still trying to find a way of making *Mary Rose* — although with whom he did not know), he busied himself with the award ceremony. But when it arrived, the evening's good cheer had a sour note.

Throughout Hitchcock's painful attempts to incarnate his romantic fantasies in a real-life situation, Alma remained strong and silent and patient — or at least such was her demeanor in public, and with their acquaintances and colleagues. What transpired at home shall never be known, but there must have been a keen tension, for Alma — who objected to the seating assignment of the Producers Guild dinner on the ground that her husband would be seated beside yet another beautiful blond actress — refused in advance to attend. She demanded that Hitchcock either ask for a new arrangement or plan to stay home. He flatly refused both requests, and Alma, furious, took the car and could not be located for hours. Just as she might have hoped, this threw him into a panic and poisoned the evening. When she finally returned nearly a day

later, he learned that she had driven, alone, up to Santa Cruz and back —
just in time to be at his side for the ceremony.

The situation is worth recounting because it reveals something about
the amalgam of need and resentment, of devotion and of demand that
characterized their relationship at this time. In this they were hardly
exceptional. The posture they showed to the world was so dignified,
and her own calculated persona of subservient hausfrau so constant, that
it is easy to forget that privately their life together was very different.
Alma's angry departure from Bellagio Road that morning was apparently for her the only thing she could do; it was an action perhaps unjustified (her husband, after all, had nothing to do with the seating plans),
but straws that break camels' backs are rarely, on their own, heavy or
exceptional. The woman seated at Hitchcock's other side might just have
been one blond too many for Alma to accept with her usual airy affect
of unconcern.

The evening had one beneficial result: Hollywood helped to bury the
bad impression left by *Marnie,* which now seemed but a momentary
lapse in an altogether outstanding career. Producers and writers and actors and editors praised Hitchcock's visual genius, the press seemed
willing to make him their darling once more, and, for a while at least,
a breach was healed. The American Society of Newspaper Editors invited Hitchcock to the nation's capital to address the group's annual
dinner, and this at once continued the favorable publicity and distracted
him from the annoying fact that, as he had found out by early spring,
the prospects of obtaining a script from Age and Scarpelli were not
bright.

On April 17 he read a (ghostwritten) paper to the journalists in Washington, who gave him a rousing response. "In just three weeks," he
said, "I shall mark the completion of ten years on television. That is a
long time to be getting away with murder, but they seem to have caught
up with me at last. I am not sure what my punishment will be, but I
suspect I shall be strapped to a chair and placed in front of an open
television set." He concluded by observing — in a possible reference
to journalists' response to *Marnie* — that "newspapers harbor a class
of people who, like me, combine movies and murder in a single calling.
I refer to the critics. . . . May I say that I rejoice that we live in a
country where the manipulation of words and images to achieve a desired effect on an audience is *my* business and not *yours.*"

By early May Hitchcock had decided to revive an old idea that had
long intrigued him — a film based on the infamous Burgess-MacLean
spy case in England. What, Hitchcock asked Lew Wasserman at lunch

one afternoon, could the emotional reaction and burden have been for the wife of Burgess? The director talked enthusiastically of the old love-versus-duty theme, complicated here by an issue of unrequited love and homosexuality. But the emotional and narrative center would be the effect on a woman of her husband's treason. Hitchcock agreed that he needed a first-rate writer to help him develop this, but he was turned down when he invited James Goldman, who was about to adapt his play *The Lion in Winter* for the screen. The story needed strong characters and a writer accustomed to handling a woman's viewpoint, and so Hitchcock took the advice of Michael Ludmer, story editor at Universal, and asked to meet Brian Moore, author of several highly regarded novels, including *The Lonely Passion of Judith Hearne*.

As it happened, Brian Moore was not at all interested in writing screenplays. Although he had adapted his novel *The Luck of Ginger Coffey,* he intended to devote his time henceforth to his fiction. "But the fact was," he remembered, "that I needed money at the time in order to be free to write novels, and the chance to work with the great Hitchcock seemed like something that should be seriously considered." When they met, the cordiality and mutual understanding were instant. Hitchcock confided that he understood Moore's Irish-Catholic background and that the religious-school setting of his novel *The Feast of Lupercal* was familiar to him from his own background. "I found him thoroughly engaging and sensible," said Moore, "but after we had discussed his idea, I decided that this was really not right for me." Hitchcock and his associates were astonished when Moore turned down the offer several days later. "In the rather perverse way of such things, of course, that convinced them that I must be the best person for the job," Moore remembered, "and at once they doubled their initial offer and said they would pay me fifty thousand dollars." Assured that the task would be a valuable addition to his credits and that the handsome salary would be earned in a matter of a few months, Moore at last accepted.

"I arrived very much against my own judgment," he recalled, "but willing to do the best I could. We met daily at his office and our relationship continued splendidly. My father came from Hitchcock's era, and so in our talks he never had to explain to me his allusions to Marie Belloc Lowndes or English Catholic schools or various aspects of Edwardian society." One aspect of their arrangement, however, annoyed the writer. He had been asked to work on a treatment first, for which he would be paid one installment of his salary; then he was to proceed to a first draft, and another installment would be issued; and so on until the final revisions. This gave him the feeling that he was a shop boy hired on approval. "But I was even more concerned when, after three or four days of our conversation, I realized that we were in for trouble. I found that he had absolutely no concept of character — even of two-dimensional figures in a story. He kept switching from the woman's to the man's point of view, and the original story idea began to shift and fade uncontrollably.''

But perhaps, Moore told himself, this was Hitchcock's working method, and since he was willing to defer to the director's infinitely superior knowledge of what made a film work, he decided to watch the Hitchcock canon — which he did for part of every day until he had seen all of his films. Their work continued throughout the summer, and somehow the cordiality survived mounting difficulties. Universal arranged for Hitchcock to have Paul Newman and Julie Andrews as the stars of the picture, but with that decision the homosexual subtheme had to be dropped, and Hitchcock further complained that the audience would be expecting Andrews to sing.

But Brian Moore knew that Hitchcock had other reasons for resenting the forced casting: "They were to be paid enormous salaries [more than 20 percent of the film's $5-million budget, and a percentage of the profits], and they were going to be the stars. Hitchcock by this time wasn't accustomed to anyone being the star but himself. And there was of course his anxiety about what their presences would do to the story. That worried him deeply and inhibited our collaboration. And the more nervous he got, the more he'd fall back on something he'd done before in an earlier picture.''

The writing of what was soon called *Torn Curtain* continued during the entire second half of 1965, even through the beginning of shooting in November. Moore liked Hitchcock, who always behaved courteously and professionally. But there was a constant anxiety during the project, and the writer very quickly realized that the film was becoming a collection of tricks from Hitchcock's earlier works. "He had a preoccupation with the most trivial details of a story — such as what airline departs a city on a given day — but oddly, this was his strength at the time, and it assured a wealth of accurate historical and social and cultural detail. But it also covered a profound ignorance of human motivation.''

As the screenplay was nearing completion, Moore realized that the woman's viewpoint and the story of Burgess and MacLean had all but vanished, and that there were only three story ideas he had provided for the picture: first, he had come up with the idea that the scientific secret Paul Newman needs (and pretends to defect from America to learn) is in a communist professor's head and must be tricked out of him; second, from an unpublished short story of his own, Moore suggested the subsidiary character of a woman who attaches herself to visitors from the West in order to win her way to freedom (in the finished film, with Lila Kedrova, the episode substitutes an eccentric, bravura performance for a potentially powerful situation); third, from his father's experience as a surgeon and from his own volunteer work during the London blitz, Moore knew that people in life do not always, as they often do in movies, die easily or cleanly — they are, he told Hitchcock, hard to dispatch. "On this point he really went to town developing the murder scene," Moore recalled. "He went further than I think he should have in that case." (Very many people who have seen *Torn Curtain* can recall only the brutal, slow killing that ends with a man's fingers twitching spastically as his head is held in a gas oven until he dies.)

"Apart from these three ideas," according to Moore, "the film is little else than a Hitchcock compendium. I told him that for truth's sake the credits should read 'Screenplay by Alfred Hitchcock, assisted by Brian Moore,' but he said he never took writing credit.''* In addition, Moore told Hitchcock quite candidly that he thought the characters weak and the narrative unbelievable, and that polishing the dialogue would help very little. "I told him that if it were a book I were writing, I'd scrap it or do a complete rewrite."

This opinion Hitchcock did not take very well, and he suggested that Moore take a short vacation in San Francisco to do a few revisions. "And so I left. And I never heard from Hitchcock again. That very day, he hired Keith Waterhouse and Willis Hall — the English screenwriters of *Billy Liar,* who were very popular then — to come over to do a rewrite." (Peggy Robertson suggested to Hitchcock that he swallow his pride and ask John Michael Hayes to come back and help with the revisions, but that advice was, of course, not heeded.)

The news did not unduly upset Brian Moore. "I realized that taking criticism or confronting disagreement was another problem for Hitchcock. As with all living legends, no one had the courage to tell him that anything was wrong. That was very bad for the poor man. And because of his own personality and background — as the lonely, frightened boy — he had a horror of confrontation with people. He wasn't able to argue something out face to face. So he did things through intermediaries, or he sent someone on a vacation and then replaced him."

Moore at this point offered to have his name removed from the film, which he thought was about to be a critical and popular disaster. To his

---

* "I never take producer credit or writing credit," Hitchcock once said. "I've been the writer of the design of the film. In other words, I sit down with the writer and lay out the whole film from beginning to end. . . . The writer goes away and elaborates on it. He'll characterize the people and write the dialogue."

surprise, however, Hitchcock asked him not only to retain credit but also to sign a waiver yielding his share of the profits from a future sale to television. At the same time, Waterhouse and Hall were demanding equal credit as writers, and thus a share of Moore's profit. The Screen Writers Guild proposed to Moore that he submit the matter to arbitration as a test case. "The decision was quick and clear. The various scripts were examined and it was determined that the script Hitchcock was going to film was the one I had done with him, and that the additions by Waterhouse and Hall were minor dialogue changes. It was all rather odd, considering that this was apparently a victory for the Guild and for screenwriters . . . it wasn't one that meant much to me in terms of my own career."

Meanwhile, the project had to proceed to its term. "I was unhappy with the script and wanted to postpone the beginning of shooting," Hitchcock said later, "but that was impossible because of Julie Andrews's schedule. I had tried in vain to free myself of her services, protesting that she was a singer and couldn't be convincing as a scientist. But the studio insisted she was great box-office. . . . Newman read the script and found it pretty bad — something I knew already."

*Torn Curtain* was something Paul Newman tried to forget ever after. "We all knew we had a loser on our hands in this picture," he said. "When Hitchcock first invited me to his house and described the story in detail, it sounded like an exciting story, so I agreed to do it. But somehow the script didn't turn out the way he'd told it, and all during the shooting we all wished we didn't have to make it. The only good thing was that we didn't have any location work, since all the European settings were built right there on Universal's lot."

And Julie Andrews expressed similar disenchantment: "I accepted for the chance to work with Hitchcock, and he taught me more about film and lenses than anyone. It was a wonderful education, but he was obviously more interested in manipulating people, and in getting a reaction from the audience, than he was in directing us. The first day of production, he announced that for him the fun was over — the creative part was finished with script and storyboard preparation — and now, he said, the rest was a bore. You can imagine how that made us feel."

"He just lost heart during the shooting," according to Samuel Taylor, who remained in contact with the anxious Hitchcock during the last months of 1965. "He had been told by the studio that he was getting the two biggest stars of the day, and he discovered that they didn't fit the Hitchcock mold or the Hitchcock method. He just couldn't get a chemistry going with them, and he got very depressed and just went through the motions." Hitchcock admitted as much later, though he never gave any indication of realizing that the true flaw was in the script itself: "We'd have done much better with that picture without Julie Andrews or Paul Newman. Bad chemistry, that was. Up front they said, 'Oh, she's so hot.' The two of them, with overhead, cost us 1.8 million dollars, which was to me a disgrace, spending all that money — and miscasting, at that! Just because they happened to be hot!"

By February the filming was complete and Hitchcock was ready to meet with Bernard Herrmann about the music. After seven scores for Hitchcock and the sound supervision of *The Birds,* Herrmann had an understanding of what helped and what hindered a picture. But Universal, unhappy with the traditionalism and what the studio executives called his lazy, derivative score for *Marnie,* made it clear that a different kind of sound track was required now — not a symphonic score, but one popular enough to include a title song and to sell thousands of records. This, they reasoned — and Hitchcock was quick to accept a recommendation that might commercially help the picture — would also help to lighten a humorless and curiously chilly, detached film.

In late March, Herrmann called Hitchcock and told him the completed score was ready for recording. Hitchcock arrived at the Goldwyn Studios, listened to the first few bars of the credit music, and burst into an angry tirade in front of the musicians and studio personnel. And Herrmann matched him — to the embarrassment of everyone present. "He had wanted a pop tune," Herrmann said later. "It's a shame — it was a good score. . . . I told him, 'Hitch, what's the use of my doing more with you? . . . I had a career before, and I will afterwards.' He said he was entitled to a great pop tune. I said, 'Look, Hitch, you can't outjump your own shadow. And you don't make pop pictures. What do you want with me? I don't write pop music.' "

And with that, Hitchcock left the recording studio, livid that Herrmann had contravened his instructions and put him in a difficult corner with the Universal executives — to whom he was more and more responsive than ever. "He became a different man," Herrmann said of Hitchcock's tenure at Universal. "They made him very rich, and they never let Hitch forget it." With this unfortunate clash between Hitchcock's persistence (dictated by stubborn commercial considerations) and Herrmann's persistence (dictated by equally stubborn aesthetic considerations), a decade's creative collaboration was broken and another sad cleavage in Hitchcock's life occurred — and at a time when there were already few associates the director could rely on for creative and emotional support. Later, when Herrmann visited Hitchcock's office in a gesture of reconciliation, Hitchcock hid behind a door to avoid being seen and escape what might have been a moment's awkwardness.

Within days, Stanley Wilson — in charge of MCA/Universal's television music department — arranged for Hitchcock to meet the Oscar-winning composer John Addison, who thereupon composed a score for *Torn Curtain* in one month. He found Hitchcock amiable but not much interested, and when Addison arranged a telephone hookup months later, during the dubbing, to play part of the music to Hitchcock in England, the only response he got was, "Good . . . fine . . . fine."

"When I saw the film," Brian Moore remembered, "it was with a chill. There were lovely moments in it, and it's obvious Hitchcock has an interesting mind. He's the film director who is most like a writer, insofar as he creates his films alone in a room — and that, for him, is the process of filmmaking. And this made him unique." Moore's analogy illuminates Hitchcock's own remarks:

I wish I didn't have to shoot the picture. When I've gone through the script and created the picture on paper, for me the creative job is done, and the rest is just a bore. . . . The most enjoyable part is in that little office, with the writer, when we are discussing the story lines and what we're going to put on the screen. . . . I do not let the writer go off on his own and just write a script that I will interpret. I stay involved with him and get him involved in the direction of the picture. So he becomes more than a writer; he becomes part maker of the picture, because the picture is being made right there with him.

None of this effort paid off with *Torn Curtain,* however. It was an inauspicious and unfortunate production despite the advertisements proclaiming it "Hitchcock's fiftieth masterpiece." As Brian Moore sadly observed, "It's a bad film. And if you know Hitchcock you know he's simply ransacked his bag of tricks here."

The film was to be released by Universal in the summer of 1966, and it so happened that the Cambridge University Film Society invited Hitchcock to England to deliver an address before the summer holiday. Glad of any chance to travel and delay promotional activities, he and Alma made the first of two trips to London that season. The Cambridge students, putting aside their critical reserve, welcomed him; they were too young, in any case, to hold the grudge of their predecessors about Hitchcock's departure from England a quarter of a century earlier. During a discussion period, the director amused his audience by suggesting that "mass hypnotism would be a nice idea for the theatre of the future. You buy a ticket and choose what character you want to be. If you want to be the villain, then you have a good time being the villain, and if you want to be the tortured woman, you can suffer." This initiated a response from the science students, and once again Hitchcock compared the film audience to a giant organ to be played, adding that electrodes in the brain could have the same effect as films — a simple surgical procedure would save him all the trouble of making movies. He tried to be witty in his Orwellian predictions, but there was a visible strain, and he seemed quite sincere in his desire to find alternatives to filmmaking.

Travel — flight, literally — seemed the only distraction that summer. By early July Hitchcock was back in New York, where on July 7, Mayor John V. Lindsay bestowed the city's cultural medal of honor on him at a City Hall ceremony. Wisely, however, Hitchcock chose to make his television appearances and to give his press interviews there before *Torn Curtain* opened, and by that time (July 27) he had moved north. At Harvard University he received the first honorary Drama Club membership in twenty years, Boston University awarded a citation, and Governor John Volpe declared July 14 Alfred Hitchcock Day in the Commonwealth of Massachusetts. Mayor John Collins of Boston practically shut down the city in his honor, and by the time *Torn Curtain* had its local premiere, everyone was so taken with the visiting television personality that criticism of the film was overriden by an outpouring of enthusiasm for the man himself.

Continuing northward, the Hitchcocks stopped to visit Samuel and Suzanne Taylor at their home in East Blue Hill, Maine, where (as Alma told them) Hitchcock seemed to relax for the first time in years. The Taylors provided elegance without arch formality; they also knew Hitchcock's gourmet preferences and served to his taste at a luncheon attended also by Walter Lippmann and Brooke Astor. Hitchcock preferred to meet the other guests by having them brought in to him, and from a safe perch he quietly held court. He told how he had several years earlier commissioned Georges Braque to design a twelve-foot ceramic tile to be installed at the end of the formal garden at Santa Cruz. Fascinated by Braque's famous bird designs in the 1950s, he had tried to bring the artist to America to supervise the installation — as earlier, taking counsel from his financial advisers, he had asked Jean Dubuffet to accept a commission. The Braque was eventually installed by others (and finally dismanted when the house was sold); the Dubuffet was never realized. Hitchcock's gift of gratitude to the Taylors for their hospitality was a specially designed, noiseless toilet for their guest quarters.

The trip continued, and on July 22 Hitchcock addressed students at the University of Toronto on "Art and the Business of Filmmaking," which was simply a new title for the Cambridge speech. The Directors Guild of Canada diplomatically chose to sidestep *Torn Curtain* after hearing the advance word, and discussion, prudently, focused on Hitchcock's British masterworks and the Selznick period — subjects Hitchcock was always ready to illuminate with anecdotes from his conversational baggage. "Selznick used to send me the most ingenious memos," he said of his former producer, who had died shortly after the Milestone Award dinner the previous year. "I just finished reading one of them the other day."

From Canada, the Hitchcocks returned to England, where Universal's London offices had arranged for him to be honored by the Association of Cinematograph, Television and Allied Technicians. Universal began a festive day by sponsoring a luncheon at the Europa Hotel on August 8, hosted by Michael Balcon, who offered a nostalgic speech in which he recalled the days when a film was a motion picture, not a package, and when an actor was a performer, not a registered company. Taking Balcon's lead, London film society had by now chosen to forget the old wounds about Hitchcock's relocation to America in 1939, and when someone suggested that he return to make a film in England, he was delighted. The suggestion did not appeal to Alma; it appalled her.

Hitchcock's luncheon speech delighted everyone and was major news in the trade papers (in fact, he would recycle substantial parts of it in two major speeches delivered in later years, after James Allardice's death deprived him of his all-purpose writer). "They say that when a man drowns," Hitchcock began, "his entire life flashes before his eyes. I am indeed fortunate for having just had that same experience without even getting my feet wet." He added that he had labored "in this bizarre trade" for over forty years, and that he had survived silent films, talkies, narrow screens, wide screens, 3-D, drive-ins, in-flight movies, and television. "And now here I am at the climax of my career — I'm an after-luncheon speaker. And speaking of television, its invention is an interesting chapter in the history of entertainment. It can be compared to the introduction of indoor plumbing — it brought no change in the public's habits, it simply eliminated the necessity of leaving the house." At the ACTT dinner that evening, Hitchcock accepted honorary membership, said that he regarded himself as a technician — one of the crew, just like them — and observed that the real intruders on their work were the actors. This brought down the house, and the invitation to come home to make a movie was repeated by several executive technicians.

By summer's end the trepidation about *Torn Curtain* had proved justified. The press in general pronounced Hitchcock's fiftieth film no cause for celebration — calling it, in various ways, a bundle of clichés. But a dramatic shift was about to occur in the director's fame and public image.

The Hitchcocks returned to Los Angeles in late August, and there

François Truffaut was waiting with interpreter and tape recorder. Over a period of fifty hours the two filmmakers discussed Hitchcock's career in a series of conversations that soon became the celebrated and influential book *Hitchcock.*\* Truffaut's interviews established Hitchcock's status as the quintessential *auteur,* or movie "author," a director who exerted unprecedented creative control over each of his films. The timing could not have been better. Hitchcock's career was indeed in crisis, and he and Universal needed to have his accomplishments codified and celebrated by a respected colleague in the industry. Truffaut, the humanist of the French New Wave, provided the honors at precisely the time when movie reviewing was graduating to the status of film criticism and when "Saturday night at the movies" was becoming "Monday morning in the classroom."

And Hitchcock, whose memory about facts and generosity toward collaborators was — in those interviews — of uneven quality, gladly accepted a beatification he never quite understood. Truffaut's sincere and devoted *hommage* — which corrected but a few of Hitchcock's many errors of memory and in effect allowed him to be more the *auteur* of that book than of any of his films — won for both of them a wide new following. It also hurt and disappointed just about everybody who had ever worked with Alfred Hitchcock, for the interviews reduced the writers, the designers, the photographers, the composers, and the actors to little other than elves in the master carpenter's workshop. The book is a valuable testimony to Truffaut's sensibilities, and to Hitchcock's brilliantly lean cinematic technique. It is also a masterpiece of Hitchcockian self-promotion.

With Truffaut's visit, Hitchcock had been sufficiently reminded of his own importance to take a longer and more serious look at contemporary films to find out what was bringing in the audiences. "That was always his criterion for a movie's success," according to Brian Moore. "Whether it was someone else's picture or his own, he could think of it as a success only if it made money."

Within a matter of days, novelist Howard Fast received a call from Universal inviting him to Los Angeles to discuss a film with Hitchcock; soon he had agreed to the task, and the daily round of discussions began. "My God, Howard!" Hitchcock exclaimed early on. "I've just seen Antonioni's *Blow-Up*. These Italian directors are a century ahead

---

\*This was not the first lengthy interview that covered all of Hitchcock's films. On February 12, 13, and 14, 1963, Hitchcock met with actor/writer Peter Bogdanovich (who was later to become a film director) for a series of discussions, which New York's Museum of Modern Art published during a season-long Hitchcock retrospective that year. Bogdanovich updated his interview a decade later.

of me in terms of technique! What have I been doing all this time?''
And with that uncharacteristic admission of the need for revaluation,
Hitchcock continued to watch every film of 1966 in his private screen-
ing room.

"After we worked out the treatment," Fast recalled, "Hitchcock gave
me a very free hand. He seemed mostly interested in working out elaborate camera movements. By the time the script was finished he had
specified over four hundred and fifty camera positions — it was that
technically detailed.'' ("An architect can put a building down on paper,"
Hitchcock said at the time. "Why shouldn't we make a film the same
way?") The film — successively called *Frenzy* and *Kaleidoscope* — was
to be about a misshapen psychopathic murderer (the son of a respected
general) who also happened to be homosexual. Hitchcock was delighted
with Fast's work on the screenplay and summoned the chiefs of
MCA/Universal. "In no time at all," according to the writer, "they
rejected the script and told Hitchcock they couldn't allow him to film
it. They told him his pictures were known for elegant villains, and that
here was an impossibly ugly one."

And for the first but not the last time, Hitchcock was so agonized by
the studio's reaction that he broke into tears. And he had Fast's sympathy: "They had belittled Hitchcock's attempt to do precisely what
they had been urging him to do — to attempt something different, to
catch up with the swiftly moving times. They insisted it might be fine
for someone else, but they took all copies of the script from Hitchcock's
office and from me." All traces of the prepared scenario vanished with
the luncheon plates on that one unhappy afternoon in autumn 1966.

As often before, Hitchcock's sorrow and anxiety were accompanied
by social gracelessness. Unaccountably, he began to resent Howard Fast,
and when he and his wife invited the Hitchcocks to dinner before their
departure from California, Hitchcock said quite calmly, "I couldn't possibly come to dinner. I'm a real gourmet, and I'd have no idea what
your wife might serve."

As the year drew to a close, Hitchcock's isolation became sadder and
more disturbing to Alma, who had the idea to ask Samuel and Suzanne
Taylor to come along for the winter holiday at Saint Moritz. The Taylors determined to make this as happy an experience as possible, and
Suzanne put special energy into the preparation of the traditional Nor-
wegian Christmas cake she had learned about from her family — a lavish, high series of almond circles and pastry — to which she attached
fifty tiny flags, each with the title of a Hitchcock film. A gala party was
arranged in the director's honor at the Palace Hotel, an event briefly
delayed when Hitchcock expressed dismay over the absence of photog-

raphers. He might have been in a creative crisis, but he had not lost his sense of publicity, and he was still his own best promoter.

The holiday was largely a gastronomic one for Hitchcock. He slept until noon, dictated the menus for the gargantuan lunches and four-hour dinners, insisted that the view from his suite was grand enough that he need not venture outside, and saw to the preparations for lavish cocktail hours. His preferences had not changed much since the 1930s, with the Bennetts. While Alma and the Taylors strolled round the snow-lined paths and the skating rinks and bundled into sleighs, Hitchcock watched them from the balcony. He joined them only once — and a spill on an icy path caused him a mild panic that then *indeed* a photographer might be present. Otherwise, he spent afternoons placing lengthy telephone calls to Universal, announcing the cocktail hour earlier each day, and insisting that it was possible to strangle a woman while using only one hand — a fact he simulated on Suzanne Taylor's neck. Later, in the course of a macabre conversation Hitchcock initiated, she said she had never understood the pathology of necrophilism, and he warmed to the subject for an hour. "Hitch was fascinated by this specialty," Samuel Taylor recalled, "for as long as we knew him."

Among all the collaborators Hitchcock enlisted, perhaps none came closer to friendship or were more loyal or patient or understanding than this couple. Samuel Taylor had created the stunning script for *Vertigo* that endowed some of Hitchcock's greatest images with dialogue and character, and he had shared the frustrating experience of working on the ill-fated Audrey Hepburn film; Suzanne Taylor was a cheerful, supportive companion and hostess. What the Hitchcocks may have appreciated most of all was the fact that the Taylors asked no questions, made no demands, never crossed the border from respectful familiarity to a presumption of emotional intimacy. And when unhappier days came, it was to them that Hitchcock would try to turn — and it was even from them, as from others, that he at last found it difficult to accept the comfort of friendship.

For virtually all 1967, very little of Alfred Hitchcock's life is known. There is nothing to suggest a period as mysterious or provocative as occurred with Agatha Christie in 1926, for Hitchcock's disappearance was only from his offices. In a period of profound anxiety and depression, he made himself a prisoner of his own feelings in his own home. In springtime he supervised the rearrangement of books in his study — the valuable first editions of complete works by Barrie and Wells and Shaw. The stability of the Hitchcock's marriage, it seems, was never more tested than during that year. Earlier, he had admitted that Alma's knowledge of him surpassed anyone's, and he made it clear that he appreciated her discretion. "I dread being alone. Alma knows that, too. . . . She puts up with a lot from me. I daresay any man who names his dog Philip of Magnesia, as I did, is hard to live with. Alma won't say."

And for most of the year, Alma did not say. When literary properties came to the studio for Hitchcock's consideration, he took them to her for a judgment, and if she felt negative about something, he rejected it. At no time was he as responsive to her as during 1967, when he kept closer to home than ever. In important protective and supportive ways, she had always been as much a collaborating mother as a patient companion; that combination of roles characterizes many relationships, and is certainly no sign of neurotic unbalance. But from this time forward, visitors and colleagues remarked that he seemed actually to be afraid of her. "Hitch and Alma were like brother and sister," according to Samuel Taylor. "Every so often she would utter a violently acid remark about someone, but it usually wasn't about a woman or about Hitch's fondnesses. It would be about someone she thought was cheating Hitch from a business viewpoint. When it came to that part of his life, she could be a scrappy little watchdog."

At the same time, she kept a dignified, almost subservient silence in public, and this had the desired effect: it gave people the impression that she was the long-suffering spouse. When he was most indiscreet in his fantasy-romances, that impression was no doubt true; at home, however, and among their closest companions, she was sharp and outspoken. Some insisted that her critical side was necessary because, as Hitchcock himself admitted, she had a lot to sustain; according to others, he, too, suffered considerably from her subtle harassment. But no wildly dramatic account emerges from this marriage, nothing to suggest that it had more or less than the tensions and eccentricities of any forty-year relationship. It is perhaps to the Hitchcocks' mutual credit that until very late neither of them complained about the other to outsiders — in public or in private — and that in some fortuitous way they were able to accommodate each other until his death.

As the year closed, however, Alma began to insist that his inactivity was doing him no good. They accepted one theater-party invitation, to the opening night of Ingrid Bergman's Los Angeles appearance in Eugene O'Neill's *More Stately Mansions*. But Hitchcock's withdrawal from social and professional interests continued, and finally Alma approached Lew Wasserman, begging him to find a project to get her husband back to work. Could he not, she asked, bring some pressure about the contract with Universal?

The Hitchcocks left for Europe with a small library of books to read, but even a month after their return in the new year there was nothing that gripped him. Finally, in their shared desperation, he agreed to undertake a film version of a novel Universal had purchased rights to that arid autumn: Leon Uris's sprawling *Topaz,* about espionage among the French, Cubans, Russians, and Americans at the time of the 1962 missile crisis. As part of the arrangement, Uris himself was to submit a first draft of a script, and while he wrote, the Hitchcocks planned their travel, for the location shooting would take them to a number of European cities.

Hitchock's mood early in 1968 was lightened somewhat by the news that the Academy of Motion Picture Arts and Sciences was going to give him, at its fortieth annual ceremonies in April, the Irving G. Thalberg Memorial Award ''for the most consistent high level of production achievement by an individual producer.'' He might have rightly guessed, however, that this was something of a consolation prize from the embarrassed Academy after years of slighting him, for although he had been nominated five times for best direction (for *Rebecca, Lifeboat, Spellbound, Rear Window,* and *Psycho*), he had been repeatedly denied the winner's gold-plated statuette. When he appeared to receive the award, he stepped to the microphone as the ovation subsided and everyone awaited a witty, offbeat Hitchcock speech — the kind they knew from television and banquets.

''Thank you,'' he said without expression, and stepped away.

Some thought this brevity bespoke a quiet, lightly veiled contempt. They were probably correct.

Hitchcock chose his usual New York residence, the Saint Regis Hotel, to announce his new picture to the press. On May 3 — between the assassinations of Martin Luther King, Jr., and Robert F. Kennedy, and just days after Lyndon Johnson's announcement that he would not seek a second full term as president — Hitchcock summoned the city's reporters and press photographers, many of whom were more accustomed, during those violent times, to covering the numerous politicians announcing various candidacies. ''I'm here to announce that I am going to run,'' he said slowly, pausing for effect, ''a picture in about a year. It has been on the best seller list as a novel for over thirty weeks, and its author is here to my left.'' He said the shooting would begin in October, and that his film would emphasize not political but emotional realities, not major stars but a respected international cast.

He then returned to Scotts Valley, where on June 9 the University of California at Santa Cruz bestowed on him an honorary doctorate ''for magnificent accomplishments in the world of cinema.'' Later that month, aware that he would need a top-notch associate producer to handle the complexities of *Topaz*, Hitchcock invited Herbert Coleman to rejoin him. During the decade since *North by Northwest*, Coleman had enjoyed a busy career in film and television, and had contributed significantly to the Hitchcock TV series after the director got over his initial resentment of Coleman's independence. They now discussed casting, and Coleman suggested that if Hitchcock wanted a bankable international cast, he should engage Yves Montand and Catherine Deneuve. But, Coleman recalled, "Hitch didn't like to be told what to do, so he forfeited both of them."

The script submitted by Uris was not going well — that was clear to Hitchcock's assistants and to those in the front offices at Universal, who were keeping a close vigil. At one point, hoping to engage him to do revisions on Uris's script, the New York office of MCA sent a copy of the book to Arthur Laurents at his summer home on Long Island; he turned it down. Once again, Peggy Robertson proposed John Michael Hayes for help with the script, but Hitchcock was adamant. By this time the film was scheduled for production in Europe, and the Hitchcocks flew to London. There the troubles began in earnest.

"He called me from Claridge's," Samuel Taylor remembered, "and said anxiously, 'I'm in bad trouble, Sam. I've got a script I just can't shoot.' I asked him why he couldn't delay until he felt there was a decent screenplay, but he cried out, 'I have to go with it now, it's in production!' In other words, the money clock was ticking — and he was very conscious of money. He didn't have the strength to stand up against the company powers when it came to money, and when the money was his, he panicked." As he had done a decade earlier on *Vertigo*, Taylor came to Hitchcock's rescue. The next morning he flew from Maine to Boston, then to London, and began writing. "*Topaz* was a dreadful experience," he recalled,

because Hitchcock threw out the screenplay entirely and had me writing scenes a few days — and in many cases a few hours — before they were shot. It was very difficult for all of us. We went on to Copenhagen and Paris and Wiesbaden, then back to Washington and New York before returning for the studio interiors. And we didn't even have a complete cast — we were still picking actors when there were only a few weeks of shooting left. The Cuban lady [played by Karin Dor], for example, was not cast until the last minute, and we went through a whole list and did screen tests of many actresses.

Casting continued in Paris, where Hitchcock hired the blond actress Claude Jade, who was recommended to him by Truffaut, her recent director. She and Hitchcock "talked in a Paris hotel about cooking," she said, "and I gave him my recipe for soufflé and told him I liked *Strangers on a Train,* and that was that." According to Hitchcock, she and Dany Robin, cast as her mother, would provide the glamour in the story. ("Claude Jade is a rather quiet young lady," he said later, "but I wouldn't guarantee [that] about her behavior in a taxi"; his cinematic imagination might have been in crisis, but his fantasies seemed as active as ever, and as typical.) John Forsythe was invited back for one of the leading roles, and the Austrian actor Frederick Stafford was engaged to play the French spy caught in the middle of personal and national loyalties.

All the details of European casting and the location shooting were problematic for Hitchcock, who believed that the slapdash nature of the script construction and shooting schedule never could make for a successful picture. When he was not anxious, he was bored, and the only diversion that pleased him was an excursion he, Alma, Herbert Coleman, and Samuel Taylor made to the Russian-Finnish border. He had just bought the rights to the espionage novel *The Short Night,* by Ronald Kirkbride, in which a major part of the action occurred at that frontier. "Hitch loved it when everyone at the border stood to applaud," Coleman remembered. "He loved being recognized, whereas many celebrities don't and cherish their anonymity when they're traveling. Hitch, on the other hand, cherished his privacy in other ways but loved being famous." Taylor agreed: "Every time we came to a village on the border, little children came and cried out, 'Heech — Heech!' and he adored it."

Returning to Paris, they found new problems. André Malraux, minister of culture, withdrew the permit for shooting on French soil because the script, which had to be approved, was judged critical of Gaullist policies. A hasty meeting was arranged with the American ambassador in Paris, Sargent Shriver, who was somewhat puzzled to find himself in the role of movie agent. Was this a matter for the embassy? he wanted to know. It was indeed, Coleman insisted, since the French government had raised it to that level by complaining that Universal and Alfred Hitchcock were producing an anti-French film. In a day the matter was resolved, but not before the temporary delay caused the director considerably more emotional upset than anyone else. The possibility of international intrigue had shifted from the story to real life just long enough to cause him anxiety. To celebrate the settlement of the matter, he changed his plans and accepted an invitation from Grace and Rainier of Monaco to dine at their Paris home. He declined, however, to visit Madeleine Carroll at her home in the same quiet cul-de-sac they were using for actor Michel Piccoli's apartment in the film.

Back in Los Angeles, the production of Hitchcock's most expensive picture to date continued with the construction of huge sets representing a Harlem hotel, a Virginia mansion, a French-government conference room, a Cuban street, and La Guardia Airport as it was in 1962. Clarence Brown (the director of *National Velvet* and *The Yearling*, among other films) loaned his local home for use as a Cuban hacienda. Hitchcock left the supervision of all this to his assistant Peggy Robertson, to Coleman, to designer Henry Bumstead, and to artist Albert Whitlock. The only details that seemed to engage him were typical: he ordered Pierre's Restaurant in Paris to ship its own pâté for a climactic luncheon scene; he twice set the revelation of secrets in a toilet; and he brought back bird trainer Ray Berwick for a hastily inserted scene in which a gull causes trouble for sympathetic spies. But Hitchcock's detachment from everything else was a cause of concern to one and all. Teresa Wright, of whom he always expressed fond memories from the days of *Shadow of a Doubt,* visited the set and was saddened to find a different man from the jovial, active director she remembered. He had not only aged, he was unhappy and distant.

Toward the end of filming, Hitchcock attempted to join in the new spirit of candor in films by including a scene between Stafford and Karin Dor seminude in a bedroom, but he was foiled when told that the actress had had surgery that made such graphicness impossible. Instead, he devoted himself to the single memorable shot of the picture: "Just before John Vernon kills her," Hitchcock explained, "the camera slowly travels up and doesn't stop until the moment she falls. I had attached to her gown five strands of thread held by five men off-camera. At the moment she collapses, the men pulled the threads and her robe splayed out like a flower that was opening up. That was for contrast. Although it was a death scene, I wanted it to look very beautiful."

The problems with the film continued to the end of shooting in the late summer of 1969 — and then into the editing process. For the first time since *Suspicion,* Hitchcock simply could not work out with his writer a satisfactory ending to the story — a story he himself had trouble summarizing, since it was being created daily, as fresh pages of script were delivered to the players. Alternative endings were considered and even shot: in one, the French spy working for Russia and the French spy friendly to America depart on separate airplanes; in another, a duel in a deserted stadium ends with the assassination of the Russian sympathizer by a sniper. But preview audiences to whom the unscored picture was shown in Los Angeles and London registered confusion about the latter version, and so from material previously shot the finale was patched together by nervous Universal executives; they enlisted the goodwill and creative assistance of the faithful Samuel Taylor and Herbert Coleman, who by this time were scarcely happier than Hitchcock with the result.

"One of the tragedies of *Topaz*," Taylor reflected later, "was that Hitch was trying to make something as if he had Ingrid Bergman and Cary Grant. But he didn't have the story for it, and he certainly didn't have the cast." And after the film had its first and only major theatrical release, Hitchcock all but disowned it: "*Topaz* was a most unhappy picture to make. The ending I put on was a duel. . . . But it didn't go down well with audiences, so they changed it. I could have fought the decision, but it didn't seem worthwhile. . . . It was a compromise, a terrible compromise. . . . And all those Frenchmen and Cubans and Russians speaking *English* — it just didn't work on any level."

Compromise or not, and in spite of the mild political contretemps, praise from the French critics persisted. On September 5, Didier Raguenet, the French consul general, conveyed his country's Arts and Letters Award, making Hitchcock an Officier des Arts et des Lettres. Among those present for the Hollywood ceremony were James Stewart, Anne Baxter, John Forsythe, Maurice Jarre (composer of the score for *Topaz*), French director Serge Bourguignon, and author Henry Miller. "I have not yet filmed my last picture," Hitchcock assured them. "*Topaz* is my fifty-first feature film, but when I [will] film my last picture has not yet been decided by me, my backers or God. . . . I want to be remembered as a man who entertained millions through the technique of film. . . . I sometimes think, though, I would have liked to have been a criminal lawyer. Think of the opportunity I would have had to be a great man in court!" But with his horror of confrontation or direct argument, he should have known he would not have been a very persuasive man in court at all.

The promotional tour for the film began on December 1. For this strenuous activity, MCA provided Hitchcock with a private jet. Within weeks the seventy-year-old director had visited 50 cities, appeared on 93 television shows, answered questions on 21 radio shows, and had given over 100 press interviews. *Topaz*, everyone at Universal reasoned, needed this much help, and by the time it opened in New York on December 19, Hitchcock was such a familiar and genial presence in the media that some important critics were even willing to defend the film. Audiences agreed with the majority of reviewers, however: Alfred Hitchcock seemed to have lost faith in his heroes. Worse, he seemed to have lost faith in his own ability to make good motion pictures. People in and out of the industry began to speak of him as "the director who used to make films like *Psycho*," or "the man who in his day had made . . ."

With the new year, Hitchcock began to look for a new project to reestablish himself — one far less expensive than *Topaz* and one that could be carefully prepared from treatment and script, so that all the difficulties of the last picture could be avoided. If he could accomplish both these goals, he reasoned, the executives at Universal could not deny him freedom in choice of subject matter.

In February 1970 Hitchcock visited the Center for Advanced Film Studies at the American Film Institute in Beverly Hills, where for an afternoon and evening he held forth, for a crowd of admiring students and apprentice filmmakers, on the history of his career, on his view of actors and audiences, and on the precise distinctions he made between surprise and suspense. Although he always insisted that his fascination with murder derived from his British background (from the English invention of the detective story and the gothic murder mystery — the tradition, especially, of Conan Doyle and Wilkie Collins), it was precisely *not*, he insisted at this conference, the intellectual exercise of the crime thriller that interested him. What he always tried to add was the emotional factor — and in fact the whodunit, as he reminded the students, was not a Hitchcockian genre at all.

There is a great confusion between the words "mystery" and "suspense." The two things are absolutely miles apart. Mystery is an intellectual process, like in a "whodunit." But suspense is essentially an emotional process. You can only get the suspense element going by giving the audience information. I daresay you have seen many films which have mysterious goings-on. You don't know what is going on, why the man is doing this or that. You are about a third of the way through the film before you realize what it is all about. To me that is absolutely wasted footage, because there is no emotion to it. . . . There is no emotion from the audience. . . . The mystery form has no particular appeal to me, because it is merely a fact of mystifying an audience, which I don't think is enough.

The added dimension of Hitchcock's best work — its moral as well as its aesthetic sense — cannot, in fact, be easily explained by referring to sociological theory or historical analysis. In part the moral sense derives from the director's "Englishness" (Nice people don't murder; it's bad form) and from his training in Catholicism (Everyone shares in man's sinful fallen state, and evil sprouts round us like demonic weeds). These two aspects come together in Hitchcock's villains, who are usually — on the surface — polite and respectable gentlemen; and there is in this motif the Cockney defiance of social convention — which was also part of the popular-artist's tool kit in the early years of this century. Hitchcock's moral sense thus reveals the shallowness of the ordinary judgment — for nice people *do* commit murder. In this regard, the Catholic sensibility triumphs. Everyone is capable of sin. Vigilance is always called for. "The world has to be watched very carefully," as MacDonald Carey says at the end of *Shadow of a Doubt.* "Things seem to go crazy from time to time."

In a quite tangible way — as Hitchcock obliquely mentioned at the American Film Institute conference that evening — his entire career, both in the content of his work and in the gradual refinement of his technique, was devoted to tearing apart the English canonization of manners. He made elegance the characteristic of the venal and the villainous personality. And perhaps because his religious training was never really integrated into his art — perhaps because the Englishness and the Catholicism caused a kind of emotional schizophrenia in him (the Catholicism he always associated with the social disrespectability he sought to shed) — his life and work were concerned with the split in his own personality. He always wanted to be accepted, and at the same time he wanted to do everything that would deny him that acceptance.

What intrigued Hitchcock about murder mysteries was certainly not the intellectual puzzle: it was the way the murderer broke with social convention while confounding society's code by remaining cultured and refined. And at the same time, the director's Catholic roots and deep moral sense as an artist insisted that this split in style and act (elegance versus crime) was the clue to the fragility of the human condition. "There's a devil in every one of us," Hitchcock said when he was besieged with questions about the moral implications of *Psycho.*

And it may not be going too far to suggest that Hitchcock's moral vision partially explains his lifelong refusal to look socially acceptable — to seem attractive or to dress stylishly. The refusal to cater to society's expectations of style perhaps betokened a latent hope that a cult of nonelegance would somehow exonerate him from the guilt that he saw masquerading *behind* the facade of fashion. Such deliberate nonconformity would correspond to that part of him that condemned the values of polite society, that rejected the world's standard of judging goodness by appearances.

A few days after the AFI event, someone at Universal who had heard Hitchcock's remarks gave him a copy of Arthur La Bern's ill-conceived novel of murder and trial *Goodbye Piccadilly, Farewell Leicester Square.* Although the director liked the scheme of the relationship between hero and villain, elegance and vulgarity in the book, he was not keen on the elongated courtroom drama, nor on the London setting. "I prefer to make movies near home," he said, explaining his insistence on remaining in California for the next project in order to avoid the globe-trotting *Topaz* had demanded. "That way I can get back to Madame at six o'clock for dinner." A short time later he would reverse this decision, but for 1970 he planned no greater excursion than to Santa Cruz. About this time, however, even that retreat began to be more of a burden than a pleasure, and at the suggestion of his advisers, to whom he confided his thoughts about selling it, he found a way of realizing a major tax benefit. Accordingly, it was not long before he turned over the country house as a gift to his lawyer and his agent (who at once sold the house and property and turned the gift into a substantial cash profit for themselves).

In May the Hitchcocks accepted an invitation from the Taylor family to attend the wedding of their son in San Francisco. Ordinarily, such invitations were ignored or politely rejected. Hitchcock's secretary, Suzanne Gauthier, remembered that he was annoyed at not being invited to many such occasions but noted that he would not have attended in any case. He wanted, it seems, to be sought out so that he could do the negating; but if others ignored him and denied him the chance to turn them down, his pain was almost palpable.

"From what he told me about his past," according to Ernest Lehman,

and from my observations of his day-to-day life during the years I was fairly close to him, I gained a strong impression that he had been and always would be, for all his fame, a lonely man who was unhappy with his loneliness but did not know how to break out into active gregariousness without suffering great anxiety.

It wasn't that people didn't *want* to be with him. They would have loved to bask in the sunshine of his wit and the wisdom of his worldly interests and the glory of his celebrityhood, but they had this unstated fear of him. Without his knowing that he was doing it — for it was his unconscious way of creating a protective wall around himself, behind which he could feel safe (though lonely) — he projected the image of a snobbish, elitist, judgmental, critical, unpleasable, aloof, superior being — none of which he truly felt about himself, and all of which was felt by would-be friends, acquaintances, and colleagues as too threatening, too frightening to risk.

Too many people felt too uneasy about the possible loss of their self-esteem to risk it by getting close to a real or imagined negative evaluation from this unconsciously intimidating gentleman. Everyone, as a result, became the loser, because everyone wanted to know so much more about this unknowable man than they got to know, and certainly he, like almost all men, wanted desperately to be known by his fellows, but didn't know how to do it.

And so there were only a few who got to know what great fun he was to be with — unless one couldn't stand dirty stories, outrageous puns, practical jokes, antiestablishment political philosophizing, and irreverent gossip about everyone from H. G. Wells to H. R. Haldeman.

The only social event of this season on the Hitchcocks' calendar seems to have been the wedding of Michael Taylor to Francesca Peck; the Samuel Taylors' personal photo album shows a jovial Hitchcock and Alma toasting the newlyweds with brimming glasses. Those closest to Hitchcock at work felt that until about this time he would often have liked to broaden the scope of his social life, but that just as often Alma kept the diversions limited. Over the years, she had gradually developed a protectiveness of their private life, and even a possessiveness about her husband — and no wonder. His attentions had so often strayed to objects of fantasy, and he sat — in and out of her presence — so often in a private haze of romantic obsession, that it is easy to understand her attempts to keep of him what she could, to limit whenever possible even innocent social intercourse, the better to prevent it from flaring into something for him more pathetic and for her more irritating. Soon, however, a series of unhappy events would forever dictate the restrictions of their social life.

For much of 1970, Hitchcock read even more avidly than usual. He went through the latest biographies, as well as the controversial fiction, plus books about international politics, intrigue, and espionage. In addition, he had an abiding interest in scientific and technical matters.

"When I mentioned that I couldn't understand how one of the jumbo jets ever gets into the air," Suzanne Gauthier said, "he gave me a detailed lecture on aviation and aerodynamics. On another occasion, I expressed some wonder about the magic of television, and he described the fine points of that, too. He was a born teacher, and he could talk for hours about a wide variety of special topics. He didn't parade his knowledge unless you asked a specific question or made a big mistake about something, but his fund of information was always surprising." And to the fund he added much that year, with extensive reading in legal history, fiction, and drama. He also continued to see almost every new American and foreign film.

By summer's end he had met several times with the chief officers of Universal, who made it clear to him that the multimillion-dollar expense for *Topaz* could not be repeated on his next film without major guarantees in script, cast, and production values. As always, Hitchcock listened to the studio heads with a mixture of quiet resentment and fear. The fear was incited not only by the gentility of these authority figures but also by their apparently greater familiarity with what audiences wanted; he knew that his success depended on following the advice of those he would otherwise have gladly ignored.

A combination of reasons financial and nostalgic thus encouraged Hitchcock to reread Arthur La Bern's inelegant novel and to see that he could make its story of a London rapist-murderer into something peculiarly his own by filming it in London, where he had lately been so well received. Even Alma had to admit that in England there was a better chance of making a film cheaper, quicker, and with less interference than in Hollywood. And the actors could be handpicked from the London theater, where training was substantial, where attention to detail was taken for granted, and where — unlike Hollywood — famous actors do not think it unworthy to accept small, well-written roles.

To generate such well-written roles from the inferior novel, Hitchcock approached Vladimir Nabokov. The Russian-born novelist and poet was exactly his own age, had also been educated in England, and had emigrated to America at the same time as Hitchcock. In addition, he had drafted an adaptation of his novel *Lolita* for director Stanley Kubrick. Hitchcock was fascinated by Nabokov's theme of an older man's passion for a young girl, and he appreciated the author's wry, dark humor. "Yes, of course I know who you are," Nabokov replied, startled at Hitchcock's formal and unassuming telephone call. Later, he confided, "I've seen very little Hitchcock, but I admire his craftsmanship. I fondly recall one film of his, about someone named Harry. His humor noir is akin to my humor noir, if that's what it should be called. Perhaps there are other reasons too." But nevertheless, Nabokov declined on the spot, under the press of his own writing schedule.

On December 31 Hitchcock called Anthony Shaffer, whose play *Sleuth* was a hit in London and New York. "I thought it was a joke," Shaffer remembered. "There we were, in the midst of a New Year's Eve party, and a man called and said he was Alfred Hitchcock, and would I be interested in doing a screenplay with him. I kept talking to him, trying to place the voice of a joking friend, but eventually I realized that it was indeed Hitchcock himself." Unwilling to commit himself without considering the novel and meeting with the director in person, Shaffer proposed that he view again Hitchcock's major films; this he did, and several weeks later he was lunching at Universal City and discussing his methods of work. By early March they had laid out the general story in a prose treatment and developed the characters and their motivations.

Hitchcock was determined to avoid the fiasco of *Topaz* and to adhere as closely as possible to his stated ideals:

"You can improvise and you should improvise," he said,

but I think it should be done in an office, where there are no electricians waiting and no actors waiting, and you can improvise all you want — ahead of
time. Sometimes, I compare it with a composer who is trying to write a piece
of music with a full orchestra in front of him. Can you imagine him saying,
"Flute, give me that note again, will you? Thank you, flute," and he writes it
down. A painter has his canvas and he uses his charcoal sketch and he goes to
work on that canvas with a preconceived idea. I'm sure he doesn't guess it as
he goes along. So I am not in approval of the improvisation on the studio stage,
while the actor is on the phone about his next picture, and all that kind of stuff.
. . . I shoot a precut picture. In other words, every piece of film is designed
to perform a function.

"Lunch was always the same, day after day," Shaffer remembered of those months, "— a small steak and salad. One day I complained, very gently, about this monotony. I shouldn't have. Next day, a fifteen-course dinner arrived, catered by Chasen's, and was laid at my table-side. Hitch, of course, had his small steak and salad." But despite the director's self-control at lunchtime, "the work stopped promptly at four o'clock every afternoon, when he ordered in a pitcher of daiquiris, and the conversation turned to Hollywood gossip, which sometimes seemed to interest him more than anything."

From the start, Hitchcock called the film *Frenzy,* although it had nothing to do with the project he had undertaken with Howard Fast. Much of the preparation involved a review of the medical and psycho-logical literature dealing with sexual pathology, and to this Hitchcock devoted himself with singular delight. "*Frenzy,*" he told people at the time, "is the story of a man who is impotent and therefore expresses himself through murder." Many have thought that the result clause — "and therefore . . ." — contains a strange logic, or one that perhaps made sense only to Hitchcock.

"It was a film he really had to do," Shaffer said. "He had lost some of his self-confidence, and he had no interest in politics. Spy thrillers were out of the question because of the recent failures he'd had, but he seemed to have this excited interest in bizarre sexual crimes. So this rather grim story of a rapist-strangler was perhaps inevitable. He had, it seemed to me, become not only mythicized — he was also lugu-brious."

Shaffer, however, kept the tone of their work light. The film was to be about a betrayal of friendship, about the cross-matched relationship between a psychotic and an angry nonhero, and there would have to be some humor in the dialogue. He kept this in mind as they went to London to scout locations and as their conversations continued at Claridge's. Hitchcock was, for a time, positively transported. He insisted on using Covent Garden's food markets for location shooting before they fell to the wrecker's ball — while they were still unchanged from his childhood, when he would go there with his father. The Old Bailey Court, which Hitchcock had also regularly visited, would also be a setting — along with the narrow alleys round Bow Street and Oxford Street, County Hall, the Coburg Hotel, pubs near Covent Garden, and, for the killer's residence, a flat above Duckworth and Company in Henrietta Street (exactly, Hitchcock pointed out, where Clemence Dane had lived). Shaffer suggested, since it was a modern story, some newer London locations, and with reluctance Hitchcock agreed to the London Hilton and New Scotland Yard. "But he was intractable about not modernizing the dialogue of the picture," Shaffer recalled, "and he kept inserting antique phrases I knew would cause the British public a hearty laugh or even some annoyance."

The location scouting and research were briefly interrupted during the first week of March, when Princess Anne, on behalf of the Society of Film and Television Arts, presented Hitchcock with the first honorary membership at a ceremony at the Royal Albert Hall attended by fourteen hundred people. Soon after, Hitchcock returned to Los Angeles to prepare for the technicalities of a longer relocation; and Shaffer wrote the first draft, met once more with his director, and completed his work before the beginning of summer 1971.

"I had a happy time with the writer of *Frenzy*," Hitchcock said. "It's a crime story, but I wanted to avoid the inevitable scene among the detectives at Scotland Yard. So we had the plot points discussed by the inspector and his wife at home over meals. And I made the wife a gourmet cook." The completed scenes between these two characters provide the comic relief of the film — the wife's gourmet cookery is disastrous, very nearly poisonous; and the obvious connection between Hitchcock the spinner of crime stories and Alma the astute listener-critic-cook is only slightly changed by the clear difference between the women's culinary skills.

The collaboration on the screenplay turned out to be the smoothest since *Psycho*, and Hitchcock's return to London for the casting and filming of *Frenzy* in the summer and fall of 1971 was in every way triumphant. He stopped first in Paris, where in mid-June Henri Langlois, of the Cinémathèque Française, awarded him the rank of Cheva-

lier in the Legion of Honor and presented him with a document signed
by Georges Pompidou, president of France. For the next two months in
England, he interviewed London stage actors in his suite at Claridge's,
and Alma scoured the shops for gifts for her granddaughters.

For the role of the psychopath, Hitchcock signed Barry Foster, after
seeing him in the film *The Twisted Nerve*. Jon Finch, who had lately
performed in Roman Polanski's *Macbeth*, was cast as the least sympathetic, most irascible innocent man in any of Hitchcock's films. Anna
Massey, who was originally interviewed for the role of the secretary
(eventually played by Jean Marsh) was finally cast as Finch's mistress;
Alec McCowen and Vivien Merchant, also widely known for their work
in the theater, were signed for the inspector and his wife. Barbara Leigh-
Hunt agreed to make her film debut as Finch's former wife and the
victim of the most detailed and lurid murder ever depicted by Hitchcock. And Elsie Randolph, the famous comedienne and musical star
who had played the amusing eccentric of *Rich and Strange*, returned to
a Hitchcock set after forty years for a small role.

"It's so wonderful to be back here!" Hitchcock said to Samuel Taylor, who was in London at the same time. "I'd forgotten what actors
could do for me! They're not only prepared, they have ideas of their
own — marvelous little bits of business! Vivien Merchant and Alec
McCowen had their scenes completely worked out before they came to
a rehearsal. And the crew at Pinewood Studios was so good!" Everyone
connected with the production agreed that, for a time, Hitchcock was in
great humor and involved himself in every detail. "He shot the film
meticulously at the start," Shaffer recalled; and Jon Finch basically
agreed: "I don't think he was that interested in what the actors were
doing, but he was always aware of the camera, and he knew when
someone was being shot too short or too long. When passersby at Covent Garden asked me who the star of the film was, I told them 'Alfred
Hitchcock.' " And Hitchcock told Vivien Merchant: "I hired you because you're an actress. You do your business, and you just let me play
with my camera."

As the shooting progressed throughout the summer, however, the
players began to notice that Hitchcock's attitude was changing. "He had
immense creative energy and a real mental zest," Anna Massey recalled, "and early on he was concerned about every detail — clothes
and colors and set dressings. But then he got slow physically. Off the
set, the only conversation that seemed to interest him was about food —
he taught me how to make a good batter — and later I realized that
this was apt at a time when we were making a film so crowded with
food." To everyone who would listen, Hitchcock spoke of his child-

hood in old London, and of the Moroccan tomatoes available at Covent Garden in both 1901 and 1971, and of the citrus fruits from Israel, the grapes from Spain, the vegetables from California, and the special produce from all over the world. He spoke briefly but for the first time in perhaps decades of his father, the Leytonstone grocer; and when a very old man came up to him at Covent Garden and said he knew William Hitchcock, Sr., there was a flicker of recognition — for just a moment — on the features of the director.

Hitchcock spoke of foodstuffs and recipes and restaurants of the world like a man speaking of various lovers; and to anyone who knew how his life had developed in America, it became clear that *Frenzy*'s food was an obsession. "Food was very important to him," as one of his earlier actresses said. "He got as emotional about food as he did about anything, and his relationship to food was almost sexual."* At this time during the shooting, as well, Hitchcock was eating and drinking more than ever — and to such excess that, as the cast unanimously remembered, he quite frequently slept through the afternoon's filming.

But his indulgences — and the film itself — were interrupted by an event as sudden as the madness of the killer in *Frenzy*. "I went down to his suite one morning," Anthony Shaffer remembered, "and Hitchcock opened the door and said quite calmly, 'Well, dear boy, it seems that Alma has had a small stroke.' " Nurses and doctors attended the small, frail woman, barely visible beneath the covers, and throughout that day it was apparent to Hitchcock's staff and to the representatives from Universal's London offices that his calm was a great performance. Alma was partially paralyzed, her speech was affected, and her cognition was temporarily erratic. After primary palliative measures were administered, it was decided that she should return to California, to her own home and her own physicians, and that a regular program of therapy should begin at once. Hitchcock telephoned Suzanne Gauthier and told her to fly at once to London to fetch Alma. The return trip, as the secretary remembered, was difficult and painful for the frightened patient, almost beyond her endurance in this sudden incapacity.

Hitchcock was very nearly incapacitated himself; the thought of Alma's death was unendurable to him, and he at once became disinterested in his work. "Suddenly he became tired and lazy," Barry Foster said.

---

*Hitchcock had told Truffaut: "I'd like to try to do an anthology on food, showing its arrival in the city, its distribution, the selling, buying by people, the cooking, the various ways in which it's consumed. What happens to it in various hotels; how it's fixed up and absorbed. And, gradually, the end of the film would show the sewers, and the garbage being dumped out into the ocean. So there's a cycle, beginning with the gleaming fresh vegetables and ending with the mess that's poured into the sewers. Thematically, the cycle would show what people do to good things. Your theme might almost be the rottenness of humanity."

''Whereas earlier he had come onto the set and said the position of certain key lights would necessitate the repainting of a backcloth because of some small shadows, he soon changed. Some of our scenes were shot by the assistant director [Colin Brewer] while Hitchcock went off to dinner with a visiting friend or a former actress from his films. And he looked forward to having us all join him promptly at teatime — but not for tea, for vodka gimlets.''

Hitchcock nevertheless rose to the occasion for three scenes in *Frenzy:* the rape-murder, with Foster as the killer and Barbara Leigh-Hunt as his victim; the camera's pullback from the villain's apartment door as he enters with his next victim, Anna Massey; and the character's search later, aboard a vegetable truck, for an incriminating tiepin in a sack of potatoes containing her corpse.

The act of murder in Alfred Hitchcock's films had always been stylized by the devices of editing and the photographic wizardry that conveyed a sense of awfulness and of shock without languid attention to detail. But *Frenzy* was designed differently, for *Frenzy* was at once a concession to modern audiences' expectations and a more personal self-disclosure of the director's angriest and most violent desires. The Covent Garden grocer, simultaneously attracted to women and repelled by them, full of desire and full of loathing for that desire, commits in this film the ultimate Hitchcock murder — an attempted rape and the strangling toward which the director's life's work had tended ever since *The Lodger.* Hitchcock insisted on all the ugly explicitness of this picture, and for all its cinematic inventiveness, it retains one of the most repellent examples of a detailed murder in the history of film. Unable to realize a rape in *No Bail for the Judge,* he had hinted it in *Psycho,* metaphorized it in *The Birds,* and, against all advice, included it in *Marnie.* Now at last — encouraged by the new freedom in movies — his imagination of this sordid crime could be more fully shown in all its horror. But this would not exorcise the desire; it followed him as an obsession right to the end of his life.

''It was quite disturbing to act the rape and the potato-truck sequences,'' Foster recalled. ''Each one took three days, and it was not a happy thing to be involved in. It was a very unsavory business, and in the rape-strangling scene we were all trying to keep a firm grip on our stomachs. Barbara Leigh-Hunt and I were so close physically, simulating everything for the camera, that we decided at once we would have to keep a sense of humor and not think too much about what was being done.''

''This was my first film,'' Leight-Hunt said, ''and I had no idea what to expect. Hitchcock had told me, when I went for the interview, that he wanted stage actors for this picture, people well known and respected, whom he wouldn't have to direct too much. He obviously looked me over very carefully, for he then suggested that I ought to have one tooth capped. I went to my dentist, who said it wasn't necessary, and Hitchcock finally agreed not to demand it as long as one particular filling would not show on film." As for the rape-strangling, she remembered that Hitchcock called her into his trailer one afternoon and said, "Barbara, about this scene — did you see *Psycho?* We're going to do it like that, but we'll shoot in sequence here. Do you have any objections to baring your breasts for the camera?" She told him that she did indeed, and that it was clearly indicated in her contract that she would not be forced to do a nude scene. "Everyone rather presumed I would finally agree to do it, but I didn't, and so a model was used for the close-ups of nudity." (The same request was put to Anna Massey, whom Hitchcock was eager to photograph walking naked from bed to bathroom, but in her case a model was also used.)

A brilliantly predesigned series of brief cuts, *Frenzy*'s rape-strangulation is a masterpiece of technical virtuosity. But although it can hardly be called, literally, pornographic (there are only one bare breast and a bit of thigh), it is also repulsive — especially in the prolonged rage of the impotent killer attempting rape. Hitchcock's closest associates — including Peggy Robertson, his most trusted and sensible adviser after Alma — told him that he was indeed going too far. "Even after all the business of the impotent frenzy of the killer and the hideous close-ups of the strangling with a necktie," according to Anthony Shaffer, "Hitchcock wanted to insert a close-up of the dead woman's tongue dripping saliva. But at last he yielded to pressure and the shot was cut." Even without that, what finally appeared on the screen was unworthy of the ordinary Hitchcock restraint and indirectness. The scene gives the impression of a filmmaker eager to push to the limits his own fantasy and to join the ranks of the more daring (but in fact less imaginative) directors, whose excesses were just beginning to fill movie screens in 1971.

The second-most-discussed sequence in *Frenzy* is the justly famous single shot in which the camera backs away from the door of Foster's upper-floor flat and descends, seemingly without a cut, to the ground level, out the building's front door, and then to the opposite side of Henrietta Street. "I used an overhead track," Hitchcock explained.

The interiors were all done in the studio. The overhead track extended a few feet in front of the [ground-floor] door, and I had the facade of the building duplicated exactly in the studio. When the camera had pulled back to the end of its track, I had a man walk in front of the camera with a sack of potatoes over his shoulder. Here there was an imperceptible cut to the same man walking past the building on location. After that I could pull back as far as I liked into Henrietta Street, and it looked like one continuous movement, beginning at the [upstairs] door. . . .

And I experimented with sound. When Anna Massey first came out onto the sidewalk, you heard the murderer's voice, "Got a place to stay?" I took every bit of sound off the track then. Dead silence. . . .

And I used the same effect in reverse: When the camera discreetly retreated down the stairs after he took the girl to his room, it went out into the street, and I brought the traffic up to a tremendous roar so that an audience would subconsciously say, "Well, if the girl screams, no one is going to hear it."

The third memorable sequence — and that which contains the classic Hitchcockian mixture of the deliberately awful and the amusing — is the killer's attempt to retrieve his tiepin from the corpse stuffed into a sack of potatoes. "The scene on the truck," Hitchcock said, "is composed of one hundred and eighteen separate shots. When we finished filming it, I sat down with my secretary and dictated a complete list of the shots. It took about an hour. Each shot was listed on a numbered yellow file card. All the cutter had to do was refer to the number of each cut and splice it all together." The episode, inspired detail for detail by the scene in La Bern's novel, is a typical example of the director's meticulous preparation.

By early October, after fifty-five days, principal photography was complete and the editing, scoring, and dubbing began. Henry Mancini, who had won Oscars for songs in two of his earlier scores, was engaged to write the music. But according to Bernard Herrmann, there was a repetition of his own unhappy break with Hitchcock a few years earlier. "Hitchcock came to the recording session, listened awhile and said [to Mancini], 'Look, if I want Herrmann, I'd ask Herrmann. Where's Mancini?' He wanted a pop score, and Mancini wrote what he thought was me."

Hitchcock turned instead to the prolific British composer Ron Goodwin. At their first meeting, Hitchcock sat quietly before taking from a hatbox an exact duplicate of his own head. (The prop was originally to have been used for his cameo appearance — attached to a dummy floating in the Thames; it was, instead, used only in the promotional trailers, and the director appeared briefly in a crowd watching police retrieve a corpse.)

"What do you think of that?" he asked Goodwin.

"Very nice," Goodwin replied uneasily. ("I mean," he asked later, "what *do* you say when someone shows you a perfect replica of his own head?'') Hitchcock was then very specific about the music he wanted: "Sparkling, early-morning music for the opening — wood-winds and glockenspiel," according to Goodwin. "If Hitchcock hadn't directed me, I would have written something with a macabre lilt to it. But he wanted no hint of the horror to come."

The finished film was magnificently structured, crisply acted, smoothly edited — and utterly devoid of any positive human feeling. (Hitch-cock's daughter refused to allow her family to see it.) It was the most typical Hitchcock film, stylistically, in years, and also the most personal.

Dinner-table sequences are always important in Hitchcock's films, and his pictures often suggest an attraction and repulsion about food and eating (and about insatiable sexual hungers) that reflect his own life. (In response to the question, "How would *you* choose to be murdered?" Hitchcock replied, "Well, there are many nice ways. Eating is a good one.") The three movements of *Sabotage* are marked by meals; the dinner sequences are crucial for character revelation in *Shadow of a Doubt, Notorious, Psycho, The Birds,* and *Marnie,* and are linked with images of nausea and vomiting in films from *Rich and Strange* to *Life-boat* to *The Birds.*

In *Frenzy,* food at last became the main character, constantly inter-rupting the audience's view, the action, and the relationship between characters. The gourmet meals so unappetizingly prepared by Vivien Merchant for Alec McCowen (including quail with grapes) are linked by association with major moments in the horror (such as by the grapes thrown down and crushed underfoot by Jon Finch). They also tie in with the dinner Barbara Leigh-Hunt buys for Finch, and with the "dinner" she becomes for her attacker: he says, "Don't squeeze the goods until they're yours," then partakes of her by rape while he "squeezes the goods" by strangulation; and then, after the grotesque human "meal," he picks his teeth with the tiepin — a detail directed by Hitchcock at the last moment. And the dialogue in *Frenzy* is punctuated with refer-ences to the (physically) starving people of the world and to the (emo-tionally) starving people of the story; the inspector talks of the killer's "whetted appetite" as he copes with inedible food.

The technique of filmmaking is expert in this motion picture, and Hitchcock used it to describe a world in which he had lost all hope. Covent Garden and its opulent produce cannot cover the hideous crimes of a grocer who appropriates his victims like food. "This is Covent Garden, not the Garden of Love," one character says; it is instead a garden of lust, and the paradise of plenty that Covent Garden represents goes gradually but inexorably to rot. ("Sometimes," says another char-

acter, "just thinking about the lusts of men makes me want to heave.")
The sour fruits of human exploitation are traded, people become one
another's food, and no decent meals are served at home; one person
buys someone a meal, another longs for a meal, another becomes a
meal. There is nothing appetizing about food or friendship, and all the
relationships are sterile or aborted by murder. *Frenzy* is, to the last
frame, a closed and coldly negative vision of human possibility.

Nevertheless, the success of *Frenzy* would very soon be tremendous.
By autumn 1971, tired, drained, and worried about Alma, Hitchcock
gathered his small staff and returned to Los Angeles. He tried to maintain a good humor but, as in his film, bitterness finally prevailed; at the
same time, his drinking increased alarmingly. At a cast party before his
departure, Hitchcock tried to amuse the British players. "But there was
a salacious, frustrated quality to his humor," according to Anna
Massey.

The players left Hitchcock's employ grateful for the opportunity to
work with so careful a technician and cinematic visualizer, but few felt
they knew him well at all. There was an impression of sadness behind
his humor, of anxiety beneath his calm exterior — and of a strange and
unpleasant sexual derailment that had at last become patent: this film
dredged up the submerged confusion between matters of the bedroom
and matters of the toilet, and between both and the business of eating.
"It's obvious," as Samson Raphaelson put it, "that there was some
kind of sexual aberration in him, but how operative it was nobody ever
knew." The truth is that it became publicly operative only in his films —
and nowhere more openly or viciously than in *Frenzy*.

By springtime of the following year, Alma had improved sufficiently
that the plans to return to England for the gala premiere could include
her. During the months since her stroke, she had received daily treatment, and her strong will and determination enabled her to make unusually rapid progress. Soon she could walk alone, with the aid only of
a braced boot, and her speech had only a slight residue of thickness.
Her husband's gait and conversation were suffering too, however — not
from a cerebral incident, but from excessive consumption of alcohol,
which by now affected him daily. The Hollywood Foreign Press Association joined the bandwagon of those honoring him "for outstanding
contributions to the entertainment field" at a ceremony that season, and
Rosalind Russell (who was gravely ill but impressively cheerful) gave
Hitchcock the Golden Globe Award and kept the evening running
smoothly.

The world premiere of *Frenzy* (the film cost $2 million — half that of *Topaz* — and soon grossed $16 million) was held by invitation in London on May 25, 1972, and was followed by a dinner in the River Room at the Savoy Hotel. The Hitchcocks, writer Anthony Shaffer, and the cast joined a generous sampling of London aristocracy and the press; and Hitchcock supervised the wine list — a 1969 Meursault followed by a 1964 Château Margaux followed by Hine brandy. At the dinner, in interviews, and in meetings with former associates (Michael Balcon, Sidney Bernstein, and Benn Levy), he was often amiable and full of memories and "impish delight," according to Billie Whitelaw, who acted in the film. But with the suddenness of a cinematic cut he could become withdrawn and aloof, and his ingestion of great quantities of liquor, wine, and brandy failed to embarrass only those who joined in his intoxication. "I'll be what Churchill said of Hitler," Hitchcock said that week, "an enigma within an enigma." As his drinking became even more public, even his closest colleagues found it hard to tolerate the enigma, hard to cope with the genius. The drinking, they might have thought, was his way of escaping the problem of Alma and of escaping the frustrations and inner rage he had admitted so fully in *Frenzy*.

Before the public premiere in London, the Hitchcocks returned to New York — which was prudent scheduling. The British press found the film wildly anachronistic, locked emotionally into a long-gone British reality and providing merely a tourist's view of modern London. (In private, Anthony Shaffer and the cast were admitting similar judgments; at various times they had all counseled various changes in the script, but to no avail: the film would present Hitchcock's attitude, Hitchcock's London, Hitchcock's Covent Garden, and Hitchcock's tone.)

But in America the response was very different. The long visit to New York in June enabled him not only to give multiple interviews in conjunction with the first screenings, but also to accept Columbia University's invitation to attend its commencement and receive an honorary degree. That event, on Tuesday, June 6, was the culmination of a serious dedication to Hitchcock's art by Andrew Sarris, a film critic on Columbia's faculty who had for a long time championed the director and defended him against his detractors. When *Psycho* was first shown in 1960, it was Andrew Sarris, virtually alone among his fellow critics, who saw that it was more than an exercise in gothicism. And as the critical debate became louder in the 1960s, it was Sarris who drew a middle ground between the factual inaccuracies and the fatuous elitism of much French criticism, and the equally snobbish dismissal of Hitchcock by those American analysts who defended only overtly "serious" films (by which they usually meant foreign ones).

That Tuesday afternoon was only the beginning of the greatest out-

pouring of adulation America gave Hitchcock in over a decade. The
next day, the *New York Times* published a photograph of him, "sardonic and imperturbable as ever, in cap and gown," as Sarris described
him. "It was as if he were making a cameo appearance in one of his
own movies, perhaps one in which even a staid academic procession
might not be all pomp and circumstance." The film's press previews
that month, and the public opening in New York on June 21, had the
critics in a whirl of unanimous praise; to the few who expressed an
unfashionable query about the nudity and extreme violence of one scene,
Hitchcock was quietly defensive: "Ten years ago we wouldn't have
been able to show that scene in the same detail and something very
crucial would have been lost: You would never have seen the killer at
work."

The publicity continued for a month, and Hitchcock's stamina was,
remarkably, undiminished by the round of activities and his indulgences
at table, although occasionally there was a dizzy spell that lasted too
long to be ignored. Alma, growing stronger, tried to temper his habits
by scolding him and limiting time with friends, but these tactics helped
not at all. Hitchcock invited Samson and Dorshka Raphaelson to a
screening of *Frenzy,* and then to dinner at La Côte Basque, where
Hitchcock confided that Alma resented even their old friends. "In the
later years," according to Raphaelson, "this once darling little woman
caused herself so much unnecessary unhappiness. They were very childish that summer of 1972, and it made us sad to see how distrustful they
had become with each other."

Ordinarily, Hitchcock's slightest remarks about Alma were expressed
only in the strictest privacy. But now, with the relaxation of liquor, his
opinions were occasionally shared even with journalists. One newspaper
interviewer found him so affected by vodka that his remarks were unusually personal: Hitchcock said that all men were potential murderers,
but that the woman is always the dominant figure in a relationship.
"That's the way it is in real life," he said quietly, looking cautiously
toward Alma's room and leaving no doubt of his meaning. "Look at
the producer's wife who has her husband cancel a television series because she doesn't like it. She could appear to be a frail little blonde
with no strength at all. But she *whines*. She's such a nag that he will
do anything, but anything, just to stop her. This little thing can probably
tear the pants off him if she has a mind to. Maybe that's me, too.
Maybe my wife dominates me more than I think." And then, in a rare
moment of self-disclosure off the screen, he spoke of his very nearly
lifelong celibate state, and of the psychology of food and sex that he
did, after all, realize: "As they get on, after five or six years, in most

married couples 'that old feeling' begins to dissipate. Food oftentimes takes the place of sex in a relationship.'' And with that he folded his hands across his enormous belly.

There were those among his associates and his interviewers that season who saw that Hitchcock was no longer the genial, amusing guest of earlier years. The change was mainly attributable not to age, nor even to Alma's recent illness, but to a fierce inner turmoil he seemed less and less able to contain. Some suggested that he retire, see to his health, spend time with his family, travel, read, visit old friends round the world. "I cannot retire," he insisted. "What would I do?" And the executives of Universal had every intention of holding him to his contract, in any case — for the business arrangement continued to make all parties very rich indeed. "I have no hobbies," said Hitchcock, "so I will just have to see where the next body will turn up."

In the fall of 1972, he and Alma were turning up at interviews in Rome and Paris and Zurich for the European openings of *Frenzy*. But they bypassed the comfortable familiarity of Saint Moritz that year. Perhaps they knew that it would have too clearly reminded them of the earlier, healthier days, when they could face each other with less anxiety.

# Fifteen

1973–1979

THE most extensive retrospective of Alfred Hitchcock's work could not have been planned for a better time. In January and February 1973, Hitchcock returned home buoyed by the reactions of people everywhere — not primarily to *Frenzy*, but to him and to his cool, deliberately enigmatic presence, which seemed so at variance with the monstrous violence of that film.

"A lot of people think I'm a monster — they really do, I've been told that!" Hitchcock exclaimed.

They don't care to be associated with me because of the nature of the work. . . . I've found women who've said, for example, "You're nothing like I thought you'd be!" and I said, "What did you expect?" And they said, "I thought you'd be very unpleasant." This has happened more than once — and I'm not talking about actresses, but about responsible women with a complete misconception, due to the fact that I deal in crime and that kind of thing. But in fact it's just the opposite — I'm more scared than they are of things in real life!

But real life, at that time, was being very gentle with him. The Los Angeles County Museum of Art (with the American Film Institute's cooperation) began its gala series "Presenting Alfred Hitchcock," which he opened on January 11 with an invitational screening of *Rear Window* and closed on February 3 with showings of *The Lodger* and *Frenzy*. In between, there were showings of twenty-one of the feature films and nine of his television shows, participation in numerous local interviews and testimonials, and telegrams of congratulations from all over the world. Even the International Alliance of Theatrical Stage Employees (the important IATSE union), Local 818, honored him with a "motion picture showmanship'' award at a luncheon on March 23. No one was more sought after in Hollywood.

When interviewers, museum archivists, university students, and television talk-show hosts summed up Hitchcock's career that season, they counted 2 feature films made in Germany, 24 in England, and 26 in America.* Of these 52, all but *The Mountain Eagle* (by now apparently irretrievably lost) could be seen somewhere; and with all the honors and retrospectives and tributes, more and more young filmmakers and older moviegoers were seeing his work turn up in art theaters specializing in early and classic cinema. Americans were seeing, for the first time in many years, *Blackmail* and *Number Seventeen* and — more to their liking — *Murder!* and *Secret Agent* and *Young and Innocent*.

"I am a prisoner of my own success," Hitchcock said with a trace of bitterness when asked about his next project.

I'm not an unwilling prisoner, but there are only certain types of films I can make. A thriller, a murder story, a film which affects the emotions of those who watch it everywhere in the world. . . . But if I made films only to please myself, they would certainly be different from the ones you see on the screen. They would be more dramatic, perhaps without humor, more realistic. The reason I continue to be what's called a specialist in suspense is strictly a commercial reason. The public expects a certain type of story from me and I don't want to disappoint them.

(Alma told Andrew Sarris, in June 1972, that her husband was eager to direct a different kind of film, but the studio prevented him.)

By 1973 Hitchcock weighed his heaviest since the days of *Rebecca* and was, as a consequence, slower. And the excessive drinking continued. "You don't suppose I waste good wine on my guests!'' he confided to a reporter the year before. "Good wine is to be drunk on one's own. Conversation is the enemy of good food and wine.'' A tenable position, perhaps, but vast numbers of people would heartily disagree. In spite of the slowness and the private indulgences, however, there was no question of retirement; Universal still prodded him to expand his new success with *Frenzy* into a winning streak that would erase forever the memories of *Torn Curtain* and *Topaz*.

Alma encouraged him to read the books that were carefully screened for his consideration by Peggy Robertson, who sorted through the pile that arrived each day at his office. That spring the best of the lot was a

---

*This reckoning counts *Under Capricorn, Stage Fright,* and *Frenzy* among the British films, since they were made in England — although under the terms of an American contract and during Hitchcock's period as an American director.

novel by the prolific English writer Victor Canning. *The Rainbird Pattern* was set in the English countryside, but that could be easily changed. More important was the dark intensity in its story of theft, guilt, revenge, murder, and deception, and its modern interest in clairvoyance and psychic phenomena, which provided seriocomic spice. More than a simple thriller, the story and its often reflective prose suggested Graham Greene's *Brighton Rock* or William March's *The Bad Seed,* and it offered disturbing meditations on theology, Christian ethics, and the inheritance of evil, interlaced with a strong plot and credible characters.

Since Universal and Alma and the press were insisting on his maintaining a "winning streak," Hitchcock contacted Anthony Shaffer, who had in fact just read the novel. "I thought it had possibilities," said Shaffer, "but I wasn't eager for the sort of version that Hitch was describing — a sort of light, Noël Coward–Madame Arcati thing with Margaret Rutherford. I thought that if we followed Canning's book and postulated the partial truth of the psychic's spiritual sensibility we could have a more complex story. But I promised to consider his suggestion. I was about to depart for the south of France for a short holiday, and we agreed to talk again soon."

But Hitchcock was evidently not ready for a basic disagreement so early in the planning, and a week later he telephoned Shaffer to say how hurt he was to learn that he had turned down the offer. "The front office tells me you're making excessive demands, that you want a share of the profits on the picture, and so forth," Hitchcock said — and when Shaffer vehemently denied that the matter had even been discussed, Hitchcock was unmoved. "He just couldn't bear to tell me straight out that he didn't want me on the picture after my disagreement. He lied to avoid a confrontation, and when I said we might still be able to work something out, he said it was too late, that he had already spoken to Ernest Lehman."

He had indeed, but for many months this was as much work as would be done. Hitchcock's life was slower and less involved than ever, a monotonous round of trips to his offices — where, his secretary remembered, he became irreversibly negligent in replying to letters, a task that he had never much applied himself to in any case. ("He almost never answered letters," according to Sampson Raphaelson. "All his life, he was a terrible correspondent.") He read at home, sat with Alma, and only occasionally invited to dinner a writer or actor from the old days. The only part of his life unaffected by age and weight and incipient arthritis was his appetite.

By October 1973, however, Hitchcock had become sufficiently bored with life at Bellagio Road to begin story conferences, and he let it be known to the press that he was at work with Ernest Lehman on a film called *One Plus One Equals One,* based on a novel by Victor Canning.

"Although I had said no to *The Rainbird Pattern* when it had been sent to me six months earlier by another studio," Lehman said,

I agreed to do it with Hitch. I guess I thought, "We did it before in *North by Northwest,* and we can do it again." By now he was a legendary figure to me, too, yet at first I felt very comfortable being back with him. However, before long I realized that the relationship was quite different. Many years had passed. We had both had successes and failures. We were [both] different people now, and he had slowed down considerably. He had none of his former stamina, and I found that I had far less inclination, in the beginning of our story conferences, to do creative battle with this legendary and physically weakened man. Much time was wasted by both of us, I think, adjusting to and handling each other's new persona.

Nevertheless, the story conferences began in early November. For the first time since the preparations for *Marnie,* Hitchcock permitted tape recordings to be made of conversations, and the almost one thousand transcribed pages of the talks with Lehman reveal a director alternately tired, disinterested, and rooted in the past — but with occasional bursts of extraordinary creative insight and energy. Most of the insight and energy came from Lehman, however, who found out at once that Hitchcock seemed to be backing reluctantly into the new production.

HITCHCOCK: I don't have any regard for *The Rainbird Pattern,* you know.
LEHMAN: I know you don't.
HITCHCOCK: It's our story, not the book's. Canning's a very lucky man.
LEHMAN: What's he going to get out of this?
HITCHCOCK: A lot. . . . You know what happens: They rerelease the book with our new title on it.*

Three days later, on November 5, Hitchcock interrupted Lehman's synopsis of the novel's plot to discuss casting.

HITCHCOCK: I'm not going to do this, Ernie — and I don't care what a fight I get into with [*studio executive*] Edd Henry — I'm just not going to do this without top performers.
LEHMAN: Would he fight you on that?
HITCHCOCK: Sure — price! But this film is going to be made by its characters!

---

*Stein and Day had recently issued *Frenzy* by Arthur La Bern ("originally published," as the cover noted in small print, "as *Goodbye Piccadilly, Farewell Leicester Square*").

Anxious to please Hitchcock and to keep the writing process moving, Lehman, on Monday, November 19, brought Hitchcock a seven-page, single-spaced outline of the picture as they had planned it. "What had *really* attracted Hitch to this movie project" according to Lehman, "was the idea of two separate and distinct stories slowly moving towards each other and eventually meeting and becoming one story. I kept insisting that audiences don't go to the movies because they're interested in unique structure — unless Hitch planned to go along with the picture as a lecturer and explain it to each audience. I felt that each moment of the film, each of the two stories, had to stand on its own, regardless of the unusualness of the structure. We sat and talked for months."

And so Hitchcock's obsession with the structure continued, rather as if two separate and opposite stories in himself were coming together, too, and he needed words to explain them and publicity to broadcast them. Apart from this concern, the transcripts of their conversations reveal an eager (and sometimes exasperated) Lehman, but an only intermittently involved Hitchcock.

On April 15, 1974, Lehman submitted for approval the first draft of the screenplay, now tentatively called *Deception*. In an astonishing burst of energy, Hitchcock responded a week later with the most detailed commentary he had ever offered on a script. Attached to each page of Lehman's draft was an identical-size piece of paper, with Hitchcock's observations on each scene and each line of dialogue. He added the opening shot of the picture in painstaking visual detail; made changes in major scenes; queried Lehman on motivations and major shots; altered a word or two; suggested clarifications; pointed out some problems of construction. From the start, no one had been quite sure of Hitchcock's basic desire to make this film — and there would be many moments in the next fifteen months when his intention was certainly questionable. But this annotated script, returned for Lehman's consideration on April 22, left no room for doubt. There was a sudden surge of will and energy, and Lehman took up the revisions happy to see Hitchcock's old fire rekindled.

On Monday, April 29, Hitchcock was honored in New York City by the Film Society of Lincoln Center, which sponsored one of the most carefully prepared and successful events in Hitchcock's honor. At a press conference held the previous Thursday, he fielded the usual questions with wry humor. He told his audience what he had told critic Richard Schickel the year before: that his personal idea of peace and serenity was a cloudless horizon, no shadows. When asked about the function of actors and technicians in his work, he drew on his cigar and said quietly, "They must conform." The press, of course, loved this sort of thing — as they did when he said that no, he would not make a film about abortion or homosexuality, now openly treated in the cinema, because "these topics aren't amusing, and the film I'm now working on is designed to be a comic thriller."

The gala itself was perhaps the major spring function in New York for the art and entertainment communities. The former Grace Kelly made one of her rare public appearances at a film event, arriving in a limousine with Hitchcock and Alma while the entire plaza burst with photographers' flashbulbs. For the program, segments of film clips had been arranged, under the headings "The Screen Cameos," "A Fantasy of the Absurd," "The Chase," "The Bad Guys," "The Hitchcock Way with Death," "A Man and a Woman," and "A State of Mind." The final excerpt screened was the entire Albert Hall sequence from the second version of *The Man Who Knew Too Much*. Each part of the evening was introduced by a Hitchcock collaborator — Princess Grace, Teresa Wright, Joan Fontaine, Cyril Ritchard, Janet Leigh, Samuel Taylor — and the audience, by the evening's end, was quite wild with excitement.

Hitchcock's remarks were appropriately — and necessarily, for he did not want the burden of going on stage — delivered on film. After reprising the James Allardice drowning-man quip, Hitchcock said how proud he was to be the guest of honor and then went on to a favorite subject.

As you have seen, murder seems to be the prominent theme. As I do not approve of the current wave of violence that we see on our screens, I have always felt that murder should be treated delicately. And, in addition to that, with the help of television, murder should be brought into the home where it rightly belongs. Some of our most exquisite murders have been domestic; performed with tenderness in simple, homey places like the kitchen table or the bathtub. Nothing is more revolting to my sense of decency than the underworld thug who is able to murder anyone — even people to whom he has not been properly introduced. After all, I'm sure you will agree that murder can be so much more charming and enjoyable, even for the victim, if the surroundings are pleasant and the people involved are ladies and gentleman like yourselves.

Finally, I think I can best describe the insidious effect of murder on one's character by reading a paragraph from Thomas De Quincey's delightful essay "Murder as One of the Fine Arts." He said: "If once a man indulges himself in murder, very soon he comes to think little of robbing, and from robbing he comes next to drinking and Sabbath-breaking, and from that to incivility and procrastination. Once begun on this downward path, you never know where you are to stop. Many a man dates his ruin from some murder or other that perhaps he thought little of at the time.''

They tell me that murder is committed every minute, so I don't want to waste any more of your time. I know you want to get to work. Thank you.

And at the very end, after a standing ovation was offered, he rose from his box seat between Alma and Grace and said simply: ''As you can see, the best way to do it is with scissors.'' Press and public appreciatively noted the ambiguity — Hitchcock had deftly referred to the killing from *Dial "M" for Murder,* to the art of editing, and to the evening's conclusion. For the following week, he could be seen and heard on every New York magazine rack and many a television program, and the retrospective cinemas and art houses, both public and academic, were showing only Hitchcock movies. His image fluttered for days on a huge banner suspended above Lincoln Center Plaza, and many people wondered if the visit of General MacArthur or the lunar astronauts had been more enthusiastically celebrated.

The tribute, as such events do, had an air of finality about it. He was being enshrined among the immortals, and Lincoln Center's previous honorees — Charles Chaplin and Fred Astaire — were, after all, no longer doing what had won them their tributes. Young filmmakers and journalists and students in New York treated Hitchcock with the awe due a museum piece that had been dragged out of cinematic mothballs, as if he were an Edison Kinetoscope.

The trip greatly exhausted him. His dizzy spells were more frequent, and now there was some alarming, sporadic chest pain. Back home, he was apparently in no hurry to resume work on *Deception* or to meet about the revisions. As a stalling tactic, he asked Lehman to write an extended prose treatment. This surprised the writer, since if a treatment were expected, it should have preceded the first draft. But he dutifully complied and took as long as Hitchcock seemed to want — which turned out to be more than three months.

The summer passed uneventfully. Anxious for frail Alma's health, Hitchcock stayed home, questioning her physical therapists and doctors, preparing the tea tray several times daily. ''If the worst happens, he can always be my maid,'' she said, most likely referring to the unimaginable: the elected or enforced end of his film career. To his staff and to executives at Universal, the Hitchcocks began to seem like any elderly couple, increasingly prey to erratic health, withdrawing socially, guarding their energies and their privacy like family heirlooms. This was not entirely in the best interests of the new film or of his health, Lew Wasserman decided, and so on the eve of Hitchcock's seventy-fifth birthday,

Wasserman hosted a lavish celebration at Chasen's. All the chief officers at MCA were there; and Cary Grant, Charlton Heston, Laraine
Day, Paul Newman, and François Truffaut toasted Hitchcock's health.
An enormous cake was wheeled in, and everyone's slice bore the Hitchcock caricature.

On August 15, Lehman submitted a 133-page treatment, and a few
weeks later sent a second draft based on it, enclosing a cover letter
expressing his eagerness to meet and get on with the final changes, since
production was now scheduled for early 1975. He expected a reply from
Hitchcock within days, but in fact none was forthcoming until November. Most of the intervening time, Hitchcock spent with his physicians.

In October the dizziness had advanced so alarmingly that Dr. Eliot
Corday advised implantation of a pacemaker. "It's really quite a simple
operation, with a local anesthetic," Hitchcock told everyone who would
listen.

But things were not so simple. Four days after the insertion of the
pacemaker, he developed a high fever and abdominal pain. It was determined that he had reacted adversely to medication administered after
the implantation, and this led to a bout of colitis. Back at the UCLA
Medical Center to treat this ailment, he responded well and was released
after a week — until even severer pain compelled him to return yet
again. The diagnosis this time was a kidney stone that was not going to
be easily passed, and so, with spinal anesthesia, it was removed trans-
urethrally. Each detail was casually described in a letter to Ernest Lehman dated November 11, when Hitchcock said he was at last comfortably settled at home and would soon be ready to work.

Hitchcock's decisions about the production — now postponed from
January until late March — seemed weak and unspirited. There were a
few meetings with Lehman, but these were uncharacteristically difficult,
and by Christmas, as the writer recalled, "we were on polite terms
rather than warm friendly terms. I found myself refusing to accept Hitch's
ideas (if I thought they were wrong) merely because those ideas were
coming from a legendary figure." Lehman's hesitation was reasonable,
for the film was becoming complex and talky — qualities especially regrettable because the story and motifs were so slight.

And Hitchcock, I think, in the years that had passed since *North by Northwest,*
had changed to the extent that he found it far more difficult to be tolerant of a
writer who acted as though he knew what he was talking about. So I probably
came across to Hitch as stubborn, difficult, unwilling to take "orders."

By the end of the final script — which took until April 1975 — Hitch had
been forced to have the pacemaker and I had been forced to accept exchanging

ideas and revisions through the mails, on an almost daily basis, rather than in person. Why through the mails? Why not in person, in his office? "It's too difficult to get Ernie to agree with me," Hitch reported to an executive at the studio, who was puzzled by the arm's-length arrangement.

There was considerable trouble and disagreement about the ending of the picture, too, for Hitchcock seemed to alter completely his conception of the main characters at a very late stage — even as late as the end of filming. It took considerable diplomacy to convince him to leave off extensive tampering.

For his cast Hitchcock selected Bruce Dern, Roy Thinnes, Karen Black, and Barbara Harris, although Universal tried to get him to accept more "bankable" and "bigger" names (like Liza Minnelli in the role of the fey spiritualist). The studio reminded Hitchcock that he, too, had originally expressed a clear intention of having major actors. But by this time Hitchcock had changed his mind: he did not want to pay the huge star-salaries that would increase the budget and thus diminish his own percentage in the film. Hearing that Hitchcock needed an actress for the role of the guilt-ridden dowager who sets the story in motion, seventy-eight-year-old Lillian Gish telephoned from New York to ask for a test; Hitchcock, however, had already firmly decided on the venerable Cathleen Nesbitt, then eighty-six. As it turned out, only she and Dern went through production without anxiety. A month after filming began, in May, Hitchcock summarily dismissed Roy Thinnes, whose manner and performance dissatisfied him; he recast the role with William Devane.

During the summertime production, it was clear to everyone that Hitchcock was more ambivalent about making this, his fifty-third feature film, than about any picture in years. Visibly weakened, he dreaded the location shooting in San Francisco and managed to get through it only with a measure of self-generated showmanship. His pacemaker activated the alarms on the metal detectors at the airports, and this he thought great good fun — much more enjoyable than one evening when there was a sudden emergence into real life of his basic terror: an unanticipated confrontation with the law. "Our driver was speeding to enable us to keep a dinner reservation," production designer Henry Bumstead recalled, "and a San Francisco policeman pulled us over. He let us go after a warning and a real movie double-take, for when he looked in the back seat there was Alfred Hitchcock — staring straight ahead, frozen with fear. Hitch didn't enjoy the dinner very much that night."

After filming at Grace Cathedral, at the porte cochere of the Fairmont

Hotel, and around a mansion in Pacifica, the company returned to Los Angeles. Hitchcock's arthritis worsened; he was drinking more to deaden the pain, and he was trying to complete a film that, in his younger years, would have been completed in no longer than six weeks. "He was in great pain a lot of the time," according to Bruce Dern.

He'd often say to me, "Bruce, I have arthritic knees." But then he'd try to smile and make a joke of it. "Wouldn't that be a name for a town — Arthritic Knees? . . . Where are you from? Well, I'm from Arthritic Knees, Nebraska." Of course, he expected us to fall on the floor with laughter, so I cracked up and he was delighted.

I had to buck him up a little every morning, to get him ready for the day's work. He was so tired and so bored with the whole thing. But when he was feeling better, there was no one better on the set. He noticed everything — a shadow on a performer's face, a bad angle for a prop, a few seconds too long on a take. Just when we thought he had no idea what was going on, he'd snap us all to attention with the most incredible awareness of some small but disastrous detail that nobody would have noticed until it got on screen.

And then he'd be bored again. "Bruce," he would say to me while we were waiting for a new camera setup, "wake me when the movie's over."

For a shot in which the gentleman villain, William Devane, was to administer a narcotic to Barbara Harris, Hitchcock was especially concerned about the detail of passing and injecting a hypodermic. "To give it a change of pace," he said to Karen Black, "do it quickly, and I'll slow it down in the cutting room. Now you see," he said, turning to everyone around him, "we're going to get four angles out of this. I want to follow the progress of everything. We've got her head swinging from side to side, in and out of the shot, then we've got her face, then his face, then the needle . . . six shots for the struggle . . . her feet twisting on the floor . . ." It was the Hitchcock of earlier years — alert, conveying to his crew the series of images that was flashing on the screen of his own mind and that he would render as cleanly as possible on the screens of the world's theaters.

Similarly, for a dialogue between Cathleen Nesbitt and Barbara Harris, he told the actors exactly how the shots would be edited. "When we start I'll stay on Cathleen Nesbitt while she says, 'If you find the missing grandson, I'll pay you ten thou—' and then I'll cut to Barbara's face for her reaction while we hear '—sand dollars' on the soundtrack." At times like that, Hitchcock amazed even his cameraman, Leonard South, who by this time had worked on Hitchcock's crew for over twenty years.

"He's still the master technician," South recalled at the time, no matter how tired he seems. To find a director with the technical expertise to match his artistic sense is very rare. He knows all the lenses, all the lights — and he doesn't need eyeglasses! Most directors these days are concerned only for the actors; they have no technical knowledge at all. But he's uncanny. He asks what lens I have on the camera, then he looks at the scene and knows what will appear on the screen. He's never wrong. . . . And he never moves his camera without a reason. When he wants to move the audience, he moves the camera, not necessarily the actors. There's still no one around like him!

There were also moments of disarming humor to relax a nervous cast who often felt neglected. In an effort to leaven an especially tense moment, Devane replied to Hitchcock's direction that it contradicted something his mother had taught him years before. No one laughed, however, and all eyes moved to the director, already in no joking mood that day. "Is that what she taught you?" Hitchcock asked, and then, after a perfect pause, added, "Have her destroyed." Everyone laughed, the anxiety dissipated, and the scene was shot smoothly.

By July, with only a few weeks of filming left, Hitchcock was exhausted and anxious. He halted the day's work promptly at four o'clock — sometimes even in the middle of a take — yet his assistants realized that in an effort to stay on schedule, to keep to the budget, he was simplifying scenes and sacrificing clarity for the sake of speed. In spite of this erratic behavior, the film was building toward a wholeness.

On the set he retained the atmosphere he had demanded for fifty years: as much quiet formality as possible. He made it clear through his subordinates that key assistants were expected to wear coat and tie. Also as usual, there was a formal line of communication, which meant that Hitchcock spoke to very few people apart from his actors, his cameraman, and his personal assistant. Instructions to lesser workers were conveyed down the line through other subordinates. He perhaps realized that he seemed, especially in the new, television-oriented Hollywood of 1975, somewhat anachronistic. But at least he was an anachronism that commanded respect; and so he insisted on the formalities of dress and manner to support him. Hardly anyone on his film called him Hitch.

Although the film's graveyard sequence was brief and demanded location shooting at the small Pioneer Cemetery out of town, it was what engaged Hitchcock's interest most in those weeks of shooting. "He usually had one set that he considered his special pride and joy," Henry Bumstead recalled, "and in this film it was the cemetery. He had us scouting cemeteries all over California for the right one. We had to put in just the right paths he wanted, and we had to negotiate with the groundskeeper to let it become overgrown for a period of months. Hitchcock knew the effect he wanted, the wonderful overhead, high-angle shot of the cemetery pursuit he had charted out most meticulously."

Throughout the production of this comic thriller, indeed, the thought of the cemetery was never far from Hitchcock's conversation or preoccupation. The press luncheon he designed — perhaps inspired by his macabre dinner conversation with the Clark Gables decades earlier — was set in an artificial cemetery, with the names of journalists and critics on tombstones, Bloody Marys for cocktails, waitresses in funereal black. He was trying to laugh at the final arbiter of human destiny — just the way he winked at the audience in the film's advertising, which showed his detached head within a crystal ball, a disbelieving smile curling round his lips.

"I am seventy-eight years of age and I would like to go to my grave with a quiet conscience," Cathleen Nesbitt says early in the picture; this line could have been Hitchcock's motto, for in spite of the criminal antics of the story and the tensions with his writer and his cast, the finished film has an air of reconciliation — even of benevolence — and an almost pacific acceptance of the end of art and life.

In mid-July there was still no final resolution to the problem of the film's title. "It will be called," he said, "Alfred Hitchcock's 'Something' — perhaps Hitchcock's 'Wet Drawers.' " Finally, on July 25 (just days before the final shot), someone from Universal's publicity department came up with a title that seemed to have the right ambiguity. The film, after all, was about a family scheme, a lost heir, kidnappers, jewel theft — and an empty grave. Not entirely pleased, but unable to devise an alternative, Hitchcock agreed to call the film *Family Plot*. ("There is no body in the family plot" read the promotional campaign.)

And there was another outstanding problem: that of his cameo appearance, which he had delayed. He looked dreadful that summer — more bloated than ever from cortisone, his face puffy and livid and his eyes veiled with a haze of pain and confusion. "I don't like these small appearances at all," he once said. "I hate it. It's an ordeal every time. But somehow I feel I have to go through with it. Superstition, I suppose." Finally he closed the set to visitors, stood as an imposing silhouette behind the door marked "Registrar of Births and Deaths" in one short scene, was photographed in one take, and painfully made his way back to his folding chair.

"By the time the film was in the cans," Ernest Lehman said, "Hitch and I were friends and fellow-conspirators again, united against studios, critics, audiences, and anyone else who hadn't gone through the creative travail that he and I had privately shared for a whole year. And then, the excellent reviews seemed to wipe away whatever was left of our differences.''

By September Hitchcock was near collapse. Throughout the autumn, he gave only token interest to his office, and to supervising the editing and scoring of the film; he could depend on those who knew what he wanted and were determined to help him — people like Peggy Robertson and Suzanne Gauthier, who were generously shouldering more and more responsibility for the daily management of the film and his office. At that time, however, they had no idea of the even greater burdens that lay ahead.

Alma's health, at the same time, was more precarious than ever; a second stroke had made walking progressively difficult, and with new setbacks her spirits began to fail. By Christmas their doctors, hoping that a short holiday would improve their morale, gave permission for them to travel to Saint Moritz. "We spend most of our time sitting comfortably in the Palace Hotel, watching it all from behind the window," Hitchcock told a reporter. In early 1976 they returned, as the doctors had hoped, refreshed.

*Family Plot,* it was decided, would have its world premiere two weeks in advance of the national opening — as the first-night offering of Filmex — the Los Angeles Film Festival. Hitchcock arrived at the Century Plaza theater complex in a Universal tour bus, the film arrived in a hearse, a choir sang a requiem, fireworks lit up the evening sky, a thousand black balloons were released, and a marching band from the University of Southern California played the familiar Hitchcock signature tune, the Gounod march. "There is everything but cheerleaders, acrobats, and a dancing bear," one writer told an inquiring newsman. And then, as if on cue, the cheerleaders and acrobats and a dancing bear arrived. Hollywood premieres, even as late as 1976, were still jolly affairs, more remarkable for their spirit than for good taste, restraint, or style. At a dinner for more than a thousand after the screening, James Stewart presented Hitchcock with a Filmex Award created especially for the director that evening. The only note of anxiety in the evening was struck by the guest of honor himself, who was drunk, though not gloomily so, at the microphone during his acceptance speech.

By the time the film opened nationally on April 9, promotional activities like this had virtually assured its success. Even most of the critics tacitly agreed that Hitchcock had earned the right to turn out a minor, relaxed comic thriller like *Family Plot.* It had a certain gentleness, they said, and in spite of Hitchcock's tortuous obsession with structure, Ernest Lehman's dialogue amused them, and Hitchcock's two brilliant set pieces — the funny-frightening runaway-car sequence and the slow, dreamlike cemetery pursuit — revealed the eye of a cinematic genius. "A witty, relaxed lark, a movie to raise your spirits. . . . Hitchcock's most cheerful film in a long time. . . . He is in benign good humor" — such was the critical consensus, although a few insisted the film was lifeless and maladroit. But the Hollywood press led the pack of admirers; and the telegrams, bouquets of flowers, deliveries of wine, and congratulatory calls were so well timed that, in one of his unpredictable reversals, Hitchcock displayed a sudden bloom of cheerful energy.

When a writer who was completing a study of his work arrived for lunch and an interview, he found a more buoyant Hitchcock than during the previous year, and for the first time the director gave permission for the publication of storyboards detailing his scene preparation. Hitchcock dipped into his memory and pulled out a variety of anecdotes about his English films, he sat in a screening room and watched a new print of *The Farmer's Wife* (which he had not seen since he had finished it in 1927), and he tried out ideas for a battery of new films. At the same time, the French continued their love affair with him. After the consul general presented Hitchcock with papers naming him a Commander of the National Order of Arts and Letters in June, there was little more that country could do to show esteem short of bestowing citizenship.

But if the press and visitors to the studio saw a smiling Hitchcock, it was perhaps because he was spending more time at the office talking about new projects, telephoning former associates about the good word on *Family Plot,* and generally avoiding Bellagio Road, where Alma's weakness had stabilized but left her a sad and quiet companion who spent most of her days watching game shows and soap operas on television and summoning nurses to tell them what they were doing incorrectly. "She didn't have much incentive anymore," Hitchcock's secretary recalled, "and he didn't know how — or didn't want — to give her that incentive. The whole situation was becoming terribly sad." Perhaps Alma was too severe a reminder of his own mortality; perhaps Alma also knew that she was no longer much professional use to him, and that when he asked her advice it was out of pity or politeness. But whatever the complexities of the matter, Hitchcock took advantage of his place in the Hollywood sun to insist that he was at work on several new projects. And so he passed the rest of 1976 and early 1977.

"One of the films I'm making," he said in the summer of 1977, "is a thriller about gangsters looking for a body, but of course the wrong body turns up. I'm not entirely sure of what's going to happen in the story'' — and no writer had been signed by August — "but there's one lovely character I've grown quite fond of,'' he confided.

She's always drunk. She's a wino — you know, on that cheap jug stuff. Then she goes to Alcoholics Anonymous, and that's when the fun starts.

There's a scene in a bar when a man tries to pick her up. At last she turns to him and asks, "Do you like sex?'' and of course he's delighted with this question and says, "Yes!'' Then after a while she turns to him again and asks, "Do you like to travel?'' And the man says he sure does, and by this time he's really getting excited. Finally she leans over to him and smiles and whispers, "Then fuck off!''

Also in 1977, Hitchcock added the fifth codicil to his 1963 will and approved the severest business dealings his agents had managed for him in years. John Trevor Story, the English novelist, had sold him the world film rights to *The Trouble with Harry* for minimal compensation. When the rights expired, Story received a letter from Hitchcock's lawyers asking him to sign a renewal document assigning all rights to Hitchcock in perpetuity, with no offer of further payment. But Story replied that he had "no intention of maintaining Alfred Hitchcock in his old age,'' and he reminded them that Hitchcock had promised to buy another Story novel, whether he used it or not, in consideration of the small payment Story received for *The Trouble with Harry*. There were forty-nine other properties to choose from, he wrote, and he admitted that he had fallen on lean times. There is no record of further correspondence.

Viewers of the Photoplay Gold Medal Awards on national television on June 18 watched Hitchcock move slowly to the stage to receive the Special Editors Award, but once at the podium, he delivered a short, deliciously lugubrious address. His humor had not yet failed him, even if his energy had. A visitor who accepted several invitations from Hitchcock in 1976 and 1977 formed a similar impression: Hitchcock found movement about his office increasingly difficult (soon he would be forced to depend on the help of a cane). Nevertheless, in early 1978 he insisted he was ready to begin work on a script for *The Short Night,* and he invited scenarist James Costigan to collaborate. Their meetings lasted only a few weeks, for it was readily apparent to Costigan that there could be no fruitful work, and no script ever began. At once, Hitchcock turned to Ernest Lehman, whose scripts for *North by Northwest* and *Family Plot* had been so well received.

"Hitch had often intrigued me,'' Lehman said,

by describing the opening sequence of a film about the British spy George Blake — the daring escape from Wormwood Scrubs Prison. When I came on the project, my first shock was to learn that he was [now] adamantly opposed to using that sequence at all; he wanted to start the film *after* the escape. My second shock was to discover that he was in love — in fact *obsessed* — with the idea that the leading man would rape and kill a woman at the outset of the picture. I insisted that no audience would have anything but hatred for such a hero. And I wore Hitch down and gradually made him realize that I was never going to buy this notion.

We had plenty of creative and interpersonal problems on that project, and many times I resolved to quit. But I always stayed on, because I didn't want *Family Plot* to be his last picture. I didn't think it was good enough to be his last picture. And there were several people at the studio close to Hitch who would whisper to me that "it would kill him" if I left the project — which was ridiculous, but I bought it.

He had painful health problems and emotional problems, and I had to live with the daily anxiety of wondering what sort of mood he was going to be in each morning, and how he was going to react to our work in progress — if indeed he was going to have any stomach for work at all. The amazing thing was that despite all the difficulties, I did manage to complete two drafts of the screenplay, and Hitch did gather a small production staff about him, and he did wire me, from a sickbed, that the script was, in his words, "very satisfactory."

We then went through all the motions of getting ready for a picture to go into production, even though it was becoming clearer and clearer to me, and I think to him, that he was in no physical or emotional condition to shoot a film, nor would he be ever again — particularly a film with as much physical action and location shooting as *The Short Night* would entail.

When my services on the project finally came to a contractual end, Hitch and I said warm and friendly farewells to each other and I went off on a two-month vacation trip to Europe. When I returned, I heard that Hitch had brought in a third writer to start *The Short Night* game all over again, to delude himself and the world into believing that he was still a picture-maker about to make another picture. I was terribly saddened.

While Lehman was away, however — and before the new writer arrived — Hitchcock had telephoned yet another scenarist, Anthony Shaffer in London. "I want to apologize for what happened about *Family Plot*," the director said, "and you know I don't apologize easily." Then there was a pause, and the sound of terror filled Hitchcock's voice. "Tony, they're all betraying me! Everyone's leaving me! You've got to come and rescue me! I'm all alone!" It was clear to Shaffer that Hitchcock was ill and disoriented; the voice was not that of the self-possessed director he had worked with on *Frenzy* seven years before, but that of a broken and confused old man who was imagining terrible harm plotted against him by close associates. His monologue rambled, senselessly, and Shaffer had to tell Hitchcock as gently as possible that he had other commitments.

Shaffer and Lehman were not the only people to be disturbed by the unhappy decline in Hitchcock's emotional and psychological health, and by his dangerously increased drinking. Samuel and Suzanne Taylor visited, and after a quiet evening, Hitchcock — normally the controlled mealtime companion — took Suzanne's arm and with tear-filled eyes whispered: "Oh, I'm so lonely, I'm so lonely . . . No one calls me anymore . . . Please tell Sam to call me!" The thought that *he* might call others — suggested to him by Lehman and by Peggy Robertson, to name just two — was of course untenable. People came to Alfred Hitchcock; he had a lifetime habit of never seeking out anyone's company or friendship.

From that time until very near the end, Samuel Taylor telephoned Hitchcock every Sunday morning — but the calls were more a duty for him than a pleasure. What Hitchcock had said was true: he was very much a lonely recluse. And he himself had carefully carved out his predicament. For years he had not responded to calls and letters and gifts and telegrams (apart from those that came from a very small group of people whose estimation was, for various reasons, important to him); finally, people just left him alone. There was the occasional call to or from England — from Sidney Bernstein — but even the executives at Universal, whose friendship was taken for granted, left him virtually to his solitude at the studio. It was, quite honestly, what they thought he preferred. The situation became just as isolated and unhappy at Bellagio Road, where the last visiting journalist was shocked to find a "desolate and depressing house filled with dusty, artificial flowers" — one of the tamer descriptions that had to be discreetly excised by Peggy Robertson when she dutifully edited the writer's manuscript, which by prior agreement had to be submitted for Hitchcock's approval.

All during 1978, Hitchcock's small staff — Peggy Robertson, Suzanne Gauthier, and designer Robert Boyle — devoted themselves to cheering him with small items of daily news, supporting him in his various infirmities, and running interference against an increasingly gossip-hungry Hollywood press who had heard the talk about alcoholism, accidents at the office, and intermittent senility. This loyal, considerate, and prudent trio were joined in their tasks by Hitchcock's personal driver, Anthony Emerzian; his duties, by the middle of 1978, included arranging for clandestine deliveries of vodka and brandy to Hitchcock's office, placing them, at his employer's insistence, in the desk drawer and bath-room cupboard, and quietly removing the remnants of the previous day's supply.

There was, however, one final attempt to keep the illusion. In early autumn 1978, after Lehman's final draft of *The Short Night* had been submitted and accepted, Hitchcock began work with his third writer. This time he would restore the original opening of the prison escape; and in addition, he would again insist on the rape-strangulation Lehman had denied him. David Freeman — journalist, playwright, television and film scenarist, and valued "script doctor" for several directors who had been in trouble earlier — was proposed as the right man to rework the screenplay. He was invited to lunch with the director in September, and for the occasion Hitchcock prepared himself by a day's abstinence.

"He was very gracious," said Freeman,

and we talked on and on at lunch about everything except the picture I thought he wanted to make — which didn't seem to interest him nearly as much as having a congenial meal-companion. Eventually, Thom Mount, Universal's ex-ecutive in charge of production, who was with us, gently steered the conver-sation to the project, and Hitchcock outlined his ideas. He asked me some questions about his films, and I must have demonstrated enough knowledge of them to impress him, which I wasn't trying to do. It was really like an audi-tion — I was being tried out for the job.

Shortly after lunch, I was told outside that I had the job — not by Hitchcock himself, of course. After an office had been set up for me in Hitchcock's bun-galow, we slowly set to work.

For his part, Hitchcock found Freeman's courtesy, good humor, and calm reassuring.

Freeman soon found that the workdays began slowly, and that much of the morning he would be on his own. Hitchcock arrived late, made a few calls to the executive offices, read the mail, and after lunch sat down with him to discuss story background for two or three hours. "He wanted to talk generally about espionage and prison escapes," Freeman said,

and his talk was wide-ranging, gossipy, and reflective — and spiced with an-ecdotes about his past films and his past life. How much of this was accurate and how much invented it was difficult to say. When he was seriously involved in preparing this script, we would talk about the characters, their past and their motivation, sometimes for weeks.

During the first several months, for a large part of the time, he was full of enthusiasm. We pored over photographs of the prison and the adjacent hospital, and the floor plans of both, and maps of the local streets and alleys in London.

We got on very well together, but after several months of this I realized that this research was no longer research. He was avoiding work.

As winter passed, Freeman had to work alone more often, for Hitchcock was absent from the office for a·week or two at a time. On some of these occasions, Freeman later learned, he had been admitted to Cedars-Sinai Medical Center for alcoholic detoxification. At other times, he had fallen at home and required a few days of rest.

After interruptions like these, he would invite me out to his house to work in the afternoons, where he was always very polite and genial — until one day in January 1979, when he asked me if I wanted a drink. I said a cup of coffee would be just right, but that was the wrong thing to say. He wanted an excuse for something stronger, and the next day he simply ordered the nurse to bring us vodka and orange juice. When she disapproved, or tried to avoid him, he struggled heroically to rise and get it himself.

Often, during the days at home, Alma joined them at the kitchen banquette, where Hitchcock read her a scene they had worked on, or he acted out a part, bellowing the dialogue and trying to prove that he was still the great filmmaker. Alma was more frail than ever, and it was often difficult to know how much of their conversation she appreciated. The best times for the Hitchcocks were the visits of their daughter; in a rare note dictated to Elsie Randolph, he praised Pat, who had been ''a great help and consolation.''

During a sustained period of lucidity, Hitchcock forced from his visual imagination his last great scene, the opening shot planned for *The Short Night:* a long, ambitious, single take in which the camera teases the audience, revealing and concealing characters and information, creating suspense with what is seen and heard. David Freeman wrote the scene just as Hitchcock described and detailed it to him, and so it remained in the final script:

It's a drizzly London evening in the fall. Wormwood Scrubs Prison and Hammersmith Hospital are side by side, with a narrow service street between them. A man sits in a car holding a bouquet of chrysanthemums. The camera is outside the car, looking at him as he listens to a voice we can't quite make out. It could be the car radio, but his ear is cocked slightly toward the flowers. The camera moves toward the windshield, still without cutting, and then descends slightly as it dollies forward, peering into the car, as if about to show us what the man is doing with those mums. But then it surprises us, and further piques our interest, by panning away, over the wet cobblestone road, toward the brick wall. As the camera climbs the rough red bricks, going steadily higher, inducing dizziness in the viewer, the voice we've been hearing becomes clearer, as if the camera were hunting it. It's an angry voice: "I'm here . . . Hurry on, now . . . Can you hear? I said I'm here!" When the camera is at the top, and before its descent, we get a glimpse of the surroundings on both sides of the wall. In our one glance, from this height, we can see that inside the wall is a prison. There's a tower, a few searchlights, and rude-looking cell blocks. On the outside, beyond the service road, we glimpse another large institution and a sign that says "Hammersmith Hospital." . . . The camera, our guide, moves down the wall toward the voice. Inside, a man dressed in prison garb is huddled against the wall, avoiding the lights and speaking urgently into a primitive walkie-talkie. "I'm here, damn it — I'm here! Now move!" The camera cuts to the outside (the very first cut in the scene), to the interior of the car. The driver speaks soothingly into his flowers. "I'm here. You'll be fine . . . Stay calm." Moments later, but only after two suspenseful interruptions which threaten the successful conclusion of his purpose, he tosses a ladder over the prison wall. From the prison side, we see the man lunge for it and he starts to climb, frantically, hungrily . . . From outside the prison, his face then appears at the top of the wall. He stares down for a moment, swings his body up over the top of the wall . . . and then falls, tumbling to the ground.

At last, in a single burst of imagination, Alfred Hitchcock had created his final scene of escape to freedom. In doing so, he had sprung himself (not George Blake) from the prison of his childhood memory. All the rest of that week, in February 1979, he was more at ease than he had been in many months. Part of him, in a mysterious and private place deep within, was at last free.

But there was another fantasy to be finalized, too — a darker fantasy, revealed in the only other scene that interested Hitchcock.

The escaped man, the protagonist of the story, seeks help from several accomplices and is at last left with a young woman who has offered to aid his escape from the country. His name is Brand (he represents George Blake); hers is Rosemary; their accomplice is Ian. Brand and Rosemary are meeting for the first time.

[*Rosemary is at the sink, making tea. He's behind her. Watching. She can sense his eyes on her back and it makes her uncomfortable.*]

ROSEMARY [*starting to chatter nervously*]: Ian and I will be driving you . . . You'll be cramped but hidden . . .

[*The kettle whistles. Rosemary pours the water for the tea.*]

ROSEMARY: There. We'll just let that steep a little. Now perhaps you'll tell me about Berlin.

BRAND: Rosemary. For remembrance.

ROSEMARY: Yes. That's right. Rosemary for remembrance.

[*He draws her to him and kisses her. She doesn't kiss back, but she doesn't push him away, either.*]

ROSEMARY: Please . . . don't . . . They'll be back very soon.
BRAND: They left you here for a bit. To be with me.
ROSEMARY: No, no. Ian needed help . . . You know I respect you so much. We all do.
BRAND: Um-hum.
ROSEMARY: We really do.
BRAND: You know how long I've been in prison?
ROSEMARY: You'll be seeing your wife soon. They've made all the arrangements. She'll be so happy.

[*He strokes her breasts.*]

ROSEMARY [*starting to get scared*]: Don't. Please don't do that. They'll be back any time now.
BRAND: There's plenty of time. It's all arranged.

[*The more nervous she gets, the more bold he becomes . . .*]

BRAND: So soft . . . It's been five years since I felt anything so soft.
ROSEMARY: Please don't do that . . . Please stop . . . I'll yell out . . . really I will. I don't care . . . Stop! . . . Please . . . don't do that . . .

[*He holds her mouth with his uninjured hand, squeezing her cheeks so she can't speak. Her voice is muffled and distorted, but growing more urgent.*]

BRAND: Stop babbling.

[*He distorts her face further, then pushes his mouth at hers, kissing her and running his hands along her body. She reaches back behind her for the cup of tea, fumbles around for it as he continues to grope and paw at her. She finds the cup and swings it forward, splashing the hot tea at him. He jumps back, but it only angers him more.*]

BRAND: Stupid cow. You'll do as I say.

[*He slaps her. She yells out, and he slaps her again. Once he starts he can't seem to stop, and he hits her several times. She gasps for breath and scratches at his face. She draws blood on his cheeks.*]

ROSEMARY: Help me . . . Stop it . . . Help me . . .
BRAND: You bitch . . . you stupid bitch. Shut up.

[*He covers her mouth with his injured hand. She bites down on his fingers, sinking her teeth into the flesh . . . He presses his thumbs into her neck, harder and harder, cutting off the flow of blood and oxygen. He squeezes and Rosemary begins to gasp for breath. She flails her arms about, desperate to breathe.*]

BRAND: Bitch . . . bitch . . . what do you think of that? What? Tell me. What?

[. . . *Her arms go limp as she collapses in his arms. Brand looks at her eyes, puts his hand on her heart, and then realizes she's dead . . . He slaps her face — in anger and desperation — but she's dead, limp in his arms. He lets the body fall to the floor, and hurries toward the living room.*]

Described in exact detail to his writer — and almost dictated word for word — this was the last expression of the darkest desire that had occupied Hitchcock's imagination for decades — suggested in his very first film, *The Pleasure Garden,* and rendered most recently and most graphically in *Frenzy*. It was from the part of him that had been "obsessed," according to Ernest Lehman, with the desire to open his film with a murderous rape. It was from the part of him that was still unfree.

The fantasies Hitchcock spun and that his screenwriters gave structure to were always geared to cinematic realization. His films depended on the emergence, from deep within him, of mysterious images — images that were often violent, at times tender. From his own secret longings and vivid imagination there came the small germs of stories — sometimes fearful and erotic, sometimes quietly comic or dreamlike. But the plots and the characters would always be subordinate to the power of the images — just as in dreams, the narrative is never quite logical or clear and is always subordinate to the images. Similarly, the residue of feelings left by dreams, like the impression left by Hitchcock's images, is more important that any half-remembered "plot."

And herein lies the unassailable genius of Alfred Hitchcock, the source of his enormous popularity. He drew so deeply from the human reservoir of imagery and dream and fear and longing that he achieved universal appeal. Had his films been simple incarnations of his own fantasies and dreams, with no wider reference, he would have perhaps won a small and devoted group of admirers. But he expressed those elusive images and half-remembered dreams in terms that moved and astounded and delighted and aroused awe from millions round the world.

In *The Lodger,* a woman shrieks in terror when her fiancé, who is a detective, snaps handcuffs on her and refers to "marriage bonds." In *Vertigo,* a beautiful, remote woman in an old cemetery clutches a nosegay and stands dazed before a tombstone; later, a man dreams of joining her in love and in death. In *The Birds,* the failure of human relationships is symbolized by the sudden, inexplicable revolt of nature itself. To select only these three is to have a rich array of icons that show how unevenly humans plumb the depths of their inner lives; other Hitchcock films are as worthy of consideration in this regard, and as full of powerful, universal imagery.

If there is anything that can be said about dreams and longings, it is that they are intensely private. Even when shared, they are hard to express. It is difficult to transmute into words the oddness of an image, the comic-grotesque distortions of inner time and space, the weird amalgams of feeling that leave people perhaps a little more aware of their deepest responses to life and a little more unsure of the artifice with which they so often cover themselves. Hitchcock's dream world somehow found form in the hugely creative and original images that went through and beyond the doors of his own individuality and found resonant echoes in countless viewers in different cultures. In giving form to his fantasies, he was exploring and exposing things not only in himself but also in others — realities more or less actual, more or less potential. He created images not of what *all* life is, but of what *some* life is all the time, everywhere, and what all life is in constant danger of becoming.

And it was precisely at this time, with images of violence and death crowding in upon him, that Alfred Hitchcock resisted — almost until it was too late — the requests for help by the staff of the American Film Institute, who had selected him as the seventh recipient of the Life Achievement Award.

# Sixteen

1979–1980

THE months after the AFI tribute in March of 1979 were an unhappy postscript to so formal an honor. Hitchcock tried to return to his office as soon as possible, where David Freeman waited for instructions on script revisions. But there were to be none.

In the mornings, Hitchcock read his mail but rarely replied. Elsie Randolph sent a warm letter of congratulations from England, and to this he responded in a wistful tone: Alma had had to make quite an effort to get to the hotel for the tribute, he told her, although they had been the king and queen of the evening. He reported his pleasure at Ingrid Bergman's spontaneity, but then his tone turned sad and fearful. He reported the death of Cyril Ritchard — his first talkie villain, in *Blackmail*. He mentioned that he was at work on a script with only three characters, and he concluded that there was not much hope for Alma, who by then had nurses in constant attendance.

In the afternoons, the faltering director occasionally summoned David Freeman, but there was virtually no work done. They sat while Hitchcock rummaged in his desk drawer for a bottle of brandy or made his way to the bathroom cabinet for the vodka. "He poured himself drinks of liquor and brandy by the beakerful," Freeman recalled, "and tilted his head backward, draining the glass in one gulp. It was then I realized his desperate need. It was clear that his degeneration would now be very swift." During the final weeks of his time on the project, Freeman listened patiently, spoke gently, and was as calming as he could be for the more and more insensate Hitchcock.

Occasionally, Hitchcock would try to talk about something concrete and present, but quickly his mind wandered. He returned in his inner journey to the studios of Islington or the streets of Leytonstone or to

Shepherd's Bush or Piccadilly. He told the few people who were allowed into the office to see him that his parents always left him alone when he was a child, and his voice shook with emotion, as if he were once again being abandoned at night. He could dip into no pool of memory and find clear relief; and he sometimes opened his desk drawer in search of a bent and yellowed card — his mother's Requiem Mass card, with her photo and a baroque Victorian-Catholic design recalling the death and funeral he had never attended but had seen only in his mind's eye. His hands shook as he gripped it, tears stinging his eyes and dripping onto the desk blotter. And he spoke of his old sister Nellie, who had died only recently and for whose memorial he had sent a small wreath. His brother, he said, came to his house in Cromwell Road only to drink his wine . . . no one ever really cared . . . he had been betrayed all his life . . . he was alone, always alone and in the dark . . . would he die? . . . *when* would he die? . . . the awful dark, when he wanted the light . . . and a cloudless horizon . . .

In a last, desperate attempt to establish some kind of direct human contact, he engaged a woman from the Universal Studios typing pool. After a few weeks she left his offices pale and needing medical care, for he gradually made ugly, intimate demands that led to a hysterical scene. The spurious office-work had at last clearly become a fumbling, futile attempt at human intimidation and exploitation. It was a hopeless and crude move to satisfy desires that had by this time become only dimly perceived memories of desire. "The Dionysian streak in him was still trying to get out," as David Freeman said.

By late April the atmosphere in Hitchcock's office was thick with depression. Suzanne Gauthier was unsure how much of his illness she could endure — how many more scenes of lunatic rage and inconsolable weeping and sudden, unusually childish tenderness alternating with senile obscenities. She and Peggy Robertson and Anthony Emerzian were not trained nurses, and it was the basic and unpleasant tasks of practical nursing that they were too often called upon to perform. The executives at MCA/Universal, meanwhile, were caught in a terrible dilemma. They could not discharge Hitchcock, for personal and professional dignity forbade so violent a gesture — and, strictly speaking, he had a contract with them. He was costing a great deal in funds and embarrassment, however, and for a few, like Lew Wasserman, personal pain.

Finally it was too burdensome even for Hitchcock to maintain the charade that there was work or that there could ever again be a film. Ironically, a colleague's death gave him the moment he needed. On May 8 there was news of the death of Victor Saville — who had known Hitchcock since 1923, when Balcon, Saville, and John Freedman formed a production company and engaged Alfred Hitchcock as a crew member. Saville had come to the American Film Institute dinner just a few weeks earlier, and he had appeared so well . . .

Peggy Robertson arrived at the office early the next morning, to tell Hitchcock gently before he heard it from the media or a telephone call. She told him that, regretfully, there was sad news — and then, without any expression, Hitchcock said he had sad news to report, too. He was closing the office. Today. She was no longer needed. With a mixture of relief and confusion and anxiety for him, for herself, and for everyone else in the office, she made her way to the executives at Universal, only to be told that her severance indeed was effective at once and that no — contrary to what Hitchcock had insisted over the years — he had made no provision for her after almost a quarter-century of employment.

The end was to be quick and complete. The office would be shut down within days. Suzanne Gauthier stayed on a short while, to help pack personal effects for removal to Bellagio Road, and then she was gone, too — and, like Robertson, Hitchcock's personal secretary was left without provision for employment or means of sustenance. "Leave me alone," he told her the last day. "I am . . . I . . . a sea of . . . alone."

For a brief time that summer, Hitchcock returned to the empty office, dictated a few mostly incomprehensible letters to a temporary secretary, and then withdrew to the house and to Alma, who like him could now move only with a walker or with nurses in attendance. In one rare lucid moment, he dictated another note to Elsie Randolph, saying that there was nothing else to wait for after all the various academic and professional honors. He and Alma were both, he said, housebound and alone, except for Pat's visits.

At times over the next months, he rejected the suggestion that he allow a priest, a friend of the O'Connell family, to come for a visit, or to celebrate a quiet, informal ritual at the house for his comfort. It had been years since he had attended worship — he had done so only when cousins visited from England — but it was not so long since he had expressed his distrust and fear of the clergy.

"I was born a Catholic," he had said a few years earlier to a boy who interviewed him during a long-distance telephone call from Saint Ignatius, their shared alma mater. "I went to a Catholic school, and now I have a conscience with lots of trials over beliefs." But for all his love of structure, Hitchcock could find no path to confront the trials, nor means to work out the struggle, in doubt and faith, and so to bring peace to his troubled spirit. "Don't let any priests on the lot," he had whispered to his office staff in the last year. "They're all after me; they all hate me." There was no way of convincing him to see a clergyman at home, either, although he imagined their presences there, too.

"There were so many resentments locked up inside him," Samuel Taylor said.

He never really had any close friends. Suzanne and I knew him as well as anyone, but even here there was a rift, as there was with everyone who ever tried to befriend him.

And yet it must have been very hard for him. Hitch was taken very seriously by the whole world — but not by Hollywood until it was too late. He was a great artist, but people in Hollywood never accepted him as such because of the content of his films. They thought he just told a good yarn. Hollywood believed the art of film lay in the content; therefore they refused to believe [that] a man who told what they considered frivolous stories could be a great artist. But after all, one could condemn Chaucer and Shakespeare on the grounds of what appears to be "frivolous content."

Hollywood never knew what a great artist was. Under the proper circumstances, Hitch should have been nominated for every Directors Guild award and every Oscar. The basic hypocrisy of Hollywood is that they don't really believe film is an art. Hitch knew all this, it was all inside him. He and Alma knew it. How painful it must have been for them to be where they were and not be fully appreciated, especially after they had left England for that reason, expecting America to provide what London hadn't. But Hollywood just made him their house clown.

Shortly after Hitchcock's eightieth birthday, in August 1979, Ingrid Bergman paid a visit. "He took both my hands," she recalled, "and tears streamed down his face and he said, 'Ingrid, I'm going to die,' and I said, 'But of course you are going to die sometime, Hitch — we are all going to die.' And then I told him that I, too, had recently been very ill, and that I had thought about it, too. And for a moment the logic of that seemed to make him more peaceful."

Just before the end of the year, the British-American Chamber of Commerce, rushing to precede a bigger honor about which everyone was talking, voted Hitchcock "Man of the Year." And then, at Christmastime, the official announcement came: the New Year's Honors List of Her Majesty Queen Elizabeth II was published, and in the Diplomatic Service and Overseas List, Alfred Hitchcock was named a Knight Commander of the British Empire.* A trip to London was impossible, and

*The idea for this honor had originated with author and critic Alexander Walker, who in October 1979 wrote to Prime Minister Margaret Thatcher and received an immediate acknowledgment promising full consideration of his suggestion.

so, on January 3, 1980, the British consul general, Thomas W. Aston, came to Universal Studios. Camera crews were present early in the day, and, with a strange aptness, the presentation of the formal papers of knighthood was held not in Hitchcock's office — which was by now completely dismantled and in forlorn disarray — but on a makeshift office set, which gave the illusion of a normal workday at the office. With the cameras and lights, it could have been a cameo appearance in one of his pictures: Hitchcock seated behind an oak desk, impassive, slightly querulous.

He had been given generous injections of cortisone, for the arthritis was causing crueler pain than ever. His pacemaker had been monitored the previous afternoon. After the formal words of investiture, Hitchcock surprised everyone — and made the men from Universal more than a little anxious — by agreeing to answer reporters' questions. "I'm happy that it came my way at the right time," he said with a trace of sarcasm. "I suppose it shows that if you stick at something long enough, eventually somebody takes note." Why did the queen's recognition take so long? "I suppose it was a matter of carelessness." Did he think being Sir Alfred would make any difference in his wife's attitude toward him? "I certainly hope so. Perhaps she will now mind her own business and do what she's told."

A luncheon followed, and a number of his business and professional colleagues toasted "Sir Hitch." Cary Grant, another Briton who had relocated, brought great cheer to the somewhat disconcerting afternoon. Janet Leigh was there, and the usual array of MCA/Universal executives, and Hitchcock's daughter and his agent. "Without knowing it was to be a final good-bye, I spoke to Hitchcock at the luncheon that day," Ernest Lehman recalled. "But none of the sadness of his last year can obliterate my memories of all the good times, the exciting times, the creative victories we had shared in the past."

On March 16 Alfred Hitchcock made a last, brief public appearance. It was the custom for the American Film Institute award winner to introduce the next year's recipient, and so he was driven back to the Beverly Hilton for a laborious but brief taping session. The producers saw to it that — unlike the afternoon taping of his acceptance speech a year earlier — he was now wearing his upper and lower bridges and that the cue cards were large enough and close enough for him to read without difficulty. He introduced the program in James Stewart's honor, but could not attend the dinner that evening.

The weeks after were quiet and uninterrupted except for the more frequent attendance of doctors and nurses at Bellagio Road. Lawyers

and agents appeared more often, too, for there were details of the vast
Hitchcock estate that required his signature — a signature, added to a
codicil on March 25, that had become all but indistinguishable by now,
completely changed from the firm, legible, schoolboy's hand of years
and years. As Hitchcock turned the many pages of his last will and
testament, he could — had he been alert and capable of reflection —
have read a summary statement of all the worldly results of his artistic
achievements.

In an estate conservatively estimated in excess of $20 million, there
were major holdings in city and county bonds issued by Los Angeles
and San Francisco, plus ownership of oil wells in four states and gas
wells in Canada. There were almost 150,000 shares of MCA stock and
2,250 head of cattle at the Hitchcock Hereford Farms, of which he was
a disinterested absentee landlord. There were major percentages of the
incomes on eighteen of his films. And there were 66 cases of wine, and
29 major artworks — oil paintings by Rouault, Avery, Sickert, Dubuffet and Dufy, Vlaminck and Utrillo; works by Epstein, Klee, Dalí,
Rowlandson, and Rodin.

Through a complicated series of trusts, Hitchcock's estate was willed
to his wife, daughter, and granddaughters. Had his sister survived him,
she was to receive a sum "not to exceed $28,000" and $25 a week for
five years after his death — "provided, however, that such payments
shall be made only so long as and to the extent that my Estate shall be
able to make such payments without unreasonably depriving my wife
and daughter." That provision would have been unlikely to take effect
in any case: the taxes paid on the estate in 1980 alone were over
$1 million.

But there was a marked omission of charitable bequests — and saddest of all, and contrary to repeated promises made to his most devoted
employees over the years, there was no provision for anyone outside the
family except for three former servants. It was a bulky, complicated,
and not entirely edifying document the lawyers took away with them in
March.

Gradually, the great final battle subsided. Arthritis had wracked his
body, but in early April the pain oddly diminished. He slept more, and
deeply, but then his liver failed, his kidney function slowed, and his
tired, enlarged heart no longer responded to the modern device he had
at first worn so proudly.

On the night of April 28/29, the doctor was called, and by early
morning the family had gathered quietly. "I retire when I die," Hitchcock had said not long before. "One never knows the ending. One has

to die to know exactly what happens after death, although Catholics
have their hopes.''

The end came at 9:17 on the morning of April 29, 1980, without
suspense, without violence. The terror, after all, had been met for years
in his dreams and in his art. It was, as so often, a quiet, scarcely dis-
cernible moment, as if he had glimpsed the cloudless horizon that was
always his image of serenity — as if his earlier, almost forgotten hopes
had finally come back to gather round and had not, at the last, left him
alone in the darkness.

# Notes
# Selective Bibliography
# The Films of Alfred Hitchcock

# Notes

Abbreviated forms refer to sources cited fully in the Selective Bibliography.

CHAPTER TWO

p. 15 "Ours was": Truffaut, pp. 17, 239–240.
16 "It must": Ibid., p. 18.
17 "a smartly": Cecil J. Rhodes, letter to DS, Apr. 7, 1981.
18 "It was": Quoted by Tippi Hedren, to DS, Oct. 1980.
18 "Always!": Lalott, p. 10, for example.
18 "They were": *Image et Son*, no. 135 (Nov. 1960), p. 11 (trans. DS). Note that Hitchcock described this event the same year *Psycho* was in first public release.
19 "I've known": Ibid.
19 "I was": Chris Hodenfield, *Rolling Stone*, Dec. 1975.
20 "I don't": Quoted in *TV Guide*, May 29, 1965, p. 15.
20 "I would": Truffaut, p. 17.
20 "as literature": Mahoney, p. 12.
21 "There the": Jay Presson Allen to DS, Nov. 12, 1980.
22 "We must": Truffaut, pp. 17–18.
22 "I remember": To DS, July 24, 1975.
23 "a well built": Cecil J. Rhodes to DS, Apr. 7, 1981 (letter).
24 "The reason": Rev. Anthony Forrester, S.J., to DS, Jan. 11, 1981.
26 "The Question": *Ignatian Record: The Bulletin of St. Ignatius College and Parish* 14, no. 4 (Feb. 1915): 43–44.
27 "In fact": To DS, Jan. 15, 1981.
27 "The method": John O'Riordan, *Ignatian*, summer 1973.
28 "With the": *Ignatian Record* 9, no. 11 (Nov. 1910): 241.

28 "If you've": Quoted in *TV Guide*, May 29, 1965, p. 15; Charles Champlin, *Los Angeles Times*, Mar. 7, 1979; John O'Riordan, *Ignatian*, summer 1973.
29 "I remember": Rev. Robert Goold to Rev. Anthony Forrester, S.J., Apr. 29, 1980 (letter dated the day of AH's death).
29 "a lonely": To DS, Jan. 15, 1981.
29 "Dread of Sin": *Ignatian Record* 11, no. 2 (Feb. 1912): 33–34.
31 "Hitchcock became": To DS, Jan. 15, 1981.
32 "They've got": Reed, p. 18.
33 "I have": Ibid.
33 "There was": Knight, p. 114.
34 "Did you?": AH to DS, July 24, 1975.
37 "At the age": Belfrage, p. 60.
38 "I would": John O'Riordan, *Ignatian*, summer 1973, p. 16.
39 "At sixteen": Hitchcock (f), pp. 1, 7.
40 "One of the": Chesterton, pp. 19–27.
41 "The romance": Ibid., pp. 161–162.
42 "very fat": Quoted in *Newsweek*, June 11, 1956, p. 106.
42 "Gas": *The Henley: Social Club Magazine of The Henley Company, Ltd.* 1, no. 1 (June 1919): 1. Reprinted in *Sight and Sound* 39, no. 4 (autumn 1970): 186–187.
43 "I was": Quoted in *TV Guide*, May 29, 1965, p. 16.

CHAPTER THREE

48 "Why did": Betts, p. 25.
49 "a third": Priestley, p. 72.
50 "It comprised": Low and Manvell, p. 31.
55 "I'm American-trained": Quoted in *Action:*

*The Magazine of the Directors Guild of America*
3, no. 3 (May–June 1968): 8.
55 "The public": George Fitzmaurice, *New York Dramatic Mirror*, Mar. 11, 1916.
57 "The players": Balcon (a), p. 16.
57 "In the days": Hicks, p. 34.
58 "In the early": Betts, pp. 43–44, 35.
59 "J.C. Graham": *Close Up,* Apr. 1929.
60 "an Alice": Balcon (a), pp. 20–21.
60 "because of": Ibid., p. 19.
61 "I'll do": John O'Riordan, *Ignatian,* summer 1973, p. 17.
61 "*The Prude's*": To DS, Nov. 8, 1976.
61 "only a": Low and Manvell, vol. 4, p. 168.
64 "It was": Joseph McBride, "Mr. and Mrs. Hitchcock," *Sight and Sound,* fall 1976.
64 "Is that": Abramson (b), p. 16.
65 "The day": To DS, Nov. 8, 1976.
65 "I had": Quoted in *Action* 3, no. 3 (May–June 1968): 8.
67 "Those were": To DS, Nov. 8, 1976.
72 "All the": Quoted in *Close Up,* Dec. 1927.
73 "he wanted": Balcon (a), p. 19.
74 "I had": Quoted in Noble, p. 5.

CHAPTER FOUR

78 "He told": Quoted in *Action: The Magazine of the Directors Guild of America* 3, no. 3 (May–June 1968): 8.
80 "I was scared": To Hedda Hopper, Aug. 17, 1958.
81 "In the ideal": Hitchcock (a), pp. 44–45.
84 "Hitchcock has": Belfrage, p. 60.
86 "It was just": Ackland and Grant, p. 35.
86 "Some people": Elsie Randolph to DS, Jan. 23, 1981.
87 "He had": Balcon (a), p. 26.
89 "A few": Quoted in Truffaut, p. 35.
90 "whose comings": Robert Barltrop and Jim Wolveridge, *The Muvver Tongue* (London and West Nyack: The Journeyman Press, 1980), p. 125.
90 "Psychologically,": Truffaut, p. 34.
93 "I was never": Quoted in *TV Times* (London), Nov. 5, 1964, p. 8.
93 "really like": Samuel Taylor to DS, Dec. 2, 1980.
93 "much shrewder": Jay Presson Allen to DS, Nov. 15, 1980.
93 "a co-writer": To DS, Jan. 23, 1981.
95 "In the twenties": Balcon (a), p. 27.
97 "they knocked": Ackland and Grant, p. 36.
98 "another personal": *Kinematograph Weekly,* May 26, 1927, p. 43.
98 "he had not": Balcon (a), p. 27.
99 "My contempt": Quoted in *Bioscope,* Mar. 17, 1927.
100 "I think": Bogdanovich, p. 12.

101 "This is": *Bioscope,* Oct. 6, 1927.
102 "The Americans": AH letter in *London Evening News,* Nov. 16, 1927.
103 "It was": Quoted in *Interview,* Sept. 1974, pp. 5, 9.

CHAPTER FIVE

110 "The best": Bob Kendall, *Hollywood Studio,* June 1965, p. 11. See also Taylor, p. 121.
111 "He never": Quoted in *TV Times* (London), Oct. 29, 1964, p. 5.
111 "I wanted": To George Angell, on *The Time of My Life,* BBC-TV, Aug. 28, 1966. Cited hereafter as Angell, BBC.
111 "more engrossed": Ackland and Grant, p. 35.
113 "My thought": Bogdanovich, p. 12.
113 "New faces!": Quoted in *Picturegoer,* Aug. 1, 1931, p. 2.
114 "champagne that": *Close Up,* Mar. 1929.
115 "Oh yes": To Angell, BBC.
115 "I set": Hitchcock (Alma), p. 69.
116 "You could not": quoted by Rev. Robert Goold in a letter to Rev. Anthony Forrester, S.J., Aug. 1, 1980.
116 "I'd been": Abramson (b), p. 13.
120 "I don't": John Longden, "The Hitchcock Touch," in *The Elstree Story* — cited at Hitchcock (b) — p. 83.
120 "I remember": To Angell, BBC.
121 "Even the": Castle, pp. 131–135.
123 "was sentimentalized": Andrew Sarris, *Village Voice,* Sept. 11, 1978.
123 "Great Britain": Low and Manvell, vol. 4, pp. 304–305.
129 "He had": Ackland and Grant, p. 94.
131 "Since this": Quoted by Elsie Randolph, to DS, Jan. 23, 1981.
133 "If you": *Film Weekly,* June 10, 1932, p. 29.
135 "My policy": *London Daily Herald,* Dec. 1, 1933.
135 "Alfred Hitchcock": Matthews, p. 136.
135 "He was": Thornton, pp. 108–109.
136 "Jessie was not": Ibid.

CHAPTER SIX

141 "It was": To DS, May 18, 1981.
141 "Certain writers": Bogdanovich, p. 9.
144 "I thought": To DS, May 18, 1981.
146 "Madeleine Carroll": To Hedda Hopper, Aug. 17, 1958.
147 "I've never": Speaking at the American Film Institute, Los Angeles, Feb. 1970; and to George Angell, on *The Time of My Life,* BBC-TV, Aug. 28, 1966.
148 "What interests": Quoted in *Sight and Sound* 25, no. 3 (winter 1955/1956): 158.

148 "There was no": To DS, Nov. 7, 1981.

149 "It had": Montagu (b), p. 90.

150 "We would": *Kinematograph Weekly*, June 13, 1935, p. 4.

151 "It's brilliantly": *Film Weekly*, June 7, 1935, p. 32.

151 "Each detail": *Today's Cinema*, June 6, 1935, p. 4.

152 "I found": Gielgud, pp. 189–190.

153 "His stage": Hayman, p. 95.

153 "Nothing gives": *Midland Daily Telegraph*, July 14, 1936.

153 "It was": To DS, Aug. 23, 1977. (Hitchcock biographer John Russell Taylor is incorrect in identifying Florence Kahn as the widow of Sir Herbert Beerbohm Tree. She was his sister-in-law, the wife of Sir Herbert's half-brother.)

153 "The eyes": AH, *London Daily Mail*, Mar. 10, 1930.

154 "I liked": Bogdanovich, p. 18.

155 "In principle": Joseph Conrad, *The Secret Agent* (Garden City: Doubleday/Anchor, 1953), p. 121.

156 "I discovered": Balcon (c).

157 "A worthy": *Kinematograph Weekly*, May 14, 1936, p. 26.

157 "He loves": Lejeune, p. 1.

159 "Some of": To DS, May 18, 1981.


CHAPTER SEVEN

163 "Hitchcock's eyes": Derrick de Marney, *New York Times*, Feb. 5, 1938. De Marney's further comments are from this article.

164 "The party": To DS, Mar. 24, 1976.

169 "The thing": Quoted in Mahoney, p. 9.

169 "I am": DOS to Brown, Aug. 23, 1937, David O. Selznick Collection, Humanities Research Center / University of Texas at Austin.

170 "Lord!": Smith.

171 "I first": Janet White, "Picture Parade" (column), *Brooklyn Daily Eagle*, Aug. 30, 1937.

171 "There it": Eileen Creelman, "Picture Plays and Players" (column), *New York Sun*, June 15, 1938.

173 "In my": Brown, p. 89.

174 "I think": Ibid.; see also Gilliat's letter in *Screen International*, no. 172 (Jan. 13–20, 1979), p. 4.

174 "I was": Margaret Lockwood to DS, Jan. 16, 1981.

175 "I had": To DS, Sept. 3, 1980.

178 "Hollywood?": Quoted in *World Film News*, Mar. 1938, pp. 4–5.

180 "I remember": To DS, Aug. 23, 1977.

180 "Oh, yes": *New York Post*, Aug. 19, 1938.

182 "We were": Quoted by Ernest Lehman, to DS, Nov. 5, 1973.

183 "which I": DOS cable to AH, Sept. 7, 1938.

183 "Joan Harrison": Jenia Reissar to DOS, n.d. (probably c. June 1, 1938).

184 "I was": Samuels, p. 244.

184 "I am": Quoted in *Film Weekly*, Nov. 5, 1938, p. 7.

184 "Penny dreadful": *Film Weekly*, May 20, 1939, p. 31.

185 "It will not": Frank S. Nugent, *New York Times*, Oct. 12, 1939.

185 "singularly dull": Howard Barnes, *New York Herald Tribune*, Oct. 12, 1939.

186 "If you": Truffaut, p. 89.

186 "The truth": *Close Up*, July 1927, pp. 8–10.

186 "It was": Low and Manvell, p. 306.

187 "The fact": Arthur Veselo, "Crime Over the World," *Sight and Sound* 6, no. 23 (1936): 136.

188 "Like most": Low and Manvell, p. 308.

188 "a quality": Bertrand Russell, *Authority and the Individual*, the first Reith Lectures (London: Allen & Unwin, 1949), pp. 58–59.


CHAPTER EIGHT

209 "We had": Hitchcock (g), p. 14.

210 "C. Aubrey Smith": Mahoney, p. 16.

210 "Los Angeles?": Quoted in *News Review*, Mar. 10, 1949.

211 "What I": Hellman, p. 43.

213 "It was": AH on *Hollywood: The Selznick Years*, produced for American TV, 1969.

214 "is ninety": To DS, May 18, 1981.

214 "We need": DOS memo to John Hay Whitney, Sept. 6, 1939.

215 "I was": Hitchcock (c).

215 "I will not": Whitney Bolton, "Hitchcock Salesman for All His Movies," *New York Morning Telegraph*, July 7, 1966.

216 "Although Hitchcock": Hellman, p. 33.

217 "in a fine": DOS memo to Harry Ginsberg and Daniel O'Shea, Aug. 23, 1939.

218 "It was no": Houseman, pp. 478–479.

218 "One thing": Joan Fontaine to DS, July 23, 1974.

222 "I was": Rosenberg and Silverstein, p. 83.

224 "The script": Speech to UA stockholders, Los Angeles, Dec. 5, 1939, p. 11.

226 "I suggest": Jan. 22, 1940.

230 "I would": Truffaut, p. 96.

231 "Hitchcock had": Quoted in *Focus on Film*, no. 30 (June 1978).

232 "I was": Reed, pp. 17–19.

235 "Who prefer": Michael Balcon, *London Sunday Dispatch*, Aug. 25, 1940.

235 "Balcon's view": AH, "Hitchcock Re-

plies to 'Deserter' Charge,'' *New York World-Telegram,* Aug. 27, 1940.

236 "Hitchcock had": Sept. 17, 1940.

237 "Hitchcock has": O'Shea memo to DOS, Sept. 10, 1940.

### CHAPTER NINE

244 "Hitchcock's material": To DS, Dec. 21, 1980.

245 "I have": Harry E. Edington to J. J. Nolan, Feb. 5, 1941.

245 "Hitchcock does not": S. Rogell memo to Edington, Apr. 1, 1941.

246 "You will": DOS letter (drafted but unsent) to AH, Jan. 29, 1941.

247 "I think we": Memo dated May 2, 1941.

247 "I think the": Lewton memo to DOS, May 7, 1941.

248 "a very": DOS memo to Lewton, Apr. 2, 1941.

249 "Don't you": DOS letter to Daniel O'Shea, Aug. 21, 1941.

249 "It seems": DOS memo to Daniel O'Shea, Sept. 4, 1941.

250 "by your": DOS letter to AH, Sept. 22, 1941 (drafted but unsent).

251 "would leap": DOS cable to Daniel O'Shea, Nov. 1, 1941.

251 "I was": Houseman, pp. 479–480.

251 "rather like": Ibid., p. 480.

253 "I cut": Truffaut, p. 106.

253 "I'm not": Quoted in *Baltimore Sun,* Jan. 18, 1942.

256 "Hitch enthused": McDonell memo to DOS, May 5, 1942.

258 "He did": Teresa Wright to DS, June 26, 1974, and Oct. 14, 1980.

259 "I was": To DS, June 4, 1974.

259 "He said": To DS, May 26, 1981.

266 "congestive cardiac": Death certificate of William J. Hitchcock, registered in Guildford, England, Jan. 10, 1943.

266 "I weighed": Quoted in *Los Angeles Herald Examiner,* Sept. 29, 1974.

267 "I am": DOS memo to Daniel O'Shea, May 15, 1943.

268 "We were": To DS, June 4, 1974.

268 "I was": Bankhead, p. 229.

268 "She stood up": Brian, p. 138.

269 "Unless we": Bosley Crowther, *New York Times,* Jan. 13, 1944.

271 "I hope": Dec. 9, 1943.

272 "I'd like": Memo dated July 10, 1943.

273 "I am quite": DOS memo to Daniel O'Shea, Oct. 16, 1944.

273 "Hitchcock taught": Fethering, p. 117.

273 "the gentlemanly": Hecht, pp. 481, 396.

275 "I won't": Quoting herself, to DS, May 8, 1975.

275 "Selznick believed": To DS, Apr. 14, 1981.

277 "Selznick thought": Bogdanovich, p. 26; see also Truffaut, p. 118.

278 "I'm not": To Richard Johnston (production manager), Sept. 2, 1944.

278 "I gave": Quoted by Anna Lee, to DS, May 25, 1981.

### CHAPTER TEN

284 "The merger": Frank S. Nugent, "Assignment in Hollywood," *Good Housekeeping,* Nov. 1945, p. 6.

285 "The whole": To DS, July 24, 1975.

290 "the great": Bogdanovich, p. 26; see also Truffaut, pp. 198–199.

292 "there are": Taylor, p. 307.

294 "The Hitchcock": Memo dated Mar. 28, 1946.

296 "Clearly there": Memo to Daniel O'Shea.

298 "Finally,": Breen to DOS, Nov. 25, 1946.

298 "This, of course": To DS, Apr. 14, 1981.

300 "In the": *London Daily Mail,* Mar. 10, 1930.

300 "He takes": Todd, p. 75.

300 "Hitchcock took": Ann Todd to DS, Jan. 19, 1981.

301 "Actors!": Clayton, p. 59.

301 "Stacks and": To DS, Jan. 19, 1981.

301 "Hitch has": Memo to Daniel O'Shea, Dec. 28, 1946.

301 "I'm getting the run-around": Memo to Daniel O'Shea, Mar. 19, 1946.

302 "I am getting increasingly": To Daniel O'Shea, Apr. 23, 1946; Dec. 6, 1946; Oct. 8, 1946.

302 "Slick and": Bosley Crowther, *New York Times,* Jan. 9, 1948.

302 "scant lack": Howard Barnes, *New York Herald Tribune,* Jan. 9, 1948.

303 "He was": Hume Cronyn to DS, June 4, 1974.

304 "Hitchcock knew": Arthur Laurents to DS, Oct. 19, 1981.

305 "Every movement": Hitchcock (e), pp. 48–51, 96–104.

306 "It was": to DS, Feb. 26, 1982.

306 "Went out": Graham Payn and Sheridan Morley, eds. *The Noël Coward Diaries* (Boston and Toronto: Little, Brown & Co., 1982).

307 "domestic harmony": Bergman, p. 190.

308 "I was": Samuels, p. 233.

309 "The thing": To DS, July 24, 1975.

310 "He got": To DS, May 7, 1975.

### CHAPTER ELEVEN

321 "But love": Highsmith, pp. 163, 228.

321 "I remember": Knight, p. 20.

322 "One day": MacShane, p. 171.

322 "The thing": Gardiner and Walker, p. 119.

322 "Our collaboration": Hitchcock (f), p. 4.

323 "full of": MacShane, pp. 174–175.

323 "These veerings": MacShane, p. 177.

325 "Sometimes he": To DS, Sept. 4, 1981.

326 "You never": in *TV Guide*, May 29, 1965, p. 16.

326 "This was": Bogdanovich, p. 30.

329 "I imagine": E. T. A. Hoffmann, quoted in Rank, p. 8.

333 "Alma and I": Hitchcock (g), p. 14.

337 "There are": Knight, p. 116.

338 "Back in": Anne Baxter to DS, Sept. 15, 1980.

339 "It had": Karl Malden to DS, May 26, 1981.

342 "the whetted": Otis L. Guernsey, Jr., *New York Herald Tribune*, Mar. 23, 1953.

342 "I was": Princess Grace of Monaco to DS, Sept. 22, 1975.

344 "This is": AH, office memo, n.d., Warner Brothers Archives, Doheny Library / University of Southern California, Los Angeles.

345 "Hitchcock was": John Michael Hayes to DS, Feb. 27, 1982.

347 "*Rear Window*": A. H. Weiler, *New York Times*, May 9, 1954, sec. 2, p. 3; see also Samuels, p. 245.

347 "The whole": To DS, Feb. 26, 1982.

348 "Every costume": To DS, July 22, 1975; see also Head and Ardmore, pp. 153–154.

351 "It's been murder": *Newsweek*, May 24, 1954.

353 "an engagingly": Frances Millington, staff evaluation for Paramount Pictures, Oct. 17, 1950.

CHAPTER TWELVE

360 "I simply": To DS, Aug. 23, 1977.

360 "The Mystery": To DS, Feb. 27, 1982.

361 "I remember": To DS, Feb. 26, 1982.

362 "In 1951": To DS, Dec. 12, 1981.

363 "Hitchcock knew": To DS, Jan. 20, 1981.

364 "What happened": Hotchner, p. 168.

364 "In the beginning": Ibid., p. 169.

365 "Look lovingly": Quoted by Reggie Nalder, to DS, Apr. 11, 1981.

366 "After four": To DS, Feb. 27, 1982.

367 "Quite often": William K. Zinsser, *New York Herald Tribune*, Aug. 4, 1955.

370 "contributes nothing": Quoted in "The Chairman of the Board," *TV Guide*, May 16–24, 1964, p. 11; see also "Alfred Hitchcock — Director: TV or Movies, Suspense is Golden," *Newsweek*, June 11, 1956, p. 106.

370 "Miss Harrison": Quoted in *TV Guide*, May 16–24, 1964, p. 11.

370 "the work": Quoted in *TV Guide*, May 29, 1965, p. 16.

371 "When I": Murray Schumach, *New York Times*, Nov. 13, 1959.

371 "Remember the": Martin, p. 71.

372 "In three": Quoted in *Variety*, Dec. 29, 1955.

372 "You can't": Haber, p. 11.

373 "The first": To Hedda Hopper, Mar. 7, 1961.

373 "When he": Head and Ardmore, p. 154.

374 "that probably": To DS, Mar. 1, 1982.

376 "We never": *Variety*, Oct. 26, 1955.

377 "implied a": Brean, p. 102.

379 "Vera Miles": *Cosmopolitan*, Oct. 1956, p. 67.

380 "It is": *London Evening Standard*, June 19, 1956.

384 "Dr. Rabwin": To Louella Parsons, Jan. 17, 1957.

385 "The biggest": Martin, p. 37.

385 "I had": To DS, Feb. 28, 1982.

386 "I suffered": To Dick Williams, *Los Angeles Mirror-News*, Dec. 9, 1957.

386 "Vera, instead": Nogueira and Zalaffi, p. 5 (trans. DS).

387 "I nearly": To DS, Aug. 23, 1977.

387 "I arrived": To DS, Dec. 3, 1974, and Dec. 2, 1980.

388 "Hitchcock and": To DS, Feb. 28, 1982.

389 "Hitchcock seemed": To DS, Dec. 2, 1980.

389 "She arrived": To DS, July 22, 1975.

390 "He wanted": To DS, July 31, 1981.

390 "She was": Aug. 17, 1958.

390 "At least": To DS, Nov. 6, 1976.

391 "Try to": Quoted by Henry Bumstead, to DS, June 12, 1981.

394 "After several": To DS, Feb. 26, 1982.

394 "What fascinated": To DS, Nov. 6, 1976.

394 "If we'd": To DS, Dec. 3, 1974. "Kim was": To DS, Feb. 26, 1982.

395 "I had": Spoto (a), p. 330.

396 "associated with": Michael Compton, *The Kiss* (London: Tate Gallery Publications, 1969), unpaged.

398 "Suspense": Quoted in *Films and Filming*, July 1959, pp. 7, 33. The reason for this sour, blunt finale to a public statement will be clear from the account of the events of June 1959.

399 "I was": To DS, July 24, 1975.

399 "within the house": Edel, p. 259.

401 "a whispered": Arthur Symons, *Studies in Prose and Verse* (London, 1904), p. 271.

401 "Hitchcock knew": To DS, Dec. 2, 1980.

402 "I didn't": To DS, Mar. 24, 1976.

403 "I hate": Quoted by Arthur Laurents and Anthony Shaffer, to DS, Jan. and Oct. 1981, respectively.

405 "I watched": To Hedda Hopper, Mar. 7, 1962 (cf. Knight, p. 118); Nogueira and Zalaffi, p. 5 (trans. DS); and Whitcomb.

407 "Due to": To DS, July 24, 1975.

407 "on condition": F. M. Rittenberg to Rudi Monta and Clark Ramsey, MGM internal memo, Sept. 26, 1958, MGM Archives.

407 "No director": Robert Boyle, *Film Comment* 14, no. 3 (May–June 1978): 33.

408 "a lot": Memo dated Feb. 17, 1959.

409 "to defer": Kenneth MacKenna to Ben Melnicker, MGM memo, Jan. 12, 1959.

409 "the enemies": MGM memo, Mar. 27, 1959.

410 "It was a shame": To DS, Aug. 1, 1981.

410 "The visual": Samuel Taylor to DS, Dec. 2, 1980.

411 "These pieces": Whitcomb, p. 24.

412 "I spent": Quoted in *CinemaTV Today*, Aug. 19, 1972, p. 4.

413 "Then she": Whitcomb, p. 25.

415 "My poodle": To DS, Sept. 15, 1980.

415 "He loved": To DS, Feb. 26, 1982.

417 "There were": To DS, July 31, 1981.

418 "A suite": Pincus to E. LaPinere, Sept. 17, 1959.

418 "I enjoyed": Quoted in *London Sunday Express*, Sept. 11, 1970.

419 "He sent": To DS, Mar. 23, 1982.

419 "It had been": To DS, Feb. 27, 1982.

420 "Hitchcock's major": Kenneth Tynan, "Shouts and Murmurs," *London Observer*, Apr. 21, 1968.

420 "I remember": Quoted in *Films Illustrated* 2, no. 13 (July 1972): 22–24.

421 "I was": To Hedda Hopper, Mar. 7, 1961.

421 "I think the thing": Truffaut, p. 205.

423 "When Tony": *Film: The Magazine of the Federation of Film Societies*, no. 46 (summer 1966), p. 13 (partial reprint of a speech to the Cambridge Film Society, May 1966).

423 "You don't": To DS, Mar. 23, 1982.

425 "Owls belong": Truffaut, p. 211.

426 "Who knows": Truffaut, p. 149.

CHAPTER THIRTEEN

444 *Sentinel* item: Reported Apr. 27, 1960.

444 "He loved": To DS, Feb. 26, 1982.

445 "Hitchcock appreciated": To DS, Mar. 1, 1982.

445 "the idol": Curtis.

446 "It all": To DS, Feb. 28, 1982.

447 "It's a": *Holiday*, Sept. 1964, p. 88.

448 "He would": To DS, Feb. 26, 1982.

448 "A SEA BIRD": *Santa Cruz Sentinel*, Aug. 18, 1961.

449 "Hitchcock told": To DS, Dec. 3, 1981.

450 "It was": To DS, June 27, 1974, and Oct. 5, 1980.

452 "She was": To DS, Mar. 1, 1982.

453 "The girl": Bogdanovich, pp. 44–45.

455 "The overall": To DS, Mar. 1, 1982.

457 "I brought": David Lewin, *Sunday Express*, Nov. 28, 1962.

458 "I always": Stephen Rebello, *Real Paper*, Feb. 16, 1980, pp. 30–31; cf. *Hollywood Reporter*, Mar. 24, 1976.

459 "Day after": To DS, June 3, 1974.

460 "One of": Diehl.

461 Federico Fellini: To DS, May 18, 1980.

462 "I arrived": To DS, Dec. 3, 1981.

464 "He told": Jon Finch quoted in *Films Illustrated* 1, no. 3 (Sept. 1971): 22.

464 "It may": Rank, pp. 4, 7.

466 "I was": To DS, Mar. 1, 1982.

469 "I didn't": To DS, Dec. 3, 1981.

470 "Her reactions": *Cinema* 1, no. 5 (Aug.–Sept. 1963): 4–8, 34–35.

471 "Somehow": To DS, Nov. 12, 1980.

476 "I needed": Stephen Rebello, *Real Paper*, Feb. 16, 1980, p. 31; cf. Samuels, p. 237.

477 "I am": Abramson (a), p. 71.

477 "I think": To George Angell on *The Time of My Life*, BBC-TV, Aug. 28, 1966.

477 "Money *per se*": Abramson (a), p. 71.

477 "I have": *TV Guide*, May 29, 1965, p. 18.

477 "one of": Abramson (a), p. 72.

478 "a human warmth": Archer Winsten, *New York Post*, July 23, 1964.

478 "pathetically old-fashioned": Judith Crist, *New York Herald Tribune*, July 23, 1964.

CHAPTER FOURTEEN

484 "The central": *London Evening Standard*, Feb. 20, 1965.

487 "But the fact": To DS, Feb. 20, 1982.

489 "I never": Quoted in *Photoplay Film Monthly* 27, no. 2 (Feb. 1976): 57; cf. Diehl.

490 "I was": Nogueira and Zalaffi, p. 4 (trans. DS).

490 "We all": To DS, May 20, 1981.

490 "I accepted": To Dick Cavett, on PBS-TV, Mar. 25, 1982.

490 "He just": To DS, Dec. 2, 1980.

491 "He had": Royal S. Brown, *High Fidelity* 26, no. 9 (Sept. 1976): 64–67.

492 "Good . . . fine": Quoted by John Addison, to DS, Mar. 21, 1982.

496 "After we": To DS, Dec. 4, 1981.

498 "I dread": Hitchcock (g), p. 14.

498 "Hitch and": To DS, Dec. 2, 1980.

499 "I'm here": Quoted in *Variety*, May 8, 1968.

500 "Hitch didn't": To DS, Aug. 1, 1981.

500 "He called": To DS, Dec. 2, 1980.

500 "talked in": *London Daily Express*, Jan. 24, 1969.

501 "Claude Jade": Leonard Gross, "Claude Jade: A Girl to Bring Home to Mother (If You Can Trust Father)," *Look*, Apr. 7, 1970.

502 "Just before": Nogueira and Zalaffi, p. 4 (trans. DS).

503 *'Topaz* was": *Films Illustrated* 2, no. 3 (July 1972): 22–24; cf. Nogueira and Zalaffi, p. 6.

503 "And all": To DS, July 24, 1976.

503 "I have": Ivor Davis, "Alfred Hitchcock Abhors Violence, Prefers Suspense," *Los Angeles Times*, Sept. 7, 1969.

506 "I prefer": *Films Illustrated* 1, no. 3 (Sept. 1971): 23.

506 "From what": To DS, Feb. 28, 1982.

507 "When I": To DS, Mar. 20, 1982.

508 "Yes, of course": Alfred Appel, Jr., "The Eyehold of Knowledge: Voyeuristic Games in Film and Literature," *Film Comment* 9, no. 3 (May–June 1973): 25.

508 "I thought": To DS, Jan. 23, 1981.

509 "You can": *Take One* 1, no. 1 (Sept.–Oct. 1966).

509 *'Frenzy'*: Samuels, p. 236.

510 "I had": Haber, p. 11.

511 "It's so": Quoted by Samuel Taylor, to DS, Dec. 2, 1980.

511 "I don't": To DS, Sept. 4, 1980.

511 "He had": To DS, Sept. 2, 1980.

512 "Food was": Anne Baxter to DS, Sept. 15, 1980.

512 "I'd like": Truffaut, p. 241.

512 "Suddenly he": To DS, Sept. 1, 1980.

513 "This was": To DS, Aug. 28, 1980.

514 "I used": Clark, p. 42.

515 "And I": Knight, p. 117.

515 "The scene": Clark, p. 43.

515 "Hitchcock came": Bernard Herrmann, *High Fidelity* 26, no. 9 (Sept. 1976): 67.

517 "But there": To DS, Sept. 2, 1980.

517 "It's obvious": To DS, Dec. 21, 1980.

518 "I'll be": David Taylor, *Punch*, May 31, 1972, p. 776.

519 "sardonic and": Andrew Sarris, *Village Voice*, June 22, 1972, p. 69.

519 "Ten years ago": Quoted in *Newsweek*, June 26, 1972.

519 "In the later": To DS, Dec. 21, 1980.

519 "That's the way": Natale, p. 32.

### CHAPTER FIFTEEN

523 "A lot": To Richard Schickel, Nov. 1972.

524 "I am": Quoted in *CinemaTV Today*, Aug. 19, 1972, p. 4; cf. Nogueira and Zalaffi, p. 4.

524 "You don't": *Los Angeles Times*, Apr. 27, 1972.

525 "The front office": Quoted by Shaffer, to DS, Jan. 23, 1981.

526 "Although I": To DS, Mar. 19, 1982.

526 "I don't": Transcript dated Nov. 2, 1973, p. 170.

528 "these topics": Quoted in *Variety*, May 1, 1974.

531 "Our driver": To DS, June 3, 1981.

532 "He was": To DS, July 22, 1975.

532 "He's still": To DS, July 23, 1975.

534 "It will": Quoted in *Newsweek*, July 14, 1975.

534 "I don't": Charles Reid, *Picturegoer*, Jan. 21, 1950.

535 "We spend": *Time*, Jan. 12, 1976.

536 "A witty": Vincent Canby, *New York Times*, Apr. 10, 1976.

536 "One of": To DS, Aug. 23, 1977.

537 "no intention": Quoted in *London Sunday Telegraph*, July 10, 1977.

537 "Hitch had": To DS, Mar. 21, 1982.

540 "He was": To DS, Dec. 30, 1980.

### CHAPTER SIXTEEN

551 "I was": John O'Riordan, *Ignatian*, summer 1973.

552 "There were": To DS, Dec. 2, 1980.

552 "He took": To DS, Apr. 30, 1980.

554 "I retire": W. J. Weatherby, *London Sunday Times*, May 4, 1980.

# Selective Bibliography

Each of the following entries is preceded by the abbreviated form used in the Notes. Many sources, particularly newspaper and magazine articles, are not listed below but are cited only in the Notes.

*Abramson (a).* Abramson, Martin. "What Hitchcock Does with His Blood Money." *Cosmopolitan,* Jan. 1964.

*Abramson (b).* ————. "My Husband Hates Suspense." *Coronet,* Aug. 1964.

*Ackland and Grant.* Ackland, Rodney, and Grant, Elspeth. *The Celluloid Mistress; or, The Custard Pie of Dr. Caligari.* London: Allen Wingate, 1954.

*Armes.* Armes, Roy. *A Critical History of the British Cinema.* London: Oxford University Press, 1978.

*Balcon (a).* Balcon, Michael. *Michael Balcon Presents . . . A Lifetime of Films.* London: Hutchinson, 1969.

*Balcon (b).* ————. "Sincerity Will Make the Film English." *Era,* Nov. 11, 1931.

*Balcon (c).* ————. "My Hollywood Star Captures." *Film Weekly,* Jan. 18, 1936.

*Bankhead.* Bankhead, Tallulah. *Tallulah: My Autobiography.* London: Victor Gollancz, 1952.

*Barrett.* Barrett, E. F. "Ivor in Bloomsbury." *Picturegoer,* May 1926.

*Bazin.* Bazin, André. "Hitchcock contre Hitchcock." *Cahiers du Cinéma,* no. 39 (Oct. 1954).

*Belfrage.* Belfrage, Cedric. "Alfred the Great, World's Youngest Filmmaker." *Picturegoer,* Mar. 1926.

*Bell.* Bell, Quentin. *Virginia Woolf: A Biography.* New York: Harcourt Brace Jovanovich, 1972.

*Bergman.* Bergman, Ingrid, and Burgess, Alan. *Ingrid Bergman: My Story.* New York: Delacorte, 1980.

*Betts.* Betts, Ernest. *The Film Business: A History of British Cinema 1896–1972.* London: George Allen & Unwin, 1973.

*Bogdanovich.* Bogdanovich, Peter. *The Cinema of Alfred Hitchcock.* New York: Museum of Modern Art / Doubleday, 1963.

*Brady.* Brady, John. *The Craft of the Screenwriter.* New York: Simon & Schuster, 1981.

*Brean.* Brean, Herbert. "A Case of Identity." *Life,* June 29, 1953.

*Brian.* Brian, Denis. *Tallulah, Darling.* London: Sidgwick & Jackson, 1972.

*Brown.* Brown, Geoff. *Launder and Gilliat.* London: British Film Institute, 1977.

*Castle.* Castle, Hugh. "Elstree's First Talkie." *Close Up,* June 29, 1929.

*Chesterton.* Chesterton, G. K. *The Defendant.* London: J. M. Dent & Sons, 1901.

*Clark.* Clark, Paul Sargent. "Hitchcock's Finest Hour." *Today's Filmmaker,* Nov. 1972.

*Clayton.* Clayton, David. "Hitchcock Hates Actors." *Filmindia,* July 1947.

*Counts.* Counts, Kyle B. "The Making of Alfred Hitchcock's *The Birds.*" *Cinefantastique* 10, no. 2 (fall 1980).

*Curtis.* Curtis, Thomas Quinn. "Honors for Hitchcock." *Herald Tribune* (international ed.), June 1, 1960.

*Davis.* Davis, Ivor. "Alfred Hitchcock Abhors Violence, Prefers Suspense." *Los Angeles Times,* Sept. 7, 1969.

*Diehl.* Diehl, Digby. "Questions and Answers: Alfred Hitchcock." *Los Angeles Herald Examiner,* June 25, 1972.

*Edel.* Edel, Leon. *Henry James: The Treacherous Years.* Philadelphia: Lippincott, 1969.

*Eisner.* Eisner, Lotte. *The Haunted Screen.* Berkeley: University of California Press, 1974.

*Fethering.* Fethering, Doug. *The Five Lives of Ben Hecht.* London: Lester & Orpen, 1977.

*Gardiner and Walker.* Gardiner, Dorothy, and Walker, Kathrine Sorley. *Raymond Chandler Speaking.* London: New English Library, 1966.

*Gielgud.* Gielgud, John. *An Actor and His Time.* New York: Clarkson N. Potter, 1980.

*Goodman.* Goodman, Ezra. "The World is Now with Hitchcock." *New York Herald Tribune,* Apr. 5, 1942.

*Grant-Whyte.* Grant-Whyte, Harry. *Between Life and Death.* Pietermaritzburg, So. Africa: Shuter & Shooter, 1976.

*Greene.* Greene, Laurence. "He Is a Camera." *Esquire,* Aug. 1952.

*Grieve.* Grieve, H. E. P. *A History of Leyton: An Extract from a History of Sussex.* Vol. 6. London: University of London Institute of Historical Research / Oxford University Press, 1973.

*Haber.* Haber, Joyce. "Hitchcock Still Fighting Hard to Avoid the Conventional." *Los Angeles Times,* Feb. 4, 1973.

*Hayman.* Hayman, Ronald. *John Gielgud.* London: William Heinemann, 1971.

*Head and Ardmore.* Head, Edith, and Ardmore, Jane Kesner. *The Dress Doctor.* Boston: Little, Brown & Co., 1959.

*Hecht.* Hecht, Ben. *A Child of the Century.* New York: Simon & Schuster, 1954.

*Heffernan.* Heffernan, Harold. "Hitchcock Views the Stars." *Milwaukee Journal,* Mar. 3, 1963.

*Hellman.* Hellman, Geoffrey T. "Alfred Hitchcock, England's Best and Biggest Director, Goes to Hollywood." *Life,* Nov. 20, 1939.

*Hicks.* Hicks, Seymour. *Hail Fellows, Well Met.* London: Staples, 1949.

*Higham.* Higham, Charles. *Marlene: The Life of Marlene Dietrich.* New York: W. W. Norton, 1977.

*Highsmith.* Highsmith, Patricia. *Strangers on a Train.* New York: Harper & Bros., 1950. Also Baltimore: Penguin, 1974.

*Hitchcock (a).* Hitchcock, Alfred. "The Chase — Core of the Movie." *New York Times Magazine,* Oct. 29, 1950.

*Hitchcock (b).* ———. "The First British Talkie." In *The Elstree Story.* London: Clerke & Cockeran / Associated British Picture Corp., 1948.

*Hitchcock (c).* ———. "In the Hall of Mogul Kings." *Times* (London), June 23, 1969.

*Hitchcock (d).* ———. "More Cabbages, Fewer Kings." *Kine Weekly,* Jan. 14, 1937.

*Hitchcock (e)*. ———. "My Most Exciting Picture." *Popular Photography*, Nov. 1948.
*Hitchcock (f)*. ———. "Why I Am Afraid of the Dark." *Arts: Lettres, Spectacles*, no. 777 (June 1–7, 1960).
*Hitchcock (g)*. ———. "The Woman Who Knows Too Much." *McCall's*, Mar. 1956.
*Hitchcock (Alma)*. Hitchcock, Alma Reville. "My Husband Hates Suspense." *Family Circle*, June 1958.
*Hotchner*. Hotchner, A. E. *Doris Day: Her Own Story*. New York: William Morrow, 1976.
*Houseman*. Houseman, John. *Run-Through*. New York: Simon & Schuster, 1972.
*Johnston*. Johnston, Alvah. "300-Pound Prophet Comes to Hollywood." *Saturday Evening Post*, May 22, 1943.
*Knight*. Knight, Arthur. "Conversation with Alfred Hitchcock." *Oui*, Feb. 1973.
*Korda*. Korda, Michael. *Charmed Lives*. New York: Random House, 1979.
*Kulik*. Kulik, Carol. *Alexander Korda: The Man Who Could Work Miracles*. London: W. H. Allen, 1975.
*Lalott*. Lalott, Marcel. "Murder by a Babbling Brook." *Hollywood Studio*, Oct. 1973.
*LaValley*. LaValley, Albert, ed. *Focus on Hitchcock*. Englewood Cliffs, N.J.: Prentice-Hall, 1972.
*Lejeune*. Lejeune, C. A. "Hitchcock, The Man Korda Cannot Sign." *World Film News*, no. 2 (May 1936).
*Low and Manvell*. Low, Rachael, and Manvell, Roger. *The History of the British Film, 1896–1906*. London: George Allen & Unwin, 1948. Also vol. covering 1918–1929, published in 1971.
*Macgowan*. Macgowan, Kenneth. *Behind the Screen: The History and Technique of the Motion Picture*. New York: Delta, 1965.
*MacShane*. MacShane, Frank. *The Life of Raymond Chandler*. London: Jonathan Cape, 1976.
*Mahoney*. Mahoney, John C. "The Americanisation of Alfred Hitchcock . . . and vice versa." *Performing Arts Magazine* (Los Angeles), Feb. 1973.
*Martin*. Martin, Pete. "I Call on Alfred Hitchcock." *Saturday Evening Post*, July 27, 1957.
*Matthews*. Matthews, Jessie. *Over My Shoulder: An Autobiography*. London: W. H. Allen, 1974.
*Montagu (a)*. Montagu, Ivor. "Working with Hitchcock." *Sight and Sound*, summer 1980.
*Montagu (b)*. ———. *With Eisenstein in Hollywood*. Berlin: Seven Seas, 1968.
*Montagu (c)*. ———. *The Youngest Son*. London: Lawrence & Wishart, 1970.
*Natale*. Natale, Richard. "There's Just One Hitch." *Women's Wear Daily*, June 16, 1972.
*Noble*. Noble, Peter. "Index to the Work of Alfred Hitchcock." *Sight and Sound* special supp. no. 18, May 1949.
*Nogueira and Zalaffi*. Nogueira, Rui, and Zalaffi, Nicoletta. "Entretien avec Alfred Hitchcock." *Ecran*, no. 7 (July–Aug. 1972).
*Priestley*. Priestley, J. B. *The Edwardians*. London: Heinemann, 1970.
*Rank*. Rank, Otto. *The Double: A Psychoanalytic Study*. Translated by Harry Tucker, Jr. New York: New American Library, 1979.
*Reed*. Reed, Rex. "Master of the Macabre." *Southland Sunday/Chicago Sun-Times*, July 30, 1972.
*Robinson*. Robinson, David. "When Hitchcock Adapted Noël Coward." *Times* (London), Apr. 28, 1977.
*Rosenberg and Silverstein*. Rosenberg, Bernard, and Silverstein, Harry, eds. *The Real Tinsel*. New York: Macmillan Co., 1970.

*Samuels.* Samuels, Charles Thomas. *Encountering Directors.* New York: Capricorn/Putnam's, 1972.

*Scheuer.* Scheuer, Philip K. "Hitchcock's Birds Begin War on Man." *Los Angeles Examiner,* Mar. 22, 1962.

*Slater.* Slater, Fr., S.J. *Cases of Conscience for English-Speaking Countries.* 2 vols. New York: Benziger Bros., 1911.

*Smith.* Smith, H. Allen. "Hitchcock Likes to Smash Cups." *New York World-Telegram,* Aug. 28, 1937.

*Spoto (a).* Spoto, Donald. *The Art of Alfred Hitchcock.* New York: Hopkinson & Blake, 1976, and Doubleday, 1979. Also London: W. H. Allen, 1977.

*Spoto (b)* ———. *Camerado: Hollywood and the American Man.* New York: New American Library, 1978.

*Spoto (c).* ———. "Hitchcock the Designer." *Print* 31, no. 4 (July–Aug. 1977).

*Spoto (d).* ———. "Sound and Silence in the Films of Alfred Hitchcock." *Keynote* 4, no. 2, Apr. 1980.

*Spoto (e).* ———. "*Vertigo:* The Cure is Worse than the Dis-Ease." In *Classics of the Cinema,* edited by Stanley Solomon. New York: Harcourt Brace Jovanovich, 1973.

*Taylor.* Taylor, John Russell. *Hitch: The Life and Times of Alfred Hitchcock.* New York: Pantheon, 1978.

*Thornton.* Thornton, Michael. *Jessie Matthews: A Biography.* London: Hart-Davis, MacGibbon, 1974.

*Todd.* Todd, Ann. *The Eighth Veil.* London: William Kimber & Co., 1980.

*Tonkin.* Tonkin, W. G. S. *Victorian and Edwardian Waltham Forest.* London: Walthamstow Antiquarian Society, 1973.

*Trewin.* Trewin, J. C. *Robert Donat: A Biography.* London: Heinemann, 1968.

*Truffaut.* Truffaut, François. *Hitchcock.* New York: Simon & Schuster, 1967.

*Viertel.* Viertel, Salka. *The Kindness of Strangers.* New York: Holt, Rinehart & Winston, 1969.

*Whitcomb.* Whitcomb, Jon. "Master of Mayhem." *Cosmopolitan,* Oct. 1959.

# The Films of Alfred Hitchcock

The abbreviations that follow are used in designating those associated in the production of each film.

> *P:* Producer(s)
> *AP:* Associate producer(s)
> *Sc:* Screenplay by
> *b/o:* based on
> *DP:* Director(s) of photography
> *Ed:* Editor(s)
> *AD:* Art director(s)/production designer(s)
> *S:* Set designer(s)
> *W:* Wardrobe and costumes by
> *M:* Musical score composed by
> *SE:* Special effects supervisor(s)
> *ad:* Assistant director(s)
> *C:* Continuity supervisor(s)
> *Int:* Interior studio sets
> *B/W:* Filmed in black and white
> *Col.:* Filmed in color

There are two dates given after each feature-film title: *prod.* indicates the year in which the film was made; *rel.* specifies the year of the first release for public screening.

# SILENT FEATURES

**The Pleasure Garden** (A Gainsborough-Emelka Picture; *prod.* 1925/*rel.* 1927)
*P:* Michael Balcon. *Sc:* Eliot Stannard, b/o the novel by Oliver Sandys. *DP:* Baron [Giovanni] Ventimiglia. *Int:* Emelka. *B/W*.
*Cast:* Patsy Brand     Virginia Valli
Jill Cheyne     Carmelita Geraghty
Levett     Miles Mander
Hugh Fielding     John Stuart
Native girl     Nita Naldi
and with Frederick Martini and Florence Helminger.

**The Mountain Eagle** (A Gainsborough-Emelka Picture; *prod.* 1925/*rel.* 1927)
*P:* Michael Balcon. *Sc:* Eliot Stannard. *DP:* Baron [Giovanni] Ventimiglia. *Int:* Emelka. *B/W*.
*Cast:* Pettigrew     Bernard Goetzke
Beatrice     Nita Naldi
Fear o' God     Malcolm Keen
Edward     John Hamilton
(Released in the U.S.A. as *Fear o' God.*)

**The Lodger: A Story of the London Fog** (A Gainsborough Picture; *prod.* 1926/*rel.* 1927)
*P:* Michael Balcon. *Sc:* Eliot Stannard, b/o the novel *The Lodger* by Marie Belloc Lowndes. *DP:* Baron [Giovanni] Ventimiglia. *ad:* Alma Reville. *AD:* C. Wilfrid Arnold, Bertram Evans. *Ed/titling:* Ivor Montagu. *Title designs:* E. McKnight Kauffer. *Int:* Islington. *B/W*.
*Cast:* The landlady     Marie Ault
Her husband     Arthur Chesney
Daisy Bunting,
a mannequin     June
Joe, a police
detective     Malcolm Keen
The lodger     Ivor Novello

**Downhill** (A Gainsborough Picture; *prod./rel.* 1927)
*P:* Michael Balcon. *Sc:* Eliot Stannard, b/o the play by David LeStrange (pseud. of Ivor Novello and Constance Collier). *DP:* Claude McDonell. *Ed:* Ivor Montagu. *Int:* Islington. *B/W*.
*Cast:* Roddy Berwick     Ivor Novello
Tim Wakely     Robin Irvine
Lady Berwick     Lillian Braithwaite
Julia     Isabel Jeans
Archie     Ian Hunter
(Released in the U.S.A. as *When Boys Leave Home.*)

**Easy Virtue** (A Gainsborough Picture; *prod./rel.* 1927)
*P:* Michael Balcon. *Sc:* Eliot Stannard, b/o the play by Noël Coward. *DP:* Claude McDonell. *Ed:* Ivor Montagu. *Int:* Islington. *B/W*.

*Cast:* Larita Filton     Isabel Jeans
Her husband     Franklyn Dyall
The artist     Eric Bransby Williams
Counsel for the
plaintiff     Ian Hunter
John Whittaker     Robin Irvine
His mother     Violet Farebrother
and with Benita Hume.

**The Ring** (A British International Picture; *prod./rel.* 1927)
*P:* John Maxwell. *Sc:* Alfred Hitchcock. *C:* Alma Reville. *DP:* John J. Cox. *Int:* Elstree. *B/W*.
*Cast:* Jack Sanders     Carl Brisson
Nellie     Lillian Hall Davis
The champion     Ian Hunter
and with Harry Terry, Gordon Harker, Forrester Harvey, and Tom Helmore.

**The Farmer's Wife** (A British International Picture; *prod.* 1927/*rel.* 1928)
*P:* John Maxwell. *Sc:* Alfred Hitchcock, b/o the play by Eden Phillpotts. *DP:* John J. Cox. *Ed:* Alfred Booth. *Int:* Elstree. *B/W*.
*Cast:* Farmer Sweetland     Jameson Thomas
Araminta Dench     Lillian Hall Davis
Churdles Ash     Gordon Harker
Thirza Tapper     Maud Gill
Widow Windeat     Louise Pounds
and with Olga Slade and Antonia Brough.

**Champagne** (A British International Picture; *prod./rel.* 1928)
*P:* John Maxwell. *Sc:* Eliot Stannard. Adaptation: Alfred Hitchcock, b/o an original story by Walter C. Mycroft. *DP:* John J. Cox. *AD:* C. W. Arnold. *ad:* Frank Mills. *Int:* Elstree. *B/W*.
*Cast:* The girl     Betty Balfour
The boy     Jean Bradin
The man     Theo Von Alten
The father     Gordon Harker

**The Manxman** (A British International Picture; *prod.* 1928/*rel.* 1929)
*P:* John Maxwell. *Sc:* Eliot Stannard, b/o the novel by Hall Caine. *DP:* John J. Cox. *ad:* Frank Mills. *Int:* Elstree. *B/W*.
*Cast:* Pete     Carl Brisson
Philip     Malcolm Keen
Kate     Anny Ondra
Her father     Randle Ayrton

# SOUND FEATURES

**Blackmail** (A British International Picture; *prod./rel.* 1929)
*P:* John Maxwell. *Sc:* Alfred Hitchcock, b/o the play

by Charles Bennett. *Dialogue:* Benn W. Levy. *DP:*
John J. Cox. *AD:* C. W. Arnold. *Ed:* Emile de
Ruelle. *ad:* Frank Mills; *M:* Campbell and Con-
nelly. *Int:* Elstree. *B/W.*

| Cast: | Alice White | Anny Ondra |
| | | (voice: Joan |
| | | Barry) |
| | Mrs. White | Sara Allgood |
| | Mr. White | Charles Paton |
| | Detective Frank | |
| | Webber | John Longden |
| | Tracy, the | |
| | blackmailer | Donald Calthrop |
| | The artist | Cyril Ritchard |
| | The landlady | Hannah Jones |
| | The neighbor | Phyllis Monkman |
| | Chief inspector | Harvey Braban |

**Juno and the Paycock** (A British International Pic-
ture; *prod./rel.* 1930)
*P:* John Maxwell. *Adaptation:* Alfred Hitchcock and
Alma Reville, b/o the play by Sean O'Casey. *DP:*
John J. Cox. *AD:* Norman Arnold. *Int:* Elstree. *B/W.*

| Cast: | Juno | Sara Allgood |
| | Captain Boyle | Edward Chapman |
| | Mrs. Madigan | Maire O'Neill |
| | Joxer | Sidney Morgan |

**Murder!** (A British International Picture; *prod./rel.*
1930)
*P:* John Maxwell. *Adaptation:* Alfred Hitchcock and
Walter Mycroft, b/o the novel and play *Enter Sir
John* by Clemence Dane and Helen Simpson. *DP:*
John J. Cox. *AD:* J. F. Mead. *ad:* Frank Mills. *Sc:*
Alma Reville. *M:* John Reynders. *Ed:* Rene Marri-
son, Emile de Ruelle. *Int:* Elstree. *B/W.*

| Cast: | Diana Baring | Norah Baring |
| | Sir John Menier | Herbert Marshall |
| | Gordon Druce | Miles Mander |
| | Handel Fane | Esme Percy |
| and with Edward Chapman, Phyllis |
| Konstam, Hannah Jones, and Una |
| O'Connor. |

(Hitchcock also directed a German version, *Mary,*
starring Walter Abel.)

**The Skin Game** (A British International Picture;
*prod.* 1930–1931/*rel.* 1931)
*P:* John Maxwell. *Adaptation:* Alfred Hitchcock. *Sc:*
Alma Reville, b/o the play by John Galsworthy. *DP:*
John J. Cox. *AD:* J. B. Maxwell. *ad:* Frank Mills.
*Int:* Elstree. *B/W.*

| Cast: | Mr. Hillcrist | C. V. France |
| | Mrs. Hillcrist | Helen Haye |
| | Mr. Hornblower | Edmund Gwenn |
| | Jill | Jill Esmond |
| and with John Longden and Phyllis |
| Konstam. |

**Number Seventeen** (A British International Picture;
*prod.* 1931/*rel.* 1932)
*P:* John Maxwell. *Sc:* Alma Reville, Alfred Hitchcock, and Rodney Ackland, b/o the play by J. Jefferson Farjeon. *DP:* John J. Cox, Byran Langley.
*AD:* C. W. Arnold. *ad:* Frank Mills. *Ed:* A. C.
Hammond. *M:* A. Hallis. *Int:* Elstree. *B/W.*

| Cast: | Ben | Leon M. Lion |
| | The girl | Anne Grey |
| | The detective | John Stuart |
| and with Donald Calthrop, Barry Jones, Ann |
| Casson, Henry Caine, and Garry Marsh. |

**Rich and Strange** (A British International Picture;
*prod./rel.* 1932)
*P:* John Maxwell. *Adaptation:* Alfred Hitchcock. *Sc:*
Alma Reville. *DP:* John J. Cox, Charles Martin.
*Additional dialogue:* Val Valentine. *AD:* C. W. Ar-
nold. *Ed:* Rene Marrison, Winifred Cooper. *ad:*
Frank Mills. *M:* Hal Dolphe. *Int:* Elstree. *B/W.*

| Cast: | Fred Hill | Henry Kendall |
| | Emily Hill | Joan Barry |
| | Commander Gordon | Percy Marmont |
| | The "princess" | Betty Amann |
| | The old maid | Elsie Randolph |
| (Released in the U.S.A. as *East of Shanghai.*) |

**Waltzes from Vienna** (A Tom Arnold Production;
*prod./rel.* 1933)
*P:* Tom Arnold. *Sc:* Alma Reville and Guy Bolton,
b/o the play by Bolton. *M:* Johann Strauss. *AD:*
Alfred Junge. *S:* Peter Proud. *Int:* Lime Grove. *B/W.*

| Cast: | Rasi | Jessie Matthews |
| | Strauss the younger | Esmond Knight |
| | Strauss the elder | Edmund Gwenn |
| | The prince | Frank Vosper |
| | The countess | Fay Compton |
| (Released in the U.S.A. as *Strauss's Great Waltz.*) |

**The Man Who Knew Too Much** (A Gaumont-
British Picture; *prod./rel.* 1934)
*P:* Michael Balcon. *AP:* Ivor Montagu. *Sc:* Edwin
Greenwood and A. R. Rawlinson, b/o a story by
Charles Bennett and D. B. Wyndham Lewis. *Addi-
tional dialogue:* Emlyn Williams. *DP:* Curt Cour-
ant. *AD:* Alfred Junge. *Ed:* H. St.C. Stewart. *M:*
Arthur Benjamin. *Int:* Lime Grove. *B/W.*

| Cast: | Bob Lawrence | Leslie Banks |
| | Jill Lawrence | Edna Best |
| | Betty Lawrence | Nova Pilbeam |
| | Abbott | Peter Lorre |
| | Ramon | Frank Vosper |
| | Clive | Hugh Wakefield |
| | Louis Bernard | Pierre Fresnay |
| | Nurse Agnes | Cicely Oates |
| and with D. A. Clarke Smith and George |
| Curzon. |

**The 39 Steps** (A Gaumont-British Picture; *prod./rel.*
1935)
*P:* Michael Balcon. *AP:* Ivor Montagu. *Adaptation:*
Charles Bennett, b/o the novel *The Thirty-Nine Steps*
by John Buchan. *C:* Alma Reville. *Dialogue:* Ian
Hay. *DP:* Bernard Knowles. *AD:* O. Werndorff. *Ed:*
D. N. Twist. *M:* Louis Levy. *Int:* Lime Grove. *B/W.*

*Cast:* Richard Hannay            Robert Donat
       Pamela                     Madeleine Carroll
       Annabella Smith            Lucie Mannheim
       Prof. Jordan               Godfrey Tearle
       The crofter                John Laurie
       His wife                   Peggy Ashcroft
       Mrs. Jordan                Helen Haye
       The sheriff                Frank Cellier
       Mr. Memory                 Wylie Watson
       and with Gus MacNaughton, Jerry Verno,
          and Peggy Simpson.

**Secret Agent** (A Gaumont-British Picture; *prod.*
1935/rel. 1936)
*P:* Michael Balcon. *AP:* Ivor Montagu. *Sc:* Charles
Bennett, from the play by Campbell Dixon b/o sto-
ries by W. Somerset Maugham. *Dialogue:* Ian Hay,
Jesse Lasky, Jr. *C:* Alma Reville. *DP:* Bernard
Knowles. *AD:* O. Werndorff. *Ed:* Charles Frend.
*M:* Louis Levy. *Int:* Lime Grove. *B/W.*

*Cast:* Edgar Brodie /
         Richard Ashenden  John Gielgud
       Elsa                Madeleine Carroll
       The general         Peter Lorre
       Marvin              Robert Young
       Caypor              Percy Marmont
       Mrs. Caypor         Florence Kahn
       and with Charles Carson, Lilli Palmer, and
          Michel Saint-Denis.

**Sabotage** (A Gaumont-British Picture; *prod./rel.*
1936)
*P:* Michael Balcon. *AP:* Ivor Montagu. *Sc:* Charles
Bennett, b/o the novel *The Secret Agent* by Joseph
Conrad. *Dialogue:* Ian Hay, Helen Simpson. *C:*
Alma Reville. *DP:* Bernard Knowles. *Ed:* Charles
Frend. *AD:* O. Werndorff. *M:* Louis Levy. Cartoon
sequence from Walt Disney's *Who Killed Cock
Robin? Int:* Lime Grove. *B/W.*

*Cast:* Mrs. Verloc        Sylvia Sidney
       Mr. Verloc          Oscar Homolka
       Stevie              Desmond Tester
       Ted Spenser         John Loder
       Renee               Joyce Barbour
       and with William Dewhurst, Martita Hunt,
          and Peter Bull.
(Released in the U.S.A. as *The Woman Alone*.)

**Young and Innocent** (A Gaumont-British Picture;
*prod.* 1937/rel. 1938)

*P:* Edward Black. *Sc:* Charles Bennett, Edwin
Greenwood, and Anthony Armstrong, b/o the novel
*A Shilling for Candles* by Josephine Tey. *Dialogue:*
Gerald Savory. *C:* Alma Reville. *DP:* Bernard
Knowles. *Ed:* Charles Frend. *AD:* Alfred Junge. *M:*
Louis Levy. *Int:* Limegrove and Pinewood. *B/W.*

*Cast:* Erica Burgoyne       Nova Pilbeam
       Robert Tisdall        Derrick de Marney
       Col. Burgoyne         Percy Marmont
       Old Will              Edward Rigby
       Erica's aunt          Mary Clare
       Det. Insp. Kent       John Longden
       Guy                   George Curzon
       Erica's uncle         Basil Radford
       Christine             Pamela Carme
(Released in the U.S.A. as *The Girl Was Young*.)

**The Lady Vanishes** (A Gaumont-British Picture;
*prod.* 1937/rel. 1938)
*P:* Edward Black. *Sc:* Sidney Gilliat and Frank
Launder, b/o the novel *The Wheel Spins* by Ethel
Lina White. *C:* Alma Reville. *DP:* John J. Cox. *Ed:*
R. E. Dearing. *S:* Vetchinsky. *M:* Louis Levy. *Int:*
Islington. *B/W.*

*Cast:* Iris Henderson       Margaret Lockwood
       Gilbert               Michael Redgrave
       Miss Froy             Dame May Whitty
       Dr. Hartz             Paul Lukas
       Mr. Todhunter         Cecil Parker
       His mistress          Linden Travers
       Caldicott             Naunton Wayne
       Charters              Basil Radford
       Baroness              Mary Clare
       The "nun"             Catherine Lacey
       and with Josephine Wilson, Kathleen
          Tremaine, Emile Boreo, and Googie
          Withers.

**Jamaica Inn** (An Erich Pommer Production; *prod.*
1938/rel. 1939)
*P:* Erich Pommer. *Sc:* Sidney Gilliat and Joan Harrison, b/o the novel by Daphne du Maurier. *C:* Alma
Reville. *Additional dialogue:* J. B. Priestley. *DP:*
Harry Stradling, Bernard Knowles. *S:* Tom Morahan. *W:* Molly McArthur. *M:* Eric Fenby. *Int:* Elstree. *B/W.*

*Cast:* Sir Humphrey
         Pengallan           Charles Laughton
       Joss Merlyn           Leslie Banks
       Patience, his wife    Marie Ney
       Mary, his niece       Maureen O'Hara
       Harry                 Emlyn Williams
       Salvation             Wylie Watson
       Thomas                Mervyn Johns
       and with Edwin Greenwood and Stephen
          Haggard.

**Rebecca** (A Production of the Selznick Studio; *prod.* 1939/*rel.* 1940)
*P:* David O. Selznick. *Sc:* Robert E. Sherwood and Joan Harrison, b/o the novel by Daphne du Maurier. *Adaptation:* Philip MacDonald, Michael Hogan. *DP:* George Barnes. *M:* Franz Waxman. *AD:* Lyle Wheeler. *S:* Joseph B. Platt. *SE:* Jack Cosgrove. *Ed:* James Newcom, Hal Kern. *ad:* Edmond Bernoudy. *Int:* Selznick Studios. *B/W.*

*Cast:* 
| | |
|---|---|
| Maxim de Winter | Laurence Olivier |
| His wife | Joan Fontaine |
| Mrs. Danvers | Judith Anderson |
| Jack Favell | George Sanders |
| Mrs. Van Hopper | Florence Bates |
| Giles Lacey | Nigel Bruce |
| Beatrice Lacey | Gladys Cooper |

and with C. Aubrey Smith, Melville Cooper, Leo G. Carroll, Forrester Harvey, Reginald Denny, Lumsden Hare, Philip Winter, and Edward Fielding.

**Foreign Correspondent** (A Wanger Production; *prod./rel.* 1940)
*P:* Walter Wanger. *Sc:* Charles Bennett, Joan Harrison. *Dialogue:* James Hilton, Robert Benchley. *M:* Alfred Newman. *AD:* Alexander Golitzen. *DP:* Rudolph Maté. *SE:* Paul Eagler. *Ed:* Otho Lovering, Dorothy Spencer. *Special production effects:* William Cameron Menzies. *S:* Julia Heron. *W:* I. Magnin. *ad:* Edmond Bernoudy. *Int:* Goldwyn Studios. *B/W.*

*Cast:* 
| | |
|---|---|
| Johnny Jones / Huntley Haverstock | Joel McCrea |
| Carol Fisher | Laraine Day |
| Stephen Fisher | Herbert Marshall |
| ffolliott | George Sanders |
| Van Meer | Albert Basserman |
| Stebbins | Robert Benchley |
| Rowley | Edmund Gwenn |
| Mr. Powers | Harry Davenport |
| Krug | Eduardo Ciannelli |

and with Eddie Conrad, Frances Carson, Martin Kosleck, Gertrude W. Hoffman, Emory Parnell, Ian Wolfe, Eily Malyon, and E. E. Clive.

**Mr. and Mrs. Smith** (An RKO Radio Picture; *prod.* 1940/*rel.* 1941)
*P:* Harry E. Edington. *Story and sc:* Norman Krasna. *M:* Edward Wand. *DP:* Harry Stradling. *AD:* Van Nest Polglase. *SE:* Vernon L. Walker. *W:* Irene. *S:* Darrell Silvera. *Ed:* William Hamilton. *ad:* Dewey Starkey. *Int:* RKO Studios. *B/W.*

*Cast:* 
| | |
|---|---|
| Ann Krausheimer Smith | Carole Lombard |
| David Smith | Robert Montgomery |
| Jeff Custer | Gene Raymond |
| His parents | Philip Merivale, Lucile Watson |
| Chuck Benson | Jack Carson |

**Suspicion** (An RKO Radio Picture; *prod./rel.* 1941)
*P:* Harry E. Edington. *Sc:* Samson Raphaelson, Joan Harrison, and Alma Reville, b/o the novel *Before the Fact* by Francis Iles. *DP:* Harry Stradling. *M:* Franz Waxman. *SE:* Vernon L. Walker. *AD:* Van Nest Polglase. *S:* Darrell Silvera. *Ed:* William Hamilton. *ad:* Dewey Starkey. *Int:* RKO Studios. *B/W.*

*Cast:* 
| | |
|---|---|
| Lina McLaidlaw | Joan Fontaine |
| Johnny Aysgarth | Cary Grant |
| General McLaidlaw | Sir Cedric Hardwicke |
| Mrs. McLaidlaw | Dame May Whitty |
| Beaky Thwaite | Nigel Bruce |
| Mrs. Newsham | Isabel Jeans |

and with Heather Angel, Auriol Lee, and Leo G. Carroll.

**Saboteur** (A Frank Lloyd Production for Universal; *prod./rel.* 1942)
*P:* Frank Lloyd. *AP:* Jack H. Skirball. *Sc:* Peter Viertel, Joan Harrison, Dorothy Parker. *DP:* Joseph Valentine. *AD:* Jack Otterson, Robert Boyle. *Ed:* Otto Ludwig. *M:* Frank Skinner. *ad:* Fred Rank. *Int:* Universal. *B/W.*

*Cast:* 
| | |
|---|---|
| Barry Kane | Robert Cummings |
| Pat Martin | Priscilla Lane |
| Charles Tobin | Otto Kruger |
| Mrs. Van Sutton | Alma Kruger |
| Fry | Norman Lloyd |

**Shadow of a Doubt** (A Jack H. Skirball Production for Universal; *prod.* 1942/*rel.* 1943)
*P:* Jack H. Skirball. *Sc:* Thornton Wilder, Sally Benson, and Alma Reville, b/o an original story by Gordon McDonell. *DP:* Joseph Valentine. *M:* Dimitri Tiomkin. *AD:* John B. Goodman, Robert Boyle. *S:* R. A. Gausman, E. R. Robinson. *Ed:* Milton Carruth. *W:* Adrian / Vera West. *ad:* William Tummell. *Int:* Universal. *B/W.*

*Cast:* 
| | |
|---|---|
| Uncle Charlie Oakley | Joseph Cotten |
| Charlie Newton | Teresa Wright |
| Jack Graham | MacDonald Carey |
| Emma Newton | Patricia Collinge |
| Joe Newton | Henry Travers |
| Herb Hawkins | Hume Cronyn |
| Ann Newton | Edna May Wonacott |
| Roger Newton | Charles Bates |
| Fred Saunders | Wallace Ford |

and with Eily Malyon and Estelle Jewell.

**Lifeboat** (A 20th Century–Fox Picture; *prod.* 1943/ *rel.* 1944)
*P:* Kenneth Macgowan. *Sc:* Jo Swerling, b/o a story by John Steinbeck. *DP:* Glen MacWilliams. *AD:* James Basevi, Maurice Ransford. *S:* Thomas Little, Frank E. Hughes. *Ed:* Dorothy Spencer. *SE:* Fred Sersen. *Technical adviser:* Thomas Fitzsimmons (National Maritime Union). *M:* Hugo W. Friedhofer. *W:* Rene Hubert. *Int:* 20th Century–Fox. *B/W.*

| *Cast:* | Constance Porter | Tallulah Bankhead |
|---|---|---|
| | Kovac | John Hodiak |
| | Gus | William Bendix |
| | Willie | Walter Slezak |
| | Alice MacKenzie | Mary Anderson |
| | Stanley Garrett | Hume Cronyn |
| | Charles J. | |
| | Rittenhouse | Henry Hull |
| | Mrs. Higgins | Heather Angel |
| | Joe Spencer | Canada Lee |

**Spellbound** (A Selznick International Picture; *prod.* 1944/*rel.* 1945)
*P:* David O. Selznick. *Sc:* Ben Hecht, b/o the novel *The House of Dr. Edwardes* by Francis Beeding. *Adaptation:* Angus MacPhail. *DP:* George Barnes. *M:* Miklos Rozsa. *AD:* James Basevi. *Ed:* Hal Kern. *SE:* Jack Cosgrove. *S:* Emile Kuri. *Dream sequence* based on designs by Salvador Dalí. *ad:* Lowell J. Farrell. *Psychiatric adviser:* May E. Romm, M.D. *Int:* Selznick Studios. *B/W.*

| *Cast:* | Dr. Constance | |
|---|---|---|
| | Petersen | Ingrid Bergman |
| | John Ballantyne | Gregory Peck |
| | Dr. Murchison | Leo G. Carroll |
| | Garmes | Norman Lloyd |
| | Mary Carmichael | Rhonda Fleming |
| | Dr. Alex Brulov | Michael Chekhov |
| | Dr. Fleurot | John Emery |
| | and with Bill Goodwin, Art Baker, and | |
| | Wallace Ford. | |

**Notorious** (An RKO Radio Picture; *prod.* 1945– 1946/*rel.* 1946)
*P:* Alfred Hitchcock. *Sc:* Ben Hecht. *DP:* Ted Tetzlaff. *SE:* Vernon L. Walker, Paul Eagler. *AD:* Albert S. D'Agostino, Carroll Clark. *S:* Darrell Silvera, Claude Carpenter. *M:* Roy Webb. *Ed:* Theron Warth. *W:* Edith Head. *ad:* William Dorfman. *Int:* RKO. *B/W.*

| *Cast:* | Alicia Huberman | Ingrid Bergman |
|---|---|---|
| | T. R. Devlin | Cary Grant |
| | Alexander Sebastian | Claude Rains |
| | Madame Sebastian | Leopoldine Konstantin |
| | Paul Prescott | Louis Calhern |
| | Dr. Anderson | Reinhold Schuenzel |
| | Eric Mathis | Ivan Triesault |
| | Joseph | Alex Minotis |
| | Hupka | Eberhard Krumschmidt |
| | Commodore | Sir Charles Mendl |
| | Walter Beardsley | Moroni Olsen |
| | Dr. Barbosa | Ricardo Costa |

**The Paradine Case** (A David O. Selznick/Vanguard Film; *prod.* 1946–1947/*rel.* 1947)
*P:* David O. Selznick. *Sc:* David O. Selznick, b/o the novel by Robert Hichens. *Adaptation:* Alma Reville. *DP:* Lee Garmes. *Production designer:* J. MacMillan Johnson. *AD:* Tom Morahan. *S:* Joseph B. Platt, Emile Kuri. *SE:* Clarence Slifer. *ad:* Lowell J. Farrell. *W:* Travis Banton. *M:* Franz Waxman. *Ed:* Hal Kern, John Faure. *Int:* RKO. *B/W.*

| *Cast:* | Mrs. Paradine | Valli |
|---|---|---|
| | Anthony Keane | Gregory Peck |
| | Gay, his wife | Ann Todd |
| | Lord Horfield | Charles Laughton |
| | Lady Horfield | Ethel Barrymore |
| | Sir Simon Flaquer | Charles Coburn |
| | Judy Flaquer, his daughter | Joan Tetzel |
| | Andre Latour | Louis Jourdan |
| | and with Leo G. Carroll, John Williams, and | |
| | Isobel Elsom. | |

**Rope** (A Transatlantic Picture; *prod./rel.* 1948)
*P:* Alfred Hitchcock, Sidney Bernstein. *Adaptation:* Hume Cronyn, b/o the play by Patrick Hamilton. *Sc:* Arthur Laurents. *DP:* Joseph Valentine, William V. Skall. *AD:* Perry Ferguson. *S:* Emile Kuri, Howard Bristol. *Ed:* William H. Ziegler. *ad:* Lowell J. Farrell. *M:* Francis Poulenc, Leo F. Forbstein. *Int:* Warner Brothers. *Col.*

| *Cast:* | Rupert Cadell | James Stewart |
|---|---|---|
| | Brandon | John Dall |
| | Philip | Farley Granger |
| | Mr. Kentley | Sir Cedric Hardwicke |
| | Mrs. Atwater | Constance Collier |
| | Kenneth | Douglas Dick |
| | Mrs. Wilson | Edith Evanson |
| | Janet | Joan Chandler |
| | David Kentley | Dick Hogan |

**Under Capricorn** (A Transatlantic Picture; *prod.* 1948/*rel.* 1949)
*P:* Alfred Hitchcock, Sidney Bernstein. *Adaptation:*

Hume Cronyn. *Sc:* James Bridie, from the play by John Colton and Margaret Linden b/o the novel by Helen Simpson. *DP:* Jack Cardiff. *AD:* Tom Morahan. *W:* Roger Furse. *Ed:* A. S. Bates. *ad:* C. Foster Kemp. *C:* Peggy Singer. *M:* Richard Addinsell. *Int:* Elstree. *Col.*

*Cast:* Sam Flusky     Joseph Cotten
    Lady Henrietta
      Flusky     Ingrid Bergman
    Charles Adare     Michael Wilding
    Milly     Margaret Leighton
    Governor     Cecil Parker
    Corrigan     Denis O'Dea

**Stage Fright** (A Warner Brothers–First National Picture; *prod.* 1949/*rel.* 1950)
*P:* Alfred Hitchcock. *Adaptation:* Alma Reville. *Sc:* Whitfield Cook, b/o the novel *Man Running* by Selwyn Jepson. *DP:* Wilkie Cooper. *AD:* Terence Verity. *Ed:* E. B. Jarvis. *M:* Leighton Lucas. *C:* Peggy Singer. *Int:* Elstree. *B/W.*

*Cast:* Charlotte Inwood     Marlene Dietrich
    Eve Gill     Jane Wyman
    Wilfrid Smith     Michael Wilding
    Jonathan Cooper     Richard Todd
    Commodore Gill     Alastair Sim
    Mrs. Gill     Sybil Thorndike
    Nellie Good     Kay Walsh
    Chubby Bannister     Patricia Hitchcock
and with Joyce Grenfell, Miles Malleson, Hector MacGregor, Ballard Berkeley, and André Morell.

**Strangers on a Train** (A Warner Brothers–First National Picture, *prod.* 1950/*rel.* 1951)
*P:* Alfred Hitchcock. *Adaptation:* Whitfield Cook. *Sc:* Raymond Chandler and Czenzi Ormonde, b/o the novel by Patricia Highsmith. *DP:* Robert Burks. *AD:* Edward S. Haworth. *Ed:* William Ziegler. *S:* George James Hopkins. *SE:* H. F. Koenekamp. *M:* Dimitri Tiomkin. *Int:* Warner Brothers. *B/W.*

*Cast:* Bruno Anthony     Robert Walker
    Guy Haines     Farley Granger
    Miriam Haines     Laura Elliott
    Ann Morton     Ruth Roman
    Barbara Morton     Patricia Hitchcock
    Senator Morton     Leo G. Carroll
    Mrs. Anthony     Marion Lorne
and with Jonathan Hale and Norma Varden.

**I Confess** (A Warner Brothers–First National Picture; *prod.* 1952/*rel.* 1953)
*P:* Alfred Hitchcock. *Sc:* George Tabori and William Archibald, b/o the play *Nos Deux Consciences* by Paul Anthelme. *DP:* Robert Burks. *AD:* Edward S. Haworth. *Ed:* Rudi Fehr. *S:* George James Hopkins. *ad:* Don Page. *M:* Dimitri Tiomkin. *Int:* Warner Brothers. *B/W.*

*Cast:* Father Michael
      Logan     Montgomery Clift
    Ruth Grandfort     Anne Baxter
    Inspector Larrue     Karl Malden
    Pierre Grandfort     Roger Dann
    Otto Keller     O. E. Hasse
    Alma Keller     Dolly Haas
    Willy Robertson     Brian Aherne

**Dial "M" for Murder** (A Warner Brothers–First National Picture; *prod.* 1953/*rel.* 1954)
*P:* Alfred Hitchcock. *Sc:* Frederick Knott, b/o his play. *DP:* Robert Burks. *AD:* Edward Carrera. *Ed:* Rudi Fehr. *S:* George James Hopkins. *ad:* Mel Dellar. *M:* Dimitri Tiomkin. *Int:* Warner Brothers. *Col.* and 3-D.

*Cast:* Tony Wendice     Ray Milland
    Margot Wendice     Grace Kelly
    Mark Halliday     Robert Cummings
    Lesgate (Swann)     Anthony Dawson
    Inspector Hubbard     John Williams
and with Leo Britt, Patrick Allen, George Leigh, George Alderson, and Robin Hughes.

**Rear Window** (A Paramount Release; *prod.* 1953/*rel.* 1954)
*P:* Alfred Hitchcock. *Sc:* John Michael Hayes, b/o the short story by Cornell Woolrich. *DP:* Robert Burks. *AD:* Hal Pereira, Joseph MacMillan Johnson. *SE:* John P. Fulton. *S:* Sam Comer, Ray Moyer. *ad:* Herbert Coleman. *Ed:* George Tomasini. *W:* Edith Head. *M:* Franz Waxman. *Int:* Paramount. *Col.*

*Cast:* L. B. Jeffries     James Stewart
    Lisa Carol Freemont     Grace Kelly
    Stella     Thelma Ritter
    Tom Doyle     Wendell Corey
    Lars Thorwald     Raymond Burr
    Mrs. Thorwald     Irene Winston
    Miss Lonelyhearts     Judith Evelyn
    The composer     Ross Bagdasarian
    Miss Torso     Georgine Darcy
    Miss Sculptress     Jesslyn Fax
and with Sara Berner, Frank Cady, Rand Harper, Havis Davenport, and Anthony Ward.

**To Catch a Thief** (A Paramount Picture; *prod.* 1954/*rel.* 1955)
*P:* Alfred Hitchcock. *Sc:* John Michael Hayes, b/o the novel by David Dodge. *DP:* Robert Burks. *Second-unit director:* Herbert Coleman. *AD:* Hal Pereira, Joseph MacMillan Johnson. *SE:* John P. Fulton. *Second-unit DP:* Wallace Kelley. *Process photography:* Farciot Edouart. *S:* Sam Comer, Arthur Krams. *Ed:* George Tomasini. *ad:* Daniel McCauley. *M:* Lyn Murray. *W:* Edith Head. *Int:* Paramount. *Col.*

*Cast:* John Robie     Cary Grant
Frances Stevens     Grace Kelly
Jessie Stevens     Jessie Royce Landis
H. H. Hughson     John Williams
Danielle Foussard     Brigitte Auber
Bertani     Charles Vanel
and with René Blancard.

**The Trouble with Harry** (A Paramount Release; *prod.* 1954/*rel.* 1955)
*P:* Alfred Hitchcock. *Sc:* John Michael Hayes, b/o the novel by J. Trevor Story. *DP:* Robert Burks. *ad:* Howard Joslin. *Ed:* Alma Macrorie. *M:* Bernard Herrmann. *W:* Edith Head. *AP:* Herbert Coleman. *Int:* Paramount. *Col.*

*Cast:* Capt. Albert Wiles     Edmund Gwenn
Sam Marlowe     John Forsythe
Jennifer Rogers     Shirley MacLaine
Miss Graveley     Mildred Natwick
Mrs. Wiggs     Mildred Dunnock
Arnie Rogers     Jerry Mathers
Calvin Wiggs     Royal Dano
Millionaire     Parker Fennelly
Harry     Philip Truex

**The Man Who Knew Too Much** (A Paramount Release; *prod.* 1955/*rel.* 1956)
*P:* Alfred Hitchcock. *AP:* Herbert Coleman. *Sc:* John Michael Hayes, b/o a story by Charles Bennett and D. B. Wyndham Lewis. *DP:* Robert Burks. *Ed:* George Tomasini. *AD:* Hal Pereira, Henry Bumstead. *SE:* John P. Fulton. *S:* Sam Comer, Arthur Krams. *W:* Edith Head. *ad:* Howard Joslin. *M:* Bernard Herrmann; "Storm Cloud Cantata" by Arthur Benjamin and D. B. Wyndham Lewis. *Songs:* "Whatever Will Be" and "We'll Love Again" by Jay Livingston and Ray Evans. *Int:* Paramount. *Col.*

*Cast:* Dr. Ben McKenna     James Stewart
Jo McKenna     Doris Day
Hank McKenna     Christopher Olsen
Mr. Drayton     Bernard Miles
Mrs. Drayton     Brenda de Banzie
Rien, the assassin     Reggie Nalder
Louis Bernard     Daniel Gélin
and with Ralph Truman, Mogens Wieth, Hilary Brooke, Carolyn Jones, Alan Mowbray, Richard Wattis, and Alix Talton.

**The Wrong Man** (A Warner Brothers–First National Picture; *prod./rel.* 1956)
*P:* Alfred Hitchcock. *AP:* Herbert Coleman. *Sc:* Maxwell Anderson and Angus MacPhail, b/o story by Anderson. *DP:* Robert Burks. *Ed:* George Tomasini. *AD:* Paul Sylbert. *ad:* Daniel J. McCauley. *S:* William L. Kuehl. *M:* Bernard Herrmann. *Int:* Warner Brothers. *B/W.*

*Cast:* Christopher Emmanuel Balestrero     Henry Fonda
Rose Balestrero     Vera Miles
Frank O'Connor     Anthony Quayle
Mrs. Balestrero     Esther Minciotti
Lt. Bowers     Harold J. Stone
Tomasini     John Heldabrand
Mrs. James     Doreen Lang
Constance Willis     Laurinda Barrett
Betty Todd     Norma Connolly
Olga Conforti     Lola D'Annunzio
Gene Conforti     Nehemiah Persoff
Gregory Balestrero     Robert Essen
Robert Balestrero     Kippy Campbell
Judge     Dayton Lummis
Det. Matthews     Charles Cooper
Miss Dennerly     Peggy Webber
Daniell     Richard Robbins

**Vertigo** (A Paramount Release; *prod.* 1957/*rel.* 1958)
*P:* Alfred Hitchcock. *AP:* Herbert Coleman. *Sc:* Alec Coppel and Samuel Taylor, b/o the novel *D'Entre Les Morts* by Pierre Boileau and Thomas Narcejac. *DP:* Robert Burks. *Ed:* George Tomasini. *AD:* Hal Pereira, Henry Bumstead. *S:* Sam Comer, Frank McKelvey. *M:* Bernard Herrmann. *Titles:* Saul Bass. *SE:* John P. Fulton. *ad:* Daniel McCauley. *W:* Edith Head. *Special sequence:* John Ferren. *Int:* Paramount. *Col.*

*Cast:* John "Scottie" Ferguson     James Stewart
"Madeleine Elster" (Judy Barton)     Kim Novak
Midge Wood     Barbara Bel Geddes
Gavin Elster     Tom Helmore
Pop Liebl     Konstantin Shayne
and with Henry Jones, Raymond Bailey, Ellen Corby, and Lee Patrick.

**North by Northwest** (An MGM Picture; *prod.* 1958/*rel.* 1959)
*P:* Alfred Hitchcock. *AP:* Herbert Coleman. Written by Ernest Lehman. *DP:* Robert Burks. *Ed:* George Tomasini. *AD:* Robert Boyle, William A. Horning, Merrill Pye. *S:* Henry Grace, Frank McKelvey. *SE:* A. Arnold Gillespie, Lee LeBlanc. *Titles:* Saul Bass. *M:* Bernard Herrmann. *Int:* MGM. *Col.*

*Cast:* Roger O. Thornhill — Cary Grant
Eve Kendall — Eva Marie Saint
Philip Vandamm — James Mason
Clara Thornhill — Jessie Royce Landis
The Professor — Leo G. Carroll
Lester Townsend — Philip Ober
Leonard — Martin Landau
Valerian — Adam Williams
Licht — Robert Ellenstein
and with Josephine Hutchinson, Doreen Lang, Les Tremayne, Philip Coolidge, Edward Binns, Pat McVey, Nora Marlowe, Ned Glass, and Malcolm Atterbury.

**Psycho** (A Paramount Release; *prod.* 1959–1960/*rel.* 1960)
*P:* Alfred Hitchcock. *Sc:* Joseph Stefano, b/o the novel by Robert Bloch. *DP:* John L. Russell. *Ed:* George Tomasini. *AD:* Joseph Hurley, Robert Clatworthy. *S:* George Milo. *Titles:* Saul Bass. *M:* Bernard Herrmann. *W:* Helen Colvig. *SE:* Clarence Champagne. *ad:* Hilton A. Green. *Int:* Revue Studios. *B/W.*

*Cast:* Norman Bates — Anthony Perkins
Marion Crane — Janet Leigh
Lila Crane — Vera Miles
Sam Loomis — John Gavin
Arbogast — Martin Balsam
Al Chambers — John McIntire
Mrs. Chambers — Lurene Tuttle
Psychiatrist — Simon Oakland
Cassidy — Frank Albertson
Caroline — Pat Hitchcock
Mr. Lowery — Vaughn Taylor
Highway patrolman — Mort Mills
"California Charlie" — John Anderson

**The Birds** (A Universal Release; *prod.* 1962/*rel.* 1963)
*P:* Alfred Hitchcock. *Sc:* Evan Hunter, b/o the short story by Daphne du Maurier. *DP:* Robert Burks. *Ed:* George Tomasini. *AD:* Robert Boyle. *ad:* James H. Brown. *W:* Edith Head. *SE:* Lawrence A. Hampton. *Special photographic adviser:* Ub Iwerks. *Pictorial designs:* Albert Whitlock. *S:* George Milo. *Bird trainer:* Ray Berwick. *Titles:* James S. Pollak. *Asst. to AH:* Peggy Robertson. *Electronic sound production and composition:* Remi Gassmann, Oskar Sala; *consultant,* Bernard Herrmann. *Int:* Universal. *Col.*

*Cast:* Melanie Daniels — Tippi Hedren
Mitch Brenner — Rod Taylor
Lydia Brenner — Jessica Tandy
Annie Hayworth — Suzanne Pleshette
Cathy Brenner — Veronica Cartwright
Mrs. Bundy — Ethel Griffies
Sebastian Sholes — Charles McGraw
Mrs. MacGruder — Ruth McDevitt
Al Malone — Malcolm Atterbury
Deke Carter — Lonny Chapman
Helen Carter — Elizabeth Wilson
Traveling salesman — Joe Mantell
Fisherman — Doodles Weaver
Postal clerk — John McGovern
Drunk — Karl Swenson
Man in elevator — Richard Deacon
Mother in Tides Café — Doreen Lang

**Marnie** (A Universal Release; *prod.* 1963–1964/*rel.* 1964)
*P:* Alfred Hitchcock. *Sc:* Jay Presson Allen, b/o the novel by Winston Graham. *DP:* Robert Burks. *AD:* Robert Boyle. *ad:* James H. Brown. *W:* Edith Head. *Ed:* George Tomasini. *Pictorial design:* Albert Whitlock. *S:* George Milo. *M:* Bernard Herrmann. *Asst. to AH:* Peggy Robertson. *Int:* Universal. *Col.*

*Cast:* Margaret (Marnie) Edgar — Tippi Hedren
Mark Rutland — Sean Connery
Lil Mainwaring — Diane Baker
Bernice Edgar — Louise Latham
Sidney Strutt — Martin Gabel
Cousin Bob — Bob Sweeney
Mr. Rutland — Alan Napier
Susan Clabon — Mariette Hartley
Rita — Edith Evanson
Sam Ward — S. John Launer
Mrs. Turpin — Meg Wyllie
Sailor — Bruce Dern

**Torn Curtain** (A Universal Release; *prod.* 1965–1966/*rel.* 1966)
*P:* Alfred Hitchcock. Written by Brian Moore. *DP:* John F. Warren. *AD:* Hein Heckroth, Frank Arrigo. *Pictorial design:* Albert Whitlock. *Ed:* Bud Hoffman. *ad:* Donald Baer. *S:* George Milo. *W:* Edith Head, Grady Hunt. *M:* John Addison. *Asst. to AH:* Peggy Robertson. *Int:* Universal. *Col.*

*Cast:* Michael Armstrong — Paul Newman
Sarah Sherman — Julie Andrews
Countess Luchinska — Lila Kedrova
Gromek — Wolfgang Kieling
Ballerina — Tamara Toumanova
Professor Lindt — Ludwig Donath
Jacobi — David Opatoshu
and with Mort Mills, Carolyn Conwell, Arthur Gould-Porter, and Gloria Gorvin.

**Topaz** (A Universal Release; *prod.* 1968–1969/*rel.* 1969)
*P:* Alfred Hitchcock. *AP:* Herbert Coleman. *Sc:* Samuel Taylor, b/o the novel by Leon Uris. *DP:* Jack Hildyard. *AD:* Henry Bumstead. *S:* John Austin. *W:* Edith Head. *Ed:* William Ziegler. *M:* Maurice Jarre. *Asst. to AH:* Peggy Robertson. *Int:* Universal. *Col.*

| *Cast:* André Devereaux | Frederick Stafford |
| Michael Nordstrom | John Forsythe |
| Nicole Devereaux | Dany Robin |
| Rico Parra | John Vernon |
| Juanita de Cordoba | Karin Dor |
| Jacques Granville | Michel Piccoli |
| Henri Jarre | Philippe Noiret |
| Michele Picard | Claude Jade |
| Philippe Dubois | Roscoe Lee Browne |
| Boris Kusenov | Per-Axel Arosenius |
| François Picard | Michel Subor |

**Frenzy** (A Universal Release; *prod.* 1971/*rel.* 1972)
*P:* Alfred Hitchcock. *Sc:* Anthony Shaffer, b/o the novel *Goodbye Piccadilly, Farewell Leicester Square* by Arthur La Bern. *DP:* Gil Taylor. *AP:* William Hill. *AD:* Syd Cain, Bob Laing. *ad:* Colin M. Brewer. *Ed:* John Jympson. *S:* Simon Wakefield. *M:* Ron Goodwin. *Asst. to AH:* Peggy Robertson. *Int:* Pinewood. *Col.*

| *Cast:* Richard Blaney | Jon Finch |
| Bob Rusk | Barry Foster |
| Brenda Blaney | Barbara Leigh-Hunt |
| Babs Milligan | Anna Massey |
| Inspector Oxford | Alex McCowen |
| Mrs. Oxford | Vivien Merchant |
| Hetty Porter | Billie Whitelaw |
| Johnny Porter | Clive Swift |
| Felix Forsythe | Bernard Cribbins |
| Gladys | Elsie Randolph |
| Sergeant Spearman | Michael Bates |
| Monica Barling | Jean Marsh |

**Family Plot** (A Universal Release; *prod.* 1975/*rel.* 1976)
*P:* Alfred Hitchcock. *Sc:* Ernest Lehman, b/o the novel *The Rainbird Pattern* by Victor Canning. *DP:* Leonard South. *AD:* Henry Bumstead. *S:* James W. Payne. *Ed:* J Terry Williams. *W:* Edith Head. *M:* John Williams. *SE:* Albert Whitlock. *ad:* Howard G. Kazanjian, Wayne A. Farlow. *Asst. to AH:* Peggy Robertson. *Int:* Universal. *Col.*

| *Cast:* Fran | Karen Black |
| Lumley | Bruce Dern |
| Blanche | Barbara Harris |
| Adamson | William Devane |
| Maloney | Ed Lauter |
| Julia Rainbird | Cathleen Nesbitt |
| Mrs. Maloney | Katherine Helmond |
| Grandison | Warren J. Kemmerling |
| Mrs. Clay | Edith Atwater |
| Bishop | William Prince |
| Constantine | Nicolas Colasanto |
| Vera Hannagan | Marge Redmond |

# TELEVISION FILMS

NOTE: All were filmed at the Revue Television Studios. All were filmed in black and white unless otherwise noted.

**Breakdown** (*prod.* Sept. 7–10, 1955; *broadcast* on CBS Nov. 13, 1955, as the 7th episode of the series *Alfred Hitchcock Presents*)
*Sc:* Francis Cockrell and Louis Pollock, b/o a story by Pollock. *DP:* John L. Russell. *AD:* Martin Obzina. *S:* James S. Redd. *M:* Stanley Wilson. *Ed:* Richard G. Wray, Edward W. Williams. *W:* Vincent Dee. *ad:* James Hogan. *AP:* Joan Harrison. *Cast:* Joseph Cotten, Raymond Bailey, Forrest Stanley, Lane Chandler, Harry Shannon, Murray Alper, James Edwards, Aaron Spelling.

**Revenge** (*prod.* Sept. 15–17, 1955; *broadcast* on CBS Oct. 2, 1955, as the premier episode of the series *Alfred Hitchcock Presents*)
*Sc:* Francis Cockrell and A. I. Bezzerides, b/o a story by Samuel Blas. *DP:* John L. Russell. *AD:* Martin Obzina. *S:* James S. Redd. *M:* Stanley Wilson. *Ed:* Richard G. Wray, Edward W. Williams. *W:* Vincent Dee. *ad:* Jack Corrick. *AP:* Joan Harrison. *Cast:* Ralph Meeker, Vera Miles, Frances Bavier, Ray Montgomery, Ray Teal, John Gallaudet, Norman Willis.

**The Case of Mr. Pelham** (*prod.* Oct. 7/8/10, 1955; *broadcast* on CBS Dec. 4, 1955, as the 10th episode of the series *Alfred Hitchcock Presents*)
*Sc:* Francis Cockrell, b/o a story by Anthony Armstrong. *DP:* John L. Russell. *AD/S:* James S. Redd. *M:* Stanley Wilson. *Ed:* Richard G. Wray, Edward W. Williams. *W:* Vincent Dee. *ad:* Jack Corrick. *AP:* Joan Harrison. *Cast:* Tom Ewell, Raymond Bailey, Kirby Smith, Kay Stewart, John Compton, Norman Willis, Jan Arvan.

**Back for Christmas** (*prod.* Jan. 13/14/16, 1956; *broadcast* on CBS Mar. 4, 1956, as the 23d episode of the series *Alfred Hitchcock Presents*)

*Sc:* Francis Cockrell, b/o a story by John Collier. *DP:* John L. Russell. *AD:* Martin Obzina. *S:* Ralph Sylos. *M:* Stanley Wilson. *Ed:* Richard G. Wray, Edward W. Williams. *W:* Vincent Dee. *ad:* Richard Birnie. *AP:* Joan Harrison. *Cast:* John Williams, Isobel Elsom, A. E. Gould-Porter, Gavin Muir, Katherine Warren, Gerald Hamer, Irene Tedrow, Ross Ford.

**Wet Saturday** (*prod.* Aug. 22–24, 1956; *broadcast* on CBS Sept. 30, 1956, as the 40th episode of the series *Alfred Hitchcock Presents*)
*Sc:* Marian Cockrell, b/o a story by John Collier. *DP:* John L. Russell. *AD:* Martin Obzina. *S:* James S. Redd. *M:* Stanley Wilson. *Ed:* Richard G. Wray, Edward W. Williams. *W:* Vincent Dee. *ad:* Jack Corrick. *AP:* Joan Harrison. *Cast:* Sir Cedric Hardwicke, John Williams, Kathryn Givney, Tita Purdom, Jerry Barclay, Irene Lang.

**Mr. Blanchard's Secret** (*prod.* Oct. 18/19/22, 1956; *broadcast* on CBS Dec. 23, 1956, as the 52d episode of the series *Alfred Hitchcock Presents*)
*Sc:* Sarett Rudley, b/o a story by Emily Neff. *DP:* John L. Russell. *AD:* John Lloyd. *S:* James Walters. *M:* Stanley Wilson. *Ed:* Richard G. Wray, Edward W. Williams. *W:* Vincent Dee. *ad:* Richard Birnie. *AP:* Joan Harrison. *Cast:* Mary Scott, Robert Horton, Dayton Lummis, Meg Mundy, Eloise Hardt.

**One More Mile to Go** (*prod.* Jan. 9–11, 1957; *broadcast* on CBS Apr. 7, 1957, as the 67th episode of the series *Alfred Hitchcock Presents*)
*Sc:* James P. Cavanagh, b/o a story by F. J. Smith. *DP:* John L. Russell. *AD:* John Lloyd. *S:* Ralph Sylos. *M:* Stanley Wilson. *Ed:* Richard G. Wray, Edward W. Williams. *W:* Vincent Dee. *ad:* Hilton Green. *AP:* Joan Harrison. *Cast:* David Wayne, Louise Larrabee, Steve Brodie, Norman Leavitt.

**The Perfect Crime** (*prod.* July 17–19, 1957; *broadcast* on CBS Oct. 20, 1957, as the 81st episode of the series *Alfred Hitchcock Presents*)
*Sc:* Stirling Silliphant, b/o a story by Ben Ray Redman. *DP:* John L. Russell. *AD:* John Lloyd. *S:* James S. Redd. *M:* Stanley Wilson. *Ed:* Richard G. Wray, Edward W. Williams. *W:* Vincent Dee. *ad:* Hilton Green. *AP:* Joan Harrison. *Cast:* Vincent Price, James Gregory, John Zaremba, Marianne Stewart, Gavin Gordon.

**Four O'Clock** (*prod.* July 29–Aug. 2, 1957; *broadcast* on NBC Sept. 30, 1957, as the premier episode of the series *Suspicion*)
*Sc:* Francis Cockrell, b/o a story by Cornell Woolrich. *DP:* John L. Russell. *AD:* John Lloyd. *S:* James S. Redd. *M:* Stanley Wilson. *Ed:* Richard G. Wray, Edward W. Williams. *W:* Vincent Dee. *ad:* Hilton

Green. *AP:* Joan Harrison. *Cast:* E. G. Marshall, Nancy Kelly, Richard Long, Jesslyn Fax.

**Lamb to the Slaughter** (*prod.* Feb. 18–19, 1958; *broadcast* on CBS Apr. 13, 1958, as the 106th episode of the series *Alfred Hitchcock Presents*)
*Sc:* Roald Dahl, b/o his own story. *DP:* John L. Russell. *AD:* John Lloyd. *S:* James S. Redd. *Ed:* Richard G. Wray, Edward W. Williams. *W:* Vincent Dee. *ad:* Hilton Green. *P:* Joan Harrison. *AP:* Norman Loyd. *Cast:* Barbara Bel Geddes, Harold J. Stone, Allan Lane, Ken Clark, Robert C. Ross.

**Dip in the Pool** (*prod.* Apr. 15–16, 1958; *broadcast* on CBS Sept. 14, 1958, as the 113th episode of the series *Alfred Hitchcock Presents*)
*Sc:* Robert C. Dennis and Francis Cockrell, b/o a story by Roald Dahl. *DP:* John F. Warren. *AD:* John Lloyd. *S:* James S. Redd. *Ed:* Richard G. Wray, Edward W. Williams. *W:* Vincent Dee. *M:* Stanley Wilson. *ad:* Hilton Green. *P:* Joan Harrison. *AP:* Norman Lloyd. *Cast:* Keenan Wynn, Louise Platt, Philip Bourneuf, Fay Wray, Doreen Lang, Doris Lloyd, Ralph Clanton.

**Poison** (*prod.* Aug. 21–22, 1958; *broadcast* on CBS Oct. 5, 1958, as the 118th episode of the series *Alfred Hitchcock Presents*)
*Sc:* Casey Robinson, b/o a story by Roald Dahl. *DP:* John L. Russell. *AD:* John Lloyd. *S:* James S. Redd. *Ed:* Richard G. Wray, Edward W. Williams. *W:* Vincent Dee. *ad:* Hilton Green. *P:* Joan Harrison. *AP:* Norman Lloyd. *Cast:* Wendell Corey, James Donald, Arnold Moss, Weaver Levy.

**Banquo's Chair** (*prod.* Mar. 25–26, 1959; *broadcast* on CBS May 3, 1959, as the 146th episode of the series *Alfred Hitchcock Presents*)
*Sc:* Francis Cockrell, b/o a story by Rupert Croft-Cooke. *DP:* John L. Russell. *AD:* John Lloyd. *S:* George Milo. *M:* Frederick Herbert. *Ed:* Richard G. Wray, Edward W. Williams. *W:* Vincent Dee. *ad:* Hilton Green. *P:* Joan Harrison. *AP:* Norman Lloyd. *Cast:* John Williams, Kenneth Haigh, Reginald Gardiner, Max Adrian, George Pelling, Hilda Plowright.

**Arthur** (*prod.* July 7–9, 1959; *broadcast* on CBS Sept. 27, 1959, as the 154th episode of the series *Alfred Hitchcock Presents*)
*Sc:* James P. Cavanagh, b/o a story by Arthur Williams. *DP:* John L. Russell. *AD:* John Lloyd. *S:* James S. Redd. *M:* Frederick Herbert. *Ed:* Richard G. Wray, Edward W. Williams. *W:* Vincent Dee. *ad:* Hilton Green. *P:* Joan Harrison. *AP:* Norman Lloyd. *Cast:* Laurence Harvey, Hazel Court, Robert Douglas, Patrick Macnee.

**The Crystal Trench** (*prod.* Aug. 25–27, 1959, *broadcast* on CBS Oct. 4, 1959, as the 155th episode of the series *Alfred Hitchcock Presents*)
*Sc:* Stirling Silliphant, b/o a story by A. E. W. Mason. *DP:* John F. Warren. *AD:* John Lloyd. *S:* Julia Heron. *M:* Frederick Herbert. *Ed:* Richard G. Wray, Edward W. Williams. *W:* Vincent Dee. *ad:* Hilton Green. *P:* Joan Harrison. *AP:* Norman Lloyd. *Cast:* James Donald, Patricia Owens, Ben Astar, Werner Klemperer.

**Incident at a Corner** (*prod.* Feb. 8–12/15–17, 1960; *broadcast* on NBC Apr. 5, 1960, as the 27th episode of the series *Ford Startime*)
*Sc:* Charlotte Armstrong, b/o her own story. *DP:* John L. Russell. *AD:* John Lloyd. *S:* George Milo. *M:* Frederick Herbert. *Ed:* Richard G. Wray, Edward W. Williams. *ad:* Hilton Green. *P:* Joan Harrison. *AP:* Norman Lloyd. *Col. cast:* Paul Hartman, Vera Miles, George Peppard, Bob Sweeney, Leora Dana, Philip Ober, Jack Albertson.

**Mrs. Bixby and the Colonel's Coat** (*prod.* Aug. 17–19, 1960; *broadcast* on NBC Sept. 27, 1960, as the 191st episode of the series *Alfred Hitchcock Presents*)
*Sc:* Halsted Welles, b/o a story by Roald Dahl. *DP:* John L. Russell. *AD:* Martin Obzina. *S:* James S. Redd. *M:* Frederick Herbert. *Ed:* David O'Connell, Edward W. Williams. *W:* Vincent Dee. *ad:* James H. Brown. *P:* Joan Harrison. *AP:* Norman Lloyd. *Cast:* Audrey Meadows, Les Tremayne, Stephen Chase, Sally Hughes, Bernie Hamilton.

**The Horseplayer** (*prod.* Jan. 4–6, 1961; *broadcast* on NBC Mar. 14, 1961, as the 212th episode of the series *Alfred Hitchcock Presents*)
*Sc:* Henry Slesar, b/o his own story. *DP:* John L. Russell. *AD:* Martin Obzina. *S:* John McCarthy, Julia Heron. *M:* Joseph Romero. *Ed:* David O'Connell, Edward W. Williams. *W:* Vincent Dee. *ad:* James H. Brown. *AP:* Joan Harrison. *Cast:* Claude Rains, Ed Gardner, Percy Helton, Kenneth MacKenna.

**Bang! You're Dead** (*prod.* July 25–27, 1961; *broadcast* on NBC Oct. 17, 1961, as the 230th episode of the series *Alfred Hitchcock Presents*)
*Sc:* Harold Swanton, b/o a story by Margery Vosper. *DP:* John L. Russell. *AD:* Martin Obzina. *S:* John McCarthy, Julia Heron. *M:* Joseph Romero. *Ed:* David O'Connell, Edward W. Williams. *W:* Vincent Dee. *ad:* Wallace Worsley. *P:* Joan Harrison. *AP:* Norman Lloyd. *Cast:* Biff Elliott, Lucy Prentiss, Billy Mumy, Steven Dunne, Kelly Flynn.

**I Saw the Whole Thing** (*prod.* July 23–27, 1962; *broadcast* on NBC Oct. 11, 1962, as the 4th episode of the series *The Alfred Hitchcock Hour*)
*Sc:* Henry Slesar, b/o a story by Henry Cecil. *DP:* Benjamin H. Kline. *AD:* Martin Obzina. *S:* John McCarthy, Glen Daniels. *M:* Lyn Murray, Stanley Wilson. *Ed:* David O'Connell, Edward W. Williams. *W:* Vincent Dee. *ad:* Ronnie Rondell. *P:* Joan Harrison. *AP:* Gordon Hessler. *Cast:* John Forsythe, Kent Smith, Evans Evans, John Fiedler, Philip Ober, Claire Griswold.

# Index

(Page numbers in *italics* indicate photographs and their captions.)